THE

TWO-STORY

WORLD

Selected Writings of James K. Feibleman

Edited, and with an Introduction, by

HUNTINGTON CAIRNS

HOLT, RINEHART AND WINSTON

NEW YORK   CHICAGO   SAN FRANCISCO

Acknowledgments

Grateful thanks are due the following for permission to reprint here chapters which first appeared in the pages of their journals: Association of College Admissions Counselors for "College Teaching" which first appeared in the Summer, 1963 issue of the *Journal of the Association of College Admissions Counselors*; the Bobbs-Merrill Company, Inc. (Indianapolis) to reprint from *Education* "The Modern Novel and Its Audience" and "Eminence of Scholarship"; *The British Journal of Aesthetics* (London) for "A Behaviorist Theory of Art"; *College Board Review* for "Needed : special climate, slower pace for superior students"; *Dialectica* (Switzerland) for "Knowing About Semipalatinsk," and "Security: The Skin and Enduring Objects"; *Giornale di Metafisica* for "An Introduction to Metaphysics for Empiricists"; *Hibbert Journal* (Oxford) for "Aristotle's Religion," which appeared in *Hibbert Journal* (LVII, 124–132); *Indian Journal of Social Research* (India) for "Institutional Conditioning," which appeared in the August, 1964 issue; *Journal of Philosophy* for "The Meaning of Comedy," which first appeared in the *Journal of Philosophy* (XXXV, 16: 421–432, 1938); *The Journal of Psychology* for "The Psychology of the Artist," which first appeared in *The Journal of Psychology* (19: 165–189, 1945); *Journal of the History of Ideas* for "The Theory of Hamlet," which appeared in *Journal of the History of Ideas* (VII, 2: 131–150, 1946); *The Kenyon Review* for "Camus and the Passion of Humanism," which appeared in *The Kenyon Review* (Vol. XXV, No. 2, Spring, 1963); *Methodos* (Italy) for "Ontology and

Ideology," which first appeared in *Methodos* (XIII, 51 and 52: 1–8, 1961); *The Personalist* for "Concreteness in Painting" and "God, Man and Matter"; *Perspectives in Biology and Medicine* for "The Role of Hypotheses in the Scientific Method," which originally appeared in the Spring, 1959 issue (Vol. II, No. 3) of *Perspectives in Biology and Medicine*; *The Philosophical Quarterly* (Scotland) for "Culture as Applied Ontology" and "On the Topics and Definitions of the Categories"; *The Philosophical Review* for "The Role of Philosophy in a Time of Troubles"; *Philosophy of Science* for "The Scientific Philosophy," which first appeared in *Philosophy of Science* (28, 3: 238–259, 1961); *The Psychological Record* for "An Illustration of Retention Schemata," which first appeared in the January, 1962 issue of *The Psychological Record*; *Rivista di Filosofia* (Italy) for "Ethics of Action," which appeared in its pages in 1958; *Saturday Review* for "The Uses of Thinking"; *The Sewanee Review* for "The Decline of Literary Chaos," which first appeared in Vol. LIV, No. 4, 666–683 of *The Sewanee Review*; *Shenandoah* for "Memories of Sherwood Anderson," which first appeared in the Spring, 1962 issue of *Shenandoah* (Vol. XIII, No. 3); *Sophia* (Italy) for "Reflections after Wittgenstein," which first appeared in *Sophia* (XXIII, 3 and 4, 1955); *Synthese* (Netherlands) for "The Psychology of the Artist"; The Society for the History of Technology for "Pure Science, Applied Science, Technology, Engineering," which first appeared in *Technology and Culture*, Vol. II, No. 4 (1961); and The University of Chicago Press for "The Social Adaptiveness of Philosophy," which appeared in *Ethics* in 1960.

Acknowledgment and thanks are also due the following publishers for permission to reprint the following studies: George Allen & Unwin, Ltd. (London) for "Aristotle's Religion" from *Religious Platonism*; Columbia Broadcasting System, Inc., for "Invitation to Learning" program "Plato's Apology," which appeared in the *CBS 10th Anniversary Series* 2, 2; 3–12, 1950; Duell, Sloan & Pearce for "The Meaning of Tragedy," "The Meaning of Comedy," "The Psychology of the Artist," "The Theory of *Hamlet*" and "The Decline of Literary Chaos" from *Aesthetics*; to Johns Hopkins Press for selections from *Ontology*; Martinus Nijhoff (The Hague) for "An Introduction to Metaphysics for Empiricists," "On the Topics and Definitions of the Categories," "The Ethics of Action," "Culture as Applied Ontology," and "Knowing About Semipalatinsk" from *Foundations of Empiricism*, for "Reflections After Wittgenstein" from *Inside the Great Mirror*, and for "An Explanation of Philosophy" (VII: 35–68, 1958) and "Activity as a Source of Knowledge in American Pragmatism" (XII: 91–105, 1963) from *Tulane Studies in Philosophy*; The National Society for the Study of Education for "An

Ontological Philosophy of Education" from their 54th Yearbook, Part 1, *Modern Philosophies and Education*; Charles C. Thomas, Publisher for "An Illustration of Retention Schemata" from *Biosocial Factors in Mental Illness*; and the University of North Carolina Press for "An Analysis of Liberalism" from *Positive Democracy*.

Contents

THE TWO-STORY WORLD

Introduction

by HUNTINGTON CAIRNS

Cultural independence in the United States was a long time in the making, but in every department except philosophy it has arrived. The arts and sciences are beginning to show the evidence of a vigorous native growth. Philosophy showed it, too, for a brief period in New England toward the end of the last century. But then the native movement died and European influences reasserted themselves. Currently most American philosophers with some notable exceptions are willing and enthusiastic followers of the English school of ordinary language and of existentialism imported from the Continent, while others are positivists who interpret the philosophy of science as the subordination of philosophy to science, also an imported product.

English followers of Wittgenstein now believe that the best that philosophy can hope for is to get rid of some of the philosophical confusions caused by the use of language, and many Americans agree with them. Sartre and Heidegger have their existentialist followers over here. They are sure that philosophy ought to be a way of talking about private anxieties, as though our very existence was a cosmic predicament, and the question asked by Hamlet, "to be or not to be" raised an issue which is still in some doubt.

The success of science has had a great impact upon philosophy. Some American philosophers influenced by the Viennese followers of Wittgenstein, and calling themselves logical positivists or logical empiricists, have reinforced the native tendency to positivism by asking that philosophy confine its efforts to serving as a handmaiden to the sciences, endeavoring only to clarify the meaning of the experimental method and to interpret its results.

In the end the classical kind of comprehensive and systematic philosophy is threatened, and the educated man who is at the same time not a professional looks in vain for philosophers who can cope with the bewildering state of modern knowledge and formulate his position for him in terms which might serve to make it more intelligible and hence also more bearable.

Only the realist tradition has kept the classical philosophy alive. The representatives of realism in the past generation, which comprised some of the most distinguished minds philosophy has known, were Samuel Alexander in England, Nicolai Hartmann in Germany, and Whitehead and Jordan in the United States. Although these men differed in many respects, they were all in the classical tradition in the sense that they were intellectually imaginative in their efforts to understand the world, they put forward complex systems rather than confining themselves to the analysis of special problems. Their philosophies were not entirely new ones; in fact, they were of ancient lineage, but they were not mere restatements. They were influenced by the thought of the preceding centuries and particularly by the scientific disclosures since the seventeenth century.

II

Professor Feibleman is the chief representative in the present generation of the realist point of view. His presuppositions are thoroughly realistic and untainted by irreconcilable elements. His thought is based on a meticulously worked out metaphysical view of the world. He is one of the few contemporary philosophers to apply the realist philosophy to all the major departments of knowledge, and to present it as a complete system. Although his writing has been extensive, his work, like Jordan's before him, has been unduly neglected, almost, in fact, to a scandalous degree. No other philosopher who has written so widely and with the insight of Professor Feibleman has been given such scant attention. But it has been the lot of not a few American philosophers who subsequently took their place on the world scene to suffer the same fate. James had little recognition until he had acquired a reputation in Europe, and Santayana was well along in his career before his merits were seen. Professor Feibleman in large part is a victim of the current repudiation of the main tradition of philosophy. If the broader understanding of philosophy should ever reestablish itself. Professor Feibleman might well wake up one morning to find himself America's leading philosopher.

Professor Feibleman was born in New Orleans in 1904 and has always made that city his home. He was educated in the public schools of New Orleans and Newman High School, at the Horace Mann School in New York, and he attended the University of Virginia for a year. His college career was interrupted by an illness, and upon his recovery, rather than pick it up again, he was drawn, like other isolated American intellectuals, to the Paris of the 1920's. He was not unprepared for the city of Hemingway and Joyce since he was already publishing poetry in the little magazines of the period, and had, with the enthusiasm of youth, identified himself with the new literary movements. With the end of the Paris phase he returned to New Orleans and entered his father's business. As was the case with two or three other provincial American cities at the time, New

Orleans was a small center of literary ferment which found expression in the *Double Dealer*, a periodical which aroused national interest. Professor Feibleman quickly became a member of the circle, and finally withdrew from business to devote himself entirely to writing. Under the influence of Julius Friend, an editor of the *Double Dealer* and his collaborator on his first book, his interests turned to philosophy. Eventually he proceeded to teaching and became a member of the Department of Philosophy at Tulane University. For a number of years he has been chairman of the department.

III

Philosophy purports to explain the world and to account for the things that are in it. In the early days of the twentieth century it was held in some quarters that its principal purposes had been achieved, and that only details remained to be clarified. But of all views ever advanced in philosophy this one had a lifespan of the shortest duration. Even as the opinion was being put forward, philosophy as a division of thought which could lead to knowledge was under attack from two deeply held contemporary beliefs. One was the onslaught upon reason and the substitution of "life," "action," "pure experience," "practical utility," and similar notions as the way to truth. The other was indirect but no less effective. While philosophers talked and reasoned, and seemed to get nowhere, science produced astonishing results which appeared to open new worlds of great imaginative possibilities. The anti-intellectualism of James, Bergson, and others wore itself out with the passage of time mainly because it could not account for the world on the basis of the human situation alone. Science itself was another matter. It was a formidable rival because its results could not be gainsaid. There was an accord among scientists with respect to the validity of their achievements which philosophy could not possibly match. After several millenniums of effort philosophy gave only the appearance of a world of perpetually warring sects, each claiming to be in possession of the truth, but all powerless to persuade the others.

Swift had satirized the same state of affairs in the fable of the spider and the bee when the discoveries of seventeenth-century science were being urgently put forward as the basis for a working view of the world. The spider claimed that he was pre-eminent because of his web, which was symmetrical, geometrical, perfect; moreover, it was all the greater because it was spun out of his own insides. But the bee observed that it was a mere cobweb, the symbol of all that is vain, insubstantial, and in need of being swept away. Its only purpose was to catch flies! As for the bee, he ranged through every corner of nature, and filled his hive with honey and wax, the two noblest of things—sweetness and light.

IV

Realism in Professor Feibleman's hands aims at the construction of a metaphysics which allows for the claims of empirical science. He does not propose to make metaphysics into a science, which is an impossible notion, but simply to utilize the results reached by science when they are illuminating, and, in any event, not to run counter to them. He labels his position realism, or more recently, ontological positivism. The classification of philosophical systems is no more than a device of convenience. They can be classified in accordance with their methods or results, their point of view, the dominance of particular schools at particular times, and in numerous other ways. Professor Feibleman adheres to the traditional division. The problem of universals has been at the center of ancient, medieval, and modern thought. If we say that "the Washington Monument is tall and white" in what sense, if at all, do "tallness" and "whiteness" exist? Professor Feibleman classifies three of the main streams of thought by their attitude toward this problem. He sees idealism as ascribing the highest reality to the realm of universals, as typified by "tallness" and "whiteness," nominalism as denying any reality to them at all and confining it exclusively to singulars, and realism as affirming an equal degree of reality to universals and concrete particulars. That is to say, he would affirm that the Washington Monument, tallness, and whiteness are all equally real. He does not see the doctrine of realism as a compromise, but as a position deeply opposed to both idealism and nominalism.

Professor Feibleman's description of the philosophies to which he is opposed is justified by historical usage and may be mentioned briefly. A defense of idealism would reject his summary and substitute the view that its main tenet was the belief that our ultimate principles are sustained by the nature of the world, a position Professor Feibleman himself would not combat. It was the idea at the core of Plato's and Hegel's thinking, neither of whom held concrete particulars to be illusory. However, not even the nominalists would dispute Professor Feibleman's characterization of them. Their principal stock in trade is the belief that universals are either merely linguistic devices or mental constructs, and in either event have no real existence. Neither argument need delay us. If words and sentences are not completely meaningless they refer to something beyond themselves, and the problem remains to determine the nature of the referent. The argument that universals are merely mental was answered by Berkeley who showed that they cannot be in the mind since our ideas are never universal but always particular. The idea of man that we frame for ourselves must be always of a particular man—white or black, straight or crooked, tall, short, or middle-sized. We cannot form an image of a man which both includes and excludes all the special traits of actual men.

Professor Feibleman has probably given more attention to the nature of universals than any other contemporary philosopher; certainly he has written more about them. He accepts Aristotle's conception that essentially they are that which may be predicated of many subjects. He is also in accord with the Platonic position that it is impossible to account for the actual world except on the basis of their objective reality. It is not possible to explain the applicability of scientific laws if we deny that the relations which exist between external objects are subjective concepts or verbal fictions. Beyond that he sees them as finite in number; as not belonging to a suprasensible world such as the mind of God, but as a part of the existing world in which the basic laws of logic are operative; as recurrent; as general; and as capable of actual illustration. By this he means that if we look at two brown tables we see their brownness, which belongs to each of them separately, but in addition, we also see their similarity, a quality we could not perceive if we were looking at just one table.

To the nominalist the problem of the reality of universals seems at best a verbal quarrel, but the issue is of great moment. If universals are real they permit us to make sense of the laws of science and the principles of mathematics and logic, rather than dismiss them as verbal fictions which explain nothing, and which fail utterly to account for the fact that they are applicable to the world of actual objects, which is the only real world the nominalist recognizes. Their reality also allows us to attempt to develop a rational ethics, aesthetics, and a system of social relations. The contention that they are not real leaves us in those fields completely at the mercy of the arbitrary. Except as a matter of opinion, no conduct can be pronounced good or bad, no poem or painting important, and no system of government preferable to any other. Any standards suggested by nominalism as a measure for such situations necessarily involve the use of universals, and hence by its logic is without real significance.

V

Professor Feibleman stresses the fact that his philosophy is finite and tentative. His purpose is to expunge from philosophy the absolutes and the ineffability which have marred a great deal of philosophic speculation.

The notion of a finite philosophy contracts the field of philosophy and minimizes the risk of neglecting the importance of the particular. It also preserves the basic laws of logic which lose significance in the realm of infinite being where contradiction is not excluded. All these matters are clear gains in the slow search for truth. In addition, Professor Feibleman suggests that there are few, if any, notions in philosophy which demand the idea of infinity to sustain them; there seem to be none which cannot be explained in terms of the finite.

From this point of view Professor Feibleman has set about the construction of an elaborate philosophical system. It is not yet complete in all applications in which he intends to exhibit it, but its theoretical basis is fully developed in its essentials. Its aim is the aim of all such systems, namely, to give a full understanding of reality, but there is an optimism about Professor Feibleman's approach reminiscent of the fruitful stirrings of American thought in the nineteenth century. "Given all the theories and facts of modern knowledge," he writes, the problem is "to find the explanatory system which could best account for them." This means that science, philosophy, poetry, history, religion, and the social sciences must all be brought together in an harmonious whole. It means also that the primary ideas of his system must be of the widest generality. A philosophy constructed on the nineteenth-century physical notions of matter, causality, space, and time could not accomplish this end. Hobbes thought that if he were given space and motion he could make the world, but he was mistaken. Ideas in science do not possess the necessary generality to serve as starting points for a comprehensive philosophical system, and a philosophic undertaking to develop such a system must perforce turn to the philosophical domain itself for fundamental conceptions.

Although Plato and Peirce have been two of the chief influences on Professor Feibleman's thinking, he has not followed their examples in his own approach to philosophy. Neither thinker put forward their thoughts in a systematic form. Plato had a clearly worked out view of the world which he wanted to communicate to his readers. He attempted by many devices, from the severely logical to poetry and myth, to lead the reader to see what he saw. Peirce threw out many reflections and suggestions on a large variety of subjects, but he never welded them together in an integrated whole. The ideas of both men can be detached in a summary, systematic manner from their writings, and Professor Feibleman himself has undertaken the task with great success in the case of Peirce; but this is far short of Professor Feibleman's conception of a systematic philosophy. He lays considerable stress upon the importance of the conception, for its significance is not self-evident. The efficaciousness of the construction of systems of philosophy has been doubted many times in the history of philosophy, notwithstanding notable attempts in that direction. If Plato was correct in his view that philosophy is primarily an act of seeing, a function of a level of intelligence, it is problematic that that vision can be conveyed in the propositions of philosophy alone. It needs the support of poetry and myth to be fully understood.

Professor Feibleman bases his system on three ideas: essence, existence, and destiny. He holds that in combination they are extensive enough to embrace the world and all that it contains. They stand for ancient philosophical ideas, but in each case their meaning has been modified and defined to meet the requirements of Professor Feibleman's own thought. Essences are ideals or possibilities, and are associated generally with Plato's Ideas. They are neither in space nor in time, and values as well as universals are part of their realm. Thus to ask, as nominalism does, where "circularity" or "goodness" is located is to raise a meaningless question. Essences are not things which are physically present in space but predicates of things and relations between them. Existence is the world of nature, of actual objects; it is in time and space. It is the circle we draw on a piece of paper, which is never exactly a circle, and hence is never circularity which is always perfect. Destiny is purpose, or in the modern term, "process." At bottom, though again with modifications, it is the classical doctrine of teleology. It is the movement of actual objects toward their possibilities.

Essence and existence are interwoven. While the latter depends upon the former for its contents, the former depends upon the latter for its effects. They share the same degree of reality. For this reason Professor Feibleman thinks of his philosophy as a two-storied world. Destiny, while as real as essence and existence, is not on a parity with them. Strictly it is a part of existence, and relates existence and essence. In less technical language Professor Feibleman is in accord with classical thought which holds that the things which have their being in time and space are partly the product of fixed laws. It is important to note that this two-storied world is a universe of realms or domains. He holds that all the world's furniture can be fitted into two rooms, one above the other, with a doorway between, and the task of his philosophy is to examine the characteristics of the various pieces of furniture in their proper setting. His method is thus classificatory and hypothetico-deductive. It differs in kind from a system such as Herbert Spencer's which, while abounding in classifications, finds the clue to all the phenomena of the world in one explanatory principle.

His view of the purpose of science, to which he has given a great deal of attention, and which is highly sophisticated, is to present us with complete knowledge of the empirical world. Its ideal is a full account of the physical world, the organism, and other elements. Philosophically he holds that science is based on the belief that the external world consists of natural phenomena which contain both uniformities and non-uniformities (chance, chaos, disorder), and that natural phenomena are approachable from different levels of analysis. The scientific discoveries of the twentieth century have inevitably had an impact upon his thought, and they are allowed for, but do not control it. His approach to science is through realism, not the other way around. Thus he avoids the mistake made by some scientifically minded philosophers of basing a system of philosophy on a generalization of an ephemeral scientific conception.

Ever since Aristotle, men have thought that the world is structured in levels. Its unity comes from the way these are fitted together, a continuum marked by inanimate matter, plants, animals, and finally men. What Lovejoy later called "the great chain of being" runs, Aristotle supposed, from the smallest species to the largest genus, from the smallest population of classifiable objects to the largest class having any members. Professor Feibleman has seen that this classification is continued in the hierarchy of the sciences, from the physical through the chemical and the biological to the social or cultural. It is, he thinks, the task of the experimental sciences to determine these classes and what belongs in them. We no longer guess at what constitutes classes and their members, we investigate them in the laboratory of the experimental scientist.

With the idea of the two-storied world as a ground plan Professor Feibleman has proceeded in several volumes to construct a philosophical system. His aim is ccmpleteness as well as consistency, and most of the major philosophical topics are accounted for without violence to their usual significance. He has, however, gone further, and also attempted to show the meaning of man's major activities when interpreted in the light of such a philosophy. This has taken him into the fields of ethics, art, religion, science, education, and human culture. The primary business of philosophy is at the theoretic level, and some philosophers are content to confine themselves to that sphere. Others, like Dewey, think of philosophy as a method of correcting specific social ills. Professor Feibleman's position is somewhere in between. His aim is to exhibit the philosophical assumptions which underlie man's major activities and the consequences which flow from the adoption of explicit or implicit premises. Although he has strong views on the nature of the good society, he is not a social reformer. His primary concern is the search for truth, and he eschews partisanship as anathema. The patient seeker after understanding cannot but fail to have his views distorted if he ventures into the fierce combativeness of the marketplace. Professor Feibleman has also extended the application of his philosophy to the individual himself. He holds the view that the man who has developed a consistent and well-grounded philosophy for himself will have a better understanding of everyday affairs and a richer life than otherwise. This is an ancient dream of philosophy, and a sound one, but we should not mislead ourselves into believing that it is possible of realization in all periods in the world's history.

VI

Professor Feibleman thinks of human culture as the set of ideas held by the members of a social group and utilized by them through tools, folkways, and institutions. He employs the phrase "implicit dominant ontology" to describe this set of ideas. Thus, he holds that idealism was the superior philosophy of the Middle Ages in Europe, in Professor Feibleman's conception of idealism, the superiority of the realm of essence to actual existence. The Church was the leading institution, and it regarded such values as heaven and the immortal soul as of greater importance than the more mundane values. In Soviet Russia the State emphasizes the means of production, the class struggle, and the values of the proletariat. This is an instance of nominalism, or the superiority of the realm of existence to that of essence. He sees the culture of the United States also as nominalistic with its emphasis on production, distribution, and consumption. One important effect of this philosophy has been to inhibit theoretical thinking and to stress the virtues of the practical. He holds the ideal goal of human life to be what he calls the natural society. This is a society capable of enduring great strains without breaking, and of consolidating gains with no loss of achieved advantages.

Culture belongs to the realm of destiny, which is to say that its principle is purpose. He sees society as a whole, the function of whose parts is the attainment of an end. In a natural or rational society the end will be a good, and the individual will have his role in the attainment of that purpose. His conduct will be guided by the rules of the plan, but they will not be oppressive. His individuality will be fostered rather than minimized because his behavior will be instructed by rational standards. Professor Feibleman's idea of destiny thus stresses the true character of social thought. At various levels it is many things—classificatory, analytical, descriptive—but ultimately it is purposive. Its final task at maturity is the statement of rational ideals achievable at least to some degree by human beings. It is this special quality of social thought which gives it its full significance. But Professor Feibleman's approach has still to meet the test of the great problems which have defied solution since the beginning of western thought. What form will the State assume in the two-storied world? On what basis will its laws be framed? How will its economic and social life be organized? In brief, is it possible to move from the high level of the two-storied world to an actual working drawing of the details of the natural society? Inasmuch as Professor Feibleman's method is both theoretical and empirical there is no logical impediment to the accomplishment of the task. That he is already contemplating its fulfillment is evident from his announcement in 1962 of a projected series of volumes which will bring his system to completion.

Culture is the subject matter of sociology, but a prime difficulty is the choice of the significant component whose analysis will lead to an understanding of the whole. Professor Feibleman holds that it is the institution, that is to say, a human group within a society organized for a common purpose, such as the family, corporations, the state, and at a higher level, the sciences, the arts, philosophy, and religion. Nominalism would have dictated the individual as the cultural isolate, with its corollary that all social organization is fictional, and idealism would have insisted upon the superior reality of society. The ultimate purpose of institutions is to aid human beings in the achievement of their ends, but with a minimum of encroachment on the part of the institution itself. The limiting qualification is plainly an ideal postulate, since institutions such as the state and religion do in fact intrude. Institutions have a career akin to the life cycle. They have an origin, they grow, and they decline. They are born from the development of the attempts to satisfy what Professor Feibleman describes as basic organic needs—hunger and thirst, sex, and curiosity. They grow in response to the abilities of the managers. They disappear when they are no longer able to meet needs and exist merely as obstacles. They flourish to the extent they propose answers; they start downward to the degree they defend an answer. At the conclusion of his carefully worked out and acute study he sees the fundamental problem of social thought as the reconciliation of consistency and completeness in a society. A consistent society is one in which the leading institution does not dominate but merely regulates; its mild control permits other institutions to make their own contributions to the whole culture. A complete society allows for the richness of difference. A fully consistent society ends in totalitarianism; a complete society, with no controlling institutions, in anarchy. He sees philosophy as assisting in the solution of this dilemma, but always tentatively and with provision for continual improvement.

VII

The goals for improvement in a society are spelled out by its notions of the good and the beautiful. Professor Feibleman believes that these values are not adjuncts to being, not chapters written in order to complete a philosophy, but indispensable parts of reality. Being is either quantitative (logic) or qualitative (ethics and aesthetics). Reality for him is structured of wholes and parts. The beautiful, then, is the bond between parts in any whole, and the good is the bond between wholes. Thus any segment of being must have its ethical as well as its aesthetic aspect. The way in which everything in the world is bonded together, he thinks, is its ethical aspect. Thus when we speak of the good we are not confined to human values, but we are primarily concerned with them because we are human. It is true also that the bonds are strongest between the members of any given type. The satisfaction of the organic needs of the individual must be conditioned by their social effects. In this way we find among humans a variety of type responsibility. The attraction between individuals is partly at least the result of their interdependence.

If the good is what is needed, then according to Professor Feibleman there is more good involved when the bond is symmetrical, when what a man needs, for instance, also needs him. This is not the case when he wishes to eat lamb chops but it is the case when he needs a friend. There are socially-approved ways of accomplishing need-reduction, and what is approved and what is not forms the content of the individual conscience. Thus the type responsibility gets broken down still further to the members of a given society or culture. The ordinary life of the individual, however, does not ever find him in direct contact with his entire society but only with some of the members of it. By sharing their morality with them, he meets them as though he and they represented the whole of society. And so he conducts himself always in consideration of all others, and this defines what in the society is considered good behavior. There may be some departure from this, either in the direction of egotism and the individual's more narrow interests, or in the direction of a wider membership in the human species or, even wider still, in the cosmos.

VIII

Plato's philosophy could accommodate the view that art was a striving toward the universal or the ideal, but it was Aristotle who made it explicit in a famous sentence when he said that poetry is more true than history. But the explanation of art as an effort to get from the world of actuality to the realm of possibilities is met by the view that the place of art is in the visible world. The function of the artist is not to depict the invisible by means of the visible, but to confine himself to what he sees. But in recent times the notion of representative art has been enlarged to include the position that the artist may turn his eye inward and report the state of his own feelings and unconscious. Professor Feibleman's philosophical realism necessarily places him in the classic tradition. The special nature of art is its harmony or beauty, which is achieved when there is a perfect relationship of part to whole. Beauty is a universal and belongs in the realm of essence. But it is even more than that. Absolute beauty is the total beauty of the whole universe of essence. Thus, the work of art is to be taken as a symbol of the absolute perfection of all being.

While this abstract discussion is conducted at the level of aesthetic theory generally, it is fully capable of application to such concrete subjects as present-day art. There are indications that nonobjective art is already in a process of change, and Professor Feibleman raises the legitimate question of the nature of its successor. Apart from being nonrepresentational, he thinks that nonobjective art has two characteristics: a canvas can be understood at once as an immediate whole, and the painter's attention has been directed more to space than to form. The classical masters had been concerned with objects separated by space, the nonobjective painter is intent on the occupancy of space. For the objects of traditional painting he has substituted colored shapes and has thus achieved an extreme generality. But there is more to the world than generality, there is also concreteness. Professor Feibleman thinks that nonobjective art has about exhausted its possibilities in the direction of generality and must therefore return to some form of concreteness. He thinks it will combine the skills of the old masters with the unitary and spatial discoveries of the nonobjectivists. It will also go further. It will restore the concrete object to the canvas, but it will be the object known to contemporary physics; that is to say, it will be porous and extremely complex. The new painter will thus explore neither the space which separates objects, nor the occupancy of space, but the space within objects. That a step has already been taken in this direction is evident from the sculptures of Lipchitz and Henry Moore which attempt to reveal the interiors of solid bodies.

Equally suggestive is Professor Feibleman's theory of tragedy. Again, it takes its departure from the realms of essence and existence. He thinks of tragedy as presenting itself as the imposition of wills and the exertion of effort rather than as principles or laws. Its special characteristic is its transient nature. But in the values which it presents, such as justice, it recognizes the world of ideals, and attempts to weave the two realms together. He sees this conception exemplified in the Greek cycle of success, hubris, nemesis, and ruin. There is first the hero's assumption that success has come to him because of his own perfection. The next step is defiance of the Gods which in turn sets in motion nemesis, or the restrictive justice of the natural order of things. Ruin is the outcome. "Thus tragedy," Professor Feibleman writes, "is the defeat following hard upon the false assumption that all which is possible is also actual, that perfection not only can be attained but has been reached." In a long and penetrating study he has applied this theory to the interpretation of Hamlet whose tragedy he sees as a failure to reconcile the world of perfection and the world of imperfection and conflict. Through his obstinate allegiance to perfection he will not make sufficient allowance for the force of actuality, and thus loses control of events, and in the end becomes their complete victim.

Comedy recognizes an ideal logical order by belittling actuality either through ridicule or confusion. Hemingway's satire in *The Torrents of Spring* is an example of the first method. "Do come home, dear," Diana says to Scripps. "There's a new *Mercury* with a wonderful editorial in it by Mencken about chiropractors." Would that do it, she wondered. Scripps looked away. "No, I don't give a damn about Mencken any more," he replied. T. E. Lawrence used the second method in replying to a proofreader's query with respect to his confused use of Arab names in *The Seven Pillars of Wisdom*: "There are some 'scientific systems' of transliteration, helpful to people who know enough Arabic not to need helping, but a wash-out for the world. I spell my names anyhow, to show what rot the systems are." There are numerous theories of comedy, but Professor Feibleman has given us perhaps the only systematic, historical, and analytical study of the subject.

IX

Modern realism, as in the systems of Alexander and Whitehead, has paid a great deal of attention to religion, and Professor Feibleman has also written extensively upon the subject. The great realist philosophers, who were still under the influence of nineteenth-century evolutionary thought, saw God as still in a state of becoming, a Being who had not yet realized his perfection. Professor Feibleman's God is the universe of all universes. He embraces both essence and existence. God is the reason for the world, and man's path to Him is through nature; but He cannot be a part of the world since the unity of the world is not one of its parts. Professor Feibleman holds that his theology does not amount to pantheism since nature is not identified with God but only with His appearances, and the world itself only with His works.

Religion in Professor Feibleman's philosophy is applied theology. It is concerned with concrete problems which do not fall immediately within the field of theology, such as the destiny of man, his freedom and immortality, and the social organization of the church. "Religion is an emergency," he writes, "in which one should keep quite calm and not allow oneself to get excited." He has written a highly personal and notable volume on the attributes that realism demands of religion. At bottom such a religion is fallibilistic, and some of its tenets would be "no dogma but fallibilism," "no feeling but humility," "no rules but safeguards," "no beliefs but inquiry." He suggests that it would be a church of the unlimited community with the figure of Socrates typifying its savior.

The general tendency of American religious thought to culminate in a humanistic ethics has been a matter of reproach, for the problems of the philosophy of religion are held to be at a deeper level, the importance of which is recognized in European thought. But the upheaval of the war, and the consequent appearance of some distinguished European thinkers on American shores, has considerably altered this picture. There is now an attempt in the United States to work out the meaning of religion in terms of metaphysical ideas, and also an effort to meet the challenge of the new philosophies of logical positivism, ordinary language, and existentialism. Professor Feibleman has only recently begun to grapple with the problems. His approach so far has been through the new theories of the composition of matter. He argues that the old materialism required God as the cause of matter and its properties, as Hobbes, La Mettrie, and Descartes recognized, and that the conception of matter as developed by the new physics does not change this situation. Inasmuch as matter is everywhere the same, God cannot be the exclusive property of any one religion. "God must," he writes, "be at the very least an object corresponding to a truth which is unaffiliated." The root ideas here seem close to Spinoza's understanding of God as the whole system of nature. Professor Feibleman's contribution is to show that modern physics has not done away with the necessity of such a conception.

X

These are the main positions of Professor Feibleman's system of thought, and it is evident that we have here a philosophy in the classical tradition and in the grand manner. When the system is completely written out it will be unique in American thought for the extensiveness of its range; only Santayana's writings approach it in this respect. Until recent days the main effort of philosophy in the West has been to give an understanding of the world and to develop a rational set of political and ethical values grounded to the extent possible on that understanding. Modern philosophy has left that track, and is lost in the endless maze of epistemology and the severely logical analysis of categories. Professor Feibleman's philosophy, while it does not neglect such matters, is a major attempt to return philosophy once again to its main course.

I

AN APPROACH TO PHILOSOPHY

AN EXPLANATION OF PHILOSOPHY

1. WHAT IS PHILOSOPHY?

To most people these days philosophy is a vague term with an uncertain meaning, having good though somewhat old-fashioned overtones but too confused, too irrelevant, and too mental, to be taken seriously. When not subordinated to religion, philosophy is thought to have become a merely academic subject, and finally science seems to have rendered it altogether unnecessary.

If such an answer is justified, then why are there still philosophers, why do men still write and teach philosophy? Are they merely foolish fellows who do not know that they are occupied with a dead field? Why is it that the physicists who were responsible for the revolution in physics all wrote philosophy; why is it that the classics in philosophy are so popular with the general reading public; why it is that as an academic subject philosophy is flourishing mightily?

Perhaps the last place to look for our answer is among the philosophers themselves, for they have no established opinions. It will have to be admitted that no statement could be made about philosophy that would be agreed upon by all philosophers, including this statement. Philosophers are seldom in accord, and this fact is well known; but what is not so well known is that this same situation can be found to hold also in many other broad human enterprises: in politics, in religion and in art, for example. Different types of government, rival religions, and various movements in art, have hardly been admired for their universal harmony. It is only in industry that cartels are formed, but the aim of business which is to make money is simple and plain, and anything but pretentious. The rule seems to be that the more fundamental the inquiry the more absolute its results; and the more speculative the question the more disastrous the practical application of the answer. Many disinterested persons have died miserable deaths in the attempt to throw open to controversy a problem regarded as settled. Have there been any wars worse than the wars of religion, say the wars between Roman Catholic and Protestant in sixteenth-century Europe, or between Moslem and Hindu in our own day?

Look at the divergence in philosophies which is current at this very moment. On the continent of Europe, existentialism is the fashion and existentialism asserts that "being" means "being unwell," in various degrees from visceral nausea to emotional anguish depending upon its advocates, with a resolution that the accompanying inability to face the making of choices should be cherished. In Soviet Russia, dialectical materialism is official, and philosophy as a consequence is founded upon the belief that all matter vacillates like reasoning and that therefore those who do the most material labor should rise to the top of society, preferably by violent means. In England and the United States, positivism is fashionable, and positivism recommends that all philosophy consists in pointing with pride to what the scientists do and otherwise in attacking metaphysics as so much nonsense. In the Roman Catholic Church, the philosophy of Aquinas is official doctrine, and it consists in reconciling with the combination of Plotinus and Christian revelation the newly recovered Aristotle of the thirteenth century, just as had been done for Islam by Averroes and for Judaism by Maimonides not many years earlier. In academic circles, philosophy is thought to consist in being grateful that when the history of philosophy accumulated and so provided a respectable profession for teachers, it incorporated the work of many men who wrote so ambiguously that constant reinterpretation is required. It should be added, perhaps, that each of these philosophies except the last has a rider which asserts that all other philosophies ought to be prohibited, or, if that is not enough, then that their advocates should be persecuted.

Admittedly, such one-sentence characterizations of contemporary philosophical positions are wholly inadequate, and are such as their adversaries might have given. Yet it is true that each philosophy always has all others as its opponents. The description is to some extent a caricature, but perhaps like caricatures brings out some of the more prominent and also more irritating features of the original. The intention, however, is to point to the extent of the divergence, for each of these philosophies has an enormous number of living adherents even though they have little else in common. Philosophy is a curious undertaking, and more striking when more closely inspected.

The philosophies described are those which have been advocated by the largest and most successful of institutions or which have won adherents by being the most admired. There are others of lesser fame which deserve at least a mention; for instance, American pragmatism which insists despite the best intentions of its founder that philosophy amounts to nothing except what it can lead us to do in a practical way. Many great philosophies of the past have sincere contemporary advocates who think that the best we can do is to bring their masters up to date. Plato, Aristotle, Spinoza, Kant and Hegel are among the favorites, but they are by no means the only ones. Serious philosophy ends somewhere after this, but the catalogue of philosophies includes much that is suspect or frowned on, and degenerates into personal attitudes and mystic cults, for each of these can count on some enthusiasts. The man who is not a success in the hurly-burly world is recommended to retire to the privacy of his study and there to take his defeat "philosophically," thus disclosing an understanding of philosophy as some sort of private consolation for public failure. An organization calling itself the Society of Master Metaphysicians existed some years ago in Philadelphia but was closed by the police for keeping the dead body of a girl, who had been a member, in the living room of a home until the neighbors complained.

Such a quick survey of the philosophical scene is quite sufficient to show what the chances are that any concert of opinion concerning the nature of philosophy could be reached. On the best interpretation it can be found that what Mr. Brown will allow (no matter who Mr. Brown is) is that what Mr. Blue is saying is after all only the Brownian philosophy bluedly—and hence confusedly—stated, inasmuch as the Brownian philosophy is the widest and truest that there could possibly be; and to this of course we could never get Mr. Blue to assent. Evidently, the broader the enterprise the less easy to define or even describe with any precision. As much difficulty would be encountered in the effort to define religion so that all religions could be included, and, though this is not so well understood, the same difficulties would arise in the definition of science. It would seem that the more universal the institution the less are we able to set limits for it or to put our fingers on precisely what it means.

The truth about philosophy is not easy to come by; for certainly if it were, men are not so arbitrarily obstinate that they would continue to disagree to the extent to which they have disagreed and still do. Those who are convinced that the truths they have discovered are not half-truths but the whole of truth are driven to such vociferous lengths as the imposition of their opinions by force; yet they would not have to do this if the evidence itself were compelling. But the failure of philosophers to agree has its good side, for one of the tasks of philosophy is the exploration of the field in which such opinions are relevant. We shall arrive at the truth sooner if we know what truth means, and we could find the true philosophy if we were able to look out for all the false ones. Perhaps this last task is endless and the truth impossible to approach through trial-and-error: a systematic survey of an infinite number of instances is by its very logic impossible. To conduct a survey, moreover, is not the sole task of philosophy though it is one. The more urgent requirement is that life, individual and social, hardly can be conducted except on a basis of some consistency, and consistency means applied (some would say implied) philosophy.

It is a paradox that abstract studies often make their greatest advances in those periods when they are supposed by their professional advocates to be utterly useless. Physics and mathematics were not cultivated for their practical value, nor brought to the pitch they reached by men eager to be of social service. The same can be said of philosophy. Evidently, the kind of intense and prolonged preoccupation that progress in such fields requires is possible only on the assumption that their applications do not exist. In this way are produced the theories which have the greatest concrete advantage. But the pendulum has swung so far that even the teachers of philosophy can think of no value that philosophy can be to men of affairs. And here they are wrong, as the study of the effects of the history of philosophy and the subject-matter of the philosophy of culture could tell them. If indeed there was no more to philosophy than its textbooks and its classrooms, the ambitious students were well advised to stay far away from it. But this is not the case.

Under such baffling circumstances what, then, are we to say that philosophy is? It might be obvious supererogation to say anything. And yet the same urge that leads a man to become a philosopher must drive him to assert his own interpretation of philosophy. The preferred opinion is that what philosophy ought to be (though what it has been on only the rarest of occasions, perhaps solely in Socrates' day) is an enterprise to lead all those who suffer from philosophical opinion so confirmed that they would impose it as the absolute truth upon their neighbors, into the more passive and safe channels of unsettled speculation.

Philosophy has been engaged in freely only by the ancient Greeks, who may have invented it, and not again until our own times. Otherwise it has been the slave of other institutions, religions chiefly. Al-Ghazzali, who wrote the *Destruction of the Philosophers,* succeeded in having it officially abolished. But three centuries later he was followed by Averroes, one of the greatest if not the greatest of Muslim philosophers. Philosophy has shown a toughness and a persistence which indicates the presence of something powerful. It is now threatened again, this time by the philosophers themselves, who wish to subordinate it to science. We would do well to put the analysis of the question of what philosophy is ahead of the statement of any attempted answer. Perhaps philosophy at its best is the method whereby we persuade both ourselves and others that in such fundamental matters the analysis of questions is to be preferred to the imposition of answers.

2. AN ANALYSIS OF THE QUESTION

The analysis of the question, what is philosophy? can be made in as many different ways as there might be answers proposed for it. Each philosopher, however, brings to his task something of the same ambition and equipment, and, if he is successful, achieves a similar result. Let us begin by looking quickly at what this approach means.

There is perhaps no one living who does not feel about life in addition to much fulfillment some inadequacy. Every comparison of similar things suggests some imperfection: deer run faster than we can, sunny days are better for plants than cloudy ones, some men survive much longer than others and are healthier. For some imperfections our efforts have been helpful; we have improved farm breeds, we have altered our environment in our own favor, we have learned to extend the span of human life. But many more difficulties remain, not only with our environment but also with our outlook. Individual desires frequently clash; the actions of many of us, if not of all, are in conflict, and we ourselves are among the imperfections. Between individuals lying, cheating and even murder, are common enough, and broader social conflicts are even worse, for war is still employed as a means of settling disputes.

All around us, then, and also within us there is that sense of imperfection, of limitation, of problems settled without the use of reason and often even in disregard of the facts. When we are able for a moment to get some distance between us and the immediate crisis, whatever it may be, we are able to see that our behavior and perhaps also the behavior of our contemporaries both individually and socially has been to some extent a piecemeal affair. We can note then that our actions and theirs are to a large measure self-defeating. But somehow there must be an understanding of the whole of existence into which the separate parts fit and can find themselves, if only we were able to grasp existence as a whole. At least we do see the old primitive questions, "why are we here?" and "what should we do?" as separate and subordinate parts of a much larger question, "what is there?"

The resultant enterprise is the one we call philosophy. It consists in the attempt to fit the various parts of our activity together into a meaningful set by way of an understanding of the whole. And it tends to see this whole in terms of perfection. Philosophy begins with a prejudice, a prejudice in favor of the excellent, the detached, the ultimate. The ambition of philosophy is understanding.

It might be objected that understanding is not confined to philosophy and that therefore it cannot be used as the equivalent of philosophy. After all, has not religion sought understanding as well, and has not art done so, and science, and even common sense? The list of enterprises which have understanding as their aim is even wider than those we have listed. Every practical undertaking, such as engineering, and political or economic systems, has sought for an understanding, too; and so even have such humbler technologies as cooking and farming.

The objection is sustained, and may help us in our exposition. Philosophy is both a separate and a collective attempt at understanding. For it consists in the presuppositions with which each of these manifold enterprises begin. That such presuppositions may be silent and unacknowledged makes no difference to their existence or their presence. Philosophy exists separately in every other enterprise also as the structure of its method. Every enterprise has some consistent method, and that method can be revealed by means of the analysis of its logic. Finally, every enterprise has conclusions which stand in need of interpretation, and philosophy can often furnish that interpretation. Thus philosophy, implicit or explicit, exists at the beginning of an enterprise as its presuppositions, is present during its workings as the logical structure of its method, and finally is required by its interpretation.

Such a claim could stand examples. Let us choose for this purpose one of the more ambitious enterprises and one of the humbler.

The ambitious one could well be that of religion. Religion usually begins with the insights of some individual, who may or may not claim divine revelation for his utterances. But no religion can secure the allegiance of many persons without becoming established as an institution. And to do so it must adopt a philosophy, either openly or in some unpromulgated fashion. The consequent theology has its presuppositions, its method and its conclusions. And if these are to be respectively defended, deepened and interpreted, considerable philosophical acumen is required.

Suppose we take as one of the less ambitious enterprises a code of law as adopted in some country. Chaos and confusion, social disaster, result if the law is abandoned and no other substituted; so it is necessary to social order, and is vigorously defended; it is, in other words, established. But is it all that a law ought to be? On what does it rest? How does it work? What can we conclude as to its meaning? These are the same questions we have been asking, and their answers call for considerable philosophy.

Thus in the separate instances of enterprises other than philosophy which seek understanding, philosophy is implicitly involved and explicitly needed. But this is not all that there is to philosophy. For this is merely philosophy in the service of other enterprises; what about philosophy itself as an enterprise? We have asserted already that philosophy is both a separate and a collective attempt at understanding. Let us see what each of these means.

Philosophy engages in criticism and in system-building. It is the critic of presuppositions. Presuppositions although first in systems are still part of systems. When they are included within systems, we call them axioms. The history of the opinions regarding the status of axioms would make an interesting book. The Greeks held them to be self-evidently true, and supposed that every axiom carried on the face of it, in addition to whatever else it asserted, the assertion of its own truth, and was thus two assertions rather than one. Modern philosophy has decided that truth is irrelevant to axioms, and that we have no way of knowing and little reason for caring whether they are true or not. What we do care about is the validity and applicability of the deductions from them.

This judgment too may be changed in time. For if the axioms are not true and we make valid deductions from them and then apply those deductions, must not our applications eventually fail? A popular argument of the nineteen twenties was that because Mussolini had the trains running on time in Italy, fascism worked; but it was not many years before he ended hanging by his heels, and fascism lay in ruins. Democracy, it seems, has worked for longer. Application is not a final proof of the truth of principles, only a strong argument in favor of them; but we must be sure that we have given application a long enough run of instances to enable it to work itself out somewhat. But it seems clear that if we apply principles many times and under diverse conditions successfully, does this not argue something for the truth of the axioms from which such highly applicable principles were deduced? In any case, philosophy is heavily involved with the axioms and with the question of truth.

The axioms of any enterprise in addition to being considered inside that enterprise, as we have been doing, may be considered also outside it. We may suppose that the axioms were themselves deductions from some more abstract system, and then seek the outlines of such a system. We may look, in other words, in the direction of ultimate axioms. At this point our argument is joined by two other considerations. Is there such a thing as an ultimate set of axioms which can lead by deduction to all of the axioms that we know from other enterprises? And does all philosophy have a single set of axioms? Finally, are these axiom-sets one and the same?

The last few problems are not easy of solution, perhaps they are even incapable of it; certainly even as problems they are not quite so simple as they have been stated. But something definitely lies in that direction, and that is why philosophy at times seems to be so simple: it is seeking for an ultimate simplicity, one that has no assumptions of its own because it underlies all other assumptions. Philosophy as the critic of pre-suppositions finally has its work cut out for it.

Philosophy is not only critical but engages also in system-building. It must put together the findings of all other enterprises by means of equipment especially designed for this purpose, and in this way seek for a general understanding. It must make up a whole explanation out of parts such that the explanation in any other enterprise or undertaking would be some part of it. Obviously, such a task, like the other, is complex and endless. Something lies in this direction, too, but far away and difficult of access. What do science and art have to do with each other? To find the answer to this question, it would be necessary first to have a precise understanding of what both science and art are, and then to posit some very much larger structure in which they were parts among many others. It is as though a man were to have in one hand the faucet of a washstand and in the other a tile from a roof. Could he from such elements ever imagine the form and function of a house? And yet that may be the task of philosophy: impossible on the face of it, and yet demanding of at least a surmise. For if we have not the equipment to make answers to such questions, it is also true that we lack the ability to refrain from asking them.

It is true of all vigorous periods such as our own when many things are being changed—the sciences proliferating at a fantastic rate, religions being revived and reconditioned, the arts putting forth their claims to existence in fresh ways—that the individual whose most urgent task is the gaining of a living may feel intensely the need to understand even what he does not know. For him at present all lines go away from the center: sex for the Freudian competes with cash for the Marxist and revelation for the Christian as the sole explanation and cause of events; and the politician, the priest and many others separately claim exclusive ascendency over him. What is he to think about things in such a world? He can keep busy and try to put aside the question, but when he does so he suppresses a craving to know how things are, which is as fundamental as his other cravings to eat and to love.

3. WHAT DOES PHILOSOPHY TRY TO DO?

So much for the ambition of philosophy; and when we try to analyze the question, "what is philosophy?" we have seen that we must include first and foremost its aims: what does it try to do? Now we must turn to the second portion of our analysis of the question, and ask ourselves, in what way does philosophy try to achieve its aims, what equipment does it bring to its task?

Every enterprise has its own technical tools, including in most cases its own special vocabulary, and philosophy is no exception to this rule. Here is where one of the most prevalent difficulties comes in. For no one would try to understand mathematical physics or biochemistry without some special training, yet everyone feels quite sure that any philosophy which is not readily available to the average educated person is somehow inadequate: it must be wanting in something as a philosophy or be badly written. The average man blames himself for his failure to understand physics, but he blames philosophy for his failure to understand philosophy. And yet philosophy is no less technical than physics or any other special branch of learning.

Philosophy is divided into a number of special areas, technical divisions for which there are names. Among these are: logic, metaphysics, epistemology, ethics and aesthetics. Every comprehensive philosophy contains all five divisions or branches, but most favor some one over the others. It will be best perhaps to glance separately at each of these.

Logic is the theory of abstract systems. These are usually approached deductively, though there are other approaches which would have to be included, such as the inductive. A system is a structure in which some propositions follow of necessity from others. The extent to which this demand is met is the measure of their consistency, and the number of such propositions—their inclusiveness—is a measure of the system's completeness. A good example is mathematics. Indeed mathematics has been described as "all abstract deductive systems." The terms in which such propositions are framed are usually those invented for the purpose and therefore have no second meaning which could lead to confusion. But logic has been traditionally worked in ordinary language and of course to some extent still can be done in that way. Logic leads to mathematics, but that is not the only application. Applied logic leads also to any orderly or systematic material.

One important area in which applied logic can be of great service is human reasoning. Logical reasoning is of course correct thinking. In the nineteenth century, logic and reasoning were regarded as so intimately connected that logic was supposed to have been derived from reasoning, and was called the laws of thought; but more recently we have returned to the view held by the ancient Greeks, according to which reasoning is only one place where logic can be applied.

We turn next to metaphysics, which is a system of ideas wider than any other existing system. This means variously the construction of first principles or the criticism of assumptions. That legal systems presuppose ethical principles was a metaphysical discovery, as was the proof that some philosophies are insufficiently inclusive. That metaphysical criticisms are made slowly and that such opinions accrue, have blinded men to the fact that they were made by metaphysics at all. The process of showing that there is no safe and rigid bottom to any discipline is a tedious and unpopular enterprise, especially to those who have to work on the assumption that there is. They have been led out of the difficulty by some professional philosophers who have contended that metaphysics is reducible to the language in which it is expressed, and, therefore, since it is not about anything else, clearly it is not about anything.

Philosophy in its constructive or systematic phase is known also as ontology. Generally speaking, ontology is positive and constructive metaphysics; metaphysics, negative or destructive ontology, although it should be remembered that criticism is analytical chiefly and so not always destructive.

The propositions of metaphysics are combinations of terms. The terms themselves are known as categories; these are principal classifications, and set the entire determination for a philosophy. Once we have chosen our terms, we have more or less decided what the philosophy which will be made up of them is to be. Familiar examples of such classifications are: "essence and existence," "form and matter," "mind and matter," "possibility, actuality and necessity," etc. The categories of classification are in effect basic attempts at explanation. To employ a single category has the advantage of simplicity, but it explains little. Two seem to do more, and three more still; there are examples of more than three but they are rare: a fourth in some way repeats what some one of the first three has done.

The relation between logic and metaphysics is a close and intimate

one, although the two studies are kept quite separate and often are engaged in by specialists who have little or no regard for each other's field.
Most logicians are not concerned with metaphysics, though there are important exceptions, but less often the metaphysicians are not concerned
with logic. Perhaps it would be better to say, that metaphysicians are less
concerned. A logician is a man who takes his metaphysics for granted,
that is, he runs it in as a set of silent and unacknowledged assumptions.
A metaphysician of any scope is one who freely acknowledges the logic
which his metaphysics assumes and employs. Hegel's logic was important
to his metaphysics, even crucial to it, as he knew; but the metaphysics
underlying Boole's logic was never mentioned, since the logic can be set
up and operated without explicit reference to any metaphysics.

Most of the great philosophers regarded metaphysics as central to
philosophy, but not all. Some have preferred to start with epistemology
and then to derive their metaphysics from it. Epistemology is the theory
of knowledge, it studies how knowledge—including metaphysical knowledge—is possible. How do we know, how reliable is our method for obtaining knowledge? Epistemologists argue that to start with metaphysics
is to take a certain philosophical method for granted, to proceed naively.
Metaphysicians reply that all epistemology and indeed all methodology
(since that is what it is) always has its hidden metaphysical presuppositions without which it could not examine the method of philosophy, that
epistemology is merely a sort of examination of the validity of metaphysical proofs, and can therefore not take place until there is some
metaphysics to examine. Kant is the chief exponent of those philosophers
who held that epistemology precedes metaphysics.

But in any case, there are the three central studies in philosophy:
logic, metaphysics and epistemology, and any philosophy which leaves
out one of the three is the poorer for it. And a poor philosophy is hardly
a philosophy, since it lacks the ingredient of inclusiveness which is more
vital to philosophy than to other studies. It is currently fashionable in
England and the United States to omit metaphysics from the trilogy, on
the grounds that it has no object and that therefore it refers merely to the
language in which it is expressed: that metaphysics is about metaphysics.
But it has been pointed out (though not to the satisfaction of those who
advocate such a position) that the metaphysical assumptions of those
who claim that metaphysics has no object are great indeed, and that therefore the argument against metaphysics is self-refuting. If the very first
statement made in this paper is correct, then there are those philosophers
also who would discontinue philosophy as a viable enterprise, and turn
its advocates toward other fields especially to mathematics, physical
science and psychiatry: to mathematics for the logic underlying meta-

physics, to physical science for having the exact method of reliable knowledge which has antiquated metaphysics, and to psychiatry for treating those who suffer from the mental illness which allows them to have the illusion that there is such a thing as metaphysics.

So much, then, for logic, metaphysics and epistemology. There still remains two divisions of philosophy to be examined : ethics and aesthetics. These along with theology are the so-called value studies.

Ethics is the theory of the value or quality known as the good. Like all values, it cannot be described to those who have not felt it, and is thus quite different from rational ideas which certainly can be explained to those who have not known them. Like the color, red, or the taste of sugar, the quality of the good cannot be conveyed to those who have not seen red or tasted sugar. But we can talk about it, and hope that the common experiences upon which we are relying for our meaning will be linked, and in this way communication will take place. In past times (and still among many today) the good is held to be exclusively human : the good is what is good for man; or even exclusively subjective : the good is what is good for *me*. But as in the case of logic that is not the Greek view, and it is not the most modern one, either. For if we insist that whatever preserves any organization whatsoever, whether a stone, a tree or a man, is good for it, and whatever destroys it is bad for it, then the good is simply the quality of the bond between wholes whatever those wholes may be.

An organization is a system of parts made up into a whole. Some organizations are loose collections of parts, some are very tight ones indeed. Aesthetics, which is the theory of that value or quality known as the beautiful, suffers from the same failure, or, at the very least, the same difficulty in communication that we have already found to be the case with ethics. What is beautiful can be pointed to in the hope that its beauty will be shared, but it cannot be communicated directly any more than any other value can.

The theory of art is a theory of the beautiful, and the connection between art and beauty has been so close traditionally that men have supposed beauty to be exclusively human, for after all is not art a man-made affair? But once again, as in the case of logic or of ethics, there are those who maintain that art is not man-made exactly but rather man-discovered and could not be brought into existence if the values that are contained in a work of art had not already existed in some sense as possibilities. The sounds of which a piano sonata are composed already existed as sounds, and their combination in the sonata was already a possibility, even though it required the intuitions of a genius to see it. But intuition is after all just what it is often called : insight, and where there is nothing to be seen it cannot occur.

Aesthetics, then, can be considered as the degree of perfection with which the parts of any organization are fitted into the whole without remainder, and so wherever there is an organization there can be beauty, whether anyone is there to appreciate the beauty or not. Appreciation is something else again. If beauty lay in the eye of the beholder, it would be possible for every connoisseur to be his own artist. Unfortunately, perhaps, this is not the case, and appreciation can only begin where the production of art leaves off; and so they are by no means the same.

In aesthetics, then, we are once again close to the ancient Greek view of things. It is easy to see why so many philosophers hold the Greeks in high esteem, for they pioneered many of the philosophical pathways, and opened up fields in a fertile way to speculation; so well, in fact, that we are still exploring many of them today. Our philosophies however fashionable and *avant-garde* often prove to be assemblies of ideas which had been discovered by the Greeks who did not, however, assemble them in just these ways.

For the Greeks, too, ethics and aesthetics lay close together. The perfection of organization is not too far from the relations between organizations; the one affects the other. There are other studies in which values are explored besides those of ethics and aesthetics: theology, for instance, the theory of the holy. But speculative philosophy has usually had to turn its conclusions in this field over to other institutions, more specifically to churches, in which they became official and hence obstacles to further speculation, except what could be conducted in the special terms of the theology adopted. Institutions which endorse particular philosophies do explore them with an intensity they would not otherwise receive, but they put an end to the consideration of philosophies which may be rivals to the one endorsed.

4. HOW CAN PHILOSOPHY HELP THE UNTRAINED INDIVIDUAL?

We began our inquiry by noting that the discord of contemporary voices in philosophy discouraged any hope that philosophers might some day agree upon the meaning of philosophy. In the next section, therefore, we decided that the answers in philosophy were, philosophically speaking, not as important as the questions. And so we decided to explore the primary question, what is philosophy itself? It was found there that philosophy can be explained chiefly in terms of its aims, and that these aims, roughly speaking, reduce to a single one: philosophy seeks the most general kind of understanding. It then became necessary to learn what tools philosophy uses in its efforts to satisfy its aims at understanding, and this called for a breakdown and description of the various divisions of philosophy.

In all three sections of the foregoing exposition, we were concerned with *theoretical* philosophy, with philosophy in search of the truth. Its aim was discovery. We are now to turn to a second broad division which is concerned with practical or *applied* philosophy. As usual in philosophy we are in another large area of disagreement. Some philosophers would shudder at the thought that philosophy has its useful side, and it must be admitted that they too have made important contributions to philosophy. But here we shall try to develop the theme that philosophy is of the utmost usefulness.

Philosophy can be helpful in various ways to the individual and to society. Let us consider first those which are of use to the individual. It should be added quickly that we are not here talking about the professional individual merely. Our discussion is directed toward the individual who has no special technical training in philosophy.

For the average individual who has other things to do and to worry about, it is not at all easy to see what any of this has to do with him. The businessman, for instance, spends most of his waking hours in getting a living, and what time he has left over is usually devoted to his family, to friends and neighbors and their interests, and to keeping up with what is going on in the world. In a period such as our own, when as a result of wars, of social conflicts and of new developments in knowledge, all the old beliefs have come unstuck, the individual feels lost and in need of help in fighting his own sense of insecurity. The more he learns about psychoanalysis, Marxism, the new physics, the chemical industry, the rise of mathematics, automation, the ballistic missile, the revival of religion, the dangers of tobacco, the overproduction of automobiles, the spread of television, rock-and-roll, the vast political parties, and the influence of oil producers, the more confused he becomes. Behind him lie the old social ambitions, ahead there is nowhere to go and nothing to do. How possibly can philosophy be fitted into such a picture?

The answer is not a simple one but there is after all an answer. For we have not been altogether fair to our businessman. He is not just a doing machine, he is also a thinking and feeling person, with all the full dignity of his perquisites, and these functions are not exhausted by his role as business partner, husband, father and citizen, however important each of these may be. True, he may go to church on Sunday there to have all his doubts and questions assuaged in the comfort of a faith; but there is more to it than that. For, although pious, he is nevertheless a separate person and to some extent different from his fellows. Now, every man in becoming a person develops a point of view of his own, overlapping with others to some extent, but also to some extent unique. There are times when he would like to know what that point of view is, and occasions upon which he longs to make the acquaintance of his own consistency. If we say here that philosophy is in a position to help him, he can answer that this remains to be shown. In the last analysis, he will have to perform this service for himself; but philosophy can furnish him with the tools.

What can philosophy do for the individual? We have listed five of the branches or subdivisions of philosophy; these are: logic, metaphysics, epistemology, ethics and aesthetics. There are accordingly five tasks it can perform. Before discussing them, it will be helpful to mention a sixth with which it is always well to begin. This sixth is the history of philosophy itself.

The history of philosophy is an account of what some of those who have given their lives to the study of philosophy have thought about it. It is, in short, a sampling of systems, assumptions and insights. A reading of some good history, therefore, will acquaint the uninstructed individual with the sort of thing that philosophy discusses. It will provide him with the experience which will make it possible for him to recognize the kind of fundamental belief or statement which is philosophical in character. For when he comes to his first task, which is the exploration and discovery of what he himself believes, he will be equipped for it.

A man's beliefs consist in all shapes and varieties of suppositions, some significant, others trivial; some profound, others superficial; some known to himself, others entirely unknown; some gained through systematic learning, others acquired through chance experience; some serving as a basis for deduction, others deduced. Is it true, for instance, that we ought to put our faith in what exists now, and gives less credence to what has passed or to what is to come? Have we not perhaps transferred our belief in substantiality of matter to those documents which relate to its possession? Do we not, for instance, slip into supposing that the United States Steel Corporation *is* the shares we hold in it? Is the evidence for immortality sufficient to justify the sacrifices we make in this world to gain it? Are the physical laws that cannot be evaded any less real than the pieces of matter we see answering to those laws? For the most part, it is fair to say, we are not well acquainted with the most fundamental of our beliefs; we are not in the habit of searching for them but we are in the habit of acting from deductions made from them. In short, it is our practice to do what we believe and to have our beliefs show in our actions, without bothering to examine, in minute detail and the fulness of consciousness, what those beliefs are and how strongly they are supported.

To most of us it would come as a great surprise were we suddenly to be confronted with an array of our beliefs. We should not recognize all of them, and we should shrink with horror from some. If we were to argue backwards from our actions to the beliefs from which such actions would follow as deductions, we would emerge into the presence of some of our beliefs, but there would still be others which were not uncovered by such a method because they had not yet had the opportunity of leading to actions. Not all beliefs are called into overt behavior; and those that are, depend for their initiation upon some event in the world of external events to trigger them.

The task of uncovering fundamental beliefs is not a simple affair nor one easy to achieve, but it will be aided if we know the sort of thing we ought to be on the lookout for. The history of philosophy can be helpful here. The sixth way in which philosophy can be useful to the individual —and the one we have chosen to mention first—is the study of the history of philosophy, for it can make the individual familiar with the sort of fundamental beliefs he is likely to find in himself when he examines what he has taken for granted and what his feelings and actions reveal. If he has made something of a study of the history of philosophy, then he is familiar with the kind of world philosophers live in, the sort of ideas they advocate, and the variety of conflicts their rival ideas engender. In the examination of the other five ways we shall have to assume that he knows what his fundamental beliefs are, although this is quite a large assumption.

Let us assume it, anyway, for the purposes of getting on with our explanation. We have, then, an individual and his fundamental beliefs. And now we are to show him how he could apply to them the material which is contained in the five standard branches of philosophy.

Logic was first, and logic has to do with consistency and completeness.

To what extent is it possible to discover among anyone's fundamental beliefs a consistent system? Obviously, a certain logical approach to the problem is to be desired. The beliefs will have to be sorted out, and those that are the more primitive and that perhaps lead to some of the others must be set aside as axioms. In other words, if possible a system will have to be found among the beliefs.

It is not always possible to discover such a system, of course, for a system is not always present. In that case, it would be advisable to fall back upon a secondary type of procedure; and then the individual would have to be satisfied if he could find among his beliefs *some* which are consistent. If belief A is consistent with belief B, and if belief C agrees with belief D, we shall have to forego the fact that A and B taken together are not consistent with C and D taken together. We have, then, instead of one consistent system two separate consistent systems, each of which is somewhat lesser in scope.

We are setting for the individual arduous tasks. He has to ask himself whether his system of fundamental beliefs is well-supported. The first test of support lies in the principle of consistency. The second and third tests lie in showing the system to be allowed by truth and fact. Does the individual find that his system of beliefs contradicts what in other systems is known to be true? Does it conflict with crucial facts? Then he will learn that it is unsound, and that some revisions are called for in it.

A brief glance at the history of such matters ought to shake us in our facile certainty that what we believe to be is. Public and widespread support for our beliefs is comfortably confirmatory. Yet look at the size of the mistakes which have been made. Astrology had a longer run than almost any other human discipline, yet it is wrong, and astronomy did not come to supplant it for thousands of years. The same statements can be made about alchemy and its replacement by chemistry. There is a simplicity about false knowledge which renders it attractive; numerology can be mastered a lot more quickly than applied mathematics as we have it today. Then, too, there is the charm of the mystery which false knowledge always carries and which the truth endeavors to dissipate. The magic and the fear of the unknown is more bewitching than the complexities of the known. Yet in addition to the ease of belief and perhaps underlying it after all, men have a keen desire for the truth, and that alone may save them. It is logic and logic alone which can be counted on in this extremity, and logic is nothing more than the cry for two kinds of consistency: consistency with already established generalizations and with fact.

The criterion of consistency seems at first glance to be a most awfully strict and rigid one. Why, it will be asked, can we not allow the individual more latitude in his beliefs? Is it not almost inhuman to be so monstrously logical? Certainly an individual who always behaves in a narrowly correct way always strikes others as insufferable. There is some strength to this objection; still, let us examine it.

Beliefs, we have seen, do not end there: they lead to feelings and they lead to actions. It is their actions here with which we are for the moment chiefly concerned. When two beliefs which are contradictory both lead to actions, the actions may either cancel each other out or bring about considerable conflict. Suppose a man believed that charity is good, and also that the giving of alms is weakening and therefore an injustice to those to whom it is given. If he were to act from both his beliefs, he would give away what he could spare, and then take back what he had given. If he believed that all wars are wrong and none justifiable, and also that a man owed his duty and perhaps even his life to his country, then the conflict would be so powerful within him that it could lead to neurosis.

But to return, the advantage of knowing what your beliefs are is that you can then find out whether they are true, and, if they are not true, exchange them for others that are. The second step is to match them against the relevant knowledge, which is for good reasons commonly accepted.

Consistency, as we stated at the outset of our discussion of how logic could aid the individual with his beliefs, is not the only requirement. There is also completeness. Consistency demands that all of the elements within a system fit together; completeness demands that all of the elements that ought to be included in a system are in it. It may happen that beliefs are consistent yet wanting in scope, they may be too narrow. It is possible to believe in very little of anything and to have that little consistent, and yet to find such beliefs inadequate. Thus the second test of beliefs has to do with their completeness: we must ask that the beliefs of the individual be both consistent and complete. Thus we shall have to ask him to stretch his beliefs over a wider area than they had hitherto covered. The well-informed man has opinions concerning a vast number of topics. But those who know little have fewer occasions on which to hold false opinions. The man who does not know the oddness of the behavior of materials under enormous speeds or high pressures is in no position to entertain false beliefs concerning the causes of such behavior. In order to discover whether his beliefs are complete even if they have proved to be consistent, we shall have to see to it that he has the proper amount of knowledge. Yet who knows enough? The world is always bigger than our knowledge of it, and the processes of gaining and testing knowledge will have to be a continuing one.

Beliefs are not static affairs; they lead to feelings and actions, and they may also lead to thoughts. We think, feel and act in accordance with what we believe; there are few who are able to believe in one way and behave altogether in another, and they are so divided as to require the services of a psychiatrist, for such split personalities are of the schizoid type. The confusion in most people is of a more modest and partial nature. At both extremes there seems to lie great peril: we may be monsters of single-mindedness or monsters of dual personality. We strive to move away from inner conflict and toward consistency, without the fear that our logicality will reach such a pitch of proportions that we will become a menace. For the single-minded man may be a prophet as well as a sinner, a Socrates as well as a Hitler, but there need be little concern that most of us are capable of so much good or evil. The earnest content of the usual thought, feeling and action betrays a want of profound belief rather than a surfeit. To believe with a breadth or an intensity sufficient to lead to extensive thoughts, feelings or actions, is given to the few: to the mathematician in the case of thought, to the artist in the case of feeling and to the political leader or the saint in the case of action. For most, it is a case of poverty of insight and conviction rather than the reverse.

The third and last criterion, then, by which the individual's beliefs must be tested is one that we may call deducibility. Another name for it, and perhaps a more descriptive one, would be fruitfulness. It is one of the tests of a set of beliefs to ask of it, how well and easily does it lead to thoughts, to feelings and to actions? A philosophy for the individual means a set of beliefs held so deeply that he does not know he holds it and yet one strong enough to influence all his thoughts, feelings and actions. So much, logic can do for the individual in the analysis and improvement of his fundamental beliefs. We can now recognize in these the outlines of his philosophy.

We turn next to the contribution of epistemology. How does he know that his beliefs are sound even after they have met the logical criterion of consistency? To answer this question, it will be necessary to examine the evidence. What is its character and how strong is it? There are many tenuous threads to follow in this connection; the theory of knowledge is not so precise an affair as logic and there are no absolutes like contradiction to be found. We shall be interested at this point for the individual in an inquiry on how his beliefs were acquired, on what they rest, and on how tenaciously he holds them.

His beliefs are so much knowledge; but how did he acquire this knowledge? The internal workings of the process of belief belong to psychology. The psychological process of the acquisition of beliefs has been little studied. We hear a great deal about learning and concept formation but hardly anything about the fate of what has been learned. Learning is not necessarily belief. I may learn that the importance of theoretical science is not understood by the members of the United States Chamber of Commerce but I do not have to believe it. The subtle ways in which we come to believe what we learn await perhaps a further knowledge of the workings of the nervous system.

For the present we are confined to saying that the ways in which beliefs are acquired can be traced to their external origins. There are many obvious sources: tradition, habit, sense experience, reasoning, acting, feeling, and what else not. In addition, other sources exist which are less obvious, and it is probable that any of the experiences of our whole life could, and many in fact do, contribute to the sum of our beliefs. The process is not a visible one nor do we necessarily know when it is happening. But there must be a point after we have acquired the understanding of a statement at which we accept or reject it. We may do both in varying degrees. For the most part, with rejection we have done with the statement; but not so with acceptance, for thereafter it will be part and parcel of ourselves. A statement, we have come to believe, may lie dormant if circumstances permit, and so for all practical purposes cease to exist, or it may call us into decisive action when relevant events arouse us to the awareness of its presence in us.

Were the sources of our beliefs such that we would do well to accept them as profoundly as we do? Are the beliefs themselves as sound as we take them to be? We do not know, and usually we take no pains to find out. Each belief would have to be examined and weighed, for again many beliefs conflict and not all tell the same story. There are some things we grow up "always having known" that just are not so. As we imbibe the "common sense" of our parents' generation and our own, we little realize that it consists in an ancient and inherited metaphysics. It is a jumble of stuff, some true and some patently false. Rain on Friday by no meteorological knowledge that we possess could possibly "cause" rain on Sunday. The healthy and wealthy are not always those who go to bed early and get up early; and so on. But on the other hand, two plus two do make four. It is not the knowledge that we know we possess and are well able to defend that is of interest here, but that other knowledge that we so take for granted that we could not imagine its being questioned at all. It will often turn out that the knowledge we regard as the most secure and unassailable is in fact the most unsupported and shaky. The discipline of epistemology is a training in the seeking out and detecting of false knowledge lurking in our beliefs.

The individual will discover at this stage in the proceedings that he has a strong tendency to continue to believe what he has always believed, that the ideas he accepts tend to persist in him. After all, he has allowed them to become deeply imbedded; they have dictated his actions, and he has come to live by them. How, then, can he give them up? Not by any mere act of will, surely. Beliefs are not acquired nor abandoned except upon sufficient evidence. We are so constituted as to believe what there seems, to us at least, to be good reason to believe, and to doubt only where there seems good reason to doubt. To be asked to believe otherwise, appears to us little short of insane. Our sanity depends upon taking certain beliefs as positive knowledge, and in putting them into practice, usually along with our fellows. We act usually in concert with our fellows or else in individual ways which they themselves would approve. A basic philosophy exists in every society, and is accepted so profoundly that its very existence is hardly suspected. Reason to believe based on evidence for belief, and reason to doubt based on evidence for doubt, are the only reliable starting points for arriving at knowledge. But such reasons are often complicated and subtle, and therefore hard to come by. We need to learn something of their properties and characteristic hiding-places, if we are to learn about how we are able to maintain our most fundamental beliefs; and we need to do this if we are to learn about ourselves.

Epistemology, then, is the study whereby we acquire the method of putting our house of knowledge in order. Even when we succeed in doing this, if we ever do at all, it is not a final or static condition. The task of mounting sentry at the gates to belief is a never-ending one. We must be continually on our guard against accepting too easily as knowledge the statements which, because they may be fashionable, clamor for admission. It is not sufficient to believe in the truth of an idea simply because there is not on the face of it any reason for doubt. There must be to the contrary positive evidence for belief. To doubt that a statement has come equipped with evidence sufficient to justify belief in it does not mean that thereby doubt is required. We believe what there is evidence to justify believing or to justify doubting, and otherwise we suspend judgment. We should never doubt simply because there is insufficient evidence for belief. Otherwise, all agnostics would be atheists, which they most assuredly are not.

We are pledged to the question, how can philosophy be of help to the untrained individual? And we are endeavoring to suggest answers to him in terms of the main divisions of philosophy. With logic as the theory of assumptions and deductions—the theory of systems—and with epistemology as the theory of evidence—the theory of how knowledge is possible —we have now methodologically equipped our individual so that he is able to take a wider view. That wider view is the one named ontology.

We are purposely omitting metaphysics here, because metaphysics is critical in the negative sense, and it is presumed that our individual has already been through that phase when he considered rival systems as he was making their acquaintance in the history of philosophy. Ontology is positive and constructive, and that is what he is prepared for first and indeed what he needs now. We shall postpone metaphysics for him, then, until after he has dealt with ontology. An ontology is a system of ideas sufficiently wide to include existing knowledge. Logic examines its nature in so far as it is a system, and epistemology examines its acquisition and retention. But in the study of ontology itself, so to speak, we have to do with the quality of its content. By the time we ask the individual to appraise his ontology, it has already been formed, oftentimes largely without his conscious planning or even help. But now we are on the threshold of an area where we need such help. For were conscious processes able to do no more than unconscious processes, consciousness itself would be suspect. The picture of the whole man is one which includes his most profound opinions, and these, we shall assume, are more systematic than unsystematic. They were formed by many influences, they were fed from many sources; information has poured in upon them. They came from the experimental sciences but not only from them, for the world is larger than any specialty, and includes what art has to contribute and what other, and lesser, disciplines can add. In the sum, this is much. Being a whole man and seeing as one, the individual must also be convinced as one; also, and he selects to see is determined to some extent by what he knows, feels and does, and so can be traced back to what he believes. This synoptic view cannot be formed in the first instance nor held together synthetically; it must be arrived at by an act of insight. Now, the history of philosophy has already shown our individual something of what such insights look like after they have been formed, verbalized, and exposed to the light and the years. He knows a little now about how to make up his own ontology, or, if he cannot, then he has learned perhaps which of the classic alternatives to adopt.

A whole man, his equipment, his peculiar perspective, his aims and ambitions, his degree of perseverance, all center upon his ontology and are immensely affected by it. Can he then afford to ignore its nature or thereafter its presence? Can he without loss avoid its contemplation? When we ask ourselves, toward the end of our life of efforts, what was it all about, we mean: what was there in the world, and what did we try to do in it? Action, of course, is what matters, but then action comes in all sorts of subtle varieties: not only crude overt action performed by the muscles, however significant these be, but also the action performed by the neural pathways, by the brain, of which, alas, we know yet so little. Feelings, thoughts—these, too, are actions but it is not enough merely to act, however incisive our actions. We must assure ourselves that what we are trying to do by our actions is worth doing and the best we could hope for, that it is, in fact, what we ought to do. And for this purpose we need to be critical of our own ontology.

To be aware of one's ontology is an enterprise of sufficient magnitude; but there is another task even more monumental, and that is its appraisal. Metaphysics is the criticism of ontology, and now our individual is to be placed in the position of a metaphysician. The piecemeal criticism of his ontology, that *is* his metaphysics. Some philosophers insist that metaphysics is the same as ontology, but that would be to claim that criticism and that which it criticizes are one and the same. Put two statements together, and you have implied a consistency which could be extended to others and so to a system. But take two apart, and devote your time to an analysis of them, to a logical and factual evaluation, and you have embarked upon a metaphysical enterprise. It should be noted that ontology is never used to mean metaphysics in this sense, but the term, metaphysics, has often been used to mean systematic ontology.

Logic looks at belief or knowledge from the point of view of its form; epistemology looks at it from the point of view of its evidence; metaphysics looks at it from the point of view of its content: how intense are its qualities, how well do they harmonize, how deeply do they penetrate, how much do they cover? Metaphysics assumes that there must be an ontology, with its own criteria of excellence, and then considers in the case of the ontology advanced by any individual how well these criteria have been met. Obviously, no other ontology can be presumed to have passed the test, for otherwise it would have been adopted and the search considered ended. It is only when none is judged satisfactory that a new start is made.

Leaf through the early chapters of most contributions to philosophy. You will find there that the author has criticized his predecessors' views in order to make way for his own; for if the truth had already been discovered, what point would there be in embarking upon a voyage of discovery; or if truth were of such a nature that it had been compounded by all those great philosophers of the past who had found safety in what they asserted and jeopardy only in what they denied, what point would there be in undermining the achievements of the past so far as these carried with them any final claims? We are forever putting our beliefs together into a system as though we did not wish to have our actions defeat each other, but we are also under the necessity of retaining a continual criticism of the resultant system.

A quick glance at some examples taken from practical life should suffice to show what the average man has to gain from the philosophy with which we have been dealing so abstractly. Would a man who had examined his philosophy and made the appropriate changes still be willing to spend all his efforts in accumulating money and at the same time maintain a stout belief in a religion which held a low regard for the things of this world? Would it be possible for him to accept the tenets of any institution which had managed to perpetuate itself upon the insight that the world was coming to an end? Would he be eager to assign a large proportion of his income to the purchase of means of locomotion more powerful than he had any use for and more able to transport him than he had places he wished to go?

It is perhaps in the possession of an unique ontology and the ability to operate upon it by means of metaphysics that the source of each notable personality lies. Logically speaking, there are two sorts of relations between a man and his fellows: similarities and differences. The similarities are large and unimportant, and the differences small but crucial. At times, men take pride in being like all others, and at other times in being more of themselves. But there never was a time when a man did not want to count in the world for something, whether that something was his own or not. And to count means always to rely upon himself and his own attributes, to have the strength of his own virtues, to make his own decisions and, if possible, also to offer his own contributions. To this end, ontology and metaphysics can aid in a way no other study can.

Our next and last task is to suggest how ethics and aesthetics can be of assistance to the untrained individual. When we come to these so-called value studies, we are, so far as the individual is concerned, in the dimly lit area of intuitions about taste. There are of course systems of ethics and aesthetics; they are suspended halfway between systems of ontology and the relevant facts disclosed by individual experience, and must check with both. If the individual should start, as most of us do, with some notions of his own about what the good is, then he can find out through the study of ethics what his choice of values will involve him in. What ought he to hold in high esteem? What ought he to seek and therefore to do? These are the questions ethics endeavors to answer. Ethical systems to be effective must be society-wide, and they are so when they are openly acknowledged and established in codes of law. We shall return to this theme shortly. Suffice to say that the study of ethics can aid the individual in becoming aware of his deepest feelings and in showing him the extent of their involvement, often a way of assisting him in their correction. The individual will no doubt have unconsciously, or will acquire consciously, some conception of the ends toward which he strives, and these ends, so far as they are inclusive enough, are his highest goods. He will be enabled to strive toward them the more directly the more he is aware of what they are. The chances of a man arriving at where he is going are increased sharply when he knows exactly where it is that he wants to go.

At the same time, the means to be employed must not be left unconsidered from an ethical point of view. The use of immoral means to gain moral ends has been both praised and condemned—praised by those having moral ends which they thought would justify the means employed, and condemned by moralists on two grounds: first, that no amount of good can make an evil good and, second, that there is no guarantee that the employment of evil means will ensure the attainment of good ends, for if the evil means fail, only evil will have been achieved.

Ethics, we said earlier, is a study of the bond between wholes and so for the individual a study of the bond between himself and other persons and things. The name for this bond is goodness, and the right is a division of the good, since justice brings things into their own proper proportion, which is to say, into their own good. It must be remembered that every actual thing has bonds with every other actual thing. When that actual thing is an human individual, it is possible for him to recall that his thoughts, feelings and actions are in some ways trivial, for they are fleeting, infinitesimal things in a large and indifferent world, but in some ways crucial, since their ultimate influence is enormous and incalculable. The degree to which the crook of a finger upsets the atoms in the star Sirius has been over-advertised, but in the social world it is difficult to estimate the final reverberations of the effect of a single individual action. Therefore, for the individual to act without forethought, to deal without reflection on the portentious meaning of such dealing, is reckless in the extreme.

Ethics is a study of power in the realm of the good as it affects all people and things that share with us the world in which we live. So far as an individual's own values are concerned, he has to consider consistency and completeness here as much as he did in logic, only here completeness takes precedence, just as consistency took precedence in logic. It would be a waste if a man worked toward conflicting ends, for then all of his efforts would be self-defeating. And this happens. But equally important is the need to avoid having aims that fall short of what they should be; and this also and more often happens. Ethics is a study of the values which ought to be included in the aims toward the achievement of which we decide to devote our lives.

Aesthetics is a study of values of another though closely related sort: the bonds between parts within a whole, bonds which are felt and apprehended as the beautiful. When parts are perfectly fitted into the whole without shortcoming or remainder, they achieve a harmony and emit an effulgence or radiance as a result, so that the beautiful is fully described as the radiance of harmony. If the whole world were to be seen in such perfection, it would be the holy; but for this it would be necessary to stand outside. Art is the production of beauty. Every man has his own theory of art, just as he has his own theory of goodness; such theories range from the estimate that art is a worthless pretense (which is also a theory) to the estimate that art is the only thing worth living for. Systems of aesthetics are apt to be society-wide also, though not in the explicit and acknowledged way that ethics is.

For the productive artist there are, of course, special aesthetic considerations, but for the appreciator of art, which each of us is at some time or other, the human attitude toward art is a complex affair. For while there are personal gains from appreciating art, the chief end is not a selfish one. Art intensifies life in many ways; one of the best known of these is the education of the senses: for instance, we learn to hear by listening to music, to see from looking at painting, and to touch from handling sculpture. But for the most part our dedication is complete and without self-interest. The appreciation of art involves a feeling of superfluous caring. In art we love without wanting anything for ourselves, and care without having to be cared for in return. The effect of this on us, though not what we were after, is of the highest and most purifying sort.

For the individual, the value studies: ethics and aesthetics, enrich all experience. The study of the good deepens and extends all of his connections, and the study of the beautiful enlarges and rounds out his appreciation of the values of things. Neither goodness nor beauty asks the individual to consider himself; for the good he must "do good" and for the beautiful he must admire: ethics calls for superfluous action and aesthetics for superfluous caring.

In general, perhaps we could say that philosophy magnifies existence for the individual. We live in as much time and space as we feel, know about or interact with. For certainly more affects us than we can affect: the forces with which we are in exchange are so much greater than we are, that our feeble influence is hardly felt; whereas we are the recipients of the effects of cosmic rays, of sunlight, and of those many bonds of society which lie beyond our power to reciprocate and which reach beyond our understanding.

It was just this understanding with which in the first place, we have claimed, philosophy is occupied. We are all affected by events which happen very far away in space, and this is true also of time: we are the inheritors of the entire past and of what has survived in it, and we are to some extent molded by all of society's plans and ambitions and unacknowledged efforts toward the future. If we are to be aware of the world in which we participate, we must know of the bonds which exist and of the forces which are at work; we must, in short, in addition to the special studies which give us the details, turn to philosophy both for a sense of the whole end and for the special tools by which to deal with our particular province of it.

5. HOW CAN PHILOSOPHY HELP SOCIETY?

No society can survive as a society for very long without some established principles and procedures. These usually occur in institutions: organizations of men and material which are usually, though not always, less than the whole of society. The principles and procedures embody philosophies;

and sometimes this is done covertly but sometimes quite candidly. There is a philosophy of democracy, and it is embodied in the Declaration of Independence, the Constitution and the established procedures of our government, such as the system of political parties; but the democratic philosophy, derived as it is from Locke and Montesquieu, has never been explicitly established. There is a philosophy of communism openly adopted in the Soviet Union, and it is contained in the writings of Marx, Engels and Lenin.

Political systems are very wide affairs indeed when they are adopted by the governments of whole peoples; but there are other and more modest institutions which are important and which have their own established philosophies, whether open or assumed. Systems of law are underscored by jurisprudence; scientific principles and procedures are studied in the philosophy of science; and philosophies of art are advocated by particular movements in art; these are well-known examples.

Entire cultures, which extend beyond societies in the same way that societies extend beyond particular institutions, have their philosophies, though there philosophy has always been implicit and hidden. A single society embraces England, France and Italy in a way which brings out the resemblances between those countries; and if we were to examine closely the consistency between the various elements which they share, we should be well on our way to discovering the philosophy of the western society. Such efforts have been undertaken, though none perhaps with entire success: the task is too enormous, and we are too close. But from a distance it is possible to discern, however dimly, the philosophy of Asia, or of ancient Greece; distance lends perspective and therefore some grasp of the whole.

Now, the individual, in addition to having a private philosophy, shares in the philosophy of larger units. He shares for instance in the philosophy of some particular institution; he shares, to a lesser extent, in the philosophy of most of the institutions within his society; he shares in the philosophy of that society as a whole; and, lastly, he shares in the philosophy of the culture to which his society belongs. He is affected by all of these, and to some small or large degree he is capable of influencing them. It it necessary for him, therefore, to know their nature and if possible to be well-acquainted with them.

There are general reasons for this, for it is obvious that we would do well to know anything by which we were so greatly influenced and with which we are so profoundly involved. But there are in addition more special and at the same time more urgent reasons, particularly concerning the institutional philosophies. For institutions often adopt official philosophies, and official philosophy can be the death of philosophy. To adopt a philosophy officially means to have discovered the final truth; and it ends inquiry into the nature of truth by claiming the possession of it: we would never seek for that which we had thought we had found. Of course, a philosophy can be officially adopted without involving such perilous steps as the claiming of absoluteness and finality; but it usually does so, as past experience has shown.

What is the solution? There is an equally vicious danger lurking at the other end. Not to establish a philosophy means for a society chaos; without some degree of establishment there can be no stable society. Hence complete freedom in this sense allows for the absence of all order and security. It is not enough to have a personal philosophy, then, but there must be in addition a social philosophy which he shares and in whose benefits he participates. The answer ought to be some sort of tentative adoption of a philosophy which would provide for the requisite stability while allowing sufficiently for alternation and change to justify continued inquiry and progress.

What is called philosophy usually is what exists in a set of textbooks in libraries and what is taught by a set of teachers in classrooms who pass on to the next generations some of the abstract thoughts of the older tradition. Philosophy, in short, is a college course. But if this were all there were to it, no man with any intelligence or enterprise would wish to undertake it as a career. This, unfortunately, has only too often been the case. The topic is largely in the hands of men who believe just this, and so it has often had to be advocated by others whose professional competence lies in philosophy but whose living is somewhere else. The Greeks taught philosophy professionally, but since the Greeks many of the great philosophers of the western world have not been in universities. Averroes, Maimonides, Locke, Hume and Berkeley, to name but a few, were not university men, and in our own day Engels was not. Philosophers have most assuredly thrived in universities, and there are great names in this list too; Kant and Whitehead, for instance.

But whether the philosopher who is truly a philosopher, which is to say a philosophical explorer and not merely a teacher of philosophy, practices his profession inside or outside the university purview, the fact remains that traditions are advanced only by those who have no respect for them. In the end, every philosophy is found wanting. It could be the epitaph of every great systematic philosopher. "Here lies so-and-so, who failed where none succeeded." And yet the social world moves by means of such systems, and without them there could be no social world.

The task of philosophy is not confined to the past and hence not to the university. If cultures are applied philosophies, as we have been saying that they are, and no less so because silently and inadvertently dealt with, then the task of philosophy is to become a laboratory for the abstract examination of possible cultures. This is a tall order, but it does seem as though our field of philosophy must be considered in this connection. The cultural question of philosophy, then, becomes this: how ought we choose to affect ourselves? What philosophical propositions can serve as cultural axioms whose consequences could be counted on to produce the kind of societies we think that there ought to be?

Admittedly, we lack the breadth of inclusiveness as yet to produce such effects. Even the experiment of trying to plan a society within the limits set by the axioms of a given culture has encountered serious difficulties. Soviet Russia has laid down for itself a goal which is well within the limits of the axioms of the western culture: a society organized unilaterally and existing for the maximization of the institution of applied science. Applied science, and Marx's theories, too, for that matter, were western cultural inventions, and whatever society utilizes them on a grand scale must come within the purview of established events of the type of the western culture.

Philosophy has many such tricks up its sleeve, and its task as a theoretical laboratory is to explore the abstract possibilities, for speculation is a sort of looking ahead at what practice could be. Its vitality as an intellectual discipline is dependent upon the scope with which it is envisaged as well as the incisiveness of its own professional tools. But we must acquire some proficiency in the use of the latter before we are ready to undertake the tasks of the former.

Thus the philosophical enterprise finds its justification in the necessity for individuals to explore their own beliefs and for societies to provide stability and progress. It could hardly be more important. And if to the plain man working for his living it does not seem to be of day to day relevance, that is because the prominence of importunateness has driven away the larger background of importance. Hunger always presses on us harder than curiosity, even though it was curiosity which led to the civilized improvements in the manner in which we satisfy our hunger. The cumulative process is never noticed yet takes its toll; we do not get much older in a day, but after many such days we die. We are no less the victim of the massing of effects for not noticing single ones as they occur. The man of breadth, then, will attend to philosophy, when to do so means living more fully the small life that we have.

6. A GLANCE BACKWARD

There is no benefit that can be achieved without the cost of some effort.

Learning often is, at least to those who have grown accustomed to it, a delight, but to those with no practice it offers all the awkwardness and the pain to be found in the unused muscles of the beginner. The concentration upon abstract ideas so intimately curious is not easy for those who have not habitually done it, and thus the prospect is a repelling one. It seems very much easier to do something else with your time. Philosophy in this respect is no different from ice-skating or the playing of contract bridge. It is only the rewards that philosophy offers, which are greater than others, that must be the inducement; for each of us has, if he could only become aware of it, a need to know.

To become keenly conscious of the existence and the strength of the need to know, is to begin the long task of attempting to satisfy it. It will be found to be like the other needs, like hunger, for instance, which can be satisfied only for a time, and which arises again in all its demands if left alone for very long. We cannot hope to know what there is to be known; very little knowledge of anything is yet the possession of the entire human race. But we can make a start in learning what is known or in prospecting for ourselves beyond the frontiers of knowledge. Learning is not a process with a marked limit; it is a way of life, and those who live in this way live more intensely and have the experience of a fuller existence.

Those who have followed the suggestions in this study, and have tried to put themselves into the discipline that devotes a small part of every day to the practice of philosophy, first learning something of the history of philosophy, then studying the nature of the separate philosophical subdivisions, and finally attempting to discover and perhaps to revise what they themselves believe to be true at the profoundest level of belief, will be astonished after a time, a year or two, say, to discover upon looking backward how far they have come. And they will be astonished, too, to discover how much the plain events of everyday life have acquired a meaning that they did not have before, and life an enjoyment they did not dream it could possess.

They began, because we all do, by holding a philosophy consisting of prejudices acquired at random through the emotions and defended by the use, which may at times even be skillful, of fallacies. But now they can be satisfied with nothing less than reasons, reasons which derive from facts carefully sifted for their value as evidence, or from other reasons which had already been well established in the same fashion by derivation from the incontrovertible principles of logic. And there will be from this a qualitative change which imperceptibly grew upon them, and will raise them in fullness to the stature of aware beings in the highest degree of what it means to be human and themselves.

THE USES OF PHILOSOPHY

Philosophy is a difficult subject that uses ordinary words in queer ways and has no practical application whatsoever.

That at any rate is what most people suppose today. And they do so because they forget that philosophy is a technical field. People who would not try to understand physics or mathematics because of the special signs and symbols employed are misled into thinking that philosophy is readily understandable because the words are recognizable. In this sense philosophy has been misleading. For the extraordinary ways in which it uses ordinary words is how it makes up its technical vocabulary.

It requires some trouble to understand philosophy, but I submit that it is worth the trouble simply because philosophy is one of the most useful enterprises ever undertaken by man. It won't build bridges but it will organize new information. As everyone knows, in our lifetime there have been tremendous advances in human knowledge. The radio, television, the airplane, Freudian psychoanalysis, the new "wonder" drugs and other biochemical marvels, the new physics and technology, including relativity physics and quantum mechanics, are just a few. Along with the new knowledge have come new challenges, such as the challenge of international trade (the European Common Market) and international Communism.

These new developments have brought new problems with them, some trivial, some grave. But most of all they have presented the average citizen with a spectacle of the greatest confusion. All lines run away from the center and there seems to be no common ground. No one stops to think that it is the business of philosophy to bring clarity and consistency into all this confusion and to give the individual somewhere to stand while all the various new theoretical and practical advances swirl around him.

The uses of philosophy are both individual and social. Let us begin with the individual uses.

The first of these is the satisfaction of simple curiosity. Man shares with the lower animals a great desire to know about things. The same urge that impels a monkey to examine a stick by turning it over motivates a man to satisfy his inquiry, but in the case of man the urge is much more extensive. Man's curiosity is extended backward and forward in time and throughout space; it includes the relations between things as well as the things themselves. It is bounded only by the limitations of the individual.

From infancy to maturity man goes through two well-recognized stages: innocence and innocence lost. It is no news to anyone that children begin life in a state of innocence, but most people forget that a child's is not an empty innocence, but an innocence full of curiosity.

I was seven years old when I saw a man die. I was playing in the front yard one summer morning watching a man on a ladder paint the side of the house across the street. All of a sudden he fell to the ground and lay there very still. His family rushed out and stood around weeping and wailing.

Since it was very strange and considerably frightening, I turned back into my house and hunted for my mother.

"I have just seen a man die," I announced.

"I know," she said. "I was hoping you would not know about that until later."

"Will that happen to me?"

She laughed. "Not for a very, very long time."

"Will that happen to me?" I repeated.

"Not until you have grown up and become a man and lived your life and grown old, and then perhaps you won't mind so much."

"But it will happen to me?"

"Yes."

"If I go on this way?"

"Yes, yes."

"Well, then," I said, "I don't think I want to go on at all. I would rather go back to where I started."

A quizzical smile came over her face. "I'm afraid that's rather impossible."

She sent me out to play again. But I only went downstairs and tried to understand my predicament. I am just in an awful fix, I said to myself, and I don't really understand how it happened.

There is nothing stronger than the curiosity of children. They are eager to learn about everything, and they routinely ask the embarrassingly fundamental questions that adults are never able to answer, questions such as: What is God like, how far does space extend, what is time, why am I here? If metaphysics has any native home, it is in the questions of children. Their state of innocence is not after all so innocent. They do know what questions to ask!

But we don't know what to answer. Yet we answer just the same, giving definite answers to what are fundamentally unanswerable questions. Our children may not be content with the stock replies formulated by dead authorities, drawn from religion, philosophy, and politics by teachers and parents generally, but they know that they must accept them, and so with a shrug they go off to think about something else.

And the rest of their adult lives are spent in the small business of everyday: running for buses, shaving and bathing, paying taxes, making a living, getting along with family, friends, and associates. This takes up nearly all of the available time. At night they are too tired to think and only want to be amused because amusement is restful. And so the childish philosophical questions are never raised again. Anyhow, there would be no point, since now they have found out exactly what has to be done to get along. This is innocence lost.

A few, a very few, however, take a third step to innocence regained. They are more sensitive than the rest, or more stubborn, I do not know which. They reject the answers that were made to their childish questions, although they do keep the questions. From this tiny group come all the productive and original people among us, the artists and philosophers who through their efforts make up the social world in which we live.

Thanks to them, human progress does not consist in finding the answers and so ending the search, but in adjustment to the search itself. At its highest, life is a perpetual inquiry. We live by the results but at bottom we are never satisfied with them, and so while we accept them in order to exist, at the same time we endeavor to continue the inquiry. All men are by nature inquisitive, but some make a profession of inquiry. A philosophy is the working tool of inquisitive men. "I would," said Democritus, "rather discover one cause than gain the kingdom of Persia." The vast discoveries connected with the atom in recent physics no doubt owe their origin to the early Greek philosophers who were the first to think about the possibilities of such discoveries.

In addition to wanting to know, the individual has things he wants to do, aims he wishes to achieve, goals he would like to reach. But it happens that unless some consistent plan is followed, he may defeat himself. He may be undoing with his left hand what he is endeavoring to do with his right, without ever understanding that this is the case. He may, for instance, want the high regard of his fellows but cheats them in order to gain it, and they in their turn may be so confused about values as to admire the success he has made in this way. Philosophy can facilitate a forward progress in achievement through action by formulating a life pattern in which the individual can measure his progress and continually correct his direction. By occasionally glancing at his philosophical compass he can keep from going off course.

Human beings can conduct their lives only in terms of some kind of framework. They are incapable of merely existing in a helter-skelter world. The framework is usually presented to them by a currently fashionable and dominant institution—a church or a state. But what is presented in this way is nothing more or less than philosophy. At some point it was the work of philosophers attempting to solve some of the recurrent problems of philosophy. The framework may be a myth, which is after all only a story told in symbols evoking emotions and regarded as true, as with a religion. Or the framework may be a kind of economic law, in which case it presents itself as the inevitable consequences of some basic facts, Marxism for instance. But in any case it is a framework, a philosophy imbedded in the nature of things and indispensable to people.

One of the most important branches of philosophy is ethics, the theory of the good. Morality is a socially adopted ethics. Men tend to think of morality as a curbing of the sexual impulse. But this is a negative side. There is a positive side which is more important and all-embracing: how one wishes to conduct oneself toward oneself as well as toward one's fellows. What ought one to do, what should one seek? These are typical moral questions. The composition of a life-plan is moral, and the following of it is, too.

Morality tends to lend depth to practice, to make of the activities of existence a wholly concrete affair having definite dimensions. The life of a man is fuller if he knows what life is. This is not to say, of course, that life should be rigid. Any comprehensive plan must have some elasticity, some allowance for revision and change. But to know in general where one wants to go—there is nothing unnecessarily confining about that. Morality is a set of laws that one sets up for oneself. Some laws are constrictive, but others add new freedom, and it is the latter kind that we are talking about. Prohibition was restrictive; it forbade everyone to drink alcohol, even the majority who knew how to control their amount. But traffic lights make it possible for everyone to cross an intersection faster than they otherwise would.

The chief business of philosophy so far as the individual is concerned is to intensify life. And what it can do for the individual generally it can do for him in connection with any one of his many enterprises. This need not be understood in any high and mighty sense. Philosophy is useful in backing up the activities of each day. Jurisprudence, or the philosophy of law, is capable of intensifying the meaning of law for the ordinary citizen as well as for the practicing lawyer or judge. The philosophy of science lends depth to the experience of the research scientist, and it seems as though all of the great scientists have had an intense interest in this direction. Einstein, for instance, physicist though he was, had studied philosophy and been influenced by it. Behind every great physicist there has stood the philosophy he acquired in his early training.

If it is the business of philosophy to intensify life, there is no place that does so as directly as in the appreciation of art. Art is in a way everybody's profession. The philosophy of art is called aesthetics. It takes some knowledge of aesthetics to appreciate the grandeur and depth that there are to great works of art. But aesthetics has another and more personal contribution to make for the individual. A study of the philosophy of art leads to an intensification of the senses. Those who have learned something of the theory of art can feel more deeply than others; they have found out how to probe the immense complexities of their experience, and as a consequence they lead a richer life.

But the use of philosophy by the individual is very far from showing the whole of philosophy's practical program. There are the social uses to be considered as well.

One great use of philosophy is to establish social organizations on some kind of permanent basis. The amount of philosophy involved depends partly on the size of the social organization.

For an institution, a charter is required in order to secure the necessary stability. In a charter the philosophy may be implicit or explicit—implicit as in the articles of incorporation of an industrial company with the common law philosophy, or explicit as in the Roman Catholic Church with the philosophy of Thomas Aquinas.

A social philosophy consists in a set of principles or laws which demand adherence to the belief in their truth. By this method they offer a stable basis which can keep the individual members together and so preserve the society. Men who hold a set of beliefs in common will endeavor to work together better than they would without it, and the more fundamental the beliefs the better the work.

A clear example comes to mind from the last world war when France was defeated and occupied by the Germans. There existed a strong underground movement of men working for the liberation of their country from its oppressors. To make secure such a difficult effort, a philosophy was needed—not just any system of ideas but one that fitted the peculiar situation. Fortunately, such a philosophy existed. In Sartre's version of existentialism reality was wholly individual and hung on the feeling of nausea which told the individual that he was an individual, and on the moment of decision which told him the ultimate responsibility for himself was his own. Now the members of the underground could not of course find many opportunities to congregate. They had lost their social self-respect through the defeat of their country in war, and each had to maintain it for himself. Existentialism was perfectly suited to the situation.

For a society something more is required, for the social organization is larger and a great many more people are involved. One thinks immediately of the American society, and of the philosophy which helped to establish it formally, a philosophy contained in the American Declaration of Independence and the Constitution of the United States. This is easily identified as the philosophy of John Locke and Montesquieu. The philosophy of the Soviet Union, as everyone knows, was deliberately chosen and formally adopted.

For man's largest organization, a culture or civilization, the philosophy is so pervasive that it is difficult to define in any particular case. But certainly in Western civilization, the institutions which it contains have so much in common that it is easy to suppose that they have underlying assumptions. The dynamism of Western civilization is well known, and so is the belief in the method of science. The perfectability of this world relies upon both, and contains its own system of ideas.

In the struggle between societies for survival or supremacy, philosophy, then, can be a weapon. We are engaged in an immense struggle with the forces of Communism in Soviet Russia and the Chinese Republic. They use philosophy as an instrument of propaganda. We use aid in various forms to undeveloped countries. We send them industrial products and farm products. Why don't we send them the philosophy of democracy as well? Not just the forms but the substance. It is not reasonable to expect other people to follow our democratic procedures without telling them why such procedures should be followed. Many countries have tried to copy the democracy which has worked so well in England, France, and the United States, but they fail because they adopted the practices without absorbing the philosophy. They *follow* democracy but they make no attempt to *understand* it. For this it is necessary to comprehend the democratic philosophy.

In addition to the philosophical imports there are, of course, peculiarly American developments, such as the multiple-party system. Why does it work so well, why is it flexible yet steady, providing for changes within a system which does not itself materially change?

The philosophers who occupy themselves with politics could help out here. They are needed to provide the revisions accompanying the minor changes in policy and principle which are bound to occur in any dynamic society. And they are needed to argue in defense of the system against those who suppose it to be wrong. We are quickly learning that the mild little fellow, the academician who teaches, thinks, experiments, or writes the pure theory of his field, may pack a punch when his theories come to be applied. We have learned this about the physicist, the chemist, even the biologist. But we have not learned it yet about the philosopher. In the struggle with international Communism, the philosophers of democracy could be potent weapons. Why don't we use them more?

II

BEING

THE STARTING-POINT OF PHILOSOPHY

HISTORICAL ORIENTATIONS

1. Premunitio

It is perhaps impossible to introduce a philosophy to anyone who has not first taken something of that philosophy for granted. The reason for this is that there is nothing that can be asserted in a general way that does not presuppose a philosophy. If, for instance, we say that the metaphysical principles upon which philosophical method relies prime that method, we have already affirmed the philosophy which rests upon those principles. No one in the last analysis can understand a philosophy who is not already somewhat in a position to accept it. In this chapter little more is attempted than the orientation of the reader toward the sympathetic standpoint from which the philosophy of axiologic realism can be comprehended. In so doing, of course, the philosophy itself is assumed as given and its categories used; but this defective procedure cannot be altogether avoided. The defects are at least held to a minimum.

Here, then, is another system of philosophy. It is well to state its purpose at the outset, and fortunately, the purpose of a philosophy is easy to state. It is to find the nature of the universe of all universes while at the same time saving the facts, to account for every type of detail in the world as well as to seek out reasons for the very existence of such detail. A philosophy is a scale-model of all that we can describe from our experience or imagine, a model based on an ontological system. All efforts at "finding nature" purport to be the final truth ascertainable at the time; and although as consistent and inclusive as possible, they allow for the possibility of their own limitations and eventual overthrow. But they need never be proved completely false any more than they can hope to be proved absolutely true, and so each may contribute something dialectically to the sum of truth. A system of ontology, then, is an imaginative work which has clung to the facts, a work of art which answers to the most rigorous requirements of the scientific method.

Ontology proper is a field of inquiry and not the name of a particular philosophy. In Bentham's definition, ontology, "the field of supremely abstract entities, is a yet untrodden labyrinth." Bentham's "supremely abstract entities" are the categories of traditional metaphysics, or, as we should say in reference to a modern logical or mathematical system, the undefined terms employed in the unproved propositions which constitute the postulates of the system. Ontology, then, is a speculative field, for there is more than one set of abstract entities claiming to be the set of "supremely abstract entities"; in other words, there are rival ontologies and none is generally accepted by common agreement. There is no official ontology; contending ontologies must support their claims on the basis of the same criteria used by other kinds of systems: consistency, completeness and applicability. Rival ontologies exist theoretically and practically, and assert both abstractly and concretely their various claims. They exist theoretically in the written and spoken words of the professional philosophers. We shall see that their practical existence is somewhat more concrete, for they exist practically as elements of cultures.

This is an essay in systematic philosophy, neither the first nor the last. A fundamental theory of realism is set forth in this work. It is a treatise of ontology because it subscribes to that theory of metaphysics in which epistemology is deemed to be a special case of ontology. "Metaphysics" is ambiguous, a term employed sometimes for ontology alone and sometimes for ontology and epistemology. Since this is a system in which knowledge is held to be a particular kind of being, it is deemed more accurate to employ ontology as a designation, although, in the sense described, metaphysics would not have been a misnomer. "Metaphysics" has vague mystical connotations and this aspect of it has recently been revived by some of the lunatic fringe of thinkers. However, we shall not altogether escape from the use of the term. Although ontology will be the chief designation, we shall use "metaphysics" from time to time to denote the combination of ontology and epistemology.

When we come to present a philosophical system based on a system of ontology, we find that we cannot start where philosophy itself begins, either in the history of philosophy, so far as we are able to trace its origins in antiquity, or in the development of the individual, as he first comes to speculate about the nature of things. For what we wish to consider is logical and coherent—both of these at once, so to speak—rather than historical and dialectical. The latter are fixed methods of inquiry, but philosophy itself is somewhat wider.

The best presentation of a system of philosophy from the viewpoint of its understanding by the reader may be an historical one. To derive a complete position step by step, in the way in which it was first discovered, is to make it easier to grasp. But while this method has certain advantages of elucidation, it has corresponding disadvantages which appear to be more serious. Had the system been arrived at logically, with first elements being uncovered first, there would have been no problem, since the logical order and the historical order would have been the same. Such a fortunate accident is rarely the case: it was not the case here. Even granted the difficulties which confront us on the other alternative, it is the system itself which must remain central; a description of origins, in addition to its limitations *as* description, may be the source of peculiar confusions of its own: nothing is altogether accounted for in any detailed recital of mere development, however complete such a recital may be. For what is being presented is, after all, a system; and a system is best exhibited *as* a system, that is, logically rather than historically. This is the consideration which finally governed here in the matter of procedure.

Philosophy is not the property of philosophers. It is implicit in the nature of things. In persons, this implicit nature is termed the content of the soul. The importance of philosophy is a matter not of discourse but of being. We are driven to place emphasis upon philosophy as a study by the importance of being, of existing things, their values and relations, and not because of the study itself. In other words, the study of philosophy is rendered important by the importance of the field of philosophy rather than the reverse. The field does not depend upon the study but the study depends upon the field.

The study of philosophy is pursued by those who have the technical proficiency demanded by an abstruse field, but everyone is profoundly involved in the philosophical nature of things and events. Many, unfamiliar with a new vocabulary or with an old one to which new meanings have been assigned, are unable to examine their own predicament. Others who may have acquired the necessary terms do not always know what their own philosophy is. The difficulties are subtle and the reasons for concerning ourselves with them far from apparent. Devotion to philosophy may lead us astray, since there are so many more philosophical views than there are true ones. It may also lead us toward the truth and its power. Neglect of philosophy is twofold in its effect. Philosophy cannot be hurt but actual philosophy, the applications or practice of philosophy, can. First, the effect of philosophy on the world is to some small extent influenced by attention to it. Secondly, to remain unaware of that which affects us is to violate elementary self-interest. We cannot afford to ignore what directly and immediately touches us.

It is only through a comprehension of the immensities of the forces which concern our existence, the remote stretches of space and the enormous periods of time, the vast regions of bodies, the unlimited number of persons and institutions, upon all of which we somehow depend, that we come to the conception of impersonal concern. All animals know how to reason and some are artful, but only man is capable of detached inquiry. Only to man has it occurred to occupy himself with seeking to know the order of the world apart from his efforts to discover his proper function in it. To desire food and a mate is animal, but to be inquisitive too is human. A system of philosophy which seeks to satisy the craving for the knowledge of order is an attempt to satisfy the higher function of the human animal.

The chief purpose of this study is expository. A system of philosophy must be understood before it can be either proved or defended. Thus indulgence is the required attitude of those who approach the comprehension of a new system, for the attempt to understand would fail without a slight inclination in favor of sympathy with it. A whole view of the system can only be gained through an acquisition of the knowledge of its details in some chronology of succession, leading to the view of how they belong together in a logical order of relations. Thus what is presented here is a positive system which, it is hoped, will be accepted both as constructive and as suggestive.

After the first section, which contains an attempt at orientation, all controversy and the refutation of rival philosophies are held to a minimum, indulged in no more than seems required for exposition by means of contrast. No doubt any position implies the refutation of its contradictory and of its opposites, and in that sense the whole work is argumentative and controversial. This cannot be avoided, yet the point to remember is that the effect intended is an affirmative one.

Of course, every such system is inferentially polemical. But this aspect is secondary. Thus other philosophies are contrasted only to the extent to which such contrast offers illustrative value of the system presented here. It is necessary to consider a new system in the light of the history of philosophy and of present knowledge. But it is far too important to defend this system against those of its contemporaries who differ from the view it represents. No philosopher writes exclusively for the present, which is, after all, already the deductive property of the philosophers of the past. The future alone concerns him, at least to the extent to which he is a philosopher. It is better to explain this than to adopt the false attitudes of pride or of mock humility. It is simply a fact that the system makes the pretension to truth—to some permanent truths, in the light of valid present knowledge, and to limited truth in the light of the limitations of knowledge at any given time, such as the present.

2.   The Proper Starting Point of Philosophy

A.   THE WORLD AND ITS ESCAPE

Philosophy surprises us in the middle of things. As children we were natural metaphysicians and asked cosmically-centered questions. And it was not until we were old enough to have acquired the requisite tools for abstract inquiry that we were able to look systematically into the problem of what it is all about. By then we had already presupposed a great deal. For in the meanwhile, if we lived at all, it was in accordance with the beliefs from which we acted; from the very inception of our existence we found ourselves in the middle not of beliefs but of actions; and in admitting to ourselves that we do have beliefs, we learn that we have disclosed a philosophy.

We must learn to distinguish between *ostensive* and *cryptic* philosophies. Ostensive philosophy is that position which is avowed; it is one which is set forth more or less clearly in the oral or written words of the professional philosophers, or in the acknowledged allegiance to some stated position on the part of the pedestrian believer. The cryptic philosophy is that position which is assumed by all feelings, by all actions and by all beliefs, whether stated or otherwise, on the part of the professional philosopher as well as the pedestrian believer. It lies behind everything that is not itself in human culture, and is assumed in all non-human nature, implicit in the nature of things. The cryptic philosophies of cultures differ the philosophy implicit in the nature of things is one of which we seek knowledge, but even to assume this is to assume a (albeit unknown) philosophy.

All our investigations in philosophy rest ultimately upon our qualitative experience and how we analyze it structurally. They depend also, of course, upon our capacity for receiving experience. But the experience which we receive qualitatively and analyze structurally is experience of something outside us; there is a world which we experience. Philosophy as the explanation of this world must rest upon its accuracy as a graph and its faithfulness in representing the whole of that world.

To become self-aware, to comprehend the human predicament, is to come suddenly upon the knowledge that as finite individuals we are divided. Everyone, the illiterate as well as the learned, has always felt that we must either seek to escape from this world or be limited to it. Neither of these alternatives is feasible, although it must be admitted that they are the ones which have chiefly governed men's thoughts and actions. Cultures have been guided by the authorized determination to live exclusively in this world or, with equal exclusivity, in some other. Neither has worked out in practice to anyone's entire satisfaction.

The third alternative, a balance between this world and some other, has never been given a fair trial. Thus the bridge between the ephemeral and the persistent becomes the chief preoccupation of the man of purpose, be he theoretician or practitioner.

We do not start out with interest in another world but with involvement in this one. The occasion for the study of philosophy is our inquisitiveness concerning existence. But existence by itself has proved incapable of yielding any satisfactory explanation of itself. Existence consists in incomplete parts for which we require a whole. That whole is furnished by the general postulate of essence, of all postulates the most reasonable and required. Since nothing in existence is complete, independent, self-sufficient or absolutely whole, the postulation of essence seems necessary to explain existence. How many different names and what diverse conceptions have been used for the idea of essence! What a myriad of heavens for the world's escape!

B. HISTORICAL BEGINNINGS

How long has such speculation been going on and how did it first arise? It is difficult to say because our records are so incomplete. Out of the estimated million years that human beings have been living on the earth, we have a meagre knowledge of only some few thousands. It is useless, then, to speculate when the data are not available. We know that to the primitive, the myth is a practical form of reasoning; that there is no such thing as an unapplied truth and that effectiveness is the only form of being; but the primitive is too advanced for our purpose. Tylor in his *Primitive Culture* asserted that the theory of ideas arose from object-phantoms under the influence of religion on philosophy. But we are even speculating when we start from the advanced cultures. Breasted has pointed out in *The Dawn of Conscience* that the ancient Egyptians represented abstract truth as the goddess, Māāt; and hence that it was through Egyptian religion that ideas (or universals) were credited with objective existence. The Greeks may have learned this from Egypt, but we do not know that they did. The earliest systematic attempts at abstract knowledge were probably mathematical. Burnet in his *Early Greek Philosophy* quoted Aristoxenos to the effect that Pythagoras was the first to carry that study beyond the needs of commerce. Mathematics, then, may have preceded philosophy historically and philosophy may have been a development of it. If this is true, then philosophy could very well have arisen through the expansion of the explanatory texts accompanying the formulae. The emphasis thus given to philosophy throws it in the way of understanding the abstract nature of logical relations better than it does the abstract nature of powers, forces or values. The attempt of modern varieties of the realistic philosophy is not only to restore logical realism but also to develop axiologic realism, the abstract and independent reality of values as well as of relations.

The study of philosophy must not be allowed to confuse the foundations of philosophy with the beginnings of philosophy. It has much to learn from a study of beginnings, but the foundations are concerned with logical rather than historical priority. The order in which things happen is not necessarily the order in which they ought to happen. If history and logic were one and the same, there would not be the necessity to distinguish between them, for then we should mean the same things by them. But we know that the difference is an important factor in our efforts at understanding. We cannot begin by accepting everything just as it occurs. We must perforce begin with what we believe and endeavor to discover what is true. Since belief is not arbitrary nor voluntary but is governed by reason and fact, the nature of things holds the key to belief. The way in which philosophy developed does not reveal the structure of philosophy. The development of philosophy must be a separate concern.

Philosophy can only have started from faith. The least faith to permit philosophy a method is faith in the logic inherent in reasoning, in the value inherent in feeling, and in the world of fact which experience reveals. Through reasoning we gain the knowledge of a logic upon which our reasoning depends. Through feeling we gain the knowledge of values upon which our feeling depends. And through experience we gain the knowledge of an external world upon which our experience depends.

These three elements are at once a set of principles and a method. The system of philosophy here termed axiologic realism, like the presentation of all philosophical systems, must begin either with a set of principles, or with a method whereby the set of principles was discovered. Which came first: the method with its assumed principles, or the principles with their deduced method? It is difficult if not impossible to say with certainty. There is some evidence pointing toward the primacy of the principles. It is impossible to consider the method itself as that upon which the method stands. Method presupposes something taken for granted, the premises presupposed by the method. On the other hand, historically the premises of the method rest themselves on the method whereby they were discovered. The basis of method is a set of logical postulates, that of method, historical development. It is impossible to have both, so we must suppose that the start is made from principles rather than from method.

C. THE INADEQUACY OF EPISTEMOLOGY

Notice that among the phenomenological first steps which the starting point of philosophy takes, knowledge as a process is excluded. Of course, the knowledge process is an element in the pursuit of knowledge; without some understanding of principles and methods and what they mean, no inquiry could be attempted. There is undeniably a process whereby knowledge is acquired. But we cannot begin the discovery of knowledge by an examination of the knowledge process, with a view to ascertaining its reliability, for several reasons.

We cannot begin our inquiry with an examination of the reliability of the knowledge process, for the knowledge process is taken for granted by the inquiry at its beginning. Since we can examine the process of knowledge only by means of the process of knowledge, to declare it invalid would be to declare our inquiry into its validity invalid, and thus to validate it by allowance. Thus we know of no way in which we can demonstrate the invalidity of the process of knowledge, inasmuch as a knowledge of such invalidity would be a piece of knowledge which would have to have been arrived at by the very process of calling knowledge into question.

We cannot begin with an examination of the knowledge process because the field which we wish to examine is that of all being. Not all being is known, though all knowledge is part of being. There is every reason to believe that more will be known in the future than has been known in the past or than is known in the present. Hence knowledge is increasing, while being is fixed. Being is wider than knowledge, and we cannot increase our knowledge of being by limiting ourselves to a study of our knowledge of being, except in a very limited way.

A third reason why we cannot begin our study of philosophy with an examination of the knowledge process is as follows. Since knowledge that is partial and limited is false to the extent to which it is partial and limited, and since empirical knowledge must of necessity always be partial and limited, it follows that knowledge must always be false to some extent; and so epistemology, the theory of knowledge, a theory of necessity involving parts and limits, affords a poor basis for the whole of philosophy. Ontology, as an inference of the whole resting on many arguments, does somewhat better, since it includes epistemology but also makes broader inferences from knowledge than epistemology itself can ever be justified in making. Thus we must pass from a comparatively narrow topic like epistemology to a broader one like ontology in seeking the proper starting-point for philosophy.

In the last analysis—and ontology *is* the last analysis—we must learn to regard the modes of being independently of the way in which we have gained our knowledge of them, for there is evidence that they do possess such independence. We must regard facts as separate from our experience of them, and universals and values as apart from the process of abstraction by which we come to know about them. Epistemology retains its interest in favor of acquaintance, but ontology ignores the method whereby we acquire knowledge of the nature of things in favor of an interest in the nature of things. To start a philosophical system with epistemology in an effort to ground all knowledge in experience is to assume an ontology, whereas in philosophy nothing ought to be assumed without explicit acknowledgment of that fact. History must not be confused with logic, and we discover the system to which we subscribe in an historical order rather than in the logical order of that system itself.

This system of philosophy, then, will be centered on a theory of ontology and on systematic researches both in ontology and related fields. The system has been reached by induction, as Bacon wished, yet without detracting in any way from its deductive structure. In the method which is employed, induction is absolutely necessary and occurs twice, while deduction also occurs twice. The starting-point of the method is inductive, and there are consequent inductive procedures; but there are consequent deductive procedures, too, and the final product is maintained by the condition of deduction: the system is inherently deductive. We can see from this that induction is historically more important than deduction but that deduction is logically and finally more important than induction.

Philosophy is ultimately the product of how we think and feel about what happens to us. We have seen that for our thoughts to be consistent they must follow the laws of logic, for our feelings to have value they must obey the principles of axiology, and for our experience to be sound it must yield to the theory of phenomenology. Of course, such a resolve leaves wide open the question of what logic is to be followed, what values chosen and what analysis of experience adopted. These three studies, together with the validity of the knowledge process to be taken for granted until a later theory of epistemology can be derived from them, give rise to an ontology which is central in importance in philosophy and upon which all branches of philosophy that remain must depend. We do not begin with epistemology but we do end by including an epistemology of the kind that our ontology calls for. Kant has at least demonstrated that no philosophy can be complete that does not go thoroughly into the questions raised by epistemology. And if the epistemology called for by our postulated ontology prove to be invalid, then, of course, either it has not been validly deduced from the ontology or the ontology itself stands demonstrated inadequate.

D. THE INEVITABILITY OF ONTOLOGY

That everyone, even the most astute technical philosopher, even the most empirical epistemologist, begins with belief, is not so familiar a proposition. We begin, it must be admitted, with a certain amount of belief rather than with doubt. For we must begin by asserting something, even if our assertion concerns only an aim or a method of inquiry; and our assertion involves belief in something, even if that something is only doubt itself. Is this belief a minimal belief, is it the least possible; or should we begin with doubt and not with belief at all? These are the questions which must concern us.

If ontology could have been avoided by fiat, it would have been, many times over. Ontology has been condemned, ignored, avoided and dismissed so often that we find it hard in these days to suppose that the scientifically-minded could still take it seriously. It has been confused with arbitrary, theological and absolutistic systems and vigorously attacked; but it may not be inherently guilty of these charges merely because they have historical justification. There is no necessity connected with mere concurrence in history; the things that happen together may or may not belong together. Be that as it may, the fact remains that ontology, like the snake seen on the wall in *delirium tremens,* will not go away merely because we might wish it to do so. Philosophy, for all the attempts at this clarification, simplification and elucidation, remains a slippery and elusive affair; and just when we think we have it pinned to the board it flies away again.

The most familiar method of attempting to escape from ontology is to appeal to some other more apparently reliable or empirical criterion for philosophical statements and beliefs. We may put down some of these at random. Philosophers have wanted to begin with sense impressions, human nature, experience, knowledge, postulates. Every one of these attempts has produced something of merit. A virtue of philosophy, evidently, is that with limited notions and strenuous consistency, partial truths which might otherwise have been understressed or overlooked still turn up. However, the original purpose fails altogether, for ontology is implied in all these efforts. We do not have to know that we are presupposing certain ontological postulates by our thoughts, our feelings and our actions, in order to presuppose them; any more than we have to know that what we are reading is prose for it to be prose. No thought, no feeling, no action, no social group or institution, nothing, in fact, that people do singly or collectively, is free from the assumption of certain generalities; and no consciousness of this truth is necessary to its existence. The only point is that here (as in all cases) there is no special benefit or virtue in ignorance.

Socrates said that the unexamined life is not worth living. He might have added that the complete examination of life is a hopeless ideal. The average man of today thinks nothing of these things after he has succeeded with the help of his family and teachers in suppressing the natural metaphysical and theological curiosity which was strong in him during his childhood. But the more aware persons, the professionals who have made such considerations their work, are equally enmeshed in the error of taking for granted more than they know. The English empiricists are no freer of ontological assumptions of which they thought nothing than are the modern pragmatists. The professional epistemologist is better equipped than anyone else to probe his own unconscious presuppositions, yet if a thinker of the dimensions of Kant was unable to do so (and it is true that he was unable, for in his efforts to construct a giant synthesis he failed utterly to see the absolute nominalism of the position that he took up when he assumed that metaphysics is a property of cognition), then there is little chance of anyone else accomplishing it. The modern logician and mathematician who is accustomed to the postulational method (which indeed he now holds to be the only reliable one) still has difficulty in understanding that behind his logical postulate-set there are postulates, and behind his mathematical system there must lie meta-mathematical systems. The first effort of everyone who comprehends the power of ontology ought to be directed toward discovering what implicit ontological presuppositions are contained in his position—with the advance warning that the returns on such a venture are apt to be poor, since they require the utmost in concentration and are largely doomed.

Yet without this effort, how can a philosopher call himself a philosopher? For philosophy in the first place, perhaps, a certain obtuseness is necessary. The philosopher is simply one who stubbornly concentrates upon his blind side. He fails time after time to see what everyone else considers so obvious that speculation about it amounts to ridiculousness. He must ask himself over and over, "Yes, but then what am I taking for granted?" And after that, "but if that is what I take for granted, what am I taking for granted in taking that for granted?" There are limits to this retrogression only because the argument is circular, but it must be pushed back at least to the point where the circularity becomes painfully apparent.

Ontology is inevitable; we may as well face up to it. And even though the ontologist himself be guilty of taking for granted some ontology other than the one he supposes, we can tell something about the consequences of applying deductions even if we only know a little about the hidden postulates from whence they flow.

METAPHYSICS FOR EMPIRICISTS

I

Definitions are in one sense arbitrary affairs, and this applies no less to the traditional terms of metaphysics than to the conventional units of measurement. They are chosen often for reasons of expediency, and only afterwards become gospel through usage. But topics are more fluid than their terms. If there were nothing new to say about metaphysics, there would certainly be no need to write about it. At the outset, therefore, we shall be obliged to define metaphysics itself as the word is to be employed here, and distinguish it from ontology to which in sympathy it is closely allied.

Ontology is the theory, or system, of being, and metaphysics is the criticism of ontology. To argue for (or against) a certain position in ontology, then, would be a metaphysical undertaking. The method is metaphysical, but what the method seeks to accomplish concerns ontology. Another way to put the difference would be to say that ontology consists in a set of constitutive categories lying beyond the regulative categories of metaphysics.

Our first task in philosophy is not to decide which philosophy is right but to see what philosophies there are; next we shall have to find standards for judging them, and only then perhaps we will be in a position to do in a calculated way, what it is traditional to do earlier but too hastily, namely, to find out the right one. Exploration must come before selection; we must find out about the mountains and the sea, the plains and the desert, before we are in a position to select the environment in which we wish to live. We must know what sort of lands there are before we are in a position to decide what is the best land there is.

Great harm has been done to philosophy in the past by failing to recognize metaphysics as a speculative field. All, or certainly most, studies in philosophy have been devoted to proving that a certain position was impregnable. Philosophers have been belligerents rather than investigators. In an area which remains to this day largely unexplored, they have chosen a position—often by simple opposition—and then proceeded to defend it as though they were more interested in being right than in learning the truth. The fact that in a final way all such studies have fallen short is no effective argument against them. Often a solution which fails tells us more about the nature of a problem than one which succeeds, and at some levels it is the problems rather than the solutions with which we must learn to live.

Metaphysics has acquired a bad name among empiricists chiefly because for so long it has had a good name among theologians. Witness the "Metaphysical Society" which was organized by clergymen in London in 1869 for the sole purpose of debating with (and refuting) men of science. It would not be too difficult to show, and in other places it has been shown, by Peirce, for instance, that metaphysics in the sense of the meaning which Plato and Aristotle gave it can be demonstrated to be far more consistent with the empirical approach than with the theological. For two thousand years western theologians have made an all-presumptive claim to Greek metaphysics, mainly through the use—or misuse—of the Platonic Ideas, the Aristotelian substance and the Stoic ethics. That there is some justification in the Greek writings for their interpretation can hardly be denied; but other interpretations can also be put forward, often with equal, or stronger, claims to justification. It ought to be possible to demonstrate to empirically-minded men that a secular metaphysics, that is to say one kept strictly in accord with logic and fact, can be constructed. Indeed the craving for explanation which seizes scientist and public alike almost requires that some system be made out of all the theories which are based on fact.

A bad name has been earned for metaphysics equally (a) by those who have made the word stand for subjective and internal processes and (b) by those who have made it identical with transcendental states of being.

(a) For the first group metaphysics has meant knowledge gained by the subject alone, through reasoning or intuiting, or by some other method which requires nothing beyond the self. Hence it is that empiricists and all those who take the experience of the world and its data seriously have come to despise metaphysics not only as of little use but even more positively as misleading. This is far from what most of the Greeks meant, far from Plato and Aristotle, for whom metaphysics or what it suggested existed apart from the mind and the senses and lay out in the external world, there to be discovered and known. It is this context of objectivity and externality that is intended here; and these terms can be read in an other than epistemological connection. It is not essential to make Hegel's mistake and to suppose that because there is a subject as well as an object every time we know an object, that the subject thereby becomes an equally important ingredient in what is finally known. The subjective viewpoint was, like every other philosophical viewpoint, originally Greek. It was the outlook of the Greek sceptics, of Pyrrho and of others. But it was not the product of the highest moment of Greek culture or of Greek philosophy at its fullest. It must be accorded a place but not the only or the most important place. For the tragic fact is that the civilization of the west took off from the decline of Greek culture and not from its height, and thus allowed itself to miss the meaning of the greatest Greek achievements.

It is better to face frankly the difficulty presented by the necessity of grasping the range of metaphysics than to disguise it by neglect, or to retreat behind some substitute, such as phenomenology or cosmology.

The experimental scientist chooses the former alternative; he dismisses metaphysics airily as a weasel form of theology. And even those scientists who live in happy ignorance of the contradiction in which they are involved by questioning every observation and every hypothesis in their daily laboratory work while swallowing their dogma straight on Sunday, prefer to suppose that either the dogma implies no metaphysics or that such metaphysical issues as it did involve were settled once and for all long ago. "What a wonderful man you are to grapple with those old metaphysico-divinity books!" Darwin wrote Huxley.[1] And if meta-

---

[1] Quoted from a letter of Darwin in William Irvine, *Apes, Angels, and Victorians* (New York 1955, McGraw-Hill), p. 198.

physics was not to be forgotten altogether at least it had survived even though very much diminished in importance, a personal rather than a world affair, a private consolation for public failure. Recently an old scientist was heard to remark to a young metaphysician of whose profession he had just learned, "But you are young to be so resigned."

What a serious error they commit who blame the scientist for his anti-metaphysical attitude! It is the aftermath of bitter experiences. He has had to come through the violent opposition of religion to the free exploration of scientific ideas and the equally free promulgation of the results. And since theologians and religious leaders have often used metaphysics as a weapon against him, he has justifiably identified metaphysics with the opposition to science. He has not understood that any one particular metaphysics cannot be allowed to represent all metaphysics, nor that any consistent enterprise, such as science itself, has its own metaphysics. But such niceties of distinction require study where they are not set forth explicitly, and the scientist is very properly too busy with his own narrower concerns to bother straightening himself out on the question of whether there is a metaphysics in which an empiricist can believe or whether his acquired prejudices were not correct.

It would be wonderful indeed if the scientist had come any nearer the truth on such a topic when the philosopher himself has behaved in so similar a fashion. The contemporary philosopher is either no metaphysician at all or he has implicitly adopted a metaphysics under another name and holds to it like a religion. The scientifically-oriented philosopher has the zeal of the convert; he hopes to win the applause of physicists by publicly castigating metaphysics. In many respects he resembles the Jewish converts to Christianity in thirteenth-century Spain, who were harder on Spanish Jews than the older Christians had ever been. The dialectical materialist, the existentialist, and even sometimes the plain logician, has an explicit metaphysics which he clings to more faithfully than he does to the search for truth. The logical positivist may devote himself to a career of anti-metaphysical propaganda or join the linguistic analyst in disguising his metaphysics under another terminology. In all such cases metaphysics itself is abjured; and chiefly because the philosopher, who is impressed by the achievements and also by the method of science, has taken the same attitude toward metaphysics he supposes the scientist would want to take. But in adopting such a course there is less excuse for the philosopher whose field it is and who therefore ought to know better.

Some few philosophers, as a matter of record, *have* known better. They have written critical metaphysics, they have even written systematic ontologies. But once again, language has helped out by providing synonyms having none of the unfortunate connotations of metaphysics. Cosmology and phenomenology are favorites for this purpose, and so are certain portions of the terminology of grammar and syntax themselves. It has been considered perfectly acceptable to write metaphysics without any dilution provided only that the dread, theologically-colored name be avoided.

(b) The second group to earn metaphysics a bad name consists of those who have given it some kind of transcendental association. The range runs all the way from the serious theologians of established churches who speak knowingly of a supernatural order in which all the elements are familiar and almost substantial, to the members of that kind of mystical disorder which is so prevalent among theosophists and other seekers after the occult. It is thought by many theologians as well as by their opponents that the term, metaphysics, implies recourse to some avenue of knowledge other than sense experience worked over by logic; revelation, perhaps, or divine insight. Metaphysics, it has been supposed by those who have proceeded against it, is not transcendental provided it is put in such a way that no traditionally transcendental language is employed.

Let us pause for a moment to examine the justice of such a case. Our method will be to contrast typical theological words with typical metaphysical ones. The transcendental language is a mixture of theology and metaphysics, but it ought to be possible quite easily to separate out the disparate elements. Among the theological words, we will choose *God, angel,* and *grace*; and among the metaphysical words, *being, universal,* and *substance.*

Now the theological terms we have chosen as representative depend wholly upon the *feelings* for evidence, and since feelings give rise to actions the theologians feel that they can point to works in support of their beliefs. It is curious to find theologians making a pragmatic argument such as this. But other arguments mean placing the proof on grounds no rationalist could accept. There is no generally agreed upon definition of God, angel or grace; all depend upon acts of faith. And since the function of reason is to defend the faith (we are speaking only of western religions), on what basis is a decision to be reached when faiths conflict, and reason, which has been declared subordinate, is powerless to become superordinate for the purpose?

It is otherwise with the metaphysical words. Universal is not transcendental necessarily, not, for instance, if we adopt the Aristotelian definition of it as that which can be predicated of many. Universals have been dismissed by empiricists as fanciful entities because theologians have claimed for them an eternal nature. The Darwinians have dismissed them on the grounds that if the fixed species were members of universal classes, the theory of evolution by gradual stages and natural selection proved that there were no fixed species. But the older theory had supposed fixed species with gaps between them. A proper theory of universals would have to include a subtheory of gradation, which would hold that between any two universals there was a universal. Thus every minute change in organic species, every infinitesimal mutation, would only mean a change from the actualization of one universal to the actualization of another lying near it on the scale. The Darwinians, in other words, have been guilty of overlooking the space between the categories, which is filled with categories. When actual organizations develop, the categories are not abolished, they are only exchanged. If this is true of organic species, it is true also of geometric forms. Circles and triangles are equally indestructible, and the very entities and processes of science are as much universals as any. Oxygen and entropy are universals in the same sense, and they could occur any time and anywhere provided only that certain conditions were fulfilled. It is not necessary to banish haemoglobin in order to get rid of hobgoblins. Both are universals but both are not true in the sense of being classes having actual members, though both are classes. It is the business of logic and mathematics, and the experimental sciences, to find out just which universals are true in this sense, namely, of being classes which either have or could have actual members.

The cases of being and substance are similar to that of the universal. A redundant definition, though a non-trivial one, is necessary in the case of being, which is, simply, the things that are. But this enables us to attribute being to more than existence, for what has existed (but does so no longer) as well as what will exist (but does not yet) surely still has being. Otherwise we could not account for the comings and goings of existence, nor, since these are characteristic of it, could we account for existence itself. Hence being is broader than existence and constitutes a condition which we need to have ready when we wish to relate the things which exist.

And we need further to explain things in existence which we hope to relate, for we can show relations only where there are similarities (A is related to B if and only if B is related to A), and there are similarities in existence only where there are also differences. Substance accounts for individuality, according to Aristotle's definition of primary substance, and so we never experience substance though it is true we know about substances. Some of the other and later definitions of substance indicate the effort that was made to include in the conception of resistance what substances reveal and the irrationality they carry.

It is clear from the above comparison that typical theological terms involve the supernatural in a way in which the metaphysical terms do not. Moreover, the theological terms are proposed in the name of faith and defended by reason, whereas the metaphysical terms require reason alone, and so appeal to logic and fact. Metaphysics in the hands of some institution other than philosophy can be turned into anything the institution wants or its devotees think it requires. It is not too difficult to argue that after all what we mean (or ought to mean) by "being" is "God," by "universals" "angels," and by "independence of substance" "grace, or the free and unmerited favor of God." But the charge that metaphysics *per se* is also connected with the supernatural is unfounded, for there is nothing transcendental about metaphysics when it is practiced by competent metaphysicians in the interest of philosophy.

The upshot of the rejection of metaphysics considered either as irretrievably subjective or as irrefrangibly theological is that it has been these, too, but does not have to be so, and, if we take the Greeks into consideration, was not always so. It is possible to have a metaphysics which is non-subjective and non-transcendental. A preferred method of procedure would be not to change the meaning of the word, metaphysics, but to restore its original meaning, and to keep the subjectivity for epistemology and the theory of knowledge, if that is thought advisable. By metaphysics, then, we shall mean here a speculative and critical study of such systems and elements as are comprised under ontology, and especially under its objective variety, working toward the development of an ontology which holds the minimal assumptions which seem essential for the presuppositions of any other enterprise.

II

The procedure to be followed in the case of metaphysics is twofold. First it will be necessary to examine the range of metaphysics as a speculative field in order to discover what ontological systems are possible. And it will be found that those which actually have been held to be true are a very small and very random sample of that vast number which could be so held. Philosophy, in the sense of an untrammeled and detached exercise in exploration, has hardly been begun. We need to regard the classic ontologies as points on a graph in order to read off others. And we may discover when we do this that the ontologies we have now are not necessarily representative; that the new ones located in this way are higher in value, greater in consistency, wider in completeness, more vivid in illustration. Next, it will be necessary to select a metaphysics and then to hold it as an hypothesis until it can be checked against logic and the relevant facts. The first task, which is to explore the range of metaphysics, can be no more than suggested at the present time, but the second, which is to advance a hypothetical metaphysics, will lend itself immediately to detailed consideration.

Assuming, then, that we have established as an hypothesis a skeletal ontology for the purposes of investigation (for otherwise it would not be possible to look, since in order to look it is necessary to know what is being looked *for*), what is the next step? We need at this point a voluminous knowledge of current enterprises, and of the mathematics they employ, the theories they have adopted, and the facts they have turned up.

We have come to our task equipped with a nose for presuppositions. Behind every active enterprise, behind every set of practices, and even behind every set of principles, there are unacknowledged abstract propositions silently assumed yet none the less effective. Every thought, feeling and action, as well as every abstract and concrete external structure, from mathematical systems to office buildings, from love affairs to civil wars, has its own set of assumptions, and no less so for not being the content of some act of awareness. Presuppositions of necessity are never part of the foreground, but are essential ingredients of background material, and furnish the strength of the foundations for any thing or process. And when they are unearthed and examined, they prove to be metaphysical in nature.

This is true of the simplest practice as well as of the most profound theories. Science, for instance, has its own presuppositions. That there is a field of investigation, called nature, and that it stands still, so to speak, are elaborate presuppositions; and there are others in this area, including the uniformity of nature of which Mill reminded us. The scientific method operates with instruments and interprets with mathematics, and these formalized procedures require some very tall presuppositions indeed. And, finally, that the conclusions of science carry their own additional presuppositions, is attested by the scientists themselves, when in their off hours they compose books of general interest devoted to the metaphysical problem as it bears on their findings.

The proper metaphysics would be the one that would furnish the ground rules and give the conditions for the interpretation of anything. The endless pressure for presuppositions must be the task of philosophy. There is, however, an additional problem for philosophy when it comes to clean its house. Ontology, as the theory of being, has its own presuppositions, and metaphysics in practicing a critical method on ontologies has presuppositions as well; but the two sets are not always consistent. Perhaps it might help to give an example. One of the presuppositions of ontology must be that whatever the ontology there are no exceptions to it. And one of the presuppositions of metaphysics is that there must be more than one ontology.

Consider still another problem. Behind every philosophy, no matter how basic, there are presuppositions which are still more basic simply because they are where they are. They in turn have presuppositions and so on. Metaphysics, as the critic of presuppositions, has to turn round then and face the same situation within its own ranks, for the criticism of presuppositions must be made from somewhere, and from wherever it is made there is a position with further presuppositions. There is evidently no escape from this dilemma other than to discover a set of presuppositions for ontology which presuppose themselves in a way which indicates to us that nothing would be gained in going back of them. When the presuppositions supposed by another set of presuppositions is identical with itself, we must recognize that we have reached the end of our inquiry in this direction.

The task of metaphysics so far as other enterprises are concerned is somewhat as follows. Given a collection of fragmentary pieces of knowledge from various sources—from the experimental sciences but also from the arts, from history and from common experience—to put them together into a system. That is to say, metaphysics is asked to make a consistency out of fact. How then is this to be done if not by means of some system of ontology? What is called for is an ontology which will account for all and only those facts which are furnished to it by other fields. Philosophy is the name for the way in which we become aware of the magnitude of inherent consistency; for if a logical agreement among phenomena were not there, how could it be discovered?

To locate and abstract the presuppositions of any one field, and then of all fields together, is neither an easy nor a brief task. It is necessary to set up a formal enterprise to undertake the beginnings, for the end is far to seek. In brief, metaphysics is a field of endeavor, and in this sense like any other going concern altogether occupied with inquiry, having its own area of investigation. Such a formal enterprise may be called speculative metaphysics.

The proponents of speculative metaphysics conceived in this fashion will have to meet the objections of those who reject metaphysics altogether as well as of those who deny any but their own. The logical positivists can be considered typical examples of the first group, while the Thomists and the Marxists will serve ably for the second. Many answers can be made to both positions, and a number already have been. We might here look quickly at one of each.

A sample of the reply to the logical positivists is to point out that the denial of metaphysics is itself a metaphysical position, and one having, moreover, its own metaphysical presuppositions. Metaphysics cannot be banished by fiat, and in some form is implied immediately by anyone who enunciates a proposition. The logical positivists either deny metaphysics altogether or hold to an avowedly nominalistic one. Nominalism is that metaphysics in which (among other things) metaphysics is denied, and so no less a metaphysics for the denial. The man who endeavors to cut the ground from under his own feet will find his failure in the fact that he needs to stand somewhere.

A sample of the reply to the Thomists and the Marxists is that the existence of more than one absolute in the arena of competing metaphysics, where the task of defense in each case takes the same uncompromising style, is a natural social phenomenon whose meaning must be sought outside all absolutes. And there is, incidentally, an outside to absolutes, and it lies in the form of probabilities. The tentative holding of relative frequencies will do very nicely. Across the screen of average distributions the totalitarian claims of absolutes are flashed with wearisome regularity. How many have been the boasts of theoretical Ozymandiases! And how many more are to come! We can only hope that increasingly often a new face will appear among the older ones, with an expression betraying only partial conviction, only half belief, only relative assurance. And we can expect that the posture of such a relativist poised for inquiry will make him ready to believe anything for which there is evidence, and to disbelieve anything previously believed if the evidence weakens or else accumulates on the opposite side. When an absolutist loses a battle he experiences a sense of moral outrage and cries unfair, as though his defeat were a crime not only against him but even against the very nature of things. There is nothing he resents half so much as being treated as he would treat others, and he will resort to any tactics to prevent another setback. When a relativist loses he concedes that every battle cannot be won, and he falls back upon the consideration of further strategy.

Anti-metaphysician and absolutist in metaphysics are equal in the strength of their conviction, and so the further assumption has been quietly adopted that metaphysician necessarily means absolutist. The situation is similar to the way in which the theist shares with the atheist an extreme degree of belief which turns them both against the agnostic, or to the way in which in the United States in 1933 the clergyman and the bootlegger united to oppose the repeal of prohibition. In metaphysics, we need a set of terms to indicate those with various *degrees* of conviction. Between the suspension of judgment and the complete surrender to belief lie many shades of conviction, and these need not only names but also studies, and they will take us, in the interest of metaphysics, into an examination of how it is that beliefs are held and to what extent and how to tell about them. And such studies will be in many different fields: in psychology, of course, but also in sociology and anthropology; in the structures of institutions, and also in those of cultures.

As for philosophy itself, a constructive approach could be undertaken. A finite ontology which would call for the least amount of axioms from which theorems could be deduced that would only just fit the facts, is a definite part of the program. And why does it seem so strange to propose a new alternative in metaphysics? We have an advanced situation to account for. None of the European metaphysics that we have been offered is suitable for the undertaking, and none of the other alternatives will do, either, for that matter. Ever since science has appeared on the scene, the philosophers have floundered helplessly in the face of it. There is a reason for this. We have seen that the British empiricists shared with the continental rationalists a common subjectivism. If a theologically-driven transcendental metaphysics is inadequate to provide a set of assumptions for science, then so is a subjective rationalism and a radical empiricism. That is to say, neither a transcendental metaphysics nor an experimental epistemology will do to account for the consistency of fact. We need instead a finite metaphysics. This is admittedly a new conception. It has antecedents in the Greek world; for instance it seems to have been what Plato suggested by his peculiar use of the dialogue form and in his reluctance to come to conclusions, and also what Aristotle was after in the limits and tentativeness of his metaphysics. We have to deal with the stubborn proposition that there are facts, and with the further, and equally stubborn, proposition that there are theories to account for the facts. And so the finite metaphysics intended to explain the consistency of fact must make a world for each of the elements: namely, for consistency on the one hand, and for fact on the other. And the first will be a world of logic and the second a world of substance, and there will be relations, of course, between them, which will have to be taken into the account.

Those who are not entirely at the mercy of ancient prejudice will see in what is offered here a new ontology, yes, but one having familiar elements of the older set, for there is nothing that does not owe much to tradition. A combination of the Platonic Ideas with the Aristotelian substance has been proposed before: it was not only proposed but also formally adopted in Islam and Christianity, by Averroes and Thomas Aquinas respectively, and by them much in the shape in which the Greek Plotinus took it from the Jewish Philo. It was Philo who first saw how religious certitude could be supported by philosophical rationalism provided the latter was read as the principles of an absolute conviction and not as the ground-rules for an asymptotic inquiry. Philo and Plotinus introduced the note of certainty into the version of Plato and Aristotle which the western religions adopted; it was not present in the original texts, and it is foreign to the spirit of Greek rationalism.

Those who are not Friends of the Ideas, as Plato called them, are in some sense outside the tradition; for whether you hold the Ideas to be apart from substance and substance an empty thing, as Plato himself did, or insist that substance is the stronger category, and so hold that the Ideas are folded into the stream of becoming, there to be regarded as the modifications of substance, as Aristotle did, or cling to some other interpretation of the relative strength and relations between the two worlds of Ideas and substance, you are still in the classic tradition. Of course, there are excesses and pathological cases which lie on the borderline. Those who are Friends of the Ideas often fall into exaggeration in deprecating the world of concrete individuals and become the prey to all sorts of mystic irrationalisms. Those who deny the Ideas in favor of the worship of matter find themselves involved with irrationalisms of another sort, irrationalisms in which nothing reasonable exists since no abstract principles are allowed to be genuine.

Ideas, under that name, and substance, too, must go; at least when we are addressing men whose memory of these terms has unfortunate connotations. In their place, we may adopt the more fashionable ones. For the "Ideas," there are a number of synonyms. Perhaps "classes" will do best, or "sets," if we choose our substitutes from logic or mathematics; and, corresponding to these, the "substances" will henceforth be "members" or "elements" respectively. Then we can build to other kinds of more complex "universals" (a term which has also been banished), such as "propositions" or "equations."

In the physical sciences, the "Ideas" will be physical, chemical or biological "functions" or "relations," while in place of "substance" we will speak of "matter" and "energy-transformations" of the same. Whenever the element is abstract, we are in the realm of Ideas, and whenever there is an affective component we are in that of substance. The equations of chemistry, for instance, are nothing more than formulas; they are completely abstract in that they refer to no particular concrete situation. And such abstract formulas are what we once would have called Ideas. The chemical elements themselves, their combinations and rearrangements, their alterations and violent reactions, are obviously concrete facts and so are what we once would have called substances. The distinction is no less ontological because it is put in other terms, and the seeking out of the relations no less a metaphysical exercise because we refuse so steadfastly to employ that word.

At some point, the retreat from proper names introduces more difficulties than it resolves. For what else can we call the enterprise which is metaphysics if we are to show the contribution which the empiricists themselves are able to make to it? The American philosopher, Charles S. Peirce, was not at once a scientist and a metaphysician for nothing. The question as he saw it was not whether the status of universals was to be accepted but *which* universals. Nobody who viewed the problem dispassionately would deny the reality to Lepidoptera or affirm it for leprochauns. We must accept the genuineness of abstractions as much as, yet no more than, we do the concrete individuals whose existence is revealed to us by sense experience. And above all we must seek the connections, trying to find evidence for them. A lay metaphysics, a metaphysics which is busily occupied in probing for the beliefs deserving of support, is not beyond the bounds of possibility. And a scientist could not knowingly reject such a study once he was able to see it in the proper perspective.

THE TOPICS AND DEFINITIONS OF THE CATEGORIES

1. THE NUMBER AND SOURCE OF THE CATEGORIES

Philosophy begins with the categories. Are they one or many; and, if one, then what is its name to be, and, if it comes to be divided, from where are we to obtain the principle which decides the first division, and what is that pair to be, and so on; and if many, then how is their order to be determined and which way are they, too, for that matter? Are we for instance to derive our categories from experience as reporting about itself, or as reporting things which lie beyond it, or both; and in any of these cases, how are we to agree on what experience reports? And the same questions could be asked for knowing. The things that we experience or that we know about, whether or not they are concerned with our own knowing, must be sorted out into some kind of order, which means taking some before the others; and which ones are we to take first, and why, and on the basis of what criterion is this preference to be decided? These are difficult but crucial questions; once they are answered, the remainder of philosophy flows in the fashion in which it was thus disposed, so that after the choosing of the categories everything else is limited by them to a special position, in accordance with which things can be seen in a certain way and no other.

Spinoza, for example, starts with one category, namely substance (for his God is merely infinite substance); and the first division is made by thought and extension (the *res cogitans* and *res extensa* of Descartes), and the rest of his philosophy is explained in terms of these. Leibniz, on the other hand, starts with many; that is, he begins with force but insists that force is not one but many, the infinite, unextended, indivisible, immaterial, simple monads, for there are as many forces as there are individuals and these are unlimited in number. The advantages are not equal of the two types of beginning; the monist has an advantage over the pluralist for he knows where he starts; and in most cases his unity is an absolute, but the pluralist has things better in certain ways, since he is not so committed and can more easily keep his system open.

The question of how many the categories are to be is not a mere matter of number; it depends in a way on the prior question of what it is that we wish to explain. The ambition of the philosopher is to get back for his beginnings to the least set of assumptions and the most primitive elements; yet he has to cope with things as they are, and this means, too, things as they are with him. We wish to construct a phenomenology which shall reflect all that is: with what elements are we to erect the structure? From which area of our experience or its revelations are we to take our categories? We do not start as naive, inexperienced creatures but in the middle of things. By the time we are old enough to come to philosophy, we have already collected for ourselves large segments of what is given; to deny it for purposes of simplicity were an hypocrisy plain to everyone.

It is easy to see how a number of focal points, seemingly fundamental, have been chosen as the proper sites on which to build governing perspectives. Aristotle was sure of substance, as sure as Descartes was of the self, as Hegel was of being, and as some now are of this-and-other; and the fact that the first was ontological, the next psychological and the third phenomenological was unnoticed; and the last was noticed but who is to say that his own undercuts the others? We want the picture that will best represent all there is, and not the temperament of those drawing the representation. The task is to purge preference and to hold an eye onto the world, looking out for its commonest properties.

The sufficiently intense study of any two or more philosophies inevitably suggests the possibility of reaching a sort of standpointlessness in philosophy. This has been dreamed of in two ways: first, by eliminating all perspectives; and, secondly, by incorporating all perspectives (the latter a sort of tensor perspective in philosophy). We could endeavor to get outside all peculiar perspectives, but this would show us the dependence of philosophy on its symbols: we would have to invent a language for the purpose in order to avoid committing ourselves. Or we could endeavor to construct a kind of super-system of coordinates whose points are systems. These are as yet ambitions rather than achievements. It may be sufficient in the meanwhile if we can become aware of just what our perspectives are and what limitations they impose upon us as well as what ranges they allow.

When we make a preliminary survey of the history of philosophy, and try to induce from it some governing principle as to the source of the categories, some estimate, in other words, of the ways in which the categories are conventionally chosen, we are profoundly dismayed. For the pattern which clearly emerges is that there is no set pattern; every item which could be obtained has been chosen by somebody as the prior in philosophy, every highway and byway has been scoured at some time and its elements raised to ontological eminence. We see the source of the categories in authority, in fact and in common sense. We see the source of the categories in every institution, in revealed religion chiefly but also in politics, economics and more recently in some one of the sciences. And not only the data of experience and the disciplines have been selected for this purpose but also every type of psychological experience itself, every subjective area, from sensation and reason to dream states, intuition, and the unconscious. When we see this profusion of sources we know that to try the second method, namely, of putting together all perspectives into a universal perspective, would be difficult.

It will be far easier, perhaps, if we adopt the first method. This calls for us to select a minimal perspective, to specify its limitations, and then to endeavor to eliminate from them as far as possible. To this end it will be necessary to assess the familiar perspectives to determine the one which involved itself the least in the outlook on which it gave. Presumably, this would be a perspective selected from some one among the philosophical disciplines. For the aim is always to take as little for granted as possible, and since we are involved in philosophy in such an enterprise whether we wish to be or not, it might be well to stop here and not look outside for some other; for it is clear that any other would involve us in two: philosophy and the other.

There has been a shift in emphasis here which had better be recognized. From a standpointlessness, that is to say, from a zero perspective, we have gone over to the side of a minimal perspective. The change, it is to be hoped, is methodological only. For the technique which employs a

minimal perspective, the zero perspective remains the ideal. The assignment calls for us to begin with a minimal perspective, and then carefully
to pare down the minimal perspective toward the limiting condition of the
zero perspective. We cannot regard the question as settled in this way,
however, for here we are only presenting the alternatives.

We are left, then, with the choice among philosophical disciplines
for a starting point. We have everything to select from that calls itself a
branch of philosophy, from logic and phenomenology to ethics and aesthetics, and even the history of philosophy. Each has in fact been selected
by some one, yet it would seem advisable to work with the most primitive, although here we are still left undecided between logic and phenomenology which have good reasons for equal claims to priority, so that it
may be a fusion will have to be made of the two. But if either one then
which one, and if one is selected then what phase of that one? For there
are many logics and the question of just what appears has not been
settled to everyone's satisfaction. These are difficult problems and they
concern the matter of approach. And if philosophers cannot agree that
they are to start from this source or that one and to derive their philosophical investigations in this wise, then we must despair of unifying
philosophy even before it has got well under way. The failure has virtues
as well as limitations, for who is to say that until the truth in this regard
has been discovered and its proofs completed all paths which may lead
to it are not to be held open?

Since the purpose of this discussion is not to set up a philosophy but
to see how a philosophy could be set up, the consideration of categorical
sources can for the moment proceed no further in this direction but will
have to take another turn.

2. A SAMPLE OF THE RANGE OF
CATEGORIES

We are now ready to propose the joining of the question of the number of
the categories, with which we started this inquiry, to the question of the
quantity of the categories; how many there are, in other words, and which
ones. We can do no more with this question than sample the range of the
categories, which is large and which thus far has never been adequately
investigated. Moreover, if we are not to fall a prey to the genetic fallacy
we shall have to neglect in our inquiries the source of the categories,
which we have treated already, however briefly. The quantity and kind
of the categories is irrelevant to the source from which they were obtained, at least for all the purposes which concern their logic and their

value. Much can be accounted for by a study of development, but such an explanation is always given in terms of occasion and not of cause; it is capable of specifying structure and substance but not being. The things which are, are while they are; and do not owe their being to the manner in which they came to be what they are.

There are a number of ways of dividing what we know, but what is it that we are dividing? If we propose to adopt a definition of the primary element, then we are at once committed to two propositions the subject-matter of which it is precisely that we wish to investigate; and we cannot afford to take for granted anything which would so determine our inquiry when what we wish to inquire into is what it is that is taken for granted. The first proposition that we wish to avoid committing ourselves to in order to investigate it is the assertion of monism.

"It is asserted that there is one and only one and that the one is—," or,

"—is asserted to be one (or the one)," or, more simply,

"—is asserted," where the one is conveyed in the singular form of the term by which the blank is to be filled. If we set up a single category, whatever name we give it, then we are so committed.

The second proposition, and an equally difficult one, is the definition of our single category. If the *definiendum* is a monism, the *definiens* must be made up of terms which themselves are left undefined and hence taken as primitive, for to define them and then to define the terms in which they would be defined would involve us in an infinite regress, hardly solved by Aristotle's suggestion that the regress could be stopped when familiar terms are reached.[1] The definition of topical categories thus is crucial to the choice of the categories themselves, and reveals itself as intimate with ontological beginnings. The question of definitions regarded from this aspect will be taken up later.

We shall be compelled then to initiate the topic with a term to stand for the *definiendum* which shall on pain of defeating itself go undefined. The term chosen for this purpose is "reality." We could describe it as the referent of that which is true in the logical sense (as distinct from both the psychological and the ontological senses), provided that we eliminated from consideration all logical implications incurred thereby. This description is intended merely to bring the term into focus and not to gain acceptance for any particular, rigid understanding of it.

For any term so chosen the question of range must at once arise, and

---

[1] 110a5.

the most elementary distinction to be brought in to assist us in laying out the range of "reality" would seem to be that between whole and part. Reality can be a name for the whole or only for a part; and if for the whole, then the whole as divisible or indivisible; and if for the part, then for parts of various sizes, for a part which is nearly the equal of the whole or for a number of parts each of which is an infinitesimally small part. Let us glance briefly at some of the consequences which flow from these.

If reality is the name for an indivisible whole, then the appearance of parts is merely an appearance. The separateness of things is an illusion, there is only the one. Such is the doctrine of *The Upanishads,* for instance, which maintains the ultimate reality of Brahma alone. In this case some conception of the unknown often is taken to be the whole: the *indefinite* of Anaximander, for instance, or the *One* of Plotinus; or something known is raised to that eminence: *water* by Thales, or *air* by Anaximenes. A variation of this philosophy would suppose that the parts, too, are real but momentary, and their fleeting reality is soon lost in the true and permanent reality of the one. Such is the Buddhist doctrine of "momentariness" for example.[2]

If reality is the name for a divisible whole, then the parts share the reality of the whole. The parts may be two, three or four or more. The most popular number is two, generally some form of essence-existence distinction, such as possibility and actuality or logic and fact. This has given rise to many subvarieties, such as objective idealism, nominalisms of several sorts, and realisms. Numbers higher than two are less often employed.

If reality is the name for a single part, then the world is divided into appearance and reality, with appearance the name for all that is not real. Various religious philosophies are of this sort. The philosophy of F. H. Bradley occurs in this connection, for example, and the doctrine of Māyā according to the Advaita Vedānta of Śamkara. In the Vedānta, spirit is opposed to matter which is unreal. Then a subvariety is possible which would attribute not unreality but lesser reality to the part or parts which is not truly real.

It is clear that if a sufficient number of charts of this type were to be constructed, and all existing philosophies plotted on them, other possible, and perhaps illuminating philosophies could be read off and their ramifications explored. It may be that the task of surveying the philosophical field is more importunate than the necessity for choosing among the alternative philosophies. Certainly it makes the most urgent demand; for

---

[2] See e.g. M. Hiriyanna, *The Essentials of Indian Philosophy* (London 1949, Allen and Unwin), p. 78.

how can we know what philosophy best suits the purpose of accounting for being until we know what philosophies there are?

Meanwhile we have before us the necessity of exploring the problem from another and in some ways more subtle point of view. We shall have to drop for a moment the approach we have been pursuing in order to try another which is quite different. We have promised in this section to take up the question of the definition of the topical categories as being crucial to the choice of the categories themselves. This we shall now endeavor to do, and in the remaining sections the problem of definition is discussed. It is to be expected that before the end of the last section the two points of view will come together sufficiently to constitute a cohesive treatment.

3.   THE PROBLEM OF DEFINITION: PLATO

Our subject-matter is the topic of the categories. Ordinarily, it would be supposed that to consider in this context the types of definitions would not be germane; and this would be so were it not for the fact that, as we shall presently note, the definition of the categories according to some procedures implies a prior selection. Thus in a sense categories are chosen sometimes in the very act of defining. Hence we must consider the latter in connection with the former.

The range of definition runs from induction to division, according to whether the method is one of ascent or descent to the *definiendum*; and to tautology, from another dimension.

We dedicate the first part of our discussion of definition to Plato's *epagogé* and *diairesis*. As in the case of most branches of philosophy, we find the earliest treatment in the dialogues of Plato, and so we give him credit for being the original source because his work has survived, when despite his great excellence chance may have endowed him with an importance out of keeping with the quality of his contemporaries and predecessors; for who knows the collected work of Heraclitus or of Democritus and how their strength may have altered our evaluations? But we are on the track of definitions of the categories, and we first take up the scent here.

The Socratic method of definition by induction or *epagogé* is employed without a formal statement of principles. It consists in two stages. In the first stage the suggestions which have been proposed are refuted by Socrates by means of the *elenchus,* leaving the speaker perplexed. In the second stage a definition is discussed by Socrates by means of tentative hypotheses, a criticism of these, resulting in consequent emendations. A good example of the first stage is contained in the little dialogue, *Meno,* on the definition of virtue, where Meno is the respondent whose proposals are rejected by Socrates, ending in clear symptoms of Meno's puzzlement.[3] Examples of the second stage are usually less well defined and more spread, as for instance Socrates' own definition of justice in the *Republic.* The term to be defined in this way is approached from below, and its meaning emerges slowly from the inquiry.

The stronger importance of the method of composition and of definition by division in the Platonic dialogues is often overlooked. The method of composition or collection is recounted briefly in the *Phaedo.* To explain a principle it is necessary to assume some other principle, chosen as the one deemed best of the higher ones, and so until one is reached which is adequate.[4] There can be no discipline for collection, whose task is to discover the Idea to be divided. "Here" as Cornford pointed out, "no methodical procedure is possible. The generic Form must be divined by an act of intuition, for which no rules can be given."[5] What is sought by the joint method of collection and division is the method by which one can naturally collect things into one and divide them into many.[6] There is a method for division. Note the emphasis on the word, natural, for Plato earlier had said that the aim is to divide things by classes "where the natural joints are" and he employs the image of a man carving meat who seeks the easiest way to divide it by not trying to break any part.[7] Definition by division, then, is chiefly a matter of classification, of dividing classes into subclasses, until we come to the lowest class of which it is a member. Plato was thinking in terms of biological genera and species, and he generalized the notion to all classes and objects.

We should start by assuming that there is in everything one idea, and if we seek we shall find it; and next we must try to divide it, and so on, until we find out just how many there are.[8] It is not wise to do as some have done, to go directly from one to infinity, but it is necessary to find out how many lie between these.[9] The best example of the method in operation is Plato's definition of angler.[10] He starts with man: man is either with or without an art; if with an art, then either with a productive or an acquisitive art; and if with an acquisitive art, then with an acquisitive art of exchange or of coercion; and if of coercion, then a coercive art of fighting or of hunting; and if of hunting, then of hunting the lifeless or

---

[3] Cf. also *Euthyphro,* 7.
[4] 101 D.
[5] F. M. Cornford, *Plato's Theory of Knowledge* (New York 1951, Humanities Press), p. 186.

[6] *Phaedrus,* 266 B.
[7] *Op. cit.,* 265 E.
[8] *Philebus,* 16 D.
[9] *Op. cit.,* 17 A.
[10] *Sophist,* 218 E-221 B.

the living; and if of hunting the living, then of living land or water animals; and if of water animals, then of water animals with wings, called fowling, or of submerged water animals, called fishing; and if of fishing, then by enclosure or by blows; and if by blows, then by fire hunting (at night) or by barb hunting (by day); and if by barb hunting by day, then by striking down, called tridentry, or by striking up, called angling. The definition of angler, then, reached by division in this way is as follows. An angler is a man with an acquisitive, coercive art of hunting living submerged water animals by striking up with barbs by day.

This, then, is the method of definition by division; and we had better look at some of Plato's comments on it, then glance at Aristotle's before turning to our own.

Plato warns us in another dialogue not to disregard species in making our division nor to make the necessary abstraction unless warranted.[11] It is, said Plato, as though one were to divide man into Hellenic and barbarian, thus mistakenly supposing them one species; or to divide numbers into one large group and the remainder, giving each group a name; when a better division would be male and female, and odd and even, respectively.[12] He suggested also that the method of division belongs to the dialectic.[13] It is indeed often hard to distinguish between them in many cases where his use of the dialectic leans heavily on division.

There are passages in which Aristotle seemed to employ division as though he thought the method entirely reliable.[14] He gave rules, for instance, for conducting the proper sort of division.[15] But curiously, elsewhere he condemns it in the very connection in which it seems to have first suggested itself to Plato, namely in the case of biological organisms.[16] What emerges from his argument is interesting, because he wishes to derive his categories empirically rather than to impose them artificially. It does sometimes appear as though Aristotle's speculative training goes against his instinct for experimentation in such a way that the latter only is able to obtrude itself now and then. The Platonic method of division into classes is assigned a small amount of importance indeed, for it is roundly condemned as "a weak syllogism" and for begging what it ought to prove.[17]

Plato's method of definition is, oddly enough, and despite Aristotle's objection, empirical in character. Plato begins by seeking a common element among all the actual uses of a term. This is good practice so long

[11] *Statesman*, 262 B.
[12] *Op. cit.*, 262 D–E.
[13] *Sophist*, 253 D.
[14] *Analytica Posteriora*, 96b15–97b6.

[15] 97a22; 1037b28–1038a35.
[16] *De Partibus Animalium*, 642b5–644a10.
[17] 46a31 ff.

as what we wish to discover is what a term has meant in use or what it has seemed to mean. But it will not do for the categories which may be neologisms or for old terms which are to be employed more precisely. In the former of these two cases the method becomes impossible; and in the latter it is what ought to have been meant rather than what was meant that is sought.

We can see that definition is not prior but to the contrary the whole weight of a philosophical position is behind each man's conception of definition. For Aristotle, like Plato, gave Socrates credit for calling attention to the importance of definition,[18] yet when the chips were down Aristotle insisted that the Platonic Ideas are undefinable[19] and that substance alone can be defined.[20] Thus Aristotle's criticism of Plato's conception of definition was not altogether detached, and his own demand for priority and intelligibility in definitions[21] could only operate within the framework of a metaphysical system already established.

These are advantages to the Platonic *diairesis* which it would be well not to ignore. It suggests a methodology for semantics in the vulgar sense, for the clarification of meaning in disputation is at present an arbitrary affair conducted by one party; whereas the method of *diairesis* could be a dialectic one, capable of arriving at mutual clarifications. It is the source of syllogism as well as of definition, first, because it relies on prior knowledge. In the instance of the angler, for example, did not the divisions (which, as Plato warned, had to be the proper ones) require of the Stranger who made them a very wide knowledge of all sorts of classes and subclasses as well as of human activities from both of which he could select what he needed, and require the same of Theaetetus so to gain his ready assent? It is the source of syllogism, secondly, because it relies on the law of contradiction. Each step in the argument is of the form

> Either *A* or *B*,
> *B*,
> Therefore not *A*.

It was Aristotle himself who admitted that the Platonic division plays a part, albeit a small part, in the method of syllogism, and in fact he calls it a "weak syllogism,"[22] on the ground that it begs what it ought to prove and always establishes something too general.

The method of division is constitutive as well as regulative, qualitative rather than structural, and not nearly primitive enough. Since de-

---

[18] 987b1.
[19] 1040a8–b4.
[20] 1031a1.

[21] 141a23 ff.
[22] *Analytica Priora*, 46a31–33.

finitions are to be used on the categories, they ought not to take for
granted a philosophy which already contains their forced construction.
Definitions to be in any way fundamental ought to be as nearly as possible without content, and shifted toward the tautology end of the spectrum of definitions. A simple substitution rule here would not work, for the
result of replacing the *definiendum* with the *definiens* would be an awkwardness of expression disastrous to context.

4. THE PROBLEM OF DEFINITION: ARISTOTLE

Before we can have a definition, we must assume the law of contradiction,
said Aristotle, for we cannot argue from a definition without "grasping
what truth or falsity means."[23] By truth or falsity is meant that while
we must consider how to express ourselves, more important still is to
ascertain "what the facts actually are."[24] Definition is "the statement of
a thing's nature,"[25] an expression signifying its essence,[26] in short its
essential nature;[27] "we have a definition ... where there is a formula
of something primary,"[28] the "double assumption of the meaning of the
word and the existence of the thing."[29] We must know of the existence
of the thing to be defined before the definition.[30]

    "We must postulate ... that something has a meaning,"[31] and its
definition will be in the "form of words of which the word is a sign."[32]
Given the laws of logic, especially contradiction and excluded middle, the
thing to be defined and the word which will stand for it, we are ready to
proceed with the definition. This consists in two steps: first we "divide
the genus into its first *infimae species*," and next we "examine the properties peculiar to the species, working through their proximate common differentiae."[33] Accomplishing the first consists in "observing a set
of similar individuals, and consider[ing] what element they have in common."[34] The second will mean working up toward the genus. A universal
term, in other words, will have for the two parts of its definition the
genus of which it is a species, and its difference from other members of
the same species.[35] And so definition is in terms of similarity and difference.[36] "The framer of a definition should first place the object in its

[23] 1012b7. See also 1012a17–29.
[24] 1030a27.
[25] 93b29.
[26] 153a15; also 154a32.
[27] 91a1.
[28] 1030a7–10.
[29] 71a14.

[30] 93b33.
[31] 1012b5.
[32] 1012a23.
[33] 96b15–22.
[34] 97b7.
[35] 1039a26.
[36] 102a8.

genus, and then append its differences."[37] The definition should not be obscure, we are warned, neither ought it to be redundant or ambiguous; it must be stated in terms that are prior and intelligible.[38]

In this manner Aristotle bids us inquire into what the "essential nature"[39] of a thing is. Definition seeks to lay bare what a thing is—its essence.[40] But there are difficulties such as the following. The reality for Aristotle resides in the individuals, "no universal exists apart from its individuals," he stated baldly.[41] Yet there is no definition of individuals, and the concrete things go undefined.[42] In another context we are told that definition is possible only "if essential form is knowable."[43] When Aristotle argued against the Platonic Ideas, he insisted that the substance of individuals could not be reduced to anything universal.[44] Yet definitions, as he insisted throughout the *Posterior Analytics,* are universal. How, then, are we to reconcile universal definitions with exclusively real yet undefinable individual substances?

Again, "demonstration develops from universals, induction from particulars."[45] It is "an inference from necessary premises"[46] and so, Aristotle said, "there is no identical object of which it is possible to possess both a definition and a demonstration."[47] What then does our judgment of essential nature rest on, merely the intuition of its essence? But this seems hardly to be in conformity with this treatment of universals generally.

The solution seems to have been attempted by distinguishing between the logical and the ontological. *Predicating* one of many, we are told, does not necessarily imply the *being* of a One beside the Many.[48] What the thing is must be an individual if it is to have a real essence, and must be a universal, a class of individuals, if it is to be defined. This is certain to be unsatisfactory, since logic is too closely bound up with the real throughout. Substance, after all, is chief among the categories.

Another and more substantive definition of definition was undertaken in terms of cause. We are assuming truth and falsity, remember, and "we do not know the truth without a cause."[49] Hence "another kind of definition" is offered, one which is put in terms of "a formula exhibiting the cause of a thing's existence,"[50] as for instance in the definition of the movement of animals.[51] Causes, then, are to be understood "in the sense of de-

[37] 139a28–30.
[38] *Topica,* Bk. VI, *Passim.*
[39] The term occurs throughout. See e.g. 97b16.
[40] 1029b15; 101b39.
[41] 1040b27.
[42] 1036a23–1039b27.
[43] 82b36.
[44] 1039a23–1039b16.
[45] 81a40.
[46] 73a23.
[47] 91a9.
[48] 77a5–10. Italics mine.
[49] 993b23.
[50] 993b39.
[51] 703a5.

finitions."[52] This almost ostensive type of definition amounts to "a quasi demonstration of essential nature."[53] It suffers from the opposite error of not being sufficiently logical. Although the purpose of a definition is "to make known the term stated,"[54] we are not supposed to add to our knowledge of anything by defining it.[55] But on the other hand neither is it a mere tautology such as might be obtained by employing a single term for the *definiens*.[56] We are treated to no formula of definition by cause, and the substitute is unsatisfactory. For if Aristotle meant what he said when he said that "definition is a 'thesis' [i.e. a 'basic truth'] or a 'laying something down,' "[57] then there is a prior knowledge in the making of a definition which can be chosen for that purpose in accordance with the first principle of the one doing the defining: and if cause is as important as it seems to Aristotle in the *Metaphysics*, where he postulates the four causes almost before he does anything else, then he will make his definitions in terms of cause. So that whatever the philosopher prefers will be what he takes as his primitive, and he will not define it but will define everything else in terms of it. Aristotle's true categories, however, are those which he took as primitive in his procedure and not necessarily those which he sets up as such. For instance, he took as primitive the movement of substances in their potential and actual states, and he explains everything in terms of these. Secondary considerations involve quantity and quality, the four causes, and the genera and species, which, although set up as categories, are yet either derived or adjunctive.

So once again we find ourselves in a condition of bafflement. We have reached the same point with Aristotle that we reached earlier with Plato. There are vast practical advantages to the Aristotelian formula for definition. As a ready rule of thumb for arriving at definitions, it is without an equal. It only gives us difficulties in the place we have come to regard as our most sensitive spot: in the area where we expect to arrive at the topic of the categories.

The conclusion of our brief survey of Platonic and Aristotelian notions of definition seems to be that both make the mistake of supposing that their definitions are primitive enough, yet in their definitions of definition and in their rules for defining both assume an entire philosophy. We began with the problem of the categories, with which we asserted philosophy properly begins. We saw that the source of the categories has been for one philosopher or another every discoverable area, and we saw further that the choice of the categories was faced with a tremendous

52 1070a22.   55 90b15.
53 94a1.   56 102a1–5.
54 141a27.   57 72a23.

range. The problem of beginning philosophy with the categories is evidently a much greater one than has been generally supposed.

5. THE CATEGORIES ANALYZED IN DEFINITIONS

We are concerned with definition here chiefly as it has to do with the categories, and this consists in taking the plunge from the imprecise language of common sense to the technical and more precise language of metaphysics. To define each of the terms employed in the definition is therefore impossible in any definite way: we know them already or we feel them, but we cannot accord them the virtues of the exactness which collectively they are expected to provide for the *definiendum*. If we use more exact terms, selected from among those which possess the requisite denotative standing, then the terms defined by them are not categories.

The whole difficulty of definition is brought on by the abstract nature of the object to be named in the process. Definition is a matter of naming, the process one of assigning a symbol to an object. Naming particulars consists in pairing symbols and objects; every actual object is unique and is assigned an unique symbol. We call *this* house by the address, "12 Nassau Drive," which is a name at least unique in the annals of Jefferson Parish near New Orleans. But when we come to the naming of more abstract and general objects we encounter special problems. Such objects are universals, that is to say, they are not individuals but classes (putting aside for the moment the question of whether such classes are finite or infinite or indefinite). Now names for universals or classes appear to be reducible to the language in which they are expressed, on the nominalistic assumption that they are lacking in reference. True, some of them are. But some are not; and nominalism serves as a useful caution in determining which these are. It may defeat our purpose to admit hobgoblins to the company of haemoglobin.

Subsidiary rules for definition issue from logic. The definition, Frege reminds us, must have a sharp boundary.[58] So much comes from the meaning of excluded middle. We learn from mathematical logic to supply it with an unlimited substitution rule, and the use of definition always involves the replacement of one name by another, although as Aristotle pointed out the second name can never be a mere term which might produce a tautology. Thus the second name must be the name for a meaning. We have, then, an equivalence with complexities of the *definiens*. Again,

58 *Philosophical Writings*, p. 159.

we learn from mathematical logic that we have the right to introduce one, and only one, new constant. Lastly, the final step of definition comes also from Frege: "the fundamental law of logic permits the transformation of an equality holding generally into an equation."[59] It would have been better to say "an equivalence holding generally into an equality." This step is made possible by the consistency of equivalence.

We are learning steadily to look behind the assumptions which are contained in the definitions we are accustomed to using, to get beneath them, to pare them down. For the problem of definition presents difficulties which go as deep as the categories with which, as we said at the start of this discussion, philosophy begins. And no matter what terms are employed in our definition, the same obstacles confront us, precipitated by the necessity of deciding what we are taking for granted in admitting those terms such as are employed in the *definiens* and there admitted as undefined lest the dread defeat of infinite regression overtake us in our efforts. Suppose that we adopt the view of modern geometry, for instance, and accept as our definition of "triangle" the phrase "a system of three non-collinear points." We might say to begin with that we know intuitively what a triangle is, by which we mean that having been raised on the study of Euclid in our elementary schools and absorbed its meaning in various practical ways, we are unconsciously familiar with the figure which is formed by connecting three points not in a straight line with straight line segments or with the figure bounded on three sides or by the figure having the sum of its interior angles equal to 180 degrees. The new definition has the merit of brevity yet suffers only to a lesser extent perhaps from silent assumptions of unacknowledged axioms such as is the case with every underived proposition. It comes to this, that we know explicitly only of proven theorems what it is on which their validity depends. We are only indulging in the remoteness induced by shorthand when we give a name to a proposition which has not been analyzed.

Here we shall regard the proper definition of definition as a correspondence between a term and the proposition to which it refers. The name is of course a symbol and the proposition a separate theorem, which, when sufficiently analyzed, can be made to reveal its systemic connection. In this sense definitions exist to be discovered and shown, as Frege asserted.[60] He even went so far as to claim that this discovery of definition is a creative act.[61] A definition requires a domain with respect

[59] *Op. cit.*, 181.

[60] Gottlob Frege, *The Foundations of Arithmetic* (Oxford 1950, Blackwell), pp. 78–9.

[61] *Translations from the Philosophical Writings of Gottlob Frege*, ed. by Peter Geach and Max Black (Oxford 1952, Blackwell), pp. 177–8.

to which it is a definition, and in definitions we must have regard for the width of the domain. Thus in a sense, before we can have a definition we must first specify the domain. When we have named and defined a thing, we still have before us the task of determining what it consists of, and a definition is the first step and no substitute for analysis. Dictionary definitions and also professional ones have existed often for centuries before the meaning of the terms, in the sense of the analysis of the object named, could be properly ascertained. Experts are still at work—and at variance—over the meaning of such words as "mind" and "light," for instance, and here the definition must depend upon the analysis. The name is employed in the meanwhile to cover an area, a phenomenon, whose familiarity compels a recognition. It is revealing that glossaries of physics exist in which the definitions of such elements are actually omitted altogether.[62]

Definition may precede analysis or follow it.[63] If definition is merely to express and confirm analysis, then it is difficult to see how the categories are definable. For if the categories are to be of any ontological signification and the point from which philosophy starts, then they must be ultimate simples and so unanalyzable. We are left, then, with this dilemma, that if we consider the categories as undefined, they remain at the level of common sense and do not enter philosophy in the technical context at all; and if we consider them definable, then definition cannot, as some say, follow analysis. It must be remembered at this point that although we have borne down on the question of definition, our chief concern is with the categories. Aristotle has asserted that in the question of basic truths "the meaning of the name is assumed."[64] Things have reached a point of development where such an easy solution is no longer feasible. We might have let it go that a definition suggests the extent of its own domain, but this will not do, either, and this for a good reason. Definitions are now so complex that they occur in terms of an entire axiom-set, such as Peano's postulates for the cardinal numbers, or Huntington's for the continuum.

Let us back away to some distance from the problem in order to view it with detachment and as a whole. From the advantage of this perspective it appears that what we are dealing with are the names for abstract and concrete objects. We shall have to find words or other symbols to stand for the names. This step is arbitrary: it does not matter

[62] *Glossary of Physics,* ed. by LeRoy D. Weld (New York 1937, McGraw-Hill). "Light" and "force" are not defined in this work.
[63] Richard Robinson, *Definition* (Oxford 1950, Clarendon Press), p. 176, also p. 191.
[64] 76a33.

what words or symbols we use provided that they are understood to be reserved for this specific employment. Having named such objects, we then propose to manipulate them prospectively in their absence by means of their names. For this purpose we need to have names which shall characterize them unambiguously. This can be done if we name the meaning of the object rather than just the object itself. The best illustration of this distinction is given on those occasions when the meaning of the object floats away from the object, weary, so to speak, of its long association, leaving the object ambiguously exposed. Words like "God" or "love" are objects named without meanings associated in any unambiguous fashion; in fact, without specific meanings at all; yet they are still held to be objects, a phenomenon of expression against which contemporary semanticists inveigh so vigorously. In the case of individuals, i.e. concrete objects, the name is apt to become encrusted with its meaning. For instance, "Franklin D. Roosevelt" is more than the name of a man, it is the symbol for intense feelings of love or hatred, of gratitude or revenge. And this is so because now what the man did has out-distanced the man, and the name stands more for a set of events which the man set going than for the individual as cut off from his environment, though all of these: the man and the set of events, are equally concrete. There is, however, no source of confusion because the bond between the actual individual named and the name never wavers.

In the case of abstract objects we need to do more than assign labels to the object; instead we name its class or its function. It often happens, if the object is sufficiently complex, that generation or derivation is called in to serve as definition. Thus in the case of Peano's postulates, we are told how to obtain the numbers, and in the case of Huntington's postulates we are given the assigned boundary conditions for the continuum. Here meaning and object are often difficult of distinction. An object means whatever it means, and our task is to discover and give a name to its meaning. There is danger of the object becoming identified with its name and so of existence sinking altogether into language, which is only one of the tools of logic. Thus we encounter delicate distinctions with which we shall have to reckon on every occasion; on the one hand, the distinction between names and the words or symbols which are arbitrarily employed for them, and on the other hands, the distinction between the abstract object and its meaning.

In the case of the categories, the objects are such as they are, and we seek to name them unambiguously in order to combine the names into axioms from which theorems can be derived to which everything revealed by experience and held to have independent being must fall under and in some way be covered. Thus the number and choice of the categories are experimental decisions on which the economy and the completeness of explanation—one might say the categorization—of everything else depends. Thus, while we should like to have a philosophical system which is final, we must regard each system as exploratory and tentative, as open and methodological, as hypothetical and probative, as the trial basis for decisions whose value is to be judged only *in situ* and not before the fact. In this way it seems that the first task is to explore the possibilities of what categories there may be before seeking to discover the best set to employ, and as we have already noted the question of range precedes the matter of choice.

III

KNOWLEDGE

KNOWING ABOUT SEMIPALATINSK

In the Introduction to his *Human Knowledge* Bertrand Russell writes as follows: "If I believe that there is such a place as Semipalatinsk, I believe it because of things that have happened to *me*; and unless certain substantial principles of inference are accepted, I shall have to admit that all these things might have happened to me without there being any such place."[1] This seems to be true in some sense, and if true to have important implications which have not been explored; but in what sense cannot be gathered merely from context; and so it is the purpose here to examine the inferences which flow from the statement.

We should perhaps begin by examining the question of the grounds for belief, since that is the point on which the argument turns. Note the form of the first part of Russell's sentence. "If I believe that . . . , I believe it because . . ." Probably in the case of Semipalatinsk if we have not been there we believe it exists because of what we have heard about it from those who have. And their language is intended to convey to us something of their experiences which we assume to be analogous to what our own would have been had we ourselves made the trip. Our belief, then, is to be determined by the functioning of empathy through language. What

[1] (New York 1949, Simon and Schuster), p. xii.

has happened to Russell presumably is that he has heard about Semi-palatinsk; that is, he has listened to sentences containing descriptions which give them a meaning. But, as Wittgenstein has pointed out, language does not lose its meaning when the referent is destroyed.[2] If Semipalatinsk were obliterated by a hydrogen bomb, "Semipalatinsk" would not thereby be rendered unintelligible. The situation has repercussions which are felt to be of the utmost concern to the stability of belief, but we are not yet in a position to say what these are.

The later work of Wittgenstein may have been intended to show how it was the demands of usage under which the great natural languages developed that enabled them to contain systems which reflect the world. They grew up by naming things or events—operations—and then inventing words to connect the names, just as there are relations in the world between the things or events named. The next step, in which philosophy consists, means learning about the world by studying these languages.

For this purpose we are going to reason backward, that is, from the facts to the specific presuppositions which would allow for there to be such facts. Now a system in which the theorems are actions and the axioms are implicit presuppositions has nevertheless well-defined rules of inference. In the case of knowing, these include the criteria which shall determine belief. We are in the perplexing situation of recognizing this and still of not being able to decide about knowing until we have decided about knowledge, and perhaps not only about what knowledge is but also about what knowledge there is. So our position is reversed: from having thought to find out about Semipalatinsk from the conditions of knowing, we have come to understand that we shall have to find out about the conditions of knowing from what we know about—among other places—Semipalatinsk.

It is clear from this, then, that we shall not go the whole way toward accomplishing our task but that instead we must learn to be satisfied with piecemeal accomplishments. For the world is always larger than any increase in our knowledge. We pursue it at a respectful distance, shedding our subjectivity along the way as best we can, and we do this by gathering alleged increments of information until what we have accumulated will stand by itself without having to gain its unity from our knowing about it in some integrated process of awareness. And when we do this we find all at once that we have made a system.

Thus a new difficulty arises. There is nothing accumulative or incremental about systems of this type, unless we consider proving additional theorems an exception, though even without these the system already

[2] *Philosophical Investigations*, I, 55.

exists. We were occupied by the cautious enterprise of creeping up on belief painstakingly collecting bits of evidence for statements that could be accepted as true, when we were surprised by the discovery that all the while we had been working inside a system. What happened, we want to know, to the question of the ground for belief, to the evidence for the acceptance of knowing?

Any thing, any event, can be pointed to. It may be an operation or an independent happening, but whatever it is it must exist in some space; and if it does then it must exist also in connection with some interpretation of Euclidean space. And this is possible because relations also have some kind of independent existence and so are available to awareness. You see the pencil lying on the book and you see more than that, for you grasp also between the pencil and the book the relation of "larger than" in one movement of apperception. We are not opening the door to hobgoblins and personal devils when we admit this claim, for to believe in things invisible we require that they be indissolubly connected with things visible in some persistent or recurrent way. We come to believe in "larger than" because of our experience with larger-than-pencil books, and of course because our experience with larger-than-pencil books can happen again. Here the tables get turned and the facts are not familiar; for it is after all the invisible part of the complex of visible-invisible that is indestructible. Pencils and books may perish, we might say almost surely will perish, while "larger than" will not. Yet "larger than," too, can be pointed to.

The point is perhaps crucial to the whole argument. Ever since Bradley destroyed the philosophical meaning of relation by demonstrating its inherent contradictions, the confusion has persisted. In the understanding of "relation" much depends upon which relation is taken as primitive, dependence, for instance, or inclusion. From the notion of "dyadic propositional function," we can with profit switch to "proper subset of ordered pairs." This, however, is another question. We debate alternatives one of which contains as a presupposition that the words to denote relations have definite references; yet in the highly controversial assertions whereby the arguments are supported, the assumption of the availability of relations to sense experience, which is so necessary to one side, is rarely maintained.

There is a borderline between the visible and the invisible worlds where decisions must be made which involve the shading of empiricism. The *neutrino* of modern physics, invented to account for the balancing of forces, is a case in point, and so at one time were other heuristic entities, such as the ether and caloric fluid. When do we depart from the sensing of relations to some other area of sense data? Belief in suspension is science in action. There is no excuse for reaching a decision about the results of a series of experiments that does not lead to further inquiry and no decision that cannot be abandoned afterwards and for reason of logic and fact. And this is no less true when the reason concerns the dim indistinguishable no man's land between logic and fact: between what is logic which is applicable to fact and what is fact containing logic in the shape of logical relations—as for instance the sense perception of an instance of "larger than." There is some instability here which threatens belief.

But if we can discover no stability *of* belief, where are we to look for stability *about* belief? "The desire to escape from subjectivity," Russell has reminded us in the next sentence to the one already quoted, lies "in the description of the world." We have thus far none before us which are ready-made and final and at the same time credible. Here the feelings of conviction stand at some distance from the axioms. For the fact is that in philosophy whenever the absolute is introduced, the abstractions become imbued with emotional fervor. Thus the relative detachment and objectivity desired in the search for the truth about the world are lost. Metaphysics ought to be claimed, not proclaimed.

We get down, then, to a matter of estimating chances. Having brought to bear all our senses and coordinating reason upon the task of attempting to discover what it is that exists independently of us, we still have to entertain the state of uncertainty; but to what degree? Knowledge is from one point of view a threshold affair: we know or we do not know, although what we know may be fractional. Proprietary feelings of conviction take charge whenever we are more than half committed. But our half commitment to knowing has a threshold mechanism: it fires or it does not fire. And how much charge, we must always ask, did it take to set off the half belief which we have in the existence of Semipalatinsk? The stimulus of energy is in this case furnished by the strength of "evidence for" Semipalatinsk, and this once again, as we found at the beginning of this discussion, turns upon the language of those who have been there and so have immediate knowledge of it.

Before we allow ourselves to be caught again in this mesh, we would do well to proceed to examine what is suggested by a phrase farther along in the quotation from Russell. The phrase in question is contained in the second part of his somewhat long sentence, in a dependent clause introduced by "unless," "unless certain substantial principles of inference are accepted." It is these principles, he asserts, that make the difference between what might have happened to him without consequences and what did happen to him that led to his belief in there being such a place as Semipalatinsk. To learn about this difference is precisely our task.

In the next step we may possibly be departing from what Russell meant by the phrase; for we cannot always tell from a phrase what its author intended but we can sometimes determine what the phrase intends. For "certain substantial principles of inquiry" let us be prepared to read "certain principles of inquiry applied to substance." We have made much less of a change than would at first sight appear and this is so for the following reason. Substance is left to us, for it is clear from other passages that Russell has specifically rejected it.[3] He understands by substance the grammatical subject merely[4] and so decides that it is not a useful notion.[5] If substance were merely a grammatical subject, however, why would he have used it as an adjective in referring to the substantial principles of inference? He has, it would seem, used it correctly none the less, and in a fashion designed to allow us to alter the phrase as we have done. There is no reason, of course, to think of substance only as something static.

Suppose that we make modifications in the definition of the Aristotelian primary substance, and ourselves understand by substance the irrational ground of individual reaction. Substance in this sense always appears in phase: as a static mass or as a dynamic event; the irreducible and irrational stuff in which to anchor chance. It is not well understood that reason somewhere requires irrationalism, lest, as with all other distinctions, there be no point in talking about reason. Existence, then, must be a world fundamentally irrational in which some reasons inhere, and hence a mixture of chance and cause. There are, of course, problems raised here; but we are not in the business of pretending that there are none that we have not solved. The inconsistency of substance furnished also a guarantee of greater completeness than would have been possible without it, yet where does that leave us with reason? Paradoxical as this may appear, we have been moving toward a description of science. Science is occupied with the task of extracting reasons from substance.

The surprising thing now is that judging from context we emerge from this discussion at a point not too far from Russell. For in the last part of the same book, *Human Knowledge,* the principles of inference to which he has referred prove to be the postulates of scientific inference. We are interested in science as a way of deciding some of the issues we have been raising, and for both Russell and ourselves science is a matter of deriving inferences from substances. Now empirical science (as opposed, say, to linguistics) does not concern itself with investigating language but with using language to describe those aspects of the world which it en-

[3] *Human Knowledge,* p. 136.
[4] *Op. cit.,* p. 293.
[5] *Op. cit.* p. 73.

counters in its procedures. Wittgenstein has uncovered some striking propositions in the course of his investigations. It is Wittgenstein's point, however, as we have seen, that in examining closely enough the implications suggested by the language of those who have named their encounters with the world, we can learn a great deal about that world. In the desire to escape from subjectivity, remember, we were warned by Russell to look for stability about belief in some description of the world. *Description* of the world; the word is important.

Where, then, does that leave Semipalatinsk? Someone, let us say, in the efficacy of whose senses we have some belief, had some experiences which they account for summarily as "going to Semipalatinsk," and these experiences were communicated to us by means of language. The language itself was for the most part general, as all language usually is, but it was rendered specific by being tied to a name, which purportedly is the name more or less arbitrarily assigned to a relatively small group of houses and streets and people occupying a particular space-time region; more specifically still, a town on the Irtysh River in Asia in latitude 50°28′N., 80°13′E. in a sandy waste at an altitude of 686 ft. A claim for the existence of substances in this connection has been clearly established; are we justified when we declare that we intend to validate them?

Solipsism is irrefutable and explains nothing, for if only my thoughts are real yet someone had described going to Semipalatinsk in one of my thoughts, this, too, would have some stability of belief as to how I had managed to describe the world. What, then, have we got to lose by trusting in the senses, and are we not obliged to take up the wager of Thomas Reid who thought we had everything to gain? For not only do substances exist in space but also relations exist among substances, so that when we trust the senses we have acquired some material which is suitable to be worked over, interpreted, and even axiomatized, by reason. In the end this shall be our principle, even though in specialized cases we shall wish to extend the senses by means of instruments and the reasons by means of mathematics, and we shall further wish to submit to the balance between these techniques only the data of such experiences as can be repeated. The method so defined will take us far from Semipalatinsk—far from Semipalatinsk yet into a method, however, in which Semipalatinsk is included, in which the conditions which make Semipalatinsk possible are set forth in such normal form that they will still be worth knowing when there is no Semipalatinsk to be known.

IV

MORALITY

THE ETHICS OF ACTION

I

Our search here, as in all ethics, is for the nature of the good and of its operation, and hence also for the approximation of its attainment. We are relying upon a general definition of the good, a definition in which all human considerations are not only encompassed but exceeded. The good is the quality which emerges from the relations between wholes. It is the ambition of every whole to become a proper part; that is to say, to fit in exactly where it ought, and it "ought" to fit where it is designed to fit. When the whole becomes a part, if that is followed by all the necessary wholes becoming parts, then we have a new whole, and moreover one which is related to other new wholes. The quality which emerges from the relation of whole to whole is the good (that which emerges from the relation of part to part, the beautiful).

Such a conception extends beyond the human; it applies equally well to ant societies or to those astronomical societies called galaxies. Now see what is implied when we examine human ethics. We have to deal with human individuals as our first level of wholes. The single human individual is the greatest lower bound of the ethical. The relation between single human individuals, even between just two, is social; and then be-

tween more: between those two, say, and another two, is how a society is
eventually constituted. And as the relations are proliferated in this manner, the good increases, and we see here, too, the good in operation.

The single human individual and his social relations was not always
the accepted ground for the examination of ethics. Those who have
wished to trace the search for the good to its source have been in the
habit of analyzing the psychological capacities. The tradition is an old
one, and received its greatest if not its first impetus from Plato. His recurrent image of "intelligence" as the charioteer driving the twin steeds
of "emotion" and "character" set the stage; and although the personages
from time to time received different names, for the most part they remained essentially the same. When the western religious tradition became
the inheritor and preserver of Greek philosophy, the list of the psychological capacities underwent a change. Intelligence remained, while
emotion spread out into an assortment of virtues and vices which were
to be sought or avoided, and character was somehow transmuted into
contemplation. Now it happens that contemplation has never been sufficiently recognized as a species of action: for refraining from action may
require an equal effort and so be a kind of action. The modern world
since the renaissance has retreated from what it supposed to be imaginary
objects into subjects which were held to be safer though they have proved
no less imaginary. And so the triad of psychological categories became
"thought," "feeling" and "will." No one has ever seen a will or been able
to isolate one for study. Investigation always begins with certain preconceptions concerning the objects to be investigated, though this is seldom recognized to be the situation by the investigator who always fancies
that he is addressing himself unhampered to the task at hand. And the
chief of his preconceptions is the supposition that there are such objects as
those he proposes to investigate, and either that there are no alternative
objects or that if there are then these are the preferred objects.

Other ways of looking at the psychological capacities exist. We would
be more inclined now to say, "thought," "feeling" and "action." When
we adopt these categories, we seem to be doing what we had said at first
ought not to be done: we are dipping below the whole individual and
appearing to include elements which are not primarily concerned with
his social relations. But that is the precise difference between the older
consideration of the psychological categories and our own. We shall look
at these three capacities as they are outwardly involved: as they are the
result of external stimuli and as they themselves issue in external results.
The psychological capacities would not exist as empirical categories were
there nothing to think about, nothing to be felt, nothing with which to
construct character—no relations, qualities or events. Thought and feel-

ing in academic psychology have come to be affairs of intelligence testing
and skin sensitivity, while action has been turned over to the behaviorists,
who have been applauded for the discovery of conditioned reflexes. It is
an elusive affair, the notion that has been alternatively described as
"character," "contemplation," "behavior," and "action." Ordinarily, one
might have supposed that "thought" and "feeling" were private functions
and so somewhat more inaccessible than "action," which takes place,
after all, right in the open. The behaviorists have been the most literal
about it, for they cut action off from its motive source and examine overt
behavior all by itself. But action may be an end-product, and non-
understandable except in terms of that by which it takes place. We have
learned, thanks to Pavlov and his followers, that reflexes can be conditioned, then reinforced or unconditioned. But what we have not learned
is, under what conditions? Under what conditions ought this or that conditioning or reinforcement to take place? Ought the dog to salivate whenever he sees wild duck? Ought the man's desire for his neighbor's wife to
be reinforced or obliterated? Can the discovery of a mechanism be made
to serve time for the ignorance as to the proper occasion for the use of
that mechanism? In terms of simple "thought" and "feeling," which are
the only categories left to us in the traditional triad, it is difficult to know
what to choose and by what criteria.

At this point we may remember that we are accepting the stock alternatives too readily. It is true that we have the capacities we have been
traditionally said to have: we think, we feel and we move. Yet there is a
hiatus between thought and feeling, on the one hand, and action, on the
other. We do not directly think and then act, or feel and then act; between
these pairs there is an intermediate function which it is necessary to
isolate for study. This function is called belief. In recent decades a great
deal of ingenuity and experiment has gone into the analysis of learning.
Yet nobody seems to have stopped to ask, what happens to propositions
after they have been learned? Presumably, after learning, a proposition
enters into the condition of belief—it is learned and then it is believed.
But what, exactly, is meant by that?

Belief is the conviction that a proposition is true, and the degree of
belief is directly proportional to the strength of the evidence for its truth.
"Conviction" contains elements of both thought and feeling. When we say
that we "believe" something, we may mean either that we "know it to be
true" or that "we have a feeling that it is true."

Beliefs may be acquired in a number of ways. They may be acquired
immediately from thought. A rational thought is a mental following of
the sequence of a syllogism together with the recognition of its inexora-
bility. The man who thinks he has sufficient evidence for the truth of the

proposition that all men are mortal, and, separately, sufficient evidence for the truth of the additional proposition that all Frenchmen are men, finds upon putting these two beliefs together that he can derive from them the additional belief that all Frenchmen are mortal, and, moreover, that he has sufficient grounds in the strength of his two previous beliefs to convey it to his new one. Feeling, of course, is not entirely excluded from the bringing of the two beliefs together, or from the strength of the connections between them, or between them and the new belief derived from their juxtaposition. For none of these feelings is ever altogether excluded from any occasion of experience. There is action, too, in the passage across the neural pathways, though it is less detectable than more overt kinds.

Beliefs may be acquired immediately from feeling. The burned child who shuns the fire has learned from allowing his hand to come into contact with the fire that fire burns and that burns hurt, and so, more briefly, that fire hurts. Thought, of course, is not entirely excluded from the connection between the sensation on one occasion, its effects, and the anticipation of similar effects upon any possible future occasion. Thought is never altogether excluded from any occasion of experience. But then neither is action, since it is by means of action or by refraining from action that the child shuns the fire.

Beliefs may be acquired immediately from action. The well-known trial-and-error method of accomplishing some aim is an instance of the acquisition of belief through action. If a cook in a restaurant were to put sugar in the sauce for the chicken on one day, and on another day spices, and were then to find that the customers preferred the one cooked in spices, he would have acquired the belief that in cooking chicken, spices were to be preferred to sugar. Thought, of course, is not entirely excluded from the comparison or from the lesson to be drawn from it, and—not to labor a point—neither, of course, is feeling.

Beliefs, then, may be acquired from thought, from feeling or from action. When we speak of either of these, we refer to a congeries of functions in which some one is uppermost but in which all three exist and from which none is absent. It is also true that belief issues in further thoughts, feelings and actions. What we believe about democracy governs later thoughts about political events. Belief also decides how we shall feel; anyone who believes that liquorice has a bad taste will experience a further feeling of repugnance on hearing that name. And, as we shall see at some length, belief leads to action; if we believe that wars should be avoided, we will do what we can to avoid wars.

We are concerned here, however, primarily with the effort to explicate the good, and we are concerned specifically, moreover, in the good chiefly as it affects human beings (for the good and ethics have a wider application than the human, but it is the human aspect of the good that we are endeavoring to analyze here). Now the good so far as it affects human beings must be regarded as an affair either of the human individual or of human society. The ethics of the human individual has been studied at length by way of the psychological capacities, and we shall not be content to continue that approach. We shall select instead the study of the ethics of human society.

Now if we refer back to the categories that we have been examining, namely, thought, feeling and action, we shall find that of the three, thought and feeling are individual affairs, while action is social. It is chiefly the business of the individual what he thinks and feels, but when his thoughts or feelings (or both) issue in action it becomes the business of others. And so we shall seek to confine our analysis to action and to those forces surrounding it which tend to bring it about. Our analysis will fall into definite parts. First, we shall examine action as such. Of what does it consist and how is it to be defined and described? Secondly, we shall study belief, on the assumption that it is belief which leads to action under certain conditions. Thirdly, we shall study the effects of action as having a bearing on further actions. These three parts can be looked at as the study of action itself, of the conditions of action and the consequences of action.

One word about method. The position is set forth here, not argued. It is not developed step by step but presented in what it is hoped will be the most approachable fashion. The only evidence in its favor must be its explanatory value. And no author is the final judge of that.

II

Pragmatism is a philosophy centered upon the notion of activity. It was built primarily on methodology, and it has an ethics. The truth of a proposition is judged by its consequences in action; that was the way in which James interpreted Peirce. But what Peirce had said was that a true proposition is one that will eventually have workable consequences. Peirce had the experimental method of the sciences in mind, and meant it to precede application. If you test a proposition, he insisted, and find it to be true, then you may be sure that in the long run its applications will be a success. James inadvertently turned this round and made application a test of truth: what works is true. The inferences of these two varieties of pragmatism to ethics were markedly different. Peirce's point was somewhat subtle, whereas James' was quite easy to understand and interpret.

The pragmatism of James fitted perfectly under the frontier philosophy of success: do whatever seems expedient; if you get away with it then it works and if it works it is true, and that is all the truth there is, anyway. Thus pragmatism in James' hands became a sort of theoretical endorsement of what people were often doing while professing the opposite. James gave us no theory of practice, merely a recommendation to act. He did not analyze action, he merely approved of it, and there was implied in his approval that it did not matter so much what we did so long as we did something. Such a philosophy goes against the feelings of what is right, against social feeling, for instance, and seems the kind of justification for our self-interest which does not quite justify. As a philosophy, and certainly as an ethics, pragmatism is a failure.

Yet that is not quite the whole story. Despite the anti-social and anti-intellectual bias of Jamesian pragmatism, one good thing was accomplished by it. It was a whole-hearted attempt to make a philosophical recognition of action, and one was long overdue. Marx had already recognized action, but more narrowly; he had insisted that economic action was determinative of all other social action, and in so doing had obliterated the distinction between occasion and cause. Economic action may *occasion* others without necessarily being the cause of them. James attempted to recognize the evidence for truth that was contained in the workability of its consequences. He went too far; but his opponents have gone too far also in rejecting the residue of reliable methodology in his treatment. It is worth examining.

Those who relate theory to practice ought to be asked to remember what end it is they wish to effect: theory, or practice. Are they relating theory to practice in order to validate theory or in order to motivate practice?

The theoretical logician recognizes not at all the evidence contained in applications. He wishes to base truth exclusively upon deducibility and to regard it in this way as absolute. But this is only to push it back indefinitely. Unless self-evidence for truth be readmitted among the logical criteria—an event which seems now extremely unlikely—we are involved in an infinite regress; for the premises from which a truth has been deduced depend for their truth upon anterior premises from which they in turn could be deduced, and so on. Not, of course, that absolutely reliable results are to be obtained in any other way. If we substitute for coherence the correspondence with fact, which is what James is advocating, we do not have an absolute proof of any kind; for obviously the consequences are possibly infinite and we cannot hope to come to the end of them, which is what would be required in order to guarantee that we should never find an exception. Thus the pure logicians advocate coherence exclusively, while the practical technologists with equal exclusivity advocate correspondence. Thus we get the strict theorist and the down-to-earth man of affairs in complete opposition, each convinced that the other is off on the wrong track.

In so thinking, both have overlooked the method of the experimental sciences which has had such brilliant results in physics and chemistry. The scientific method begins with correspondence and checks the evidence contained in this fashion by means of coherence. What corresponds to the facts is then tested for consistency with the use of mathematics, and then applied in practice by means of prediction and control. Where in this logical structure of methodology does the Jamesian version of pragmatism find its place? That a proposition works when applied in practice is no conclusive evidence for its truth. But let us not go to the other extreme and assume that workability is evidence for falsity, either. The fact is that workability *is* evidence for truth; it is not conclusively evidence, to be sure, but it is evidence all the same. The evaluation of the strength of the evidence depends upon the amount of the workability. We conclude from this that workability is evidence for truth well enough, it is simply not conclusive evidence; and the evaluation of how much the evidence is worth is an extremely complex affair; it depends upon many factors, among which are: the strength of the evidence itself, the size of the problem and the number of other factors engaged.

Having cleared from our path the intellectual prejudice against action, brought about, perhaps, by the perfect abstraction of deduction and the vulgarization of pragmatism, the way is now clear to make a philosophical analysis of action. We should begin with a definition, and so we will.

Action is motion among concrete objects involving their alteration.

The definition will bear some examination. The adjective, concrete, is introduced to distinguish from abstract objects those to which we mean to refer. There is no movement among abstract objects, and if there were it is hard to see how it would involve their alteration. There are properties of concrete objects which when we examine them reveal their abstract nature, properties such as redness, roundness, aboveness; but we will be concerned with them in this context only so far as they are properties. Their alteration always involves exchange: when action on them takes place, they disappear and are replaced by other abstractions. The red wall is painted blue, the round ball is mashed flat, the book is taken from above the table and put under it.

The objects in this definition must be material objects, then; actual material objects. For, clearly, we are not speaking of possible objects, since they would be abstract. And we are not speaking of objects which are actual without being material, for then there would be no action among them. The philosophy of action has to be immediate and substantial. You cannot say that matter does not exist and still hold that existence matters. But you cannot say, either, that *only* matter exists and still hold that all that exists matters. Of what will the difference consist? What exists besides matter we have already mentioned: the properties of matter which are not themselves material, such as redness, roundness and aboveness. Action among concrete objects that involves their alteration, when it is social produces artifacts. An artifact is a piece of material which has been formed for some human purpose; an artifact is an human production, and it always starts with a "raw" material, that is, with something in nature which is non-human. An artifact, then, is something made by man.

Let us pursue the analysis of social action a little further.

Consider the three psychological capacities with which we began our inquiry: intelligence, the will and the feelings, or, as they have often been called, the intelligible, the sensible and the affective. We fasten, as usual, on the last: the *a*ffective is the passive form of the *e*ffective, and it is the active form that we need, since action is active. Now suppose that the effects of our actions are felt upon human beings instead of upon inert objects; suppose, in other words, that other human beings are the concrete objects which are to be altered in our example of action. The thought and the feeling of human individuals, and perhaps also their own subsequent actions, become in this instance the alterations effected.

Actions which are felt by human beings may effect their thought as well and hence their action eventually if not immediately. And so action in society becomes quickly compounded even when it is without plan. When it is planned, then it develops that many individuals working together in concert can accomplish things, i.e. perform actions, not open to the single human individual or even for that matter to the uncoordinated group. Thus the final ground of ethics so far as human beings are concerned, no matter what the secret thoughts or feelings of the individual may be, is society. The ethics of action means the ethics of how society shall be affected.

We have studied the problems of abstract objects *in abstracto* for so long that we have forgotten their role in the actual world. We learned about them there; then we removed them in effigy, so to speak, in order to think about them. This is a mistake Aristotle never made, except when he began to speculate on their ultimate status. He reversed the error, then, and refused to admit that what he had been treating as concrete had any abstract standing at all. In addition to the properties we have named, there are others which are not so readily perceptible. Redness is more obvious than roundness, but it is possible to perceive roundness provided you know what it is that you are looking for, and, somewhat more elusively, also aboveness. We have in these three properties a declining series of obvious properties, of abstractions *in concreto*. There are still others, lower down on the spectrum of obvious observability, until we reach the unobservable, which are still effective. By observable here, of course, is meant observable by anyone who is in the proper perspective. In addition to the crude observations at the level of ordinary material objects, there are the mental objects: aberrations aside, John could see the image which is now before Tom's consciousness—say the face of Tom's dead brother—were John to occupy Tom's perspective, that is to say, were John to have identical memories with Tom and Tom's reason at that particular moment for recalling one of them. The mood of a social gathering, the climate of opinion, the atmosphere of a culture, these are felt though they are not seen; and how exactly they are felt even, it would be hard to say. The causes of action are often unseen, for there are definitely effective unseen elements in the seen world, and their philosophical importance at most times goes unrecognized. How the unseen objects become altered when there is action among them, is at present a problem too complex for the simple methods of our analysis; we are only sure that they do become altered from time to time.

Suffice to say that motion among concrete objects involves their alteration in some often non-understood ways. Indeed motion among concrete objects could hardly fail to involve their alteration. Unless we are speaking of motion in a vacuum never proceeding as far as its walls, which may be the exception, we cannot move without disturbing the air through which we move and without causing small gravitional perturbations. These are, of course, alterations, however tiny.

Now let us carry the same elements into the social picture. All social action involves production, destruction, or both. Anything that the individual does in a social way alters the fabric of society somewhat. The production may involve the building of artifacts, or it may involve the construction of more complicated structures, such as institutions or even whole societies. Societies as well as material tools have been remade from top to bottom as the result of deliberate planning, but there is no record as yet of the building in such a way of an entire culture. Usually, however, only material tools and institutions are deliberately planned, and even then the life and adventures of the tool or the society exceeds the expectations and the plans of its inventors or founders. The more common case is the on-the-spot invention of the artifact or the gradual and unplanned growth of the institution.

We have been describing social action in its positive phase, but it has a negative phase as well. Many acts of production involve destruction, and often social acts are willfully destructive. Ethical considerations arise in the estimation of the balance of production over destruction in any instance of social action. The building of any artifact which is efficient in accomplishing an human purpose is good, and the destruction of any such artifact evil. The exception may be the case of weapons of war, which have as their purpose the destruction, or at the very least the inhibition, of further social organization. A machine gun is more efficient than a bow and arrow, but the end for which it is efficient is an anti-social end, that of killing human beings.

The measurement of the production over the destruction in an instance of social action is not always an easy thing to accomplish. Nazi Germany was a highly organized Germany, and, within the limits of the goals set, efficient. But the organization of Germany by the Nazis involved the disruption of most of Germany's foreign relations and the eventual partial destruction of Germany itself, and so must be considered on balance more evil than good. Democracy is a far less efficient method of political organization, on any superficial scale; it moves often slowly and clumsily, it is riven with differences. But the fact is that it organizes *more,* and in this sense is more efficient. The free individual enters freely into the social arrangement of democracy, because he has a stake and a voice in it, and so the whole man is part of it; whereas in fascism, this is true of only a small part of the population, and only one side of it and not the best side. Government not only by consent but also with choice would appear to be the preference among existing alternatives.

The issue between production and destruction must take into account the fact that in all actual instances there is good as well as evil involved. The most horribly evil act probably has some small side effect which is good, and so with the greatest good and its attendant evil. The avoidance of conflict is called consistency when it is found among abstract structures; but when we come to concrete instances where values also exist, another consideration must be raised, and it is that of completeness. Among the values, completeness wars with consistency. When premises grow too narrow, values take charge. In society, there are individuals wanting different things of the same sort, each, let us say, legitimate. One man prefers Italian cooking, another French. One man prefers the tango, another the waltz. Thus far, very well, for we can have both (though assuredly not at the same time). But what about the resolution of the political conflict as one wit proposed it (assuming that he was not serious): we can have, he said, both capitalism *and* communism, capitalism for those who can afford it, and communism for those who need it? If we cannot satisfy every man with the same values and can in many instances have only one set of values, on the basis of what criterion shall we choose? Since society as a whole is involved, it had best be those values which are of the greatest service to society. The selection is not an easy one to make but is rendered no less the correct one for that reason.

It would seem, then, that ethically speaking the purpose of the human individual is the service of society, whether through artifacts, institutions or both. And it would further seem that the purpose of society is served by the voluntary increase in its own size, provided always that whatever the size the same individual values are being pursued. This would make of the good a public and social value for human beings, and the measurement of individual goods the extent to which they eventually issue in something public and beneficial. Thus the ethical consideration requires us to concentrate upon the question of action. We have tried to say what action is; what we need to know, in addition and for ethical reasons, is, what does it follow from and what follows from it?

III

Action follows from belief.

It will be necessary at this point to revert to an earlier discussion, in which it was declared that thought and feeling are forms of reaction and that none of the three, neither thought, feeling nor action, quite covers the ground that is covered by belief. We there introduced the idea of belief, and explained briefly what is meant by it. Belief, it was said, is the conviction that a proposition is true. When we say that action follows from belief, it is not the case that action follows *only* from belief. We are speaking now rather of any kind of concerted or planned action. Action at lower levels may be the result of simple stimulation, of course. A man who is tickled or hurt does not stop to think, and if he is hungry, he does not stop, either; but what if he is amused? If he does have time to stop and think, in most cases this takes the form of a quick overhaul of his store of beliefs, in order to see whether he has one already that will fit. What is meant here, then, by action following from belief is something a little more involved, a little more sophisticated, socially effective action which is more or less deliberate, where at least something of the sort is intended.

Belief is the conviction that a proposition is true, and conviction, we said, involves both thought and feeling. How much conviction, for there are no doubt strong convictions and weak ones? The spectrum of conviction must run from the merest suspicion that such and such may be true, all the way to absolute certainty. Belief is not bestowed whimsically or for no reason but always after thought and with evidence. There are always good-seeming reasons for belief. A man may believe that he is being persecuted because wherever he goes he is followed by little green men, but this is not his fancy; it is the result of evidence, for he thinks he has seen the little green men. And this is no less so because he has not. In short, the conditions for truth do not have to exist, it is only the case that the requirements for truth have to be met. One who believes does so on what seems to him to be sufficient evidence whether it exists or not.

We have, then, the truth-conditions and the evidence for belief; these may or they may not be the same. And then we have also the belief itself. Now we have said that the degree of conviction varies, not that the belief varies; but the belief varies, too, and it varies with the amount of feeling in the conviction. A conviction contains as elements thought and feeling, we have asserted. But the thought does not vary; the thought is the thought—it is the feeling that varies from weak to strong. One could have a weak conviction of belief, which would mean that the component of feeling was weak, or one could have a strong conviction of belief, which would mean that the component of feeling was strong.

And the degree of the feeling depends somewhat upon where the feeling takes place. There is a saying that one believes something with "the top of one's head," which is to say, not much; and the conviction of belief in such a case has as its component of feeling only the one which accompanies consciousness, so that when the belief is not being thought of, the conviction of its truth fades. Out of mind, out of feeling. But at the other end of the belief spectrum there are beliefs so profound that to challenge them is to challenge sanity, and the conviction of their truth is so strong that one may not be even aware of its existence. No doubt, as belief becomes confirmed and secure, the feeling sinks below consciousness and toward the lower end of the nervous system, away from the cerebellum and toward the celiac ganglia. The firmest beliefs are those which can rise to consciousness only with effort, for they come from the visceral center of the physiological organism and occasion awkwardness whenever they emerge into the psychological level. What such belief means has only been suspected and almost never investigated.

The emphasis on belief shows only a rough correspondence to truth, yet it is clear that were there no truths there could be no belief, either. For a belief means at least thinking—and feeling—that the truth is being had; and if in many cases altogether and perhaps in all cases to some extent there is a discrepancy between belief and truth, that only emphasizes the necessity all the more. Belief *means* the conviction that a proposition is true. And all efforts at learning and all techniques of investigation are designed and employed with the sole purpose of increasing the known truths, or, in other words, of building new beliefs or in amending or reinforcing old ones. And what, then, is the meaning of the truth on which belief so largely depends?

We are now some distance from the topic which we undertook to explicate. Action follows from belief, we said, and so we intended to pursue the study of the ethics of action; but now we find ourselves faced with the antecedent of belief, and we say that belief follows from the truth as its conviction. We will take one glance backward and then pass on. Truth is the one-one relation between a proposition and the relevant facts (correspondence theory) or it is the consistency of a proposition with the propositions from which it can be deduced (coherence theory). Science says it is both, as we have already noted, and proceeds to attempt to weave the two together by subjecting a proposition first to one criterion and then to the other, always allowing correspondence to assume the final authority in an instance of doubt. If the propositions taken as premises in the case of coherence were themselves first tested by correspondence, a junction could be effected. Back of the truth, there is the dim outline of a system of such truths such that when the collection of true propositions is complete, then its members can be shown to be consistent. It has been noted by others that if "the weather at the poles tends to be colder than elsewhere on the earth's surface" and "anger temporarily diminishes the use of the ability to reason" are both true, then the statement that "anger temporarily diminishes the use of the ability to reason" follows necessarily from the statement that "the weather at the poles tends to be colder than elsewhere on the earth's surface." The prospect of a system of truths is set forth in ontologies and argued in metaphysics. Thus lying dimly in the background of beliefs are the shapes of metaphysical topics and speculations.

The metaphysical theories which provide for the kind of belief which leads to action are thus required for action, as little as this appears to be so to those who are engaged in the heat of action. Those who would end with a certain kind of action, namely, the action which promotes the social good, must begin with the proper metaphysical theory. Not just any theory will do provided it is metaphysical. The idealists first, and then the nominalists, have had their day in affecting action. The pragmatic justification for realism, which has not yet been tried, is contained in the fact that it seems difficult if not impossible to interpret action in any other way. We would not make alterations in our own position or in those of other objects did we suppose them to be either altogether unreal or else figments of our own imagination. The chair that you move, the man you convince, will be in some way other than they were before you exerted yourself on their behalf. There has been realism before: the realism of

Plato's second philosophy, but never carried into practice, and the scholastic realism which had no adequate social theory. But metaphysical realists need a theory of activity, one which can be as eminent in its standing as pure contemplation has been, and the avoidance of evil. In short, the criticism of metaphysics demands that if you intend to do good things you need to assume inadvertently if not profess explicitly a system of metaphysics, which is an ontology.

Starting with ontology in the line of progression, we come next to truth, then to belief and finally to action. Action is related to truth through belief, which faces both ways.

It is easy to see how this works out in practice. If the propositions believed true are not true, yet because they are believed lead to action, the action will either be in vain or else self-defeating. If we move among concrete objects with a view to their alteration, it is always with the understanding that the concrete objects are thus and so and we wish them otherwise. Now if they are in fact not thus and so, our movements among them will involve their alteration in unintended ways or not at all. If a drunken man believes a window to be a door, his actions as a consequence will land him in the hospital and perhaps end his life. We can only strive to bring things nearer to the heart's desire, if we know where they are in the first place; in this way (though perhaps only in this way) fact is essential to poetry.

IV

We have seen that action follows directly from belief and indirectly from truth. We have now to ask what it is that follows from action. Remember when the assertion is made that actions follow from belief that they do so within a wide penumbra of other considerations, such as—and chiefly—truth. We are concerned here only with the truth relevant to our main theme, which is the relation between the good and action. The good, we decided earlier, is that quality which emerges from the perfect relation of wholes. The truth relevant to the good would then be the proposition having a one-one correspondence with the relations of wholes. And the beliefs from which action follows, in so far as action is relevant to the good, would be the action which follows from what we know about the relations between wholes. We would, in short, by our actions, seek to increase the relations between wholes in order to make them perfect and so to occasion the quality which is the good.

This could occur in two directions. It could occur by intensity, that is, by making more perfect those relations between wholes which exist already. And it could occur by extensity, that is, by making the relations between wholes so perfect they merge as parts and so form larger wholes, between which the perfection of relation could, in turn, be pursued. It can readily be seen, too, that the latter is only a further and more advanced instance of the former, that extensity is the step after the completion of intensity. Hence the ethics of action requires that all action taken shall be in pursuit of the good, where the good is understood in the terms just explained.

We are now in a position to apply these findings to the ethics of social action. First of all, the individual is a whole containing parts, but the relations among its parts shall not concern us, even though being valid parts and so themselves wholes to their parts they no doubt have their own ethics. But we are looking at them from a somewhat higher perspective, from that perspective in which the whole individual shall be considered, and in this perspective it is the relations between individuals that become the object of consideration. It is the beliefs concerning the action which would tend to perfect the relations between wholes and so lead to such action, which is the concern here. What follows from social action is a better society. In this connection we shall recognize any acts of privacy that are not preparation stages for publicity as acts wrongly aimed; for in this context we are not able to neglect the glaring fact of the immorality of private anything, where by private we mean anything that cannot or should not develop into a public affair. Everything ethical can and should be, eventually at least, public and open.

The result of social actions, then, in so far as they are ethical, is a good society. We have said what we mean by the good; we should add what we mean by society. A society is an organization of social institutions, and a social institution is a group of human individuals organized around a central purpose in some established fashion, and furnished with the appropriate tools or artifacts. Human ethics is itself bound up in some important way with the fact that it is the highest of all social realities. The principle of consistency governs the organization of society, but the principle of completeness, which is part of ethics in practice, or in other words morals, is felt as a quality and known as a requirement by each and every member of the society in the form in which it exists as a dominant theme. Completeness is the requirement that the society shall contain all the necessary values; and since many of these are incompatible, action is required to actualize them in turn and so to contribute to the completeness. For the quality which emerges from the perfect relation between wholes takes precedence over the relation, and, when the perfection itself is being closely approached, over the wholes as well.

Society has a curious way of bringing about its desired results, of achieving those ends with itself which it seeks to encompass. It builds artifacts, and then reacts to the artifacts in unpredictable ways. We have seen much earlier that the effects of action are production, and now we are speaking about the products. An artifact is anything made by man, and usually the result of the efforts of a number of men. Once the artifact is produced and finished, it takes its place, so to speak, in society and plays a role there, often indeed a crucial role. Everything from hairpins to skyscrapers to languages is an artifact, and societies are more often than not altered by artifacts in unexpected ways. And since the resultant ways are ways of behavior and have a further result in the effect of the behavior of men on each other and so on the degree of the good which is actualized, the artifacts themselves have an ethical value, and no moral considerations can be complete without counting on them.

V

Where does our discussion leave the psychological capacities with which we began? We saw that thought, feeling and action together constituted an incomplete analysis, for neither thought nor feeling leads directly to action yet action is not entirely uncontrolled. Belief was then suggested as the proper interpositional function. From our thoughts and our feelings operating in terms of stimuli from the external world, we arrive at beliefs about it, and then we act in terms of these beliefs.

It follows that there are no such things as private thoughts or feelings, since these lead to beliefs and beliefs lead to actions, and there are no private actions. The innermost thoughts of the most self-contained individual may either lead him to action or (what is oftentimes equally efficacious. socially) to refraining from action, and thus to social effects. Ethics is not individual, then, but social in its effects, and if in its effects then in the events leading to the effects, also. Morals are concerned with how a particular ethical code exists and is practiced in a given society. It may be adopted inadvertently and applied unconsciously, and its whole train of consequences may seem to the individual merely the way in which the individuals in the society behave in conformity with their fellows. But the degree of our awareness of it does not fundamentally determine its presence or absence, and our very awareness of it may not seriously affect the nature of its constitution. We do not believe, or disbelieve, without reason but only on evidence, and so even knowing how morals are made up cannot change the morals: we must act in accordance with our beliefs, and for these we ourselves are the switching circuits. Evidence comes in to us from the world of objects, becomes transformed into belief, and then issues back in effects on the objects. Belief, it could almost be said if one wanted to take up the extreme view (which may, for that matter, be the right one), is the subjective way in which objects affect objects. And so our good or evil nature depends in part on what circuits we get caught up in (the older language would have it, "depends on circumstances"), and in part on what equipment we have with which to operate the switches. In part only, though an important part; for despite the existence in us of a "good feeling," it may be too weak to issue in action; and despite the existence in us of the habit of reasoning about experience, our thoughts may be inadequate to the matter at hand. Leadership, then, might consist in the exercise of an impulse to right action as a result of correct belief resulting from sensitive feelings and complex thoughts. But the weakest individual is capable of some action and so of exerting a moral effect, and he is capable of training himself, too, in sensitivity and reasoning. As with so many practical enterprises, so in the case of the morality of social action, it happens that what we wish to achieve cannot be worked on directly. The gaining of money may be the result of the learning of business methods, or, perhaps, of industrial techniques far removed from the end to be sought. The desire to help the sick may require first long years in which the learning of the Latin names for anatomical elements is the task which is set. The man who wishes to be good in the ethical sense must work not on his feelings alone—for that may prove impossible—but on his beliefs. It is what he holds true that he believes and what he believes that he practices; and so the search for the good eventually resolves itself into the anterior search for the true. What we think there is in the world determines what we shall try to do about it.

How far do our beliefs check with the truth? Alas, no man is ignorant, in the sense of knowing nothing, or of having an absence of beliefs. The mind is that part of nature which peculiarly abhors a vacuum, and so instead of no beliefs if there cannot be true beliefs there are false ones. A false belief is not a belief held to be false, for this would be impossible and a contradiction; it is a belief held to be true which, as it happens, does not accord with the facts. If you believe in ghosts you believe it is true that there are ghosts, and you avoid dark rooms and solitude and empty houses accordingly. Your belief is unassailable; that is to say, each belief has exactly one Achilles' heel, and it consists in undeniable evidence to the contrary. This is often difficult to obtain. Yet the search for the truth, or what is more matter of fact, for the correction in terms of the truth of what we believe already, may be what every one of us can do in the long run toward improving his ethical contribution to society, and so through it toward furnishing whatever the whole of the nature of existence requires of its smallest parts.

V

RELIGION

GOD, MAN AND MATTER

I

Formal materialism is not inconsistent with a belief in God. The Marxists are official atheists, but there is nothing inherently atheistic about materialism. Indeed the association of God with matter is an old one. The history of philosophy is strewn with the work of men who were materialists and who at the same time believed in the existence of God. The same Xenophanes who said that "everything comes from earth and everything goes back to earth at last" said also that "there is one god, among gods and men the greatest, not at all like mortals in body or in mind."[1] Aristotle was certainly one who divided his beliefs between matter on the one hand and God on the other.[2] And it is possible to see in Aristotle also why it was impossible for any thinker to analyze matter at that time. Matter was impenetrable and it was one of the things of which it could be said that they could not be understood as they were in themselves, and

[1] Freeman, Kathleen, *Ancilla to the Pre-socratic Philosophers,* Fr. 23 and 27. Oxford. 1948. Blackwell.
[2] For matter as one of the four causes, see *Metaphysics,* A, 10. For God, see *Metaphysics,* λ, 7.

so it became necessary to shift the investigation to their causes.[3] And so the science of first principles became the science of original causes. And much later that same Hobbes who in the Introduction of his *Leviathan* makes such a plain statement of materialism did in the twelfth chapter of that same book affirm his belief in God.[4]

In the next century, La Mettrie, the author of *L'homme machine,* was a materialist who at the same time believed in God's existence. It is La Mettrie's point that while the materialist can believe in a supernatural God who is the cause of the material universe, this will make no difference to him in practice. For it does not mean that God can be invoked to discriminate among the parts, and therefore can be employed to justify one type of morality over another.

The only use to which such knowledge can be put is not to choose a certain line of behavior but to comfort us with the knowledge that the positing of a cause for the material universe rules out the possibility that all is chance and accident and that therefore our lives have no meaning. It is a general comfort rather than a particular guide.

Descartes's categories were God, mind and matter. But now we should make only one strong revision. In view of the remoteness of God and the vastness of the universe it seems arrogant and foolish to consider the human mind in the same dimension. We should be disposed now to say that mind is a property of some kinds of matter, that mind is epiphenomenal, a property of the high organization of matter as it is found in the central nervous system and brain. But God and matter still hold their authority as metaphysical categories. Matter and its properties have a cause and this cause is God.

But while some of the materialists believed in God, most of the religions have been uniform in their denunciation of materialism. Since science seemed to grow out of materialism, religion has opposed the growth of science as well. Yet it is science which has called the turn on the composition of matter, making it easier to reconcile God with materialism.

A great deal has happened in science since matter was understood as it was by Feuerbach and Engels. Matter is no longer a simple, inert stuff which resists analysis and has to be reckoned with only in the round, but has become recognized instead as a highly dynamic agent capable of

[3] *Metaphysics,* A. 2.
[4] See also *The first Grounds of Philosophy,* VII, 1. Reprinted in *The Metaphysical System of Hobbes.* M. W. Calkins (trans.) Chicago. 1948. Open Court.

sustaining the most complex activities. Thanks to the new knowledge, we are now in a position to distinguish between the *analysis* of matter and the *causes* of matter. The analysis of matter is the business of the investigations of physics, and the causes of matter may be assigned to the speculations of theology.

We are in a position to say now thanks to physics that matter is complex. There are more than forty subatomic constituents. Even now the question of the relation between them has left many vexing problems. A satisfactory model for the structure of the atom has not been found. The powder model has replaced the earlier orbital model, but now the powder model too is almost obsolete. The nature of the short-range forces which hold together the atomic constituents, for example the electron and proton, are not understood. It has also been suggested that there may be analytical levels and causative forces at work below those which experimental analysis has yet succeeded in reaching. More evidence of complexity comes from the plasma state of matter which has been added to the traditional three: solid, liquid and gas. When matter is in an excited or plasma state, what is the nature of such an energy-level?

Matter is in addition to its complexity averagely distributed but rare. Astronomical studies of distribution give a low average density for matter in metagalactic space. Calculating the amounts of matter within the stars and between the stars as roughly the same, it is not difficult to arrive at a figure for average distribution, with empty space predominating. But it is important to recall that nothing can be done without a material base. No matter, then no action and in fact no existence. Matter may be only the means by which ends are envisioned and approached, but they are the necessary means.

Given the chemical studies of the stars, it appears as though the same stuff prevails throughout the universe. Studies of stellar birth and decay support the theory that the same processes are at work there as here. The energy which moves matter and into which matter can be transformed seems to be the same wherever we look. The evidence of the integrative levels, the way in which atoms combine into molecules, molecules into cells, cells into organisms and organisms into societies, shows the same basic units in stone, paramecium, trees and men. Organisms, instruments, and even meanings do nothing more than exemplify some of the many enormous capabilities of matter. Evidently we live in a material world.

We have now a new and more subtle materialism to deal with since science has illuminated its composition. But this does not affect the relation of God and matter, which remains much the same. If God as the cause of matter is required by the older materialism, so He is also by the new.

The causes of objects and events in the material world are looked for in the material world. But the cause of the material world considered as a whole cannot be looked for within that whole but must lie outside. The idea of the world self-caused is in a sense unacceptable, for if the cause of the world is in the world it does not disclose itself, and is not evident in the parts. Then, too, "in the world" means "among the parts," and if a part or many parts can be said to be the cause of the world, then which part or parts and in what manner? But even if the cause of the world were the world itself, we are confined to a tiny part of it and the knowledge that the other parts had had the chief role in causing the world would be no help. Again, if the parts can cause the whole, then it is a whole such as we have never known, and do not know any more for the assertion of such causation. So we have recourse to a cause for the world which lies outside the world. God is the name for the cause of the world, and we do not know anything more about God in this way, since as Bacon said He is not represented in the world,[5] except that arguing from the existence of the world to the cause of the world existing God too must exist. God, then, is the reason for the world.

The reason for the world would require that the world, for which a reason had been found, possessed some sort of unity, some similarity among differences. There is a sense, then, in which everything within the world is some part of it. The parts exhibit similarities and differences among themselves. The similarities show the parts to be parts of the whole, and the differences enable the parts to be parts within themselves. Thus although from this perspective the similarities are superior to the differences, yet the differences are necessary to the similarities. For things must first have some property which enables them to be distinguished before the property which enables them to be related can be recognized.

It is easy to see now that God as the cause of the world cannot be a part of the world. The whole cannot be introduced among the parts with a view to discriminating among them. That is what Heraclitus meant perhaps when he said that while men hold some things just and others unjust, God holds all things just.[6]

Nature is the name for the world of matter. If we assume that nature has a cause, then it must lie outside nature since it is not to be found within nature. The cause of nature we will call the supernatural. Nature itself is a visible theophany. But such a statement is not open to the

[5] Bacon, F., *Advancement of Learning,* Ch. II.
[6] Kirk, G. S., and Raven, J. E. *The Presocratic Philosophers.* Fr. 209. Cambridge. 1957. University Press. P. 193.

charge of pantheism, since it does not equate nature with God but only with his appearances, and the world only with his works. And where there is being, there God has been. "Faith requires us to be materialists without flinching," Charles S. Peirce said.[7] Where there is something there is being, and matter is something. Matter is scarce but it is a sign of being —perhaps it could be said that it is the only sign of being.

How is man's attitude to God changed by the picture of the material world in the new materialism provided by science? We shall have to preface such an inquiry by asking how man fits into the material picture of the world. Presumably, as material objects among other material objects, and no less so for being very good examples of the high degree of complexity of which matter is capable. If it is true that every integrative level introduces new qualities, and new grades of sensitivity, and with them new ranges of behavior, then the aspirations of the human individual offer good evidence of the tremendous capabilities of matter when properly organized. For it is not matter, mere matter, in the old sense of a simple impenetrable stuff, that we have been talking about, but matter which has been formed, which can be formed, and in which the forms can be changed or exchanged. A formal materialism similar to Aristotle's conception but revised extensively in the light of physics, chemistry and biology is what we have to deal with now.

Man is an animal but one with a sharp degree of self-consciousness and an active relation with material objects which he is able to alter and which in turn alter him. He has won a round in his struggle with matter by changing the shape of material objects in such a way as to enable him to direct some material objects against other material objects in a manner and with a size and force he would not have been able to accomplish by himself. He has conquered other animals, but not all organisms, and in particular not all of the smallest, and he has not conquered himself.

The human individual is a natural animal. The cause of nature is also the cause of existence. It is not possible to have any experience of the supernatural by natural means. Any experience within nature is a natural experience. Man in his normal state experiences only the natural.

But, it is claimed, the supernatural can be matched by the abnormal state of the individual. The argument continues by asserting that some abnormal states are exalted, when the individual is able to reach beyond his natural experience. Then he can experience the supernatural. The

[7] *Collected Papers of Charles S. Peirce.* Cambridge Mass. 1931. Harvard University Press. 1.354,

experience of the supernatural cause is also the experience of the cause of his own existence, since it is the cause of all nature and hence also of his nature as it exists. But there is a difficulty with the argument, for nature is wider than its normal states, and includes the abnormal. An abnormal state is a degree of disorganization of the material organism of the individual human animal. According to the vertebrate paleontologists man is one of the Platyrrhine Primates, and made his appearance as a tool-using animal during the later Pliocene, some million three hundred thousand years ago.[8] In an animal with such a protracted development and dependent to a large extent upon environing circumstances, abnormalities are bound to occur with relative frequency. The abnormal although a deviation from the normal is sure to be as common an occurrence. Thus abnormal states are in a sense if not normal at least expected, and accountable in ways familiar in nature. Human behavior—the whole of it —can be regarded from the animal point of view, and the human individual considered an animal with added properties. He has overcome his struggle with the other animals by establishing a continuity of aim and activity extending from one generation to the next often in an unbroken chain for many generations. Thus human culture, with its economic security, its churches and arts and sciences, is a social affair, and this helps to soften the hardness of the fact that he has not learned ultimate survival. Death still exists.

But what about the life span of the single human individual? It is short and often painful. But it can be put into the proper perspective, at least, for purposes of understanding.

Consider the individual who may be alive now. He did not exist for billions of years. He will not exist again for billions more. His life expectancy of less than a century constitutes a brief interruption in an otherwise ordinary state of affairs which he does not remember with regret but looks forward to with fear. Yet he does not think of what will be in terms of what has been, nor expect in any way to encounter the same conditions again. However, while there is no certainty there is a strong probability that death is only a restoration.

But an individual who contemplates his existence as it might be after his death in terms of what it must have been before his birth is sure to understand that being lacks the pervasiveness and the persistence of non-being. He would conclude that ultimate security lay in identification not

[8] An estimate of 1,750,000 was made by J. F. Evernden and Garniss H. Curtis as reported in the *National Geographic*, 12, 568 (1961). See also Dr. Kenneth Oakley as reporting to the British Association, *The Sunday Times* (London) for September 3, 1961. Revised to 1,300,000 by W. Gentner and H. J. Lippolt, in *The Sunday Times* (London) for November 26, 1961.

with being but with non-being. As Plato pointed out, the opposite of being is not non-being but difference and positive otherness.[9]

How are we to treat this? Most people die happy in the faith provided for them by some religion. Most faith means a belief in some theory of what will happen to them after death. Now in the absence of knowledge the faith is stoutly maintained, for that is what faith is: belief without knowledge. It enables people to die, however, in some comfort, secure in the belief that their future is assured. Few are capable of facing the fact without flinching that the body putrefies and decomposes, and that we do not know what the soul is. For if the soul is the same as consciousness, then it depends upon the body, and if it is not, then small comfort if it survives. But consciousness is so ephemeral it can be lost without death. Accounts of immortality are as vague as they are certain, and their definiteness is directly proportional to the absence of knowledge. For we do not seem to believe quite as firmly in other connections where we do in fact have reliable knowledge. Certain knowledge when we have it does not seem so reliable. Thus it is fortunate for certainty that faith is a matter of ignorance. As Augustine said, we must first believe in order that we may know.

The result is the discovery that faith is comforting, and any faith is as comforting as any other. Every one of the competing world religions, large and small, old and new, can boast of having comforted many adherents and to have given aid to them in proportion to their faith. But this does raise the question of truth. Is there a truth corresponding to the faith of each religion? If so, it is a partial truth in each case and the claims of the religion to be absolute are over-stated. But this no religion can admit.

In addition to the question of truth, there is the question of morality with respect to differences in faith. Statements for which there is no evidence when parading as knowledge may be termed false knowledge. The question which has never been answered, and indeed hardly ever raised, is the following. Is there any immorality involved in encouraging or allowing ignorant people to die happy when their happiness has been secured at the expense of false knowledge?

It does seem idle to suppose that God could be the exclusive property of any one religion. Matter is everywhere the same. God must be at the very least an object corresponding to a truth which is unaffiliated. What is wrong, then, is not the belief in God but the use to which such a belief is put. If all exclusive claims are abdicated and God not expected to side with one part of the universe against another, if the cause of the

---

[9] *Sophist,* 275**B**.

universe is not considered the cause of one part of the universe more than another, then the belief in God can be retained by all as equally necessary.

Such is the complexity of those small corners of the world with which we are familiar that the truth about the universe as a whole is almost sure to surpass the human capacity for understanding. But although the truth therefore allows for a faith, it is a different kind of truth, namely, one arrived at by reason operating on matters of fact. The limitation is perhaps that religion as such has always looked back for its security to a fixed creed adopted in the past, whereas the religious interest can never be satisfied, so long as it remains alive, with anything short of the search. We are ourselves material parts of the world and we live among a small number of other material parts by whose aid we seek the knowledge of a great number of other parts. Thus fundamental inquiry is a variant of the religious interest. The truly religious life is a life of perpetual inquiry, and for this we need a renewal of religion, one which will provide for all human interests and also satisfy the intellect,[10] one which will emphasize the great questions which the human predicament raises, without endorsing any of the answers which through its acceptance might threaten the inquiry.[11] Some bits of matter are so highly organized that they can respond sensitively both to the existence of a common world of matter and to the probability of its having a cause. Man, in short, is that peculiar kind of material object which seeks the knowledge of God.

ARISTOTLE'S RELIGION

The question whether Aristotle's philosophy was that of Platonism or that of a position opposed to Platonism has been greatly debated ever since Porphyry wrote his *Commentary* to Aristotle's *Categories* in the third century. It is still being debated today. The assumptions underlying the present work include the proposition that Aristotle is the leading Platonist. There is very little in Aristotle's metaphysics and ethics and psychology that was not first in Plato. Aristotle did two things: he arranged the ideas of Plato in orderly fashion, and he opposed the early

[10] Bradley, F. H., *Essays on Truth and Reality*. Oxford. 1950. Clarendon Press. P. 446.
[11] Feibleman, J. K., *The Pious Scientist*. New York. 1958. Bookman Associates.

Neo-Pythagorean interpretation of Plato made by the nephew who inherited the Academy in Aristotle's day—Speusippus.

There are, however, very many ideas in the discussions of religion in Plato that are not to be found in Aristotle, or, if found, are not given anything like the same emphasis. Chief among these, perhaps, is the idea of immortality, second only, perhaps, to the upholding of the conventional religion. The difference between Plato and Aristotle is the prevailing note of scepticism in Aristotle which exists also in Plato but which is more consistently maintained in Aristotle. Scepticism in religion is the healthy principle that the evidence is not to be exceeded. In the *Phaedo* it is exceeded, and it is exceeded in the *Laws,* although not so in the *Euthyphro* or the *Apology.* In Aristotle the principle is always present, and if he is misled it is the facts that have misled him in most cases. For temperamentally Aristotle is a partial sceptic.

A supporting piece of evidence is Aristotle's fondness for Euripides. Aristotle quotes him more than the other poets, more than Aeschylus for instance. That Aristotle was familiar with the plays of Euripides, the number of references to him in the extant work of Aristotle attests: there are some twenty-nine direct references and some seven indirect. Moreover, although Aristotle was not above endorsing the ridiculing of a side of Euripides that he did not like,[1] he also quoted him often with approval.[2] Euripides is frequently made to speak for the poets,[3] although, it is true, not on specific points of religion. No doubt the influence is there. But Aristotle formulated his own religious ideas under the naturalistic side of Plato; and although they are often in agreement with the Euripidean outlook, the influence would be difficult now to show. But the point is that scepticism, like faith, is never dead; only, where the object of faith changes from religion to religion, the object of scepticism is always the same, namely, religion. And the caution to believe about religion no more than reason and fact would allow was learned by Euripides, possibly from Xenophanes, and passed on, possibly, to Aristotle.

Admittedly, Plato was more concerned with religion than was Aristotle, if the number of pages devoted to religious questions are any indication of interest. Aristotle's theology is a topic which does not seem to have troubled him overmuch. "Aristotle says excellently that we should nowhere be more modest than in matters of religion. If we compose ourselves before we enter temples ... how much more should we do this when we discuss the constellations, the stars, and the nature of the gods,

---

[1] *De Sensu,* 443b30.

[2] E.g., *Ethica Nicomachea,* 1142a2; *Magna Moralia,* 1209b36; *Ethica Eudemia,* 1244a10; *Politica,* 1277a18,

[3] E.g., *Magna Moralia,* 1212b27; *Politica,* 1252b8.

to guard against saying anything rashly and imprudently, either not
knowing it to be true or knowing it to be false!" The words are Seneca's
but they do sound like Aristotle's.[4] Aristotle's own words are, however,
no less emphatic. The common sense based on reason and fact which he
maintained in the face of other topics did not desert him in religion.
"Our forefathers in the most remote ages have handed down to their
posterity a tradition, in the form of a myth, that these bodies [i.e. the
heavenly bodies] are gods and that the divine encloses the whole of
nature."[5] This Aristotle accepted, but he could not accept much more,
for he goes on to add, "The rest of the tradition has been added later in
mythical form with a view to the persuasion of the multitude and to its
legal and utilitarian expediencey,"[6] such as that the gods have human
form. Aristotle has left us a fragmentary account only; but in those of
his works which have survived we can detect the outlines of a set of beliefs
concerning nature, God and man, and the relations between them, which
is at least not inconsistent with his general position. Aristotle's chief concern seems to have been with nature and with man, in that order, and to a
far lesser extent with God. He has left us books, for instance, devoted to
nature, such as the *Physics,* and others devoted to man, such as the *De
Anima,* but none which is altogether devoted to God. We have to reconstruct his views on God from comments scattered throughout the
other books.

First, then, as to nature. Nature is "the immediate material substratum of things which have in themselves a principle of motion or
change."[7] Aristotle's metaphysics begins with the categories, and his
categories are those of *physical* nature: substance first and then the modifications of substance: quantity, relation, quality and the opposites, and
motion. Matter (*hulé*)[8] is that aspect of substance which is capable of
taking on form. Form (*eidos*) is the shape specified in the definition of
the things.[9] Form for Aristotle is always immanent form. The formal
and the material are causes of change, and so are the efficient cause,
which sets things in motion, and the final cause, or that toward which
things move. Every actual thing comes-to-be and passes-away, and in
these processes of becoming makes the potential actual and the actual
potential again.

The universe is eternal. "The same things have always existed," in
the sense that "actuality is prior to potency."[10] The change from potency

---

[4] Sen. *Q.N.*7.30. See *Select Fragments* in *The Works of Aristotle,* ed. by Sir
David Ross (Oxford, 1952, Clarendon Press), p. 87.

[5] *Metaphysics,* 1074b1, Ross trans.   [8] *Ibid.,* 190b24.
[6] *Ibid.,* 1074b5.   [9] *Ibid.,* 193a30.
[7] *Physics,* 193a28–30.   [10] *Metaphysics,* 1072a5–10.

to actuality could come about through art, nature, luck or spontaneity.[11]
There is a first movement that is not moved by anything else,[12] and it
occupies the circumference of the world.[13] The final cause is a last term,
so that the process is not infinite.[14]

The next category in the order of the understanding of nature is that
of human nature. The transition from the inorganic to the organic in
nature takes place by way of the soul. "The knowledge of the soul ...
contributes ... above all, to our understanding of Nature."[15] The soul is
"the first grade of actuality of a natural body having life potentially in
it," i.e. "of a naturally organized body."[16] It is "the essence of the whole
living body."[17] There could be no separate existence of the soul unless it
could act;[18] but instead it is the cause of thought and movement.[19] The
soul is inseparable from its body";[20] "it is not a body but is something
relative to a body."[21] It is part of nature[22] and itself has many parts:[23]
sensation and knowledge are within the soul;[24] while the mind, "that
whereby the soul thinks and judges,"[25] "is in its essential nature activity,"[26] and "seems to be an independent substance implanted within
the soul and to be incapable of being destroyed."[27] The soul, then, does
not survive the body, but the mind does, but still the mind is not the
person. As Guthrie says, "The description of the thinking part of us in
De Anima, iii, 4 and 5, makes it clear that there can be no survival of
individual personality and no room therefore for an Orphic or Platonic
eschatology of rewards and punishments, nor ... for a cycle of reincar-
nations."[28]

We have next to consider nature and God together. The world of
nature is a world of physical and biological existence. It is uncreated and
eternal; it was not created by God but has always existed and will
always exist. "God and nature create nothing that has not its use."[29]
Philo insisted that "Aristotle was surely speaking piously and devoutly
when he insisted that the world is ungenerated and imperishable, and convicted of grave ungodliness those who maintain the opposite."[30] Sextus
Empiricus reminded us that "Aristotle used to say that men's thoughts

---

11 *Ibid.*, 1070a5.
12 *Physics*, 242a19.
13 *Ibid.*, 267b8.
14 *Metaphysics*, 994b9.
15 *De Anima*, 402a5.
16 *Ibid.*, 412a28–b5.
17 *Ibid.*, 415b11.
18 *Ibid.*, 402b10.
19 *Ibid.*, 432a17.
20 *Ibid.*, 413a4.
21 *Ibid.*, 414a20.

22 *De Anima*, 403a28.
23 *Ibid.*, 433b1–4.
24 *Ibid.*, 417b23.
25 *Ibid.*, 429a21.
26 *Ibid.*, 430a17.
27 *Ibid.*, 408b18.
28 Guthrie, *The Greeks and Their Gods*, p. 370.
29 *De Gen. et Cor.*, 336b30–35.
30 *Politics*, 1326a32.

of gods sprang from two sources—the experience of the soul, and the phenomena of the heavens."[31] The world of nature is the work of the gods.[32] He was also quoted as having insisted that "the world itself is divine, a reasonable immortal animal,"[33] that "the world itself is a god."[34] Nature consists of an actuality of separate individual objects together with their potentialities of matter possessed by forms, continually changing in terms of opposite qualities. The world of nature is one of substance and becoming, of concrete individuals together with their modifications, engaged in continual motion. However, "the world refuses to be governed badly."[35] Nature depends on God[36] who introduces order into the unlimited. God arranged that coming-to-be should itself come-to-be perpetually, the closest approximation to eternal being under the condition that not all things can possess being at the same time,[37] the opposites, for instance. God holds the universe together;[38] and he does so, moreover, by being loved.[39] The relation between God and the world of nature insofar as it is active is one prompted by the world. God is the supreme object of desire; he moves the world by his active intellect. He is passive toward the world but the world is prompted to be active toward him by moving, and this means by seeking his perfection. God, then, is the Unmoved Mover.

We have sketched briefly Aristotle's conceptions of nature, the soul and the relations of nature to God. We have now to look at his conception of God (or of the gods).

Men imagine gods and their way of life to be human, he said.[40] Some people say that there are gods but in human form, but they are "positing nothing but eternal men."[41] Xenophanes said that the One is God but this can be neglected entirely as being a little too naïve.[42] There is one prime mover and so there is only one heaven,[43] according to Aristotle; but since he spoke, like Plato, indifferently of "God" or of "the gods" and posited a different god for each of the fixed stars, it is difficult to tell whether he ever decided how many gods there are—one or forty-seven or fifty-five.[44] The God-like property of the heavenly bodies rests on their immutability, which is evident to the senses. "For all men have some conception of the nature of the gods, and all who believe in the existence

[31] *Metaphysics*, 1072b14.
[32] *Politics*, 1252b24.
[33] *Metaphysics*, 997b10.
[34] *Ibid.*, 986b25–28.
[35] *Ibid.*, 1074a32.
[36] *Ibid.*, 1074a12. But see also *Physics*, 259a.
[37] *De Caelo*, 271a33.

[38] *Select Fragments*, ed. by Ross, p. 88.
[39] *Ibid.*, p. 84.
[40] *Ibid.*, p. 86.
[41] *Ibid.*, p. 94.
[42] *Ibid.*, p. 97.
[43] *Metaphysics*, 1076a4.
[44] *Ibid.*, 1072b14.

of gods at all, whether barbarian or Greek, agree in allotting the highest place to the deity, surely because they suppose that immortal is linked with immortal and regard any other supposition as inconceivable."[45] "God is thought to be among the causes of all things and to be a first principle."[46] God is removed to a great distance,[47] and, "as a brute has no vice or virtue, neither has a god";[48] his state is higher than virtue. That God even now possesses the good does not mean that anyone gains.[49]

Homer appropriately called Zeus king, for he is the king of the gods.[50] Like the good, God is better than the things that are praised.[51] "The gods surpass us most decisively in all good things."[52] God is "a living being that partakes of knowledge"[53] yet " 'intelligible living being' could not be a property of God."[54] Aristotle is very clear in rejecting the personal anthropomorphic gods. The gods "do not make contracts or return deposits," they do not perform "liberal acts," they have no money.[55] "God has but does not use the capacity to do bad things any more than a good man.[56] The activity of God is immortality, i.e. eternal life."[57] God is eternal, self-dependent, a living being, most good.[58] It would be silly to suppose the gods active or productive, for what would they do or produce? But they are alive, and there is only one thing left for living beings who are neither active nor productive: they are contemplative.[59] God has no external actions over and above his own energies, but this does not take away from his perfection.[60] "The activity of God, which surpasses all others in blessedness, must be contemplative,"[61] since he is neither productive nor active. "Thought is held to be the most divine of things observed by us."[62] God thinks about his own thoughts;[63] God's thinking is a thinking on thinking,[64] and he thinks eternally.[65] We assume the gods to be above all other beings blessed and happy.[66] God enjoys a single and simple pleasure; for he does not move, and

[45] *De Caelo*, 270b5–12. Cf. *passim* for the evidence of the senses concerning the existence of the star-gods as "primary bodily substance."
[46] *Metaphysics*, 983a8. Ross trans.
[47] *Nicomachean Ethics*, 1159a5.
[48] *Ibid.*, 1145a25, Ross trans.
[49] *Ibid.*, 1166a22.
[50] *Politics*, 1259b13.
[51] *Nicomachean Ethics*, 1101b30.
[52] *Ibid.*, 1158b35.
[53] *Topica*, 132b11.

[54] *Ibid.*, 136b6–7.
[55] *Nicomachean Ethics*, 1178b10–15.
[56] *Topica*, 126a34–36.
[57] *De Caelo*, 286a9.
[58] *Metaphysics*, 1072b28.
[59] *Nicomachean Ethics*, 1178b8.
[60] *Politics*, 1325b28.
[61] *Nicomachean Ethics*, 1178b21.
[62] *Metaphysics*, 1074b16.
[63] *Ibid.*, 1072b19.
[64] *Ibid.*, 1074b34.
[65] *Ibid.*, 1075a10.
[66] *Nicomachean Ethics*, 1178b8.

pleasure is found more in rest than in movement.[67] God is happy by reason of his own nature.[68] God's actuality is pleasure.[69]

Such activity is ceaseless and eternal, nevertheless is drawn toward a goal and the goal is its God. All that is not God is form and matter; no matter, then no form; but God is the only form existing without matter. Since God has no matter he cannot change; he is perfect and so has no reason to change. He is instead the eternal cause of all the change in the world, the unmoved mover, the pure actuality. But though he does not change he is continually active, and his activity consists entirely in the thought of what is highest and best: he thinks about himself and so about his own thoughts, and this is pure enjoyment. As we are sometimes, so he is always.[70]

About the role of man in relation to God in theological terms, Aristotle is clear. To praise the gods is to refer them to our standards, which seems absurd.[71] Praise involves a reference to something else; and to what else would you refer the gods? Instead, it is better to call them blessed and happy.[72] God cannot be injured and therefore cannot be wronged;[73] yet one should honor the gods[74] for they are absolutely honorable.[75] The religious life is the rational life, the holy life is the life of reason. "If reason is divine, then, in comparison with man, life according to it is divine in comparison with human life."[76] Expenditures connected with the gods are called honorable—votive offerings, buildings, and sacrifices—and similarly with any form of religious worship.[77] "It is enough with the gods, as with one's parents, to give them what one can."[78] The philosopher is dearest to the gods. For if they have any care for human affairs, as they are thought to have, it must be for what is best and most like them, i.e. reason.[79] "Now if there is any gift of gods to men, it is reasonable that happiness should be god-given because it is the best."[80] Since God is pure form and we grasp pure form only in the mind, we approach closest to the condition of God when we reason. Faith for Aristotle meant degree of belief, and degree of belief was determined by the force of demonstrative reasoning.[81] Faith as opposed to or divorced from reason was a later and non-Greek conception.

---

[67] *Ibid.*, 1154b26.
[68] *Politics*, 1323b23.
[69] *Metaphysics*, 1072b16.
[70] *Metaphysics*, 1072b14–15.
[71] *Nicomachean Ethics*, 1101b19.
[72] *Ibid.*, 1122b19.
[73] *Topica*, 109b33.
[74] *Ibid.*, 105a5.
[75] *Ibid.*, 115b32.
[76] *Nicomachean Ethics*, 1177b30.

[77] *Ibid.*, 1122b19.
[78] *Ibid.*, 1164b5.
[79] *Ibid.*, 1179a25–30.
[80] *Ibid.*, 1099b11.
[81] For an excellent discussion of "faith" in Plato and Aristotle, see H. A. Wolfson, *The Philosophy of the Church Fathers* (Cambridge 1956, Harvard University Press), Vol. i, Ch. VI.

Reason is the divine part of the human being. To be "immortal as far as we can"[82] means to think the most abstract thoughts, for "the faculty of active thought" alone seems "capable of separate existence."[83] In short, there may be a survival of the disembodied reason, which may mean simply the reunion of human reason with the divine reason.

The moral order is a social order; man is an animal as well as rational, and so for practical ends he needs to have an ordered society. The family is necessary for sexual reasons and the state for economic ones. The state is served if there is the widest diversity of interests, but strict justice must be administered, and for this constitutional law must be held supreme. But all this means a concession to natural conditions and does not represent man at his highest and best. Moral virtue demands the good life of practical conduct, but the best life is the intellectual life which searches for knowledge for its own sake.

As the Greeks saw it, the religious problems are centered about nature: nature, God and man, and the relations between them. God is remote from nature, whereas man is imbedded in nature; but neither God nor man can be understood apart from nature. The very remoteness of God is measured in terms of nature, although it is of concern chiefly to man and neither to nature nor, for that matter, to God. God, for Aristotle, is remote and draws us toward him because of what he is, not what he does, though we can and should imitate in a small way what he does. God is remote, contemplative and quiet, utterly charming, and unconcerned with practical human affairs, a sort of immortal prototype of what Aristotle must have wanted himself to be. The philosopher is most like the gods in that he reasons most of mortal men, and he is therefore dearest to the gods as well.[84] Thus we are left of the religious problems chiefly nature and man, which are entirely naturalistic concerns. Aristotle did not devote many pages of his extant works to the topic of God or the gods. But what he has to say on the topic is in accord with the indigenous Greek religion and with the religion of Plato's realism. It is not in accord with the Orphic idealistic tradition and therefore had little if any influence on the Neo-Platonists.

It was in fact to be many centuries before Aristotle was to have any influence on the western religions. His effect was first felt in any force in the thirteenth century—some seventeen hundred years after his death. His philosophy was incorporated into the Jewish religion by Maimonides, into the Moslem religion by Averroes, and, slightly later, into Christianity by Aquinas. When the western religions did incorporate the works of

---

[82] *Nicomachean Ethics,* 1177b30   [84] *Ethica Nicomachea,* 1179a25–30.
[83] *De Anima,* 413b24 ff.

Aristotle, it was his metaphysics and his ethics rather than his specifically religious ideas which were found the most congenial. A Neoplatonic idealism was combined with a kind of nominalism: these have more in common than either has with realism. Aristotle's own religious ideas are too thoroughly Greek, too metaphysically realistic, too naturalistic, too anti-Orphic,[85] too rational, to be anything but incompatible with a transcendental, supernatural and revealed religion, which all three of the western group are. This antagonism, which is inherent in Aristotle's religion, has usually been passed over; and the inconsistency of adopting his metaphysics, which is consistent with his religious ideas, while at the same time rejecting those religious ideas, is simply ignored.

Aristotle's religion, in short, is one of naturalism, whereas the three western religions, which in the thirteenth century adopted his metaphysics in combination with Neoplatonism, were committed to supernaturalism. It is no small wonder that they omitted and overlooked Aristotle's own religion; the wonder is that granting its existence they were able to reconcile their beliefs with his metaphysics without it.

[85] *De Anima*, 410b28.

VI

AESTHETICS

A BEHAVIORIST THEORY OF ART

I

In this chapter an attempt will be made to construct a theory of aesthetics by employing a theory of human behavior which has been extended from the theory of animal behavior as developed by Pavlov, Watson, Hull and Skinner. By "behavior" then will be meant here the movement of individuals so far as it has any structure, and by "need" what a material object can supply to an individual which is necessary for his or his species' survival. The theory supposes that all behavior is an attempt to reduce some one of a number of organic needs, and that such reduction is necessary to the individual's welfare.

Animal behavior can be accounted for by supposing that it is appetitive—behavior in accordance with needs. When a stimulus is introduced from the outside—usually some material object which appears to offer need-reduction—the animal makes responses intended to reduce the need, usually in two parts: a preparatory response leading to a consummatory response. The consummatory response offers the reward of need-reduction which reinforces the pattern of behavior.

Human behavior can be accounted for by assuming that the individual is an animal with added properties. The human additions are many, but I shall single out chiefly three.

1. The preparatory responses are more elaborate. A man does not lean over and lap up water when he sees it, as a dog does. He pours it into a container and then drinks from the container in accordance with the customs of his particular society, and all this usually after constructing reservoirs, purification plants and an elaborate system of underground conduits and indoor plumbing.

2. There is a feedback from the material objects which have been altered by the behavior. A horse tends to behave on every occasion just as it behaved in the past on a similar occasion. Not so man. With the use from childhood of chairs, he loses the use of muscles which enable him to sit with his heels flat on the ground, after the manner of East Indians.

3. Responses to stimuli may be considerably delayed. Behavior patterns of any elaborate nature are not usually retained for any length of time among the lower animals. But the human response to stimuli may occur many years after the stimuli. A young business man may learn of excellent commercial opportunities in another country, yet wait several years before exploring them.

All human behavior, then, like all animal behavior, can be accounted for as a series of responses to stimuli. The responses are made in terms of needs, or of drives to reduce the needs. The chief needs are thirst, hunger, sex, curiosity, activity and survival. The human individual has developed the first three—the primary drives—in terms of the preparation for responses, and the second three—the secondary drives—in terms of education, science and religion. Thus while the human behavior is similar to that of the lower animals it is also far more complex and constructive. Both the complexity and the constructiveness can be seen in the transformations which human individuals effect in material objects. Let us call such material objects "artifacts" and define them as objects which have been altered through human agency. They are of two kinds: tools and signs. "Tools" are material objects employed to move other material objects. "Signs" are material objects employed to refer to other material objects. "Symbols" are signs with attached qualities.

There are lower animals which fashion material objects, such as the beaver and its dam or the bird and its nest. But with man the case is stronger. He has succeeded in surrounding himself so completely with altered material objects that it can be almost said that he has transformed his environment. One reason for the existence of such objects is that he has learned to anticipate his needs and provide for them. He stores water and food, marries, establishes scientific laboratories, builds cities and joins churches. Wherever he may look he will find himself surrounded by the material objects which he has changed so that they may help him to reduce his needs. That is in a sense what human culture, what civilization, is: a collection of such objects, the calculated sources of need-reductions.

There is nothing degrading in the consideration of human individuals as animals with needs similar to those of other animals. While it is true that human individuals are not dogs conditioned to salivate to a bell by ringing it at the same time that they are given food powder, still they may be men conditioned to respond to the beauty of a landscape by being presented with a picture in which its most beautiful features have been intensified. It is certain that if works of art did not satisfy some human need they would not be made. Works of art are material objects in the world, they owe their existence to human agency, and they have their effects on need-reduction in the human individual.

The thigmotaxic response to the work of art is the sensitivity to confronted objects, in consideration of their perfection. The universe is large and its unity can best be apprehended through feeling. The appropriate feeling, as we shall presently see, is one of exaltation. The permanent objects in the world are both large and far away. The individual needs them for their permanence which he wishes for himself, and so he reaches out for them in his longings, and experiences a drive toward them. But he cannot reach them and could not touch enough of them if he could. And so he falls back upon a substitute technique. The unity which is apprehended through feeling is beauty, and it can be symbolically represented in a nearby object which he can reach and touch: the work of art. Beauty is the reflection of far-away objects, which reduces them to unity whatever their size and distance. The need for art is the need to be included through feeling in the whole in which all things are parts. The need for far-away objects is what the work of art reduces. As an object the work of art is nearby and as such is a surrogate for objects which are not. It symbolizes for the individual within the reach of his feelings the immensity of existence which lies beyond his reach.

Thus art and the individual are connected in at least two ways. The first is the way in which the individual artist stimulated by something in his environment responds by making a work of art. The second way is the way in which the individual who is not an artist stimulated by something in the work of art responds with appreciation. The artist is primarily responsible for altering a material object in such a way that it is regarded thenceforth as a work of art. And the appreciator is stimulated by the work of art to make a certain response. We shall deal, then, first with the artist and the artistic process, secondly with the work of art itself as it leaves his hands, and thirdly with the art appreciator, reserving a few words for a last look at the entire involvement.

II

What is it in the environment that stimulates an artist? Obviously, it is not the whole environment but only some part of it. But which part? What are its characteristics?

Taxially what orients an artist to a particular material object is a quality it may suggest to him so that he sees how he could in another object exhibit a similar quality as the quality of the relations between its parts, that is to say, as the quality of its internal relations (beauty).

Perhaps art arose as a secondary development of physical technology. Men who made for themselves crude tools, such as chipped stone arrowheads and clay pots, may have seen the comparison between those well done and those better done. The delight in the difference may have exceeded the utility of either. Hence there may have arisen the notion of things excellent for their own sake, that is to say for the sake of the excellence rather than for the sake of the thing, and the product was the first work of art: superfluous beauty probably first produced and afterward recognized as a by-product of craft excellence.

Scientific empiricism is new but empiricism is very old. The artists always were empiricists. Every discipline in fact has its own empiricism, which may here be defined as the derivation of abstractions from sense experience. Every abstraction has to justify itself by such experience. In science what is abstracted is naturally occurring relations and these can be represented in equations. In art what is abstracted is naturally occurring qualities and these can be represented only in other material objects in which they can be featured in a way in which they were not featured in the material object in which they were found, namely, as the bonds between the parts. Something in a face, say, or a landscape orients an artist in such a way as to compel him to react toward it. It releases in him a need for perfection. Somehow he sees in the form to which some accessible material object lends itself an element of perpetual novelty. He knows nothing exists like that—but it could. And if he succeeds it will. Aesthetic apprehension is a fusion of feeling, thought and action, all operating together in a single organic response centered on an image.

Imagination of this sort is a kind of analogical thinking. Strictly speaking it is neither inductive nor deductive, though it more nearly resembles the inductive variety. Analogical thinking needs both empathy and the facile ability to combine, separate and recombine very disparate elements, to which profound belief can serve only as an impediment. The releaser is the sensitivity to confronted objects, in consideration of their perfection, which is stronger in the artist than in others and precipitates him into action. The response to the stimulus of beauty is the work of art.

The activity of the artist is a species of human doing, an activity intended to transform some material object in the environment into a form in which the quality of internal relations is put forward as a symbol of the internal relations of the universe. Qualities in this context have a suddenness which is a result of the character of their presentation. It is by means of such featured qualities that naturally occurring relations can be bonded.

Art raises the question of the distinction between the artificial and the natural. The artificial is only the natural rearranged in order to concentrate certain of its properties—in the case of art, certain of its qualities. The natural contains all possible aspects, including beauty and ugliness. Art is more single-propertied; the artificial is either beautiful or ugly. And it requires the services of an artist to call attention in the artificial to the beauty of the natural. Every insight means that some subtle component of the external world has been apprehended. In this sense nothing is peculiarly subjective if it is true. But an artist depicts things in the condition in which we could wish everything was; so that if an artist builds better than he knows, it may still be because he knows and can express his knowledge best only by building. When mysticism does discharge into logical channels, as it does in the controlled imagination of the artist, there are powerful effects. Thus it stretches the individual's limited being out toward the wider being of the universe, through a common quality.

What the artist does is to ready through his consummatory response a preparatory response for others. The artists are life-givers. Without them existence would be empty and without significance, meaningless, a mere hollow round of habitual actions to satisfy primary needs. But the arts carry the secondary needs, they show the individual how to reduce our needs to know, to do and to be. They make nearby sources of need-reductions out of infinite yearnings, proximate rewards for needs which had extended too far in space and time beyond man's limited powers. To experience lawfulness—to know that something is right, to construct a symbol of such knowledge in a material object, and to feel some measure of surrogate survival—such is the need-reduction accomplished by the artist.

Making a work of art is "qualifying" an object, undertaking an extended qualification as a preparatory response, in view of operant learning. A technique must be known, a material object aggressively transformed, and a generalized being adequately represented. Qualitative research is a form of need-reduction for the artist as part of his need to survive, to put himself in touch with the long-range properties of existence, and in this way to associate or identify himself with the universe as a whole.

Art is the only true acceptance. That is why it may be a mistake to think of art too narrowly in connection with the beautiful. For the artist does not try to make more beautiful the beauty he encounters but he tries also to find beauty in the ugly, for it is the ugly which illustrates more graphically that beauty is the qualitative infinite in nature. Religion asks why, philosophy asks what, and science asks how. Only art does not ask; instead, it rejoices. It likes things as they are however they are, and strives to include them, the ugly as well as the beautiful, the evil as well as the good.

From the philosophical point of view art is the practice of phenomenology. It involves the reading of meanings by means of the appearances. There are signs on the surfaces of material objects not ordinarily seen, signs of inner significance and of outer value. The inner significance is an essential quality susceptible of much condensation. The outer value comes from the suggested similarities of remote and otherwise dissimilar items. The qualities of far-flung relations indicate a unity of being by discovering the qualities of relations which had not even been thought to exist.

Such analogies are new discoveries—they require new languages. Unless an artist speaks a new language he is hardly worth listening to. If he employs in addition a new syntax, our joy at comprehending him at last will be in proportion to the difficulty we experienced at first. In this sense every artist strives toward an ideal language of his own devising, and many obstacles are encountered in getting from one ideal of this kind to another.

III

What is a work of art? The deliberate apprehension of beauty in a material object. We have already seen that beauty consists in the quality of the bond between the parts of a material object, but this needs elaborating somewhat. Beauty is the quality which emerges from the perfect relations of parts in a whole, it is the quality of internal relations. The artistic method consists in apprehending in a material object the quality of such relations. Beauty is in readily accessible form when the qualitative correlate of the relation of consistency in a material object dominates the appearances of that object. Where the quality of internal relations is featured in a material object (as it is in a work of art), it symbolizes a unity in which every separate part is represented as a necessary part of the whole.

A work of art, then, is a material object made for the quality of its internal relations. But let us consider such objects with respect to the representation involved. Another element then enters. A work of art is a material object in space and time and has to be understood against the background of other material objects in space and time which are not works of art. When the quality of internal relations is featured in a material object, as it is for instance in art, there is a symbolism involved of the unity of the universe in which everything—including, by the way, the appreciator of art—is represented as some necessary part of the whole. But such symbolism involves qualities in the present derived from possibilities which are only described.

That art has a formal quality can hardly be denied. We have grown so accustomed to the achievements of logic and mathematics that when we say formalization we seem to refer only to abstractions, but the question occurs whether there are not other kinds of formalization. To formalize could mean to render as precise as the material to be included would allow. Then we should have to admit that in art we are rendering something precise, but we should need another kind of precision to handle another kind of subject-matter, in this case values. To render values precise presents a problem of formalization in art. We shall have to find for it a different logic—provided we are to be allowed to use the word "logic" at all.

Thus we could speak of dream logic as the reason why scenes are juxtaposed in dreams in ways which are inconsistent with actual time and space relationships yet exhibit their own type of consistency. The consistencies of qualities have not been studied and dreams have been considered chiefly with respect to their psychological content. In a dream it is possible to walk out of one room and into another without difficulty, where in actual life the adjacent room may have been miles, and decades, away. But there was in the dream—and the dream will of course justify this on its own ground—some reason for joining these two rooms. They may for instance have figured in important episodes in a man's life which are quite closely connected despite many superficial differences.

A work of art, then, may be an example of dream logic come alive in a material object. In a work of art the artist tried to capture in a material the impact of an intuition. He never completely exhausts the intuition although he approximates it as nearly as possible in words, in clay, in the actions of characters, in the movement of human bodies, in

sound or in architectural structures. Works of art are equivocal as the
logic of dreams is equivocal. Only in this way is it possible to obtain the
tensions which will invoke the proper values. In dream logic we cannot
formalize without residue, but we can suggest the presence of what is
omitted. The formalization of dream logic in a work of art makes of the
formal work of art a system which includes in an important way what is
excluded or omitted in other ways.

In art what is present is not merely present but represents the absent
in the present. Just as a universal represents absent as well as present
objects, so the work of art stands as the prerogative instance of a supreme
quality, that member of a class which can represent so completely the
other members as to be, qualitatively at least, identical with the class.

The relation of a work of art to what it represents that is absent
requires further analysis when we remember that the work of art also
represents what is present. The distinction is similar to what objective
idealists call the possible and epistemological realists the potential. Works
of art can now be further defined in relation to their environment as "the
qualities of negative constructions." By "negative constructions" I mean
configurations of objects and events representing other material objects
which do not exist and other events which do not happen. It was Proust
who said that "The pleasure an artist gives us is to make us know an
additional universe." (*Letters*, 228.) Art is negative in the sense that it
stands in exclusion from the positive contents of actual existence and in
contrast with them. Art is the picture of possibilities.

Art exists in order to verify the authenticity of alternatives, through
an endorsement of the genuineness and intensity of each of them by
means of the use of a model. A statue, for instance, is a configuration in
bronze of a man who does not exist as an organism. A novel is a configuration in language of human events which do not happen in any existing society. By the "qualities" of negative construction I mean the total
effects of each of such objects or events considered as wholes. Works of
art are negative constructions which are made, in fact, with a view to
producing just such qualitative effects.

A work of art is a selection of possibilities which are not actualized
except in symbolic form. The work of art is a surrogate of the representation. There is no such Wonderland as Alice inhabited, no such individual as Hamlet. In this sense they are both negative with respect to
actual existence, and if they exist at all it is in the form of qualitative
effects which because they are symbols are more powerful than the qualities of their actual and positive counterparts. Works of art are concrete
only with respect to their qualities, and otherwise exist only as lower
forms of matter, such as clay or stone, or marks on paper. But as qualities

they enjoy a persistence which would not be the privilege of their actual and positive counterparts. Hamlet has a different sort of existence from that of the live King of Denmark but one which lasts much longer.

IV

Works of art are material objects transformed through human agency, things made. But what is more, they are things made for a reason. The purpose of art is appreciation. The unconditioned response is the response to beauty, the "all-well" signal. The appreciation of art is a conditioned response, learning by means of the feelings something of the depth of the external world through the qualities peculiar to the objects disclosed to experience. The individual who is sensitive to natural beauty can be shifted to substitute works of art, with the result that the quality of his response is intensified. The art is useful because it is stronger and more concentrated. Works of art may be considered preparatory responses providing the permanent possibility of conditioning. Art appreciation is active self-conditioning. The man who has been conditioned by works of art will retain his intensity of appreciation when he returns to the contemplation of nature. In this way his aesthetic conditioning is an enrichment.

In animal psychology there are certain experiments in which electrodes are implanted in the brain of an animal and the animal given a switch, a foot pedal say, so that he can stimulate himself as he wishes, on the ground that he will do so if the resultant sensation is pleasant and not if it is not. In the work of art, conceived as what Mill called matter, "a permanent possibility of sensation," the human individual is "given the switch" when he is allowed access to the work of art, either through ownership or availability, concert hall or art gallery. The analogy should not of course be carried too far. The animal experiment belongs to physiology since it is not conducted with the intact animal, but the human individual confronted with an art object belongs to psychology because the individual *is* intact. I am not suggesting, either, that the values involved are the same. But the situation is similar in type. In both cases, an animal is allowed to stimulate himself if he wishes.

Works of art as artifacts constitute stimuli. We build them ourselves, it is true. But then they stimulate us. An artifact of this sort is a calculated and direct source of need-reduction. All artifacts serve need-reductions, but most of them do so indirectly. A stove does not reduce hunger but it cooks the food which does. But a work of art may reduce a need directly. It is not used to facilitate the servicing of the need by another material object but accomplishes this itself. Building a work of art is a preparatory response, but appreciating it is consummatory. The equipment of art plays an indirect and secondary role: studios, art galleries, theaters, symphony halls are parts of the preparatory response as much as the work of art itself is. But the work of art has a dual function to perform, for works of art—poems, paintings, concertos, novels—are preparatory responses providing permanent possibilities of need-reduction.

The moment a work of art is finished and takes its place as something existing separately, the activity of the artist is replaced by the passivity of the appreciator. For the appreciation of art is passive in relation to the activity of art. It exerts a force upon anyone entering its field of attraction who is equipped to take up the proper perspective. Appreciation, then, becomes an act of submission, a decision to be influenced or affected. The appreciator will feel what the work of art demands of him that he feel.

Responses to works of art consist in the more advanced sort of feelings which for want of a better word we call exaltations. Exaltation is the feeling of uplift. It is simple in that it consists of a single, uncomplicated feeling, entirely without parts, as any quality inevitably must be. But it exists at a higher level than simple sensations such as taste or smell. Implicit in the force of a feeling is a representation of the world. There is something external corresponding to the feeling, and no less so when the feeling is one of exaltation. What the work of art stimulates in the appreciator is the world-quality of exaltation suggesting it as a property of the world without change.

The appreciation of art, then, is a response to the stimulus provided by a work of art. What is to be obtained from the work of art is the quality of pleasure which comes from loving the world as it is. Not the passive "entertainment" of pseudo-art but an invitation to participate in the quality whereby things are related, which the artist has managed to elicit from the object. Art appreciation is an active enterprise, requiring effort on the part of the appreciator. Superficial feelings occur like waves on the surface of awareness, but deeper ones lie at deeper levels. They call for exertion in order to be reached. It is necessary to face in their direction such capacities of attention as we have at our disposal.

The necessary degree of formalization may occur as a result of the exigencies of rigorous communication whereby the artist informs his audience. There is a sense in which a work of art is the formula for a perspective. A formula of this sort tells us how to take up a new perspective on value, how to freshen up an old perspective, how to acquire a more penetrating perspective, or how to include more in our perspective.

Works of art suggest to the appreciator more than he is capable of experiencing without their aid. They point beyond the limits of experience, and bring "immortal longings" to man. Thus they remind him of his participation in being, which however small and temporary is none the less authentic, and offers as much of a hold on being as anything has. The purpose of art is not to give pleasure, though assuredly it may do that, but to intensify the senses and give depth to experience. Those who appreciate great art have learned to live more intensely. They have learned to know that there are in the world qualities corresponding to their most intense feelings.

Art is an effort to intensify feeling as another way of understanding the sources of being, self-conditioning by artifacts making possible a further penetration of the external world. Because of the artist we are able to see more deeply into the nature of things. Matter has at tremendous depths enormous complexities and powerful qualities, but they do not lie wholly on the surface. And if physics through the study of elementary particles can show us something of the complexity, art through the study of the conditions under which beauty arises can show us something of the quality. As consistency is to the mathematical system, so beauty is to the object of art. And as the consistency becomes more difficult the more complex the mathematical system, so beauty becomes the larger the greater ambition embodied in a work of art.

From the viewpoint of the appreciator the feelings quickly tire, and the more intense the more quickly. What stimulates is novelty. Thus the work of art must possess the property of perpetual novelty. The great work of art is capable of presenting to the appreciator a sort of permanent surprise. It is ever fresh, ever new. It is not common to find the world-quality disclosed in such an humble context phenomenally revealing itself as the similarity of diverse elements, and it is always unexpected, because feelings which resist resolution stubbornly remind us of their existence as feelings. A work of art is a stimulus in a given place that has its effects elsewhere, and appreciation reacts upon cognate experiences in the individual.

V

It is time now to step back and view the artistic process in the round.

The method of art consists in reacting to the quality of internal relations by building a material object with a view to featuring them, in order that the process of self-conditioning through exposure to them will be available to others. Such exposure is known to have certain affective and stimulating properties, through the intensification of the senses and the deepening of experience.

Thus in terms of entire man there is a feed-back mechanism at work. What he makes, makes him. The stimulus-response system begins with an interaction but ends by spinning off a product. Nature and man interact to produce the work of art, and then the work of art assumes a permanent form. It takes over when there are no further changes in it, and henceforth continues the function of stimulating man in a certain way which we have endeavored to describe. The only protest which man can make to this now one-way process is through habituation. Too much stimulation from the same object evaporates the effect of the novelty and leads to an eventually negative stimulation. The cumulative effects of exposure too prolonged are deadening.

But then there are always new works of art. Studios are needed as well as art museums, and artists as well as curators. It is the new which keeps the old alive. The artist who is our contemporary is capable of reviving for us an interest in the classics of art by giving us a new perspective from which to view them. In art we are always standing still while the influences go rushing by. We withstand the impact of the past only to be carried off headlong into the future. We exist, however, at that point between past and future where the current is most intense, and we can feel in our bodies the tremendous passage of forces which lie beyond us, which are of a tremendous beauty, but which we can hope to feel only so much as our limited sensibilities permit.

PHILOSOPHY
OF ART

THEORY OF COMEDY

Comedy is a unique field of investigation. It is an intrinsic value, and as such comparable only to other intrinsic values. As intrinsic it cannot be explained away or reduced. There are no words to describe logically the intrinsic aspect of any value—it just *is*. All that logic can hope to do is to effect an analysis. Such a logical analysis must consist in the tentative segregation of the field itself and in the exploratory attempt at definitions. It is this task to which we must address ourselves.

Comedy is one kind of exemplification that nothing actual is wholly logical. Expressed as the truism that nothing finite is infinite, that nothing limited is ideal, this truth appears to be self-evident. Yet such is not the case. Self-evidence is an *a priori* judgment, and has often been disproved in practice. It is a notorious historical observation that customs and institutions rarely enjoy more than a comparatively brief life; and yet while they are the accepted fashion they come to be regarded as brute givens, as irreducible facts, which may be depended upon with perfect security.

All finite categories, the theories and practices of actuality, are always compromises. They are the best possible settlements which can be made in the effort to achieve perfection, given the limitations of the historical order of events. Thus the categories of actuality are always what they have to be and seldom what they ought to be. It is the task of comedy to make this plain. Thus comedy ridicules new customs, new institutions, for being insufficiently inclusive; but even more effectively makes fun of old ones which have outlived their usefulness and have come to stand in the way of further progress. A constant reminder of the existence of the logical order as the perfect goal of actuality, comedy continually insists upon the limitations of all experience and of all actuality. The business of comedy is to dramatize and thus make more vivid and immediate the fact that contradictions in actuality must prove insupportable. It thus admonishes against the easy acceptance of interim limitations and calls for the persistent advance toward the logical order and the final elimination of limitations.

Comedy, then, consists in the indirect affirmation of the ideal logical order by means of the derogation of the limited orders of actuality. There are, of course, many and diverse applications of this principle. It may, for example, be achieved (1) by means of direct ridicule of the categories of actuality (such as are found in current customs and institutions), or it may be achieved (2) by confusing the categories of actuality as an indication of their ultimate unimportance, and as a warning against taking them too seriously. Comedians from Aristophanes to Chaplin, from Daumier to the Marx Brothers, have been occupied with the illustration of these approaches. The first is the method employed by Ring Lardner; the second, that employed by Gertrude Stein. A good example of (1) is the satire in Hemingway's *Torrents of Spring*[1] on the contemporary outlook of the literary generation. "Do come home, dear," Diana, the girl in the beanery, says to her man, Scripps. "There's a new *Mercury* with a wonderful editorial in it by Mencken about chiropractors." Would that do it, she wondered. Scripps looked away. "No, I don't give a damn about Mencken any more," he replied.

A good example of (2) is contained in one of T. E. Lawrence's replies to the proofreader's queries concerning the *Seven Pillars of Wisdom*. To an objection that his translation of Arabic names was full of inconsistencies, Lawrence replied, "There are some 'scientific systems' of transliteration, helpful to people who know enough Arabic not to need helping, but a wash-out for the world. *I spell my names anyhow, to show what rot the systems are.*"[2]

Students of comedy are fond of pointing out the element of surprise which enters into every comic instance. Something is expected and does

---

[1] P. 131.

[2] *Seven Pillars of Wisdom*, p. 25 (italics mine). See in this connection the whole of Lawrence's answers to the proofreader as excellent examples of true comedy.

not happen; the result is comedy. A man sits down but the chair has been snatched away and he falls on the floor. As crude as this is, it is true comedy. But the attempt to hold comedy down to the failure of expectation follows from the wrong interpretation of what is involved. First of all, comedy does consist in the absence of something which is expected, but it can also consist in the presence of something where nothing is expected. Always, however, the situation must illustrate the absence of what ought to be, if it is to reveal comedy. The unexpected indication of the absence of perfection (the *ought*) constitutes the comic situation.

Corresponding to the unexpected something and the unexpected nothing in the above analysis are the types of humor known as understatement and exaggeration. Understatement shows vividly the absence of something which is expected. It does not ridicule current estimations in order to show their limitations, but achieves the same end by other means. The beautifully simple means employed consists in the failure to take current estimations seriously on just those occasions when they are most expected to be taken seriously. Charles Butterworth, the screen comedian, is a master of this kind of comedy. When on one occasion he was shown a very elaborate statue, so large that all of it could not be included in the camera's focus, he observed approvingly, "Very artistic." Again, when introduced to a woman who wore orchids and ermine, Butterworth said, "Oh, all in white."

Exaggeration shows the presence of something where nothing is expected. Exaggeration is more common than understatement because it is so much easier to effect. Exaggeration ridicules current estimations by pushing the emphases to their apogees. Exaggeration takes the evaluations of the day, so to speak, at their word, accepts them as almost the whole truth. The features which the cartoonist singles out for attention are made to stand for the whole face. Charlie Chaplin's shoes, the cascade of knives which flows from Harpo Marx's pockets, the grammatical errors of Lardner's people—the list is practically endless. One familiar form of exaggeration is the grotesque. The grotesque is that form of exaggeration which occurs under the species of the ugly; and it works by combining the most unlike parts into a single whole. The half-animal, half-human gargoyles of Gothic architecture are examples. The fact that the creatures consisting of a combination of plant and animal parts, or of animal and human parts, unities of different kinds of life, seem more grotesque than those made up of inanimate combinations, has its own meaning. The higher we go in the series of organizations, the more subtle and tenuous but also the more important the differences. Hence the combination of higher with lower animal forms appears grotesque. The grotesque also conveys the idea that while all is ultimately one, this One is not made up of a random collection of parts thrown together helter-skelter but consists in a graded hierarchy of levels. The grotesque, too, then, as a form of comedy is a qualitative call to order. Both understatement and exaggeration point the moral that by exceeding the ordinary limits of actual things and events, the arbitrary and non-final nature of these limits can be demonstrated. Thus comedy is an antidote to error. It is a restorer of proportions, and signals a return from extreme adherence to actual programs, insofar as these programs are found to be faulty. Thus indirectly comedy voices the demand for more logical programs.

Needless to say, this kind of ridicule does service to the ideal, to the truth of an ideal society, by jesting at things which in the current society have come to be taken too seriously. Customs and institutions, in virtue of their own weight, have a way of coming to be regarded as ultimates. But the comedians soon correct this error in estimation, by actually demonstrating the forgotten limitations of all actuals. In this sense the clown, the king's jester, and the film comedian serve an important function. This function is to correct overevaluation, by exhibiting current evaluations in the light of their shortcomings. The corrosive effect of humor eats away the solemnity of accepted evaluation, and thus calls for a revaluation of values.

Inasmuch as comedy deals chiefly with current evaluations, its specific points bear always upon the contemporary world. The butt of its jibes may be shortcomings which have enjoyed a long and rather persistent history, or they may be merely evanescent and fashionable assumptions which are doomed to a short career. In either case they are usually highly contemporaneous. For example, the desire of insignificant men to appear important, as when Bacchus puts on the lion's skin and club of Hercules, in Aristophanes' *The Frogs,* illustrates foibles which can easily be shown to have been a weakness of human nature throughout historical time, and which still holds true of members of our own society.

Yet there are many contemporary allusions in the same play, some of which are now identified as having been aimed at known historical figures of Aristophanes' day, while others are permanently unidentifiable. When actual things and events have vanished, comedies which criticized them begin to date. *The Frogs* is valuable to the extent to which its criticisms remain applicable. Despite this saving element of atemporality, in the main it is true that classic comedies require extensive footnotes giving historical references, in order to render particular satires intelligible.

Thus the contemporaneity of comedy is one of its essential features. Sherwood Anderson is speaking for all comedians when he exclaims, "I want to take a bite out of the now." Comedy epitomizes the height of the times, the *zeitgeist*. Hanging upon the vivid immediacy of actuality, it touches the unique particularity embodied in the passing forms of the moment. A criticism of the contradictions involved in actuality, it must inevitably be concerned with the most ephemeral of actuals. Since its standpoint is always the logical order, it deals critically with the fashions of specific places—because they are not ubiquitous, and with those of specific times—because they are not eternal.

We have seen that some comedies criticize customs and institutions which are no longer viable, while others go deeper to those which are still effective. Following upon this distinction, it is possible to divide comedies into the romantic and the classical varieties. Romantic comedy deals with that which was actual but is now remote; classical comedy deals with that which is always true and therefore perennially actual. Needless to add, the division is not an absolute one, and most instances of comedy contain elements taken from both varieties. Yet the division is important. We can perhaps best make it clear by further comparison between the classical and the romantic. Classical comedy is comedy that tends toward an absolutistic logical view. In classical comedy, the ideal of the rigorous logical order is unqualifiedly demanded by the criticism of actuality. No sympathy is felt for the extenuating circumstances which render that goal difficult of attainment. This uncompromising demand is the criterion of what is classical. It manifests a severity of outlook which marks particularly great comedy, and tends to be of permanent worth.

Nothing, however, is ever completely classic, and there is found throughout all comedy, even the loftiest, a strain of sympathy for the uniqueness of actuality, a nostalgia for the lost particularity of actual things and events, especially when these belong to the past. The mournful regret that remembered events cannot be recaptured in all their frightful but fluid vividity is the hallmark of the romantic. The romantic tends to relax a little from the uncompromising demand for the logical ideal, and to identify its interest somewhat with the irrevocable uniqueness of elements flowing by in the historical order. *Trivia* by Logan Pearsall Smith is replete with romantic comedy, though touched here and there with classic insight. " 'I have always felt that it was more interesting, after all, to belong to one's own epoch: to share its dated and unique vision, that flying glimpse of the great panorama, which no subsequent generation can ever really recapture. To be Elizabethan in the Age of Elizabeth; romantic at the height of the Romantic Movement ...' But it was no good: so I took a large pear and ate it in silence."[3]

The romantic consists in a partial identification of interests with lost

[3] *More Trivia*, p. 92.

or perishable unique actuals. Since these must soon belong to the past, romanticism implies that perfection lies, or should lie, in the past rather than in the future. Thus romanticism is a form of primitivism. Romantic comedy points out that although passing actuals should have been better than they were, they were better than what has taken their place. The classic, on the other hand, like all true rationalisms, is directed toward the future; since what can happen is a wider category than what does happen, and classic comedy criticizes actuality in order that possible things and events in the future might be more perfect. Thus romantic comedy is shot through with nostalgic regret that *certain* actuals (i.e., specific ones in the past or present) cannot be made better than they were or are, while classic comedy takes the same observations of certain actuals but concludes from these observations that *all* actuals should be better than they are. Where romantic comedy is concerned with a segment of actuality, classic comedy is concerned with all actuality.

Comedy is properly part of the study of aesthetics. But it will be observed that this would restrict comedy to works of art. This cannot be done, since comic elements are contained in much that lies outside the arbitrary aesthetic field. As we have already defined and further explained comedy, there is a comic aspect inherent in every actual thing and event. A short digression will be needed, therefore, in order to show just what is the artistic element in all its field of investigation with which comedy deals. This can best be done by exhibiting the logical structure which works of art share with other systems.

Every piece of knowledge, whether it be a thing or an event, a tangible object or an abstract system, possesses a formal structure. This formal structure consists in a set of primitive propositions or postulates which are arbitrarily set up, in a chain of deductions which are rigorously drawn from them, and in a necessary conclusion. This is not the way in which the structure has been erected historically, but the logical form which it has by virtue of what it is. Perhaps the most familiar example of formal structure is the system of Euclidean geometry. Here the number of postulates is simple and few, the deductions rigorous and the conclusions demanded. As a result, the system enjoys a remarkable generality of application.

This kind of analysis is a common one throughout the realm of abstract systems, such as those of mathematics and theoretical science. But what is not equally well known is that the same analysis can be made of events; nevertheless it is true for them also. Every event possesses some formal structure. An event may be abstracted from its context in the stream of actuality, and considered as a self-contained system, having its own postulates, deductions, and necessary conclusions. The mere fact that the postulates may be implicit rather than explicit, and the deductive actions following perhaps a matter of instinctive or even automatic reaction, does not alter the fundamental formal validity of the structures. A man who chooses to go to the movies, a lost dog which manages to find its way home, and a river which winds its way to the sea, are equally good examples of the principle that all actions are purposive, and as such must be served by mechanisms which are analyzable into strictly logical systems.

What is true of abstract systems and events, with regard to their formal structures, is also true of works of art. For works of art also have their formal structures, though these are perhaps not so candidly expressed. Indeed it is the very difficulty presented by the problem of abstracting the formal structures of works of art which has led critics to suppose that no such thing exists. Nevertheless, it remains true that without their formal structures nothing actual could be. Works of art are sometimes admitted to have organization of a sort; but what such organization could consist of without formal structure cannot be imagined.

As a matter of fact, a close inspection of any work of art will bear out the truth of this contention. In some art mediums the form is more apparent than in others. For instance, the theme and variations scheme of most musical scores has a logical form which lies fairly obviously at the surface, and may be easily discerned by most appreciators. Indeed it is well known that any thorough musical appreciation must be grounded in an understanding of the form of the composition. The theme, or themes, announce the postulates, and the variations illustrate the deductions which are drawn from them. In the novel much the same holds true. The characters and situations as the reader finds them at the outset are here the postulates; the actions and interactions of the characters are the deductions drawn; and the climax presents the necessary conclusions toward which everything else has moved. What is true of music and fiction is true of every other kind of work of art; the effectiveness is always closely identified with a rigorous logical scheme, which is present even if never presented as such.

In abstract logical disciplines, all claims for the *a priori* and self-evident truth of postulates have been abandoned. In their place there has been substituted what is known as the postulational method. This amounts to nothing more than a recognition of the arbitrary selection and objective existence of postulates, which must rest not upon their self-evident truth but upon the fruitfulness of deductions made from them (i.e., the generality of their possible range of application) together with the self-consistency of the system of deductions itself. Now, what does this mean in terms of works of art? It means simply that the subjective claims of intuition and the creative claims of the artist must be somewhat abated in favor of the deductive aspect. Induction and the artistic process are not to be abandoned, since there is no other method known for the discovery of works of art, but the fact is to be recognized that such inductive processes rest upon the prior assumption of a logical scheme in terms of which the inductions are made. Postulates are chosen by the artist by means of induction; necessary conclusions are drawn from them by means of deduction. Thus although the insight of the creative mind is an indispensable tool in the production of works of art, it yet remains true that the process, as well as the final product of the system itself, is strictly logical.

In this connection, it may be remarked parenthetically that the genius of the artist lies largely in the choosing of postulates. Once they have been chosen, he may exercise his ingenuity in determining where the proper deductions can be drawn. In a highly organized work of art (i.e., one which is technically perfect), all possible deductions are drawn. For here aesthetic economy has demanded that the postulates be kept few and simple, and therefore the number of possible deductions severely limited. The best of Bach's fugues are illustrations of the latter type of works of art.

The criticism which comedy makes of all actual things and events is aimed specifically at their formal structures. Formal structure is alone responsible for the paucity of actual value; and it is this lack with which comedy expresses dissatisfaction. But warning must be issued against a grave danger which lurks in this fact. It is a mistake to suppose that ridicule leveled at the limitations of any actual system is being directed at the idea of system itself. To make fun of some man dressed for an afternoon wedding is not to make fun of formalism in dress, but might indeed be a plea for stricter attention to appropriate proportions in formal dress. To deride our government's shortcomings is not to deride the necessity for some sort of government but is rather a demand for better government. Theories and practices are criticized not because they are theories and practices, which in one form or another must always have their place, but because they fail to be sufficiently wide and inclusive. Comedy, we must remember, upsets the categories of actuality only with the purpose of affirming the logical order. The literal nonsense of Gertrude Stein calls for the establishment of wider conventions in prose than those which her own prose came to destroy.

In short, it is not the content (i.e. the value) which is being criticized in comedy, but the limitations put upon that value. Criticism of formal structure means criticism of the fact that the content contained in formal structure is not unlimited content.

There is nothing which does not have its tragic as well as its comic aspect. Comedy and tragedy are both members of the same class of objects, and are known to bear some close relation to each other. It will aid, therefore, in the understanding of comedy to contrast it with tragedy for points of difference, and to compare them for points of similarity. In order to make clear what we are talking about, it will be best to begin with definitions. We have already defined comedy as an indirect affirmation of the logical order by means of the derogation of the limited orders of actuality. What is required now is a definition of tragedy which can be set over against this definition of comedy. Tragedy, as we have seen, is the direct affirmation of the logical order by means of the approval of the positive content of actuality. Tragedy is content to endorse the threads of the logical order as these are found running through the historical order.

Tragedy affirms the infinite value of the world through the endorsement of the remorseless logic of events. This blind faith in the triumph of the logical order over the contradictions and evils of actuality survives the observation that in any limited time the logic of events may be accomplishing more harm than good. According to Dorothy Norman, Alfred Stieglitz has related an anecdote which illustrates very well this aspect of tragedy. "When someone asks him what he understands by the word 'justice,' Stieglitz replies, 'There are two families, equally fine. They go to a hillside, and there they build their farms. Their houses are equally well built; their situations on the hillside are equally advantageous; their work is equally well done. One day there is a storm which destroys the farm of one of them, leaving the farm of the other standing intact. That is my understanding of the word 'justice.' "

Among the best examples of tragedy are the Greek dramas of Sophocles and Aeschylus. In the *Oedipus Rex* of Sophocles, the hero unintentionally sets off a chain of circumstances, of which he is himself the unhappy victim. Unwittingly, he sets up a postulate for action, and is himself enmeshed and crushed in the deductions which follow. He kills his father in order to become the husband of his mother, and then banishes himself from his own kingdom—all without his own conscious knowledge or consent. This play is a true illustration of the dramatist's recognition of the inexorable march of the logic of events, of the logical order as it operates through the medium of history.

There are many points on which comedy and tragedy may be contrasted, which will serve to explain them both in a more thorough manner. Comedy is an intellectual affair, and deals chiefly with logic. Tragedy is an emotional affair, and deals chiefly with value. Comedy is negative; it is a criticism of limitations and an unwillingness to accept them. Tragedy is positive; it is an uncritical acceptance of the positive content of that which is delimited. Since comedy deals with the limitations of actual situations and tragedy with their positive content, comedy must ridicule and tragedy must endorse. Comedy affirms the direction toward infinite value by insisting upon the absurdly final claims of finite things and events. Tragedy strives to serve this same purpose, but through a somewhat different method. For tragedy also affirms the direction toward infinite value, but does so by indicating that no matter how limited the value of finite things and events may be, it is still a real part of infinite value. Logic being after all the only formal limitation of value which is the positive stuff of existence, tragedy which affirms that positive stuff is greater than comedy which can affirm it only indirectly by denying its limitations.

Comedy is by its very nature a more revolutionary affair than tragedy. Through the glasses of tragedy, the positive aspect of actuality always yields a glimpse of infinite value. Thus tragedy leads to a state of contentment with the actual world just as it is found. According to tragedy, whatever in this finite world could be substituted for the actuality we experience, would still have to be actual and therefore to some extent limited. It would have to be finite to be available for experience, and would not be the infinite value toward which we always are working. The historical order of actuality, wherever and whenever it is sampled, yields a small amount of positive content which must be a fragmentary part of actuality. Thus, tragedy seems to say, since any segment of actuality is bound to be a fragmentary part of infinite value, why change one for another? Better to stress the fact that whatever small fragment of value we have, it is as much value (though not as much *of* value) as any other fragment? Why then, it asks, be dissatisfied?

Comedy, however, is occupied with the termini of things and events, their formal limitations, as opposed to tragedy, which is occupied with their positive stuff or content. If it is only the limitations of actuality which prevent actuality from containing infinite value, those limitations should not be suffered. To justify the demand for their elimination, it is only necessary to point out that they are limitations. Comedy leads to dissatisfaction and the overthrow of all reigning theories and practices in favor of those less limited. It thus works against current customs and institutions; hence its inherently revolutionary nature. Actuality may contain value, so comedy seems to argue, but it is capable of containing more of value; and it is necessary to dissolve those things and events which have some value in order to procure others which have a greater amount. Better to stress the fact that however much value any actual situation may have, it is prevented from having more only by its limitations. Why, then, be satisfied? In periods of social change, we may expect to see the role of comedy assume an increasing importance, although, to be sure, both the comic and the tragic aspects of being are always and eternally omnipresent.

It has been pointed out by Bergson and others that comedy bears a closer resemblance to real life than does tragedy. This is true, and it is very obvious why it should be so. The contradictions and disvalues of actuality wear a greater vividity than do truths and values. In our daily occupations, we are confronted more frequently with the intense aspects of existence than we are with the diffused aspects. Error, ugliness and evil, are, after all, colorful. Truth and value, as found, for example, in the systems of mathematics and the feelings of ecstasy, are wonderful; but they are likewise rare. Everyday life knows much more of the partial and extremely limited side of existence, and it is only a truism to say that this side is more familiar. Fortunately for the progress of humanity, familiarity is no index to value; what we are forever condemned to pursue are just those fleeting glimpses of infinite value which come to us so seldom. But it is comedy which wears the common dress.

Comedy, then, criticizes the finite for not being infinite. It witnesses the limitations of actuality, just as tragedy witnesses the fragmentary exemplifications of the logical order. Tragedy affirms continuity by showing how it exists in every actual thing and event. Tragedy shows the worth of every actual, down to the most ephemeral, and so is always close to the permanent value of the worshipful. Comedy comes to the same affirmation, but inversely and by indirection, just as one might affirm beauty by criticizing the ugly. Comedy catches the principle of unity in every finite thing; tragedy attends to the principle of infinity.

It should be remembered that our contrast of comedy with tragedy tends toward a misleading oversimplification, as all analysis, of necessity, must. There are subtle relations between comedy and tragedy which reveal them to have more in common than do the rough comparisons we have had to make. Often indeed the connection between comedy and tragedy is so close as to render them hardly distinguishable.

An excellent example of comedy in this sense is afforded by the episode of Alice and the Cheshire Cat, in Carroll's *Alice in Wonderland*. Alice had been nursing a baby, when suddenly, much to her dismay, it turns into a pig. She puts it down and it trots off into the woods. Alice walks through the forest, "getting well used to queer things happening," when with no warning the Cheshire Cat reappears exactly where it had been before. In the midst of this series of marvels, the Cat's conversation assumes the most casual, conversational tone.

" 'By-the-by, what became of the baby?' said the Cat. 'I'd nearly forgotten to ask.'

" 'It turned into a pig,' Alice answered very quietly, just as if the Cat had come back in a natural way.

" 'I thought it would,' said the Cat, and vanished again."

Here comedy, too, turns upon the logical order of events, but what events! Through the exposition of their connectivity, limitations are unexpectedly exposed and the comic aspect brought into predominant relief. Or the connectivity is emphasized as one of continuous value, and the tragic aspect triumphs. There is comedy in actual situations whose limitations have been laid bare. There is tragedy in the inexorable march of actual situations, because what value is contained in them will not be denied. Both comedy and tragedy emerge from the same ontological problem: the relation of the logical to the historical order. We may see the actual situation as comedy or as tragedy; for in fact it is both.

THEORY OF TRAGEDY

All art has its tragic aspect, but then so has every ordinary event; hence we are bound to seek for art a more definite knowledge concerning the nature of the tragic. We experience tragedy in our personal lives and we witness tragedies on the stage; but do we mean the same thing when we speak about the tragedies of ordinary life and the tragedies represented in works of art? If so, what is the element they have in common? Through the answers to these questions the essential meaning of tragedy may be found. We are safe in assuming, for the purposes of this study, that some experience of the tragic in both its occurrences: as an element of art and also of ordinary life, is familiar to all persons. Yet the meaning of a thing, that which is essential to it, is not always to be found in the common-sense definition, for common sense is apt to be too general; or in the artistic definition, for art is apt to be too special. We are here making the assumption (for which, as we shall learn, there are good metaphysical reasons) that the two meanings of tragedy as given in ordinary life and in art are special cases of a grander principle.

With the understanding of this assumption, we may proceed abruptly to the statement of the hypothesis which is to be accepted as the basis of the present argument. The hypothesis, which is in the form of a definition, is as follows: Tragedy is that aspect of artistic value which is concerned with the qualitative presentation of the acceptance of the content of actuality. The remainder of the study will be devoted to exploring the meaning and implication of this definition.

By tragedy is meant the qualitative reaction to limited value, taken just for its value and despite its limitations. Tragedy depends upon the fact that values as actual affairs cannot persist forever, for it does not matter that values are fated so long as they *are* values. What is, is, when it is; and this irrespective of how long it may or may not remain what it is. Every actual thing is both valuable and logical. Its value has disvalue; its logic has contradictions. Thus it is doomed; and indeed history is the record of doomed things. Everything must come to an end in finite time; all individuals, families, empires and whole civilizations, however long their span of time, they must know defeat and eventual death and decay. We argue from a knowledge of the past to the expectation of the future; that is the reasonable thing to do. But value always transcends logic, and love, being a manifestation of value, reaches beyond reason: we love the things we have and we do not wish them to die. We know that they shall die; yet we love them, all the same, and we are willing to fight for them. It is a hopeless fight, and we shall undoubtedly lose them in an end which may be near or distant. But we fight for what we love, doggedly, blindly, against all adversaries, though we may know in a way, or feel, that we are certain to go down in defeat.

Tragedy is self-contained and self-sufficient; it calls for nothing else and requires nothing more. Tragedy is chiefly a qualitative affair; it presents itself as force, value or power, rather than as principle, law or analysis. It acts as a whole and not through the agency of its parts. Lastly, it is the content of existence, the positive part of actuality which we meet in our experience, that tragedy qualitatively accepts. In tragedy, the conflicts, the logic and the structure of existence are there only to point up the bafflement, and hence the limitations, of positive value. Nothing actual exists forever; everything eventually runs into conflicts and contradictions and hence must perish. The perishing comes as an indication that value is not unlimited, and because it is not unlimited it must come to an end. Tragedy is the recognition of the fact that even limited value (and all actual value is limited value) is *value* just as much as unlimited value would be, only it is not as much *of* value. The tragedy is that no values less than infinite value are allowed to remain actual more than a limited time.

Actuality in the round is neither as good nor as bad as it is sometimes painted. Actuality is the world of action and reaction, the realm of those things which affect and are affected; and in this world there is harmony as well as conflict, logic as well as irrationality. Tragedy concentrates upon the consistent elements. Value has its structure; and since we are concerned with positive value in tragedy, we are also concerned with the extent to which that structure is valid, even though this part of our concern is indirect. Thus tragedy requires for its values a certain degree of consistency. The requisite consistency is furnished in actuality by the remorseless logic of events. In a limited time, the logic of events cannot be demonstrated, and that is why tragedy in art so often hangs upon a protracted time-span. The *Oresteia* of Aeschylus pursues its postulates through several generations with the aid of a dramatic trilogy, and in this wise the logic of events makes itself evident; for it is always possible that the postulates of a set of actual circumstances may take a whole generation to establish, the deductions another generation, and the conclusions still another. In Sophocles' *Oedipus Rex,* the protagonist is the unhappy victim of the chain of circumstances which he himself had started. He sets up the postulate for certain action, and is himself enmeshed and crushed in the deductions which follow. He kills his father in order to become the husband of his mother, and then banishes himself from his own kingdom. Tragedy is a logical affair, otherwise it could not be accepted qualitatively as a value; for illogical things present themselves qualitatively as disvalues.

The logic of events may be compared to the syllogism laid down along the time-line moving from the past to the present and into the future. Postulates have been established by events in the past; in present events deductions are drawn, wittingly or unwittingly, from those postulates; and everything concerned works toward conclusions as consequences in the events of the future, conclusions of which we may be unmindful but which operate effectively none the less. By following the chain of events through the time-span in which their logic will be revealed, tragedy is able to recognize the inevitable end of the values involved in those events. Thus tragedy reaffirms the inevitability of logic by emphasizing the effect which the logic of events exercises upon its own inherent values. Thus tragedy is involved in the present or in the future, just as reason is. And, also like reason, it requires more than the present to demonstrate its character.

If logic and consistency are secondarily involved in the axiological considerations of tragedy, it may well be asked why there must be a conflict in tragedy and why positive aims must end in defeat. Both conflict and defeat affirm in different ways the actual limitations on value, in spite of which the value must be accepted and even defended. We fight for what is good and true and beautiful not because we think or hope that these things will exist forever; on the contrary, we know they will not.

We fight for them because we know they are valuable, and because we know that whether or not they are banished from actual existence they will nevertheless have their being forever; and we fight for the retention in existence of the values of being. Nothing of value can ever be destroyed simply by being removed from actuality. What is actual is always possible, and what was actual or what may (or may not) someday be actual is still possible; essence is a larger and more inclusive category than existence. In recognition of the higher status of value, actual values have their limited cycle and eventually meet with disaster; and those who fight for the good and the true and the beautiful, provided that the fight goes on long enough, are sure to be brought to eventual failure. But through the very disaster and defeat, the infinite nature of value is once more confirmed. We cannot lose in the final sense, just as in a more proximate sense we are not apt to win. Values will be lost from existence but may return eventually.

The tragedy is, then, that particular exemplifications of value cannot be continued indefinitely in existence.[1] Struggle always has its tragic aspect, since there must be a vanquished whenever there is a victor, and tragedy is the victory of the vanquished. Actuality is a mass of major and minor struggles; every actual thing is fragmentary, and every fragment is engaged in a constant striving to complete itself. In this effort it meets with the opposition of other fragments which are engaged in the same pursuit. The contradiction of actual conflict results, a conflict from which currently only one victor can emerge; but there is a consolation prize for the loser: the values on his side, whether lesser or greater than those of his opponent, retain their essence even though not their existence, and hence it will always be possible that they will come into existence again. Hence every tragedy is a fairy story for the values which exist happily ever after, even if not for the carrier of the values who sooner or later must die. His solace is the promise of the return of the values which he cherished, even though this is to be accomplished with the aid of other carriers.

The two ontological universes of the possible and the actual are involved in the meaning of tragedy. Tragedy represents one aspect of the strain between the universes; that what is actual and therefore also possible cannot remain actual, and also that what is possible but non-actual cannot become actual. The first aspect of the strain is an ontological impossibility, in that nothing actual is wholly valuable and non-contradictory; thus it must eventually fall a prey to its logical and axiological

[1] Cf. Francis S. Haserot, *Essays on the Logic of Being* (New York, 1932), p. 443 *et seq.*

shortcomings. Things live by means of their value and consistency, and die as victims of their disvalue and inconsistency. There has been nothing actual which was ever known to be lacking in shortcomings and limitations. The second aspect of the strain, namely that what is possible and non-actual contains no ontological prohibition against actualization, at least none against those possibilities which are not essentially non-contradictory. Thus in tragedy there is always the note of faith and the note of hope. In the most heartbreaking tragedy there is always the feeling that somehow it is well with the victims and that being is essentially good and right and even beautiful. But despite this positive note, the fact is that the possibilities are not actual and we do not see how they shall become so. Their failure to become actual, continued into the immediate future, is a tragic fact.

Tragedy weaves the two ontological levels together; it runs threads from the possible to the actual and from the actual to the possible. It recognizes elements of the eternal and unchanging in the temporal and the changing; it bids a regretful farewell to those values which are being lost from the world that we know and confidently expects their return on some as yet unspecified occasion, from the assumption that there is at least nothing illogical in such an expectation. Thus it tacitly but emphatically recognizes the being of some level other than that of the actual world of action and reaction, and depends upon an interaction between the two universes. Tragedy is metaphysically realistic in its admission of the being of two universes of ontology. If the values conflict here below, if the inconsistencies abound, if justice is seldom done, tragedy at least recognizes that the values, the consistencies and true justice belong to another kind of world: though it says nothing in detail concerning such a world and its order, and thus avoids theology and cosmology except by remote inference and subsidiary implication.

An illustration of how tragedy weaves the two ontological orders together is given in the Greek conception of the cycle of tragedy; success, hubris, nemesis and ruin. In this conception, man is defeated because of his assumption that through perfection he has managed to raise himself from the level of the temporal to the level of the eternal. Success at the temporal level is followed by defiance of the gods, as by one of themselves. But this divine insolence is followed by the retributive justice of that nemesis who is the guardian of the natural order of things; and after nemesis there is complete ruin. Thus tragedy is the defeat following hard upon the false assumption that all which is possible is also actual, that perfection not only can be attained but has been reached. Similarly, we are furnished with another example of the interweaving of the two ontological orders if we consider the distinction between the romantic and the classic from this aspect. The classic is the pursuit of the eternal values for their own sake, as though they were inclusive of the temporal; the romantic is the pursuit of the temporal values for their own sake, as though they were themselves eternal. In this way we are enabled to view the tragic hero, the defender of lost causes, either from the romantic or the classic perspective.

We have defined tragedy as that aspect of artistic value which is concerned with the qualitative presentation of the acceptance of the content of actuality. We have noted that tragedy affirms the ideal axiological order by this acceptance. How, then, does it happen that when tragedy is confronted with a situation involving disvalue, it behaves in exactly the same way? The answer to this apparent dilemma is that the highest and most symbolic instance of the acceptance of value in actuality would be the acceptance of the smallest amount of value. But the smallest amount of value is not value at all but disvalue. From the point of view of positive value, the smallest amount of value is the largest amount of disvalue. We see this illustrated graphically in mathematical analysis, when we plot negative values for y on the scale of rectangular coordinates, and find the amounts growing larger for $-y$. We see it illustrated, too, in the trial of Socrates as recited in the *Apology* of Plato, when Socrates replies to his accusers after he has been unjustly condemned to death, that they must suffer the penalty of villainy and wrong while he abides by his award: "Perhaps these things are fated and I think that they are well." (*Apology*, 39B.) Thus the very highest affirmation of eternal and positive value must consist in the embracing of the largest amount of disvalue in actuality. Tragedy, we may now say, consists in the direct affirmation of the ideal axiological order by means of the acceptance not only of the positive content but also of the disvalues of actuality.

We have discussed the logic and the ontology of tragedy. Readers who are oriented toward human values to such an extent that nothing makes sense without them, will want to know something concerning the relation of the tragic to the human. This topic involves a further discussion, this time one on the epistemological, the psychological and the ethical meaning of values. We shall want to return to the perspective from which we started, however, and this will be done by relating tragedy to other aesthetic elements. In the meanwhile we have committed ourselves to a specific point of view by the very order in which the topics relevant to the meaning of tragedy have been treated. If the definition of tragedy, and its other logical and ontological aspects, can be considered without reference to our knowledge of tragedy or our reactions to it as human beings, then obviously tragedy itself must be to some extent independent of such considerations. That is indeed the position advanced here. Tragedy is, as we have already seen, a thing in itself independent to some extent of all other things. From the human point of view, it is something objective and external. As such it does have an effect upon human beings, however; and it is this effect that in the following paragraphs we shall consider. There is an epistemology of tragedy, and more pertinently, there is a psychology; and though neither of these topics is central to the meaning of tragedy, both well may be important in the actual practice of tragedy.

The knowledge of tragedy is gained to some extent just as is the knowledge of any other item. Tragedy from the viewpoint of epistemology is an object, and the knower of the tragic is the subject. The subject is not entirely devoted to the knowledge of tragedy, since there are so many other things to be known, and the object of tragedy is not entirely occupied with the subject since there are so many other subjects. Thus the relation is one which can be switched on and broken off without entailing the disaster of either subject or object in the case of tragedy. The tragic object is what it is whether or not the subject is standing in the position of knower. We may term this position a perspective. Tragedy always occupies a perspective, and we may assert that every object has its potential perspective. When this perspective is occupied by a subject, there takes place the knowledge of tragedy, occasioned in the subject by the object. Knowledge, the knowledge of tragedy, then, is a result of the occupancy of a perspective.

Everything in the world is limited and fated, as we have noted earlier. Each thing in a sense travels about with its own perspective. When this perspective is occupied by something capable of knowing (and in the highest degree known this something is a human being), there is knowledge, the knowledge of tragedy. The truth of tragedy is the one-to-one correspondence between the view from the perspective of tragedy and the tragedy itself, plus the coherence which is the consistency of a given tragic view with the tragedy of other views. The ability to stand in the perspective of tragedy is for a subject a question of his equipment. Not everyone has the necessary equipment. To one without sympathy and the code of a certain obligatory behavior of children toward their parents, for instance, the tragedy of *King Lear* might very well be meaningless. Yet that would be no argument for the essential meaninglessness of *King Lear*. Tragedy would be tragedy even if there were no one capable of occupying the perspective necessary in order to gain the knowledge of it.

In formal art the elements of tragedy are intensified, so that the knowledge of tragedy is more readily gained from it than from everyday life. Yet the knowledge of tragedy is not confined to art but may be acquired through pedestrian events. The death of a nobody who may have had important ambitions is tragic, even though the tragedy had been apparent only to his wife and children; assuming that not enough persons crossed his path who would have been able to glean his moral by occupying the perspective which would have made the knowledge of his tragedy available to them. Tragedy is charged with the capability of exercising a certain effect; it is an object full of potentialities for subjects; and when a subject, that is to say, a knower, wanders into its perspective either deliberately or by chance, or perhaps even unwillingly, it works its influence upon him. The subject does not have to stand in the perspective of tragedy, but when he does he has to know it, just as a certain logic is inexorable but only to those who have accepted its postulates.

The psychological aspects of tragedy differ from the epistemological in that the former are concerned with the effect of tragedy upon the person rather than with the way in which the knowledge of tragedy is obtained. In order properly to consider the psychology of tragedy, we must reverse the subject-object order which we have found obtains in the knowledge process, and consider tragedy as the subject of the psychological effect and the person as the object upon whom that effect is exercised. Immediately it becomes obvious that there are more subjects than objects. Tragedy is tragedy whether it is observed or not; tragedy is not exclusively human, but there is, of course, human tragedy.

That tragedy does exercise a psychological effect has been known for some time. Plato observed that people enjoy their weeping[2] and Aristotle said that the tragic pleasure is that of pity and fear,[3] a statement which Plato had made more specifically in the *Laws* but which Aristotle elaborated into his famous doctrine of the effect of tragedy as one of purgation through pity and terror. Plato did not say enough; Aristotle went too far. The Aristotelian explanation was perhaps occasioned by the feeling of exhaustion combined with satisfaction that accompanies the enjoyment of a good tragedy. This, however, is the after-effect, not the effect. The effect of tragedy is rather what Edmund Burke declared it to be: a matter of sympathy. The conflict between value and existence, evident in tragic events whether enacted in ordinary life or depicted on the dramatic stage, has its effect upon the human individual in the sympathy which it evokes in him. We may here go further than Burke in declaring that the response of the person to the stimulus of the tragic is one of empathy, the quasi-projection of the self into the contemplated situation. All positive feelings are substantial connectives; and in the feelings prompted by the apprehension of a tragic situation, we know ourselves to have the capabilities and the limitations which make us the brothers of those who are suffering. When a character in a drama, or a person in actual life, is confronted in his aims by the more powerful aims of other elements of his environment (which includes of course other human individuals with their aims), we know that there but for the accidents of circumstance go we; hence symbolically we are defeated in his defeat and we die his death, at least in spirit. We feel for him as we assume he must feel for himself; and we are rent by his failures and consoled only by the knowledge that the values for which he stood cannot perish utterly but always may return. Thus dwelling within the divine part of man is his sense of tragic value, a sense to which his reasonings as well as his feelings guide him.

The after-effect of which Plato and Aristotle speak is the enervation that comes from dealing with the qualitative nature of things. To touch essentials is an exhausting experience; it makes us feel better, but also it makes us weary. The very intensity of the feeling might be expected to do that. With the exhaustion, however, there also flows wisdom. We may be tired out by the intense witnessing of a tragedy; who could help it after enduring even in representative form the trials and the death of the hero and the transfiguration of the values for which he stood? We may be weary, but we have also grown a little more understanding. The vicarious experience, which is sympathy with the tragic, has taught us something; we have learned to be aware that while we, too, must pursue the values in existence, there is for us also a fundamental contradiction in actuality, a conflict of values and existence, and the temporary but otherwise complete triumph of disvalue to which some day our efforts must succumb. Thus tragedy has an educative worth, and those who have not been allowed to experience tragedy by having the tragic happen to them in some measure fall short of being wise; their position is made possible only by a certain understandable blindness.

Those, too, who have not learned to appreciate tragedy as it exists in the arts also lack something; they have not been able to view tragedy objectively and in high concentrations. Their lives are not as rich as they might otherwise be; their experiences will not be intensified as the experience of tragedies might have intensified them. To possess feeling and comprehension for the arts and to exercise these means to live a deeper and a fuller life. For some ethical theorists, the good life is the beautiful life; yet no one can touch beauty without being hurt somewhat, without experiencing the tragic. Such theorists went too far, so far as strict ethics is concerned, yet surely there is something valid in what they have maintained.

Tragedy is related to practical ethics in that it teaches us by example to seek the good. The assumptions of tragedy involve the postulate that nothing evil has any possible future, whatever its successes in the present of actual existence may be. The good, on the other hand, represented by the contemplation of events as they ought to be through viewing the actual or symbolic enactment of things as they are, has a future however remote and a being however tenuous. Knowing this about the good, who could resist the desire to pursue it? In this wise, the psychological and the educative aspects of tragedy are closely linked with the ethical. The values of which we spoke in our definition and explanation of the nature of tragedy are none other than those of the good and the beautiful, together with the rational value of the true. What applies to both the good and the beautiful applies to the good.

As for the beautiful, we must remember that tragedy is an aesthetic topic; and we shall expect that the tragic has more peculiar relevance to the beautiful than it has to the other values. Such indeed is the case. We have noted that tragedy exists in actual life as well as in art; yet tragedy-as-art is an intensification of tragedy-as-life, and so we shall take our aesthetic considerations of tragedy from the field of the arts. The beautiful involves the harmony of parts in the whole: when anything has this property of perfect relatedness, it is said to be beautiful. We have, in a way, already referred to the specific aesthetic aspects of tragedy in the definition given at the outset of this study. What is perfect is more acceptable; and the *value* of the perfect relation of parts to whole is that of the beautiful.

In a perfect tragedy, everything falls into place. The circumstances that lead the protagonist to do what he does; the logical deductions in action with which as a result he gets himself involved; the forces of antagonism, or perhaps of an antagonist, that thwart him, as, in accordance with the dictates of the shortcomings of actuality we should expect that something or somebody would do; his struggles which are so unavailing, and his final disaster or death which was so obviously inevitable; these are the parts of which a tragic whole is made. Other examples could be adduced, but in the end the effect is the same, and we almost shrink as the impact of the sheer beauty of the logic of tragic events makes itself evident in all its power and in all its glory. What happens is not always so beautiful, though it may be; but out of the pieces of what happens, the dramatic artist forges a portrayal of what ought to happen. The perfect intentions and actions of the tragic protagonist who fights for the good, for some specific justice or success, the efforts of the hero who fights no less well because he knows that the cause for which he fights (whatever it may be) is foredoomed to eventual failure, are rarely justified in the short run and rarely betrayed in the long run, being more concerned with value

than with victory; and the spectacle of such logic in the smooth functioning of its parts is very beautiful indeed.

That tragedy is only an aspect of artistic value is, of course, obvious:
besides tragedy there is comedy, which has also an artistic value. The
meaning of tragedy can be made somewhat more evident, perhaps by
contrasting tragedy with comedy. In the terms in which we have defined
tragedy, comedy is that aspect of artistic value which is concerned with
the qualitative presentation of the shortcomings of actuality. Both
comedy and tragedy are expressed qualitatively; but where tragedy is
concerned with content, with values *qua* values, comedy is concerned
with the limitations on those values. Comedy proposes that what is funny
is a thing not being what it ought to be, and emphasizes the ludicrousness
of the shortcomings of things in actuality. Comedy is indirect, tragedy is
direct. Seen in psychological terms, comedy is the more intellectual of the
two, and tragedy the more emotional; comedy is detached and contemplative, and does not require that we put ourselves in the position of
those in the comic situation. Where there is laughter, there is apt to be
little sympathy except in the grand sense. But where there is tragedy,
there is participation rather than contemplation. Tragedy asks us not to
contemplate but to take part, at least in projected empathy with the
tragedy of the situation. Comedy views the present with regret and condemns it at least in symbol for not being better than it is. Tragedy views
the present as the helpless child of the past, with certain virtues of its own,
which are virtues irrespective of what they have come from or what they
lead to; but doomed nevertheless. Comedy thus points to reform, in
showing what the conditions of actuality are that stand in need of improvement; it calls for action, for planning, for effort. Tragedy, on the
other hand, points to acceptance, in showing what there is about actuality
which though limited is valuable; it calls for faith, for belief and for hope.
Tragedy is the deeper, comedy the more critical and therefore the more
penetrating and keener. But despite the uses of comedy, it is tragedy that
we must lean on at the last, for the simple reason that after our improvement is accomplished and our amendments executed, there is a residue
of the unfulfilled, a remainder of what could be but is not, a failure and
an end and a defeat, constantly reminding us how the things for which
we fight must perish for a little while, and how we can only hope that they
will come again because we know that if certain things are good they
must be good regardless of whether they exist or not. Comedy and
tragedy are complementary aspects of existence; the former emphasizing
logic, the latter values; both are required if we are to enjoy and to benefit
by the artistic view of the nature of things.

Tragedy has cosmological and even theological aspects. We have already noted that while tragedy is always tragic, it does not always have to close in absolute disaster and defeat, for there is always a kind of triumph inherent in the fact that the values which are removed from actuality do not go out of being but are always possible, and therefore can never be utterly destroyed. The Greek tragedies, particularly those of Aeschylus, contain the idea of the perfectibility of the actual universe. If God is all good and all powerful, a combination which, in the light of the existence of evil seems inconsistent, then He will in the future improve his style. To quote from Gilbert Murray's translation of *The Suppliants,*

> *"Oh, may the desire of God be indeed of God!"*

The perfectibility of the universe, a property more likely to exhibit itself in the remote future, but indicating a perfection toward which we can work in the present, has been restated for us, this time in terms of the logic of probability, by an American philosopher, Charles S. Peirce, in his notion of the unlimited community. Chance, said Peirce, begets logic, and the likelihood of the laws of nature asserting themselves in human events is very high. Hope in the future rests on statistics which can be mathematically demonstrated. Tragedy, unlike comedy, is positive, and its positive character is more than justified. For the tragic, which is content to affirm and embrace the limited values of actuality in the sure faith and knowledge that they *are* values, is willing to face death and dissolution gladly and even gloriously, though the circumstances in which they occur be small and ignominious indeed, because it is only the values which can triumph ultimately; and we shall have a share in their triumph posthumously as evil slowly but surely is abated, as contradictions are resolved and the ugly transformed. The greatest art is tragic art, and the greatest art is that which transcends art itself.

The common goal of the values and of their analysis into truth is one which can be approached through many avenues. In the theater, for instance, we may think of the work of Chekhov or of John Webster, as that of the greatest artists. But the plays of Aeschylus and Shakespeare can hardly be bound down within the confines of art. For these men, the art of the theater was a means only and not an end. Art so universal is also cosmological and even theological. In the hands of Aeschylus, Prometheus is translated from his position as a culture-god in the Greek Pantheon to that of the God of Reason. Zeus was, as Aeschylus saw, the first rational god. Similarly, Shakespeare took what would in rational terms be considered merely a gentle melancholy, a sort of sweetly disillusioned viewpoint, and showed it to be peculiar to the contemplative human being in his actual life in so far as that life is forced to be one of action.

Shakespeare demonstrated that man with all his limitations is yet a forthright portion of the cosmical universe, a segment of undeniable being, existentially expressed. It is this fact which lies at the heart of tragedy.

We are now in a better position to understand the statement made at the outset of this study. There is no distinction between the meaning of tragedy as it occurs in ordinary life and in art except one of greater intensification in the case of the latter. Art deliberately points up the values which in ordinary life exist in somewhat more diffused form. The cosmological meaning of art is the meaning which includes both the lesser meanings which tragedy has in art and in ordinary life. The ultimate beauty of the universe becomes dramatically exemplified by the acceptance of the disvalues of actuality as themselves somehow good; and this is the meaning of tragedy. This definition of tragedy might be essentially retained as a true proposition concerning certain aspects of the nature of all things.

VIII

ART CRITICISM

CONCRETENESS IN PAINTING

The argument of the following pages endeavors to suggest what might be the next development in painting after abstract art. Recently, nonobjective art has replaced representative art. In the latter, the object was present, whereas in the former it is absent. But traditional representative art did not fully represent; the object was held to be the same as its appearance, unity was sacrificed to obtain richness, and space was sacrificed to objects in space. The nonobjectivists discovered unity and the properties of space, but they overlooked the new knowledge of the object which the physical sciences might have placed at their disposal. In the next development in art, full concreteness may replace the extreme of abstractness of the nonobjective school. It will have to incorporate the resources of the old masters and the lessons learned by the nonobjectivists, in a new approach to the object divested of its mere appearance and laid open by the new knowledge which the physical sciences are in a position to contribute. Full concreteness has never been represented, and art for the first time is in possession of the equipment with which to approach this goal.

It happened first, probably, when Cézanne tried to endow the work of the impressionists with the technique and the profundity of the old masters. After that, the immediate future was decided; and the direction toward increasing abstraction established. Cézanne wished to add to the colors of the impressionists the strength of the traditional painters, and he wished to free the forms somewhat from their academic confinement. This called for a certain measure of abstraction. The work of such men as Feininger, Gris and Léger calls for a still further measure. Cubism was another step in the same direction, and the abstractions of Picasso were still another. The object began to fade; until, finally, it was destined to disappear altogether. From the abstractions, in which the object was represented in only the most dimly suggested sort of way, to the absence of the object altogether, was a very short step. And the nonobjective "school of New York," which liberated the painter from the need to represent the object at all, was the result. Nonobjective art, therefore, is only the logical inheritance of an extended development reaching forward from the impressionists.

What are the characteristics of nonobjective art?

First, unity. The whole canvas can be grasped as an immediate whole and needs no prolonged reading. There is in nonobjective painting an all-at-onceness which both makes itself available to the appreciator and overwhelms him with its effect, as though with implosive force.

Secondly, space. Nonobjective art studies the properties of space as the paintings of previous artists had studied form. The classical painters were intent on solid objects *separated* by space but not *occupying* space. In nonobjective painting there is spatial occupancy. It is space as space, rather than space as adjunctive to objects, which chiefly concerns the nonobjective painter.

The two properties exist, of course, together, and the total effect is that nonobjective art strives to obtain unity by continuity in space and continuity by extensibility. Under the old dispensation, continuity was achieved by unity; under the new, unity is achieved by continuity. That is to say, instead of a continuity composed of infinite divisibility and infinite extension, we have the propagation of properties across space.

There can be no question of the tremendous impact of the large canvases produced by the abstract expressionists and the abstract impressionists alike. A crisis occurred in art for the same reason that crises always occur: the actual consequences of an established set of premises had become exhausted. To go on with the old masters would have meant to continue repeating in academic art the designs which had grown stale from repetition, a thing which they themselves had never allowed to happen. Nonobjective art undertook to supply the new premises. Bare of representative meaning and stripped to the minimum of content allowed by the requirements of the greatest degree of generality attainable through the simplest kind of particularity, nonobjective art succeeds in representing the last and most meaningful of all contentual statements, that of pure universality. In divesting itself of the object, the "school of New York" has divested itself also of what is individual, of what is dated, and of what is specific, and has replaced it with extreme generality, with statements holding only a faint trace of qualification and the least stain of embellishment possible in a formal language. The colored shapes on the nonobjective canvas are the formal symbols of an abstract system of communication and consist in signs invented for the purpose and limited to the reference they convey to themselves. The broad strokes of affirmation of Rothko, the small detailed weavings of insinuation of Pollack, and the rectangular assertions of decision of Mondriaan, are all variations on the semantics of self-reference. It comes to this, that abstract symbolism in art is qualitative self-reference.

Such effects, of course, were not achieved without some finality of revolt; there is a sacrifice of orthodoxy. A deliberate and orderly withdrawal from the sum total of resources available to the painter was demanded and supplied; for instance, the depiction in two dimensions instead of in three, and the abjuration of the use of that knowledge of perspective which had been commonplace since the fifteenth century—the century of Brunelleschi and Uccello. A kind of narrow scholasticism was adopted which sought to achieve depth by means of the renunciation of breadth. The arbitrary confinement to narrow limits meant that the huge suggestiveness of the concrete object was charged with divergence and interference and, hence, had to be excluded. The result was a permanent contribution: nonobjective painting. Freedom from the old academic restrictions, new conceptions of space and of unity, are not to be forgotten.

The value of art is to be found not in its effects but in its achievement. The role played by the appreciation of art is as extraneous as is the psychology of the artist to the object of art. Neither the audience nor the artist can ultimately be taken into consideration, which must center exclusively upon the work of art itself. Thus, to complain about the effects of the abstractive tradition from the impressionists to the nonobjectivists is to introduce a topic essentially irrelevant. It may, however, serve to illuminate something of the inadequacies of the tradition, and for that reason it is introduced.

The effects of art are felt throughout the society, to which the artist is responsible for supplying a certain measure of new insights into the visual world.

This world has hitherto been peopled with the ordinary objects of common sense: the objects available to a population engaged in hunting, fishing, agriculture, manufacture, and trade—in all of which pursuits there was direct contact. But the world of the average man has been radically altered. It has been altered chiefly by the technological applications of theoretical science, and the result is that the average man now lives in a world where he does not come into direct contact with the objects of common sense; he lives in the city and his contacts are mediated by a number of complex instruments which he understands hardly at all: the automobile, the airplane, the television set, the radio, the telephone, the atomic engine. He is treated not by herbs gathered in the garden but by drugs manufactured in chemical industries; he understood herbs, but he does not understand antibiotics. Where his understanding fails to follow the amazing complexities of his technological culture, advertising and the mass media of popular journals undertake to enlighten him.

The result is that the average man lives in a limbo of slogans and formulas, of pat explanations and clichés, all of which have been designed for him by experts especially employed for the purpose: the journalists of popular science, the public opinion consultants, the apologists for contemporary art. He never quite attains to the high abstractions of science and mathematics or philosophy, yet he has been robbed of his ordinary world, of the objects of common sense experience. He lives, therefore, an empty and meaningless life, suspended in spirit between an abstract world which he cannot understand and a concrete world from which he been removed. He needs desperately to have concreteness restored to him, and in this need the painters could help. At the present he is fed by them not with the insights into the world of the common objects among which he continues to live, but with abstractions which lie well beyond his comprehension. What he requires of the artist, and does not receive, is a tremendous new concreteness—a concreteness which uses all of the resources of science and of every other enterprise in order to place man back in his own world with its objects widened and deepened. Nonobjective art, in other words, fails to furnish to the society which produced it exactly the values which that society so desperately lacks: full concreteness.

These contentions contribute to the main argument a serious interest in the next stage of artistic development. Will the immediate future supply what the present misses? In a certain sense, the "school of New York" marks the end of an artistic development rather than the beginning. It is a *reductio ad absurdum*: there is no way for it to go beyond where it has already gone. What further steps could be taken in the direction of abstraction beyond the elimination of the object? The end of that direction is the canvas in two colors and one form, or, more dramatically, the canvas in one color, or the blank canvas. These steps have been taken.

The program of nonobjective art stemmed from the deliberate effort of certain artists to isolate themselves from all the influences of their time, except one. They voluntarily gave up everything that had been learned about painting in the past, and they gave up, too, all the constructive possibilities which lay in the new developments outside of art in their own time. They accepted only the fashionable notion of abstraction as they understood it from the contemporary scientists. The result was a set of serious limitations and displacements along with the advantages.

The unity of the canvas, the all-at-onceness, was gained only at the cost of a certain over-simplification. When the nonobjective artist boasts that all of the values of his canvas can be encompassed in a single glance, he is admitting that there is not very much there. Gone are the multiplicity of levels of meaning, the profundity, the depths that require frequent repetitions of viewing. When a single glance suffices, no second glance is likely. There is the danger that, unwittingly, decoration has perhaps been substituted for art.

If the unity turns out to be an insufficient gain, much the same can be said of the new knowledge of space. The traditional painters had studied the space *between* objects, and the nonobjective painters studied the space *without* objects; but what about the space *within* objects? For objects, too, occupy space, and they do so in a way which distorts space and is peculiar to themselves. The space without objects derives from the space between objects, which is empty, and not from the space within objects, which is full. Thus, there are properties of space which result from spatial occupancy unknown to the nonobjective artist, who therefore does not study all of the properties of space but only those of unoccupied space.

Thus we see that despite the influence of depth psychology on some of the abstractionists, nonobjective art is not subjective. The subject dreams in pictorial images, including the images of geometry; and nothing appears to the subject that was not first in the world of appearances. Those who suppose that abstractions are subjective have not reckoned with the resistance of such abstractions to all efforts to make them other than they are. Nonobjective art has freed itself of objects, of representation, only to find that it has thereby accepted the limitations imposed on it by the nature of abstractions. These have their own set of conditions which must be met or deliberately avoided: symmetry, repetition, a certain simplicity which represents itself as complexity, and a requirement of variety that conceals the intricacy of design. And then, too, of course, there is in abstraction an object, one which is no less so for being a queer sort, and it is a segment of the pure quality of substance itself—substance defined as the irrational ground of individual reaction—and hence easily imposed upon by every sort of representation.

If art is the qualitative side of consistency, then abstract art might be described as the representation of the pure quality of consistency. The nonobjective design wishes to take its place, so to speak, as itself an object in the midst of the world of objects, thus adding to the number of discrete individuals; and the nonobjective painting is the effort to help it toward achieving this end. But this object, which is an approach to absolute chaos, is represented in the abstraction by a turning back to more primitive and less sophisticated conditions, to the formlessness of pure universal form which does not wish to commit itself to the form of any particular. From the ambition to depict only the objects of ordinary experience art has, as it were, freed itself and, in dedicating itself to the specific, has also become involved in more advanced types of symbolism in which the universal uses the particular by shaping it to its own ends.

The influences at work on the artist are not only those of art. The artist is to some extent a product of the art of the past and of the fashions of his artistic contemporaries. But other influences are also at work—influences coming to him from other disciplines in the society in which he lives and works. There is little question, for instance, that the most powerful institution in contemporary western civilization is science. Traditionally, the painter has endeavored to acquire any and all of the knowledge of his day that he thought might help in his painting. The artists of the renaissance were interested in science for what it might contribute to the solution of their artistic problems. Like Leonardo, they studied anatomy for its value to the painting of human posture and movement. They were not in revolt against science and in fear of it as a threat to art but, instead, relied upon it as an aid.

Yet, the nonobjective artist prides himself upon his ignorance of science and, if he thinks about it at all, it is only to hate and fear it, without encompassing the possibility that it might be turned into a powerful ally. If we look at nonobjective art not historically in terms of the painting that went before but in terms of the leading values of the culture in which it has developed, we note that it has been heavily influenced by physics and chemistry. Or, rather, the artist not familar with physics and chemistry has, nevertheless, been heavily under their influence.

The art of painting, like all other originative and productive enterprises involving intuitions, is not entirely a conscious process, and the effects of the physical sciences on the artists were not wholly conscious and deliberate; at the same time they can hardly fail to have been strong. The physical sciences are abstract; that is to say, they have started with the world of ordinary experience but have soon departed from it into a world in which the objects and events lie at deep analytical levels. The representation of abstractions in art has been in the same direction as the mathematical abstractions of the world of physics: away from concrete objects as these have been available to ordinary common sense. Thus, nonobjective art is not non-representative art; it is, rather, art in which particular sets of abstractions have been represented. In short, nonobjective painting is not nonobjective at all: it simply has exchanged the familiar objects of common sense for the unfamiliar objects of the world of abstractions, as seen, for instance, through the electron microscope and the reflecting telescope.

Science knows what it is about, but the effects of science on art have to a certain degree been disastrous. The results are somewhat empty and poverty-stricken, being insufficiently filled with the richness of values. The effort to escape from nature into a world of abstractions neglects the nature of abstractions: the fact that they were *abstracted*. It is not possible, in other words, *not* to be a form in nature. The uniform effort to avoid form is itself a certain kind of form, because it is the result of a certain principle of uniformity. Pollack's paintings endeavor to attain to a kind of qualitative chaos, a state of perfect disorder. They could as well have represented a photomicrograph of cat cortex, or the paths of the molecules in a heated gas enclosed within a rectangular vessel. With a little patient searching among photographic plates of distant galaxies, one might find that the paintings of de Kooning and of Tobey are representational after all. The chaos of chance is as much a design as is any deliberate formal order; and to adopt a uniform principle of procedure, such as the elimination of the known visible object, is to achieve a uniform result which has its counterpart in some unknown but not invisible object.

Nonobjective painting simply rejects the forms encountered in ordinary experience in favor of those to be found in the kind of extraordinary experience that occurs in the scientific laboratory. It is a matter of complete indifference that neither we nor the artists have at our disposal the scientific objects corresponding to their representation in nonobjective art; for even in the case of the traditional old masters we rarely have a chance to compare the painting with the original object; we only recognize in the painting that there was an original object, on the principle that the painting was a representation of sorts. Philip IV of Spain is no longer around to allow us to compare his appearance with the painting of him by Velasquez. Since the heads of states of today neither dress nor groom in that fashion, we have only our faith in representation to tell us that

Philip IV looked anything even remotely like that. Similarly, we do not recognize the object in nonobjective painting, because we accept the principle that the painting is not a representation of sorts.

Yet, perhaps this principle must be disallowed. How could one demonstrate that for a given painting there was no such thing as a corresponding object anywhere in the universe? What we lack is not the object but the representational *intention* of the painter. A nonobjective painting is a canvas painted by an artist who proceeded on the assumption that there was no representation because he himself was not deliberately representing an object. But since when do results match intentions? And if they do, then how is anyone to know? The work of art is to be distinguished sharply from the psychology of art, even though it is clear that, if there were no artist, there would be no art. We cannot sell a copy of the artist with every painting that he composes, and if we could, it might not be of very much help, because it is not settled that the artist himself knows and can explain exactly what it was that he sought to accomplish in a particular painting.

Despite the often confused aims of the nonobjective artists and the unhealthy effects of sudden critical and commercial success, nonobjective art has registered a powerful effect. We have only to appreciate it when it is at its best and, ignoring the dreadful work of the camp followers, wonder what is to happen next. No one with any intelligence would predict what will happen; but it may be possible to perceive something of what ought to happen. There is a sense in which whatever happens is what ought to have happened under the circumstances, else it would never have been able to happen. However, no harm is done by inspecting some of the elements that might contribute to the next step in painting.

It seems to be the time, then, to move in the direction of the representation of full concreteness.

Once more, the object must become the center of visual interest, only this time with two added features which, were it not for the intervention of nonobjective art, would never have been available; for full concreteness now means (1) that the space within objects is to be explored and not merely the space between objects, and also (2) that a new richness of objects is possible.

1. Thanks to the study of space, the painters have learned a lot about how to depict it. Space is no longer adequately represented by the space between objects, for the nonobjectivists have not been concerned with that; they have been concerned with the properties of space itself— how it could be stretched, for instance. In the large canvases of the

"school of New York," space is stretched to the uttermost and lies upon the canvas in an agony of revealment. Objects having this space within them as well as around them are now available. New geometries have brought new properties of space to light; but they have not yet been used by the artist. Then, too, sculptors like Lipschitz and Henry Moore have studied the interior of forms in a way which the painters could well adapt to their own medium, for they have, even more than the sculptors, techniques capable of disclosing the interiors of the forms of solid bodies.

2. The nonobjectivists have relied a lot upon the spatial properties of different colors, that some advance while others recede. Scientific studies, observations taken from chemistry and biology, could well suggest new dimensions in the interior of bodies, and a new richness of representation would result. The traditional painter had to be content to work with appearances and never sought to probe beneath them except in terms of such suggestions as he could discover on the surface. There were no other means at his disposal. Today the situation has altered considerably thanks to the researches of the physical sciences. New organs in the human organism, new conceptions of organic cells, new structures at the molecular level, and enormous new constituents and forces at the atomic and nuclear levels, have demonstrated that the material object of whatever degree of organization is both porous and extremely complex. The porosity opens up the object to the view of the painter, and the complexity shows him the many dimensions now available for representation. Material objects as we know them are everywhere dense in a way that was not suspected before and therefore not taken into account by the great painters. It is possible to combine the old object with the new knowledge of space, to use color to depict intensity, to hollow out the object and to show its interior, its profusion.

In short, the abstract painters who were diverted by the scientists could now move in another direction in order to show the qualitative infinity of the concrete object rather than its abstract character. Science deals with abstractions, and the abstractive character of solid objects is a poor subject for the artist. But the qualitative infinity of nature is not a poor subject; to show it is his very aim and goal, and the end of all his efforts. The richness and diversity of the properties of solid objects have hardly been explored. When the painter was confined to the objects of common sense, he could still perform wonders; but what greater wonders have been opened up for him now that we know something of the complexity of the object and its many redoubtable facets!

If, as we have noted, the sculptors are pointing the way, then, in another sense, the architects, too, are somewhat ahead of the procession. The paintings of the current period resemble nothing so much as the architecture of the last period. Modern architecture, however, is in the process of getting away from its severe and unadorned surfaces, its un-embellished planes and angles. Taking a suggestion from Moorish art, which was forbidden representation but which still found abundance of design in elaborate geometrical patterns, recent architecture has revived the grille and has embarked upon a new effort to intensify a surface by subdividing it, to procure continuity in this way rather than by extending it. Paint is intended to be brushed on canvases, and canvases are made to receive it. Every corner of a canvas ought to be hard at work.

The painters have now at their disposal a new approach to the representation of full concreteness. The dialectic of artistic progress moves from the representation provided by the art of the old masters, through the opposition embodied in nonobjective art, and on to the representation of full concreteness. Just as abstract art depends upon the academic art that went before, so the art of full concreteness must depend upon abstract art and revolt against it much as it had itself revolted earlier. The sterile nature of academic art compelled the search for a method of restoring that ancient power it had so degraded, and the abstractionists found that method. And then abstract art, in its turn, but in a much shorter time because it is a much smaller movement, ran afoul of its own shortcomings and so brought about the need for a substitute which would utilize the discoveries of both its predecessors, yet go beyond them. And so in the same way that abstract art overcame and superseded academic art, the art of full concreteness should replace abstract art, and for similar reasons; for abstract art, too, has become academic and sterile in its turn. It is only necessary to look at the paintings done in the provincial art schools, and in the art departments of regional universities, to become convinced of the truth of this statement. It is time in the course of the development of American paintings for full concreteness, and the fully concrete work of art should combine the individuality of representation with the universality of abstraction in a unity made possible through the exploration of spatial occupancy.

By "full concreteness" is meant not the banality of representation of the old masters limited to appearances, nor the vacuous actuality represented by the abstractions of the nonobjectivists, but, rather, an art that would take advantage of all the techniques and skills of the old masters and the new lessons in unity and in spatial properties of the non-objectivists. It would be an art that would take advantage, too, of the new knowledge put at everyone's disposal by the physical sciences of the abundance and richness of properties of material objects not hitherto known. Thus, the representation of the objects of our ordinary world would not be limited to the ordinary; or, put in another way, the objects of our ordinary world would be enriched with all of the properties they possess and which the artist alone can make it possible for us to appreciate. The qualities of the scientific abstractions do not give rise to abstract art—they have indeed never been treated in art—but they could give rise to an art so powerful that mankind would be gifted with a new insight into the unimaginable depths of the material world and a new abundance of life; and all this made possible by the greatness of the artist.

IX

PSYCHOLOGY

SECURITY: THE SKIN AND ENDURING OBJECTS

If it is true that every tissue need is associated with a particular organ, then I wish to examine now the thesis that the skin is the organ of security and the source of the need to (continue to) be. I propose to study first the role played by the skin as the organ of the need to be, then the religious need as the need for ultimate security, and finally the relation between the skin and the religious need. To do this I shall have to show how cutaneous innervation leads to religion, and how religion relies upon cutaneous innervation.

THE SKIN AS A BOUNDARY LAYER

The outer layer of the organism which separates the individual from the external world is the skin. It is, however, not precisely defined; for external material objects impinging upon the skin vary enormously, while the skin itself is not permanent so far as its constituents are concerned. The epidermis replaces itself on the average about once a month. This renewal of structure makes possible a continuity of function which has never been adequately explored.

In the dermis and epidermis and around hair follicles are free nerve endings, exteroceptive receptors sensitive to warmth, cold, pressure, and pain. Coordinated stimulations give both the topography of the body and orientations toward external material objects, probably by means of mechanoreceptors, receptors sensitive to mechanical deformation reporting light touch.

Various elements belonging to the external world are brought to the surface of the organism. This is the somatic frontier, past which such elements could have a decisive effect. It is there that the crucial alternatives exist: some external elements are beneficial, others harmful. The organism responds to its own evaluation of the elements as belonging to one of the two categories by means of approach and avoidance behavior. Hence the approach of curiosity or escape and defense reflexes and the avoidance of pain are all actions taken after evaluating skin responses.

The generic drive of aggression involves "risking one's skin," but the body's defenses can be considered entirely in terms of the sense of security coming from skin stimulations, expected and unexpected.

Expected skin stimulations report security, as for instance the contact experienced in the soles of the feet when walking, or in the contact of buttocks with chair seat. Balance is not entirely assigned to the inner ear but is aided by touch on symmetrical sides of the body.

Unexpected skin stimulations report insecurity. Insufficient importance has been attached to the fact that the skin entirely covers the body. The integrity of the organism is somehow guaranteed by the skin, and thigmotaxic responses can be interpreted as alarm responses.

There are known to be no more than four varieties of cutaneous sensations: pain, touch, cool and warm. These are the skin senses, and we shall be concerned here with all four, but in different ways. It will be necessary to treat pain by itself and then the others in a group. The reception of pain occurs in the free nerve fibers. The pain receptors are part of the fine fibers of the superficial cutaneous plexus. By varying the rate of electrical stimulation, pain reception can be broken down into contact, itch, prick, bright pain, and ache. But these require other stimuli and are not elicited alone. Specificity is a product of the entire sensory mechanism, central as well as peripheral. The pain receptors can be activated by mechanical, chemical and thermal stimuli.[8]

An unvarying stimulus almost never causes more than a single impulse in the nerve, the adaptation being exceedingly rapid; but in the nerves of cutaneous and muscular tissue a volley of impulses can be produced. Adaptation, however, occurs more rapidly in tactile than in muscle receptors. Tactile receptors require a stimulus of mechanical deformation.

In man the skin as a sensory organ plays a special role. More sensory nerves pass through the spinal cord in man than in other mammals. Then, too, the loss of hair in man enables the skin to take on a special significance, since it must serve as the warning of touch, in a way not available to chimpanzees and gorillas, for instance. The tightly stretched skin makes it an excellent recorder of muscular and limb movements.[10] Thus the outside of the naked body is closely linked to the greatest of human aspirations, as will be shown.

Although many of the broad areas of the cortex function together in adjusting the organism to its environment, it is the parietal lobe which is chiefly involved with the cutaneous receptors. Thus the exteroceptors serve as alarm devices for the central nervous system, alterting the organism to threats of danger. What is less well known, however, is that the same system is employed to send messages of opportunities of safety. In neurophysiology a great deal more work has been done on pain than on pleasure.[3] The same type of signal is always employed, but sometimes with a different meaning and at a higher level of signification. Pain is a signal of danger, but touch, cool and warm may be pleasurable or reassuring.

It is perhaps significant in this connection that different messages are not transmitted over the same pathways. Each type of sensation employs a specific type of end organ, even though the nerve impulses themselves are not specific and the specificity relies on the entire sensory mechanism, central as well as peripheral. Touch, cool and warm are sufficient sensations to convey the impression of security through contact. It is with signals of safety presented through contact that we will be chiefly concerned here.

The alerted guardian of the need to be is the pattern of cutaneous innervation. It is from nerve endings in the epidermis and dermis that signals of attraction or repulsion are sent, and approach or avoidance behavior initiated. For security responses the skin is cued by touch. But the skin can also be affected by what happens centrally. Consider for example how ghost stories "make the skin creep" and "give goose pimples." Fear may cause the individual to break out in perspiration. In humans the skin fits more tightly and is more firmly connected to the tissues beneath and so is more integrated with the rest of the body than is the case with many other animals, such as the rabbit.[5] As a result skin injuries are more serious and healing less effective. Also, skin grafts between individuals are not interchangeable, and so it is fair to say that the skin is the guardian of the uniqueness of the individual. There are other carriers of uniqueness, such as, and chiefly, the genotype, but the skin is the frontier defense of uniqueness. What is brought into contact with the skin, then, has a special meaning for the individual. It must be interpreted as contributing to security or as a threat to integrity; to be repeated as an experience in the former case, or to be avoided at all costs in the latter.

The skin is not only the physiological frontier but also the psychological. Thorpe lists "care of the body surface" as one of six "positively identifiable instincts."[13] The care of the body surface, "skin comfort," is insurance of somatic well-being so far as external threats are concerned. Scratching, preening and grooming are recurrent forms of behavior and also available as displacement behavior even in the human individual. The restoration of cleanliness, as for instance by bathing and the use of clean clothing, is an effort to protect the psychological frontier and to insure the continuance of being through the symbolic expression of the absence of threats to security. As birth and death are represented as a journey from earth and to earth again, so cleanliness, as the absence of dirt, or earth, is a sign of life. So far as death is a threat, then, keeping clean is a form of avoidance behavior.

I have sought to establish the role played by the skin as the organ of security. But the skin does not function merely in connection with the need to be. It has a role to play in the other drives.

Water and food cross the skin frontier with willing assistance. These are approved by the skin in the process when they are touched or tasted. The mouth is a continuance of skin surface, and the tongue is an organ of touch. Then, too, everyone knows that it is more fun to eat food with one's fingers than with implements, such as knife and fork or chopsticks. At picnics and other "nature" celebrations, when the individual for refreshment drops down with his fellows to the fundamental ground of non-human nature, it is usual to eat without tools, i.e., through contact with the skin of the fingers. Drinking from running brooks is more fun than drinking from cups. But contact with water is not confined to the mouth; bathing is a sensual pleasure.

In the case of sex, most forms of the preparatory response of titillation involve the touching of skin, at sensitive points especially but also everywhere. The contact with the skin of prospective sexual partners acts as a very effective stimulant. Skin changes and skin odors are reinforcers in this kind of behavior.

The cortex is the organ of inquiry, but the method of inquiry most in favor currently is that of empiricism, according to which knowledge is a product of sense experience, and in such experience the skin senses play important if not crucial roles. From one point of view, then, empiricism makes the need to know depend for reliable knowledge upon the criterion of contact.

For the need to do, the part played by the skin is no less considerable. Activity involves muscular exertion, and the skin being stretched as tightly as it is furnishes an effective index to such activity. Activity, like the other needs, has a goal object, in this case the alteration of a material object. Contact with that object is established through the skin.

Since the relation between the drive for being and the skin is the chief topic of this study, it will require special consideration.

If I have now succeeded in establishing the role of the skin as an organ of security in the drive for the continuance of being, it will be necessary to look at the same relationship from another point of view, that of religion.

RELIGION AS A CUTANEOUS INTEREST

The activation of a need is the result of the presence of a need-reducing object. After a sufficient degree of arousal, the need becomes a drive. Not all responses are overt, of course. There are in the human organism enormous covert response resources. There is at least a potential response for every actual stimulus. The range of stimuli is a function of the depth of awareness.

The limits of the individual are defined by the outer layer of skin, the epidermis. Those who have studied man, from whatever point of view, have sooner or later concerned themselves with boundary conditions. From the religious as well as from the scientific interest the problem appears to be the same, namely, how to account for the individual's relations with what lies beyond him. Let us consider for instance the viewpoints of two widely separated authorities, a mediaeval Christian and a modern biologist. For Nemesius of Emesa, "man's being is on the boundary between the intelligible order and the phenomenal order";[12] while for Portmann, the limits of the biological indicate that he who lives on the borderline has been on the other side, a point at which the biological impinges upon the unknown.[10]

All the external relations of the individual are material. The relations between two subjects, two consciousnesses, is never immediate but always mediated, and the mediating agent is a material object, something connected with both, such as a touch or a sound-wave. For the individual, who is a subject, lives not only nor chiefly in a world of subjects but also in a world of material objects by which he and his fellows are vastly outnumbered. His current concern is with available objects of both kinds:

nearby objects, such as other human individuals, and the material objects within his reach upon which he is dependent for his immediate survival. But his more extended interest is for ultimate survival, and for this his concern is with the large-scale and far-away material objects of an unavailable environment. The nearby objects are represented by themselves: he can touch them and in this way determine whether they act as reinforcement or threat. But the far-away objects are too remote for touch of pain or pleasure. They could bring reassurance because of their permanence and reliability: the stars for instance always shine, but he cannot close with them; and he constructs nearby things which are the symbols of far-away objects.

We may define the "short-range self" as that aspect of the self which is concerned with immediate survival, and the "long-range self" as that aspect which is concerned with ultimate survival. The skin serves the former directly and the latter indirectly. Pain is an alarm signal for the short-range self; but contact with symbols is necessary for reassurance in the case of the long-range self. For the short-range self pain alone suffices, and is negative; but for the long-range self there is an active seeking of reassurance through selective contact: the long-range self involves complicated signalling systems: contagious magic, sacraments, ritual contact with symbolic objects. In addition to touch, cool and warm, the short-range self is reassured through the *absence* of contact. A skin *not* in contact is a skin *in*tact and therefore an indicator of the absence of threat to the whole organism.

The primary needs are those of the short-range self, the secondary needs are those of the long-range self. The aim of the primary needs, then, is immediate survival, but the aim of the secondary needs is ultimate survival. The former can be reduced through the attainment of short-range goals and the assimilation of objects in the immediate environment, but the latter require long-range goals and the assimilation of objects in a remote environment. It is possible to drink, eat and copulate only with objects in the neighborhood, but knowledge of galaxies so far away in the universe as to be measurable only in light years is common in astronomy, while theology envisages gods beyond the universe. Aristotle's God is so remote as to be unconcerned with human affairs but the God of the Judeo-Christian religions is very much concerned. Activity can reach out either by movement, as in travel through outer space, or by symbolic representation, as in the nearby signs of far-away objects, such as religious talismans and icons, so that much more of being is encompassed than otherwise.

Largeness in space usually means remoteness in time. The individual who from birth onward is dizzily engaged in rushing toward extinction, looks forward to as well as back upon "those far-off divine events" in which he aspires to participate. In the setting of religious goals evolution can hardly be ignored, since man faces in many directions. He is himself confined to one small strip of existence. He lives for a brief-enough period within the boundaries defined for him by his skin, on a portion of the surface of a single planet; but as his perceptions and thoughts extend outward from him so he aspires after them and wishes himself more widely connected in space and time.

So much for extension; but there is an intensive direction as well. The religion I have been describing is characteristic of the West; in the East the oriental religions have in common that intensive cultivation of the short-range self via the ego is the best method of getting in touch with eternal beings and universal powers. The mysticism of the "inward way" has its exceptions in the East and its minority advocates in the West; as for instance in the East with early Buddhism and before, the Lökayatikas and the Cärväkas, and in the West with Hebrew[4] and Christian mystics.[14]

Salvation through concentration on the self is a negative approach to the concept of the skin, which has been here proposed as a boundary for the spiritual path. It avoids contact by retreat within consciousness itself and away from the exteroceptors, on the assumption that the being of the self itself, the bare consciousness, is the ultimate interoceptor. The ecstatic state of the mystic is one in which knowledge is received.[1] The spirit with its vantage point in the ego is the special organ of knowledge in this tradition. Correspondingly, the preparatory stage is one of detachment, but the mystic is nevertheless able to distinguish between friendly and hostile elements among those which lie beyond himself. In the end, the mystic way is a method by which the individual surpasses himself quite literally: by passing out of himself for ease of access to the remote goal-object—around the boundary of cutaneous innervation rather than through it. In this way the boundary problem is still recognized but differently regarded.

THE SKIN AS A RELIGIOUS INTEREST

These two factors: cutaneous innervation and the religious impulse, have been known for a long time, but they have not often been connected. The evidence involves a particular kind of reading of how the human organism behaves and what such behavior means.

The distinctions recognized here are not those with which in prehistoric times the associations started. For while now the religious effort is invoked in the service of ultimate survival and the secondary needs, in the beginning of man's cultural career religious efforts were called out in aid of the immediate survival and the primary needs. The forces of magic were used to insure the fertility of crops and women. Both kinds of survival, being useful, were more closely related than is ordinarily supposed. The practice of early religion was the practice of magic, and served immediate survival. The religion of the primary needs connected with magic is an immanent religion. Only later did ultimate survival enter the picture and religion become transcendental.

It is indeed a very short distance from the emblems and implements of sympathetic magic, with its imitative and contagious varieties, to the relics and symbols of the transcendental "world" religions. Let us consider magic first and then religion in order to sharpen the comparison.

Magic, according to Frazer[2] is either imitative or contagious. In imitative magic, things which resemble each other in one respect will resemble each other in all respects and will therefore share the same fate. For instance, to make an image of a person then damage it with a sharp stick, is to compel that person to suffer the same injury. But it is the other branch of magic that most vividly illustrates the role of cutaneous innervation in the reduction of the need to continue to be. In contagious magic, things which have been once in contact are always in contact. Thus the control of hair or nails which have been severed from a human body suffice for the control of that body itself.

Now let us look at the material symbols as employed in transcendental "world religions." Here we can see we are dealing with yet another version of sympathetic magic, this time a combined version involving both varieties. For in transcendental religion, things which are brought into contact with the same thing are brought into contact with each other. The symbol *resembles* the object symbolized. By touching the symbol, one comes into *contact* with the object symbolized. The cross represents Jesus, the claret and wafer of the Eucharist His body and blood.

The transcendental "world" religions are not as much concerned with proximate goals and immediate needs as they are with remote goals and ultimate needs; and so the sacred symbols have lost their element of compulsion, having been transformed instead into nearby representations of imponderable and impossibly distant objects which are neither in whole or part characteristically apprehensible by the senses and at the very least are permanently out of reach in every way.

The primary needs: for water, food and sex, are those which call out short-range religion for their reduction. Short-range religion is devoted to fertility of crops and women; it has an immediate practical value. Its

results are produced by for instance totemic ceremonies, involving painting the skin to represent the totem, mimetic dances, and the use of
imitative and sympathetic magic which compel the effects desired. Prayer
in this connection has to do with favors sought, with supplication.

The secondary needs: for knowledge, activity and survival, call out
long-range religion. Long-range religion is devoted to the immortality of
the soul; it has an ultimate preferential value. Its results are invoked by
membership in a church, by ritual observances, by sacrifices and pen-
ances, by abstentions—activities which solicit effects without compelling
them. Prayer in this connection either registers an emotional acceptance
of the material world (adoration) or through similar emotions seeks to
produce certain minor alterations in it (supplication).

Ultimate survival is a matter of long-range religion. The individual's
greatest effort is to find a secure foothold in a shifting world. The short-
range self in time proves inadequate, and ultimate security lies outside
him. He must include the world, allow it to include him, or associate
himself with it as equals. Now, it is far too large for any hope that he
might include it or even be taken into partnership. Therefore he must if
possible allow it to include him as his only chance for ultimate survival.
But the world also is too far-away, too big and too permanent for his
limited spatial range, small size and brief life, and so his choice of a
personal surrender will have to be conducted by surrogate: a nearby
symbol will have to represent for him the large and far-away object: a
sacred relic he might touch or a rite he could perform.

Thus the need for a supernatural religion is a natural phenomenon.
The transcendental religions were designed not to provide an escape from
the short-range self but rather to establish connections guaranteeing
security for the long-range self. If man as an animal would exceed himself, that is only because of his intense desire for life, which is habit-
forming. The more of a grip the individual obtains upon his existence
the more he wishes to perpetuate it, and this need is so pressing that all
of his forces are spent in the effort to obtain its reduction. The unbearable
urge to maintain life is nearly exhausted by the effort at immediate survival but spends itself altogether on ultimate survival in the craving for a
life beyond death. Always there is more unknown than known, and identification with the large, far-away object which at least in some sense may
spell ultimate survival—super-identification—is replete with mystery.
Thus the material objects and habitual procedures—the sacred things and
sacraments—which are to put the individual "in touch" with his remote
goal-object must match occult with occult. It is not for nothing that
"sacrament" was the accepted rendering in Christian Latin of the Greek
word for mystery.

In nearly all religions, contact is established through ritual, either by special cult only or throughout daily life. In the Greek popular religions, the importance of touch in ritual is obvious,[7] and so it was with the ancient Jews, whose observances were very many.[9] Consider for instance the use of unleavened bread and the ritual of the *seder* or ordered meal in the festival of the Passover, or the festival of the Tabernacles in which the Jews eat their meals in a rustic booth and in which a branch and some willow sprigs are moved by hand to indicate the omnipresence of God. These practices and others like them are still current among orthodox Jews. Another good contemporary example is that of the sacraments of Roman Catholicism, with the water of Baptism and the oil of Extreme Unction.

In general, ritual observances with their variety of contacts are procedures intended to invoke either the immediate survival of the short-range self or the ultimate survival of the long-range self—as we have seen, either the fertility of crops and women or the immortality of the soul after death. The same two basic interests run through the "world" religions of civilization as through the cult practices of more primitive cultures: the need to be is either the need to be now (immediate survival) or the need to continue to be in some part forever. Need reductions in both cases consist in the contact of skin and sacred object or skin and object employed in ritual cult practice. Such cutaneous encounters signal that security has been reinforced and that the meaning of immediate or of ultimate survival has been transmitted to the person, so that in this way he can record his belonging. To the extent to which he touches the emblem of God, he makes contact with the Godly. Touching a sacred object or participating in a cult practice furnishes the necessary reassurance that the individual is partaking of its meaning.

The god or gods who can assure such security are far-away and in themselves unattainable. But they can be reached through surrogate objects with which it is possible to come into immediate physical contact upon any stipulated occasion: water, oil, a ring, a cross, bread, wine, or whatever talisman or sacred symbol is designated by the particular ritual for the particular occasion. All religious objects whatever their differences serve the same generic purpose. Contact with them, either by bringing them into connection with the skin of a believer or by bringing the skin of the believer into contact with them, is beneficial. And this holds true whatever the object, whether it be a black stone in Mecca for the Moslems, a wall in Jerusalem for the Jews, or the thaumaturgic arm of St. Francis Xavier for the Christians.[6]

We cannot hope to discover the spiritual nature of man by looking inside him or outside him exclusively. It is the effort of man to aggrandize himself in its special phase as the direction toward ultimate survival, manifest in his religion primarily, which carries for him what is now ordinarily designated as the spiritual. Man's individual hope is that something of his uniqueness can survive materially: he wishes this for the immediate future in order that he may have the time and energy to make further plans. The plans themselves will set forth elaborate preparations for undertaking an attachment to something more permanent in order to share the permanence. Religion is based on the faith that permanence is contagious. Thus while sporadic and intermittent contact with immediate objects interpreted literally enables his skin to perform its organic function of protecting the individual's immediate survival, regularized contact with symbolic objects representing the large, the faraway and the permanent, reassures him and reinforces his feeling of ultimate safety and survival. The spiritual belongs to the frontier of cutaneous innervation, precise and yet so far-reaching, where the individual marches with the world.

REFERENCES

[1] Bennett, Charles A. *A Philosophical Study of Mysticism.* New Haven 1923. Yale University Press.

[2] Frazer, Sir J. G. *The Golden Bough.* 12 vols. London 1926. Macmillan.

[3] Fulton, John F. *Physiology of the Nervous System.* 3rd ed. New York 1951. Oxford University Press.

[4] Heschel, Abraham J. "The mystical element in Judaism," in Finkelstein, Louis (ed) *The Jews: Their History, Culture, and Religion.* New York 1949. 2 vols. Vol. I, Pp. 602-621.

[5] Medawar, P. B. *The Uniqueness of the Individual.* New York 1958. Basic Books.

[6] *New York Times* for Tuesday, May 14, 1963.

[7] Nilsson, Martin P. *The Greek Popular Religion.* New York 1940. Columbia University Press.

[8] Peele, Talmadge L. *The Neuroanatomical Basis for Clinical Neurology.* New York 1954. McGraw-Hill.

[9] Pfeiffer, Robert H. *Introduction to the Old Testament.* New York 1948. Harper.

[10] Portmann, Adolf. "Biology and the phenomenon of the spiritual," in *Spirit and Nature: Papers from the Eranos Yearbooks.* New York 1954. Pantheon. Pp. 342–370.

[11] Radhakrishnan, S. *Indian Philosophy.* London 1948. Allen and Unwin.

[12] Telfer, William (ed.) *Cyril of Jerusalem and Nemesius of Emesa.* Philadelphia 1955. The Westminster Press.

[13] Thorpe, W. H. *Learning and Instinct in Animals.* London 1956. Methuen.

[14] Underhill, Evelyn, *Mysticism.* New York 1955. Noonday Press.

THE PSYCHOLOGY OF THE SCIENTIST

1. THE PREPARATION OF THE SCIENTIST

The practice of the scientific method is in the hands of those who have trained themselves for such work. It is meaningful that neither provocative facts nor significant theories in science occur to those who have become concert violinists. An absorbing interest in a field leads to a preoccupation with it; what marks the professional off from the amateur is more than the payment of money; it is the performance of excellent rather than mediocre work, and the devotion of full time rather than part time to it.

Thus devotion and commitment turn the tables on the psychological explanation and make of it an effect rather than a cause. If we wish to understand the scientific method we must see it as an independent process in all its uniqueness, a method which can be followed, but followed or not remains a method, and not primarily as a psychological process in which it stands on the same footing with all other activities of the human mind. To know a horse and a cow means the same thing as regards the knowing but not as regards the difference of the horse from the cow. As independent, then, the scientific method allows no effects to issue from the psychological knowing as such, and the subject aware of the method follows it and does not lead; in other words, the scientific method uses the subject in order to get itself put together as an object; but is for this reason no less objective than the horse and the cow which do not. The psychology of the practicing scientist is a circuitous route taken by the combination of many concrete objects and many abstract logics from the conglomerate of the world under one set of conditions in which the regularities are hidden to get itself back into the world under another set of conditions in which they are revealed as a new object in which the abstract and the concrete are united.

(a) *The scientist and his method.* The method of science, the natural world which it investigates, and the conclusions at which it arrives have been discussed elsewhere. The description is usually kept impersonal in order to concentrate on its logical and empirical aspects. We are now obliged to add to the picture the person of the investigator, and in particular his psychological processes. What is the behavior of a scientist when he is engaged in the practice of the scientific method? More particularly, what goes on in the mind of the scientist, and what is the subjective end of the making of discoveries?

When an investigator pursues a science, he ostensibly behaves like a scientist. Now the behavior of a scientist, like the behavior of any other individual, has its inner and its outer aspects, that is, what it feels like to him to be doing what he does and what it seems to us that he does. The two aspects do not exactly match; we are not dealing with a mirror image nor, as Hegel said, with a double gallery of pictures. There is at all times a slight divergence, and neither comes up altogether to the other. The inner psychological world is derived with some reservations from the outer, and makes its individual corrections accordingly.

To be a scientist, psychologically speaking, means to turn oneself over to the scientific method in order to be used by it for its own purposes; to devote as much of oneself as one can to such thought, feeling and action as will serve to further the purposes pursued in the exercise of that method; in short, to behave as closely as possible in the ways demanded by it. For the demands are outer demands, they are made of the man, when he becomes a scientist, by the impelling nature of that discipline he means to serve, and do not issue from himself except as the response to a stimulus. Thus in a sense a scientist is the route taken by a segment of nature to get itself resorted and reordered, to get the knowledge of itself separated out and the controls established. He is himself a tool, an instrument, a device necessary to the working of a certain technique. He is a part of the scientific method because he practices it.

However, it is not this outer or behavioral aspect of psychology that we mean to cover in this essay. The behavioral sciences have never succeeded in making the overt description of psychological events adequate to the inner aspect, for all that sciences have held this to be what is called for by correspondence with the physical sciences. And this is true because of the emotional or qualitative coloring of those events; and it is true too despite the promise held out by the analysis of language as evidence of the inner aspects of psychological events. Languages contain more meaning than the individual users had put into them separately or had intended them to carry; and this traffic exists if in no other way than in the form of connotations.

Individual thought, feeling and action, then, are to be the elements employed, and the method the introspective method of the practicing scientists as interpreted by the logical structure of the dialectic of scientific method already established. It is necessary to know what a man has set out to do before we can hope to understand how he has gone about doing it. Thus in the analysis of the psychology of the scientist we rely upon the anterior knowledge that he is in effect following the scientific method.

(b) *The selection of science.* Perhaps we should begin our analysis by asking why a man chooses a science as a career in the first place. Can this question be answered with the information currently at our disposal? All intelligent people begin life with an intense curiosity. Others may possess this instinct, too, but it remains with the most intelligent the longest. The brain as an organ exists for the satisfaction of the need to know, just as the gonads exist for sexual satisfaction and the stomach for hunger. The intelligent are the most curious; they will not be put off as easily as the others; which may mean of course that they are merely the most stubborn. For there are no ultimate answers that are permanently satisfying. Religious questions, such as what is the reason for the world; artistic questions, such as what is the beautiful; philosophical questions, such as what is there; and scientific questions, such as what are the contents of the universe, are equally hard to answer. All must be satisfied with the most proximate and progressive guesses. But why would the questions, the types of problems engendered, and the answers that have been made in one field interest a beginner more than those in another field? Curiosity characterizes equally the religious man, the artist, the philosopher and the scientist; we know why a man becomes some of these, therefore, but not too well why he becomes one rather than another. Why would a man choose science as a career? It could only be because of his interest in the world of nature. Most young people who later become scientists have constructed electrical devices, collected rocks or mollusks, examined trees, trained mice or dogs, or in some other similar way evidenced an interest in things as they are. The pace of such interest is irrelevant to the intensity of its eventual development; some scientists grow up slowly, others with lightning speed. What is important is the dawning comprehension that this is what must be done. A desire to become absorbed in some area of interest could be at its inception almost casual; but then the desire to go deeper into an area in which one was already absorbed is more likely to be self-conscious and deliberate.

(c) *The training of the scientist.* So far as the scientist himself is concerned, his training as a scientist starts from his possession of the native capacities for reasoning, for the having of sense experiences, and for acting. These are sharpened and extended by repetition and channeling; by his experience in laboratories and in the field, with instructors and with texts. His sense experience is extended by means of instruments, his motor precision by means of habit, and his reason by means of mathematics.

The scientist begins his career as one might say all children do: with a state of innocence. It is thus that he enters the classroom and the laboratory. This is the first stage of his training; the second stage consists in innocence lost; that is when the knowledge which has been gained thus far in his science by others is indoctrinated in him. Then there is the third stage—if he is worth his salt—of innocence regained. It is this last stage which for his purposes is the most important. For innocence which is regained is a knowledgeable one, and rests now on his growing comprehension of how very little is known in his field and how very much yet remains to be done. Qualitatively, the third stage has something of the character of the innocence he had as a child, yet held now somewhat differently by him as an adult fully in control of himself, self-consciously and deliberately confronting the facts which lie before him. The facts, and, one might add, the accepted theories and the new hypotheses, too.

Just how the latter is accomplished has been a baffling problem. What is it that equips a man for the discovery of hypotheses? The evidence all lies in the twin directions of philosophy and disparate fact. A training in philosophy means two things; it means becoming habituated to generalization, and it means the acquisition of a readiness to make wide guesses as to the answer to a given problem. Philosophers are facile generalizers, they move easily among abstractions, and, moreover, among abstractions which are more inclusive than those of mathematics and allowed to sweep over a wider domain, for they must include not only the quantitative and the structural, as is the case with mathematics, but also the qualitative. The philosophers dream, so to speak, of abstractions in the solid state. Now, it is not enough to have imagination: it must be a *controlled* imagination, an imagination which can be called out to some extent at least at will, and harnessed to a particular inquiry. Here is where the facts come in. They are never as widely selected as the philosopher might require, but are confined instead to a particular domain which is deep but narrow. It takes imagination to discover provocative facts, but more imagination still to discover their connections and causes. Thus a training in philosophy is for an experimental scientist able to bring about the kind of atmosphere in which hypotheses become easier to discover. He must keep the proper distance between himself and his work, between his passions and his experiments.

Who knows what secret pieces of equipment contribute their part to the success of the productive scientist and make possible his life discovery? He must know certainly how much remains to be explored, and he must have supreme confidence in his own abilities to make a start in it however infinitesimal in extent. He looks backward to his predecessors who have made his contribution possible and on whose work he will build, and forward to successors who will build on his work. Just as the neurotic individual, the man with acute yet unfocused anxiety, is only exaggerating an ordinary characteristic which he has made into a disease by carrying it to abnormal lengths, so the scientist is only the old Adam, as Musil wrote, with the courage and initiative of the hunter, the freedom from scruples and morals of the soldier, and the patient bargaining for advantage and respect for measurement of the merchant, only now transformed from practical vices into intellectual virtues. Many observers have noted that while great geniuses in science advance it greatly, little scientists are able to advance it a little, and the bottle washers in science have their place as much as the supreme theorists.

The discovery of hypotheses requires imagination as much as the observation of nature requires sensitivity. The patience to observe and the quickness to discern a provocative fact in the observed field is matched only by the ability to put such facts together however disparate and to leap to an imaginative hypothesis. At this point the scientist is required to combine his sharpened faculties, and by devising and executing experiments calling on thought extended into mathematics, feeling extended into instruments, and action extended into the turning of one material against another, in the effort to add support or refutation to the hypothesis. Finally, the test of his hypothesis which requires it to find its consistency with the existing theories of his science, calls on his ability to calculate, to move easily among the abstractions of mathematics. Prediction and control are practical tests calling for more action and are often the prerogative of others, yet they too are scientists, applied scientists, and can find their place in the scientific hierarchy.

Thus thought, feeling and action, which were the subjective faculties of the ordinary person, are in the scientific dialectic objectified and formalized together as the capacity for the practice of the scientific method, which is a sequence of actions in which thought and feeling are effectively blended. The training of the scientist must include an objectification as well as a sharpening of all these specialities, calling on the entire man in a way perhaps equalled in the past only by the fine arts. Training in such terms means specialized training as usual, but it means also, in a way which has never been sufficiently comprehended, preparing the social background for the reception and rewarding of such attainments. But here we are at the border of a topic which is more suitable to another essay.

(d) *The attitudes of the scientist.* The characteristic attitude of the research scientist consists in the feeling that he should believe only what there is reason to believe in virtue of his experiences with fact and with logical consistency, and this attitude is the one which provides him with the greatest amount of freedom. We shall break down this attitude into what appears to be its four components. These are *productive scepticism, fallibilism, detachment,* and *humility.*

The name, *productive scepticism,* has been adopted for doubt leading to discovery, in order to distinguish it from mere negative scepticism. Scepticism is not necessarily negative, as those enamored of dogmatisms of various sorts would have us believe. It is the guardian of reason. It stands at the entrance to belief and inspects the credentials of the applicants for admission. The passport is fact and it must bear the visa of logic. Scepticism does not say, "do not believe"; it says merely, "do not believe without reason." Clear and justifiable belief, or faith in reason and fact, has nothing to fear from scepticism.

The men of the seventeenth century were profound sceptics, and it was in the seventeenth century, we must remember, that science took its first big leap forward. They adopted the attitude of refusing credence to whatever lacked evidence, and the result of their determination has astonished the world. Scepticism was of course equally an element of the thought of ancient Greece. We can see it in the Socratic questioning and before that in the fragments of the pre-Socratics: it is this strain of thought that was formulated by the sceptics themselves and carried to its furthest edge by Pyrrho of Elis. There is a close connection between the periods in which rational thought and inquiry is pursued most avidly, and the flourishing of a healthy scepticism.

Productive scepticism has a positive end and this is the fostering of freedom. The kind of inquiry which is furthered by the active imagination is possible only in an atmosphere of freedom, and freedom is guaranteed by philosophical doubt. The freedom to adopt new beliefs is a function of the freedom to doubt all beliefs. Only a discipline which can lead to falsity holds the promise of leading to significant truth. Bernard Shaw said somewhere that religion is always right and science is always wrong, and that is why he preferred science. Freedom allows for discovery, for change, for improvement, for progress, which are of the very essence of scientific activity.

Scepticism has been charged with eclecticism, with the prevention of the completion of systems, and with similar defects. Under the attitude of scepticism, the tolerance of the half-truths of rival positions must be encouraged. There cannot be an equal amount of truth in all theories, especially in contradictory ones, but apart from the latter distinction there is some truth in all theories. What appear to be contradictories often turn out to be merely contraries or opposites, and the conflict of those who seek to impose their truths on us is not necessarily a contradiction of their theories but only of their ambition for their theories.

Then again, how can we judge before we know? The hallmark of ignorance is the haste with which the judgment—perhaps we had better say the prejudgment—is made. To withhold opinion until such a time as the knowledge requisite for rationally arriving at an opinion can be acquired, requires strength and great tolerance, without which, it might be added, there would have been no science.

The second component in the attitude of the scientist is *fallibilism*, so named by Peirce. This consists in the caution that all formulations are subject to error. It is of course the contradictory of theological *in*fallibilism. And it means that short of logical and mathematical tautology there can be no absolutes in science. Everything, not only the hypotheses in science which are frankly tentative but also the laws which are considered established and even the method of discovery itself, cannot be considered to be placed beyond the reach of inquiry, of challenge, of doubt. It means that in science there are no authoritative persons or statements, no one and nothing which can be rendered inviolate to questioning and to reason. Thus it serves to insure that no earlier discoveries in science can block the road to inquiry or stand in the way of later formulations.

Men who make significant and even crucial contributions to science are not necessarily for that reason reliable on all counts. As late as 1904, Wilhelm Ostwald refused to accept the validity of the atomic theory in chemistry, and this was a century after Dalton had established it there. Those whose lives are led in the wake of the discovery of great ideas in science are apt to be convinced that there are no more great ideas to be discovered, and that all that remains to be done is to work out the consequences of what was discovered.

The third component of the scientific attitude is *detachment*. The scientist as a person must keep himself, his preferences and prejudices and temperament, as much removed from his experimental investigations as possible. The ideal is one which is destined never to be attained absolutely, nevertheless it marks a limit toward which the scientist must work. The personal bias or interest of the experimenter in the outcome of his experiments must be eliminated as much as possible, and this can only be done by candidly recognizing them, knowing that they exist and making the proper allowances. Objectivity is the goal, subjectivity the starting-point; and the degree of success achieved will play a role in the final results obtained. The chief aid in reaching the proper detachment is the scientific method itself; for if it is utilized and followed properly, the very logic of its procedure must ensure that the subject does not inject himself too much into the picture. Thus the effort at detachment can consist in concentration on the method. Psychologically speaking, detachment requires a selfless devotion to science, so that it is felt that the scientist exists for science and not science for the scientist. The increase of knowledge must be held as a goal worthy of attainment in itself and not for what practical or personal goods it can accomplish.

The fourth and last component in the attitude of the scientist is *humility*. The human world is an infinitesimal segment of the natural world and one that grew up in it and issued from it. The natural world thus contains all that the human world contains, but is larger, deeper and richer. Thus the efforts of the scientist to probe the natural world are handicapped by the feebleness of his equipment and the vastness of the world within which he stands. Hence the necessity for a scientific attitude of humility. The recognition of the extent of ignorance is the beginning of wisdom. Unlike those who profess to know, he must profess to wish to know; for those who know never need to inquire, and science is above all a method of inquiry, not an established set of facts or even of principles. To seek to know means to discover something and then to try to learn more; and the additional seeking often upsets the original knowledge and reveals it to be the opinion that it was; and so conditions the further achievement of knowledge, which is forever suspect in the same way. And so the reliable part of the knowledge of science is the method of science and not its findings. The method requires that the scientist accept science if at all as a religion then as the religion of the humble role, the seeker after knowledge and not the knower, the man of perpetual inquiry.

(e) *The motivation of the scientist.* We have noted that each of the basic tissue needs of the individual can be traced to an organ: hunger to the stomach, sex to the gonads, and curiosity to the brain. The need to know is no less strong than the need to copulate and to eat, and for all that it may be merely important while they are importunate. Doubt is the same kind of discomfort and signal to inquire that is felt by those in need of a mate or of food. Reason is as much of an instinct as the others, and as necessary for survival. If we accept the fact that food is necessary for the survival of the individual and sex for the species, then we must accept also the fact that these are short-range satisfactions, urgencies of the moment compelled at the moment and completed in it. But to provide for food in the future, to marry and carry on the kind of stable arrangement that will provide not only for procreation but also for the rearing of children, is not of the moment but of the future. And here we enter the kind of world in which possibilities are scanned and plans are made. And it is here in this world that we need to know more than we know if we are to do more than we are doing. Inquisitiveness is the providential faculty which forges ahead to prepare the ground for the practicalities of the future, it is the pioneer of the human spirit.

It could be argued, then, that in addition to the drives for feeding and breeding, the organism has also an insatiable curiosity to learn about the world in which it finds itself, so that inquiry constitutes the third most fundamental human drive. For the scientist is still a human being. Like most of us, he is driven to reproduction and restored by rest. Astonishingly enough to the layman, the scientist feeds and breeds and works as though there were no death and sleeps as though there is no day. He is tempered into a scientist by his adventures at the fore-edge of observationally-sustained knowledge. He undergoes the strains of the pioneer, he suffers the misunderstandings of the discoverer, he endures the loneliness of those who seek for the sake of understanding only. In the discovery of hidden facts and of new laws there is a kind of ecstasy, which together with the recognition of his fellow-seekers is his only reward, and it is enough. For the passion to know which grips him is no ordinary passion and is satisfied by no limited amount of knowledge. It feeds on itself and multiplies and leads him onto ever greater efforts. Thus the scientist is in a sense a religious figure: he seeks the knowledge of the real in measureless quantities, and is content with nothing less.

(f) *The activity of the scientist.* The scientist to a certain extent is busily engaged in bringing about his own world of experience. By means of instruments in the laboratory and even in the field he is able to confront himself with new types of sense experience. What he can see through the microscope and telescope or photograph by means of the electron microscope or hear by means of radio astronomy represent values akin to sensations within the ordinary range (these after all are what he is capable of apprehending) but come to him coded from hitherto inaccessible areas. Thus he controls to a certain extent the type of experience which shall occur to him and he confronts himself with the necessity for making particular interpretations.

This is not always planned. It is possible to hear scientists at foundation laboratories refer to their interim activities as "love making," by which they mean stirring around in the laboratory until something occurs to them as a hunch or an hypothesis. Thus chance is evidently given an opportunity to develop what it can—but always within the range of the limits prescribed by previous training.

The scientists themselves are divided into types. There are many, but we may select two. There is the imaginative investigator, the man in search of mighty hypotheses. He is a rare creature. The meticulous investigator is far more common, the cautious plodding sceptic engaged in uncovering errors, busily checking the work of other men, repeating their experiments, testing their findings, and in general going over pioneered ground in a very minute way. Both types of scientists are of course equally needed, for the work of science requires specialists, and no sequence is completed by the labors of a single individual.

When we observe the scientist at work we are able to witness only one of his two chief activities. We see him in motion among his apparatus, but we cannot perceive him thinking. For before he picks up a test tube or adjusts an ultracentrifuge and after he has left them, he is engaged in exercising his mind upon the general scheme in which these instruments play only a part. The motion made by thought is not observable, yet it is there most surely, and without it there can be no science. It constitutes one of the two indispensable habits of the experimentalist, without which we are in no way to estimate his professional activities.

2. OBSERVATION AND EMPIRICAL DATA

The impression made upon the scientist by the external world is one which he passively receives. From this point of view his senses are helpless in the hands of the data. The chemist must accept the dictates of his taste buds when they are confronted with an alcohol or an oily substance; the eyes of the physicist are largely at the mercy of the needle of the voltmeter or the tracing of the recording pen. The data corresponding to the senses have an integrity which resists all efforts to make them other than they are. A color, a smell, a movement, a pointer-reading, are beyond his power to change them, and so he must accept them on their own ground. The nervous system is like a camera which receives, enters, records and stores the impressions made upon it by the phenomena which reach it from the external world.

Thus far the reception of the data has been described as passive and so it is, but an active phase also exists. The process is active to the extent to which the mind of the observer is able to select that part of the external world from which he wishes to receive his sense impressions. He is able to turn his attention like a camera upon any object that he chooses, and there to hold it fixed with great single-mindedness of purpose. Tremendous attention is his forte, and for this considerable training is required. The acuity characteristic of the observations of a scientist is a product not of peculiarly superior physiological organs but rather of profound concentration. A scientist is not one who can see better but one who can watch more intensely. Here the imagination of the scientist plays its first part. The scientific imagination, which is at this stage a kind of tiny induction, goes to work at the very start in helping to select the area of the environment from which it is intended to make a further selection, this time in terms of interpretation. To observe, then, for a scientist, means to secure the reflection of an individual fact, one which promises to be provocative of further inquiry. It represents the active effort to become the passive and easily influenced subject of a series of significant sense impressions. An impression in the case of a provocative fact is a question, and in areas approached in this spirit it is difficult to think of anything to ask. Thus all of the intellectual powers are called out in the exercise of each one. The significant similarities are those which are located in regions characterized by extreme difference. The conditions under which discovery is best brought about are those conducive to the grasping of relations between disparate elements hitherto not suspected of being related. Hence the need for training in the recognition of similarities among diversities, and the methodology of analogues.

It has often been noted that the separate senses constitute a distance hierarchy. The sense of sight reaches out farther than the others; the observer can see farther than he can hear, and he can hear farther than he can smell; and so we come down the list of senses through touch to taste. And so the observer is able to watch motions in his instruments, detect changes in his pointer-readings, and interpret photographs of the tracks of subatomic particles or of the behavior of cells in microphotographs. It is the very asymmetry of the senses in their role as distance receptors which renders their coordination significant; when they agree, their agreement must indicate the presence of something which is both objective and unified, because individual, to occasion the agreement.

But sensation, however coordinated, does not indicate anything by itself for the scientist. He has in addition the capacity for action and for thought which are employed in this connection. Action plays an important role in mediating between observation and concept formation. To act when confronted with a material individual means for the scientist to manipulate it. He may do this in one of two ways; he may change his position as observer, or he may change the position of the object. When he changes his position as observer, he is able to observe other features of the object hitherto concealed. He may walk around it, turn his instrument to another corner of it, or construct a new instrument of observation in order to observe another facet. Each of these instances is accompanied by another range of sensations; the observer can see, hear, touch, smell or taste another set of qualities, which he is then able to coordinate with a previously observed set, thus bringing the other dimensions of an object or its solidity roundly into view.

When the investigator changes the position of the object by his actions, he may again do this in one of two ways; he may merely manipulate the object in order to alter its position without disturbing its internal relations, or he may alter it by deformation. In the former case, he places it in a new set of relations which affords him a new perspective, and in the latter case he engages in a far more complex operation of dissection or analysis. In the former case, his observations do not disturb the object crucially, while in the latter case they may. They are, taken together, degrees of disturbance and interference, and have their own type of interference as well as advantage. But in either case, as in the two former cases, he has aided the coordinated sensations by bringing them up to the stage where concept formation is made possible.

The addition of thought to sensation and action takes the investigator up to and within the limits of concept formation. He enters into this stage by naming. Thought here precedes naming but it issues in naming, which is its result. Before entering upon a discussion of the intellectual reaction of naming, it will be best to recapitulate. The investigator senses a challenging material object which he conceives as an individual as the reports of his various senses converge upon it. He manipulates the object; he encounters it as one material individual does another; he then thinks about what the meaning of his action and sensation produces. Thus he acts as a whole man in acting as a scientist; and while his thought here plays a subordinate tertiary role to the subordinate secondary role of action and the leading primary role of coordinated sensations, it is nevertheless present and an integral part of the combination.

What we shall want to know, as we pause at this point and look back at the complex reactions which have already been described, is what prompts a scientist, psychologically speaking, to behave in such a way? The experimental method of natural science requires that there shall be nothing in the mind of the investigator that was not first in the external world. The scientific method is inherently an *ex post facto* method. First a material object, and only then a reaction to it, finally a class name suggested by the material object acting in its capacity as the member of a class. Sensation-manipulation-recognition; this is the order of observation. And the recognition takes the form of naming.

Naming means assigning words to objects exclusively, so that whenever a certain word is used it will stand for a certain object. The objects themselves may be abstract or concrete. Abstract objects are universal, concrete objects individual. The scientist as scientist is concerned exclusively with the naming of abstract objects, and this only if it is done in strict accordance with a rigorous method. Thus for him naming means finding the universal suggested by concrete individuals. By "universal" here is meant trans-finite class, i.e. a class which may have an infinite number of members. A class known to be finite is not a universal; but on the other hand the infinity of class-membership does not have to be asserted for universals. The name itself is a sound, an arbitrarily chosen sign to indicate that every such material object is a member of a universal class. But the class it names is not arbitrary; it is as real as the material individuals which are its members. For it is their resemblance we are taking seriously and their differences we are ignoring as unimportant. The name "atom" was first given to a material particle which was considered irreducible, and this property—at the time its only known one—was included in the name: "a-tom" = cannot be cut (divided, analyzed).

Concrete objects are individuals—material objects. Scientists investigate them by means of observation, and in a later stage of the scientific method by means of experiment; but it is never the individuality of the material object that the scientist is concerned with, only its typicality: if there is this material object as indeed there seems to be, then there must be others like it, others of its type, so that the material object plays a role in science which is crucial, but a role still only insofar as it can suggest that there is an abstract class of which it is a member. A crucial feature in science of the encountering of a material object which is in need of a name for purposes of reference is that it is never the individual material object itself, never that particular one, which is being named. It is rather the class, so that the material object together with its name marks the actual comprehension of the fact that others of its class must also exist. In science we should never need to name an object if it were the only one; for it will perish as they all do and in most cases pass from memory, and does not therefore need any treatment in communication. A scientist in a laboratory dissecting a rat is certainly not a man whose entire concern is with that particular rat considered as a unique material object, although that is what the rat is. His concern is rather with that rat insofar, and only insofar, as he is justified in regarding it as typical; what he learns about *that* rat is true of the *class* "rat" and so will constitute part of the ordered body of knowledge which will render unnecessary the dissection of all rats, on the ground (reliable but assumed without proof) that the properties he has discovered in *his* rat are the properties of all such material objects and so the properties of an *abstract* object, namely, the *class,* rat.

A scientific statement is always a general statement. There would seem to be several objections to this contention, and so we shall need to examine them. The earth is a unique object with a specific name, but this happens to be the result of an accident of circumstances. If we could get at enough planets to examine others we should have a unique name for this particular one only for extra-astronomical reasons, such as that we happen to live on it; for it would then be for science the properties of the class of planets and not this particular member of that class that held our interest. And indeed we wonder as scientists just how far we are entitled to estimate the properties of the class from this member. Outside of the scientific purview, human beings are at present uniquely named, and culture objects, like cities, whose role is memorable. It is in all such cases what the material individual (Socrates, Paris) stood for, and not what it is inherently in itself, that counts in the naming. In the case of science, we are in the same connection concerned with the class of outstanding individuals and capital cities; Socrates and Paris as such have no scientific standing, however much meaning they may have in other connections— value connotations, for instance—which lie outside science. Within the scientific purview it is the class that counts but the class only as exemplified, instanced, and discovered by the encounter with material individual members. This is the initial, the primitive, meaning of empiricism; that the investigator shall certify no class without encountering with all of his faculties at least one material individual which is a member of it.

That the name, as name, goes beyond the single material individual which suggested it has a meaning for concept formation: the name is a psychological concept as well as a methodological name. Memory has played a role here: the name might not be just a word arbitrarily chosen (though it might): the name might be a class name chosen in full recognition of its place as the species under a genus; that is to say, there might have already been other class names of similar material individuals which had a family resemblance as belonging together under a common genus. The name "horse" is the name not only of a certain class of material individuals (though it is that well enough) but of a class of material individuals known to have something in common with other material individuals having other names, such as "cow" or "dog"; it is, in other words, an "animal." The name has singled it out as a recognizable class; it has also placed it in a zoological hierarchy.

Many far more complex examples could be given. The naming of a particle the "anti-proton" is involved in a far more elaborate system of concepts, or in other words, of theories, than the mere name *qua* name might suggest. At this point concept formation turns into theory construction and calls for separate treatment.

3. INDUCTION AND THEORY CONSTRUCTION

We have seen that concepts are formed by assigning names to abstract objects. Theories are constructed by combining concepts. But before we are in a position to undertake the discussion of theory construction from the psychological point of view, we shall have to consider the psychological process of induction.

We left the investigation in the previous section at the point where the data were received by the conscious mind and, where necessary, named. We shall now undertake to follow them on their further psychological adventures.

(a) *The revision in the unconscious mind.* The data received by the conscious mind are turned over to the unconscious part of the mind for revision. It is there that they are combined and distributed and in general wholly assimilated. The role played by the unconscious mind in the scientific process is very important. It occupies what may be described as a fallow period, because the unconscious mind works while the scientist himself may be entirely unaware or only dimly aware of its working. For this reason we are entitled to speak of the process of induction arrived at in this way as slow induction, because such inductions come when the scientist is not aware of them and are held for some time, so that the dawning of the awareness takes place gradually. This is the only way in which induction can be slow, for a theory is under construction whenever it is suddenly acquired by the unconscious, and only slowly dragged into consciousness. The scientist is often unaware that this process is going on within him, although at times like this he may feel like doing little else. If he does anything it tends to be irrelevant or trivial: straightening up the laboratory or casually reading. Helmholtz said that his best ideas came to him when he was walking slowly up a wooded hill. Intense thought simply cannot be observed, and so the scientist may appear to others to be doing little or nothing.

The truth is that some activities are visible where others are not; and some take more time than others. An induction from observation to hypothesis may take only a second to happen in the investigator's mind, thus requiring neither a visible occasion or much time. On the other hand, the laboratory experiment carried out by the same investigator in order to test his hypothesis requires the patient use of instruments; it may be observed and be quite prolonged. It is what we ordinarily assume the scientist "does with his time." However, we must not be led by our senses into supposing that what can be observed and needs much time is any more important than what cannot be observed in this case and may happen in a flash. Without the hypothesis to be tested, which was arrived at in this way, the experiments designed and conducted to test the hypothesis would never have been executed. The psychology of scientific discovery, the movement of illumination and doubt, although opposites, are equally intense. Illumination is ecstatic, doubt is painful; the ecstasy comes from the harmony of the inner and outer, the doubt from their diremption; but they are very close together and alternate rapidly in the period before the adoption of an hypothesis.

This second period which consists of revision in the unconscious may be best described as one involving chaos. Within the unconscious of the scientist there is much of puzzlement and confusion; but there can be no act of clarification where there is no confusion. What emerges may be clear, for it is the task of the mind to clarify the confusion. The construction of a theory can take place only from the situation in which the data are placed in new relations and new connections between things emerge, and this step is actually made possible by chaos and confusion. In chaos all things rub shoulders with all things, and hence new connections may be detected by chance and seized upon for clarification.

What appeals to the investigator about a particular idea more than others which may occur to him at the same time? What leads him to adopt it as an hypothesis? Its impression must be sympathetic: its seeming naturalness, its ease of comprehension, its simplicity, its economy. The kind of appeal which Euclidean geometry has over non-Euclidean, which is possessed by mechanical models in physics and by geocentric theories in navigation. Hypotheses may be chosen, in other words, because of prejudices in their favor, prejudices which, however, are those dictated by the demands of a rigorous method and which call for the elimination of extraneous considerations: religious beliefs, predetermined concepts, anything which may in fact militate against the issuance of a supposition which experiment and calculation may be able to disallow.

A very long time and an immense preparation may go into the making of a productive theory. The actual act of discovery, however, takes place in a very brief spell. There is a period of incubation which we may call the unconscious fixation. J. J. Thompson once remarked that the discovery by a scientist of new ideas just when he did not suppose that he was thinking about them depended upon his having thought about them often in the past. Many scientists have from time to time attested to the character of this experience. Hadamard, the mathematician, goes so far as to recommend that scientific problems be dismissed from conscious attention in order to be solved by the unconscious; most of us, according to him, think better in this way, and the genius most of all. Theory construction is the name for what occurs, induction is the way in which it occurs; psychologically, the process strikes the object as a feeling. Thinking in this way without words to the novel association of ideas involves qualities in a peculiar context which remains to be analyzed.

(b) *Scientific imagining.* In science we must learn the conventions before we can afford to be unconventional. If we do not know the conventions, then we are not in possession of the equipment in terms of procedures; and if we do not introduce innovations, we have not employed this equipment to advantage. In the testing of hypotheses as well as in their discovery, imagination is the single indispensable factor. The discovery of hypotheses usually means the recognition in a flash of novel and seemingly far-fetched relationships. The method of discovery is the sudden association of elements which had not been hitherto related, not hitherto *seen* as related, that is. To operate the imagination on a scientific subject-matter requires a working knowledge of details in the field to be explored, and a facile imagination. In other words, the unconventional usage of conventional material produces new knowledge. Imagination, one might say, requires that the set of qualities and relations which are actual be assigned no reality superior to any other possible set of qualities and relations. In this way, the ideal world can obtain a hearing in images, more nearly on a par with perceptions in the actual world. For the fact is that a considerable amount of imagination is a prerequisite in most important acts of discovery. We can only hope to find what we can suppose might be there. The scientific imagination is a partly controlled operation. In science we have to imagine *logically,* we have to suppose in terms of system. The scientific imagination according to Peirce does not dream in qualitative terms but rather in terms of explanations and laws.

The extent to which we need imagination in scientific discovery has been very surprising and often confusing. The sudden perception of similarity and differences among actual things and events requires effort. It was pointed out long ago by Heraclitus that "nature loves to hide," and the key to the understanding of natural events has often been found by imagining what this might be and then searching—successfully—for it. A lucky hit would be strange indeed in a world filled with random phenomena. But where there are no entirely unique facts, and where all facts are examples of general principles, this could easily be the case. Such propositions do often have to be supposed.

The scientific imagination works at its highest only in two contexts: in the construction of theories to account for empirical results, and in the choice of axioms for mathematics. The evidence of things unseen is not in this case faith but rather predictions or deductions from axiom-sets. We commit an act of faith when we predict events or choose axioms, and this must be done by means of the imagination.

It is important at this point to indicate the precise division between induction and theory construction. The investigator can go only so far by combining concepts suggested by observation. The limits vary from instance to instance. The question is, do the observations suggest the method of combining or merely the concepts? Both; but the latter less surely. There is a vague and undefined area in which theory construction fails without the assistance of induction: imagination comes to the aid of construction, but the investigator may shift easily back and forth between them in this dimly lit area without knowing that he is doing so.

Imagination is a kind of thinking. It is neither entirely deductive nor entirely inductive. It has an inductive aspect and it can be used deductively, but it is in itself analogical; it works by the method of analogy, requiring understanding and the facile ability to combine, separate and recombine very disparate elements. Imagination is rendered impossible by belief, which makes the elements too rigid and impermeable. In imagination what we do is to think *through* the structures and not *around* them, to penetrate them and work inside as well as outside them, and for this purpose they must be fluid and transparent.

We may be able to illuminate the function of the imagination in science if we compare science with art in this regard. The scientist is in search of relations, the artist of values; and so what the scientist imagines must then be put to the truth-test of comparison with facts, while what the artist imagines is itself the value he seeks. In the past the artist has been assigned the imagination as his exclusive possession, while the scientist has been deemed a sort of superior mechanic. But the scientist is not a robot any more than the artist is altogether a divinely inspired creature who is set off from the rest of mankind and sacred, having nothing whatsoever in common with other mortals. The scientist uses his imagination within the structure of a circumscribed method, and the artist has a circumscribed method just as well as his special imagination. There are no known mechanical methods which have operated successfully in the discovery of mechanisms, and the scientific imagination is an indispensable part of the method of scientific discovery.

Little if anything is understood about the workings of the imagination. It lies between unconscious chaos and conscious order as the end-process of the revision in the unconscious. The remainder of its explanation is a matter of the earliest dawning of a conscious reaction.

(c) *The conscious reaction.* The perception by the scientist of the new hypothesis is an exciting experience. The sudden enlightenment which consists in the grasping of the new relations takes place at the moment when some order in the chaos of the unconscious spills over into consciousness. It is for the scientist a period of exalted sensibility. It is a period of quick insight and high excitement. This is the phase of genuine discovery. He has become aware in an immediate flash of insight of how things could be. The data from the external world which were received and reshuffled have been put back together in a possible new order.

The conscious reaction is the sensation of tremulousness in the face of a newly arrived hypothesis. For the scientist the hypothesis came, he does not know how, and so an adjustment to its existence must be made. One scientist described his feelings of recognition as divided into steps, somewhat as follows. "First you don't even dare to tell yourself that you have an hypothesis; then you do tell yourself. Next you tell your wife (she will forget), and afterwards your technician (he will not talk), and finally you write it down on paper tentatively."

After the first rush of excitement occasioned by the awareness on the part of the investigator that there has been the discovery of an hypothesis, there are two qualms which overtake him. First, he suddenly understands that he has gone too far: his new idea is not yet a theory but only an hypothesis, since there has been no support for it. The theory remains to be constructed. In the emotion of discovery he has regarded it as a theory; in the testing which is to come, he will regard it as an hypothesis. Here the roles played by the proposition, or equation, are reversed temporarily, and, in contradistinction to the logic of the scientific method itself, the theory for a brief spell precedes the hypothesis. The sudden caution which overtakes the investigator following his discovery immediately corrects the reversal of roles and re-establishes the logical order, which does not always correspond with the psychological order but eventually does control it.

Secondly, as to the certitude with which he regards his newly discovered hypothesis, there is the qualm which comes as an addition to the substitution of the role of hypothesis for theory and suggests to him that perhaps his hypothesis were it to be established as a theory would be only a statistical theory and not a causal one. What he has discovered in the conscious reaction to his act of imagining is a probability and not a certainty even if subsequent experiment and calculation were to support it to the fullest. And here, too, there is a reversal of roles, for just as it has been noted that probability measures relative frequency, so now inverse probability measures degree of belief. In the earlier formulation studying the properties of the objective logic of the scientific method, it was learned that inverse probability is an error; but here, where the concern is with the psychological correlates of that method, inverse probability acquires an altogether different meaning and is not to be ruled out. It frequently happens that what objectively constitutes an error, subjectively amounts to a truth; and vice versa. Psychologically speaking, then, it is fair to say that the statistical probability which is a matter of objective relative frequency, is, subjectively considered, a matter of ignorance. Thus the kind of interpretation made of probability, typified by von

Mises, is justified in the psychology of the scientist though not in science itself.

4. THE ADOPTION OF HYPOTHESES

The last stage in theory construction consists in the conscious and deliberate expression of the new insight. This could consist in the private formulation of the hypothesis, the semi-public recording or the public announcement. This last part of the process, for which the preceding parts may be said to have existed, is predominantly a matter of the keenest consciousness. The elements which have been received from the external world and which have been rearranged in a new order are now restored in a new form to their original condition of objectivity.

In this form the hypothesis is promulgated as an objectively-formulated proposition, perhaps as a mathematical expression, in preparation for submitting it to fresh data for testing. This is the stage in which the separation is made between the mind of the scientist in which the hypothesis was discovered as an intuition (logically an induction) and the hypothesis itself existing independently of the act of its discovery. Thus we might say from an objective orientation toward the psychological processes of scientific discovery, that the trained mind of the productive scientist is the indirect route taken by sets of data in order to get themselves interpreted in ways in which the laws which are operative in them could find suitable expression.

The objective formulation secures the method of science in its true aim. For our entire conception of the scientific method relies upon the hypothesis that the contents of repeatable experience can be interpreted as results of the properties of the data of experience.

Psychologically, hypotheses occupy that ambivalent area which is composed of belief and doubt and where, while belief predominates, doubt is very much in the picture. It is a proposition held tentatively, that is to say, consciously, and not admitted to full belief. Belief accounts for its being held at all, and doubt accounts for its being held tentatively. It is indeed the doubt which dictates the tests; the investigator tries to disprove his hypothesis, and belief only becomes stronger should his efforts fail. An hypothesis, then, is a question, where the answer will perforce involve a long series of operations; and so it requires an emotionally painful stage of puzzlement, of bafflement and perhaps to some extent of anxiety. The ambivalence is very much to the fore here, and feeling swings back and forth uncertainly between belief and doubt, at the mercy of every allegedly relevant submission of evidence and changing as each bit turns up; so that doubt itself and not merely belief if taken alone would constitute some kind of emotional release and rest. The holding of an hypothesis is a necessary stage in the scientific method, a crucial one in fact, yet psychologically a temporary one which the investigator longs to bring to an end in relatively settled acceptance or in final rejection.

Yet the hypothesis initiates a series of operations for the investigator: it tells him which way to direct his experiments, his calculations, his predictions and his efforts at the control of phenomena. They are guide lines, and once established even in their temporary state they take the investigator in tow and become themselves the leaders of the movement of inquiry which he has no choice but to follow and, so to speak, obey. The hypothesis suggests an explanation of concepts already well known, the existence of entities and processes not yet known, or the ideals in terms of which their knowledge may be acquired. For each of these there is a corresponding operation, of which more later. The psychological criteria are based upon emotional appeal: how good does the explanation seem, how strong a compulsion to further inquiry does it carry, what imaginative vistas does it open up?

Thus the holding of an hypothesis accomplishes two forward-looking purposes for the experimenter. It acts as a powerful stimulus to his imagination, suggesting its own kind of verification; and channels his inquiries sufficiently to initiate a specific line of investigation. In other words, it gives him the necessary content and form to constitute a complete cycle of the application of the scientific method. He derived it from observations of the natural world by means of the process of induction; he is now obliged to submit it to that same world, only under other circumstances, this time of his own devising, in order to see what further support he can find for a discovery which by its method asserted nothing necessary and was tenuous at best. How he does so we shall next examine.

5. EXPERIMENTATION

Speaking very generally, every phase of the practice of the scientific method carries with it its necessary professional preoccupation and consequent over-emphasis. The observer, the experimenter, the calculator, the applied scientist, each thinks that the phase of science in which he is most interested and therefore at his best is the most crucial and significant phase. For the botanist and zoologist, observation *is* science, for the quantum physicist experimentation, for the astrophysicist calculation, and for the applied scientist prediction and control. Now it must be confessed that for those on the side lines, for the lay public, experimentation holds this position clearly. A scientist to the non-scientist is one who experiments. There is more than a grain of truth in this opinion. For what distinguishes the scientific method of inquiry from all other methods is precisely the role played in it by experiment. It is the active and dynamic part of science. Observation is passive by comparison even though it requires some activity; but experimentation is so to speak permeated by activity, it is activity all through.

The prominence of activity in experimentation enables the investigator to decide issues through the use of motor centers which have been raised by sensation and worked over by thought. Experimenting, then, means the whole man at work; for neither sensation nor thought drop out when movement takes over. It is a simple matter of action leading the other faculties rather than of replacing them altogether. And to the extent to which the faculties are properly coordinated, the results will be to some extent successful. An experiment is an intellectual act performed by a man of unusual observational powers. His peculiar skill may lie in the area of manual dexterity; he may be at his best in constructing mechanical devices, or he may have wonderful motor control: one scientist, for example, is said to have been able to thread a sheet of writing paper without having the needle or thread show on the other side. So perfectly coordinated are the faculties, however, that the peculiar skill of an experimenter may be in imagining how crucial experiments could be conducted and not in doing them, which in his case may be left to others; and here the intellectual imagination rather than action is the leading faculty.

Science engages all three human faculties: thought, feeling and action, and, moreover, all three working together. Science is the only form of inquiry which uses the whole man, with the possible exception of art. In science, feeling operates through observation and induction leading to the discovery of hypotheses, and again in the search for supporting evidence for hypotheses; action takes place in the laboratory or the field; and thought works in the interpretation of the data. To experiment for a scientist means to enlist the aid of one piece of matter in eliciting the properties of another, the cyclotron and the properties of the meson, for instance. Such properties are of course concealed from the unaided perceptions of ordinary common sense. An investigative instrument is an extension of some human capacity: a time exposure on a photographic plate made through an optical telescope is an extension of the human eye, an ultra-centrifuge is an extension of human movement, and an analog computer is an extension of human thought.

All experiments are conducted with particulars, and all experiments with particulars are for or against the acceptance of universals. Actual things and events either do or do not support concepts; and so the intellect once again predominates. In the arts, while all three of the human faculties are employed, it is the feeling which governs. In the sciences, while all three of the faculties are also employed, it is the intellect which governs. In the dialectic of the procedures of science, understanding leads to action and action in turn illuminates understanding. The action of experiment is indispensable but it should not be forgotten that such action functions as decision theory with respect to hypotheses, which are universal propositions in the form of equations.

Experimentation is a large field of interest, and it may be even further subdivided than has yet been suggested. For instance, there are specialists corresponding to each of the four steps in the carrying out of an experiment. Some scientists are more adept than others at readying specimens for experiments. The cutting of thin sections, the arrangement of control groups, the preparing of slides, the selection of sites, often require great delicacy. Others are better at inventing or operating instruments: at determining just what sort of device is needed to make a particular test or at seeing to it that the instrument to be used is running properly. Still others are superior in operating the testing instruments: they do not mind the detailed maintenance and supervision, the long hours of vigil that are often required, and they are excellent at detecting and preventing disturbances in the instrument which might arise from flaws that develop during its operation and cancel the effects of the test. A last group is superior at reading results: the painstaking work of collecting the data on dials or in changes in laboratory animals, which must be caught and recorded at once.

Whatever the area of specialization, one ability must be in the possession of the practicing scientist and that is concentration. A scientist is a man who works, eats, sleeps and dreams his adopted profession. Problems arising in experiments, either from planning experiments or from executing them, cannot always be settled off the cuff, and may indeed require prolonged hours of conscious or unconscious thought. Everyone intimately connected with a research scientist, such as his associates or the members of his family, are the victims of his preoccupation; for conscious thought may be restricted to his legitimate working hours but not so the unconscious thought, which carries with it as an almost necessary prerequisite the condition that he be doing something else. Pure science, like the fine arts or philosophy, calls on the entire man and calls on him all the time; no one can engage in one of these fundamental forms of inquiry unless he turns himself into an investigative instrument and regards all other aspects of his life as ancillary.

Thus far we have considered the activity of the scientist in experimenting as though the entire affair were a matter deliberately controlled and executed. To a large extent this is true. It is not the whole story, however. There is also the question of chance. Accidents which are productive do not occur of course to just anybody, but only to those with a prolonged training in a particular field of endeavor. Pasteur once observed that it was only the prepared mind that chance visited. The scientist, equipped as he is with a deductive knowledge of the structure of his particular field, submits himself in his laboratory daily to a number of unpredictable factors. The actual world being the mixture of order and disorder that it is, unexpected factors are bound to enter into every operation. He cannot be expected to anticipate everything that he is going to encounter; indeed if he could, experimenting would be unnecessary.

The laboratory scientist has a great many decisions to make, and he makes them by means of the knowledge that he has or in view of the hypothesis that he has adopted. Chance enters as an important factor into many of his most crucial decisions, often in a way that he is unable to see himself at the time. That Darwin was invited on the voyage of the *Beagle* was a lucky circumstance. The discovery of radio activity by the Curies and of penicillin by Fleming are also cases in point; and a number of other instances could be adduced, so that the phenomenon is familiar enough to the scientist. But there is no known method of training by which such accidents can be increased. Good fortune, as someone observed, comes only to the fortunate.

An even stronger piece of evidence of the importance of the deductive background in the psychological makeup of the experimental scientist is furnished by the instances of simultaneous discovery. There are famous cases, such as the discovery of the infinitesimal calculus by Newton and Leibniz, or the independent discovery of oxygen in 1774 by Priestley in England and by Scheele in Sweden, but today the rate has increased. In chemistry, for instance, so many men are engaged upon similar problems that discovery must be followed quickly by publication not only in order to disseminate information and to share it with other workers in the field but also to establish priority.

Simultaneous discovery is only partly the result of accident. Men with similar training engaged upon exploring a field which is in the same stage of development are likely to come upon the same hypothesis or to encounter the same significant data. The frontiers of a science are common to the pioneers in the science, so that the activity of scientific inquiry is perforce a social enterprise. This is not to say of course that individual initiative or private inquiry counts for nothing. Genius is still unique, and the relation between the great powers of discovery possessed by the exceptional scientist and the majority of men occupied with the same interests is one of constant interaction. We could hardly hope for much from science without the labors of both groups. Still, the difference between them does exist. And in addition there are the bottle-washers of science. Not all scientists are geniuses, not all have conducted crucial experiments or discovered important laws. The laboratory assistant makes his own contribution to science, no less genuine for being small. The character of the progressive application of the scientific method is such that while the great scientist advances science markedly the little scientist advances it a little. This is made possible by the dependable nature of the method itself; the genius of science is in its method. How this was laid down, therefore, is a matter of intense interest; for it must have been laid down by the aid of the psychological abilities of men of genius, an enterprise to which, however, lesser minds have contributed their mite.

The psychological collective, in which scientists both great and small have their place, is reflected in the repository of the objective achievements of science. That is why scientific activity bears a greater and greater likeness to a convergent series. We have reached the beginning of our own kind of organized, as opposed to random, inquiry. Group attacks upon problems in science, such as the atomic research in the United States during World War II, are becoming a familiar feature of the scientific landscape. The parcelling out of the pieces of a problem among the members of a team engaged in a cross-field inquiry, and similar enterprises indicate clearly the growing deductive nature of scientific research. Induction, insight, hunches, hypotheses, are being fitted into a definite place in the larger deductive picture; and while experiment and appeal to individual facts must always remain the bedrock of empirical science, it is the building of the abstract deductive structure which appears to be the growing end in view, and this is as evident in the psychological preparation and psychological activities of the scientist as it is anywhere else in the scientific institution.

Perspective distortion. Scientists are not only scientists; they are also human beings. The intrusion into their findings of other considerations should not, therefore, be too surprising. The only way to solve the problems raised by this fact is to measure their extent and make the proper allowances.

The scientific experimenter is also an observer whose observations for a number of reasons interfere to some extent with the subject-matter to be observed. In the act of observation, the means often condition or defeat the end. When the mechanism of observation distorts the observation itself to the extent that nothing of that which is observed can come through, then we have reached the limiting case and we know that here at least observation serves no useful purpose—certainly not the one for which it was designed. For the observer in the practice of science does not wish to learn merely about his own observations, unless the science in which he is working is psychology and the observations those to be made upon himself. In every other science, the psychological factors must be held to a minimum. Every individual has had his own peculiar development and hence possesses a psychological constitution which differs to some extent at least from all others. It should not be too surprising, then, to learn that every scientific observer occupies a psychological perspective which is peculiarly his own. It is important not to confuse the observer with the information he receives from his experiments. The psychological bias of the observer will no doubt affect his readings and so will change from time to time in accordance with the thousand and one influences at work upon him. But the information is such as it is. It does not change because he receives it, and indeed he receives it because it does not change.

The account given here is obviously an oversimplification. There is no such thing as an experimenter who is absolutely free of psychological bias. He is never sure of his observations or calculations. He may think he sees what he hopes to see, and he may be working from theories which he had aspired to prove. The edges of his thoughts and actions in the laboratory are never clearcut, and through their penumbral borders may creep all sorts of extra-scientific considerations from which he had supposed he was free. It is often through the very planning of an experiment that there enter frustrating elements which do not appear in the carrying out of the experiment itself.

Thus psychological bias and experimental error are factors of deviation which condition all scientific work. They can be reduced and held to a minimum but probably never altogether eliminated. The observer can carry them properly if he keeps in mind that the psychological factor is a surd which must be counted in every scientific formulation. The predicament of the observer, who is always so situated that the readings he takes must be always considered to be those of a coordinate system, is compounded when he fails to make the proper allowances.

6. CALCULATION

That stage of the scientific method at which the results obtained by experiment are studied and the hypothesis supported by them shown to be consistent with the accepted body of knowledge in the given science, is psychologically a matter of calculation. The operation itself is usually a mathematical one. We owe to Peirce the illumination that mathematical calculation is itself an observational science even though a peculiar one. He called it "ideal experimentation." Much the same interpretation was made by Planck, who called it "intellectual experiment" and considered it many ways more subtle than any other kind.

All deductive reasoning consists in first making a graph, either in the form of a mental image or on paper, and then in observing the graph just as though it were a concrete object like a beehive. The scientist next makes the appropriate changes in the graph and then notes the results of his changes. There is perception and experiment in this kind of deductive exploration, only it is concerned with images or with signs rather than with the concrete objects which lie in the actual world and outside the mind. The applied mathematician (for that is what the calculating scientist is at this point) does not always know what the properties of his results will be. If this were not the case, the discovery of ingenious theorems would not be both difficult and rare, for he could anticipate what he would get. The failure of anticipation here indicates the need for both manipulation and observation. He manipulates his graph: he alters his axioms, deduces from them by means of his rules of inference, and observes the resulting theorems. If he does not by means of this experiment obtain the results that he sought, then he must try again. He is, in short, experimenting.

Thus while inductive discovery accounts for most of the advances in science, deductive discovery is also a potent weapon against many types of problems. We are here of course concerned chiefly with the psychological aspect. There is no room in the proportions of this essay to discuss fully the psychology of thought. Moreover, we are concerned with it here only insofar as it is peculiar to the operation of the scientific method of inquiry, where we have termed it deductive discovery: employing propositions about existing items and conditions to formulate premises, and then to deduce from those premises propositions about other items and conditions which may or may not exist but which are considered possible, and then to direct the search for such items and conditions in existence, with a view to understanding their occurrence, to predicting their frequency and to controlling their effects. The confirmation of the sequence of thoughts would consist in the discovery of the facts corresponding to or illustrating the thoughts. Thus deductive discovery is a way of making predictions about what will be found empirically. A very important warning is in order here. The fallacy of rational dogmatism lies in wait to defeat the efforts of those who suppose that the truth about empirical fields can be ascertained by means of thought alone. Such thoughts are

suggested by the data obtained through observation, and they are referred
back to the actual world for empirical verification or disconfirmation.

The study of abstract structures, logical systems derived from the
external world by means of observation, induction, hypothesis and experiment, is, then, still a variety of the observation of nature. The thought
of a scientist in grasping a law, that is to say, in comprehending that the
law which he recognizes and before which he stands mentally, is at the
same time if not an absolute truth then at least a proximate one and as
close as any experimental scientist is ordinarily able to come to such a
truth, to the inner reflection of an outer reality which is just as secure as
the reliability of the material facts to which it had to correspond to
establish itself as a truth.

The psychological process of calculation, which is that of mathematics, can never be altogether free from empirical fact, that is to say,
from representation. The more advanced the science the more abstract; so
that physics, for example, has come to be known as "mathematical
physics," when it is inherently no more mathematical—and no less so—
than any other empirical field. Whatever exists, as Plato insisted, is subject
to the art of mathematics. However, it is true that manipulation depends
upon abstraction. Mathematics is a kind of shorthand, and in this language combinations and rearrangements are possible that otherwise would
be awkward and unwieldly. Thus the scientist, who at this stage of the
method is engaged in calculating, depends upon the degree of abstraction
which it is possible to achieve. The concepts of the given science must be
amenable to mathematical treatment, which is to say, must be sufficiently
abstracted empirically. But with these conditions met, the task is to
manipulate the empirical abstractions mathematically as though they
had no empirical reference whatsoever. The process is one of withdrawal
and return: withdrawal from the empirical level to make the manipulation
at the mathematical level possible, and then return to the empirical
level with the conclusions to be applied. Psychologically, the mathematical scientist benefits from the circumstance that he does not have to
bear in mind the reference of his symbols. The process of calculation
takes place in the same way whether the symbols are purely abstract
and without meaning, as in pure mathematics, or containing empirical
reference, as in experimental science. The only difference is how the
symbols were derived in the first instance and how they shall be applied
afterwards.

7. PREDICTION AND CONTROL

At this late stage in the scientific method, the scientist has come, so to speak, to the end of his road. The stages in the scientific method could be conducted by a series of investigators, and frequently are; but as frequently they are steps taken by a single investigator. Theoretically, all six steps could be conducted by the same man. With prediction and control, however, the situation alters somewhat; for the kind of temperament which experiments may be the kind which also calculates, a condition forced by the fact that experiment, as we have noted, involves some degree of calculation, and calculation itself is a kind of experiment; but the kind of temperament which experiments and calculates is rarely the kind that predicts relevant events and endeavors to control them. Pure scientists look down upon applied science as a vulgar consequence of an elegant inquiry and usually will have nothing at all to do with it. Applied science and technology seem both crude and cheap, a practical affair with which pure science as such has nothing to do. And of course the applied scientist retaliates in his attitude and criticism: the pure scientist to him is a hopeless dreamer from whom nothing practical could ever come.

Pure scientists often forget that a theory which has been successfully applied in practice does not thereby cease to be a pure theory. Pure laws are no less pure for being utilized. The compromising attitude of the pure scientists may well have a purpose, however. It may be the occupational disease which provides the isolation necessary for their productivity. For it stands to reason that a pure scientist who kept his eye upon practice would never produce anything which could be applied in practice. And this paradox governs the relation between pure science and practice. What has made the pure scientist so successful is just this removal from the sphere of practice, and the result has been the development of theories which have had an enormous effect.

The reverse attitude, of course, also prevails. The applied scientist, the technologist, and the industrialist look with some scorn upon the pure scientist who often seems to them an impractical and hopeless dreamer. This was more true before the discovery of atomic energy than it has been since, although the term of opprobrium, "pencil chemist," is still used for the chemists who work at a desk by those who work in the laboratory. The contempt of the practical man for the theoretical thinker is perhaps as old as the world, for it is usually impossible for men of affairs to envisage how the affairs with which they deal might some day be altered almost beyond recognition by the theoretical work which they cannot understand. Practical minded men have in mind never more than current practice, and always assume that practice in the future must be much the same. And so it will be, in periods when no theories are being developed. The common sense by which the practical minded man is guided may be nothing more solid than an ancient and long accepted metaphysics, but if it be old enough and regarded as fundamental, it is enough to make all contemporary metaphysical speculation seem idle. And so it is with old theories in science, so far as the man of practical affairs is concerned.

Both points of view are of course wrong. What the pure scientist discovers the applied scientist applies, and this is no less true because of the existence of a time lag which correlates neatly with the amount of abstraction involved: the more powerful the theory the greater the time required to discover its application. However, the prejudices of the pure and applied scientist toward each other may represent necessary occupational equipment. If the pure scientist is too much concerned with practice, he will never get his work sufficiently removed from practice to discover anything which may be practiced; and if the applied scientist is too much concerned with theory his work will fail to be practical also. Both the theorist and the practitioner need the removal of the theorist from the practical scene. But the facts show that the human benefactor needs to apologize to no one, and pure science is in no wise hurt by its applications.

A word must be said here about planned investigation in group research, the organization of research teams to attack particular problems in science, so-called "operations research." Experience has shown that to attack practical problems in applied science by this procedure can be very successful. Witness the development of the atomic bomb by the Manhattan Project during World War II. There are advantages in such an approach, and they lie chiefly in the degree of concentration on a practical problem that is made possible. The method is established now in industrial laboratories, where it serves industrial purposes, the purposes recognized by technological requirements. But is it capable of producing the high inductions which lead to very abstract and universal laws, such as the work of Planck or of Einstein, or Newton or Gauss? This at least remains to be shown. And the curious paradox remains that if operations research fails in this direction, then what is produced individually (pure science) is needed for what is produced socially (applied science); the group method of research teams having to wait until individual genius produces the kind of theory which can be directed to the solution of practical problems by groups of investigators specifically assigned to solve them. And this may well be the case.

The interests of the applied scientist stem from a different motivation than do those of the pure scientist. Where the pure scientist is engaged in the attempt to satisfy the need to know; sheer inquisitiveness as to what there is, the applied scientist had dropped back to the two more primitive needs: the need to satisfy hunger and the need to satisfy sex, the two needs which are responsible for the continuance of the species. Thus the applied scientist asks *how*: how can we improve our crops, our buildings, our cities, our health, how can we best provide for the future of our children? The pure scientist asks *what*: what is matter, what is life, what is our history? The natural world in which we live is the beginning and end of both types of investigation, but the emphasis differs sharply.

Psychologically, the applied scientist may not be as far removed from the pure scientist as the foregoing discussion would seem to indicate. For with his investigations the scientific method in one respect at least has swung full circle. The investigating pure scientist began his procedure with the observation of nature; prediction and control call once more for the observation of nature, only this time for purposes of application; and if the nature that is under observation the second time differs operationally from the nature that was under observation the first time, it does not differ materially: there is only one natural world, and the matter and energy in space and time, the events, which compose it the first time are also those which compose it still the second time. Some bits of the external world have been turned against other bits through the skill of the scientist, and he is now able to observe a somewhat altered world; and others similar to him are able to seize upon these potential alterations and to use them for specific human purposes: to grow more food, to heal wounds, to protect themselves from the inclement elements. The route runs from nature and through a special process which has been devised for its investigation and partial control, then back to nature once again. And just as the pure scientist stands more and more in awe of what he contemplates in all its signal vastness, its multidimensional infinity, so the applied scientist is more and more impressed with how the little knowledge gained in this way can be used to change the world in which all of us live, the social world of culture and civilization.

THE PSYCHOLOGY OF THE ARTIST

The psychology of art is a field which lies within the province of psychology rather than art. For the psychological aspects of art are not the whole of art nor even the most important part, at least so far as art itself is at stake; and, while they are not the whole of psychology, either,

they are at the same time more at home with psychology. In the psychology of art, we are dealing with psychic processes in so far as the human
being is concerned with art. Yet although it is the human concern with
art which is chiefly responsible for the discovery or the making of works of
art, the human concern with art is not art; it is merely human concern.
Art, like everything else, is ontologically independent of its origins. Hence
the psychology of art is more psychological than artistic. A work of art
in no way resembles the man who made it or the method by which it
was made; and it may differ radically also from its own self in its earlier
stages of composition or construction. The things with which a topic is
related must be separated from that topic in order to be understood in
their proper relations with it. The psychology of art will throw some light
upon the meaning of art, which is here our main interest.

Inasmuch as there are two psychological functions in connection
with art and we intend to treat only of one, it will be best to begin by
making a sharp distinction between them. The psychology of art may be
divided into the psychology of art expression and the psychology of art
appreciation. The first deals with the psychological processes that take
place when a work of art is made. The second deals with the psychological processes that take place when a work of art is enjoyed. Since the
appreciation of art does not throw as much light upon the meaning of
art as the expression of art does, it is with the latter that we shall occupy
ourselves.

I

The psychology of art expression rests upon facts and theories in both
psychology and art, and these theories find their basis in, and the various
facts bear witness to, a principle which they hold in common and which
lies deeper than they do. This theory has to do with the unity of men and
nature and with the status of abstract possibility of all occurrences in the
human and natural worlds. The world which man has made as well as
man himself are integral parts of that larger world which we call nature.
Since man is part of nature, anything that he makes out of bits of his
environment must be part of nature, too. Now, we usually take the
human viewpoint on the things that catch our attention, and indeed it is a
little difficult to see how any other viewpoint could be available to us. We
are human beings in an irretrievable way, and no matter how we twist
and turn we cannot escape the narrowing consequences of that fact.

Yet if we eliminate that question as being of little value, we still find
that from the human viewpoint several perspectives are possible. We may

take up (1) the frankly human perspective, or (2) the quasi-non-human perspective. Let us see what each of these involves.

1. We can take the perspective which never allows us to forget ourselves. According to this perspective (and we must never lose sight of the fact that *all our* perspectives are essentially human), the spectacles through which we view the world must themselves be kept constantly in the field of vision. We must insist upon seeing our eyes as well as that which our eyes see, and this fact must be constantly repeated to ourselves in a never ending series of inverted returns. It is, we may as well confess, a little difficult to see what is gained by insisting upon confusing the mechanism with the purpose which the mechanism is intended to serve. The eyes are obviously not what we wish to see but only that by which our seeing is made feasible. A smooth mechanism is one which does not intrude itself upon its function, in the same way exactly that a good organ within the somatic organism never makes its particular presence known: we are never conscious of our liver, say, until the occurrence of some liver disorder. A condition of well-being is one in which we are able to forget our bodies altogether. Hence it is that which lies within the perspective and not the perspective itself that we wish to study.

2. We can take the perspective which allows us to forget ourselves almost altogether. According to this perspective, we can separate ourselves from our processes of perception and view the world and man's place in it apart from all egocentric considerations. We can so to speak take the god's-eye view, or at least the cloud's-eye view, and from this perspective see the world together with man and all his works as a comprehensive whole in which he plays his part but in which we from our perspective and for the purposes of that perspective play no part at all. This perspective, let us pretend, is nature's perspective which we have been allowed for the moment to use. It may make it possible for us to see ourselves and some of the things with which we play in a new light and from an angle which we had never envisioned before. And we may return, then, to our old familiar perspective with a fresh comprehension which we would not otherwise have been able to gain. In what follows, it will be the second perspective which is as consistently as possible employed. And when we come to a description of the psychological processes themselves, we must bear in mind that the second perspective is still the one we have chosen to take up, and that as a result we are endeavoring to study the artist's mind as an integral segment of the natural world and not as apart from or opposed to it.

The psychological process of art expression, then, is the method whereby nature produces art through the utilization of the objective human perspective. From the viewpoint of nature, the artist is a mechanism employed by nature to achieve her end which is the making or discovery of a work of art. It may be asserted that art is simply an extra complication of nature. For since man, the artist, is part of nature, and the materials out of which works of art are made are parts, too, the resultant works of art must themselves be natural objects. Because there is nothing unnatural about works of art, it is not legitimate to speak of the opposition of nature and art, as though they were contraries or opposites, or inimical to each other in any way. The only reason to speak of them separately is the necessity to refer to those parts of nature which are not works of art and to those which are. A work of art is that part of nature which has been turned into a work of art.

If works of art are natural, it follows that they are not supernatural. According to the postulate which asserts that everything in nature must have some natural explanation could we but find it, a work of art may be a rare object but is too common to be regarded as in any way a miracle. Those whose keen sense of appreciation makes them capable of the most exalted emotions when confronted with a very great work of art are apt to regard their experience as having something of the miraculous about it. But the fact that such experience is of the highest kind does not mean that it is a supernatural experience. For it is not. Any experience which can be reproduced at will is not a supernatural experience, and the work of art, however great, remains there and is continuously capable of exciting exalted emotions in the equipped appreciator. Great artists are not common but they continue to occur among us, and so the artist and his products may be among the highest expressions of human society without having to be supernatural. Thus it is misleading to speak of artistic expression and the making of works of art as any kind of "creation," as is so often done. Creation is usually understood to mean a process which has something of the divine about it. For those to whom everything is somehow touched by divinity, art is not to be singled out.

The denial of the divinity of artistic expression and works of art is apt to occasion the wrong impression. It is supposed that if the artistic process is not divine, then it must be merely mechanical. But this, too, is erroneous. No artist and no one familiar with the psychological processes which accompany the making of a work of art would be willing to accede to this contention. If art were entirely a mechanical affair, works of art could be reproduced mechanically and automatically, that is, without the continual assistance of the feelings of the artist. It is true that works of art can be produced occasionally by accident, such as indeed has taken place through the action of rivers on drift wood, for instance. But this is a natural process working without the usual human agency, it is not a mechanical process. In the future, no doubt, a mechanical method will be found for the exact reproduction of works of art. But we know of no way in which we can institute a process or a mechanism which will without further aid produce (not *re*produce) works of art. No two works of art are alike, and hence there is nothing mechanical about them.

The process by means of which works of art come into existence must therefore lie somewhere between the miraculous and the mechanical. What is that process? We have one clue already, for we have seen that a work of art is entirely a natural affair. But what exists in nature potentially does not have to be created or mechanically produced; it only remains to be discovered. The making of a work of art is thus in one sense a discovery, and that which is discovered has had its own nature laid bare and no longer depends upon something else. Hence the work of art, once made, is no longer dependent upon the artist who made it. However, since the artist is intimately bound up with the *process* by which the work of art is made, we must look within the artist for the key to the nature of the artistic process.

The artist does not exist in a vacuum and he is not the product of a vacuum. He exists as a member of society and he is a product of his own date and place. Thus what he produces is colored to a great degree by what has produced him. The contrary situation is not essential to his efforts to occasion in a work of art a value which shall not be occasional. History does not determine value. It is quite possible, as we have noted, that an accident of circumstance might be responsible for the making of a work of art whose value is unchanging and permanent, independent of all circumstance. Thus we can see that the artist, like everyone else, is determined by his environment. What is this environment? It is an affair of empirical levels, for there is the physical environment, the biological, the psychological and the social. Each of these is greatly subdivided but for present purposes we shall not need to probe any further. The physical environment is a very important one to the artist. It includes climate, geographical features, etc. What the artist senses is highly significant to his art, and his sensations are dictated largely by what exists to be sensed in his physical environment. The biological environment includes the fauna and flora by which he is surrounded. What diet exists for him, what pets, what animals to serve him, what infectious diseases, what parasites, how densely populated the area, what decorative and useful plants, etc., are all relevant questions so far as the artist is concerned. The psychological environment includes the beliefs which are current in the artist's own social group and which its members directly or indirectly communicate to him. What ideas does he encounter and which of them does he believe? How much impression does the atmosphere of opinion and the color of currently preferred values make upon him as an artist? The psychological environment is even more important in some ways than the other environing levels we have already mentioned. Lastly, there is the social environment. It makes a whole with the psychological environment and is difficult to distinguish from it, but there is a difference. The social environment includes the culture as a whole together with the structure of the ideas (the *eidos*) and the values (the *ethe*) which dominate it. It includes, as an item of special interest, the works of art which society has deemed great and held as classic. The social or cultural environment is the highest psychic force which is brought to play upon the artist and it influences him in ways of which he is not even aware. Thus his efforts to be absolutely and completely original are foredoomed to partial defeat, just as his fears that being subject to influences means he can do nothing that will survive his own life and times are groundless.

The breakdown of the environment in which the artist lives reveals elements that are not peculiar to the artist but concern everyone. The elements here referred to are the sheer phenomena of the real world as it appears, the qualities of the external world that confronts the senses. The artist is peculiarly susceptible to these, but even for him the task of properly perceiving them is an enormous one. D. H. Lawrence observed of Cézanne that he had a forty-year fight to get to know an apple fully and a jug or two not quite so fully.[1] Thus it is not difficult to understand that to the average man the phenomena pass for the most part unperceived. The elements of the phenomena are highly important to the artist because the artist is more than normally sensitive to the factors both ponderable and imponderable in his environment and because the imponderable factors are suggested to him by the elements of the phenomena. When discussing the sensitivity of the artist with which the artistic process begins, we must not allow ourselves to forget the complex of forces which through that sensitivity have had their effects upon him and left their marks.

The artistic process begins, then, with the sensations of the artist. These of course are excited in him by the qualitative data of the external world. Art is therefore a reaction as well as an expression: a reaction of the artist to the world as well as an expression of the artist's own personality. The same qualitative data are available to everyone. What makes one man an artist and another not is still an open question. Certainly, however, we do know that the artist is more than ordinarily sensitive and that as a consequence his experiences make an unusually lively impression upon him. They matter to him very deeply, perhaps the

---

[1] *The Paintings of D. H. Lawrence.*

most deeply where they concern him the least directly. In fact, the attitude of the true artist may be characterized psychologically as one of *superfluous caring*. He not only experiences the qualities of the external world but he also feels *for* them. Most persons whether they realize it or not are only half awake to the qualities of the external world. The colors, smells, sounds, tastes, textures and pressures that confront the individual make only a half-hearted impression upon him where they make any. The conventional artist, that is, the mediocre artist who receives some prominence in his own day because of the fact that he is readily understood by his contemporaries, is one who calls attention to qualities which have always been faintly or dimly felt by everyone. The *avante-garde* artist, the pioneer in new forms, is one who has undertaken the task of opening the sensations of people to elements in the world around them which they have never before felt.

In addition to qualities, the artist is also sensitive to shapes and patterns, forms which exist in the external world. Such qualities and forms as the artist observes have a special aesthetic meaning for him. The average man lives also by the qualities and forms he observes, but to him they usually have some more pedestrian reading. They mean things to be utilized; raw products to be manufactured, articles to be distributed, advantages or obstacles, friends or foe, etc., etc. But to the artist they do not mean any such thing, at least in so far as the artist is an artist (for every artist is also to some extent many other things: a citizen, a father, a hungry man, etc.). But as an artist, he is not concerned with the utilitarian aspects of what he senses but only with the artistic or aesthetic aspects. And these remain in the realm of qualities and forms *as such,* the realm of elements of phenomena.

The artist begins by appreciating and understanding classic works of art which may fall within his purview. This step is quickly followed by the desire to make a work of art which shall be of his own devising and discovery. The admiration of another's style leads to the imitation of it and then to a new private vision. A sensitivity which can be so highly excited by what exists in the external world has a self-generating property; without additional external experiences it is able to proceed a certain way on its own momentum. For the artist, excited by what *does* exist, goes on to suppose what *could* exist and to be responsive to it. Such a supposition is what is called the imagination, and when employed in a high degree by the artist, the artistic imagination. The artistic imagination is a matter of intensity of awareness. To be able to manipulate the values sensed and the relations known, the individuals and events we learn about, is to have imagination. Thus imagination consists in the qualitative aspect of assuming what could be from what is, both actually and potentially. The man with a vivid imagination is one who can call upon mental images of things as they could be (and in his opinion ought to be) by placing together in new contexts and associations the elements of the actual world with which he was already familiar (but dissatisfied). The scientist as well as the artist possesses imagination to a high degree, but what distinguishes the artist from the scientist is the type of element with which he is chiefly concerned. The imagination of the scientist is concerned chiefly with the universal relations of phenomena as represented by abstractly expressed laws of possibility. The imagination of the artist is concerned chiefly with the universal values of phenomena as represented by concretely expressed, possible objects.

Having distinguished between the imagination of the artist and that of the scientist, we may return to an emphasis on the difference between the imagination of the artist and that of the ordinary man. Once again, what distinguishes the artist from the ordinary man is not the possession of an extraordinarily lively and sensitive imagination. The ordinary man is perfectly capable of imagining things to be other than they are; but while he does so in a more or less desultory fashion, the artist goes on to do something about it: to paint a picture, model a head, or compose a quartet, devoted to things as he thinks they should be or at any rate might be. Thus what characterizes the artist, what starts him on his way, is not his possession of an imagination, for everyone has that, but his possession of *intense* imagination. The artist takes off from experience but so does everyone else, and it is the way in which he uses that experience that characterizes the artist. His peculiar use of his experience is the fact that he is not confined or limited to it but gets control of it in such a way that he discovers something new with it; and it is his high concentration of imagination which makes this possible. Gilbert Murray has pointed out that intensity of imagination is the hallmark of the artist, and that it does not require so very much experience. "Almost the first characteristic which one notes in what we call 'a man of genius' is his power of making a very little experience reach an enormous way."[2] James Joyce left Ireland when he was twenty years old. In 1943, the year of his death at the age of sixty-one, he was still writing about the place of his birth and his early years. The artistic ability is the power to wring an act of experience dry, to extract from it the last drop of meaning and the last little bit of value, which in sum always proves to be greatly more than anyone else had ever suspected there might be in it.

We have arrived at the fact that it is intensity of imagination which makes the artist possible, and we know already that this imagination

[2] *The Rise of the Greek Epic,* 4th ed., p. 251.

works with the material of experience, with data which the sense experience of the artist has allowed him to gather from the external world. The final product of this process is something which once again issues into the external world: the finished work of art which the artist has made. But we have not yet answered the question, How do artists manage to arrive at the discovery of works of art? This is the central problem of the psychology of art. It is admitted by everyone that works of art have their own peculiar order, organization and even internal logic. It is equally admitted that the artist plies his trade intuitively—through feeling, emotion or imagination, as it is called. How does the imagination of the artist manage to discover the elements of order which are forged into the work of art? These are questions which have required in the past and which will continue to require in the future more than a little investigation, but something approaching an answer may be hazarded.

In the first place, imagination has more than intensity as a dimension. It also has breadth. The breadth of imagination is the extent of the field over which it ranges. Intensity and breadth of imagination are the coordinates by means of which the value of imagination can be estimated. Breadth of imagination refers directly to the external world. In fact it means just that: how much of the external world is being included in an act of imagination. The artist works through love, and love does not end with its object but reaches through that object to embrace the entire universe of being. Thus when the painter covers a canvas or when the poet types out a sonnet, he is endeavoring to get into the frame or on the page a great many more values than could ever be literally depicted within so narrow a compass. He is trying to symbolize a large segment of existence. The breadth of imagination in a given work of art can be estimated by the number and size of the values to which the work can be said to have reference. Breadth of imagination is characterized by a sweep of inclusiveness which we cannot fail to recognize in the achievements of the man of genius. The personality and acts of Raskolnikov have for Dostoyevsky and those of Don Quixote have for Cervantes an axiological richness of direct reference far in excess of what can be narrowly attributed to the meaning of the student-murderer or to that poor excuse of a knight on horseback. The truly great artist is able not only to feel the abundance and variety of the values which have been actualized in the world but even to add the feeling of some of those values which could be and ought to be actualized; and he is able to do this within the limits of the small span of operations made possible by the single work of art. But the breadth of the imagination is not the only coordinate which refers to the external world, for the intensity of the imagination does so, too, even though its reference is not as readily evident. Intensity of imagination is an objective affair with the artist. True, it seems to take place within the artist, but we must not lose sight of the fact that it is stimulated in him by things outside him. He has that faculty of imagination which allows him to envisage the things he senses and perceives as existing in new relations. He is one, as Wordsworth so keenly observes of the poet in his Preface to the *Lyrical Ballads,* who is as much affected by the absence as by the presence of things. And he strives to make privately viewed things, or images of things, into public objects, in the light of the way in which he has imagined they could be or ought to be. The sense of style possessed by the artist is actually a sense of the fitness of things, a sense of due proportionality; and since nothing exists for him quite in the way in which he imagines it could be or ought to be, he strives to make it so by means of some image-malleable material.

In the second place, the function of imagination involves more than one psychological level in the artist. The bulk of the artistic imagination takes place in the unconscious or psyche (soul) of the individual. That is to say, the storing and discharge of aesthetic energy takes place in the psyche and not in the consciousness of the artist. The psychological life of the human individual is comparable to the iceberg which is always more than three-quarters submerged. The consciousness floats like a film upon the surface of the unconscious and hardly more than represents the multitudinous activities of the whole psyche. The discharge of the psyche at the level of the unconscious spills over into consciousness, but the storing of its contents does not involve consciousness at all. The inherited and acquired wisdom of the human race—called common sense—is the subject-matter with which the artist deals. He is a myth-maker, a worker in the *sensus communis* who renders our implicitly accepted social beliefs objective through the feeling for their forms. What is technically known now as the unconscious was formerly called the soul. The soul is not merely a storehouse for implicity accepted beliefs and myths; it is also a workhouse where the activities of the psyche which lie below conscious-ness take place. For that there are such activities as unconscious mental processes no modern psychology would permit us to doubt. The artist's inspiration, then, is a manufactured article, produced by the soul from the raw material of experience.

The relation between the conscious and unconscious parts of the psychological realm, between the *nous* and the *psyche,* between the mind and the soul, is still unknown. So far as the psychology of art is con-cerned, however, what we can claim to know is that the artistic process involves them both. The psyche or unconscious or soul alone would not be capable of producing a work of art; nobody has ever become an artist or executed a work of art in a light sleep, though many have tried. The actual writing of *Kubla Khan* was done in the full possession of consciousness, as were De Quincey's lucubrations on opium eating. The modern effort by the surrealists to portray the content of the unconscious under the influence of the Freudian exaggerations is done in a calmly and coldly calculating and thoroughly conscious way. But then the consciousness alone would be equally impotent. Not everything about a work of art can be deliberately planned, and it is the unplanned elements which often intrude themselves that make a work of art great. No artist has ever been entirely rational and none has ever succeeded entirely in the business of guiding the making of a work of art from start to finish. He may begin the process, but somewhere along the line he felicitously loses control, or at least fails in his efforts to exercise full control. Hence it is fair to conclude that the artistic process extends over both the conscious and the unconscious realms.

II

We have now seen something of the tools of the artistic process (the data of experience and the imagination) and also of the places in which the process takes place (the *psyche* and the *nous*). Let us next turn to an examination of the successive steps of the process itself.

Four active stages may be distinguished in the making of a work of art, so far as the psychological aspects of the situation are concerned. These may be described as (1) the reception of the data, (2) the revision in the psyche, (3) the conscious reaction, and (4) the making of the object. It will help to look at each of these separately.

1. The impression which natural objects make upon the mind of the artist is one to which we have previously paid attention. It should be stressed, however, that the imagination of the artist is a faculty which is already present in his reception of the data that come to him from the external world. The apprehension of sense impression is in one way a passive process. The senses are helpless in the hands of the data. If we look at a blue wall, smell a rose perfume, touch a concrete surface, hear an alto flute, or taste a salt mackerel, we are powerless to alter, change or avoid the blue sight, the rose odor, the rough touch, the shrill sound or the salt taste. The mind of the artist is a sensitive mechanism like a photographic plate which receives, enters, stores and records the impressions made upon it by the phenomena of the external world. In quite another way, however, the apprehension of sense impressions is active. For the mind is able to *select* that part of the external world from

which it wishes to receive its sense impressions. We are able to focus the camera containing the photographic plate upon any object we choose. It is in this latter, active connection that the imagination of the artist already plays a part. For the artistic imagination gets to work first in helping to select the area of the environment from which it is intended to make a further selection, this time of the impressions. The composer of music will direct his attention toward sounds rather than any other sense data, and among sounds he will seek for the kind he prefers; although of course, having selected them and directed his sense organs toward them, he is helpless in their hands and cannot avoid hearing whatever noises enter into the pinna and meatus of his ears.

The reception of the data does not have to be a fresh experience upon every occasion. By data itself is meant the raw experienced material of the external world; but this may have been received upon some past occasion and stored in the memory, and the imaginative act of receiving the data may often be merely a matter of recalling it from memory. The characteristic emotional quality of the reception of the data is the feeling of surprise, and this may occur as much from an act of memory as from a fresh experience. The surprise comes from the fact that the recipient did not expect the data to be exactly what it was. The data always has with it some element of novelty; and so freshness is a concomitant quality of the reception, whether it be a new reception from the external world or a recollection. We are always a little startled by our memories, since we do not ever know exactly what they will bring back to us. In one sense, every reception of the data whether from raw experience or from memory, is a first reception; and in this sense it is not untrue to say that every reception is a reception of data from raw experience.

2. The data received by the conscious mind are next turned over to the psyche, or the unconscious, for revision. It is there that they are actually combined and distributed and in general wholly assimilated. The part played by the unconscious in the artistic process is so large that it may be said to be the chief part. But the duration of its functioning has been described as a fallow period, because the unconscious works while the artist himself may be unaware or only vaguely aware of its working. The artist is usually not aware of its entire functioning, although he may at this time feel like doing little else. If he does anything, it tends to be something irrelevant, and often physical, and usually simple: fishing, sawing wood, or perhaps even desultory reading. From the public point of view it is a period of sterility because the audience is not able to detect in it any act of productivity by the artist. Lay persons are not able to see that this in in a way the artist's most productive time. For it is undoubtedly true that appearances are here deceiving.

This second period of revision in the psyche may be described as one of chaos. Within the soul of the artist all is confusion. What emerges may be clear, for it is the task of the artist to clarify the confusion; but there can be no act of clarification where there is no confusion. A work of art can issue only from the placing of data in new relations and the seeing of new connections between things, and this step is actually made possible by chaos and confusion. In chaos all things rub shoulders with all things, and hence new connections may be detected by chance and seized. Of course the chaos must have present within it the seed of order, else it is merely chaos. But that is what it means to have the chaos existing within the soul of an artist. Nietzsche, who understood the artist so very well, observed somewhere in *Also Sprach Zarathustra* that it is necessary to have chaos within one in order to give birth to a dancing star, a kind of poetic description of a very essential stage in the artistic process. The artistic soul is a female base, a sort of meeting place and breeding ground where values assemble, unite, and give birth to something new. It is what the chemists call a culture medium, a very thick, largely neutral, field, one in which catalysis is made possible on a statistical basis. A very great many typewriter keys have been completely worn out in the effort to describe what is essentially indescribable, namely the soul of the artist. Except for the tendency toward regularity, which is by nature an affair of statistical probability, and which is felt emotionally by the artist as a longing to bring order into the world, the disorder in the artist's soul has no features except its featurelessness. The properties of chaos will not stand enumeration. But the necessary and essential function which this particular chaos performs is obvious. It makes new combinations possible and hence new artistic insights.

3. The perception by the artist of these new combinations is an exciting experience, one of which he is keenly aware. In the field of chaos the new relations and values sought are suddenly seized, to be utilized in the making of the work of art. This seizure takes place at the moment when the artistic process spills over from the unconscious area into the consciousness. The act is a sudden one, dynamic, and even frenzied. When the artist grasps a new vision, he feels like the pioneer and the discoverer which he unquestionably is. It is for him a period of exalted sensibility. He has had a new revelation and his state for the moment at least is one of unspeakable joy. It is something like that divine madness of which the ancients spoke, a period of quick insight, galvanic action and high excitement for the artist. That "inspiration," which is held to be the sole and sufficient equipment of the artist by so many laymen, is another name for the immediate perception of new relations and values which takes place on this occasion.

The witness of artists concerning this stage in the artistic process is not far to seek. We have abundant evidence at hand of what it feels like to be inspired in this particular fashion. Perhaps the most graphic descriptions come from two composers, Mozart and Beethoven. Mozart, for instance, declared that he did not hear the separate parts of a musical composition (which after all take some time in order to be played) one at a time and successively but rather all together (*"gleich alles zusammen"*),[3] and Beethoven confirmed this by declaring that the artist sees his whole composition in a single projection (*"in einem Gusse"*).[4]

Thus the artistic process which took place chiefly in the unconscious (*psyche*) hands its product over to the conscious mind (*nous*), and the conscious mind receives it in a state of heightened excitement. There can be little doubt that such is the faculty which the artist exclusively possesses, and this is important to bear in mind provided only that we bear in mind also the fact that the conscious stage is the end-product of a process which began in the unconscious.

4. The actual external and public act of making a work of art follows hard upon the conscious reaction to the perception of new relations in the psyche. There is not much that can be said about this last and final stage in the process. Nearly everyone has seen some artist at work, writing down words or notes, carving in stone, or painting on canvas. This last part of the process, for which the preceding parts may be said to have existed, is predominantly a matter of the keenest consciousness though not entirely so. The unconscious spills over, as we have seen, and in spilling over colors the work of the conscious mind. An artist is often if not always surprised to view his finished work, and he may wonder at it and not be entirely able to recall elements in the work which he does not remember having executed, or remembers only vaguely. For the finished work of art does not exactly resemble any of the elements that went into its composition any more than it exactly resembles the aggregate of them. A finite whole is at a higher axiological level than any of its parts or the sum of its parts. The phenomena of the external world which the artist first received have undergone a radical revision and alteration; and the mind, as well as the psyche to which it belongs, has acted as a tool which the finished product leaves behind. Even the artist, a chaotic creature possessed with the striving for order, is eventually an alien before his own work of art—which when finished may be said logically to be no

---

[3] Quoted in Julius Portnoy, *A Psychology of Art Creation* (Philadelphia, 1942, privately printed), p. 27. In this doctoral thesis there has been assembled much important documentary material concerning the artist's own impressions of what he holds the artistic process on its psychological side to be.

[4] *Op. cit.*, p. 32.

more his own than it is anyone else's. In the making of a work of art, however, the whole artist has been at work, with his soul, his conscious mind, his terrible intensity and devotion of effort, his whole being. And he experiences a feeling of relief, of letdown, of emptiness, as well as of accomplishment, when a particular work of art is completed and done.

III

We have now, after examining the psychological tools with which the artistic process is conducted, enumerated and considered the four psychological stages in the production of a work of art. Our task is not yet completed, for we have to consider the logical analysis of the psychological process. The time is almost gone when it was erroneously believed that psychology could throw light upon logic. In the nineteenth century it was falsely supposed that logic was a branch of psychology. The advent of a new logic and the abandonment of the subjectivistic metaphysics has led us to see that logic cannot be a branch of psychology since it applies to more things than enunciated or thought propositions, and since the logic of propositions itself is not entirely a mental affair. Logic is close to ontology, and has relevancy to world conditions, whereas human psychology is confined to the theory of the psyche alone. Thus logic is broader than psychology; and where logic can throw light upon psychology in so far as thinking is or endeavors to be logical, psychology can throw no light upon logic but only upon the logical elements in the process of reasoning. Psychological processes are by no means confined to logic, because not all psychological processes can be reduced to reasoning. But in so far as reasoning, and hence its logical elements, is involved in the psychological processes, a logical analysis of psychological procedures is elucidatory and helpful.

In the psychology of artistic expression, logical form exists as a kind of structural framework. For the making of any work of art, there are (1) postulates, (2) a method, (3) applications and (4) a conclusion.

1. The postulates of a work of art are those ideas or feelings or both which the artist decides he wishes to express. They are not always conscious, they are never fully conscious; and they are not necessarily all adopted at once. A painter may see something in a face which he wishes to use, a composer may hear a combination of sounds, a choreographer may see a group of work-movements, or anyone of these persons may merely have a feeling which stimulates him to some kind of particular expression. The choice of acceptance of postulates is, in the terminology of logic, an inductive procedure. The logical choosing of postulates

usually means that a deductive system has been seen in an inductive flash. It takes place, in the terminology of psychology, by means of intuition. The highest performance of artistic insight is required to fulfill this first step. It is where genius first comes into active play.

It is important to add, however, that artistic intuition or insight is no bolt from the blue. Hard training and complete devotion are prerequisites. Indeed, the elementary steps in the process are all but impossible to trace. What makes a man want to become an artist to begin with? Apprenticeship to art, once a man has decided that this is the career for him, may be somewhat irregular but is none the less arduous and prolonged. He must practice concentratedly and at great length in studying the greatest of his predecessors, in imitating their work, and then in trying to do something tentatively on his own. Thus by the time, when as an adult and professional artist, he comes to choose the postulates for a particular artistic enterprise on which he wishes to embark, he has behind him, upon which he not only can draw but does draw during every moment of his active life as a practicing artist, long successions of inductive and deductive procedures. He has already seen and tried a good deal and also drawn conclusions from what he has seen and tried. It is a familiar fact that conspicuously great insights in the field of art do not come to capable politicians or manufacturers or scientists, or indeed to anyone except artists. Thus it would be idle for the present purposes to attempt to say which comes first in the artistic process, induction or deduction. In the actual choosing of postulates, induction is first, but then such inductive steps are based upon a long deductive as well as inductive background.

The inductive step which consists in the choosing of postulates is a leap to the conditions which shall determine the making of a given work of art, which thus far only exists as a plan in the artist's mind (but which already exists as a logical possibility in the external world, else its making could never take place). Once the postulates are chosen the artist is to that extent no longer free; he cannot arbitrarily do whatever he wanted to do but only what the postulates allow him to do; he has by accepting them set up his own restrictive conditions. Of course, it is true that he can do whatever he wishes to do, subject to change without notice; but in making any radical changes which involve violations of his postulates he is in effect abandoning those particular postulates in favor of another set. For he cannot execute an orderly work without the consistency which adherence to postulates assures, and he must be confined within the limits set up by the adoption of one set or another.

Let us suppose that a novelist plans a new book. He has decided on the scene, the date, the plot and the characters together with their relationships to each other. These are his postulates and by them he must be guided. The characters must act in a way consistent with their period and perform according to their own peculiarities. The novelist was free in the beginning to write about anything that interested him. He could have chosen to compose a historical novel about any date, place and people; or a detective novel, with equal latitude; or a contemporary novel; and so forth. But his choice was an act of self-binding; and now, having chosen, he finds himself no longer free. He must abide by the demands of the rules which he has established for himself.

2. The adoption of a method of artistic expression is part of the acceptance of postulates. Although absolutely essential, in that there can be no work of art made without some method, the method is theorematic; for *what* is to be done takes logical as well as temporal precedence over *how* it is to be done, and the selection of postulates must follow this order. This is true of method in what we shall here term the narrow sense. The selection of a method in the broad sense actually precedes the selection of postulates for any particular work of art. For when a man decides on a career in a particular art, that decision means that he has chosen his method in the broad sense. He may, for instance, decide to become a graphic artist, and among the graphic arts he may choose to specialize in etching. Thus he chooses his method in the broad sense. But then he is confronted with the task of doing one etching at a time, and each time he must choose his postulates: what is the etching to be about? He selects a person or a scene which in his opinion will be a very exciting subject for an etching. He had, we recall, already chosen his postulates, and now he faces the task of choosing his method in the narrow sense. How is this particular problem at hand to be approached and by what means? That is the problem to be solved next, and it is entirely a question of approach, of method in the narrow sense.

The task of adopting a method logically is a matter of induction, just as was the choosing of postulates. Like the choice of postulates also, the induction to a method is only possible to those possessing a long deductive and inductive background, based on training in the particular field. The method may also be conceived as confining and restrictive to a certain degree, even though it is specifically devoted to means and constitutes a tool whereby the end desired may be sought and perhaps reached. Thus the method is liberating as well as restricting in that it finds a way to do what is desired.

The psychological term for induction is intuition. The correct method for the special occasion (i.e., method in the narrow sense) is decided in a flash of insight. This takes place in a half controlled, half uncontrolled, way, partly in the conscious mind but also partly in the psyche or unconscious. We do not always know what led us to see that a certain way of doing a particular work of art was the only proper way of doing it, given the end we wished to achieve. But we know that once having seen it we are bound by it. And so we understand that our method forms an integral part of the postulates we have adopted and from which all procedure must start.

3. The applications of the postulates according to the method consist in the actual steps taken to produce the work of art. These may be, as we have said, the modeling of clay, the writing of notes of music, the writing of lines of poetry, the applying of paint to canvas, or any other specific procedures involving physical action and intended to produce an independent and public product. This is the part of the process which may be viewed objectively. An artist seen at work is generally an artist engaged on this stage of his project. This step is confused in the lay mind with the whole process, whereas it is merely the third step in a series.

The applications are physical but they are also susceptible to logical analysis. It is the very fact that they do constitute a *third* step in the process which makes it possible for us to view the temporal succession of this process with the tools of logical analysis and to see that the applications are largely a matter of deductions. Given the postulates and the method, only a certain number of possibilities exist; and these are actually and physically drawn in the making of a work of art. The drawing of such deductions may be an easy affair or a difficult one, a brief task or one of long duration. The determination of just what deductions may be drawn given the postulates and the method is not always so easy as it sounds. Only a genius of the stature of a J. S. Bach can tell exactly what variations a theme will lend itself to, and only a poet of the size of Dante can determine what events will be permitted to certain characters and scenes. The deductions may be drawn in a hurry or they may take years to work out. Voltaire's *Candide* was written in a few weeks, but Flaubert took many years to pare down the writing of *Madame Bovary*. Both works of art are of great value, and such value is not proportional in any way to the time spent on their composition.

Those who view logic in the old, narrow way experience some difficulty in seeing any objective and actual physical action as related to propositions. The whole of logic is held by them to be identical with the logic of propositions. Of course, it is by propositions that we analyze logic. The business of logic as an abstract affair does not require any charades; we do not need to produce a boy holding a bird in order to explain for logical purposes what we mean when we say, "The boy holds the bird," though indeed such would be the actual reference. But when we deny the validity of the logical content of the actual boy actually holding the actual bird, we deny that our theoretical logic has any practical applications, i.e., that logical propositions are true outside of the realm of theoretical logic itself. But assuredly it is so, else there would be no use to logic. Hence the theoretical deductions from the logical postulates and method adopted for the production of a given work of art are actually used in what we have termed the applications, which themselves therefore consist in actual deductions.

If an artist did not have a certain plan in mind, he could never execute a work of art. But what does it mean to have a "plan in mind" if not the conception, however vague, of a set of postulates, a method, both theoretically held, and a determination to work them out in practice deductively? And of what use would the plan be were it not to be worked out in the objective and external world as a set of purposive actions? Any such purposive action, following a certain order and with a certain end in view, may be said to be a planned action. And where its postulates, method and aim include general propositions, it may be said to be deductive in nature. Hence the matter of applications, or in other words, the execution of a work of art, is primarily deductive.

4. The conclusion of the artistic process consists in the finished work of art together with its meaning. When the last application has been made, the work of art stands completed, a whole thing, destined perhaps to lead a life of its own in the social world. Its meaning may not be easy of access or of abstraction, yet it must exist.

Logically, the conclusion is the last deduction to be drawn. It must follow from the postulates, be made possible by the method, and be akin to the applications. In the novel it would be exemplified by the final unraveling of the plot. In sculpture, it would be those last, finishing touches from which the meaning of the whole often emerges. The conclusion of a work of art is hard to come by, for it is not constituted by the last note in a symphony or the last word in a play, but rather by the whole which the last parts complete. The situation is similar to that of a picture puzzle where the entire picture is meaningless until the very last piece has been put into place. It is *not* similar to a chain before the last link has been added. The conclusion of a work of art does not depend upon the most recent or the most advanced steps taken but upon *all* the steps taken. It is that for which the whole exists and not merely that which comes at the end. This is the most obvious in musical compositions, for assuredly the coda does not carry the meaning of the whole, which instead depends upon every part: upon the announcement of the theme, and upon each one of the variations. But the conclusions, despite this peculiarity which is one characteristic of all candidly axiological organizations, is deductive by nature since, though it follows from the whole rather than from the last part, it does, after all, follow logically—as an implication in the actual exemplification of a general proposition by an actual particular proposition.

IV

We have now considered the psychological tools with which the artist works, the psychological stages in the production of a work of art, and the logical analysis of the psychological process. We are obliged to add some final remarks on the process as a whole.

It will be remembered that we have observed four stages in the psychological process and also four stages of logical analysis. The question obviously arises of whether the four psychological stages are closely related to the four logical steps. The answer is that to some extent they are related, although the correspondence is not exactly one to one, as we might superficially be led to expect. The best explanation of the relationship will be given by comparing them in detail for points of similarity and difference.

The first pair to be compared, then, is: "the reception of the data" (psychological) and "the postulates" (logical). These are of course very close. The reception of the sense data from the objective and external world (which includes the artist's social environment as well as his physical, chemical and biological environment) carries in with it certain propositions which the artist henceforth holds in his psyche or unconscious to be true. This is another and longer way of saying that his beliefs come to him from the external world. To view them as postulates rather than as received data is to make the distinction between values and their logical analysis. The relationship is a very intimate one indeed, for the bonds between an axiological whole and its logical part are closer than those between things which are strongly similar.

The second pair to be compared is: "the revision in the psyche" (psychological) and "the adoption of a method" (logical). The connection between them is not so obvious as it was between the previous ones. The confusion within the artist may be said to be a necessary concomitant of his search for a method, since here we see quite plainly that, while we have distinguished a method and the other postulates, there is no absolute division between them, and a method is an integral part of that which is to be accomplished by the method. When something definite emerges from the psychic chaos, it takes the form of the way in which the problem can be executed; the artist grasps suddenly not only what is to be done to produce a particular work of art but also how it is to be done. Hence the revision in the psyche and the adoption of a method are closely related, though not quite in the same way as the reception of the data was related to the postulates. For the revision in the psyche is the emotional turmoil from which the logical definiteness of the adopted method is produced.

The third pair to be compared is: "the conscious reaction" (psychological) and "the applications" (logical). The conscious reaction is what drives the artist to make the applications, which is only another way of saying that when the artist sees what is to be done he begins to do it. Consciousness, we might say, is the instrument which enables action to follow what in the content of the unconscious it is believed ought to be enacted. When the artist commences a work of art and proceeds with its execution, he does so because his beliefs as to what should be done and how to do it have risen to the level of awareness whereby he is enabled to do it. Thus the relationship between conscious reaction and applications is much the same as we found it to be between the revision in the psyche and the adoption of a method; the former is the feeling from which the specific determination of the latter is produced.

The fourth and last pair to be compared is: "the making of the object" (psychological) and "the conclusion" (logical). The artist in making a work of art of course regards every part from the point of view of its contribution to the whole. Hence throughout his labors he manifests a constant concern for the finished product, which we have already noted logically to be the conclusion. In other words, the psychological processes which go on while the artist is actually occupied with the making of a work of art lead inevitably to that last deduction which we have termed the conclusion. Thus the relationship between the making of the object and the conclusion is primarily a consequential one.

We are now as a result of our studies in a position to understand the artistic imagination a little better. Some outstanding features immediately present themselves. One feature is that the artistic imagination does not depend on facts so much as it does on logic. Indeed it takes off from facts about things-as-they-are but soon departs for the realm of things-as-they-ought-to-be or could-be. The case for the artist rather than the seeker after facts is, paradoxically, well presented by—of all people— the historian, Herodotus, when he remarks that: "As for the tale of Abaris, who is said to have been a Hyperborean, and to have gone with his arrow all round the world without once eating, I shall pass it by in silence. This much, however, is clear: if there are Hyperboreans, there must also be Hypernotians." (Bk. IV.) The facts of the artistic imagination consist in whatever have been accepted as postulates, whether factually true or not—usually not. Once the postulates have been accepted and a method adopted along with them, the artist must follow his logic which is no less inexorable for not being based on facts. The world of the artist is not only a never-never land, it is also an if-then region; it is conditional and hypothetical, so that one thing will follow if another be accepted.

Another feature of the artistic imagination is that it is no less imaginative for being logical. We are enabled to analyze the wildest products of the imagination because of the logic that is in them; but that logic did not ever prevent them from being wild. The affective part of imagination is a value affair, an affair of feeling, insight, emotion. The logical part is one of analysis, element, relation. There is no conflict between them; each complements and needs the other and each makes the other possible. Conflict arises only when it is supposed that either could exist without the other or could take the place of the other; and this conflict chiefly occurs in theory which is erroneous and in the studied application of erroneous theory according to a fixed and conscious formula, more rarely in intuitively guided practice.

From a functional point of view, perhaps the most significant feature of the artistic imagination is that it consists in a kind of aesthetic judgment. The artist is required to do more than merely to grasp new possibilities of relations and values; he must in the act of imagining seize upon *important* new possibilities of relations and values, that is, upon right relations and meaningful values. The artist could, conceivably, imagine anything. But the situation does not long remain one involving such vagueness of generality. For he does in fact imagine something. This something which he imagines entails a selection from among all the possible things which he could have imagined. He selects the one he does on the basis of aesthetic preference: it is better for his artistic purposes than were others not selected. Hence imagination involves judgment.

The field of application in this connection has of course its own natural limits. These are set up for it by the distinction between form and content. Too great an emphasis upon content leads to sentimentality in art and to a kind of formlessness which approaches the limits of not-art. Undue emphasis on method may lead to a rigidity and even to a superficiality which approaches the same confines. The absolute effort at abstraction leads toward a content-less art. The absolute effort at slavish reproduction leads to a pure representation which must compete with mechanical reproduction by the camera. Between these extremes lies symbolism, a method which employs both degrees of representation and abstraction but achieves a qualitative symbolism which is more artistic than either extreme. The paintings of Braque and Miro are examples of extreme abstraction; the sculptures of Jo Davidson tend in the direction of extreme representation; while the canvases of Cézanne furnish instances of the successful performances of the method of symbolism. The method of symbolism employs the artistic imagination upon a sound basis of perception plus imagination, without the loss of logic and aim. This means that the aesthetic judgment is best able to fulfill its requirement of due proportionality in the production of works of art. If this last statement be interpreted as a defense of academic work in art or as a rejection of all innovation, then it is being misunderstood. Due proportionality does not mean conservatism, or the golden mean conceived as a middle-of-the-road, compromise policy. It involves giving the imagination full sway but within the wide limits of logic rather than of some more restrictive formula.

The proposition that the artistic imagination consists in a kind of aesthetic judgment has important implications, so far as the nature of the psychology of aesthetics is concerned. The act of judging is subjective but that which is judged must be objective, although this has from time to time been denied. Spinoza, for instance, was explicit in asserting that he did not attribute to nature either beauty or deformity, order or confusion. But if artistic imagining involves judging, then it cannot be true, as he goes on to assert, that "only in relation to our imagination can things be called beautiful or ugly, well-ordered or confused." The position upon which aesthetic judging depends claims, to the contrary, that only in relation to the imagination do things make the *impression* of beauty or ugliness, orderliness or confusion, and that their condition of actually being so, whichever they are, does not depend in any way upon the impression they make. The artistic imagination selects from among possible things according to their aesthetic worth, and this involves beyond a doubt some sort of aesthetic judgment.

The impact of the world upon the artist stimulates him to the production of works of art. After the process has been gone through, there is a change to be observed all around. The artist is no longer the same but older and wiser and emotionally a little more used up as well as a little more educated. And the world is the better for containing a new element which is the work of art. Since the work of art did not exist before its making except as elements and a possibility, it is something new. But in a sense also, what is discovered is not new; what is new is the discovery. Human "creations" are after all only discoveries. Thus the artist is a pioneer, and his field of pioneering is that possible world of what could exist. We can only hope to find what we can suppose there could be. The greatest artist is he who looks for and finds the greatest beauty.

Culturally speaking, art is an all-or-nothing venture. It cannot be done halfway. The fairly good artist is not, like the fairly good business man, doing something fairly well. Art will not stand for compromise; the man who temporizes is badly hurt and has nothing to show for his pains. Bad art, even fairly bad art, is much worse than no art at all. The artist cannot approach his task, one might say his dedication, with any reservations. If what he has to give to art is not enough, he is the loser and there is no gainer. He has to have something important to give and he has to give it all. He must be prepared to give everything and to expect nothing in return, on the assumption that if he receives nothing it will be well.

It is a truism that an artist cannot hope to be great who lacks technique. Art has a technical side, which includes some kind of acquired predisposition plus a long apprenticeship to the method and materials of art. But the greatness of an artist is measured by the breadth of his interest more than by the excellence of his technique. Bad technique can be partly overlooked, limited interest never can be. This is the main difference between a major and a minor artist. Given the same technique, the major artist is the one who concerns himself with cosmical themes, as for example in the plays of Aeschylus. The minor artist is more parochial in the selection of his thematical material and is frequently preoccupied with matters of style, as for instance in the novels of Hemingway. By this criterion, Chekhov, for instance, verges on greatness, Shakespeare, like the Greek dramatists, achieves it, while Flaubert and Dickens fall short of it. Breadth of interest is closely related to that concern on the part of the artist for the qualities and form of the external world which do not concern him so far as his survival and physical well-being are at stake and the survival and well-being of his family, neighbors and social group. The artist, in other words, has both interest in and love of the external world, but for its own sake and not for what it can do for him. This concern and interest and love is what we have earlier termed "superfluous caring." The hallmark of the true artist is his superfluous caring.

What it means to be an artist is evident in the personality of an old artist, a man who has, so to speak, been filled up and emptied many times, worn out with superfluous caring. Temporarily, however, the psychic figure of the artist is not improved by giving birth to a work of art. The chaos which remains in the psyche of the artist is left over, like afterbirth, in the making of a perfect thing. Even if he is a great artist and well recognized as such, this does not alter the internal circumstances which accompany the production of a work of art.

But the fate of an artist, so far as external circumstances are concerned, does not depend upon the value of his work so much as it does upon the recognition of that value by his contemporaries. If he is exploiting the values which have received favorable current regard, he will be applauded; if he is celebrating values which have been received with favor in the past and which have retained a sort of sentimental and nostalgic worth according to current evaluations, he will be applauded; but if he is attempting to actualize values which have not as yet been even recognized in current evaluations, the chances are that he will be either ridiculed or ignored—preferably the former, though probably the latter, for in the case of the former any kind of attention may turn eventually to understanding and appreciation. The nature of the public reception of the work has of course its due effect upon the psychological makeup of the artist himself. He may become disproportionately discouraged or egocentric and arrogant. Since contemporary recognition of great art is far from the rule, he is more apt to be discouraged; and many artists are given to much complaining about their unhappy lot. The predicament of the living artist is that of any reformer, for the artist, in his desires and efforts to depict things other and better than they are, that is, as they ought to be and could be, is a reformer.

The artist is apt to dramatize and overemphasize the tragedy and pathos of his role. But any idealist who at the same time must live in the world is in a sense in the position of cutting the ground from under his own feet: he depends upon social relations in order to continue his existence so long as he must eat, wear clothes and live under some kind of shelter; and yet he remains discontented with the imperfect society which produces such things for him. So far as the good of the artist and of everyone else is concerned, however, this is to be swallowed and borne, not dwelt on in any self-pitying way. The artist in most cases does lead a thankless existence; but despite the truth of that circumstance, his whinnying still has a disgusting sound. He should and must learn to bear his slights, his pains, his neglect, in silence, in dignified silence. Even if he knows in his heart that the silence which greets his work is like that of an unpaid debt and will probably not continue after his death and the subsequent recognition of his work, he can do little except bear it—for bear it he must if it is not to weigh him down and crush out of him his art-producing capabilities.

The artist has an important role to play in society. He himself lies directly in the path of the route which nature takes to produce a work of art. Hence his psychological faculties, which must be attuned to the sensitive and yet powerful task of furthering the artistic progress of nature, are complicated in the extreme. It is unlikely that these faculties have been fully explained here, but if something of their peculiarities has been laid bare so that further investigators may have a clue, the attempt to describe them has not been undertaken in vain.

PHILOSOPHICAL BELIEF: A DIALOGUE

In this dialogue, a theoretical position with respect to the nature of individual and social beliefs is illustrated by a set of interviews. It is necessary to begin with a statement of the theoretical position presented by means of definitions. However, nothing more final is intended by them than the formulation of an hypothesis. The report of the interviews is based on notes made at the time, supplemented from memory.

PRELIMINARY DEFINITIONS

Every individual has a security system consisting in a set of retention schemata. There is always a private retention schema and a public one. By "private retention schema" is meant an unconscious set of experientially acquired and emotionally accepted and endorsed dispositional states. The private retention schema has a core of stability and a peripheral area of change; it requires and receives occasional reinforcement.

By "public retention schema" is meant a system of social beliefs interpreted as rules of procedure whereby cognition is enabled on the one hand to apply its fundamental categories to sort out the data subsequently disclosed to sense experience and on the other to guide behavior.

The elements of the two schemata are rarely sorted. The private schema is peculiar to a given individual; the public schema common to all members of a given culture. The two schemata together constitute the beliefs of the individual. But there is no dead storage, as in a computer; some of the beliefs must be revised from time to time as new information is received or new relations between bits of stored information detected.

The retention schemata are the results of continuing inquiry. When there is too little or too much belief, a pathological situation results. To borrow an analogy, a liquid schema would not allow sufficient retention; a solid schema would not permit the slightest revision; a colloid or plastic schema would provide for both. When there is no belief except inquiry, even of a provisional nature, then there is no integrity, no order, no direction. When beliefs are entirely settled, then the consequent absoluteness makes for a rigidity which is non-adaptive.

The following experiment in mental health was undertaken to determine whether an overly rigid set of retention schemata could be broken and active inquiry restored.

THE SUBJECT

The subject was a German emigrant thirty-five years of age, educated at Heidelberg. He had gone into the furniture business in Düsseldorf, was married to a Jewish girl and the father of one child. When the Nazis came to power, he emigrated with his family to New York where he succeeded in making a connection with a business similar to his former one. He was highly successful in business both in the country of his origin and in that of his adoption.

A healthy man of average size with a commanding presence, his attitude indicated an assumed superiority. He had little patience with disagreement. Preliminary conversations revealed an excellent memory and a considerable preference for the German intellectual background which he had acquired through education and experience. In the University he had been interested primarily in philosophy, and he continued to read philosophy exclusively, and he interpreted Greek philosophy altogether through German premises. He gave an impression of a powerful personality, without, however, its usual charm.

PRELIMINARY DISCUSSION

The subject was first encountered on a number of social occasions. He seemed unimpressed by a common philosophical interest but was willing and even sometimes eager to continue philosophical discussion, the discussion of which, however, was to inform the author, not enlighten the subject. Although an amateur, he regarded himself as more than the equal of all non-German professionals because he was German. He made it perfectly clear that he had nothing to learn from non-Germans.

All references to prominent British and American philosophers he accordingly dismissed with a shrug. The Germans were authorities, and everything else had been learned from them. Each reference to a particular non-German philosopher was traced by him immediately to an earlier German. Bertrand Russell, for instance, he said owed his metaphysics to Leibniz, his theory of knowledge to Meinong, and his logic to Frege. He knew that the American pragmatists, Peirce and James, had derived their doctrine from Kant. This led to a discussion of Kant.

FIRST INTERVIEW

A. [*the author*]. Have you read Hegel's criticisms of Kant?

S. [*the subject*]. Hegel's points are more telling than those of others who have tried to demolish Kant's position. Nevertheless they can be answered. I don't think Hegel really understood Kant.

A. Kant is not easily understood, is he?

S. Not easily, no. I began his *Critique of Pure Reason* when a student, and I have not failed to read in it at least once every day since.

A. Do you think it that important?

S. I certainly do. It answers all the philosophical questions that had gone unanswered since the Greeks first raised them.

A. What about the friends of your undergraduate days, did they agree with you about the importance of Kant?

S. Not all, certainly. Many of them did, I should say a bare majority.

A. And friends made since then, your business acquaintances, for instance?

S. Very few of my friends share my enthusiasm for Kant or for philosophy, especially in America. With my business associates I have never had the time to discuss such matters. There was always business to be conducted. However, I could not help noticing that most Germans are Kantians whether they know it or not.

A. What do you make of the fact that Kant's parents were Scotch people who had settled in Germany? The family name was "C-a-n-t" before Immanuel Kant changed the spelling.

S. Kant was born in Germany, and he gave the highest expression to the German spirit.

[*The private retention schema of the subject has been constructed by employing the commonly accepted interpretation of Kant's* Critique. *There was no disposition to question it. The private and public retention schemata largely overlap; the subject is not psychotic.*]

A. What about the philosophers since Kant's time?

S. They could have saved their trouble. There has been no need for them.

A. Including the German philosophers?

S. Yes.

A. Husserl and Heidegger as well as Hegel?

S. Yes, they were not good Kantians.

A. But what about the problems of a philosophical nature which have occurred as a result of social events since Kant's day?

S. They could be solved by the proper application of Kant's system. We do not need new philosophers; originality in that field has been rendered superfluous. But we do need Kantians.

A. You mean qualified Kant scholars who could apply Kant's philosophy to contemporary situations?

S. Yes, that's what I mean.

A. Are there no problems that such an approach could not solve?

S. No.

A. Is it not possible that by getting outside of Kant's framework another and more insightful position might be undertaken, one which is perhaps more inclusive because of the new scientific knowledge which has developed in the last century and a half?

S. There are other positions, certainly, but they are less inclusive rather than more. They resemble the pre-Kantian philosophers. It is not reasonable to behave as though Kant had not lived.

[*Since for the subject, all inquiry into philosophical fields had long been terminated, and the subject had been alerted as to the importance of reaffirming this, there was no point in pursuing the topic further at this time.*]

SECOND INTERVIEW

The second interview took place a week later. The subject seemed anxious to resume the discussion.

S. The last time we talked you said nothing as to your own philosophical preferences. Are you a Kantian?

A. That depends on what you mean by a Kantian. I think that Kant made a considerable contribution, but I am inclined to view his philosophy critically as he himself claimed to view all other philosophies. I think there are flaws in his work.

S. There are no flaws. One either accepts Kant or one does not.

A. Surely a man as intelligent as you has other interests. Even if we were to agree about Kant's importance there would be other things to talk about in the domain of ideas. What other intellectual interests do you have?

S. Only one, mathematics. Particularly geometry—topology and the like.

A. Was this in Heidelberg?

S. It began in Heidelberg but like my interest in Kant, it has persisted.

A. You read mathematics now?

S. Yes, when I can find the time. I try to keep up by subscribing to some of the journals.

A. But surely learning mathematics by yourself is most difficult. This is a drill topic, like logic. One needs to have it explained, and then one needs to be rehearsed. There is a good deal of rote learning involved. Isn't the classroom the best place?

S. Of course it is. Especially if you plan to become a mathematician or to apply mathematics in a particular way, such as in mechanical engineering. I have found out, however, that there are two levels of understanding in mathematics. The one we have been talking about is for the man who wishes to operate it. He must be able to solve equations, derive formulas and the rest. For him there are few short cuts.

A. That's not your type of interest?

S. No, I am content with the second level of understanding. I want merely to grasp the concepts, not derive the formulas. It is possible to comprehend what the mathematicians are doing without being able to do it one's self. I can watch, for instance, while a geometrician solves what is for him at least a simple problem: finding the locus of the midpoints of a set of parallel chords of an ellipse; and I know perfectly well what he is doing, but I could not do it.

A. Is that satisfactory to you?

S. Yes. It has to be. Because that way I understand many of the more complex problems and their solutions. What I want most is to *understand* mathematics, not to do it.

[*The next question was a leading one. It would be no good if he could see where it was likely to take him. He was blinded, however, by the obscuring strength of his own dogmatism. He was an absolutist with respect to his own knowledge, and could not entertain the thought that it might contain contradictions.*]

A. You are familiar, of course, with the non-Euclidean geometries?

S. Indeed. Riemann and, to a somewhat lesser extent, Lobachevsky have made powerful and distinctive contributions.

A. I thought that the geometries of Riemann and Lobachevsky were equivalent. Riemannian geometry treats of convex surfaces while Lobachevskian deals with concave. Why do you say, "a lesser extent"?

[*Riemann was German, Lobachevsky Russian.*]

S. The Riemannian plane is the surface of a sphere, the Lobachevskian plane the interior of a circle. In astronomy, it is only the convex surfaces of stars and planets which are available to observations by our instruments. The convex inner surfaces are not.

[*Since it appeared that there would be another interview, it was deemed expedient to terminate the present one on this note.*]

THIRD INTERVIEW

A. I have been thinking that you are a superior sort of citizen to have your high quality of interests. There are not many business men who do.

S. That is true. Making a living is one thing, and one's private life quite another. Considerable ingenuity is required in industry. I see no reason to sink below its requirements when I have leisure time.

A. The tired banker in New York tries to find a sentimental musical comedy in the evening.

S. I know that, yes. Sometimes I have to go with him for business reasons, and when that is necessary I do not express any opinion contrary to his. I always pretend to find the musical entertaining. When I am alone it is different. I try to find a good performance of Bach or Mozart. Nothing later than the eighteenth century. I do not want to be entertained, as they say; I want to be enriched, I want to be elevated.

A. Kant, Bach, non-Euclidean geometry—you lead a full life.

S. Now or never.

A. I would like to return to Kant for a moment.

S. A pleasure.

A. There was no non-Euclidean geometry in Kant's time. For Kant, geometry was Euclidean.

S. Just so.

A. But did not Kant go further than that?

S. What do you mean?

A. Correct me if I am wrong. It is my understanding that Kant asserted that Euclidean geometry is the form of the human mind.

S. I don't think that Kant anywhere says it exactly like that, but it would follow from what he does say in the *Critique*, especially from B 120 and B 207.

A. You know Kant well enough to remember the line numbers!

S. I have an excellent visual memory. At least what you are saying is for Kant true of space; and since space is the outer form of the intuition and Euclidean geometry the only study of space, it would follow. But see also A 25 = B 40. In A 165 = B 206, Kant seems to admit that what geometry asserts belongs to the pure intuition. There are some relevant comments also in the *Dissertation.*

A.   Aren't you in trouble?

S.   How do you mean?

A.   Let me ask you this. Do you believe in non-Euclidean geometry as firmly as you do in Kant?

S.   I don't see that the acceptance of the one involves the rejection of the other . . .

A.   What if it did?

S.   But it doesn't—it can't.

A.   Are you that sure? The parallel postulate which Euclid accepts Riemann rejects. In fact, Riemann accepts the contradictory of the parallel postulate, does he not?

S.   Yes.

A.   Well, then, if they are logically equivalent contradictories, how can the geometry which includes one of them only be the form of the human mind? What happens to the other? And if the form of the mind were to include both, would this not involve it in accepting a contradiction? And in that case, what would happen to logic?

[*At this point, the subject grew angry and appeared quite disturbed. He turned pale and began to breathe heavily. There was a long pause.*]

S.   Do you realize what you have done to me?

A.   No, what have I done?

S.   You have disturbed things I had thought were settled for once and all. It is very upsetting and I resent it. Now I shall have to go home and rethink the whole problem over again, I should have known better than to argue with Americans!

CONCLUSIONS

When the subject was first encountered, he was secure in the solidity of his retention schemata. The pathological symptom was the ascendency of the private schema over the public schema, resulting in over-determined behavior (in this case the insistence on superior personal authority among non-German nationals) and the emotional acceptance of the public schema. But there were no conflicts. The chief feature of his private retention schema was the peculiar way in which it incorporated elements of the public schema. He was a German national; therefore in his view reliable knowledge issues from German authorities. Those he selected were from the fields of philosophy and mathematics. It was clear that he would not have considered objections emanating from other sources, as for instance from authorities who were members of other nationalities. To effect a breach in this solid front, a weakness had to be found in his own schema and he perforce confronted with it. It would have to be an internal contradiction in the schema.

The retention schemata are stored in a way which makes them available to releasing mechanisms. The weakest elements are capable of firing only vague inclinations to action, and consist in convictions quite easily disposed of, but the strongest have a compulsive character and carry an emotional charge. Strength of retention also means resistance to change. Retention schemata therefore must be disintegrated before fundamental inquiry can be reopened. Doubt is an interim affair, but it can replace belief in the service of inquiry. Belief is shaken only when contradictions or conflicts appear. Contradictions in retention schemata are found either as between elements of the schemata and external fact or theory, or within the schemata. In the present case, the former would not have served; the latter was supplied.

X

SOCIOLOGY

INSTITUTIONAL CONDITIONING

The single individual of the species, *Homo sapiens,* is a social animal, very strongly conditioned by those activities in which he participates with his fellows. Such participation takes place at very many levels. I shall be concerned here especially with the interaction between the human animal and the artifacts of his material culture. By the individual I will understand the human organism with its basic tissue needs as determined by its genotype. The genes which the individual receives from his parents when considered in their totality make up the genotype. The needs themselves are the primary ones: for water, food and sex, and the secondary ones: for information, activity and security. Corresponding to each of these needs there is an organ: for the primary group, kidneys, stomach and gonads respectively, and for the secondary needs, cortex, muscle and dermis.

The phenotype is conventionally understood as the product of the interaction between genotype and environment. But what is the character of this environment? It is emphatically not, except in a minor sense, non-human nature. Throughout his lifetime the individual is bombarded continually with stimuli which seem almost intent upon activating him in some way or other. Of many of these he remains unaware, but with some he is conscious that he has a deliberate choice. However, if he is to survive with all his sensibilities intact, he must acquire a certain measure of stability both internally and externally. Internally, the process consists of the formation of a philosophy consisting of a set of beliefs and habits both weak and strong. Externally, the process consists in the establishment of institutions. So equipped, he is ready to react mechanically for the reduction of most of his importunate basic tissue needs, and in this way be left free to pursue more important aims.

The individual spends most if not all of his time in one institution or another, beginning in infancy with the institution of the family and working out the greater part of his adult life in the institution to which he contributes the bulk of his professional labors and which in turn earns him the funds for his support. The institution broadly speaking can be likened to a Skinner box in which man is the animal conditioned and the institution is responsible for the type of operant conditioning. Such conditioning of course varies greatly from institution to institution; what does not vary is the process of institutional conditioning itself. Before we can explain this, however, perhaps it will be best to get clear just what is meant here by an institution.

Beginning with individual man, there is a hierarchy of participation in which man and materials share equally, first the individual himself with his social beliefs and dispositions, then the social group of which he is a member, then institutions of which social groups constitute parts (though not indeed the whole), then cultures (or civilizations) in which institutions are members. Since we have already set forth what is meant by an individual, the social group would be next in order. A social group is a collection of individuals organized around a central purpose. If the purpose is very narrow and limited then the social group is independent but temporary; but if the purpose is broader and more pervasive then the social group is more permanent but only at the cost of a dependence on institutions of which it comprises one of the elements. A mob intent on lynching is a social group. We shall have to see in more detail what makes up an institution.

By an institution I mean that subdivision of society which consists in social groups, established by means of a charter, together with their customs, laws and material artifacts, and organized around a central aim or purpose. The social group is the collection of individuals who agree to work together within the institution to achieve its central aim. A charter is a set of principles and procedures written or unwritten which give the institution its measure of stability. The formal adoption of a charter is called establishment. Artifacts are of two kinds, tools and signs. Tools are material objects employed to move other material objects. Signs are material objects employed to refer to other material objects. Signs are usually employed in combinations. Artifacts constitute the material components of culture.

The elements which are used in the construction of the institution: the organization of the social group and the various kinds of signs and tools (artifacts) all are material objects which have been changed and arranged by the human individuals themselves. Never the less, these objects of material culture exist independently of those individuals and usually outlast them. They constitute the external inheritance of the species *Homo sapiens*. As we shall see, once the institution is constructed, the individual is as much affected by it as it was by him. For those human effects on the institution which brought it into existence were social, whereas the effects of the institution on its members are individual—it is individual man versus institution.

There are a number of kinds of institutions. Some are service institutions which furnish goods and services to all other institutions, and they in turn are subdivided into the constitutive and regulative types. Examples of the constitutive type are: the family, transportation, communication, economics. Examples of the regulative type are: the state, the military, the judicial. There are in addition the higher institutions which are in the main devoted to varieties of inquiry. Examples are: the sciences, the arts, philosophy, religion. All societies have these institutions, but usually arranged in some sort of hierarchy.

The society is always colored and dominated by some one institution, called the leading institution, for instance the church in mediaeval Europe, and business in the United States. Institutions organized into societies make up cultures, although the individual in some limited senses belongs directly to the culture and not necessarily only to the institutions which compose it. For one thing, he belongs to and has relations with segments of non-human nature with which he deals directly, and only indirectly through institutions. However, in the main he belongs primarily to one institution and secondarily to many others. He belongs to the institution to which he is committed through his profession, although he rarely ceases to be also a member of a family, a citizen of a state, a taxpayer to a government, a mailer of letters and a traveler.

I have set forth now what I mean by an individual in the biological sense, and what I mean by an institution in the sociological sense. It remains to show the nature of the interaction between them. It will be necessary to discuss first the effects of the institution on the individual and then those of the individual on the institution.

It is important to account for the existence of such phenomena as institutions from the point of view of the single human individual. Why does he need institutions? Evidently, the individual must engage in elaborate programs of social cooperation if he is to provide a continuous reduction of his basic organic needs. This is the origin of his membership in the institution. For the social group cannot operate without an elaborate structuring of tools and signs. His correspondence for example may be extensive but not sufficiently so to justify him in conducting his own postal system. However, if he is to participate taxwise in the institutional construction of such a system so that it is available to a vast population, the effort and expense can be justified collectively for the individuals supporting it. And what is true of such a communication system is equally true of the standing arrangements for all his organic needs.

The important fact to note in this analysis is that man is conditioned by the material culture he has produced in institutions no less inadvertently because he has produced it. This is true of tools. Consider for instance the effects tools have on men in many ways, from skills to occupational diseases. The pianist, who spends his life mastering the technique of interpreting the music of the great composers written for the piano, has nothing like the effect on the piano that it has on him. The worker who contracts cancer from painting radium on the dials of watches is in a way a victim of his trade.

What is true of tools is no less true of signs. Men have been moved emotionally to violent action by the connotation of words as much as they have been conditioned physically by adaptation to the use of tools. Emotionally-loaded words like "the flag," "revenge," "honor" and the like have been responsible for the enthusiastic and on the whole voluntary death of many men. Formal education is less manual than verbal; the laboratory aside, it is conducted almost entirely by means of words and word-combinations. The learning process is a process of systematic conditioning in which the individual cooperates.

In addition to formal education, there is the more subtle and elaborate process of conditioning which begins at birth when the infant is conditioned by the institution of the family, and accelerates to a maximum when a man is learning a profession and entering it as a career, namely, in the period of youth and manhood.

The pecularity of man among the primates is that in him the responses exceed the stimuli. Man is the animal that would surpass himself. Thus it is that institutions have come into existence. The result of organ deprivation and stimulus cue is often elaborate. In response to his need for water, for instance, he has marshalled all his forces: social cooperation, and the production of material artifacts of both kinds: tools and signs. The result is access to more water than he needs in the present in order to insure his need of water in the future. Consider the construction and operation of the complex water supply of a modern metropolitan center, for example. Thanks to the degree of foresight involved in the directional component of activation, with its planning and construction in anticipation of future needs, the intensity of a drive remains minimal in many cases.

There are, then, two types of occasion in which the individual interacts with institutions. The first of these is the type of occasion in which the institution is constructed in the first place. The second is the type of occasion in which the individual responds to a stimulus from the institution. Statistically, the second far outnumbers the first. Institutions are rarely constructed, but their continuing effects upon many individuals are common. The human individual responds to whatever there is in his environment which can activate a need, and the institution for all practical purposes *is* his environment. Considering that the institution and the environment—at least the available environment—is the same, no wonder that the individual reacts to it. He must do so insofar as he reacts at all.

And then, if our hypothesis is correct that in man the responses exceed the stimuli, it is as true that his effects are felt in alterations to the institution as that need-reductions are conducted in terms of it. But here the statistical proportions reverse. Individuals conform to the demands of institutions far more often than they change them. The institution shapes the man more frequently than the man the institution, although both types of event occur. Man is primarily and predominantly institutional man. If it is true that bipedalism, tool-making and communication were responsible for the transition from earlier species to *Homo sapiens,* it is equally necessary to remember that institutions are socially-established arrangements whereby the artifacts of culture, including material tools and material signs, are habitually employed in well prescribed ways, and the entire structure passed on through a process of external inheritance to the individual members of successive generations.

Thus along the entire course of his development through all of the various stages marked by age grades, from infancy to senescence, individual man makes and is made by institutions.

The introduction of the individual to the institutions among which he will spend the greater part of his adult life is one which occurs with no great ceremony. He has already prepared himself in many cases for the principal one by means of which he will earn his living, and he has become a member of the other more or less automatically. He registers to vote and so begins to take part in politics, he marries and so enters into the compact of the family, he joins a golf club, he buys a car. The chances are that he was already a member of some religion, usually that of his parents.

From now on, the stimuli for his basic tissue needs will be institutional, and both his preparatory and consummatory responses will be made to them. He will become an occupational man, subject to the occupational hazards peculiar to the institution of his choice and aimed chiefly at the rewards obtainable thereby. He will in this case, however, just as much as with the lower animals make the responses he is stimulated to make. And these can be manipulated institution-wise. For instance the drive to survive can be turned from aversive to excitatory behavior by revising the concept of death from punishment to reward. An occasion for anxiety when considered the end of human survival, it can be a drive-reduction when considered the beginning of survival of another sort, based on the immortality of the soul. Thus from punishment to reward is an easy conceptual step which can be taken even in the absence of evidence either way provided there is a sufficient degree of belief.

An institution is a Skinner box on a much larger scale. By means of it the proper stimulus is furnished to the individual who responds accordingly and so reduces his needs, usually one per institution. The law of culture is that the response exceeds the stimulus in at least a sufficient number of cases to insure the development of the apparatus providing the response, with the consequence that subsequent stimulations are more refined and are met with more elaborate responses. The apparatus is externally inherited from generation to generation of individuals. Hence we have anciently established churches, for example, stable governments, classics in art, and progress in scientific investigations.

The evidence that the individual's drives are more vigorous and more demanding than can be provided for by the preparation of apparatus for their reduction is contained in the series of disastrous wars and revolutions resulting from the generic drive of aggression, which usually sweeps away all of the constructions which had been so sedulously invented and so carefully preserved through decades, through centuries and even millennia. Nothing internal to the individual or external to him is stronger than his drive to dominate the environment, particularly in its negative phase in which it can be reduced only through destruction. Whatever the Eumenides can provide for human comfort and security, that the Furies can destroy; and in relatively quiet periods when the only human needs seem to be for knowledge and security, the need to do, under the violent aspect of the need to destroy, is almost forgotten, and men tend to think of themselves as men of good will, oblivious to the fact that when the good will is dominant there is also an ill will which is recessive.

In most advanced cultures, institutions are well defined and distinctly differentiated. The same man is not a carpenter by day and a physician by night. Considerable preparation, involving usually years of concentrated training, is necessary before an individual can take any important place in an institution. Even where the apprentice system prevails, much time elapses before the apprentice is considered a mature and professional craftsman. And so the process of conditioning operates in terms of reinforcement. The habit of performing certain institutional tasks: that of the surgeon in medicine or that of the trial lawyer in the legal system, for instance, must be deeply grooved before expertise is recognized. The role played by the individual in an institution becomes that with which he is identified not only by others but also by himself. He turns more and more into the image of what he has decided to do as he continues to do it. The individual becomes through the role with which he is identified an integral part of an institution.

The behavior prescribed for the individual within an institution is in terms of ritual. Ritual behavior constitutes the reinforcement of roles. The artifacts requisite to the ritual furnish the reinforcing stimulus and the conditioned reaction acts as a reinforcing agent. The more the individual behaves like a surgeon the more he becomes a surgeon, in a way which is dominant over his role as a man. The recessive lesser roles he plays in other institutions do not receive the same strength of reinforcement.

We have already noted that established institutions have more effect upon the individuals who have roles in them than the individuals have upon the institutions. Nevertheless institutions do change and develop, and when they do it is partly the result of the behavior of individuals. When individuals conform to stable institutions in traditionally prescribed and equally stable ways, this can be called stereotyped behavior. But when individuals alter institutions in an excess of endeavoring to conform to them, then this is the human version of adaptive behavior. That part of the individual's response which exceeds the stimuli is felt by the institution as an influence for change. I call this species of adaptive behavior "effective behavior." Novelty and originality enter in this way.

Effective behavior may be considered in two of its aspects: the intentional consciousness, and decision-making.

In the period of youth, or the early twenties, the appearance of a material object (or artifact) is suddenly suffused with its own possibilities and as a result an internal determination develops in the individual. This is the intentional consciousness. Its degree of determination in terms of temporally and spatially distant goals would perforce require that the individual behave in his institution not entirely in ways predetermined by its prescribed roles. The external inheritance, which is so evident in the long-established institution, may be subtracted from, or, in the type of case in question, added to; and indeed it must be so in human society. Culture does not stand still; only primitive societies with their paucity of differentiation do that. And so institutions are dependent for their maintenance upon the adaptability of the individuals composing the social group of the institution, and at the same time are dependent for their progress upon the effective behavior of the exceptional individuals whose possession of a strong intentional consciousness makes him more a source of effective behavior than of adaptation.

A decision procedure within the context selected for consideration here is a method of determining the appropriateness of practices within the framework of a given institutional structure. We may consider the type of the institution as a domain having a phenomenology and a kinetics. The phenomenology consists in the institutional cues and tropisms. The kinetics will be divided into kinematics and dynamics respectively; the abstract relations between individual and institution in terms of the moves the individual could make, and the movements themselves. The decision theory involved in this set of interactions is the determination of the relations between the individual and the institution with its various dynamic possibilities. The decision domain consists in all denumerable individual moves within the institution.

Of an important and even crucial character is the question, is a desired result obtainable? For this question, which theoretically can be resolved into one of adopting the correct methodology, there exists no algorithm. The multiple variations of individuals and of environing situations would make difficult the discovery of any special process for solving problems of this type. It is even doubtful whether there is any universally valid decision procedure for institutions, since this would have to be at the cultural rather than the institutional level and we know of no supra-cultural determinants; but there can be for domains of the institutional size. These would vary with the type of the institution, however.

The kind of conditioning the individual receives from the institution depends of course upon the type of institution. I will choose for illustration three examples of institutions corresponding to the secondary needs, which are for information, activity and security. The corresponding institutions would be: a university, an army and a church.

Educational institutions are those in which knowing is dominant, while doing and being are recessive. They offer culture in the form of learning, reinforced by repetition and intensification. The individual enters a university because he is information-oriented. The intensity of his generic activation has risen to a point sufficient to produce curiosity, and the direction of his activation has become specific enough for the selection of knowledge as a goal-object.

In a university, the phenomenology consists in the well-formed relations between information and education: some acquisition of information but more of methods of information-retrieval. The need to know is itself only partly reduced, but channels are established between cortical hungers and drive-reduction centers of an institutional character: the classroom, the library, etc. The candidate for a degree is informed how to decide between the various alternatives when a problem with respect to knowledge is presented. Most of the information is of the signalling-system variety, and consists of relations between the signs themselves rather than between signs and other material objects. The kinematic necessities of such information are assigned intuitively and the dynamics effectively begun. Teaching and scholarship studies do not have to be delayed but can begin immediately, though information is transferred to cortical storage where it awaits recall. Further decisions will have to be made when recall becomes appropriate to meet particular situations encountered in connection with other institutions.

Military institutions are those in which doing is dominant, while knowing and being are recessive. They offer activity in the form of fighting, reinforced by training and hardening. The individual enlists in an army because he is activity-oriented. The intensity of his generic activation has risen to a point sufficient to produce exertion, and the direction of his activation has become specific enough for the selection of destruction as a goal-object.

In an army, the phenomenology consists in the well-formed relations between activity and discipline: some practice in activity such as close-order drilling but more in the acquisition of the care and use of weapons. The need to do is itself only partly reduced, but channels are established between muscular hungers and drive-reduction occasions of an institutional character: war, invasions, etc. The candidate for promotion is informed how to decide between the various alternatives when a problem with respect to battles is presented. Most of the activity is of the sign-relation variety, and consists in "war plans" with various countries: sign-relationships indicating controlled activity of the aggressive variety. The kinematic necessities of such activity are dealt with strategically and the dynamics effectively postponed. The necessary techniques are assigned to cortical storage awaiting invocation. Further decisions will have to be made when recall becomes appropriate to meet particular situations encountered in the field in connection with other institutions.

Religious institutions are those in which being is dominant, while knowing and doing are recessive. They offer belief in the form of praying, reinforced by dogma and renunciation. The individual enlists in a church because he is security-oriented. The intensity of his generic activation has risen to a point sufficient to produce piety, and the direction of his activation has become specific enough for the selection of identification as a goal-object.

In a church, the phenomenology consists in the well-formed relations between security and ritual: some surrender to chastity and sacrifice but more to the care of sacred relics. The need to be is itself only partly reduced, but channels are established between dermic hungers and drive-reduction centers of an institutional character: liturgical services, etc. The candidate for elevation is informed how to decide between the various alternatives when a problem with respect to conversion or a sceptical adherent is prescribed. Most of the security is of the symbolic variety, and consists in representations of larger and more permanent, and usually far-away objects or beings. The kinematic necessities of such security are assigned formally and the dynamics effectively rejected. Skin sensitivity is the guardian of being *qua* being and security as a result is a matter of selective contact, as in contagious magic or the manual performances of sacraments. The necessary commitment is recorded and thereafter regarded as a dedication. Further decisions will have to be made when recall becomes appropriate to meet particular situations encountered in the laity in connection with other institutions.

It is obvious from the foregoing sketch of the individual and his relations to three institutions that his secondary drives function much in the same way as his primary ones, which are the needs for water, food and sex. Each has its appropriate organ and with that organ the need-activation which is occasioned by organ-deprivation. But need-reduction is never with human individuals a one-time affair. Man has foresight and he makes plans. His most elaborate plans are to take such action in the present as will provide in the future for the need-reduction which he can anticipate by abductive inferences from the past and present. As his needs have been and are, so they will continue to be. The primary needs are importunate and the secondary needs important, but the importunateness is a matter of immediate aggression and the importance a matter of eventual or ultimate aggression. The generic need is to dominate the environment, and so to aggrandize the ego that in a world populated by large-scale objects it can hope to survive. Particular needs are specific ones under the generic need for aggression.

And so the institutions come into existence in order to provide for the needs. But they become articles of the external inheritance and like all objects organic and inorganic have careers of their own. They change in ways unprovided for which are in the main unforeseen and unpredicted. And as they change they effect changes in the individuals whose adherence is an expression of a dominant need. Thus there takes place a continuing though discrete series of interactions in which the institution is altered though slowly by individuals and the individual is transformed though much more quickly by institutions. Individual man in any developed culture, that is to say, one in which functional differentiation has reached a considerable degree, is Institutional Man, as such a product of institutional conditioning.

Although as I have said the individual devotes most of his life to the service of one institution, usually that one in which he gains his livelihood, he is also a member of others. The same individual belongs perforce to many more than three institutions and plays important roles in each of them. He pays his taxes and votes, he does his military service, he is a husband and father, he pursues established channels of recreation, such as golf, fishing or card-playing. He spends his life within institutions, and he is seldom free from conditioning or reinforcement by some one of them. The environmental variables which operate to control the individual's behavior exist largely as properties of institutions.

Stimuli of one sort or another penetrate the organism without being noticed; they may even pass through consciousness without receiving much attention. He is in a sense unaware of them. The vaguer and more general the stimulation the more is this likely to be true. Institutional conditioning is largely unconscious conditioning. And what lies beyond the individual's deliberation also lies beyond his control. And so in many cases where he thinks he is exercising an arbitrary choice it happens that he is merely acting in response to stimuli. Institutional Man is man under the control of institutions unaware of their influence upon him. In this way a necessary uniformity is imposed upon the individual which insures that the actions as a result of their deliberations will be guided by deeper motives which are socially prevalent and which therefore will not be inclined to upset the customary ways of thinking, feeling and acting which are necessary to the preservation of the society.

For the individual, the development of the institution has advantages and disadvantages. The principal advantage is the maintenance of channels for the preservation of the effects of long-range behavior. Were it not for institutions, individual human behavior would have to be random and sporadic in its effects, and there would be no way in which to augment it with the effects of the behavior of others. Whatever need an individual is engaged in reducing, there are institutional ways of behaving and co-ordinating behavior, whether in educating the children which results from the individual's reduction of his sexual needs, or in the sale and distribution of the farm products from which he makes a living.

The disadvantage of the development of the institution is the anonymity and conformity it imposes upon its members. When it happens that no one individual is essential to the institution, then the individual sinks to the level of membership and gains nothing in personal distinction or dignity from the association. Every individual is in some of his characteristics absolutely unique; no two individuals begin with the same genotype and hence each develops a distinctively different phenotype, but this individuality the institution tends to mask and obliterate. In rare cases does originality and distinctiveness triumph over the institution, and it can do so only through an institutional alteration.

Institutions are the chief agencies for the accomplishments of those individuals who can triumph over the limitations institutional conditioning imposes. It is as though the institution as such presented a challenge which only a few individuals could meet. The few individuals are those exceptional and powerful originators who compel the institution eventually to adapt to them. The others are those vast numbers who in return for an humble adaptation to the requirements of the institution receive support from it in proportion to their stability within it. There is no help for the situation. Belonging carries with it a certain assurance and so a certain security. The individual believes and does what the institutionally established charter and prescribed ritual require of him, and in return obtains from it the security he needs.

It is clear, therefore, that for *Homo sapiens* institutions are necessary and institutional conditioning is here to stay until the next development in man.

XI

CULTURE

THE SOCIAL ADAPTIVENESS OF PHILOSOPHY

Our task is the understanding of the existence of philosophy in culture primarily as this concerns culture and only secondarily as it concerns philosophy. Men will not be happy, poverty and wars will not be abolished, until there is a better comprehension of the nature of the conditions of their living together, until they know what social groups are like in themselves, how institutions are composed, and even the nature of entire societies. Our theme is that the possession of a philosophy as such is essential to the continuance of all social organizations. To show their constitution in this regard is another matter. These are the tasks of social science, and it is no help to suppose that we have solved them already.

History is the account of past cultures; it is the study of cultures conceived developmentally. The flux of cultures may be likened to a number of broad rivers, each containing side currents and eddies, some flowing on the surface, others lying at much deeper levels. The surface currents are perceived most vividly and seem to be the only ones; these are the currents of political and economic events. But far below, and with longer cycles exercising pulls, lie the currents of the *ethe,* the philosophical currents. How to probe and chart these more powerful subsurface influences is one problem in the analysis of cultures.

Philosophy, not as expounded abstractly by philosophers but as imbedded in human cultures where it furnishes the necessary consistency, is the variety of cultural influences with which we are here concerned. Yet the argument here is that something akin to what the philosophers study abstractly as technical philosophy—under the headings of logic, ontology, epistemology, ethics, and aesthetics—exists concretely in human societies as assumed by them and in this silent form determines their structures and activities. Such a function is not explicit but implicit, not overt but covert, not recognized by those who live in cultures or even by those who make them but assumed by all types of social organization and by all social actions. Despite the highly diverse number of artifacts and events which are included in what we term culture, there is a certain consistency at work in it; otherwise we should find it difficult to recognize the existence of culture itself or to differentiate between different types of cultures. Given the variety of enterprises and activities, the arts and the sciences, the practical techniques, the customs and institutions which together make up a culture, it is difficult enough to claim a common frame for them; yet we do know that in some ways, at least, the religions of India have more in common with other things Indian than they have, say, with the religions of Europe. Nothing less than a systematic metaphysics—an ontology—could function as a set of axioms so broad that every aspect of culture assumes it. Ontology, then, can be said to be that which furnishes the consistency of culture. A culture is, roughly speaking, a kind of concrete system; but what is a system if not a consistency of elements? Now when a system is so large that we call it a culture, the consistency has to rest on some very wide base, nothing less, in fact, than an ontology. We call the ontology of a culture its implicit dominant ontology because it is assumed and often unknown, and because in this guise it tends to dominate everything else. On what other base could one rest the consistency which is found between the individual members of a society, or between the social groups and their artifacts, or between both and the institutions in which they are engaged together?

Implicit dominant ontologies become social philosophies when they are adopted by societies as the result of some kind of shock—a social revolution, say, or a defeat in war. A social revolution always brings with it new sets of assumptions as, for instance, occurred in the transition from the Middle Ages to the Renaissance in Europe, a familiar enough change whose lines can now be traced through the Reformation, through the discovery of experimental science, through the growth of industrialism and the rebirth of learning, through the rise of the cities and of democracy. And it meant that nominalism had replaced idealism as the assumed philosophy. Again, Christianity would never have triumphed to the extent that it did without the destruction of Rome by the Goths. The Roman ethos rested on military power, on physical force; when this was dissipated by a counterforce, it left a vacuum, together with the assumed stipulation that the new power would have to take some other form.

Social philosophies are abandoned when their fruitfulness as a source of theorems capable of supplying practical consequences is exhausted, when such practical consequences issue in crippling contradictions, or when a stronger philosophy with a greater foundation in fact is encountered. Unfortunately, concrete evidence for these contentions is wanting: cultures which die leave no record of their deaths for there is nobody to write about them. The ancient civilizations of Indo-China or of Central America were flourishing ones and disappeared in ways quite unaccounted for. But it is possible to see in old and continuing civilizations the necessity for new and invigorating assumptions before fresh outbursts of energy could be achieved. This is the case certainly with contemporary China where new hope was stimulated by the adoption of new principles. When a culture loses its beliefs it loses with them its ability to survive, as was the case with the American nomadic plains Indians after their defeat by the incoming Europeans. Only in the last few decades has the rapid decrease of the Indian population been reversed.

The implicit dominant ontology is a concrete ontology yet a transparent ontology. It lies deeply imbedded in cultures and permeates every corner of them, and the bare bones do not protrude. A certain amount of searching is necessary in order to detect its presence. It comes closest to the surface and may be discerned best in five places: in the rational social unconscious of the human individual, in the hierarchy of institutions, in customs, in the kind of art which is prevalent, and finally in questions of taste as exhibited in the adopted set of preferences.

The first place in which the implicit dominant ontology comes close to the surface is in the rational social unconsciousness. The rational social unconsciousness of the individual consists of those beliefs which he holds in common with other members of his society without in the least knowing that he holds them. They are the basis of his sanity and are maintained implicitly. They do not rise to the surface of consciousness, but whatever does so is a logical consequence of them. When confronted with them the individual is likely to express surprise that anyone would ever question their truth as though they were held by all members of all societies. Thus a good test to determine whether a belief belongs in the rational social unconscious is to suggest its opposite or contradictory. The thought that this is "inconceivable" is evidence for the presence of a fundamental belief.

In these terms, for instance, the majority of members of the western cultures are materialists. Most professional philosophers are subjective idealists rather than materialists thus revealing a sharp cleavage between the philosophy professionally held and the philosophy widely practiced. Few among us (other than professors of philosophy) really believe that our knowing makes a difference to the things that we know. We shall revert to this divergence in a later connection.

The second place in which the implicit dominant philosophy comes close to the surface is in the hierarchy of institutions. Most cultures have the same set of institutions even though these may have been developed to quite different degrees and may be quite different in character. What distinguishes cultures is the order in which their institutions are arranged. The dominant institution is the one at the head of the list, and it carries a great deal for the culture in the way of leadership, aristocracy, and implicit ontology. The philosophy of a culture furnishes to it its most fundamental beliefs, and is carried not as a philosophy explicitly but as the assumptions underlying the values taken for granted by the leading institution.

In the Middle Ages in Europe the Church was undoubtedly at the top of the institutional hierarchy, whereas in the United States in recent decades business has enjoyed this favored place. In Soviet Russia science, and especially applied science, occupies a privileged position. Needless to say, in most cases such a hierarchy is not deliberately constructed but happens, except in the case of Soviet Russia where the elevation of applied science was carefully planned.

The third place in which the implicit dominant ontology comes close to the surface is in the type of custom which is adopted. The technique of abstracting from concrete social events the philosophies which are implied by them is not always an easy matter, though this does not furnish any evidence against the contention that such philosophies exist and in such a manner. If there is any consistency to customs (and there always is when they have been long established) then this consistency suggests a certain ethics and so a particular metaphysics. Conduct presupposes belief. We act from what we hold to be true, no less so because we may happen to be ignorant of our beliefs. And we will be ignorant if the beliefs are at all fundamental. Only crucial actions, actions which have allowed no time for rational thought, will bring out our beliefs; but they are there always in custom.

In a culture such as the Chinese in which ancestors were worshipped as divinities, with appropriate ceremonies conducted regularly as early as the Shang Dynasty (1766–1122 B.C.), it would be difficult to suspect that any completely transcendental beliefs could have survived. Custom is capable of embodying philosophies in the form of beliefs so basic they may furnish the reasons for life or death. When courtiers sent to the eldest son of Shih Huang Ti a forged letter purporting to come from his father, the Emperor, and ordering him to commit suicide, he obeyed immediately (210 B.C.). Chinese culture survived because of an emphasis on the institution of the family, and emphasis on social ritual with its implied ethical standards, and behind this ethics an ontology clearly assumed.

The fourth place in which the implicit dominant ontology of a culture comes close to the surface is in the art which the culture develops as peculiarly its own. Art does not have to do with didactic beliefs, of course, but rather with qualities, with the symbolic expression of beliefs. But there is no reason to suppose that the beliefs do not show here also, no less so for having been arrived at in an indirect fashion and with different means of expression. The arts cut deeply, and what rises by their means to the world available to awareness has welled up from profoundly immersed forces deeply influential in the culture.

It would be difficult to divorce the method of Cézanne, who insisted that what he was trying to paint were sensations in the presence of nature, from the empiricism of the experimental scientists of his day, who were endeavoring to accomplish the same ends in a more rational and even a mathematical language. The subjective philosophies of India are apparent in their tension dances in which the attainment of bodily control counts for so much, as indeed it does also in so many religious observances, such as Yoga, in the same culture.

The fifth, and last, place in which the implicit dominant ontology comes close to the surface is in the set of preferences which the individuals in a given culture exhibit. Examination of the popular set of preferences, shows the philosophy of the culture at work, and reveals what it has been. In contrast with this, examination of the special set of preferences of the professional philosophers shows what the philosophy of the culture is becoming. These signs are not always infallible but they are rough guideposts where otherwise we have none. It takes some time for the philosophy of a culture, which is imbedded in it through the implicit dominant ontology, to make its way to that superficial place in the culture occupied by matters of taste; but this is in some fashion the surest, even though it be the last, manifestation.

If two men, two friends let us say, agree to pass up an invitation to the opening of an art gallery in order to attend a professional baseball game, they are exhibiting the mutual possession of a set of preferences. But in doing this, they are doing more. For the preference, which they show by sharing, hooks up through consistency with many other such preferences which they hold in common with many other such people. And so we come to the discovery of the foundations of a consistency which is society-wide, and we find in the end that it is nothing less than a philosophy.

The association between societies and philosophy is a very intimate and a very necessary one. Societies either find the philosophies they need to justify what they want to do, or they are activated in certain directions by the philosophies which they had adopted for other reasons. In either case philosophy is influential and serves the basic function of a rational justification. Such justifications are not merely "rationalizations" after the fact; they are often predetermining factors. When we remember that the establishment requisite for any continuing program conducted by a social organization calls for a philosophy of some sort, and that a whole society and even an entire culture (though vast) is just such a social organization, we can then see the necessity of having a philosophy. The philosophy need not be announced, promulgated, or even recognized in order to exist and be effective. Philosophies are pervasive in a kind of culture space; they are the essential ingredients in a complex and adjacent background which make all simple social relations quite complex as to their total meaning and which interact with them.

It will be useful to consider three highly diverse examples.

In the first example the social situation is that of occupied France during World War II, and the philosophy is that of existentialism. Sartre was active in the underground resistance to the Germans, and his modified version of Kierkegaard enjoyed a considerable vogue. To a people who had been defeated in war decisively and quickly, without in fact offering much of a struggle, and who were therefore without a national self-respect and without a community, a philosophy which offered an extreme subjectivism and with it the supremacy of feelings of revulsion was most welcome and sustaining. A limited philosophy, granted, but one eminently suited to a limited situation. It would be difficult to imagine any other philosophy, even one with a broader scope and a more embracing set of truths, that could have served the purpose half so well. No people needs to feel the support of an enduring philosophy more than one whose social ties have been sharply broken.

In the second example the social situation is that of medieval Europe, and the philosophy that of scholastic realism. Many persons are apt to forget that Thomism came at the end of the Middle Ages and not at the beginning or even in the middle. The philosophy of St. Thomas (an amalgam of many disparate elements. Christian, Greek, Roman, Alexandrian and Arabic) was more summary than explanatory. It was a philosophy designed for a holding operation—for which purpose, it should be added, it was highly suited. In the medieval synthesis all questions had been decided, and everyone and everything could find the place assigned. Culture had come to a rest at last, without forward movement and without any problems except that of how to apply the ideas upon which all agreed. This was the compensation for the absence of curiosity and the hope of improvement. The faint glow of new values and new interests on the horizon could dimly be seen, but they only served notice that it was time to tighten the grip on what had already been settled.

In the third example the social situation is that of revolutionary Czarist Russia, and the philosophy that of dialectical materialism. Russia in 1910 was a country marked by a depressed majority but with a definite leaven of intellectuals. She had been defeated by the Germans, and her people were confused and embittered but full of energy. Her intellectuals turned political revolutionaries and furnished the spearhead for the adoption of a philosophy engendered by the economic revolution. Marxism is a philosophy of dynamism, one filled with urges to violence, with admonitions of progress, with ideas of becoming. It has many loose ends: it lacks a political system for a stable society, an explicit ethics, a terminal date for its period of transition and for the establishment of its ideal, and rules of order for guidance in the calm waters after the storm has passed. It is a call to action and a philosophy of social change. As such it was held by those anxious to engineer a revolution to be the best practical philosophy that could have been adopted for the dynamic growth-phase in Russia.

It is important to note that in all three examples, despite the fact that more divergent ones could hardly be found, there is a common adaptability of the philosophy to a given phase in the development of the society. We are not concerned in this essay with the truth of philosophies but with their relative social adaptiveness. Given the particular stage of development of a given culture in a particular time and place, there is one and only one philosophy which is suitable for it. This philosophy may or may not be explicit. In the past it has usually not been, but in the case of Soviet Russia it was.

When we isolate the philosophy of a culture, we are, so to speak, penetrating to its essence logically considered; (its essence axiologically considered can only be felt and cannot be analyzed structurally). A philosophy is what a culture means; only, we have in the past had too narrow a conception of philosophy. Abstract systems of philosophy could be promulgated which would be far more complex than any that we have before us now. And we shall have to reach such a degree of complexity if we are to understand the kind of philosophy which can underlie vast and elaborate cultures. What type of relationships are there that philosophies could assume for events? Simple Hegelian triads, and complexities consisting of triads piled on triads? But this is too simple, a complexity consisting of more instances of the same simple structure rather than one consisting of different sorts of structures themselves complexly interrelated. The probabilities are that the kind of philosophy requisite for the kind of culture we should wish to see established is of an order of complexity not yet envisaged by the philosophers. At present, philosophies are far simpler than the components they endeavor to embrace and explain, components such as art and science and mathematics, for example; and these simple philosophies will not do for the establishment of more complex cultures with higher grades of value.

How different are the fates which await philosophies when they are confronted with very diverse social situations! Philosophies very close together in feeling may end in applications remarkably far apart. There are serious similarities between Jainism and Hegelianism, but quite different destinies awaited them because the social soil in which they were planted contained quite different elements. Subjective idealism *is* the culture of India; but in Europe, with Bradley, say, it becomes a sort of academic declaration of independence from practical concerns. Again, the similarity between the Yogācāra school of Buddhism and the Greek sceptical school founded by Pyrrho of Elis gives no hint of the religious acceptance of Yogācāra in India or of the western atheism resulting from the sceptics. A culture cannot be sustained without a philosophy. The strength of a culture is the strength of the philosophy it naturally assumes. We do not know very much yet about how such philosophies are adopted or abandoned or even about how they operate. But we do know that cultures exhibit the property of consistency among their several parts, and we do not know of any assumptions less than a philosophy which could support a consistency so wide holding among parts so diverse.

Culture imposes its own consistency upon the elements within it; and where the elements are intractable to a given canon of consistency, the full force of interpretation is turned upon them. For instance, Christianity, whose own method is pacific, was transformed into an aggressive religion which practiced conversion by the sword in Central and South America where the Spanish encountered the Indians. The need for consistency must be very great when interpretations of a contradictory nature appear this necessary. Again, a philosophy conformable with the religious view that the end of the world is at hand would surely have to be different from one asked to support the hope that the Church as an institution will last forever; Tertullian is not the same as St. Thomas. From the crisis of such an emergency as the Goths to the inheritance of the Roman Empire marked a transition which surely required a change in philosophies, which is to say a change in fundamental beliefs even as to what was revealed.

Philosophy is in fact a kind of summatory recording. It is what we find that we have when we put our heads together; that is to say, the wisdom that can be derived from our separate callings. What do the sciences have in common with each other, and they with the arts, and so on? The semi-autonomy of interrelated fields incidentally should get rid of the self-regarding fallacy of considering the object of one's own interests to be central to all others. But this, too, has its average cultural function. From one point of view, social and political philosophies consist in the finding of elaborate reasons for explaining what men do on instinct. For instance, every expansion of a people, by war and conquest or by cultural diffusion, is the aftermath of an increase in population. Increase the birth rate, and the result is a pressure on expansion by whatever means; and man, being a rational, which is to say a resourceful, animal, the means are always found, and more often than not at the expense of neighboring peoples. All this has deep roots in meaning; and what we do individually as a result of a policy of survival may be comprehended statistically in the assumption of a system of metaphysics, of an ontology. We do not live alone, and collectively we do not amount to a mere collection of individual selves; there is also the culture, and the culture includes a complete philosophy if it is a complete culture.

Those who practice philosophy—the professional philosophers of the classroom and the texts—are talking and writing about the things men live by, but they do not talk and write about them as though men lived by them. Philosophical themes in the hands of professionals are far less related. Consider the conventional divisions of western philosophy: ancient, medieval, and modern. These divisions are the recognitions of distinct cultural changes, recognizable in types of philosophical interests both as to methods and as to results. There was a Greek philosophy, there was a medieval philosophy, and there is a modern philosophy. Plato's philosophy is characteristic of the first culture; Aristotle as seen through the eyes of Plotinus, of the second; and Hume, say, of the third. A concern with nature dominated the first culture, a concern with religious revelation the second, and with human sensations the third. The contests between philosophical schools (the fact for instance that philosophers spend more time defending or attacking a philosophy than they do in developing one) resembles nothing so much as the state of war between nations. Philosophers, too, have to maintain their standing armies; but they could easily show that all philosophies serve their useful turns and thus that enmity is unnecessary as a sign of enthusiasm.

When will the world learn to discriminate between those who discover philosophies and those who advocate or communicate them—between the philosophers and the teachers of philosophy?

Limited philosophies do in fact apply better than broad ones to limited social situations. But we have to be sure that we mean by a limited social situation one which is limited in every sense. When we speak of the glory of Greek culture, we mean the culture advanced by the society of a single city-state, Athens. Now, despite early expedient victories, Athens was actually defeated in its two most notable wars: those with the Persians and with the Spartans. But the Athenian ideals were not limited and the aspirations to which they gave rise were equally wide so that these ideals finally issued in the conquest of Asia by Aristotle's best pupil. Greece was eventually annihilated as a state and absorbed as a culture; but the philosophy has survived, as those of us who have come under its influence are well aware. In the Chou Dynasty in ancient China (1122 B.C. to 221 B.C.), there was much intellectual activity, but wars between feudal Chinese states were conducted according to well-established rules so that prestige was involved more than bloodshed, and battles became more a matter of elaborate maneuvers than of mutual slaughter. Culture was advanced, religion rudimentary, theoretical speculation much encouraged. It was in this period that Chinese philosophy began to be developed.

Leadership, in the grand sense, as it concerns active affairs, consists in intuitively discerning what system of abstract ideas will best suit what concrete social situation. And it is best to prepare the range of available philosophies well in advance of their employment. Thus the social role of the productive philosopher is a value-neutral one: he may discover the ideas upon the basis of which a culture may operate, but he does not discover the occasion for the adoption of a system of ideas by a culture. This latter task is a special one and ought perhaps to be studied by the members of a profession specially equipped.

It may be that the task of discovering the perfect culture has to be pursued separately from that of discovering the perfect philosophy. In the end, however, the two are one; and all of us, regardless of the seemingly separatist nature of our special activities, whether we are engaged in selling shoes, running for political office, or carving sculpture, contribute what we can to a sum-total in which the distinctions that once belonged to the disparate parts are obliterated, and culture cannot be differentiated from the implicit dominant ontology which goes to make up a whole out of its disparate elements.

The men who discover the stuff of a culture are usually buried in it and so not noticed by the others; but if they are noticed then it is for something else, some flamboyant side-effect which manages to conceal the future important influence of what they have accomplished. The clash of rival philosophies goes unheard by the multitude who look to the idols of the moment rather than to the recognition of the forces that truly prevail in society; and though the voices of philosophy go unheard they are partly explained by their relative social adaptability. If all philosophies are partly true in what they assert, then it is their truth which is being employed in societies and not that part of their falsehoods which consists in denials and limitations.

CULTURE AS APPLIED ONTOLOGY

I

The smallest human isolate is a culture, not an individual. The test for valid isolation is the prospect of survival: the individual cannot live alone, a culture can. Philosophy in the old sense of a subjective study involving supernatural or transcendental knowledge was inimical to the physical sciences; but this is not true of philosophy in the new sense and it is not true of the social sciences. We shall see what these two propositions involve, for they result in the proposal to set forth a certain theory concerning the relations of that part of philosophy named ontology to those large-scale items of the social field called human cultures, more specifically in the use of ontologies as instruments of cultural analysis. The term, ontology, has acquired an unfortunate reputation among scientists because of the theological endorsement by which it has been identified with a particular theory of ontology long considered official in certain quarters. But the field of ontology is wider than any particular theory comprised within it. Since the association with theology is not the meaning of ontology intended here, it may be well to begin with a definition and description.

Ontology is the widest system in any finite set of systems. It would perforce have to be an abstract body of knowledge and make the claim to truth. This could be either a tentative or an absolute claim. Its own terms of description are the categories of traditional metaphysics. The definition of Bentham, that the field of ontology is "the field of supremely abstract entities," refers to these categories, or, as we should say in modern logical and mathematical systems, the undefined terms employed in the unproved propositions which constitute the postulates of the system. There is no official ontology, and contending ontologies must support their claims on the basis of the same criteria used by other kinds of systems: consistency, completeness and applicability. Rival ontologies exist theoretically and practically, and assert both abstractly and concretely their respective claims. They exist theoretically in the written and spoken words of the professional philosophers. We shall see that their practical existence is somewhat more concrete, for they exist practically as actual elements of cultures. But before we can be more detailed we shall have to explain what we mean by cultures.

Culture is the common use and application of complex objective ideas by the members of a social group working with tools, folkways and institutions. Such complex ideas are held subconsciously by the individual members, and are manifested socially by the myth of the leading institution of the culture. The complex ideas are said to be objective because they issue from the external world and are referred back to it. Another name for them is the implicit dominant ontology. They are ontological because they refer to ultimate problems of being, and they are dominant because they take precedence over all the thoughts, feelings and actions of the social group which holds them. Thus every culture has its own implicit dominant ontology, but the environing conditions for every culture differ, and each finds itself in a definite climate, terrain, with different types of neighbors, etc. Thus a culture, let us say in a revised definition, is the actual selection of some part of the whole of possible human behavior considered in its effect upon materials, such as tools and institutions, made according to the demands of an implicit dominant ontology and modified by the total environment.

Ontologies are empirical affairs, then, since they are elements of analysis of actual cultures. They are found empirically in two places: in the subconscious of the individual and in the social order of institutions.

Belief, at least the kind of fundamental belief from which we act, is unconscious and rarely rises to the level of awareness. The unconscious beliefs held by individuals reveal themselves in critical actions. When individuals are forced to decisions without having had time to consider, their actions are the consequences of beliefs which are held so deeply that they themselves are unaware of holding them. In other words, the unconsciously maintained propositions are the postulates for the actual deductions which consist in sudden and decisive moves. What individuals do may be better (or worse) than what they consciously know to do.

Beliefs are common to the individuals of a given culture. They exist within each individual yet they are social for they exist within all the individuals of the culture.

There is no doubt that we are all susceptible to the power of certain conceptions of which we are for the most part unaware. The first principles we accept are so pervasive that we do not consider them at all but everything else in the light of them. In short, we live inside a system of ontology which is altogether taken for granted, and this is what we have called the implicit dominant ontology.

It requires a tremendous effort of concentration after prolonged preparation in dealing with abstractions of this sort, for the individual to be able to make himself aware of his unconscious ontological beliefs (for that is what they are).

With the term, implicit dominant ontology, in addition to Hegel's "community of conscious life," we have recognized the existence of a community of unconscious social life. The infant is ethically neutral: we are not born with a knowledge of good and evil or with a conscience. We are taught it by the acquisition of a set of conditioned reflexes. These may be psychological as well as physiological. Habit patterns of thinking and of emotional attitudes are also stimulus-response mechanisms.

Ontologies exist also in candid social form. An implicit dominant ontology is found in the myth of the leading institution of the culture. The institutions within a culture are arranged in some order of importance, and this arrangement differs from culture to culture. Thus the order is revealing. The first division of cultures is institutional, it is not the class struggle but the institutional struggle that is the most significant. The culture is dominated by the institution it places first in order. For example, the Church was the leading institution in the Europe of the Middle Ages, while economics and politics are the leading institutions of Soviet Russia. In the Middle Ages the implicit dominant ontology fostered by the Church included the superiority of certain absolute values over the human values, original sin, and the partially evil nature of man due to the fall: the idealistic philosophy based upon a realm of essence superior to actual existence. In Soviet Russia, the implicit dominant ontology fostered by the state includes the superior reality of the means of production, of the class struggle, the superior values of the proletariat: the nominalistic philosophy based upon a realm of existence superior to essence. It may be difficult if not impossible to analyze the content of one's own myth without getting outside the circle of belief of which that myth forms the center. For everything in a culture is affected, from the merest details of economic life to the most grandiose conceptions of the professional philosopher. The term, myth, as we use it is intended to convey no opprobrium, it means a symbolic account containing a theory of reality (or *eidos*). It is revealed in the folkways as well as in the order of institutions, and it is pervasive through the quality which is termed the ethical.

II

The foregoing discussion of culture and ontology and their interrelations suggests certain methodological considerations. The classic conceptions of philosophy are swept away, for philosophy can no longer be limited to the abstract speculations of the professional philosophers. Such men are the theoreticians but the theories they develop can be applied. Their procedure is untouched, it is merely reinterpreted. What is new is the research and development at the empirical level. We have not been thinking along lines which would make of the subject-matter of the cultural anthropologist and the historian a fertile field of data for the hypotheses of the empirical ontologist. Therefore we shall need to say a few words about the empirical problem and its approaches, and then try to show what this adds to the work of the speculative ontologist.

The organization of things and events *qua* organization is also evidence of the force of ontology in existence. Those organizations whose postulates include false ontological propositions (and this must be true of every actual organization to some extent) are those which must suffer diminution, degradation and perhaps extermination. An organization exists and acts according to the forces of its ontological postulates. To act inconsistently is to act illogically; to act astructurally is to act unmathematically; and to act against the postulates is to act anti-ontologically.

The empirical ontological problem, then, can be formulated as follows. Given the institutions, tools and folkways of actual cultures, to find the ontologies which underlie them. This involves investigation into the details of an actual cultural situation, an assignment at once easier and more difficult than it sounds. Cultures are all of a piece and will give the same ring when struck in any vital spot. But on the other hand considerable equipment on the part of the investigator is presupposed: a knowledge of the varieties of cultures and of types of ontologies. The task requires painstaking inquiry into, for instance, the graded meanings of the leading institution and its myth. It relies upon the use of the projective techniques furnished by empirical psychology, to interpret the implicit dominant ontology in the subconscious of the individual. For the ontology there reveals itself indirectly, never directly. The investigator has to back up, so to speak, from the encounter with the details of actual conditions in a given state, nation, tribe or country, to reconstruct an ontology whose application could have given rise to such conditions. He will have to subtract the environmental factors, which are brute and irreducible, constituting the framework within which the choice and application of beliefs was made; and he will have to reconstruct an hypothesis on the basis of the solid remainder. Of course this mechanism must not be misunderstood as operating too consciously. Cultures were not developed by logicians armed with postulate-sets. And they must not be interpreted dogmatically simply because they can be analyzed in this way.

So much, then, for the empirical side of ontology. The speculative ontological problem can now be reformulated as follows. Given the actual applied ontologies as empirical elements of analysis, obtained by the above method, to set up a comparative study for the purpose of seeking a better theoretical ontology. By "better" here is meant one which is more consistent and more complete, and which therefore would be when applied capable of producing a fuller culture. The "better ontology" will not result from a mere choice of the more preferable among the implicit dominant ontologies but will rather be an imaginative construct suggested by them, embracing what they have of value and truth and eliminating their shortcomings. The history of philosophy is the chronological recital of a succession of theoretical ontologies whose practical role does not seem to have been well known. All we get are social interpretations of the effects of the times upon the philosophers. We do not get the dynamic interaction of the societies and philosophies. Theoretical ontology has a practical application, which does not, however, make it any less theoretical. There is nothing more practical than the use of abstract theory, as recent advances in technology have dramatically illustrated. The great philosopher is a culture-maker in the grand sense, but he must work with the materials and depend upon the findings of the empirical ontologist. In this sense too, the cultural anthropologist and the sociologist are field workers in ontology; and philosophy, to the extent to which it is held down to actual human cultures, is nothing more nor less than social science.

III

Thus far we have been viewing the relations between ontology and culture from the perspective afforded by culture. In other words, we have been considering the cultural functions of ontology. But we can turn the picture around and look at it from another angle. We can view the relations between ontology and culture from the perspective afforded by ontology, and consider the ontological functions of culture. Where culture has been our chief concern, ontology will be substituted.

The fundamental theory of ontology involves inquiries which can in a certain sense never be answered with any finality or absoluteness. Yet actual cultures are themselves the frozen answers to ontological problems. Unless such answers are made tentatively, they tend to block further inquiry. This is the sense in which philosophy can act as a liberating force, as Russell pointed out. It sets us free of fixed abstractions which we have been accepting as implicit beliefs. But the forces of tradition, which are the conditioned habits of cultures, are against change of any kind. In short, cultures inhibit further inquiry by giving final answers to ultimate questions.

We see this at work in the process of education. It has often been observed that young children are natural metaphysicians. Within the narrow limits of their vocabulary, they do ask penetrating questions, such as how far does space extend or who made God. The end product of the process of education, however, transforms such basic inquiry and smothers the hunger it represents with the petty behavior patterns of our complex society: the rat race which consists in paying taxes, going to church, earning a living, running for street cars. The authorities who administer this system have the temerity to consider the ultimate problems adequately solved. Thus far the only institutions devoted to the necessity of keeping an open mind on tentative answers to such problems are the mathematical and empirical sciences and the fine arts. The scientists and the artists are the only ones who are able to save or else recapture what Einstein has somewhere described as "the holy curiosity of inquiry," an attitude paradoxically so foreign to the established religions.

Most human cultures, then, mean inhibited inquiry. Although cultures are themselves the results of inquiry, their practice is to stand in the way of further inquiry. If curiosity is almost as basic as food and sex, frustrated inquiry may be almost as disastrous to society as frustrated sexual desires are to the individual. The difficulties of actual societies may to some extent be characterized as neuroses resulting from blocked inquiry. But the fact is that individuals and human cultures do not live on the unsolved problems of philosophy but on incorporated and institutionalized solutions. Individual life is simply impossible otherwise, or so it appears. It is the purpose of what Emerson labeled perpetual inquiry to insure that such acceptance is never irrevocable. For an individual or an entire culture can progress only to the extent to which change is allowable, and improvement is permitted only when the final truth is held to be unknown. Militant faith in bad solutions may be hasty philosophy but it is also traditional practice. We do not have a long tradition based on the acceptance of the postulate of an independent truth or of the unaffiliated search. To be a realist, it is mistakenly thought, one must be a Platonist. To be religious means to most people to embrace the dogma of some existing church. Whom do you follow? that is the universal question.

But it may be that our failures and frustrations are due to an ambition for which hitherto we have not found the proper methodology. We ought to start by taking tiny steps toward ultimate goals, implementing final causes by more efficient methods. We ought to investigate the natural society. The cultural domain comprises the laws and the structure of the natural society. Some work toward the discovery of these has already begun, but it is in a tentative stage only. Grimm's Law which describes the shift in pronunciation of cognate words, imported into Europe from Asia, the mutes moving forward two places, is an example of a cultural law. Another has been suggested by Bryson. The rate of change in any culture is a function of the complexity of the culture, so that the greater the complexity the faster the change. Murdock and others in the cross-culture survey at Yale have discovered more than seventy institutions and folkways which appear, on historical evidence only, to be invariants for all cultures, primitive as well as advanced. The loosest subdivision, the ethnological, is indistinguishable from the highest, which is the subdivision of social psychology. At the highest empirical subdivision we reach the lowest level of theoretical systems: ethics is the highest subdivision of the cultural domain. Above ethics lies ontology.

Speculative ontology seeks to discover the perfect ontology, which is the implicit dominant ontology of the natural society. The result of this is the discovery of better ontologies. The theoretical ideal is the aim of every practice. The social is the highest of the integrative levels, and so it makes no sense to speak at once of the physical or the chemical as empirical and of the psychological or social as normative. There is such a thing as a natural society possible, and indeed it is only to the extent to which any actual society deviates from the natural society that it becomes the product of inhibited inquiry. The task of discovering the perfect ontology is a speculative one, its application the corresponding task of "finding nature" in the social field. In other words, the natural society would be an expression of the perfect ontology.

Every institution in a culture, and many folkways, represent specific answers made to ontological questions. Since we have not reached absolute and entirely satisfactory answers, we are interested in the questions. Therefore the first empirical assignment of the ontologist is to work back from the institutions and folkways of various cultures—from the specific answers, in other words—to the abstract formulations of the questions.

Then the movement is to be reversed and go forward again to the hypotheses of better answers. This is the empirical side of scientific culture theory considered in its synoptic aspect, and such aspect proves to be nothing less than applied ontology.

The aim of the theory set forth here, which has been to establish the claims of the search for truth, is out of the ordinary. To declare such claims officially established would be to defeat the search. The seal of officialdom or of authority would be as fatal to the realism of the position advanced here as it has been already to other philosophies. We have been occupied mainly with a methodology, in an attempt to save speculative ontology from vagueness and to point out the ready-made existence of empirical ontologies to be studied in the field. To bring the speculative and empirical branches of ontology together, after the manner of mathematical empiricism, would be to discover for ontology a way in which it could be used for the prediction and control of actual human cultures.

XII

SCIENCE

THE ROLE OF HYPOTHESES IN THE SCIENTIFIC METHOD

Much spadework has to be done before that stage of scientific procedure at which hypotheses enter the picture. And no doubt experiments are conducted without benefit of hypotheses in many instances. Yet only with the hypothesis can a line of investigation be pursued. The role of hypotheses in the scientific method is examined here under the following headings: definition and description; character; criteria; occasions; discovery; and function.

1. DEFINITION AND DESCRIPTION

A hypothesis is a proposition which seems to explain observed facts and whose truth is assumed tentatively for purposes of investigation. It is a leading question put to nature, a guess designed to suggest the sort of inquiry by which an answer might be reached. The success of the method of hypothesis depends upon the delicate balance between conjectural and empirical elements. We have to construct guesses as to how things are before we can make the observations necessary to determine whether our guesses were correct. The hypothesis, then, is a proposition suspected of being true but lacking the requisite support of evidence, a suggestion that new and necessary relations may exist and should be investigated. A good hypothesis is one that offers a possible explanation or that ascribes an adequate cause.

In other words, a hypothesis is a preconception of what investigation will disclose. It must be a matter about which there is both doubt and some inclination toward belief. Where there is no doubt concerning the truth of the idea, there is no willingness to submit it to the test of experiment. No one would try a proposition already convicted on conclusive evidence, and no one would test a proposition whose truth is not doubted. Without the inclination to belief, there would be no disposition to look into the degree of truth of the hypothesis. For if the hypothesis should be confirmed, it could be used as an instrument in further inquiry. And without the large element of doubt, the proposition would be a simple matter of belief, not a scientific hypothesis.

2. CHARACTER

Every theory or law in science must have begun its career as a hypothesis. Something suggestive in the subject matter compels the framing of a hypothesis as a possible explanation. Thus, in order to determine the character of a hypothesis, it is necessary only to read back from a theory or law to its more tentative, probative formulation. Of course, the formulation may have become more abstract and precise; experimental and mathematical evidence may have strengthened its claim to truth; it may even have achieved mathematical expression. But what has changed radically as it has moved from the status of hypothesis to that of theory and then to that of law is the increased support it receives.

Thus a hypothesis represents a temporary state between two non-hypothetical conditions—rejection or acceptance. No hypothesis is intended to remain a hypothesis forever; it cannot occupy a permanent slot in a science. It is a proposition on trial until it is confirmed or disconfirmed. Then it will be either elevated to the status of theory and passed along to another type of consideration or dismissed as false and unworthy of further consideration in any connection.

Besides being tentative, hypotheses are heuristic in that they (a) may suppose generalizations not yet tested or otherwise investigated; (b) may suppose entities not yet observed or isolated; (c) may suppose processes not yet observed or isolated; (d) may suppose properties not yet observed or isolated; and (e) may posit ideals in terms of which specific inquiries can be conducted. This classification is rough and incorporates a certain amount of unavoidable overlapping.

(a) The generalization is the kind of hypothesis we usually have in mind and the kind that has been discussed thus far. It is usually a statement about a universal, expressed perhaps as an invariant relationship between variables or as a set of conditions. The first proposal that perhaps epithelial tissue is constituted chiefly of keratins did not mean that insoluble proteins of the scleroprotein class—containing large amounts of leucine, cystine, and tyrosine radicals—were to be found in *some* instances in the epidermal layer of skin; it meant rather that the keratins are the chief ingredients in *all* epidermal layers of skin and in *all* horn, hair, nails, feathers, and hooves. We are concerned with the degree of truth of our hypothesis and its capability of being elevated to the status of theory and perhaps of law, but we are concerned also with a larger area which our generalization may help to explain. To say, then, that a generalization is "heuristic" means that it furthers explanation, that it elicits other generalizations or facts which we might not reach without its aid. A hypothesis is a guide to a fresh view-point, to novel observation, and to original experiments.

(b) Hypothetical or heuristic entities are quite common in science. We find them in physics among the subatomic particles, many of which were inferred before they were experimentally demonstrated. The recent discovery of the antiproton has led to further speculations in the same direction—to the supposition, for instance, that corresponding to every physical particle there may be an antiparticle and that there may be antigalaxies, and even such a thing as antimatter. Antiprotons and antineutrons were, in fact, first proposed and later produced experimentally as a result of investigations conducted with the bevatron accelerator at the University of California. On the other hand, the entities proposed by Freud—the ego, the superego, and the id—have never been observed, but they have aided in the understanding of the unconscious.

(c) What is true of entities is also true of processes: they may be hypothetical and unobserved, yet a great aid to explanation. The biological process of maturation and the economic operation of "conspicuous waste" are of such a nature.

(d) Supposed properties not yet observed or isolated may, when investigated, lead to new knowledge. William Gilbert in the sixteenth century experimented with magnets and observed that a freely suspended magnetic needle pointed north and south in directions roughly comparable to the geographical poles and that the angle of the magnetic needle dipped through an angle that varied with the latitude when pointed toward the North Pole. From these facts he made an induction to the hypothesis that the earth had the property of an enormous magnet.

(e) A postulated ideal is familiar in the sciences. The scientific "ideal" does not connote anything peculiarly mental. Patterns of perfection set limits; they are models and nothing more. They serve an operational purpose. It often seems necessary to posit ideals in order to investigate actualities; for then standards are provided for measuring degrees of approximation in actual cases. Carnot's conception in 1824 of a theoretically perfect engine which loses no heat by conduction and no work by friction is one of the best-known examples. An ideal elastic would rebound with undiminished speed after colliding with the walls of its container. The equation for an ideal gas states that pressure *times* volume equals quantity *times* time. The ideal "black body" of thermodynamics is the hypothetically perfect heat radiator.

One important characteristic of hypotheses is that they usually extend beyond ordinary observational levels, by means of an extension of the senses accomplished with instruments or by means of abstract symbolic functions accomplished with mathematics. Thus, while hypotheses start from common-sense levels and may have been suggested by observations of that character, they do not directly refer to those levels but rather to conditions far removed from them. From the Ptolemaic hypothesis to the Copernican to the Keplerian to the Newtonian to the Einsteinian, the degree of abstractness continually increases, even though each attempts to account for much the same kind of phenomena (although, it is true, not the same range). Scientific observation certainly begins at the ordinary common-sense level, but its aim is perfectly abstract mathematical formulation: the representation of empirical statements in tautological form. The hypothesis is the first step in this direction; it takes off from familiar data, perhaps, but it does get off the ground.

We have been discussing hypotheses as single generalizations or single entities, but they rarely occur singly. Since hypotheses are discarded so rapidly, every scientist must have a great quantity at his command. And since they must account for the same phenomena and must share areas of common agreement, they constitute families of explanations. Nests of hypotheses may occur to a single investigator, or they may be collectively brought to bear on a problem by a group of investigators. In either case, rival explanations of the same crucial phenomena or provocative facts have to be tested and those found wanting discarded. Many are called, but few are chosen. The life-span of a hypothesis may vary from the flicker of an instant to many years. A hypothesis may occur to an investigator in the process of sorting out possible explanations and, because of obvious limitations and inadequacies, be instantly given up. Or one may be announced by him in a technical journal and then, because of the difficulties confronting its investigation, await years for the decision regarding its final disposition.

3. CRITERIA

What are the proper criteria of good hypotheses? A good hypothesis offers a possible explanation. This requirement must be broken down into six lesser but more precise statements.

(a) A good hypothesis adequately explains the observed facts. The classic example is the hypothesis of gravitation—suggested to Newton in 1665 by small objects falling toward the earth and extended by him to account for planets remaining in their orbits. Obviously, if the uncovering of crucial or provocative unexplained facts gives rise to the hypothesis, it must be cast in the form of a principle of explanation or, alternatively, in some form from which it might be possible to deduce a principle of explanation.

(b) A good hypothesis offers the simplest explanation possible under the circumstances. A modified form of Occam's razor is applicable here. Economy of explanation is one of the guiding principles of science. Einstein's theory of relativity is simpler than Whitehead's, and so it was chosen.

(c) A good hypothesis offers an explanation that is as complex as necessary under the circumstances. This is the counterprinciple of Occam's razor and, although it has no name, is to be found in Kant's *Critique of Pure reason* (A656). It could be called "Kant's shaving bowl." It is simply the demand for completeness of explanation: a good hypothesis is broad enough to cover all the observed facts. Gibbs' phase rule in chemistry—a formula for classifying all heterogeneous systems in equilibrium—is complex enough to cover all the observed facts. However, a qualification must be noted here. All abstract formulas are stated as general propositions to cover an infinite population of instances; thus, in the very act of meeting the requirement of covering the observed facts —always, of necessity, a finite number—they go far beyond them.

(d) A good hypothesis can be brought into agreement or disagreement with observations. In other words, it is cast in such a form that it lends itself readily to investigation. A theory that the metagalaxy has outer limits would be difficult and perhaps impossible ever to verify. Hypotheses referable to an empirical subject matter but, by their nature, insusceptible of verification have no place in science. On the other hand, impossibility of verification is difficult to demonstrate. Not so long ago the proposition that there are craters on the other side of the moon was a favorite example of an unverifiable hypothesis; now, since the invention of the rockets and the firing of the first artificial satellites of the earth, the same proposition becomes potentially verifiable.

(e) A good hypothesis is strong enough to compel inquiry. It must be sufficiently intriguing to urge the investigator to try to verify it. He will try if it is the kind of hypothesis that, once verified, would suggest many further experiments. It would be difficult to deny such a claim to Darwin's original hypothesis of the origin of species by natural selection. Some hypotheses are so provocative that they open up entirely new lines of investigation; these are apt to be tested before others.

(f) A good hypothesis extends inquiry. Some hypotheses suggest more than their own immediate confirmation and lead on to investigations beyond the limits of their confirmation. When William Gilbert introduced the concept of mass by setting up a function between the magnetic strength of a lodestone and its mass, he launched a hypothesis which was taken up by many physicists who came after him, notably by Kepler, Galileo, and Newton. Bernard's hypothesis of 1885 concerning the constancy of the internal environment of the organism was succeeded by Cannon's theory of homeostasis, with its profitable influence on many aspects of physiology and medicine. Darwin's evolutionary hypothesis gave a tremendous impetus to developmental studies in many biological fields.

4. OCCASIONS

Hypotheses are never introduced *ad hoc* but always for reasons. However, quite diverse occasions function very well as reasons.

(a) Quite commonly a hypothesis is developed when problems are encountered which cannot be solved on the basis of existing theories and when unexpected data are turned up which the old, established laws cannot explain. Harvey discovered that the heart deals in a minute or two with as much blood as there is in the entire body, which suggested to him that, since the heart keeps on pumping, the blood must somehow travel from the arteries to the veins and so back to the heart. This single, unexplained fact of the volume pumped induced him to discover the hypothesis of the circulation of the blood, which he announced in 1628. Again, the Fitzgerald contractions and the Michelson-Morley experiment could not be accounted for by Newtonian mechanics. A new hypothesis broad enough for both had to be developed.

When rival theories are in conflict, a temporary sort of settlement may be reached through some wider hypothesis. Copernicus was confronted with the established Ptolemaic theory and the theory of Nicetas, who—according to Cicero—thought the earth moved. He therefore in 1530 proposed the hypothesis that the stars were fixed while the planets in the solar system, including the earth, were in motion. The so-called unified field theories can perhaps be described as hypotheses, although they are already mathematical and incorporate the results of much experimental work. A number of these—the theories of Einstein, S. N. Bose, Vaclav Hlavatý, and Heisenberg—contend at the present time for the unification of physics.

Experiments may seem to disclose conflicting data; here, too, resolution through the positing of a hypothesis is called for. The evidence for light as a stream of particles seems irreconcilable with the evidence for light as a wave phenomenon.

(b) Hypotheses are devised as bridges from raw data to an explanatory principle which accounts for them. Heisenberg's principle of indeterminacy was an attempt to get from the raw data to the explanatory principle even at the cost of accepting the apparent conflict between the data; and Bohr's principle of complementarity, by extending the difficulty to the world as a universal condition, shows how far explanatory principles can be carried in such an instance. Either the raw data or the explanatory principle may fail of establishment to some degree as a result of the reliance upon the other. Either the data are accepted and the explanatory principle is presumptive, which is the usual case, or the principle is accepted and the data are inferred. Young's experiments with interference phenomena at the turn of this century, with the resultant supposition that light must consist of waves, constitute an example of the former. Freud's principle of an unconscious mechanism moved by the proposed entities "ego," "superego," and "id" exemplifies the latter. Whichever side the established evidence falls on, the other side will always be presumption.

(c) Hypotheses often are discovered by chance. Malus' discovery of the polarization of reflected light and Curie's discovery of radium are now famous instances. Galvani touched the leg of a frog with a piece of metal entirely by accident. And it was an accident in a laboratory which precipitated the discovery of the wave property of matter by Davisson and Germer. Chance discoveries such as these are possible only to investigators with a broad deductive background in a particular science. A man in one field of inquiry does not accidentally make a discovery in some other. Prolonged preoccupation with a particular subject matter seems to be a much overlooked prerequisite of all chance discoveries. In short, the probability of serendipity is a function of the number of observers and experimenters with deductive training and long absorption in the science. The chance discovery here, from the hypothetical point of view, was not the substances but the inference from observations that new and hitherto unknown substances were involved in the phenomenon. The number of unknowns in any situation being what they are, it would be impossible to rule out chance occurrences, and some of these are bound to be happy occasions; the experimenter cannot foresee everything that might happen, and so he cannot see, either, what might suggest further exploration.

(d) The exploration of practical problems may be the occasion for the discovery of hypotheses in pure science. A significant amount of pure science has come out of industrial laboratories where the solution of problems in applied science was being sought. Much of our knowledge of the carbon compounds issues from the search for patentable products. Practical application of scientific knowledge involves a knowledge of science; hence expediency, far from driving out principles, requires them. The hypothesis of atomic fusion resulted from efforts to improve the efficacy of the atomic bomb as an instrument of war and of atomic energy for the practical purposes of a world at peace.

In addition to the above occasions when hypotheses arise, on many other occasions they are not present and do not seem to be needed—for example, when observations are explored by means of various precise methods, such as group theory in quantum mechanics. Newton's contention that he framed no hypotheses could be interpreted to mean that he did not appeal to explanatory principles far removed from the data, such as, for instance, metaphysical principles would be. His careful experiments to show by means of the prism that white light contains all colors only made explicit a proposition which must have implicitly suggested his investigations in a given direction. Then, too, in such cases the various, relatively minor consequences of previously established theories (which were once hypotheses but are no longer) are being worked out. Hypotheses, if successful, lead to operations and experiments which sometimes do not seem to require further hypotheses. But such a situation soon runs its course in consequences both theoretical and practical and cannot continue indefinitely without further stimulation; and so the more familiar rhythm involving occasional hypotheses is eventually restored.

5. DISCOVERY

There is no inevitable mechanism which, once set in motion, must carry the investigator from immersion in the data of his science to hypotheses. Experience is necessary for the discovery of hypotheses, but it is not a sufficient cause; often experience leads the investigator nowhere.

Hypotheses may be discovered by induction from individual instances or by deduction from more inclusive theory. The former is by far the more familiar procedure. Laboratory experiments usually suggest inductions; work at the desk is more likely to produce deductions. Fleming's inference that an antibacterial substance might be the microorganism responsible for contaminating one of the plates on which he was studying mutations among staphylococci is an example of a hypothesis discovered by induction from data. A deductive hypothesis would be, for example, a constructed mathematical model not yet tested against empirical data.

A hypothesis induced from one instance is no weaker than the same hypothesis induced from several thousand. A hundred interferometers would not have made the null results of Michelson-Morley's experiments to detect the ether drift more null or suggested any more than they did to Einstein; and a hundred contaminated plates would not have suggested any more to Fleming than did the one which led to the discovery of penicillin. Instances count only when we are trying to support or verify a hypothesis—but this is a different, and a later, kind of induction.

The ideal of science is system; every science wishes to put its findings in order, and at present all known types of order are deductive. The role of hypotheses is to suggest the missing axioms from which theorems in agreement with observation can be deduced. A hypothesis and the facts to which it refers stand in the same logical relation as the axioms and the theorems which can be deduced from the axioms. In choosing a hypothesis, the experimenter is reaching inductively for something which is to stand to the experiments which are to test it in the relation of an axiom to its theorems: he intends to employ it for purposes of deduction.

Accordingly, hypotheses are more often than not inductively discovered, but they are not inductive *by nature*. Induction in this connection is the choosing of axioms for deductive purposes. A hypothesis is a proposition proposed for consideration, and as such it is neither inductive nor deductive. Induction refers to the manner in which a proposition is suggested by data disclosed to experience; deduction refers to the manner in which a proposition fits into a scheme of propositions. Thus there is no such thing as a hypothesis inherently inductive or one inherently deductive; there are only hypotheses inductively or deductively discovered. Although the discovery of hypotheses calls upon the rarest of human faculties, imagination, and the presence of a hypothesis of some sort is the *sine qua non* of the scientific method, it remains true that hypotheses are intended to fit eventually into a deductive scheme or else to be abandoned as worthless.

Hypotheses, then, are usually the results of inductions. More rarely, they may be arrived at deductively, as we have noted above. From a broad theory a deduction may be made to some proposition which can be tested for agreement with observation while the theory itself is receiving mathematical treatment in order to demonstrate its consistency. Thus hypotheses are arrived at deductively further along in the chain of investigation rather than at the beginning. Confirmations of the special theory of relativity continued to be made experimentally in order to test lesser hypotheses long after the mathematical consistency of the general theory was accepted.

6. FUNCTION

The purpose of hypotheses is to lead the investigator to new knowledge; the aim is to move from suggestions which are uncertain to information which is more reliable. Hypotheses are self-liquidating: if they are successful, then they remain as hypotheses no longer.

The hypothesis was suggested by data, and it will be tested by more data. It is, then, a way of bridging from samples of data to other samples, usually from small samples to large samples (and never the same samples). Samples of data are, of course, collections of individual cases. Now the curious thing is that no way has ever been found for getting from individuals to other individuals except by way of a general proposition. Archeologists excavate stones which can be interpreted as the foundations of a large palace on a site in the southwestern Peloponnesus, and they argue that this may have belonged to King Nestor of Homeric times. The inference from the present-day remains to a former state of glory rests on the general proposition that when buildings are destroyed by fire, their stone foundations remain indefinitely. Hypotheses, being general propositions, always extend beyond the data, no matter how large the collection, as was noted above. They are statements about populations indefinitely large and perhaps infinite, and are not limited to any collection, however great. For the rule holds that no number of individual instances will ever exhaust a universal proposition, and a universal proposition is one that can be predicated of indefinitely many.

In the case of hypotheses which pertain to individuals, it is equally true that such hypotheses are not limited to the individuals. For it is *types* of individuals and not the individuals themselves that are being considered and proposed for investigation. The anatomy of a rat would interest few unless what is true of that rat could be assumed true for most and perhaps all. The investigator will not concern himself with or preserve that specific rat, but he will retain what he has learned of the type. Thus the hypothesis suggests new lines of evidence prompted by the investigation of old types, and it helps the scientist imagine relevant types which he can then devise experiments to discover.

In this fashion a hypothesis tells the investigator what to look for and where. It defines a field of data as instances of a generalization, so that confirmation or disconfirmation is rendered feasible, for there must, after all, be something to confirm or disconfirm. No scientist ever undertook an experiment without having before him some notion, however vague, of what he hoped to find. A pilot or exploratory experiment conducted in order to probe into or run over a range of possibilities constitutes a hypothesis, which is no less one for being implicit or unacknowledged. That it was not formulated clearly and explicitly is no evidence that it was not there. For why else would he have chosen this experiment rather than another? Implicit hypotheses, operating as assumptions dimly understood, are still hypotheses. Every theory we entertain and every law upon which we rely began as a hypothesis at some point in its development.

Of course, the fate of most hypotheses is to be investigated and rejected. Therefore, it is essential to any investigator to have on hand a vast number. An able investigator fertilizes his deductive knowledge and technical skill with imagination to produce hypotheses in abundance. One or more may survive the first tests. And often a discredited candidate turns out to have been of some value, for important discoveries often emerge from investigations undertaken to explore some hypothesis which later proved to be false. The hypothesis of the ether is one such. Investigation did not disclose its presence but did lead eventually to the special theory of relativity.

PURE SCIENCE, APPLIED SCIENCE AND TECHNOLOGY

1. THE THEORY OF PRACTICE

It is not the business of scientists to investigate just what the business of science is. Yet the business of science is in need of investigation. If we are to consider the relations between science and engineering, the relation between pure and applied science will have first to be made very clear;

and for this purpose we shall need working definitions. Once stated, these definitions may seem an elaboration of the obvious and an oversimplification. But the elaboration often seems obvious only *after* it has been stated, and the definitions may have to be simple in order to bring out the necessary distinctions.

By "pure science" or "basic research" is meant a method of investigating nature by the experimental method in an attempt to satisfy the need to know. Many activities in pure science are not experimental, as, for instance, biological taxonomy; but it can always be shown that in such cases the activities are ancillary to experiment. In the case of biological taxonomy the classifications are of experimental material. Taxonomy is practiced in other areas where it is not scientific, such as in the operation of libraries.

By "applied science" is meant the use of pure science for some practical human purpose.

Thus science serves two human purposes: to know and to do. The former is a matter of understanding, the latter a matter of action. Technology, which began as the attempt to satisfy a practical need without the use of science, will receive a fuller treatment in a later section.

Applied science, then, is simply pure science applied. But scientific method has more than one end; it leads to explanation and application. It achieves explanation in the discovery of laws, and the laws can be applied. Thus both pure science and applied science have aims and results. Pure science has as its aim the understanding of nature; it seeks explanation. Applied science has as its aim the control of nature; it has the task of employing the findings of pure science to get practical tasks done. Pure science has as a result the furnishing of laws for application in applied science. And, as we shall learn later in this essay, applied science has as a result the stimulation of discovery in pure science.

Applied science puts to practical human uses the discoveries made in pure science. Whether there would be such a thing as pure science alone is hard to say; there are reasons for thinking that there would be, for pure science has a long history and, as we have noted, another justification. There could be technology without science; for millennia, in fact, there was. But surely there could be no applied science without pure science: applied science means just what it says, namely, the application of science, and so without pure science there would be nothing to apply.

Logically, pure science pursued in disregard of applied science seems to be the *sine qua non* of applied science, while historically the problems toward which applied science is directed came before pure science.

It has been asserted, for instance, that Greek geometry, which is certainly pure, arose out of the interest in land surveying problems in

Egypt, where the annual overflow of the Nile obliterated all conventional boundaries. Certainly it is true that the same concept of infinity is necessary for the understanding of Euclidean geometry and for the division of farms. Be that as it may, it yet remains true that the relations between pure and applied science are often varied and subtle, and will require exploration.

Let us propose the hypothesis that all pure science is applicable.

No proof exists for such an hypothesis; all that can be offered is evidence in favor of it. This evidence consists of two parts, the first logical and the second historical.

The logical evidence in favor of the hypothesis is contained in the very nature of pure science itself. Any discovery in pure science that gets itself established will have gained the support of experimental data. Thus there must be a connection between the world of fact, the actual world, in other words, which corresponds to sense experience, and the laws of pure science. It is not too difficult to take the next step, and so to suppose that the laws, which were suggested by facts in the world corresponding to sense experience, could be applied back to that world.

The second part of the evidence for the applicability of all of the laws of pure science is contained in the record of those laws which have been applied. The modern western cultures have been altered by applied science, and now Soviet Russia and China are following their lead. Indeed so prevalent are the effects of applied science, and so concealed the leadership of pure science, that those whose understanding of science is limited are apt to identify all of science with applied science and even to assume that science itself means technology or heavy industry.

One argument against the position advocated here would be based upon the number of pure theories in science for which no application has yet been found. But this is no argument at all; for to have any weight, it would have to show not only that there had been no application but also why there could be none. Yet a time lag between the discovery of a theory and its application to practice is not uncommon. How many years elapsed between Faraday's discovery of the dynamo and its general manufacture and use in industry? Conic sections were discovered by Apollonius of Perga in the third century B.C., when they were of intellectual interest only, and they were applied to the problems of engineering only in the seventeenth century. Non-Euclidean geometry, worked out by Riemann as an essay in pure mathematics early in the nineteenth century, was used by Einstein in his theory of relativity in the twentieth century. The coordinate geometry of Descartes made possible the study of curves by means of quadratic equations. It was in Descartes' time that the application of conic sections to the orbit of planets was first noticed; later the same curves were used in the analysis of the paths of projectiles, in searchlight reflectors, and in the cables of suspension bridges. Chlorinated diphenylethane was synthesized in 1874. Its value as insecticide (DDT) was not recognized until 1939 when a systematic search for moth repellants was undertaken for the military. The photoelectric cell was used in pure science, notably by George E. Hale on observations of the sun's corona in 1894. Twenty-five years later it was found employed in making motion pictures. It often happens that the discovery of a useful material is not sufficient; it is necessary also to discover a use, to connect the material to some function in which it could prove advantageous. Paracelsus discovered ether and even observed its anesthetic properties, and Valerius Cordus gave the formula for its preparation as early as the sixteenth century. But it was many centuries before ether was used as an anesthetic.

Presumably, then, pure scientific formulations which have not been applied are merely those for which as yet no applications have been found. In the effort to extend knowledge it is not strategically wise to hamper investigation with antecedent assurances of utility. Many of the scientific discoveries which later proved most advantageous in industry had not been self-evidently applicable. This is certainly true of Gibbs' phase rule in chemistry, for instance. It often happens that for the most abstract theories new acts of discovery are necessary in order to put them to practical use.

2. FROM THEORY TO PRACTICE

It should be observed at the outset that applications are matters of relevance. The line between pure and applied science is a thin one; they are distinct in their differences, but one fades into the other. For instance, the use of crystallography in the packing industry is an application, but so is the use of the mathematical theory of groups in pure crystallography and in quantum mechanics. The employment of mathematics in pure science means application from the point of view of mathematics but remoteness from application from the point of view of experiment. Some branches of mathematics have been so widely employed that we have come to think of them as practical affairs. This is the case with probability or differential equations. Both branches, however, considered in their mathematical aspects and not at all in relation to the various experimental sciences in which they have proved so useful, are theoretical disciplines with a status of their own which in no wise depends upon the uses to which they may be put.

Procedurally, the practitioner introduces into his problem the facilitation afforded by some abstract but relevant theory from either mathematics or pure science. The statistical theory of extreme values is a branch of mathematics, yet it has application to studies of metal fatigue and to such meteorological phenomena as annual droughts, atmospheric pressure and temperature, snowfalls, and rainfalls. The discovery of the Salk vaccine against polio virus was an achievement of applied science. Yet Pasteur's principle of pure science, that dead or attenuated organisms could induce the production of antibodies within blood serum, was assumed by Salk; so the immensely important practical applications would not have been possible without the previous theoretical work.

It is clear, then, that we need three separate and distinct kinds of pursuits, and, perforce, three types of interest to accompany them. The first is pure science. Pure theoretical sciences are concerned with the discovery of natural law and the description of nature, and with nothing else. These sciences are conducted by men whose chief desire is to know, and this requires a detached inquiry—which Einstein has somewhere called "the holy curiosity of inquiry" and which Emerson declared to be perpetual. Such a detachment and such a pursuit are comparable in their high seriousness of purpose only to religion and art.

The second type is applied science, in which are included all applications of the experimental pure sciences. These are concerned with the improvement of human means and ends and with nothing else. They are conducted by men whose chief desires are practical: either the improvement of human conditions or profit, or both. Temperamentally, the applied scientists are not the same as the pure scientists: their sights while valid are lower; they are apt to be men of greater skill but of lesser imagination; what they lack in loftiness they gain in humanity. It would be a poor view which in all respects held either variety secondary. Yet there is a scale of order to human enterprises, even when we are sure we could dispense with none of them; and so we turn with some measure of dependence to the type of leadership which a preoccupation with detached inquiry is able to provide.

The third type is the intermediate or *modus operandi* level, which is represented by the scientist with an interest in the solution of the problems presented by the task of getting from theory to practice. As Whitehead said, a short but concentrated interval for the development of imaginative design lies between them. Consider for example the role of the discovery of Hertzian waves, which not only led to the development of radio but also brilliantly confirmed Maxwell's model of an electromagnetic field, specifically the existence of electromagnetic waves, with a constant representing the velocity of light in two of the four equations.

The conception of science as exclusively pure or utterly applied is erroneous; the situation is no longer so absolute. When scientific theories were not too abstract, it was possible for practical-minded men to address themselves both to a knowledge of the theory and to the business of applying it in practice. The nineteenth century saw the rise of the "inventor," the technologist who employed the results of the theoretical scientist in the discovery of devices, or instruments, of new techniques in electromagnetics, in chemistry, and in many other fields. Earlier scientists like Maxwell had prepared the way for inventors like Edison. In some sciences, notably physics, however, this simple situation no longer prevails. The theories discovered there are of such a degree of mathematical abstraction that an intermediate type of interest and activity is now required. The theories which are discovered in the physicists' laboratories and published as journal articles take some time to make their way into engineering handbooks and contract practices. Some intermediate theory is necessary for getting from theory to practice.

A good example of the *modus operandi* level is furnished by the activities and the scientists concerned with making the first atomic bombs. Hahn and Strasmann discovered in 1938 that neutrons could split the nuclei of uranium. Einstein and Planck had earlier produced the requisite theories, but it was Enrico Fermi, Lise Meitner, and others who worked out the method of getting from relativity and quantum mechanics to bombs which could be made to explode by atomic fission.

3. TECHNOLOGY

There has been some misunderstanding of the distinction between applied science and technology; and understandably so, for the terms have not been clearly distinguished. Primarily the difference is one of type of approach. The applied scientist as such is concerned with the task of discovering applications for pure theory. The technologist has a problem which lies a little nearer to practice. Both applied scientist and technologist employ experiment; but in the former case guided by hypotheses deduced from theory, while in the latter case employing trial-and-error or skilled approaches derived from concrete experience. The theoretical biochemist is a pure scientist, working for the most part with the carbon compounds. The biochemist is an applied scientist when he explores the physiological effects of some new drug, perhaps trying it out to begin with on laboratory animals, then perhaps on himself or on volunteers from his laboratory or from the charity ward of some hospital. The doctor or practicing physician is a technologist when he prescribes it for some of his patients.

Speaking historically, the achievements of technology are those which developed without benefit of science; they arose empirically either by accident or as a matter of common experience. The use of certain biochemicals in the practice of medicine antedates the development of science: notably, ephedrine, cocaine, curare, and quinine. This is true also of the pre-scientific forms of certain industrial processes, such as cheese-making, fermentation, and tanning.

The applied scientist fits a case under a class; the technologist takes it from there and works it out, so to speak, *in situ*. Applied science consists in a system of concrete interpretations of scientific propositions directed to some end useful for human life. Technology might now be described as a further step in applied science by means of the improvement of instruments. In this last sense, technology has always been with us; it was vastly accelerated in efficiency by having been brought under applied science as a branch.

Technology is more apt to develop empirical laws than theoretical laws, laws which are generalizations from practice rather than laws which are intuited and then applied to practice. Empirical procedures like empirical laws are often the product of technological practice without benefit of theory. Since 1938, when Cerletti and Bini began to use electrically induced convulsions in the treatment of schizophrenia, the technique of electroshock therapy has been widespread in psychiatric practice. Yet there is no agreement as to what precisely occurs or how the improvement is produced; a theory to explain the practice is entirely wanting.

Like applied science, technology has its ideals. Let us consider the technological problem of improving the airplane, for instance. For a number of decades now, the problem to which airplane designers have addressed themselves is how to increase the speed and the pay load of airplanes. This means cutting down on the weight of the empty airplane in proportion to its carrying capacity while increasing its effective speed. If we look back at what has been accomplished in this direction, then extrapolate our findings into the future in order to discern the outlines of the ideal, we shall be surprised to discover that what the designers have been working toward is an airplane that will carry an infinite amount of pay load at an infinite speed while itself weighing nothing at all! This of course is a limit, and like all such limits, is an ideal intended to be increasingly approached without ever being absolutely reached.

Conception of the ideal is evidently of the utmost practicality and cannot be escaped in applied formulations. Yet the existence of such a thing as a technical ideal is fairly recent and is peculiar to western culture. The ideal of a general character envisaged in this connection is that of fitness of purpose and of economy; no material or energy is to be wasted. Roman engineers built bridges designed to support loads far in excess of anything that might be carried over them; their procedures would be regarded as bad engineering today. The modern engineer builds his bridge to carry exactly the load that will be put upon it plus a small margin for safety, but no more; he must not waste structural steel nor use more rivets than necessary, and labor must be held to minimum. The ideal of technology is efficiency.

Although technologists work in terms of ideals, they are nevertheless more bound down to materials than is the applied scientist, just as the applied scientist in his turn is more bound down to materials than is the pure scientist. Since the technologist is limited by what is available, when he increases the going availability it is usually at the material level. The environment with which a society reacts is the available environment, not the entire or total environment; and the available environment is that part of the environment which is placed within reach of the society by its knowledge and techniques. These are laid out for it and increased by the pure and the applied sciences. Only when these limits are set can the technologist go to work. For example, discovery of the internal combustion engine which required gasoline as fuel turned men's attention to possible sources of oil. The applied scientist found ways of locating oil in the ground, while the petroleum technologist made the actual discoveries. In the hundred years since Edwin Drake drilled the world's first oil well near Titusville, Pennsylvania, in 1859, the technologists have taken this discovery very far. Oil is now a natural resource, a part of the available environment; but it can hardly be said to have been so a hundred years ago, although it was just as much in the ground then as now.

Another kind of technologist is the engineer; engineering is the most down-to-earth of all scientific work that can justify the name of science at all. In engineering the solutions of the technologists are applied to particular cases. The building of bridges, the medical treatment of patients, the designing of instruments, all improvements in model constructions of already existing tools—these are the work of the engineer. But the theories upon which such work rests, such as studies in the flow or "creep" of metals, the physics of lubrication, the characteristics of surface tensions of liquids—these belong to the applied scientist.

The industrial scientific laboratory is devoted to the range of applied science, from "fundamental research," by which is meant long range work designed to produce or improve practical technology, to immediate technological gains from which manufacturing returns are expected, for instance, the testing of materials and of manufactured products. Technological laboratories have been established in the most important of the giant industrial companies, such as DuPont, General Electric, Eastman Kodak, and Bell Telephone. The work of such laboratories is cumulative and convergent; applied science in such an institution is directed toward eventual technological improvement, the range of applied science and technology being employed as a series of connecting links to tie up pure science with manufacturing. University and foundation laboratories often serve the same purpose, but with the emphasis shifted toward the theoretical end of the scientific spectrum.

The development of technology has a strong bearing on its situation today and may be traced briefly. In the Middle Ages, there was natural philosophy and craftsmanship. Such science as existed was in the hands of the natural philosophers, and such technology as existed was in the hands of the craftsmen. There was precious little of either, for the exploration of the natural world was conducted by speculative philosophers, while the practical tasks were carried out by handicrafts employing comparatively simple tools, although there were exceptions: the windmill, for instance. There was little commerce between them, however, for their aims were quite different, and the effort to understand the existence of God took precedence over lesser pursuits.

Gradually, however, natural philosophy was replaced by experimental science, and handicraft by the power tool. The separation continued to be maintained, and for the same reasons; and this situation did not change until the end of the eighteenth century. At that time, the foundations of technology shifted from craft to science. Technology and applied science ran together into the same powerful channels at the same time that the applications of pure science became more abundant. A craft is learned by the apprentice method; a science must be learned from the study of principles as well as from the practices of the laboratory, and while the practice may come from applied science the principles are those of pure science.

There is now only the smallest distinction between applied science, the application of the principles of pure science, and technology. The methods peculiar to technology: trial-and-error, invention aided by intuition, have merged with those of applied science: adopting the findings of pure science to the purposes of obtaining desirable practical consequences. Special training is required, as well as some understanding of applied and even of pure science. In general, industries are based on manufacturing processes which merely reproduce on a large scale effects first learned and practiced in a scientific laboratory. The manufacture of gasoline, penicillin, electricity, oxygen were never developed from technological procedures, but depended upon work first done by pure scientists. Science played a predominant role in such physical industries as steel, aluminum, and petroleum; in such chemical industries as pharmaceuticals and potash; in such biological industries as medicine and husbandry.

A concomitant development, in which the triumph of pure science over technology shows clear, is in the design and manufacture of instruments. The goniometer, for the determination of the refractive index of fluids (used in the chemical industries); the sugar refractometer, for the reading of the percentages by weight of sugar (used in sugar manufacture); the pyrometer, for the measurement of high temperatures (used in the making of electric light bulbs and of gold and silver utensils); the polarimeter, for ascertaining the amount of sugar in urine (used by the medical profession); these and many others, such as for instance the focometer for studies in the length of objectives, the anomaloscope for color blindness, and the spectroscope for the measurement of wave lengths, are precision instruments embodying principles not available to the technologist working unaided by a knowledge of pure science.

4. FROM PRACTICE TO THEORY

In the course of pursuing practical ends abstract principles of science hitherto unsuspected are often discovered. The mathematical theory of probability was developed because some professional gamblers wished to know the odds in games of chance. Electromagnetics stimulated the development of differential equations, and hydrodynamics function theory. Carnot founded the pure science of thermodynamics as a result of the effort to improve the efficiency of steam and other heat engines. Aerodynamics and atomic physics were certainly advanced more swiftly because of the requirements of war. Air pollution, which accompanies big city "smog," has led a number of physical chemists to investigate the properties of extreme dilution. Hence it is not surprising that many advances in pure science have been made in industrial laboratories: from the Bell Telephone laboratories alone have come the discoveries by Davisson and Germer of the diffraction of electrons, by Jansky of radio astronomy, and by Shannon of information theory.

Technology has long been an aid and has furnished an impetus to experimental science. The development of the delicate mechanisms requisite for the carrying out of certain experiments calls on all the professional abilities of the instrument maker. Such a relation is not a new one; it has long existed. The skill of the Venetian glass-blowers made possible many of Torricelli's experiments on gases. Indeed, glass can be followed through a single chain of development for several centuries, from the early microscopes to interferometers. The study of electromagnetics was responsible for the later commerce in electric power and the vast industries founded on it. But, contrariwise, thermodynamics grew up as a result of the problems arising from the use of steam in industry. We cannot afford to neglect in our considerations the economic support as well as the social justification which industry has furnished, and continues to be prepared to furnish, to research. The extraordinary rise of pure chemistry in Germany was not unrelated to the industry constructed on the basis of the aniline dyes, as well as cosmetics and explosives, during the nineteenth century.

The harm to practice of neglecting the development of pure theoretic science will not be felt until the limits of installing industries by means of applied science and technology, and of spreading its results, have been reached. Science can to some extent continue to progress on its own momentum together with such aid as the accidental or adventitious discoveries of pure science in technological laboratories can furnish it. But there are limits to this sort of progress. Thus far the communist countries of the east have taken every advantage of the scientific developments achieved in the capitalist countries of the west. But after all, the applied science which the west has been able to furnish has been the result of its own preoccupations with pure science and with theoretic considerations which lay outside the purview of any practice. Industrial laboratories may occasionally contribute to pure science, but that is not their chief aim; and it is apt to be forgotten that such industries would not exist were it not for the fact that some centuries ago a handful of scientists with no thought of personal gain or even of social benefit tried to satisfy their curiosity about the nature of things. The restless spirit of science, never content with findings, hardly concerned with the applications of findings, is always actively engaged in pursuing methods in terms of assumptions, and must have some corner of the culture in which it can hope to be protected in its isolation. A wise culture will always provide it elbow room, with the understanding that in the future some amortized inquiry is bound to pay dividends. The ivory tower can be, and sometimes is, the most productive building in the market place.

Of course, applied science and technology cannot be independent of pure science, nor can pure science be independent of applied science and technology. The two developments work together and are interwoven. Gilbert discovered that the freely suspended magnetic needle (i.e., the compass) could be a practical aid to navigation at the same time he proposed that perhaps the earth was a gigantic magnet.

Problems which arise in the midst of practical tasks often suggest lines of theoretical inquiry. But there is more. Pragmatic evidence has always been held by logicians to have little standing. A scientific hypothesis needs more support than can be obtained from the practical fact that "it works." For who knows how long it will work or how well? What works best today may not work best tomorrow. A kind of practice which supports one theory may be supplanted by a more efficient kind of practice which supports quite a different theory. Relativity mechanics gives more accurate measurements than Newtonian mechanics. That use does not determine theory can be easily shown. Despite the theoretical success of the Copernican theory as refined and advanced by Kepler, Galileo, and Newton, we have never ceased to use the Ptolemaic conception in guiding our ships or in regulating our clocks. However, if the practical success achieved by the application of certain theories in pure science cannot be construed as a proof of their truth, neither can it be evidence of the contradictory: workability is no evidence of falsity, either. Newton is still correct within limits. Practicality suggests truth and supports the evidence in its favor even if offering no final proof. The practical uses of atomic energy do not prove that matter is transformable into energy, but they offer powerful support. Hence, the use of a scientific law in the control of nature constitutes the check of prediction and control.

5. CROSS-FIELD APPLICATIONS

We have treated all too briefly the relations of theory to practice and of practice to theory in a given science. We have also mentioned the productive nature of cross-field research. It remains now to discuss a last dimension of relations between science and practice, and this is what we may call cross-field applications: the employment of the practical effects of one science in those of another.

The applications of science have been greatly aided by the cross-fertilization of techniques. Radio astronomy, which has proved so useful in basic research, being already responsible for the discovery of "radio stars," and for adding to our knowledge of meteor streams and the solar corona, owes its inception to a borrowed instrument. Cross-field application has a long history, dating at least to the early half of the eighteenth century when distilleries in England brought together the results of techniques of producing gin acquired from both chemistry and theories of heat energy. Perhaps the most prominent instance of this is the way in which medicine has drawn upon the physical technologies. The use of the vacuum tube amplifier and the cathode ray oscillograph in determining the electrical potential accompanying events in the nervous system, the entire areas covered by encephalography and by roentgenology show the enormous benefits which have accrued to medical studies and procedures. Scintillation counters, developed and used in physical research, have been employed to measure the rate at which the thyroid gland in a given individual removes iodine from the blood stream; to measure the natural radioactivity of the body; to determine the extent of ingested radioactive compounds in the body; to assay the radioactive iron in blood samples. Chemistry has been an equally potent aid to pharmacology, which would have hardly existed in any important sense without it.

Other instances abound, and indeed multiply every day. In 1948 the Armour Research Foundation sponsored a Crystallographic Center, of interest to pharmaceutical corporations because of the crystalline nature of some of the vitamins. The invention of automatic sequence controlled calculators and other types of computing machines has seen their immediate application to atomic research and to military problems of a technical nature. Medical knowledge is being placed at the service of airplane designers, who must estimate just what strains their aircraft will demand of pilots. Perhaps the most graphic illustration of cross-field application is in scientific agriculture. Here hardly a single science can be omitted: physics, chemistry, biology—all contribute enormously to the joint knowledge which it is necessary to have if soils are to respond to management.

The cross-field applications of science usually work upward in fields corresponding to the integrative levels of the sciences. Applications found in physics will be employed in chemistry or biology, those found in chemistry will be employed in biology or psychology, those found in biology will be employed in psychology or sociology, and so on. The use of physics in biology has in fact brought into existence the science of biophysics, in which are studied the physics of biological systems, the biological effects of physical agents, and the application of physical methods to biological problems.

The cross-fertilization of applied science, the use of techniques, skills, devices, acquired in one science to achieve gains in another, has effects which tend to go beyond either. They add up to a considerable acceleration in the speed with which the applied sciences affect the culture as a whole. In the brief space of some several hundred years, western culture has been altered out of all recognition by the employment of applied science and technology to purposes of industry, health, government, and war. Much of the alteration has been accomplished by means of the cooperation between the sciences. We now know that the shortest route to an effective practice lies indirectly through the understanding of nature. If there exists a human purpose of a practical kind, then the quickest as well as the most efficient method of achieving it is to apply the relevant natural laws of science to it.

THE SCIENTIFIC PHILOSOPHY

1. THE PHILOSOPHY IN SCIENCE

Science is a comparatively recent affair, but the alternatives at our command in philosophy are old ones. The range of Greek philosophy seems to have an astonishing stability. The philosophy of religion was used for centuries to bolster religion. It is some indication of the rapid growth of the prestige of science that now the philosophy of science is used to bolster philosophy.

The philosophy of science is not a topic which has been settled nor is it one which can be settled easily. It is a speculative field of inquiry, to which there will be, and indeed need to be, many contributions. Some writers endeavor to interpret science in terms of a given philosophy, while others try to show that no philosophy is needed in the understanding of science. Poincaré, for instance, assumed that philosophy is what we impose conventionally upon our scientific schemes, thus approaching the philosophy of science from the standpoint of philosophy rather than of science; and Mach argued that philosophy disturbs the economy of science which seeks agreement between thought and observation, a sort of biological function requiring no interpretation.

The philosophers have always been interested in science, for philosophy itself was indistinguishable from science in ancient Greece. The scientists by contrast have always held different opinions about philosophy, but their succession of attitudes constitutes a recognizable cycle. The first efforts made by the scientist are in the interests of getting science free of philosophy. It is felt by the scientist that only what can be properly distinguished can be properly related; otherwise there would be only a confusion of science with philosophy, and confusion is an improper relation. Once, however, a science is on its feet and has successfully defined the difference between itself and philosophy, good relations can be established.

Our supposition will be that by examining science carefully enough it is possible to discover in it a full philosophy. What science means in philosophy is what we wish to explore, and this can be found out only by examining science—not by examining philosophy. But philosophy cannot be excluded, either, for it is a specific philosophy that we wish to discover, namely, the philosophy of science; and so we are obliged to look for it in science where in fact it operates.

The wrong kind of philosophy is the kind which is brought in to furnish an interpretation only when science falters: when it cannot determine the nature of life (vitalism), when it sets up a negative or a subjective principle (the principle of indeterminism), or when it cannot decide between rival hypotheses (light as wave or as particle). Philosophy is not a substitute for science nor an explicit aid to its endeavors. The philosophy of science cannot go against what the scientist does; but then he ought not to be confined to it, either. Science cannot be examined with the tools of science; science possesses the language to describe its operations but not to interpret its descriptions. We need to talk about science in terms to elicit the meaning of science.

There are two kinds of theories: those which do and those which do not lend themselves to experimental investigation. We shall call the former scientific theories and the latter philosophical theories. Now it so happens that scientific theories are the theories which guide research, while philosophical theories furnish the background against which the scientific theories are selected. Thus although in scientific procedure philosophical theories never overtly appear, covertly they make their presence felt. The right kind of philosophy, then, is the philosophy inherent in the scientific situation and standing in need only of elicitation.

It should not be supposed, however, that our troubles are so easily over. Two problems present themselves immediately in the philosophical examination of science: what exactly does the scientist do in his laboratory, in the field, and at his desk, and what is the meaning of what he does? Obviously, the scientist does many individual things: he observes, he manipulates concrete objects, and he comes to conclusions about them; but it is just the description of individual things which has always given the most trouble in philosophy. The history of philosophy is more often made up of attempts at analyzing universals; the account of individuals has been until lately much neglected. It will continue to be exceedingly baffling. The new situation disclosed by the philosophy of science is the difficulty of analyzing individuals.

Efficient causes are what work in an area of inquiry, but it is some final cause that has laid out the area. And it is in terms of the invisible final cause that we must interpret the workings of the efficient causes within the area. If we wish to observe what the scientist is doing when he is behaving like a scientist (for presumably he is not always one), and then to draw some inferences as to what his doings mean, we must remember that insofar as the various bits of his deliberate behavior in this connection are integrated we may suppose that he is following a plan of action, and it is the meaning of this plan that we are after: what, in short, are the assumptions behind the pattern which he aims at in his actions? He does not say, he only acts. The silent method represents actual procedure clothed in logic. Often the most intuitive scientists are left unaware of the structure which underlies their professional actions. There is, however, a system behind every system except logic. Metaphysics, which in its structure is synonymous with logic, is the metasystem.

The first thing to observe, perhaps, is that the experimentalist in one sense always behaves in the same way. If a chemist sets up a reaction and awaits the results, it is because he expects that the results obtained will be repeatable. An experiment, then, is an appeal to reason; it is intended to reveal some segment of the orderliness in nature. It is logic carried out in the area of action; that is to say, we study the action in order to determine the logic, actually, in logic itself, an instance of the fallacy of affirming the consequent, and defensible only as an inductive procedure. Were this not so, there would be no point in experimentation for it would tell us nothing.

It is folly to assume that only the methods of science are reliable, for there are also reliable *results*. We cling to the method over the results because we know that in many cases we shall improve upon the results and then abandon them, whereas we shall not abandon the method. But the results also have a certain measure of constancy, enough to justify us in drawing inferences concerning them.

We have now two areas in science to be considered: the method of science and its results. There is a third to be added: on what basis are we justified in setting up the method to obtain the results? Behind the method, and assumed by it, lies a set of presuppositions, or axioms. We shall find when we examine these that they are philosophical by nature.

Science does not set forth its own presuppositions. Therefore, what its presuppositions are it is difficult to determine, and the speculations concerning them constitute a separate inquiry. Put otherwise, empiricism itself does not tell us how far we are entitled to extrapolate empirical findings and still regard the conclusions themselves as empirical; but this is a serious question, too, and it belongs to the philosophy of science. The search for the metaphysical presuppositions of science, the logic of the method of science, the epistemology of the scientist, and the ethics of the conclusions of science, all belong to the philosophy of science and are equally subject to revision, as is the case with topics in any speculative field.

Clearly, then, we shall need definitions both of philosophy and of science in order that it may be well understood in what senses these words, which have been employed so widely and so freely, are to be taken here.

First, then, as to philosophy.

Philosophy is a system of ideas more general than any other. There is no accepted definition of philosophy. More strongly yet: there is probably no proposition in philosophy which would be uniformly accepted, including this one. This has the disadvantage that we do not know which philosophy ought to serve as the philosophy of science if science is to be correctly interpreted; but it has the advantage that various interpretations will come forward in a speculative field, and some illumination of the meaning of science is bound to result.

2. THE DEFINITION OF SCIENCE

There is, of course, no official definition of science, either; neither scientists nor philosophers have agreed among themselves what science is nor how it should be defined. The task remains, however, and so what is proposed here is a number of alternative definitions, in the hope that each may have an explanatory contribution to make and that some one may be more appealing than the others.

Science Is the Experimental Search for Natural Law

A working definition, but too brief for many purposes. The prospect of a search successfully undertaken would have to be included. Again, nothing is said about natural law. Then, too, where are the static principles underlying the activity?

Science Is the Activity of Extracting Reasons from Substance

The world involves disorder as well as order. The ultimate irrationality of substance is necessary to keep the domain of existence from collapsing into the domain of essence, and hence in making an idealistic rather than a realistic philosophy responsible for science. For we must believe in the reality of the actual world if we are to look into it for evidence of law. Yet once again we are involved in the difficulty of not knowing from the definition of science just what the method is. We know that the practice of scientific method is an activity and what the activity is intended to accomplish. What we wish to know in addition is how this intention is carried out.

Substance is the generic name to cover both matter and energy. Matter is static substance; energy, dynamic. Realism in practice means learning how to turn matter (and/or energy) against itself in an effort to accomplish ends beyond the reach of bits of matter acting alone. Matter, as we have found out from surveys of the astronomical universe, is a scarce element and correspondingly precious. It is not the only thing in the world but it is the necessary substratum. Matter is part of being, and we learn about being (even though not about the whole of being) when we learn about matter. There are, of course, also rules, formulas, laws. The uniformity of matter provides the characteristics of matter which lend themselves to study. The definition, therefore, contains a large measure of truth but it is not entirely adequate, for it fails to reveal the important and necessary relations between substances and laws.

The Aim of Science Is to Construct Tautological Propositions Which Refer to Facts

Here we are a little closer, perhaps, than we had been to an analytical definition. The emphasis is on the aim of science as it should be in such a connection, and the logical nature of the investigation is brought into the consideration. The method of science, however, is implied rather than stated, and very precise directions are not given. How are we to know from this definition that the laws which science succeeds in constructing in the light of this aim includes laws of probability, and that the tautological propositions striven for are rarely achieved in empirical terms? How do we know, either, that the facts mentioned are not those of ordinary experience usually but instead data obtained at high analytical levels?

Science is that division of culture which conducts the search among substances, through the method of observation, hypothesis and experiment, for tendencies, laws and causes, leading to the prediction of events and the control over phenomena, at advanced stages of development involving mathematically-formulated tautologies to account for instrumentally-discovered data leading to the knowledge of natural laws.

This definition is intended to avoid the shortcomings of the others. Partly it does so, though not altogether. But the definition is in classic form; it is framed in terms of genus and difference. The disciplines of culture devoted to the search for truth and its applications are: art, philosophy, religion, science and the practical techniques. The definition seeks to show wherein science differs from the other disciplines.

3. A PHILOSOPHY FOR SCIENCE

Induction is so important in science that at times there have been tendencies to characterize science in this way, as for instance by Whewell. Our point of departure is simple observation, but we get away from it very quickly. We start with the assumption that all knowledge can be derived from the data of sense experience. Notice that we are not talking here about the sensations themselves but rather about axiomatized experiences: the data hypothesized into elements. The method includes the memory of similarity and difference, worked over by reason. We shall get away by means of the two primitive logical relations. These are: class membership and class inclusion, to be derived.

The transient sequence of differences (sometimes called "existence") contains actual individual objects or events. These can never be entirely accounted for in any regularity or uniformity of description, such as is given in the account of them as members of classes. They are members of classes, but they are not merely members of classes, for there is always a remainder, however infinitesimal in quantity, and there is always an element of the quality which defies complete description. We must take into account the fact that while transient things come into and go out of existence, grow and decline, there must be an existence in which this series of events can take place. Thus the transient sequence is a spatio-temporal field in which events succeed one another, and in which everything falls under chance as well as law. The evidence of the recurrent order is characterized by repetition, but the repetition is never entire; events are never identical. This gives rise to a kind of rhythm: the transient sequence is a world of clocks or of waves. It is a rich world of difference.

Completeness as well as consistency requires that we must be sure that all the phenomena are accounted for before closing the record. This can never be accomplished altogether, and so we are left with the prospect of consistency and with a completeness which is allowed to increase because incompleteness is acknowledged. Hence the limitations of any monolithic culture or of any wholly consistent individual: they are generally proved false by what is true without.

Of course the differences among discrete material objects and events are never absolute. Groups of irregularities are taken care of by the theory of probability, where they approach but never reach the total state of regularity. In this sense (and only in this sense), then, all concrete universals are trivial in that they are hardly worth speaking about. Only generality is non-trivial. Empirical propositions, which are never more than immense probabilities, are bounded on the bottom by contradictions (logically false propositions) and on the top by tautologies (logically true ones). This must make generality abdicate from some of its larger claims. The identity of the infinite set with the subset of all its elements forbids us to speak of the widest system; so that logically we can talk only of proper subsets, and of approximations and percentages.

The recurrent order of similarities (sometimes called "essence") contains similar elements, i.e., elements absolutely identical in part. But they differ in their structure with regard to degree of complexity: names, elementary propositions, systems. We can here, as in the case of the transient sequence, distinguish between a field and the objects in the field. The objects we have enumerated have their order in logic. Here we find a logical order, not an historical one. But here, too, the strictures of evidence apply. Mere abstraction is not sufficient ground for those endless extrapolations, of which the classic philosophers have been so guilty. Corresponding to every truth there is unlimited falsity. What are the elements of logic, then, and how are they to be found?

We can revitalize philosophy, in other words, only by revising its claims downward. We introduce an axiom of finitude. The change in philosophical method can be explained in a word. What is proposed is to substitute the procedure of interpolation for that of extrapolation. When we write "all men are mortal," we do not need to include necessarily an infinite number of men, though of course we may. "All" here means "every one and only those." In any case we should be hard put to it to prove that the number of men, including the dead, the living and the as-yet-unborn, is, or is not, infinite. We may mean by our proposition, then, merely an undeterminedly large number.

The characteristic signature of the finite philosophy is the preservation of the second universe but only as a very much shrunken affair, as a recurrent order of finite similarities. This calls for an abatement of its transcendental claims. The position not being a subjective one in which propositions are identical with propositions known, its extension beyond the grounds of empiricism and logic is held unjustifiable, and even damaging to the cause of truth. Whitehead pointed out that Sheffer's stroke function founded logic on inconsistency, and that inconsistency involves the finite, as Spinoza saw in the second definition of his *Ethics*. The limitations on the second universe have been shown in its function as a field of classes, but limitations exist also among the classes. There are two kinds of classes: those which arise from empirical elements, and those which arise from relations between empirical elements. "Horse" is an instance of the former, and "divisible" of the latter. Now let us consider both in connection with the infinite. We cannot say that the number of horses is infinite for we do not have the requisite empirical knowledge. But we could say that the "divisible" are infinite, for if we take as an example the rational numbers we will find that they are infinitely divisible: between any two rationals a third can always be found. We cannot, in other words, assert infinity of elements selected from the transient sequence, while of some of the elements of the recurrent order we can.

Whatever we learn about the transient sequence of differences must remain the base-line. Existing things, actual individuals, concrete objects, become mere episodes in the theory of descriptions. This is the truth requirement. From elements found at the base-line, we erect our structure of the recurrent order of similarities. This order, we remember, contains such types of objects as classes, propositions, and systems. Classes are combined in propositions and propositions in systems. The first task is the formation of classes. This is a matter of naming groups of objects by their similarity or partial identity. We combine classes into the first level of complexity of propositions, which have been called elementary propositions. The meaning of the elementary proposition is to be found in the analysis of the theoretical method of their verifiability. We are moving up in abstraction from classes to elementary propositions, but we can at all times still refer back to the transient sequence for confirmation of the results of our manipulations.

There are no theoretical limits to the verifiability of empirical propositions. We can for instance project a method of testing for the metagalaxy. A system whose elements are galaxies of various sub-orders makes sense in terms of conceivably empirical terms. Similarly, the sense of metaphysics ought to provide for a carefully and empirically constructed system within the limits allowed by logic; namely, one whose elements are referable to a conceived empirical set of inter-related world-orders.

Such a conception involves more than the transient sequence of differences. We have learned that we cannot support universal propositions one moment longer than their elementary constituents lend themselves to continual testing. We cannot say, "all men are mortal," unless we can continue to predict successfully that such propositions as "John Q. Doe will die" are true. This means then, that we construct our abstractions painfully by correspondence with details; to borrow an analogy, we work in chorographic rather than geographic terms, having only finite ambitions with respect to it, and not being charmed by needless proliferations concerning the eternal and ubiquitous, nor ruling these out, either, when, as and if they can show reasons.

It is one thing to assert the being of a recurrent order of similarities considered as a field of objects of an abstract nature which if they change must change with comparative slowness. It is quite another to show what are the elements of this field. It is not empirical, though constructed of empirical elements; it is logical—more, it is a kind of ramified logic: metaphysics. That is to say, the field of the recurrent order is composed of logical and mathematical systems into which are poured the elements of propositions which are empirical. We have extended our inquiry into the empirical field of differences by means of instruments; and into the logical field of similarities, by means of mathematics. Philosophy of science appears as the system of the two orders.

We do not, in other words, need to admit to philosophy anything more than the world of facts and the limitations of logic. But when we have examined these and shown how they fit together, we shall find that we have discovered a philosophy for science. For that is what the relations between the facts, and the logic called forth by the facts, involve. It is true that we have to account for a world of particular objects, but not of any objects in particular. "My world" is a logical world because logic, so to speak, is everybody's solipsism. It is Wittgenstein's thesis that we never talk about more than limited portions of the world. This is only a way of saying that we do not operate in an unlimited world but only in terms of systems; and this can be deliberate, though more often the systems are assumed. Philosophy, then, is not something we understand but something by means of which we understand. It is not the objects we see from some perspective; rather it gives us a perspective from which to see objects.

The recurrent order of similarities has its own autonomy. This is provided for it by the ways in which the elementary propositions are combined. Logic has its own rules, and the order of similarities is the domain of logic. Complex propositions are made up by combining elementary propositions according to logical rules. The meaning of complex propositions is to be found in their logical definitions. The complex propositions become combined into systems according to mathematical rules. Thus a process which began with names for differences ends in systems of similarities. We must set about to discover the metaphysical laws which the logical laws obey, for they do not follow further logical laws. Or rather we may say that the further logical laws which the logical laws obey are laws we are obliged to call metaphysical.

4. INTRODUCTION TO THE AXIOMS
OF SCIENCE

Logically speaking, there are only two starting-points for the acquisition of knowledge: induction and deduction. The former is suggested by what is revealed to the senses, and the latter by what is disclosed through reasoning. The results of these two movements are in the scientific method extended and combined by empirical and mathematical investigations respectively, and finally formulated in abstract systems. Now it will be necessary to show how a philosophy similar to the one outlined in the last section underlies this method.

The scientific method is a logical sequence of acts considered together as the guide-lines for a behavioral structure. In endeavoring to discover the principles upon which the scientific method is founded, it is necessary to begin by remembering that the method consists in a succession of concrete individual actions, and that therefore any abstract analysis must of necessity fall short of a full description. The axioms upon which the method rests are not laid down deliberately as presuppositions by the investigator in a conscious manner, but rather are assumed by the method which he practices. They come into existence not because they are known, assumed or even recognized afterwards, but because the method is itself followed by investigators: the method itself could not exist were the axioms not in effect what they are.

The problem of the axiomatic presuppositions of theoretical inquiries is one which has been around for a long time. It is clear that the method must start somewhere and with something. And what is that something is our problem, and whatever we find in this way we shall have to treat as axioms, and these in fact are what axioms are. And if science taken as we find it has a method and a field in which to operate, then that field, too, must have its axioms; and even the results must have their axioms, too, for science does produce results and must have them, however impermanent they may be. The scientific method does not operate in the laboratory for nothing, but to discover empirical laws, and not half-laws, either, though that is what may be found; and if that is the case it is not because half-truths are sought but because truths are only half-found.

No one has yet shown how to axiomatize a qualitative concrete act so as to retain the qualities; and so an approach of quite a different sort from the present one may be required. Mathematical systems run to the order of a dozen axioms or less, together with a couple of rules of inference. Perhaps a vast and complex social phenomenon like experimental science may require many hundreds of axioms; it is hard to say. Gazing through the depth of complexities involved means supposing that one has seen vistas of systems so enormous that the human mechanism for handling them has not yet been envisaged. Our present schemes are obviously too simple. We can only hope that they may serve a purpose as stages on the way.

5. PHILOSOPHICAL AXIOMS OF SCIENCE

Science is divided into three parts; these are field, method and law. There is the *field* in which science operates: the external world of natural phenomena. There is the *method* by which the field is studied, together with its laboratory, instruments, techniques, and operations. Finally, there are the *laws*: the level of abstractions, of causal or statistical laws. The three parts, of course, belong together under the scientific enterprise. Science itself is a *method*; it investigates the *field* to find the *laws*.

There are separate sets of axioms for each of these areas, and for brevity we shall undertake to set forth only those which are peculiar to a given one. For instance, we shall discuss (a) metaphysical presuppositions of the field, (b) the logical axioms of the method, (c) the epistemological assumptions of the scientist, and (d) the ethical principles of the laws. Obviously, there are also metaphysical axioms for the method, the scientist and the conclusions; and epistemological axioms for the field and the conclusions, and so on.

(a) The metaphysical presuppositions of the field are such as we might expect from a study of the method. In this work the actual conduct of the scientist when he is behaving as a scientist, that is, when he is practicing the scientific method, is taken as central, and all else derived from and oriented about it. For instance when the scientist undertakes observations, hypotheses, experiments, he is assuming that such-and-such a world exists and can be studied in just this way. The axioms following are samples.

Nature consists in identical substances. The most basic of the substances are matter and energy, which exist at the integrative level of the physical, though it would be possible to list many others, such as any of the entities or processes considered empirical: chemical compounds, organisms, societies, in fact all varieties of matter; and electromagnetic forces, valency, life, all varieties of energy. For each kind of material or energy, there is an identity with itself, as required by the conservation laws, which recognize that something is conserved of substance: matter-energy. The conservation laws are in conflict with that interpretation of quantum mechanics which describes external reality as mere waves of probabilities. Meyerson's "principle of identity" is provided for; and identity is here understood to be self-relation, relation to self. Both maintenance of form and repetition of form are involved in identity. Electron, hydrogen, cell—these are the names of universal classes of material entities, not the names of individual material entities; they are the forms that matter takes, and so the names of "materials"; but as predicates they may be freed from their subjects, as Hegel said, and so have their being as universals, possibilities for matter. But to assert the reality of universals is not to do so widespread and at will; for the business of science, according to Peirce, is to discover *which* universals are real; the scientific method is capable of validating echinoderms over poltergeists.

The similarities of substances are infinite. This is the axiom which recognizes the existence of continuity. Mill's "uniformity of nature" is provided for. Material entities and energetic processes fall into well-defined classes, and so make the discovery of empirical laws possible. The existence of reason in nature depends upon the existence of similarities.

The differences of substances are infinite. This is the axiom which recognizes the existence of chance, change, disorder, chaos. Chance is the intersection of causal lines; without chance nature would not contain differences as well as similarities. Thus the whole of nature cannot be encompassed in any theory of order or by any set of empirical laws; there is always the surd element.

Causality depends upon the integrative levels. Causality is the principle of consistency for energy, for the interaction among substances. It requires the existence of a structured hierarchy of levels. Effect is generally one integrative level higher than cause (Bohm's law). It is the hypothetical principle in action, if *A,* then *B,* for the concrete order. Causality operates in terms of mechanism. In nature, the purpose is always achieved, and in terms of its mechanism we see *how* (so that an overt purpose is always a misunderstood mechanism). Final cause is broken up into a succession of efficient causes, and so is implicit in them.

Causal law is explanatory. Whenever in a chemical experiment the investigator approximates the prescribed conditions, he can anticipate producing reasonably reliable results. Thus chemistry is evidence for the absoluteness of causal laws. *Statistical law is descriptive* of the same area covered by causal law and therefore a subclass. In science, the investigator is content with description only when he cannot have explanation.

In opposing causal laws with statistical laws, some investigators think they have got rid of causality and are dealing now only with aggregates of particulars. But to the extent to which the aggregates of particulars constitute aggregates which perhaps even behave differently from the particulars themselves taken separately, causality is still a factor. Planck defended causality by means of the example of entropy: the second law of thermodynamics is an absolute causal law. But it is difficult to see how the science of chemistry is not replete with such examples, although set on a more modest scale. Is not the formula for the electrolysis of water a causal law? Given pure samples and proper conditions, it does not happen that such a procedure fails. Then is not any predictable reaction an instance of a causal law? It is difficult to see how there could be any valid science without some reliance upon this principle. Parameters represent the causality underlying probabilities. A perfect gas is an absolutely complete chaos of perfectly elastic molecules in rapid motion conflicting with each other in every possible way. Peirce's principle that disorder generates order is relevant here.

Judged by the success or failure of theories, those devoted to discreteness fare better in empiricism, while those devoted to continua fare better in logic. The atomic theory has won an overwhelming success in physics, and so has the calculus in mathematics. The continuum has been smuggled back into physics as the concept of the "field": electromagnetic field, gravitational field, for example. Atomic theories in mathematics take the form of combinatorial logic. The atomic theory in philosophy, which began with Democritus and reached its fullest expression with Leibniz, led nowhere. The theory of continua in empiricism had its most successful expression in the theory of the ether, which has on the whole been equally unsuccessful.

(b) The logical axioms of the method are derived from the method considered as a logical structure laid out along a time line, in short, a logic of events. One or more scientists, working alone or in succession, carry out the steps and they do so precisely, though not necessarily with any deliberate recognition of the sequence. Our task is here to show the logic involved, the bare bones of the structure, and hence the inner essence of science, upon which only could a valid philosophy of science be based.

The scientific method so far as its presuppositions are concerned may be regarded as a method of welding together Plato's world of forms with Aristotle's world of substance. The world of substance is first explored, then a model of the Platonic world is constructed in mathematics, and the properties of the actual world are explored by means of observation, hypothesis and experiment. Then the former is brought as far as possible into conformity with the latter. The hold of science on empiricism needs to be an ineluctable one but does not need for that reason to be heavy. It must always be there but it can be in the terms prescribed by referentiability, and not require a continual reference to actual fact. The investigator does not have to stand transfixed with his hands forever attached to an instrument in a laboratory, provided the instrument is always there ready to confront the hypothesis with relevant data. Differential equations for which it is feared no solutions can be found are often furnished with model solutions.

Observations lead to concept formation. Observations are hardly random, and, when undertaken to discover invariants, even less so; the usual sort of exploratory scanning apart. It is not possible to make observations of unique entities: there are none. But the recognition of types is a special sort of searching. For concepts to be scientific formulations, they must be, on the one hand, abstract, and, on the other, held down to just those entities and processes which can be exemplified in the concrete and the individual.

Inductions are made to theory construction. In general in their theories the scientists take charge of quantity and action, while the philosophers content themselves with studying the relations of qualities. Bohm wishes to add qualities to empiricism for the scientists. The philosophers will have to treat also of quantity and action, especially if they wish to take account of scientific method, its presuppositions and results.

Tests of hypotheses for correspondence are instrumental. The observations made with instruments invariably conflict with the findings of the unaided senses. Most of what is observed could not otherwise be observed at all. Hence a new world is opened up by the invention of each new device. The beginnings of genuine science are imbedded in observations made with instruments in order to achieve exactness and penetration. The senses unaided reach only so far as ordinary experience can take them; extensions of the senses are required for the verification of elements of analysis.

Instrumental experiment, in undertaking the verification or falsification of hypotheses, links up the individual with the universal. Hypotheses are universal propositions, but every experiment observes a particular or a group of particulars. The particulars in such a case are particulars under the universal. The sampling of particulars (individuals) from the standpoint of the universal proposition are made for its purposes. Thus both domains are assumed: hypothesis, in the domain of logic, and experiment, in the domain of substance.

Experiment involves the principle of analogy, because of its inductive nature. Sampling relies upon the validity of analogy: what is found to hold in some cases may be found to hold also for similar cases.

The tests of theories for coherence are mathematical. There is in science progress toward more inclusive theory. Scientific theories are often abandoned (phlogiston, for instance), but they are more often subordinated (Newtonian mechanics by relativity mechanics). The logic of scientific method is governed by the relation of inclusion. It is the aim of science to construct a system which includes all lesser systems, to syllogize, as Peirce put it, from one grand major premise.

The constants of nature are also related, and this brings them within the limits of a continuity upon which inclusion must necessarily depend. There are many examples.

The tests of laws for applications are conditional. Detailed comment on the logical axioms will not be undertaken here. Scientific method is applied logic, and applied logic is distinct from pure logic, the logic of abstract objects (logic proper), and also distinct from concrete logic (the logic of actual things and events). There could be no applied logic were there no pure logic to apply and no concrete logic to elicit. The process of elicitation—which is the scientific method of inquiry—can never be complete, because the actual world is not entirely logical. The principle of diversity, $x \neq y$, implicit in logic since Aristotle, has never been stated by logicians but has been continually encountered in practice by empiricists. When reason goes beyond experience, it must do so by means of logic and must always preserve the willingness to re-examine its assumptions (i.e., axioms). But on the other hand, as Kant saw, science relies upon analytic judgments only so far as synthetic judgments require (*Crit. Pur. Reas.*, B 17-18). We must not be led astray, however, as Kant was (*Ibid.*, Bxiii) by the importance of the role that reason plays in science. Reason may ask the questions of nature and the investigator undertake to elicit the answers, but it was nature in the first place which suggested the questions.

(c) The epistemological assumptions of the scientist fall into three main divisions. The field of nature becomes in epistemology the *knowable,* science is looked at as the process of *knowing*, and the laws are called *knowledge.* Through the activity of knowing, the knowable becomes (in part, at least) knowledge.

The epistemological assumptions of the *knowable* is the first of three divisions by which the relation between the knower and the object of knowledge, through the process of knowing, is graded. Here we are concerned with the balance between knower and world to be known.

The external world is independent of the knower. Scientific method conducts its search for scientific laws as though these were independent of the scientist. The investigator does not create the scientific laws, he only discovers them. Bodies must have attracted each other directly as the square of their masses and inversely as the square of the distance between them long before Newton was born. Millions of years before the advent of human beings there must have been stars and planets; but obviously these facts were not observed, at least not on the earth, and the regularities remained unknown. Thus there were knowable phenomena but no one to observe them, and knowledge, but no one to possess it. For there to be knowledge, there must be the awareness of phenomena, and the phenomena must exist independently of the awareness. The world, in short, does not conduct itself in strict conformity with its being known; yet it is knowable for all that, else there would be no knowledge.

It has seemed to many investigators, Peirce and Whitehead for instance, that the objectivity and independence of the scientific subject-matter is undeniable. Whitehead put it best when he argued that the scientist is not investigating his own sense impressions. He is investigating the properties of the world as these impinge upon his sense impressions. They resist his will to make them other than they are, as Peirce said, and so he must learn how they are.

The uniformities of the external world are knowable. We do not have knowledge of the entire external world but only of that part of it which is orderly. Disorder is felt, but we lack the techniques for recording it. We can only make records of the uniformities.

We seem to have two kinds of knowledge: knowledge of individuals acquired through sense experience, and knowledge of universals acquired by means of language. It is the latter which constitutes communicable knowledge; the former must of necessity remain private. Thus in any formal sense it is the uniformities of nature which are constituted in knowledge. In the comment on a later axiom we shall explore the further consequences of this situation.

The principle of causality has been defended on epistemological grounds despite the position of Hume. We do at least perceive events which are distinguishable as occurring together, as Hume admitted, and we perceive this again and again so that the repetition of the pattern of the content of perceptions can be accounted for only in some such manner, and it could be argued that in the routine of perceptions there is this element which helps to make the perceptions themselves possible.

The non-uniformities constitute interferences in knowing. Science abstracts from disorder, non-uniformity, chance and chaos. To the extent to which these stand in the way of the search for uniformities they constitute interferences. It is often extremely difficult to separate out the repeating patterns, and requires great ingenuity to isolate the causal chains. Probabilities are the evidence of the attempts to extract the last modicum of uniformity from non-uniformities. The statistical expressions of averages of behavior endeavor to reduce to order the irregularities which stand in the way. Behind them, however, are the shadows of parameters, on the logical side, and of the ultimate irrationality of substance, on the other. Substance, as the irrational ground of individual reaction, resists at the last all efforts to break it up entirely into elements of order. If the domain of logic cannot be altogether derived from the data disclosed by experience, even though its elements can, then the domain of substance cannot be altogether dissolved into logical relations, although much of it can.

The mind and the external world are similar. Our conceptions of the material object are subjective; but not entirely so. For we would never have such subjective conceptions were there no material object to have them about; moreover, we adjust our conceptions to conform to the object as we learn more concerning it.

From Galileo to Planck, men have relied upon the principle that reason and nature share common properties. If the human being, with his mind, is a natural product, this affinity ought not to appear too surprising. As Peirce once pointed out, Galileo's appeal to the natural light of reason, *il lume naturale,* is an appeal to instinct. It is because man has a natural inclination toward the comprehension of natural processes that he can understand nature at all. For Planck, logic is not alien to what the sense impressions reveal but instead coincides with them to some extent, thus giving man an insight into the structure of the world. The human mind, being part of nature, must have some natural affinity to truth. Galileo's "natural light of reason," like Meinong's theory of congruence, presupposes such an affinity. The correspondence theory of truth which is assumed by the experimental method of verification allows for a wide range of possible errors; corresponding to every truth, there is in fact an infinity of possible errors. Hence were there no "natural light of reason" or situation of congruence, it is difficult to understand how there would be any specific achievement at all.

The epistemological assumptions of knowing are marks of the growing separation of knowledge from both the knower and the world-to-be-known. Through the operations of the knower acting upon the world-to-be-known, knowledge arises; and it is knowledge only to the knower, not to the world otherwise; nevertheless, although in the possession of the knower, it is marked off from him by the assumption of a different character, that of knowledge itself. Objective to the knower, though in a different order than the world from which it was derived, knowledge is still close to the knower in being known, and close to the world in being itself a segment of the world. And its derivation and possession by the knower gives him his special place in the world.

As knowledge increases, the knowable recedes from the subject. The scientific procedure begins with the common experience of subjects but soon moves on from the data derived from such common experience by penetrating to analytical levels lying far below them, and proceeds with the investigation of such analytical levels as are more and more independent of the subject's ordinary experiences. Empiricism is not subjective. The appeal to sensation is an appeal to material objects whose existence has been verified by sensation, not an appeal to the sensation itself.

The contribution of empiricism to knowing is completeness; the contribution of mathematics to knowing is consistency. Philosophy can no more afford to forget the first than the second. But it has, and it has done worse: it has sought for spurious empirical consistency in the unity of the knowing subject: Kant's celebrated "transcendental unity of apperception." Scientific knowing spins away from the subject as its instruments become more precise and penetrating. The interposition of instruments marks one definite dimension of recession of the investigating subject *qua* knower from the knowable material object. Planck cited the replacement of the ear by the vibrating membrane. The replacement of the eye by the electronic detectors in scintillation counters has led to a gain of from ten to one hundred million in the closeness of pulses which can be discriminated. The colorimeter, the photoelectric cell, and many other devices are capable of receiving impressions, discriminating them and making records to a degree of fineness inaccessible to the human sense organs.

The order of discovery differs from the order of nature. Were nature altogether orderly, there would be no conflicts. But instead, animals eat other animals and galaxies collide. The investigator approaches the natural world perforce as it is, and endeavors from his encounters to separate out the natural order. But logic is not history; and his encounters are themselves historical episodes, whereas the data discovered in this way belong together logically. Thus from the temporal succession and the spatial distribution of events he is obliged to seek the elements of their logical structure. That is why mathematical calculations have to be added to instrumental observation, before the conclusion can be properly framed.

The sensations can be experimentally planned. The Greek philosophers tried to bring thought, feeling and character together in the investigation of knowledge. They succeeded in making reason dominant over feeling, and failed to introduce action into the investigative trinity by substituting action for character. The European philosophers failed in another way: the British empiricists, Locke, Berkeley and Hume, thought that knowledge could be gained through sensation alone, and usually through one sensation at a time. The continental rationalists, Descartes, Spinoza and Leibniz, thought that knowledge could be gained through reasoning alone.

Since Kant we have known better, although Kant, too, failed because he admitted conceptual material into sense experience only at the cost of making both utterly dependent upon the investigator. We assume in science that objects in the external world have properties akin to sense qualities, and that they are related in ways akin to logical relations.

The scientific method turns Kant inside out by externalizing the senses and reasoning by means of action. A scientific experiment is a planned action designed to produce a certain experience. Feeling, thought and action skilfully blended comprise the psychological equipment. But these three components are combined *externally*, in the performance of a complete cycle of scientific method. When the triad of psychological capacities is combined *internally,* action has a tendency to turn into its opposite, inaction, with the consequent self-control representing the action and the combination of inaction with thought and feeling resulting in religious mysticism rather than in science. But when the triad is combined *externally,* it fixes on experiment as the supreme synthesis, and science results. The senses and reason that failed to meet inside the subject, and from there to make possible the task of coping with the world, have been able to meet outside the subject and in the world by means of instruments to objectify the senses and mathematics to objectify the reason, and in this way to cope with the world by turning particular material portions of it (e.g., instruments) against other material portions.

The experiments of science are designed to enable the investigator to check his hypotheses against data disclosed by experience. The validity of experience means that we can repeat his experiences and express the findings in a formula which will enable other investigators to obtain them. Scientific method is merely a formalization of the way in which the investigator gets the results of combining his actions and thoughts by planning his sensations. The investigator has the ability to integrate his movements which are made simultaneously or successively for the purposes of compounding them. If this is true of movement, how much more, then, of the senses? He plans to bring about certain sensations from the framework of himself as observer, on the ground that, as for instance in the case of relativity physics, nature is conceived as the sum of perspectives. If the physical world consists in relations between tensors of space-time, then the world of the observer is a segment of space and time selected from the space-time continuum of four dimensions. The knowing subject, in science, is simply the object known (the knowable world of nature) as felt, acted upon, and thought about, from a certain framework.

Structures result from producing sensations. The result of producing sensations is not merely sensation-complexes, as Mach supposed. The moment we observe our sensations we are in the domain of thought. And the objects of our thinking, the abstract structures of science and mathematics, say, are not subjective. They are not merely collections or summaries of sensations. Hence reality cannot consist quite simply, as Mach asserted, in sensations directly observed. What we discover by means of planned sensations are pointer-readings and other index guides which the investigator fits into abstract structures expressed in equations, and these are something different if not always something more than the sensations disclosed by themselves. And this remains true even though, on the other hand, the abstract structures the investigator tends to endorse in empirical science are just those for which effective support can be found among the relevant sensations.

The epistemological assumptions of *knowledge* are the last of the three grades into which the knowing process has been divided. Knowledge has by this time separated itself from the world to be known and from the knower, although retaining the characteristics of both; only now it has its own peculiarities, and its own advantages and shortcomings, which contribute to its estimate, so that it has to be considered on its own account as an independent entity and not merely as something arising in the relation of two others.

The knowledge of relations multiplies faster than the knowledge of qualities. At the common sense level of experience the investigator is confronted with qualities and relations. Consider, for instance, all that ever enter into the field of his vision: colored shapes. The qualities record themselves on his sensations; but as a scientist he is on the track of sets of relations which he can then combine into structures. Thus the relations as they enter into technical knowledge tend to combine faster than qualities. For it is only later and at more advanced stages in the knowledge of abstract structures that they result in the emergence of new qualities. Hence the difficulty presented by the necessity of interpreting data.

Knowledge is limited by the techniques employed in obtaining it. Since Locke, the question has been before us of the extent to which the knowledge process limits (conditions, colors, determines, falsifies) knowledge. Another phrasing of this same question is to ask to what extent the instruments employed in observation interfere with the observed material. If the interference were total, knowledge would be impossible and the scientific method productive merely of illusion. There is no reason to be sure that this is not the case, but there is some evidence for suspecting that it is not. As we have noted earlier, knowledge is limited by the perspective from which its readings are taken; yet the determination of the degree and kind of this limitation is another matter. A datum which has been discovered has had its own nature laid bare, and no longer depends upon its discoverers for its role in knowledge. From this point on it leads a life of its own.

The most recent occasion for the revival of this question is the issue brought to the fore by Heisenberg's Indeterminacy Principle. The inability to ascertain with accuracy both the position and the velocity of a particle may be an instance of a general condition which prevails through nature, as some have supposed; or it may be that here investigators have encountered an instrumental limit in one direction only, so that the principle is not a general one but merely a reification of limitations. The latter view is the one adopted here. The limits of knowledge are not held to represent correctly those of nature, except insofar of course as the scientist's own investigative powers are themselves held to be natural. The line is drawn where the observer together with his instruments interfere with what is to be observed. For the observer is not concerned with investigating his own reactions to phenomena (which are left to psychology) but rather the interactions among phenomena which his reactions to them report.

We are apt to confuse partial knowledge with false knowledge; they are not the same. We may know, for instance, some of the elements of a mixture and not all, in which case our knowledge is partial and incomplete; yet surely it is not false, for the elements of which we do have knowledge are genuine elements of the mixture. All philosophies derived from Kant are faced with this dilemma, for in positing the conditions of knowing as interfering with the acquisition of knowledge and in further positing a real world as unknowable in itself, he seems to have laid upon knowledge the characterization that it must be forever unreliable. This view is here rejected. To engage in the scientific method at all as a way of acquiring knowledge of some degree of reliability, we must have a genuine support for the view that what we are doing is not merely investigating our own investigations or even our own limitations and perspective.

Language is never completely adequate to represent the world. To say that knowledge is genuine is not, however, to say that it is absolute or final. The method of science requires two kinds of inquiry; there are those who look for tidy schemes, and there are those who look for facts which upset the tidy schemes. A science would be poor which attempted to do without either. Science proceeds on the assumptions that there is an external world, that it is governed by laws, and that our knowledge of this world and of its laws can be approached in closer approximations by successive applications of the method. If it is never reached in any final sense, that is no condemnation of it.

The knowledge of nature is itself a segment of nature; but as nature is governed by the conditions of substance, so the knowledge is governed by the conditions of logic. Therefore knowledge, though we acquire it through the study of nature, is not reducible to nature; it remains instead a segment separated for its own purposes. That is why the formulations of empirical science have continually to be revised.

That language is never adequate to represent the world completely does not mean that it cannot do so partially. Two corollaries are required to the present principle. One is the principle of the open system; the other is the principle of fallibilism.

Bergson and many others have argued for the open system, since knowledge is never perfect; but there are grave difficulties confronting such a conception. Insofar as a system is open, it is not a system; and insofar as it is a system, it is not open. A system has the two properties of consistency and completeness; a system having the property of completeness would not be open; there would be nothing for it to be open *to,* no elements that were relevant remaining outside, no parts not included. However, these statements apply to logical and mathematical systems which are perforce abstract and ideal. A scientific system by contrast is an empirical system; which means never ideal nor entirely abstract, and so never complete: not, in short, even altogether a system. And so it must be kept open in the hope of improvement, and improved in the light of the abstract and ideal models of logic and mathematics. We have already noted how the non-uniformities of the external world constitute interferences in knowing.

The principle of fallibilism was first advanced by Peirce who established it on the ground that error could never be excluded altogether from any empirical system. Thus doubt must be an irreducible element of any formulation of knowledge. But this is a disguised subjective form of the same principle as that of the open system. For what if the method of doubt could itself be doubted? On Russell's theory of types, this is impossible; but the argument advanced by Fitch (1952) for the retention of self-reference in philosophy seems the more tenable.

(d) The metaphysical presuppositions of the field of science were concerned with an area which lay outside the purview of the scientific method proper. The logical axioms of the method and the epistemological assumptions of the scientist were contained within that method. With the consideration of the ethical principles of the law, we are once again outside that method and in the world affected by its conclusions. This is perhaps a more tenuous area than the first, too, because just as the method of science in its strongest outlines does not change, so the metaphysical presuppositions which imply that method do not change, either. The conclusions of science, the findings which result from the successful application of its methods, do change, however, and they change often, just as often as the repeated exercise of the scientific method calls for revisions and alterations. Hence the ethical principles of the laws or results of science must be as tenuous as those results themselves.

The name for the area dealt with in this way is applied science. Applied science is the application of pure science to the solution of practical human problems. The method of science is not applied, however; the results of the successful applications of that method are. In short, scientific laws as applied to human problems is applied science. Ethics enters the picture to the extent to which the effects on human society brought about by the application of scientific laws to practical human problems are in themselves right or wrong, good or bad.

Pure science is of course ethically right and good. Pure science is the search for truth, and the truth in itself cannot be anything other than right and good. (How could the truth be wrong, or bad?) The aim of pure science, if not pure science itself, transcends particular human societies and cultures. Applied science, however, is culture-bound, and serves the needs and purposes of a particular culture. Applied science, indeed all science, has a social and cultural effect, intended or not, and science is often blamed for such effects and condemned for social irresponsibility.

The fundamental question of the ethics of the laws of science is not yet settled; and this concerns the selection of the ethics to be employed in making the estimate. Since our criterion throughout has been the scientific method itself, this method has thrown up its own metaphysical presuppositions, its own logical axioms, its own epistemological assumptions. Does it produce by the same analysis its own ethical principles? This question cannot be answered except in part. To some extent it is certainly true that it does, and what this is can be discerned quite clearly.

Science insofar as it is applied endeavors to provide for the good life to be lived in this world. Applied science does not provide for immortality or for the soul directly but rather for the material life to be lived here and now. Better food production, better health conditions, better housing materials and designs, better transportation, better communication, for those alive in the present.

Science insofar as it is applied endeavors to supply the means and not the ends. What men ought to do individually, socially or even culturally, is no concern of science; but how they achieve the ends they set themselves certainly is. Better food, health, housing, transportation and communication for what? Science does not say. It furnishes the means; the ends to be selected are left to other social institutions to decide.

The primary effect of science in society is to intensify social behavior outside of science. It does this by applying to social situations the tools and techniques of pure and applied science. Such intensification is without regard for the moral consequences; more efficient methods of life-saving, but also more efficient methods of killing: anaesthetics and antibiotics, but also poison gases and ballistic missiles. More often than not the first effects of any new instrument are bad; the earliest practical airplane was used for bombing before it was used for commercial transportation, and the atomic bomb was used at Hiroshima before the construction of the first American plant for the production of atomic energy at Shippingport, Pennsylvania.

The secondary effect of science on society is to orient the society toward science. Much if not most of the time and space, the matter and energy, available to the society is devoted to science, and this direction tends to be total. Science as an institution gradually preempts the rights of other institutions; all institutions are affected, some favorably for a while; but the only institutions that do not suffer are those which are entirely devoted to the means of the society, transportation and communication, for instance. Institutions which, like science itself, are devoted to the ends of the society, suffer irreparable harm, the arts and religions, for instance.

This orientation of the society toward science as a secondary effect is a result of the primary effect. Science, with the collusion of society, draws that society up into itself and directs it around itself until science is society-wide and the society as a consequence exists only for the support of science. However, in so doing, society drives a cleavage between pure and applied science, saving the latter and discarding the former as having no social effect, not seeing that the social effect of pure science is there and efficient but indirect, mediated by the applied science it produces for society.

By eliminating pure science, society eventually also eliminates all science; for the source which led to applied science ceases to flow; and applied science, which drew its sustenance from pure science, being only, as we have seen in an earlier section, the applications of pure science, comes to an end as a result. Hence in the dialectic of science and society, society first benefits from the rapid progress of science and only afterwards suffers, when it brings the science which has had such a powerful effect upon it of both good and evil, to a close.

XIII

POLITICS

AN ANALYSIS OF LIBERALISM

FALLACIES OF IRRATIONAL INDIVIDUALISTIC LIBERALISM

Liberalism has occurred as an actual program only in a brief flicker between the reign of absolutisms. In our day, it occurs in the comparatively short interval between faith in the revealed truths of Christianity and possible faith in the dogmas of communism. By these two absolutisms, liberalism is considered a condemned error. It is specifically condemned by Catholic Christianity. It is specifically condemned by communism. But what is liberalism? Should it be defended or annihilated? In order to determine the answers to these questions it will be necessary first to make an analysis of liberalism. This analysis will reveal that liberalism has been conceived irrationally and is therefore contradictory and fallacious, but that a rational form of liberalism is possible and necessary.

Liberalism may be defined as the freedom of individual thought and action. According to the doctrine of liberalism, the individual is to be left free to think whatever he wishes to think, and to do whatever he chooses to do. Two observations must be made immediately. The first is that freedom of *thought* is something of which no individual can be deprived, inasmuch as thought is a private affair and must therefore remain free. It is seldom possible to tell what a person is thinking about, and more difficult still to dictate the psychological order of his reasoning. Therefore freedom of thought need not be argued here. It is rather with the freedom to express thoughts that the doctrine of liberalism is concerned. The second observation is that *complete* freedom of action is a contradiction. If one wishes to murder a neighbor while he wishes still to live, freedom of action is obviously not possible for both persons. Freedom of individual action, then, must always assume a residual basis of social law which is held to a minimum but operative wherever there is a possibility of conflict between individual courses of action.

Liberalism as defined above, and as historically formulated by the English utilitarian school of Bentham and the Mills, is irrational. It rests upon the theory that only atomic individual particulars are real and that society is but a fictional convention to represent the collection in free association of real atomic individuals. In order to expose the contradictions contained in this irrational individualistic liberalism, it will be necessary to break it down into its constituent assumptions. These are: (1) that the individual's own capacity for reasoning constitutes his final court of appeal; (2) that there is no other guide to individual thought and action except conscious experience; (3) that there exist no universal laws superior to the individual; (4) that consequently no social organization is superior to the individual; and finally, (5) that since there is no certain knowledge possible, individual opinion must always govern. Let us consider each of these assumptions separately.

1. To maintain that the individual's own capacity for reasoning constitutes his final court of appeal seems to be an affirmation of the authority of reason, but is actually just the reverse. The thesis of the absolutism of individual reasoning is based upon confusion of reason with reasoning. The individual's reasoning refers to an independent reason (i.e., an independent logical order of existence), else it could not be. To consider the reasoning of the individual final is to make the errors of reasoning into something ultimate, since without an independent referent, there would be no way in which errors in reasoning could be detected. But that errors in reasoning are, in fact, detected, is evidence of the existence of an independent reason, an independent truth in terms of which error can be judged.

The final appeal to individual reasoning rests upon a failure to make the necessary distinction between the logical independence of ideas and the psychological process of reasoning. Thinking, which is a psychological process, must not be confused with thoughts, which are the apprehension of ideas by the mind. It is indeed the mind which apprehends ideas, but independent ideas are what the mind apprehends. Thus independent reason or logic, and not individual reasoning, must be the final court of appeal. True rationality rests upon the awareness of an independent reason, and upon the recognition of both success and failure in the individual's attempt to apprehend the conditions of reason through the process of reasoning.

2. The second assumption of individualistic liberalism is that there is no guide to individual thought and action other than conscious experience. The doctrine of the sole reality of conscious experience as the individual's guide is only another way of stating the philosophy of radical empiricism or positivism. We may sum up one objection to it here by asserting that it does not allow any reality to the actual world, and hence gives no objective basis for the judgment of the individual upon his conscious experience. Hence the doctrine eventually reduces to a solipsism which cannot be proved or refuted but which few persons have ever sincerely held.

The appeal to individual conscious experience was made by Descartes, who saw that to prepare the ground for such an appeal it was necessary to start with doubt. He attempted to begin by doubting all but his own existence. But what Peirce has pointed out in this connection remains true, that "no one who follows the Cartesian method will ever be satisfied until he has formally recovered all those beliefs which in form he has given up."[1] We cannot doubt simply because we choose to do so. Doubt is possible only when we have been given sufficient reason. "Let us not pretend to doubt in philosophy what we do not doubt in our hearts," says Peirce.[2] But if we are not able to start with universal doubt, our beliefs cannot be guided wholly by conscious experience.

Yet neither can we start with universal belief. The fact is that we are no more free to believe than we are free to doubt, both demanding logical justification. If belief without sufficient reason were possible, there would be no more basis for accepting one belief than for accepting another. Consequently the beliefs of the individual would be in a constant state of flux, and his mind would be a confusion of beliefs many of which would be contradictory, accepted or rejected only according to the current of whim or caprice. But this is a description of insanity. Indeed our sanity does depend upon the fact that we do not accept or reject beliefs without reason. We are free to believe only what we have reason to believe, which is to say that we are not free to believe except what reason allows.

[1] *Collected Papers*, 5.265.
[2] *Ibid.*

So much for conscious experience as a guide to individual thought. But the same is true when conscious experience is offered as a guide to individual action. Freedom of belief and freedom of action are in fact inseparable doctrines, since actions usually follow from beliefs and each person acts according to what he believes. The failure of belief leads to the failure of action, and contradictory beliefs lead to contradictory actions. Ideas are apprehended intrinsically as feeling, logically as thought, and expressed objectively as action. They do not in any wise have to be conscious in order to exist and to have their effect. We are not free to do whatever we choose to do—at least not when our actions lead to contradictions. The truth shall prevail in the world of actuality simply because contradictions eventually prove themselves obstacles which cannot be overcome. Thus the same conclusion holds for action as for thought: namely, that we are free to do only what we have good reasons to do, which is to say that we are free to do only what an independent logic allows.

3. The contention that no universal laws exist to govern the individual is refuted by the truth of the laws of logic. Certainly the individual is not free to believe in ultimate contradictions. Moreover, the whole body of scientific and mathematical knowledge can be offered in refutation. No individual is free to believe, for instance, in any but a one-way process for the radioactive disintegration series of chemical elements. Certainly the individual is governed as to his belief. The contention that no universal laws exist to govern the individual's actions is likewise impossible to maintain. If the individual were always free to act, there would be no need for consistency in our actions, and no searching for rational plans. What we would do would be—whatever we did. But since here, too, sanity is challenged, universal laws must be admitted to exist.

4. Irrationalism prohibits the allowance of real social organizations superior to the individual. For this philosophy admits the reality of individuals, who, after all, do exist on the physical level as well as other levels, but denies the equal reality of the relations between individuals. If social organization did not govern individuals, men could not exist in a state of society. The division of labor, which makes society possible, and which exists even in primitive societies, depends upon the subordination of the individual to social plans. The old nominalistic explanation of social organization as a mere summatory convenience does not account for the *necessity* of social organization where men are living in collections. From the social point of view, complete freedom of individual action must lead to inevitable contradictions. The chaos resulting from the lack of authority on the part of social organization would allow the contradictions to inhibit all individual action. Thus the fact of the reality

of social organization is attested by the mere presence of individuals in the condition of society.

5. It is doubtful whether anyone sincerely believes that no knowledge is possible and that opinion alone governs, yet this is an assumption of the appeal to individual reasoning as the sole authority. Science exists for the purpose of transferring ideas from the status of hypothesis to the status of law, from the realm of opinion to that of knowledge. When an hypothesis is suggested in science, reason to doubt it as well as to accept it may exist. No hypothesis is accepted as law without sufficient empirical allowance, plus the proof by self-consistency within the given system; but once such demonstration has been forthcoming, the agreement with regard to it is almost unanimous. If, then, later experimentation provides sufficient evidence to doubt the law, it is discarded, or subsumed by a more general law. This ideal of science is most closely approached by the science of physics. To insist upon the impossibility of knowledge and the primacy of opinion would be to challenge the validity of scientific method. Since the method of reason is supported by the method of science, the claim of invalidity for scientific method would be unreasonable. Therefore insofar as science is admitted, knowledge is also admitted to be possible, and opinion admitted to exist only in order to become knowledge.

Subjectivism is irrefutable, yet untenable. The adherence to opinion and the denial of objective knowledge amounts to the adoption of the subjectivist position. To deny that there are any "irreducible and stubborn facts" which resist the individual's desires, and to assert that the world, including all other persons, has been created by the individual's mind, is a position which is safe from logical refutation while remaining inadmissable to enlightened common sense.

We have examined liberalism in its traditional formulation sufficiently to conclude that, as such, it is untenable. Liberalism stated entirely from the point of view of the atomic individual is irrational through and through, and therefore completely invalid. Thus we must turn next to the question of whether a rational social liberalism is possible.

POSSIBILITIES OF RATIONAL SOCIAL LIBERALISM

Can there be a rational social liberalism? Nineteenth-century liberalism, as an explicit affair, was the doctrine formulated by Locke, Bentham, and the Mills, and thus extremely irrational and individualistic. It has frequently seemed necessary to those who have wished to challenge reigning laws, customs and institutions because of demonstrable limitations, first to indicate their subjective nature. Social reformers find it necessary to remind themselves that such laws are man-made in order to feel quite sure that, despite their age and authority, they can be man-destroyed. Yet they always wish to establish the objective validity of the laws they offer in place of the old. The complete denial of the validity of law is hardly the way in which to question prevailing laws. It is necessary only to recognize that all laws are equally independent but not all equally limited. When less limited laws are being substituted for more limited laws, the question of the independence of law should not be involved.

When humanitarian social legislation appeared in the nineteenth century, it did not come as the result of the old irrational individualistic liberalism. Indeed how could it, since the traditional liberalism had set its face against such legalism? But as John Dewey points out, in that century there were already the beginnings of a rational social liberalism evident in social legislation, not due to the accepted version of liberalism. He says that

> Benthamite liberalism was not the source of factory laws, laws for the protection of children and women, prevention of their labor in mines, workmen's compensation acts, employers' liability laws, reduction of hours of labor, the dole, and a labor code. All of these measures went contrary to the idea of liberty of contract fostered by *laissez faire* liberalism ... Gradually a change came over the spirit and meaning of liberalism. It came surely to be associated with the use of governmental action for aid to those at economic disadvantage and for alleviation of their conditions.[3]

Such is the change from individualistic to social liberalism, as it took place historically, forced by the logic of economic events. Explicitly, the new understanding of liberalism was formulated and vigorously defended by Thomas Hill Green and his followers. Green was an objective idealist, which is to say, something of a rationalist, and he opposed the old liberalism on ethical grounds. The good, he asserted, is not something subjective and individual, but something absolute, and thus the individual is helped in its attainment by and through the perfection of society. As John Dewey says, Green "asserted that *relations* constitute the reality of nature, of mind and of society."[4]

But if relations are real, then laws are real, which means that not only must the perfection of society be the true concern of the individual but also that the authority of social laws must be recognized. But such recognition lays an injunction upon belief. Is freedom of thought, then,

---

[3] John Dewey, *Liberalism and Social Action* (New York, 1935), pp. 20–21.
[4] *Ibid.*, p. 24.

inconsistent with this conception? Definitely not. On all questions where knowledge cannot be segregated from opinion, liberalism must prevail. In short, *freedom of thought is required more for hypothesis than for law.* Insofar as the true relations or laws of existence are discovered, their questioning would be idle and unreasonable. If an hypothesis is put forward as a suggested explanation of anything, its proof or disproof must wait upon evidence; and until such evidence is forthcoming, it can neither be believed as law nor doubted as error. Until reason to believe or doubt is forthcoming, it must occupy an interim realm. It is only toward such hypotheses, toward opinion, then, that the attitude of liberalism is possible.

An important exception must at once be made here. From the formulation of rational social liberalism which we have just been presenting it would seem as though laws once discovered could never again be doubted. This is not true, and rests upon a misunderstanding of the realistic liberal doctrine. The liberal attitude is absolutely excluded only from absolutely ideal laws. The absolute, ideal and logical conditions of existence cannot be questioned; they are just as they are and as they must be. The laws which are discovered by human beings in their search for truth, are approximations of the ideal law. When a science abandons, or rather subordinates, one law to another more general, it is in process of approximating always closer and closer to this ideal law. And insofar (but only insofar) as discovered laws approximate to the ideal, liberalism is compelled to fall away.

When all the sciences reach the same degree of success that has been obtained in physics, the ultimate rule of reason over belief will become apparent, and there will no longer be any claim made for complete freedom of individual opinion. Once the social sciences are in a position to state some of the laws of social conduct, the reason for actions will be apparent, and the conflict of actions arising from conflict of individual opinion will be greatly diminished. Thus the ideal of society (approachable, albeit remote) involves the complete abolition of freedom of thought and its replacement by adequate reason for thought. Inasmuch, however, as such a state of affairs is incredibly remote, a residual rational liberalism is essential to any progress toward it. The proper mode of the attainment of this ideal lies in scientific method. One measure of the success of science in this regard is the ground remaining for freedom of thought within a given subject matter. For example, freedom of thought on questions involving physics is already difficult for the non-professional; whereas such freedom of thought on questions involving politics or any other division of social science is the common and often jealously guarded prerogative of the man in the street. Liberalism must remain, however, and be required for hypotheses, for any state of affairs short of the complete establishment of law.

Rational social liberalism must continue to prevail indefinitely, yet there can be nothing *absolutely* permanent about the formulation of a rational social liberalism. Such a liberalism is required only until the laws of all the sciences, including the science of society, come to be known, and it would be meaningless thereafter. But since at the moment no social theory occupies the status of law and all occupy the status of theory or hypothesis, liberalism must now apply unconditionally to all social studies. The goal of the ideal society is, of course, one in which all the laws of society are known, and in which the attitude of liberalism is not required. Of course this ideal is indefinitely remote and difficult of approach, so that little more can be expected than the very gradual establishment of social law and the correspondingly slow reduction of liberalism. Thus the criterion of progress in the social field as in all others is the extent to which the liberal attitude can reasonably be diminished, and not the reverse. Liberalism is strictly limited at both ends: it cannot be absolutely applied to all fields, since some laws have already been discovered by some sciences; yet it cannot be absolutely abolished short of the complete establishment of law. So far as the social sciences are concerned, liberalism is the attitude of hope assumed in the face of ignorance. It is thus actually an expedient measure taken as the best way to promote its own abolition.

The interim nature of rational social liberalism is inherent in the fact that human beings live in the historical order of actuality and are part of the actual world. They aspire to the complete reign of order, to the establishment of the logical order of possibility, yet are held down by the irreducible element of actuality and the partial nature of their own historical being. The predicament is recognized and made the basis for attack by those who oppose liberalism in all its forms. "A liberal," says that arch Catholic reactionary, Léon Daudet, "is a man who reveres God but respects the devil. He aspires to order and flatters anarchy in every domain."[5] The description is one which liberals may fairly accept. The liberal, in other words, is one who wants to apprehend God yet give the devil his due. Philosophically, this means that the liberal wishes to achieve infinite value while remaining actual. But is this not true of all human beings? And does it not amount to a definition of the human being in all his aspiration and struggle? We may aspire to God, but to suppose that we can leave the devil behind altogether is to end by ceding everything to the devil, who takes a sure revenge whenever he is cheated

[5] *The Stupid XIX Century* (Eng. trans., New York 1928), p. 54.

of his portion. Those who have gone to such extremes of asceticism and renunciation as the Christian St. Anthony must recognize the truth of this assertion.

The point of liberalism in this regard is that without a certain amount of anarchy from time to time, the prevailing order can never become a wider order. This alternation from order to anarchy to order is part of the dialectic of actuality. Anarchy is necessary to increase the inclusiveness of order, and is evil only when taken as an end in itself. The liberal, then, is simply one who is not satisfied with any limited order but who wants always to keep open the possibility of greater order.

Individualistic liberalism cannot be saved, but must be supplanted by social liberalism. Does this mean that individualism has no validity whatsoever, and that it too must be overthrown? Not at all. It may be asserted definitely that individualism has an important place under the doctrine of social liberalism. Major advances in the apprehension of ideas, in science or wherever, are most frequently accomplished by individuals. Now, it is true that individuals do not work completely in isolation, and that their work should not end with them. The individual as a unit is only part of a social whole; but he is a real part, and as a part irreducible. Insofar as it is individuals who serve society, the advance of society is impossible without the retention of a certain amount of freedom of thought, expression and action on the part of individuals.

Since liberation of the capacities of individuals for free, self-initiated expression is an essential part of the creed of liberalism, liberalism that is sincere must will the means that condition the achieving of its ends. Regimentation of material and mechanical forces is the only way by which the mass of individuals can be released from regimentation and consequent suppression of their cultural possibilities. The eclipse of liberalism is due to the fact that it has not faced the alternatives and adopted the means upon which realization of its professed aims depends. Liberalism can be true to its ideals only as it takes the course that leads to their attainment. The notion that organized social control of economic forces lies outside the historic path of liberalism shows that liberalism is still impeded by remnants of its earlier *laissez faire* phase, with its opposition of society and the individual. The thing which now dampens liberal ardor and paralyzes its efforts is the conception that liberty and development of individuality as ends exclude the use of organized social effort as means. Earlier liberalism regarded the separate and competing economic action of individuals as the means to social well-being as the end. We must reverse the perspective and see that socialized economy is the means of free individual development as the end.[6]

[6] Dewey, *Liberalism and Social Action*, p. 90.

The old liberalistic doctrine of Bentham and the Mills assumed that liberty was the inalienable inheritance of the individual. But realistic social liberalism does not allow this to be held true. Realists, from Thomas Hill Green to Charles Peirce, have understood that liberalism is a goal and not the heritage of individuals.

> They [Green and his followers] served to break down the idea that freedom is something that individuals have as a ready-made possession, and to instill the idea that it is something to be achieved, while the possibility of the achievement was shown to be conditioned by the institutional medium in which an individual lives. These new liberals fostered the idea that the state has the responsibility for creating institutions under which individuals can effectively realize the potentialities that are theirs.[7]

Thus we see that for the individual to serve society there must be freedom for the individual, not as an atomic and self-contained unit, self-sufficient and absolutely free, but as a part of a larger whole, requiring as a part the necessary latitude to best perform its function for the whole. In this sense freedom becomes the irreducible minimum of liberalism under the realistic socialistic doctrine: the freedom to find the law and to follow it. Without the existence of an absolute and independent system of laws, which can be sought for and always approximated closer and closer in actuality, the conception of freedom has little meaning.

For realistic social liberalism is neither an ultimate nor an end, but exists for the sake of something else; and the recognition of this fact constitutes its chief virtue. When the end for the sake of which it exists is attained, it may be discarded. All men desire to know the truth, and they recognize that this way lies the good life; but truth concerning the social field is not yet known. Until it is known, freedom of thought and expression is required for the sake of the hypotheses which must be formed in the search for that truth. When a social utterance (e.g., a political opinion) is voiced, and its contradictory is also voiced, we must be prepared to permit them both, although knowing that conflicting assertions cannot both be true. We allow them and reserve judgment, but only until such a time as we have a criterion for choosing between them. On that day, liberalism with regard to contradictory utterances may well be diminished, since there would no longer be any purpose served by allowing false assertions that are known as false, and demonstrably so, to be made.

The aim of liberalism which has made science possible is to preserve the pursuit of science by whatever means, until social science can obtain

[7] *Ibid.*, p. 26.

agreement in the social field, and make future opinionate differences on social matters an impossibility. As the abolition of the need for liberalism through the discovery of law is included in the ultimate goal of society, so the maintenance of a rational social liberalism is included in the proximate goal of society. We may conclude that if liberalism be understood as the old irrational individualistic liberalism, it may be abandoned, but that understood as rational social liberalism it must be retained.

ONTOLOGY AND IDEOLOGY

Abstract philosophy is what is conventionally meant by philosophy, while the philosophy of history, which deals with cultures as organizations having a career, is quite apart from it. The two studies have rarely been brought together. But the fact is that there exists also a concrete philosophy, which is philosophy as imbedded in culture, and, in this connection, cultures, it may be held, are applied ontologies.

Before the nature of applied ontology can be explored, some definitions are in order.

By "ontology" here is meant a system of ideas more general than any other. An ontology can be stated explicitly or exist implicitly. Explicit ontology is ontology as known and taught in books, journals and lectures. Implicit ontology is what exists concretely imbedded in cultures. In this state it can be (a) permeating, or (b) separate but included. (a) The permeating type of implicit ontology is what has been elsewhere called the "implicit dominant ontology."[1] It exists throughout cultures as their principle of consistency. The consequences of being and of behaving in terms of the consequences of an ontology are so large that they become invisible; but this means that they extend beyond vision, not that they do not exist. It is everywhere in a culture, and no more in one action or condition than in another. (b) The separate but included type of implicit ontology is commonly known as ideology.[2] By "ideology"

---

[1] Cf. my *Theory of Human Culture* (New York 1946, Duell, Sloan & Pearce), chapter 4, B; *The Institutions of Society* (London 1956, Allen & Unwin), pp. 176, 276.

[2] See e g Karl Mannheim, *Ideology and Utopia* (New York 1952. Harcourt Brace), pp. 179, 277.

is meant a culturally adopted metaphysics. Thomism in Roman Catholicism, for instance, or Marxism in Soviet Russia; or the subjective idealism of Hitler's national socialism in Nazi Germany. Both implicit dominant ontologies and ideologies are socially established ontologies, the former by acts in which the ontological implications are unrecognized and the latter by acts performed in the full recognition of what is entailed.

Ontologies operate in cultures, then, as implicit dominant ontologies or as ideologies. If we are to understand the relation of ontology to ideology we shall have to know more about cultures.

Let us begin the analysis of cultures with the hierarchy known to the philosophy of science as the integrative levels: the physical, chemical, biological, psychological and cultural strata of the world of nature. Each of these levels includes but also depends on the ones below it. If the integrative levels are as complex as we suppose, if, that is to say, molecules are composed of organizations of atoms, cells of organizations of molecules, organisms of organizations of cells, and cultures of organizations of organisms, then human cultures must be the most complex object known. It is composed of structures which are germane to its own level.

Two more conditions must be recited in order to further the analysis of cultures.

One of these is that the elements of analysis of cultures are not equivalent to the integrative levels. The analysis of any integrative level yields as its elements of analysis its own proper sub-levels. Thus societies, institutions, social groups, human individuals, and artifacts, are the elements of analysis of the integrative levels of the cultural.

Another condition is that each included level appears in its own independent form as it exists on its own level but also as transformed into objects of the included level. Thus when physical objects become parts of cultures they remain physical objects but they have acquired in addition the properties of artifacts or tools; chemical elements retain their place in the periodic table of the elements but they add another role when they are used in industrial and medical technologies; biological objects are no less organisms because they also serve as sources of food, as pack animals or pets. What is added to psychological objects when they become parts of cultures will become evident later in the discussion. In the sense of transforming but including objects from levels below it, culture becomes the sum of integrative levels.

By "culture" here is meant the organization of society and its works, and by "society," an organization within a culture. Thus we speak of "western culture" and within it of the French society, or, more currently, the French nation. A society is a hierarchy of institutions. It remains only to define institution. By "institution" is meant the behavior of men and materials in accordance with a charter.

The argument has now brought us to a point where it should be possible to show how ontologies operate in cultures both as implicit dominant ontologies and as ideologies.

(a) If it is true that ontology permeates cultures as their principle of consistency, we shall be obliged to show such consistency existing in each of the cultural elements of analysis. The implicit dominant ontology is readily detectable in places where it rises to the surface of cultures, more specifically in societies as (1) the hierarchy of institutions; in institutions as (2) the creed of the leading institution; in social groups as (3) fashions in arts and technologies; in human individuals as (4) the quality of customs and the character of unconscious beliefs; in artifacts as (5) sets of preferred items.

1. Every culture has approximately the same set of institutions, with only rare exceptions, but they are not always arranged in the same order of importance. The arrangement, therefore, is significant and should tell us something about the ideas which dominate the culture. In a religious society the church is the dominant institution, in a war-like and aggressive society the military occupies this position. Even such service institutions as communication and transportation can move around; they occupy a much more important place in our society, for instance, than is usual. The acceptance by a society of the relative positions of institutions in the hierarchy is evidence of consistency, to the extent, let us say, of the absence of institutional conflict and competition.

2. The creed of the leading institution may contain the philosophy of the culture, as some of Locke's and Montesquieu's ideas are built into our Declaration of Independence and Constitution, though in such a case the language is that of the institution: legal or political language, rather than philosophical. The evidence for consistency here is the permeation of other institutions and even of non-institutional phenomena by the practice following from some of the articles of the creed.

3. According to this theory, fashions in art, such as surrealism or non-objective painting, and fashions in technology, such as the current vogue for miniaturization, are indicative of the dominant philosophy, though again not in professional language. Evidence for the consistency of practical interests with theoretical conceptions can hardly be escaped here.

4. Qualities are difficult to describe, and the qualities of customs no less so. The somewhat stuffy customs of nineteenth-century England are still remembered, and make an interesting contrast with the very casual manners of twentieth-century United States. Both produce atmo-

THE TWO-STORY WORLD

spheres in which the individual lives and by which he is influenced with respect to his most fundamental beliefs. His thoughts, feelings and actions insofar as they betray a conformity with customs can hardly fail to reveal a consistency.

Individual beliefs when profound exist below consciousness, stored in the memory. The more profound the beliefs the less the individual is aware that he holds them. His individual beliefs are the result of his own private history, and may be rational or irrational. But the beliefs concerning the nature of reality, which he holds in common with the other members of his society, are rational, because they are the very basis of his rationality, and social because they are the ground for what he and the members of his society think, feel and do.

5. What does it mean in terms of sets of preferences to have a national sport, or to prefer cricket to baseball? How are we to measure the causes, of which belching after meals as a sign of politeness, or suicide after public failure, as in Japan, are the results? Customs pass over into sets of preferences when they are particularized, but the two are not the same. Consider, for instance, what it must feel like to live in a primitive society where when one meets one's mother-in-law one must avert one's eyes. After a time, such actions become niceties in their execution, and are preferred to other alternatives as a matter of individual and arbitrary choice. Consistency discloses itself here as social approbation.

Generally speaking, the consistency of a culture indicates the establishment of a philosophy. A culture is an interpreted system of philosophy in which social events are substituted for the variables. The philosophy of a culture, then, is the culture made self-aware *qua* culture. A society exists as a conceptual symbiosis: an association of dissimilar human individuals to their mutual advantage by means of a commonly-held set of beliefs, institutions and customs.

The commonly-held set of beliefs allows for a certain definite range of philosophies, philosophies allowable within the limits of an established implicit dominant ontology. The range of philosophies in any given case specifies the width of the culture, i.e., its completeness. The uniformity of philosophies within a given culture defines its consistency. The range of philosophies within the western society in the last two centuries: Kantianism, Hegelianism, British idealism, logical positivism, ordinary language analysis, existentialism, all lie within the broad purview of subjective nominalism, which has been since the Renaissance the philosophy of western culture. The differences between philosophies specify the completeness of the culture, always providing of course that the consistency extends beyond the completeness; for there must be a sufficient remainder of uniformity over difference to insure the cohesiveness of the culture.

(b) We turn now to the question of how ontologies operate in cultures as ideologies. The history of the development of ontology is the story of its separation from magic and religion and its transformations into secular speculation and ideology. Metaphysics began with the Greeks. Ideology was initiated by the formal approval of the philosophy of Thomas Aquinas in the Roman Catholic Church, and later by the adoption of dialectical materialism in Soviet Russia and China. Ideologies are deliberately adopted enabling invariants, chosen in order to give direction to the culture. Their choice is itself indicative, and any complete analysis would have to be pushed back to the question of why one ideology was chosen rather than another. We have already noted in looking at the integrative levels that lower sets of conditions are what make human cultures possible. The laws as well as the materials of the lower levels are required; physical structures, chemical compounds, biological farm products. On these we erect the more complicated structures from which higher values emerge. Thus the presence of an ideology as a fully self-conscious ontology, explicit rather than implicit but no less dominant, when dissected reveals an underlying layer of assumptions in terms of which the ideology was chosen from a number of others. And these assumptions can be shown to constitute the axioms of an implicit dominant ontology which is therefore no less effective when disclosed as an ideology than when it is permeating and supposedly non-existent.

How does one society manage to be so much more active and successful than another? Why is it that one society enters into history in a way that others do not? What, in short, makes one culture dynamic while another remains static and quiescent? Social dynamism results from fixing standards of pleasure on artifacts whose effects are intended to be higher than can be reached by the means necessary for their mere enjoyment, and this remains true whether the artifacts be altars or automobiles and intended to produce asceticism or surfeit. In the effort to attain to the condition required by these standards, the society takes no time out for enjoyment at all but spends itself in the effort at reaching. The pleasure consists in working toward the goal of pleasure and not in the attainment of the goal itself.

Now the pleasure at this level consists usually in the exercise of power or the surrender to it. In the exercise of power artifacts become instruments, inducements to conformity and obedience: immortality to be gained at altars and social prestige in automobiles. The possession of power determines who shall enter into history, and thus what shall be remembered. For "entering into history" two factors are necessary: the possession of power, and the breaking of the rhythm of social life.

The possession of social power is a matter of the freedom to wield economic and political control in the exercising of limiting freedom. This new surge of power comes from new techniques or from new instruments, as for instance the Roman phalanx or the American atomic bomb, or from new ideas, as for instance Marxism in Soviet Russia.

The people who establish and maintain a social rhythm are, so to speak, never heard from individually. Their society has no effect outside its boundaries. Those who break the rhythm are the heroes and martyrs of the new social order. The breaking of this rhythm means a change in the logic of events: axiomatic events turn the society toward new deductive directions, with the result that different theorematic consequences occur. These reverberate spatially to other societies and temporally to later societies.

Those who believe that philosophy and culture are one do so in terms of truth and consequences. Absolute belief entails drastic action, such as murdering people who refuse to accept a religion: as when the Spanish conquerors offered the Indians a choice between the cross or death. When it is held that an abstract philosophy ought to be the concrete philosophy of a culture, men are willing to substitute force for persuasion in order to put it into effect.

Ideologies as applied ontologies are wholly formalized systems governing societies. They liberate as well as restrict. They liberate so far as they can provide consistency for a culture, and they restrict so far as they fail to be complete (i.e., sufficiently inclusive). All begin with a residue of restrictions just because they are systems. At the outset when the theorems of action have not been fully deduced from the axioms of belief, ideologies liberate more than they restrict. But toward the end when their development has seen the development of most of the possible theorems, then they restrict more than they liberate. At this point, nominalistic philosophies, art, and similar social activities come to the fore, in an effort to break up the old order and to make way for newer and more complicated ones.

A culture is in the process of growth when the individuals within it contribute to it more than they receive from it, and in the process of decline when the individuals receive from it more than they contribute to it. In decline, a mortal uniformity can be observed, such as we see today in Spain where a single institution has vanquished every other and established a monotony like that of death itself. Dogmatism has so conquered reason that Spain has developed neither science nor philosophy, and has made a smaller contribution to western culture than any other European country. Too busy fighting the Moors, the Spaniards did not have time to engage in the Renaissance and never saw the Enlightenment. Their virtues as a result are merely personal, and their public activities are taken care of entirely by religion and are the same for every one.

An official ideology always rides upon the surface in full view, but it can be undermined by other forces. For the possession of an ideology does not do away with the effectiveness of a subterranean implicit dominant ontology, and the dynamics of social and cultural change can be accounted for better by the latter than by the former. Either the implicit dominant ontology is in conflict with newly uncovered facts or newly discovered theory, and consequently weakened; or institutions are challenged and replaced by Outstanding Individuals acting in their own right and cognizance. In either case, surface emotion substitutes for custom in the individuals whose membership in the mob has replaced their institutional affiliation, and the mob becomes easily led into the action of impulse or panic. The foundations of the established order are slowly eaten away once the cement of the implicit dominant ontology that has held them together is eroded.

Animals are adapted to their environment: the horse is an animal of the steppes, the shark an animal of the sea, the monkey an animal of the jungles, and man an animal of the cities. There, conditioned by his own cultural environment, he works out the set of variations made possible by the establishment of a particular theme. The black mass is celebrated in France as well as the mass, and an independent and separatist communism is promulgated in Jugoslavia as well as orthodox communism in Soviet Russia—Huysmans in addition to St. Thomas, and Tito in addition to Stalin. When conditions grow worse than can be supported, then the barbarians grow stronger at the gates. Not only the Goths and the Visigoths, but also the lower integrative levels with their simpler and stronger conditions, are always waiting just outside. The jungle outgrowths which eventually over-run the city furnish the boundaries to its outskirts during the city's most flourishing years.

There is something very logical about the offender against culture being locked up in a culture-world. The ordinary conformist is rewarded by the culture with the keys to some escape hatches. He needs the artifacts of culture if he is to have the experience available in a less restricted world beyond the culture confines. Hence the amateur skin-diver, the jungle explorer, the mountain climber. His contacts with the non-culture world—his summer vacations at the beach, in the forest or upon the mountains—are ways in which he keeps his cultural batteries charged. It is a fitting punishment, therefore, to the offender that he be locked up in a culture-world and in prison surrounded altogether by man-made objects, deprived of any contact with the non-culture world of nature. The world itself is wider than any conception of it; and that is why no ideology can hope to do more than serve as the justification for a developing stage in social affairs. It was brought in as an explanatory establishment; it must be dropped or forced out when another stage is in process of preparation, for then a new explanation is needed and hence a new act of establishment.

The philosopher prepares the way, and his activities constitute a preparation of the ground by means of free speculations concerning the possibilities; and hence he influences the choice of ranges. The empirical search for the truth of the Perfect Ontology requires him to investigate what ontology would result from what the most successful cultures have assumed as their implicit dominant ontologies or have established as their ideologies. Then the explicit ontology which corresponds closest to the implicit dominant ontology would be constructed abstractly and tested for completeness and consistency. The result would be the Best Available Ontology, which if not the Perfect Ontology would serve as the nearest approximation to it.

XIV

HISTORY

THE ROLE OF PHILOSOPHY IN A TIME OF TROUBLES

Explicit philosophy in its broadest aspects and as it concerns human beings may be defined as the attempt to discover the unchanging truths about the nature of things that change. Thus it has an actual existence in minds and in the tools of communication between them. Implicit philosophy is nothing less than the true nature of things, the possibility or conditions according to which things have their being. The truths of which we seek knowledge are independent both of that search and of our knowledge; yet to the knowledge also we have given the name of philosophy. Pursuit is practical; philosophy, theoretical. Applied philosophy consists in all our practical actions insofar as these may lead to or follow from some theoretical attempt to discover truth.

Philosophy in some one of its modes turns up in every effort of the actual world, and the actual world is involved in a constant round of change. Everything that we know about changes if it exists; and an important feature of the stability of the concrete world, upon which so much of our conviction of security depends, consists in those things which change most slowly: the regularity of astronomical orbits, the reaction of chemical elements, the organic impulse toward the perpetuation of life. But in the world of human affairs conditions are altogether different. The rate of change there seems vastly accelerated. Civilizations rise and fall at an alarming speed. States come to prominence and then decay just when they have been taken for granted. Even the individual's career is unpredictable; a response today differs from that with which he would have met the same situation a few years ago, or perhaps even yesterday. So it occurs to many of us to conclude from this comparison that human action, in contradistinction to the course of events in the physical world, is irrational, unpredictable, and insecure. Where is the dependability which the pursuit of implicit philosophy promises but which explicit philosophy never delivers?

We are apt in this state of frustration to be overlooking or forgetting one proposition, containing immense philosophical implications, of which mathematicians since Newton and Leibniz have made us keenly aware. This is that rate of change is not itself a changing thing. It is often possible to discover a functional constant in change, usually the rate at which the change is taking place. But the rate of change of things which are changing swiftly differs only in quantity from the rate of change of things which are changing slowly; it does not differ in change. Despite the fact that physical conditions are altered more slowly than social conditions, they do nevertheless change. And since rate of change is an invariant between variables, all change, social as well as physical, is governed to some extent, at least, by functionally evident, unchanging relations.

In this study we want to consider two things together: the nature of the pursuit of the unchanging, and its relation to the nature of the period of violent change. Stated as a problem, what is the function of philosophy in a time of troubles?

The sequence of social life, the flow of human affairs as a whole, set into the world of the action and reaction of all existing things, is what we term history. The course of events is by no means uniform. We speak of periods when "history is being made," and of dull periods when "nothing happens." It seems to us who are part of the process that time moves slowly or swiftly. Such comparisons are relative, of course; but relative differences are absolutely different. Since we can detect the existence of time only by the relative change of things in time, and since things in time evidence time itself only to the extent to which they bring about or suffer change, we may conclude that when time seems to move swiftly and things happen to us in quick succession, it is because social change is occurring more rapidly than usual, and, conversely, when time seems to move slowly and nothing at all happens to us in a long while it is because social change is occurring more slowly than usual. We may for convenience name the periods of relatively slow change, stable periods, and those of relatively rapid change, unstable periods.

We are logically forbidden by the rules of definition to explain the fact of change by change itself under another name, wherefore we must seek to account for social change analytically in that which changes. Since human individuals are the agents of society, the social situation is altered by individual action. The solution of our difficulties is contained in the character of human motivation. Nobody will dispute the fact that human action follows from belief when we include in the category of belief all biological acceptance: everything that is "believed" by the organism, from consciously held opinion to propositions which are incorporated in the physiological organism and revealed in behavioristic response. But we are concerned here of course only with those beliefs which can lead to voluntary actions. Obviously, the acceptance of belief must precede the actions which follow from them; in the sense in which we have defined belief, we must have our beliefs before we can act at all. But beliefs are accepted from among many propositions which are advanced; hence they must in one way or another be chosen. Thus social events would seem to fall into two distinct periods: those when beliefs are chosen, and those when actions are taken. The first consists in the establishment of theories; the second in the application of practices.

Examples of the two basic divisions of social life abound in history. Christian theology was chosen as an acceptable theory during the first two centuries A.D. It was applied as a practice during the next thousand years. The theory of biological evolution was accepted as a belief after 1851. It is at present being applied as a practice by the geneticists. The principles of science were discovered in the days of classic Greece; they have been elaborated and applied as a practice ever since, in the tradition which has carried on continuously from ancient Alexandria through Byzantium and North Africa to modern Europe and America.

One outstanding feature is inescapable in these examples. The period of theory and of the adoption of belief is apt to be short and violent, whereas the period of application and of practice is apt to be long and comparatively calm. Since this alternation of stable with unstable periods seems to be the characteristic pattern of social history, we may assume that the short violent period followed by the long period of calm, taken together as a unit, has a structure which can be analyzed to show cause. If, as seems obvious, there is a close affinity between the logic of events and actual structures, then we are justified in considering the whole of an historical unstable-stable period as the working out in practice of a logical system. A logical system consists of a set of postulates plus the deductions which can be drawn from them, the set of postulates to be as compact as possible, the deductions to be self-consistent and widely applicable. If we were to lay such a system down along the timeline of successive social events in history, we should expect that the postulates being first would fall into our short and violent period of instability, and the deductions into our longer and calmer period of stability.

It is now clear that this correspondence between logic and history, between the choosing of postulate-sets and violence on the one hand, and between the working out of deductions and calmness on the other, is consistent with the statements which we have already established. For we said that there were some periods when theories were chosen by belief and others when actions followed from their acceptance, and we identified the former as subject to transience and sudden change and the latter as subject to duration and slowness of change. The theories chosen by belief are postulate-sets, and the actions following from their acceptance are the deductions implicit in various practices.

From the social point of view, two different kinds of activity are required; one when we try to change our beliefs and another when we try to act upon them. Before new beliefs can be chosen, the old ones which have been demonstrated to be inadequate, together with the customs and institutions which have served to guard them, must be overthrown, a process involving the extreme disorder of social revolution. In the chaotic atmosphere brought about by this state of affairs, constructive philosophies are constituted and compared. At the time of the abandonment of an old order, new theories stand out in abundance, and the choice confronting society is brilliant but difficult. Although it must adopt new beliefs, beliefs which will begin a new era when all seems hopeful and everyone's attention is fixed upon the indefinitely large possibilities of the future, they cannot be chosen without reason. The postulates selected do not have to be self-consistent to be rational; they may even appear irrational. Their true rationality can only be tested by their deducibility. But their future regulation of an extended period of history makes the day of their choice a grave and momentous occasion.

It is otherwise with the period of application, the exploration of actions which should follow as deductions from the accepted postulates. Then the greatest efforts are directed toward rendering social life all of a piece, for actual deductions are naturally conducive to integrity. Despite the fact that the process has its flavor of adventure in the searching out of unknown implications, the general tone is one of contraction and conservation. Philosophy as a vital constructive force containing the blueprints for a new order is not needed. The critical faculty of philosophy is the one to which society appeals in this part of its development. The basic issues and the fundamental beliefs, which a vigorous philosophy would have come to challenge, and perhaps to replace, have long been regarded as safely settled. Society wishes only to be told how to move along the path which it has decided to follow, without swerving or stopping. To the furtherance of this purpose, new ideas are superfluous and new techniques alone are required.

It is no paradox that the philosopher is secure in stable periods but finds the most interest in unstable ones. In stable periods the postulates for action come to be accepted at such a deep level of belief that no one is even aware of their existence as postulates. Actions are thought to spring altogether from conscious reasoning based on common sense, on the accepted ethics of custom, or on "what we know to be right." It is in this period that philosophical inquiry is regarded as the property of professional men. An academic pursuit, having no relevancy to the vital problems of the real world of practical action, it is relegated to the classroom where it can serve to elevate the minds of the young. Philosophy is restricted less by the prohibition against the expression of new philosophies or by the reassertion of older points of view than by the profound acceptance of some one philosophy as the common understanding of the nature of things. The approach to practice on the part of the philosophers is confined to the negative service of criticizing the lack of that self-consistency which actual deductions are supposed to have. In stable periods, then, all philosophical activities are allowed to continue unabated simply because they are regarded as unimportant. The disadvantage of stable periods is that philosophical inquiry is apt to be curtailed by the restrictions which a framework of absolutely accepted philosophy imposes. No matter how tentative and liberal such a system may be, once its principles are accepted as postulates for action by a society, it becomes intolerant and dogmatic. It identifies itself with the whole of the final truth and regards any challenge to its authority as a challenge to reason itself. Unfortunately, a world dominated by any given philosophy does not provide the atmosphere in which the spirit of philosophical inquiry can grow.

The unstable period we may identify with the time of troubles, a period of violent change when old doctrines are abandoned and new postulates selected. It is a morning not only of freedom but of chaos as well. Along with the release from sanctified absolutisms and implicit dogmas goes an uncertainty and an indecision that is neither comfortable nor welcome. But what a profusion of theory is offered to the minds of men! What powerful values are glimpsed for the first time! What feverish activity takes place! Working side by side with the opportunists who seek to preserve an old order for the sake of its traditional and established benefits, are the men of the future: those intellectual pioneers who are seeking to carve out a new universe of vast theoretical speculation. Every enterprise is conducted at high speed and on a hazardous basis. In no other time is there so much suggestiveness. Nothing is any longer safe from inquiry; issues regarded as settled which formerly it were heresy if not insanity to doubt are once more called into question. The speculative mind probes everywhere but always in danger of being confronted with prohibitions, always just about to be silenced by the constituted authorities who feel the ground reeling under their feet. In such periods of transition, the teaching of philosophy is apt to be disrupted, but the teaching is easier to disrupt than the pursuit. The real disadvantage is that the pursuit itself is likely to be rendered publicly impossible. But there exists still the freedom from restrictions imposed by the framework of an accepted philosophy. All old beliefs are uprooted; nothing is undeniable; first principles are challenged again; possibilities are stirred up from the bottom. Philosophy, usually in some religious or political dress, is once more a necessary article.

Although the philosopher himself may remain unrecognized, a forgotten man, this is of no importance to philosophy. The fate of any individual, be he philosopher or any other, is merely an incident; the fate of an accepted explicit philosophy is an epoch; but implicit philosophy itself as the nature of things is free of fate and consonant only with destiny. Thus from the point of view of philosophy, in the sense that it is incapable of change since there is only one truth, man lives for philosophy and not philosophy for man. The nature of things is not subject to revision. In a time of troubles, consolation is only a by-product of knowledge. The chief aim of first causes and final ends is not personal but universal. Truth can only be properly pursued with a view to its general application. Every man who feels for humanity as a whole is something of a traitor to his narrow class. He does not deny the value of those with whom he is identified but seeks to go beyond them; his interests are beautifully cosmical.

To embrace the conception of the unlimited community of Peirce—that selves are only vicinities through which we must pass on our way toward ever larger organizations of being, in the search for the largest organization with which we can safely identify our interests—means to struggle to improve the course of events yet never to be hurt by what happens. But the social world has hovered desperately between the dogmatic mysticism which maintains that nothing that happens matters, and the equally dogmatic philosophy of practical action which maintains that only what happens matters. The truth of the doctrine of the unlimited community lies in a unique combination of these seemingly irreconcilable positions. What happens matters so long as we are powerful to alter the course of events in the slightest fashion. But when we are no longer able to intervene with good effect, then the being of an unlimited community alone matters, just as it is and without our efforts. For where we cannot help it is good to understand and to love. In that humming cosmopolis which is the universe, we are at least neighborhoods, and share its unlimited community of interests.

Thus it comes about that when a philosopher who chances to live in the midst of a time of troubles decides to do something for his contemporaries in terms of philosophy, he is lost. His own times have already been served by the philosophers who have preceded him. He may be part of the present, but his work belongs to the future. It is only the extreme separation of theory and practice which enables their interrelations to develop into anything. Philosophy can imply a certain kind of experience, just as experience can suggest a certain kind of philosophy. But a considerable change and the time in which it can occur are needed for the transition between the abstract and the concrete. Hence theory and the practice to which it leads, like practice and the theory to which it leads, are never contemporaries.

The purpose of philosophy in a time of calm deduction is to criticize the contradictions among deductions when these are inconsistent among themselves or with the postulates. This it can do through the exercise of the duty of philosophers to maintain alternative truths and to advocate logical principles of consistency. But the purpose of philosophy in a time of troubles is to see to it that better postulates are chosen for belief. This it can do through the exercise of the duty of philosophers to maintain the widest truths and thus to keep them in the foreground of attention.

Philosophy is another name for immutable truth, and a time of troubles is the fate which comes upon the social world when the actual philosophy which it has adopted reveals in its practical application contradictions which prove insupportable. Something less, but nothing different is to be expected, except perhaps the ameliorative influence which would follow the awareness of such an expectation, until the day when the knowledge upon which we base our actual philosophies becomes one with that philosophy which we call truth. To comprehend the nature of social change is to prepare ourselves for it somewhat and to meet with less violence in the difficulties of adjustment. But there will be social change until there is only philosophy, which is only another way of saying that there exists an indefinitely remote limit to the nature of things in terms of which there is change. It is crucial that there can only be actual change because there is possible exchange. The time of troubles is thus only one more illustration of the real being of that realm of philosophy, where nothing can be altered and where everything is true.

XV

LITERARY CRITICISM

CAMUS AND THE PASSION OF HUMANISM

In the world of literature it often happens that great men have profound feelings and superficial thoughts; the most able do not let matters rest there but go on to dramatize the feelings, out of which they elicit another kind of thought that results in an art which is anything but superficial. It was not always so, however, and there are many instances of failure. Good novelists, like Mann, wrote such bad philosophy, and good philosophers, like Santayana, such bad novels. Each had a field of competence on which he could fall back in case of trouble: Mann was an important novelist and Santayana an important philosopher. If we try to judge Camus from the same point of view and with identical canons, we experience considerable difficulty. Camus was responsible for a kind of literary philosophy and for vaguely philosophical novels in such equal amounts that it is difficult to say in which category he belongs. In his novels he borrowed plentifully from others: Defoe, Simenon, Gide, Kafka, Hemingway, and Faulkner. Except for *The Plague,* his novels are quite short and unpretentious, more like novelle or long short stories, and do not seem either original or impressive. In his philosophy he relied upon existentialism, particularly upon the version advanced by his contem-

porary, Sartre, with whom he broke personally and from whom he
thought he had departed doctrinally. He was neither a great novelist nor
a great dramatist; his work is too non-specific and undramatic. For the
most part, he was rational but at the same time superficial, often reasoning closely about what hardly matters, pages which sometimes give off
the appearance of philosophy but deal with trivial generalities, the
finished work amounting only to weak philosophical essays and glimpses
of plans for fiction. It is difficult to see anything of permanent worth in
all of this if we confine our judgment strictly to his writings in their
proper categories. Camus did not advance the cause of either the novel
or philosophy, and these are the two fields to which he devoted most of
his attention. And yet there is a tremendous value in Camus which is
worth recognizing and saving.

Perhaps, for clues, we may best look to the philosophical movement
in which he awoke to find himself immersed. It would not have been easy
to escape the influence of existentialism. At once we find differences in
the way Camus interpreted what he found. For he was the only positive
existentialist who did not understand existentialism in Christian terms.
The existentialists are either positive and religious, like Marcel and Tillich,
or negative and atheistic, like Heidegger and Sartre. Heidegger comes
closer perhaps to making a contribution in positive terms, for Heidegger
is a philosopher while Camus was not. Heidegger's contribution is theoretical, as any philosopher's usually is. The most notable exception is
that of Socrates, who was able both to expound his philosophy and to
live by it. The contribution of Camus was made in action and expression,
both concrete—as concrete as they could be made. The example of a
man of action who can also dramatize his values, because he is something
of an artist, and set them forth in theory, because he is something of a
thinker, ought to be tremendous. He leaves us in no doubt as to what the
values mean as well as to what impact they can have. His hope evidently
was to represent the essence of what the western culture has stood for and
what ought to be saved in it.

Camus was above all a humanist. And humanism is ordinarily associated with rationalism. Men of good will are always expected to be
reasonable men. But, in the usual practice, humanistic rationalism is too
narrowly conceived. Men of good will, who are both humanists and
rationalists, tend to forget that reason has two demands, not one. A
system of ideas, to be rational, must be both consistent and complete. To
be consistent, no two of the ideas included within the system can be
contradictory; to be complete, all of the relevant ideas must be included.
But no system can include all ideas and still be consistent, as one logician
has proved; so that the excluded ideas press at the door and make their

existence felt out of all proportion to their importance merely because they are outside the system. It happens that men of good will think only in terms of consistency. The completeness passes them by, and so they have earned reason a bad name among irrationalists: for a narrow reason improperly applied may fail and thus show reason inadequate.

There are always men who remain outside any system and oppose it, and they are thought for this reason to be unsystematic. Some of course are, but there are others who are aware only of its inadequacies and remain standing close by with the missing elements in their hands. That is why, perhaps, the idea of the absurd held such a fascination for Camus. He saw as absurd every impossibility, and recognized in it a call for the rationality of completeness. If anything impossible has to be accounted for—and it does, since the impossibility of anything is a fact about that thing—then we need a wider system of rationality. What is new is the discovery that such an interest can become so absorbing that it turns into a passion. Camus was one of the first to become aware of the intensity it could contain and the damage it could do. In the preface to his plays he tried to explain this. "For the dramatist the passion for the impossible is just as valid a subject for study as avarice or adultery. Showing it in all its frenzy, illustrating the havoc it wreaks, bringing out its failure—such was my intention."

"Bringing out its failure." But to show the failure of the passion for the impossible: what does that imply if not a preference for the possible? And the possible is the reasonable, the rational. Camus' method here is an effective one. The best way to refute a position is to accept it and then from the inside to reveal its limitations. As the keystone of a philosophy to be applied in practice, the impossible can lead only to disaster; and Camus used his dramatic powers to disclose this by showing it in practice, for he was a dramatist who was also intelligent enough to be aware of the ideas which were involved in the values he was testing.

Camus, then, was a rationalist, but he was also keenly aware of the limitations of all the rational systems by which men had lived and were endeavoring to live still in his own day—including the proposed new system of Marxism, of which the limitations were immediately evident. For Camus was also a humanist who did not wish to leave his humanism to the mercies of a cold and limited rationalism.

There is nothing more disastrous in human affairs than absolutes. Those who think that they have the truth in any final form are always willing to impose it on others; they may even consider it their duty to do so. A wholly ordered system is the equivalent in logic of an absolute belief. There is no room in it for change, since neither its assumptions nor its consequences can be altered in the slightest. But the trouble with wholly ordered systems is that while rigid they are apt to be incomplete. In which case their consistency is not enough. Marxism has that kind of commitment. A partially ordered system is not complete and so lacks the security which wins unswerving adherents who are willing to make converts to their point of view by physical force. Humanism can survive in democracy because democracy is only partially ordered; with all its logical limitations, it has the virtue of not lending itself to absolutes or to political imposition.

Camus' concept of humanism was a finite affair, but it had the passion usually associated with irrationalisms. For his revolt against all limited orders was made in the interest of a wider order, based on world-wide humanism. Only by a benevolent world-government could an adequate world-order be established. But it has been obvious to many for some time that both the intellectual equipment and the emotional climate for such an arrangement are lacking. Men are not ready to get together in one central organization for the entire world, which, given the immense progress in communication and transportation, their technology and personal interests demand. What instead?

Camus replied by showing that irrationality is one legitimate moment in the rhythm of rational existence. Here was a beginning which had been seriously overlooked. It could lead after some preparatory stages to the establishment of true foundations for liberal democracy, the only system of politics discovered thus far which is capable of providing the individual with the maximum of personal liberty. The precondition discovered by Camus is serious and the aim of a firm liberalism worth achieving, but many other considerations intervened, and a number of subordinate steps were first necessary.

One of these steps is the recognition that integrity is individual. Here is required, then, a defense of liberalism. Not liberalism in the new social meaning but liberalism in the old personal meaning. "After a certain age," said Camus, "every man is responsible for his face." For this very reason that Camus' approach was affirmative, he had to account for the negative side of existentialism and arrange to deal with it. Very few people can stand the thought of death, and men have devised religions to provide for it, but the existentialists could not stand the thought of life.

There is an explanation from history for their aversion. The decline of Europe in a series of world wars and deliberate atrocities had left sensitive man alone, guilty, and without support. Camus was acutely aware of what this meant: "at a certain level of suffering or injustice no one can do anything for anyone. Pain is solitary." And death. Man's birth is necessarily a social situation, but often he dies alone. He can die alone because he must, but he cannot live alone because he need not. In the world of Nazi-occupied France, and in the demoralization which followed liberation, solitude was often compelled by the situation. The individual was condemned to stand alone and to face himself directly and in isolation, and he found this intolerable. The comparison of Frenchmen in the underground during the German occupation of France with the Russian nihilists in Czarist times occurs more than once in the writing of Camus. Just as he felt the sin of separation experienced by the sensitive individual who is cut off from his fellows, so he also recognized "the profound joy experienced by the man of action in contact with a large section of humanity." There is no morality for man by himself; human life is social. Interference with a man's political freedom, however, tends to cripple all his other endeavors and to stifle his very being. It is interesting to examine what a man needs in order to have any firm direction. For one thing, some knowledge of history; without this knowledge there cannot be a sense of history—a feeling that the future will at least in some ways resemble the past, and that one stands halfway between them, capable of assisting historic forces toward their destiny. When Camus suggested that the twentieth century is more than most a century of slavery, it was only because of his imperfect knowledge of history. Slavery has always been the rule, freedom the exception; usually, revolutions do no more than exchange masters in the name of freedom.

But there are dangers to freedom as well, even though they are rarely recognized. Thus it happened that after the second World War only the victors grew bitter: the existentialists in France, the angry young men in England, and the beatniks in the United States. But the losers were quite happy. The Germans and Italians, with their integrity guaranteed to them by the victors, were busy with an industrial renaissance and had nothing to worry about. For the victors, there was only a sense of despair growing out of new responsibilities, and the prospect of struggling with a fresh adversary in Soviet Russia who had emerged as the result of cleavages: freedom, threatened again.

In France and elsewhere, then, man was growing up to an awareness of the dependence on society which for the individual had always existed. The sin of separation was felt keenly and expressed by the rising generation in the name of the others. Those who think in social terms think of life; those who think in individual terms think only of death. Camus was horrified at the thought of death. He thought of "mankind as people sentenced to death." This was an outlook from which social life, destroyed in France in the second World War, could not be reconstituted. Under what auspices could society arise again and the individual safely identify his interests with it?

The artist is always a prophet. He is a prophet in general because he can foresee the possible, and he is one in particular because he can foresee the probable. And he does both by serving as an implosive center for the most sensitive forces of his own times in a way which issues in works of art of an axiologically predictive nature. Being more aware than ordinary men of these forces which are shaping the future, he is more able than they to predict what will come. The time had arrived to clear away tradition and to make a fresh start. In whose name was this to happen?

Mindful of his influences, Camus declared for the presupposition-less life; nothingness, Sartre would have called it, and Camus here, as usual in his thinking, owes much to Sartre. But the position of Camus was more affirmative than Sartre's. Presuppositionlessness, standpoint-lessness, is nearly nothing but not quite nothing; it is a tiny location, a point of view which can easily be moved. A subjectivism without a sub-ject is the least amount of something that anything can be, but it is yet something. Not being a philosopher, Camus set forth all of this by in-ference rather than explicitly. He certainly never used these terms. But the orientation is apparent in everything he said and did. For the starting point is the single human individual and the properties of the world he is able to observe from its universality. The particular properties of the human individual are those which face inward. But there are others which face outward, and it is the latter set whose universality has to be determined. It is to the glory of Camus that he was able to do so affirmatively, and the story of this preferment takes us to the examination of another subordinate step.

In order to establish the presuppositionless position from which he wished to take off, it was necessary to question not only certain things but everything. In *The Rebel,* Camus undertook to show by means of examples taken from many disciplines and many events that everything encountered in human life is absurd. All distinctions and differences re-cognized by man are human, but even man is not taken in by human distinctions and differences. He cries aloud for something more than is met only by what Camus elsewhere called "the unreasonable silence of the world," and in the confrontation of the human need with this silence the absurd is born. Whether a good man is rewarded or an evil one punished seems more a matter of chance than of design. The chosen people endure longer only to suffer greater hardships and ostracism, and the members of one religion do not live longer or fare any better than those of another. If God or nature has a preference, it is expressed only materially through the misfortune that occurs from a transgression of natural laws. But what of moral laws or of divinely ordained prin-

ciples? If only there were such laws and such principles!—for then, if
they were known, how simple it would be to obey them and so not to sin.
But there is no word except that which is given to science to discover,
and this, it is contended, is on a wholly different plane. And so there is the
silence which Camus found so "unreasonable."

The absurd is the contradictory in practice. Consider the admini-
stration of justice, for instance. This involves action. But as Camus explained about his efforts in the theatre, "I merely wanted to show that
action itself had limits. There is no good and just action but what recognizes those limits and, if it must go beyond them, at least accepts death.
Our world of today seems loathesome to us for the very reason that it is
made by men who grant themselves the right to go beyond those limits,
and first of all to kill others without dying themselves. Thus it is that
today justice serves as an alibi, throughout the world, for the assassins of
all justice."

The European is capable of murder like everyone else, and can even
plan mass exterminations. Genghis Khan is not alone with his pyramid
of skulls. But it is to the credit of the European that he, like the classic
Greek, is capable also of metaphysical rebellion and can even feel it as a
threat. So for instance with the humanist who comprehends the essentially inhuman nature of beauty, as Camus does in *The Myth of Sisyphus,*
and the corollary of beauty, that detached aspects of subjective truth do
not add up to the objective Truth. The only unity lies in nostalgia; otherwise, for individual man everything flies apart. As with life in the underground, not too different for Dostoyevsky under the Czarist police and
Camus in France under Nazi occupation, down is up and up is down.
Under such circumstances it is clear enough that everything is absurd.

For most this was a counsel of despair. But not for Camus, and
herein lay his genius. His rebellion, he said, was metaphysical, and he
defined metaphysical rebellion as one against not only the whole of the
human condition but the entire cosmos, "the whole of creation." And
what does such wholesale rejection mean? Ordinarily, something puerile
and amateur, or, at the very least, primitive. Whether life is worth living,
Samuel Butler wrote in his *Notebooks,* is a question for an embryo, not
for a man. But metaphysical rebellion, as Camus called his rejection *in
toto* of being, is saved because it is not final and in the end produces an
affirmation through its very promulgation. For there is yet to be accounted
for the fact of the rebellion itself.

It requires a pretty immense effort to conspire in a rejection so large,
and Camus was committed to the effort, which exists even if nothing else
does, and can only be exercised by being accepted. I accept the total
rejection, he said, and thus he made an affirmation even though it was

made inadvertently. The tremendous positive affirmation contained in that idea of rejecting the whole world when combined with the actual rejection itself amounts to a monstrous absurdity, the final absurdity which is destined to take care of all absurdities. And it gives Camus the ground upon which to stand in order to make a fresh start. For he was very much alive and he would not surrender to death—he would not, for instance, commit the suicide that the immensity of his rejection seemed to require.

For Camus, absurdity, contradictions, produced the most intense feelings. Life is absurd, he cried—and I am that alive! The absurd, then, was not the end of everything but a call for greater logicality, the recognition of the existence of a wider logic. Camus' own logic is peculiar, a logic of the absurd. The usual conception of absurdity arises from the juxtaposing of ideas which have no reason for belonging together. But the absurd as understood by Camus was quite different. He recognized the universal property of the absurd. But at the same time he did not reject logic; he did not alter it but only wished to change its conclusions. He drew a perfect syllogism and arrived at a conclusion which was the contradictory of the valid one. All men are mortal, and Socrates is a man, yet for Camus Socrates is immortal. Such a procedure would not be absurd to anyone who was not equally logical. Indeed, one must be immensely logical to see absurdity in these terms.

Thus the absurdity which led the existentialists to reject life is the same one that led Camus to reject suicide. He was an existentialist who accepted life without any support, transcendental or otherwise. As a result, he discovered not perpetual life but perpetual youth. He refused to accept the evil nature of things as they are and became a personal idealist, but one who made the effort to bring together the abstract and the concrete, to live his philosophy and to extract philosophy from life (rather than life from philosophy, which is impossible), to endow his fiction with depth and thereby render it more intense and effective, or at least to show others how this could be done. Life is meaningless but precious, all existence is absurd but worthwhile.

And so he arrived quite simply, without intellectual agony, at the presuppositionlessness which he had sought. Presuppositionlessness involves absolute universality. There can be no compromise, no stopping short. Identification with one's own society is for the individual hardly enough. There remains left out in this way the rest of humanity. Thus social identification must be total. And even this is not enough. The drama of mankind is played out against a background of the cosmos, as the ancient Greeks knew so well. The human individual and his society are parts of nature; they fit without remainder into the natural world.

Camus saw in this "delicate equilibrium between humanity and nature, man's consent to the world." Personal integrity can in this way be pursued under circumstances of social disintegration. And personal guilt can in the same way be exonerated: only so much liberty as is compatible with the liberty of others.

What then did Camus accomplish? The understanding of human nature has been prevented by the prejudices of man in favor of his own virtues. We can learn more of what is positive by concentrating on the perspectives presented to us by those thinkers who have looked from the negative side, philosophers like Schopenhauer, rather than the eternal optimists who confuse what-is with what-ought-to-be, and so much suppose that what-ought-to-be is that they prevent what-is from becoming what-ought-to-be. The firm philosophical foundations upon which a society can rest securely cannot be imposed only from above. They must emerge from the difficulties of experience with inadequate ideas, with insecurity, and as a result of a struggle from below.

Camus would have individual man be the first to know the truth about himself, for such truth is value-free; it is no more ugly than it is beautiful, and it leads to beauty in the end. The truth for individual man is a hard truth. It is that he must serve society without necessarily demanding as a precondition society's support. The human dilemma is one that demands the subordination of the individual to the aims of society, but at some distance from society. Only the strongest and most resolved can accept such terms without flinching. For just think what this means in practice to the individual who would be true to himself while serving society. He may be in it and yet not of it, and even under these conditions he must be for it. Camus was sure that a reunion of any sort between the two could only be temporary, and that happiness is like an accident which has lasted: both will end abruptly, and the one fundamental condition for the human individual is that this diremption which was inevitable must not change anything. For it is the totality of being which is integral and permanent, and not the association of any of its parts.

So much for the nature of things; but what about action? Camus tried to discover what to do by examining the situation that prevailed in his own times. The nature of the European crisis was clear enough. It consisted in the impossibility of finding a rational justification for moral values. These values were neither religious nor political. What could they be, then? Economic, as the Marxists declared? Technological, as the Americans assumed in their practice? As for the rational justification, it has not been the kind most people have demanded, even though some sort of justification is always necessary. There is in the European, as there has been in few others, a necessity to base life on intellectual foundations. As noted earlier, however, rationality does not necessarily imply absolutes. The thinking of the genuine rationalist always contains an element of uncertainty. Since it is the case that belief calls for action, absolute belief demands death. Yet we never know the truth of anything with sufficient certainty to kill anyone about it or to die for it.

The European need in its latest crisis was to discover for all mankind how intellectual justification of sufficient strength could rest upon a rational system made up of probabilities alone. Although Camus was not a philosopher in the technical sense, he was a dramatist and an artist and a man of considerable character, and so he sought to symbolize the need by avoiding the peril of despair in the midst of a national disaster which offered little else, employing philosophy only to lend depth and intensity to literature. In the end he succeeded in discovering that there are passionate grounds for defending democracy, that there could be an intensity to the democratic life. He did this before disappearing under a welter of omissions and less defensible errors. He overlooked science altogether, a neglect which he shared with Sartre, although in the end the mystery of being is inherent and apparent in the laws disclosed through the study of every material thing. He thought that a man of good will ought to be able to expect better from his contemporaries; as though there had ever been such a thing as times of good will. The trouble is that societies have never lived up to the good intentions of their declarations, while men of good will lack the power to execute their intentions. The society calls men of good will to account, but there is never anyone to call the society.

THE THEORY OF *HAMLET*

I

The beauty of the world and the excitement of life for the adventurous empiricist in the field of theory is heightened by the fact that nothing has been done finally: even the stalest of problems offers a fresh and a glorious opportunity. Where little has been attempted, much remains to be done; where much has been attempted and something accomplished,

much remains to be done better. But it would be difficult, outside the
field of science, to find any problem which has been settled perfectly and
irrevocably, once and for all; and even within science those who are able
to count upon a kind of ultimate inquisitiveness refuse to accept absolutely any solution to a given problem, even though the degree of the
probability of their acceptance begins closely to approach absolute
acceptance as a limit. In the case of literary interpretation in general and
of Shakespearean interpretation in particular, the amount of controversy
has been gigantic; and in the case of Shakespeare in general and of
Hamlet in particular, it is perhaps still larger. In *Hamlet* the nature of
the subject-matter, the corruption of the text, and the implicit philosophy of the scholars and commentators—for the most part that
philosophy which has ruled out all philosophical interpretation as illicit
—has meant that the problems confronting interpretation have, as it
were, conveyed their own peculiar kind of bafflement, a bafflement which
differs in kind from those presented by other literary difficulties of works
by the same author or in the same period.

There is, for instance, the problem of discovering and defining
Shakespeare's philosophy, and there are the subordinate problems of
discovering and defining the philosophy set forth in each of the various
plays. The many-sidedness of Shakespeare's outlook has been hitherto
regarded as its chief feature. The repeated attempts to read Shakespeare
as the advocate of this or that philosophy have gone down to ignominious
defeat before the quotation of this or that contradictory passage. So
Shakespeare has been described as a man who held no philosophy—or
as one who held all philosophies. But, of course, neither of these alternatives makes the slightest sense. The unity of the plays within themselves and as a solid body of work is inconsistent with the view that
Shakespeare had no philosophy. To have no consistent outlook would
mean to have discovered chaos in literature, and this assuredly no one
accuses Shakespeare of doing. On the other hand, to assume that Shakespeare held all philosophies means the same thing; for a chaos of nothing
is the same as one of all things, unless we assume that all the philosophies
are arranged in a system such that one prevails over the others.

Why is it, we may ask at this point, that work which embraces a
number of conflicting meanings appears to convey a greater sense of the
fullness and abundance of life than does work which presents only one
meaning?

"Do I contradict myself?" asks Walt Whitman, "Very well, then,
I contradict myself. I am large, I contain everything." The author whose
work embraces conflicting viewpoints is a source of great self-justification
to the narrow partisan, who is able to find his own viewpoint reflected

by a master and to ignore the others. The author, declares our partisan, saw the light of the truth upon one occasion, at least, and we may all rejoice in that. The rest is interpreted as the same truth in exotic dress, or else is dismissed on chronological grounds as early improvisations or senile concoctions—but dismissed, in any case. Thus we have the spectacle, not without its uses, of warring criticisms occasioned by literary interpretation, and the spectacle of single-minded assertions and denials in the enterprising game of cross-purposes.

Those who find, however, that Shakespeare's work embraces a number of contradictory meanings are apt to be the same scholars who emphasize the contradictoriness of the meanings in favor of the truth of one or another of them, while neglecting to observe the importance of the notion that the conflicting meanings are also *embraced*. The conflicting meanings are caught up in the embrace—of what? Presumably, in the embrace of some more inclusive meaning. But just what is that inclusive meaning? The answer must wait for a thoroughgoing study of the philosophy of Shakespeare. Those who have proffered answers to this question have agreed upon the term, humanism, without understanding that this does not decide the question so long as humanism itself is open to many interpretations. Our special problem in this study is the philosophical theory of *Hamlet,* and we shall see the term humanism, occurring here also. But the larger question must for the moment be exhibited in a lesser, albeit a still complex, one: what is the meaning not of Shakespeare as a whole but of that part of Shakespeare which is exhibited in the play, *Hamlet?*

Here the interpreter meets at its fullest a further difficulty which confronts all interpreters of Shakespeare. Analysis is a task which for most ordinary purposes is easily distinguished from the altogether different task of appreciation. The temperamental differences between critics and appreciators makes the distinction between these undertakings a light accomplishment. Yet Shakespeare at his best—and he is certainly at his best in *Hamlet* even if not only in *Hamlet*—has a fascination which adds to rather than detracts from the difficulties of the mechanism of analysis. While we are reading a particular passage in *Hamlet,* or in any other of the great plays, we find ourselves persuaded, so charming is the language. How can we quarrel with one who writes so well, with such a curious combination of the utmost both in economy and profusion? Those who are conquered by the effect of the whole have little inclination toward the dissection of the parts. Yet that is just what the understanding of the play requires. And to return to the play as an appreciator after the appreciation has for the time being been surmounted in order to make an adequate analysis possible, is to experience an effect which is almost overpowering. To understand Shakespeare, and to feel him, too, is almost to prompt the cry of "enough—too much."

It is well, then, to remember that the embracing of meanings which conflict seems to the limited critic to be accomplished only at a price, which price seems to him to be the unity of the whole. Most advocates of partisan and narrow positions are advocates of half-truths, who assume that their half-truths are the whole of truth. Thus they are not wrong, except in the claims they make for the field of applications of their partial truths. We can find no solution by easy sublation, either; for to submerge the half-truths altogether in the higher unity of the meaning of the whole is to lose them at the lower level where as half-truths they are indeed true. What Shakespeare could do, and what gives him his peculiarly universal appeal, was to sublate half-truths by a greater truth while maintaining them at the lower level as half-truths. In order to illustrate the misinterpretation by critics of these half-truths, let us sample some of the most typical of Shakespearean interpretations, before proceeding to an exposition of the theory which prompted the composition of this approach.

II

A great bulk of Shakespearean criticism falls into the nineteenth century, when psychological interpretations prevailed. To the critic of Shakespeare born into the nineteenth century, with but few exceptions the tragedy of *Hamlet* was a tragedy of the things of the mind, and all the events of the play were held to be subservient to the development, or disintegration, of Hamlet's mind and, as a consequence, also of his character. The struggle takes place between one resolution and another, between intellect and will or between will and action; whatever conflict be chosen for the analysis of the Prince's character, it is always cast in psychological terms; and this psychological conflict in Hamlet himself is always understood to be the chief motive of the play. The most important critics of the nineteenth century were English and German. Apart from the languages in which they wrote, there are no fundamental differences between them, and, on the contrary, they had in common the subjective or psychological interpretation of the meaning of the play.

Among the English critics, we may single out as typical of the best the remarks made by Coleridge and Hazlitt. For Coleridge, "the character of Hamlet may be traced to Shakespeare's deep and accurate science (*sic*) in mental philosophy . . . In Hamlet he seems to have wished to exemplify the moral necessity of a due balance between our attention to the objects of our senses and our meditation on the workings of our minds—an equilibrium between the real and the imaginary worlds. In *Hamlet* this balance is disturbed; his thoughts and the images of his fancy are far more vivid than his actual perceptions, and his very perceptions, instantly passing through the *medium* of his contemplations, acquire, as they pass, a form and a color not naturally their own. Here we see a great, an almost enormous, intellectual activity, and a proportionate aversion to real action consequent upon it, with all its symptoms and accompanying qualities." Hamlet's mind, "unseated from its healthy relation, is constantly occupied with the world within, and abstracted from the world without," a character giving utterance to soliloquies which "spring from that craving after the indefinite."[1] In short, as Coleridge explains in a later book, Shakespeare in *Hamlet* "intended to portray a person in whose view the external world and all its incidents and objects were comparatively dim and of no interest in themselves, and which began to interest only when they were reflected in the mirror of his mind."[2]

There is no need to expatiate upon the subjective, psychological and mentalistic preoccupation which is so evident in Coleridge's analysis. There are many philosophical assumptions here which presumably Coleridge, like most of his generation, took so fully for granted that he was not aware of them. One instance will suffice to show this. The "real" and "imaginary" worlds of Coleridge, as he explains in context, are the mental and the physical, the world of concepts and images, on the one hand, and the world of actual things, on the other. But these are epistemological terms, so that the contrast, in its importance, amounts to a reduction of the ontological to the epistemological. There are three worlds, not two, to all except the crudest of nominalistic empiricists. There is the world of the subject, which is mental, and there is the world of the object, which is physical; but these are both epistemological worlds. There is also the ontological world which is independent of both subject and object, the world of universals and values. The critics of nineteenth-century Europe shared with its philosophers an implicit belief in the sole reality of the two epistemological worlds, a belief which went so deep that it was never even called into question. Then, again, the play, *Hamlet,* we must remember, is a "tragicall historie," and history can occur, even in the case of a single character, only somehow objectively out in the world. Since there is an interaction between Hamlet and his world in that each has an effect

[1] Coleridge, S. T., *Notes and Lectures upon Shakespeare* (New York 1868), IV, p. 144.

[2] Coleridge, S. T., *Seven Lectures on Shakespeare und Milton* (London 1856). p. 141.

upon the other, the history cannot be entirely a matter of what went on in
Hamlet's mind. We cannot, in other words, justify the reduction of the
scope of the play from the historical order, as exemplified in the events
which took place at the court of the King of Denmark, to the psychological order, as exemplified in the events which took place in the mind
of one person, albeit a central one, at the court of the King of Denmark.

It would be useless indeed to seek relief from this intense psychol-
ogizing by taking refuge in the interpretation of Hazlitt. For Hazlitt
merely shifts the meaning of the play from Hamlet's mind to our own.
The speeches and sayings of Hamlet are "as real as our own thoughts.
Their reality is in the reader's mind. It is *we* who are Hamlet."[3] Whoever
has suffered the melancholy mood, the withdrawal, in brief, the problems,
of Hamlet, is himself Hamlet. Of course, this is only another way of
saying that the greatness of the play rests upon the sympathetic reactions
which it arouses in the spectators, and that the universality of the problem of *Hamlet* accounts for its appeal. If it says anything more, it is that
the meaning of the play is exhausted by the appreciators' understanding
of the mental problem of the central character. Such an interpretation
obviously confuses the appreciation of *Hamlet* with the meaning of
Hamlet. Otherwise, we are left with the spectacle of a play whose meaning
is exhausted by the struggles between various ideas and impulses which
take place in the protagonist's mind, and which are accorded no reference
and in fact no meaning outside that mind.

There is undoubtedly a great similarity between the English and the
German commentators of that period. Apart from occasional insights,
which to some extent always seem to contradict the central theses advanced, the main theme of *Hamlet* is Hamlet, for the Germans as well as
for the English; and, further, in the man, Hamlet, the psychological
states are solely and exclusively important. It would be foolish to argue
that Hamlet's mind can be left out of the play, for this is far from the
truth; but it is quite another thing to argue that everything can be left out
of the play except Hamlet's mind. Hamlet's mind is occupied with real
problems, that is to say, with problems having an objective reference.
What is the problem which occupies Hamlet's mind, and what is its
objective frame of reference? Before we can attempt answers to these
questions, it will be well to glance at some of the German interpretations,
since in the nineteenth century the Germans devoted so much thought
and energy to Shakespeare.

A very great deal of thought and energy was expended, that is true;
yet it is doubtful whether it added up to much. German thought in the

[3] Hazlitt, W., *Characters of Shakespeare's Plays* (London 1817), p. 104.

nineteenth century was too deeply under the influence of the nominalistic Kantian philosophy to produce anything in the way of literary criticism that could avoid the spell of subjectivism which Kant had cast over all his fellows. Goethe has chided his countrymen for failing to understand that the external relations of the play, that is, those things which do not depend upon the central character but upon accidents, are as important as the internal relations, that is, those things which depend solely upon the central character.[4] By distinguishing between internal and external relations, and further by insisting upon the external relations, Goethe went a long way toward counteracting the intense subjectivism of the German criticism, but to no avail. Goethe himself saw the whole play as the depicting of "a great deed laid upon a soul unequal to the performance of it,"[5] and those who came after him tended to revert to the subjectivistic view.

For Herder, *Hamlet* was a tragedy "which is to lead us into the very soul of Hamlet."[6] For Schlegel, *Hamlet* was "a tragedy of thought inspired by continual and never-satisfied meditation on human destiny."[7] For Gans, it was "the tragedy of the Nothingness of Reflection, or . . . it is the tragedy of the Intellect."[8] The names as well as the comments could be repeated many times over, but the intense subjective interpretation remains the same. The German critics seem unable to get away from the mentality of Hamlet, the central character of the play, a psychological part of the play which they tend to confuse with the whole. Despite the corrective influence of occasional insights into the detached and objective meaning of *Hamlet* (insights which would seem to indicate that with the proper metaphysical orientation much might have come from the same writers of inestimably greater value than what actually did come), the burden of the Germans was that the meaning of the play is entirely directed toward and wholly exhausted by events in the mind of its central character. This would not have been an explanation or an accounting which could have satisfied the contemporaries of Shakespeare, any more than it could have satisfied, say, the classic Greeks; and it no longer satisfies us. We are willing to accord Hamlet's mental problems their due importance in the scheme of the whole, but that importance is not equal to the whole scheme, as older critics have supposed.

The German psychological interpretation of *Hamlet* was revived for

---

[4] Goethe, J. W., *Wilhelm Meister*, trans. Carlyle (Boston 1851), I, p. 353.

[5] Goethe, *op. cit.*, p. 294.

[6] Herder, J. G., *Literatur und Kunst*, p. 12.

[7] Schlegel, A. W., *Lectures on Art and Dramatic Literature*, trans. Black (London 1815), II, p. 192.

[8] Gans, E., *Vermischte Schriften* (Berlin 1834), II, p. 270.

a last flicker of life in the second decade of the twentieth century, though this time in a new guise under the auspices of the Freudian psychoanalysts. According to this interpretation, Hamlet is a man who has repressed the cause of his own hesitancy. He maintains a strong sexual attitude toward his mother, in terms of which much can be explained. The hesitancy, as well as the sex feeling, is due to the attitude toward his father as a rival for the affections of his mother. Ophelia is the sufferer from his reaction against all women, which occurs as a result of his filial experiences. In all probability, Shakespeare himself attempted to get rid of the same difficulty, one which he would have had if he had not written the play.[9] It is, of course, despite the difference in emphasis, which removes essential reality from the mind where it had been supposed to dwell by the thoughtful Germans and English of the nineteenth century, and places it in the gonads, on the assumption that the only genuine psychology is abnormal psychology, and that therefore abnormal psychology is completely explanatory of psychology in the normal range—it is, we may say, an incorrigibly psychological theory, since it, too, assumes that the problem of the play, *Hamlet,* is something entirely indwelling in the body and mind of the character, Hamlet. We are still concerned with a play which is supposed to center about the psychological motives of its chief character, though these motives are no longer conscious but subconscious, and motives prompted no longer by the spirit but now by the flesh. We have gained by this change a novel turn of criticism, but in thus attempting to get at the meaning of the play we have failed utterly to divest ourselves of the subject.

The psychological theory which we shall have to consider next is that of the late English critic A. C. Bradley. According to Bradley, the key to *Hamlet,* the play, lies in the psychological character of its leading figure. The character of Hamlet will explain whatever meaning the play possesses. Hamlet, says Bradley, is an intellectual, and as such he is naturally grieved at his father's death, horrified by his mother's overhasty and incestuous marriage, and also naturally unbalanced by the appearance of the ghost. The events which do happen in the play are those which would happen, given the effect upon the character of a sensitive intellectual prince of the more or less devastating events which already have happened.[10] Bradley assumes, of course, that the problem of Hamlet is the problem of his character, and that his character explains

9 Jones, E., "The Oedipus-Complex as an Explanation of Hamlet's Mystery: A Study in Motive," *American Journal of Psychology,* XXI (1910), pp. 72–113. Also Sharpe, E., "The Impatience of Hamlet," *International Journal of Psycho-Analysis,* X, (London 1929), pp. 270–79.

10 Bradley, A. C., *Shakespearean Tragedy* (London 1904), pp. 89–174.

the play. Naturally, it can be admitted that the play has a character meaning all its own, and furthermore that the character meaning is just what Bradley says that it is, without thereby precluding the possibility that the play as a whole, including such a character and such events, may have a further meaning which has nothing specifically to do either with this character or with those events, but may be much broader than either or than both taken together. The shortcoming of Bradley's interpretation is that it does not interpret very much. It does not venture and hence it does not gain. We may admit what Bradley has to say—all, that is, but its limitations—and still wish to prepare ourselves for a search into the meaning of the play as a whole. Subjective or psychological explanations are apt to be narrow, and the one at present under consideration is no exception to this generalization.

It has occurred to some timid souls that it would be a daring thing to dislike *Hamlet* and boldly to say so. *Hamlet* is admittedly strong medicine. To be repelled by the play is not an unusual experience; but to state the dislike and to assume that such a statement constitutes a profound criticism, is to have the courage merely of cowardice. The best known of the criticisms of this kind are concerned with psychological questions bordering on that of character. Eliot, for instance, asserts that the play is unsatisfactory because the emotions of Hamlet are in excess of the dramatic situations which are presumed to have evoked them.[11] Eliot has a pontifical habit of preparing us for a tremendous conceptual mountain, only to bring forth a casual, observational mouse.[12] His criticism is not a basic one, even if it were true; and, in addition, he is far from having proved it. Hamlet's emotional sprees admittedly are tremendous, but so are the events which call them forth. As Shakespeare himself points out, the events which occur at court have gigantic repercussions.[13] Prince Hamlet's emotions are supercharged, but the events which happen to kings and queens, princes and prime ministers, are always great events. Tragedies which influence the lives of so many people are not trivial tragedies, and there is no reason why their effect should be thought of as limited to the production of trivial emotions. Hamlet's reactions are only natural in view of what is involved.

Much the same comment could be made upon Stoll's suggestion that the characters in Shakespeare's plays mark a refinement over the

[11] Eliot, T. S., "Hamlet and His Problems," *The Sacred Wood* (New York 1921), pp. 87–94.
[12] An observation made by Professor Leonard F. Dean, in conversation.
[13] *Hamlet*, III, iii, pp. 22–23. See also *loc. cit.*, pp. 11–22.

> Never alone
> Did the king sigh, but with a general groan.

hand-me-down plots. Character is always that which would work itself out in practice, were it not for the fortuitous elements in events. In this connection may be mentioned again the caution of Goethe, who said that in the interpretation of *Hamlet* the external relations of the play must not be sacrificed to the internal relations of its protagonist. Werner even goes so far as to suggest that the hero of the drama should be studied from the viewpoint of the tragedy as a whole, and not the reverse.[14] Many of the psychological and subjective theories of the interpretation of *Hamlet* are ingenious and all are interesting, but in the end they lead to a bankruptcy which suggests that the answer does not lie here and that we should somehow look beyond the subject.

III

There are such things as non-subjective theories of the meaning of *Hamlet*; and we shall, in fact, examine some of them.

The first is, surprisingly enough, to be found as an exception among those same nineteenth-century Germans against whom we have so vigorously inveighed for their intense subjectivism. The exception is Karl Werder. Werder launched a keen attack upon those subjectivistic critics who had blamed Hamlet's inward deficiences for creating an obstacle to his own actions in the play, and who had further assumed that the stumbling-block of such deficiences, together with the confusion consequent upon it, constitutes the theme of the play. Werder insisted that the objective nature of Hamlet's problem itself precluded the performance of his revenge on Claudius for the murder of King Hamlet. What was required of Hamlet "simply was not *possible,* and this for reasons entirely *objective.* The situation of things, the force of circumstances, the nature of his task, directly forbid it, and so imperatively, that he was compelled to respect the prohibition, if he were to keep his reason; above all, his poetic and dramatic, aye, and his human, reason. The critics have been so absorbed in the study of his character, that the *task* imposed upon him has been lost sight of. Here is the fundamental mistake."[15]

Werder goes on to argue that against the social and political background of Hamlet's day, or perhaps even of Shakespeare's, the murder of Claudius by Hamlet, followed by Hamlet's seizing of the throne, would have been condoned neither by the courtiers nor by the masses of the people, unless indeed there had been some way in which Hamlet could

[14] Werner, H. A., *Über das Dunkel in der Hamlet-Tragödie.* Jahrbuch der deutschen Shakespeare-Gesellschalt, (1870), V. p. 40.

[15] Werder, K., *Vorlesungen über Shakespeare's Hamlet* (Berlin 1875), p. 32.

have proved that his motive had been revenge, and his actions called for by the previous murder of his father by Claudius, a proof which would not be sufficiently supported by Hamlet's contention that he had learned of the earlier deed from the ghost of his own father. Therefore the action of the play, including Hamlet's own hesitation, is a purely objective result of circumstances and conditions prevailing in the social world at the time that the mandate was forced upon him.

Can we rest content with this theory? No, we cannot; not, that is, unless it turns out to be sufficiently comprehensive. And it fails on this score, since it does not adequately explain Hamlet's psychology. The solution to the shortcomings of theories which are excessively subjective assuredly cannot consist in a theory which overlooks the subjective realm altogether. Hamlet's thoughts as revealed by his speeches and actions, and particularly by his soliloquies, cannot be successfully overlooked, as they are in Werder's theory. There is also another and a more serious sin of omission; but since the omission appears obvious in the context of a later objective theory, we may proceed to examine this later theory, and to allow the criticism of it to reveal the second shortcoming which both objective theories have.

The later objective theory is that which is offered for our consideration by the contemporary Marxists. The Russian critic, Smirnov, sets forth a Marxist interpretation, based on the assumption of the economic determinism of history. Hamlet, according to this interpretation, is a character not of an earlier Denmark, but of Shakespeare's own day in Elizabethan England. He is a character enveloping within the fictive frame of his problems the socio-economic dilemma with which Shakespeare correctly felt his own person to be confronted. Shakespeare lived at a time when the corruptions of a declining feudalism were beginning to manifest themselves. He was disgusted with them, naturally enough. But, as a true humanist, he was equally disgusted with the socio-economic force which he saw was rapidly rising to the fore; and he viewed with dismay the increase in naked self-interest revealed by the efforts at primary accumulation of the rising bourgeoisie. Hamlet had no faith in the masses because of their political immaturity. He was repelled by the practical philistinism of the bourgeoisie. Shakespeare could find no solution to this choice of evils; he expressed himself in the character of Hamlet, who took refuge from the impossible choice in madness. Hamlet is a man of action delayed by the necessity of choosing between equally distasteful alternatives; a humanist who is able to discover in his own situation no humanistic alternative.[16]

[16] Smirnov, A. A., *Shakespeare: A Marxist Interpretation* (New York 1936), pp. 61 ff.

The Marxist interpretation makes up for one of the deficiencies of the Werder interpretation, for the former does attempt to embrace and explain the subjective field of Hamlet's mind in terms of the socio-economic events which cause it to be what it is. The Marxist theory of *Hamlet,* however, falls into the group of familiar fallacies which we have come inevitably to expect from the Marxist interpretation of anything; Smirnov confuses occasion with cause, and he reads the accidents of history deterministically. On the first score, there is little doubt that Marxist theory has done scholarship a great turn by pointing out that while the economic level of social events is not the highest yet it is the most reliable, in the sense that it is the level on which all other social events rest. The economic level, in other words, furnishes the occasion to other levels, but not the cause, since the distinction between occasion and cause is a perfectly valid one. An event may have one or more occasions, but it can have only one cause; occasion is historical, while cause is logical. The socio-economic events which have occasioned Hamlet's lapse into madness may be, as Smirnov says, the occasions of that madness; but the assumption of Smirnov's theory, to be good ortho-dox Marxism, has to make the further claim that the socio-economic events are also the cause of the madness; and this is something else again. Cause is always at a certain level; things can only be caused by something existing at their own level, they may be occasioned by things existing at practically any other level. Socio-economic events assuredly do not exist at the psychological level, nor does the psychological level have anything more in common with the socio-economic than occasions.

On the second score, we find another fallacy which is not extremely different from the first, and indeed flows naturally from it. This fallacy has to do with that part of Marxist theory which is described as historical determinism; it is in brief, the theory which asserts that the way things have happened is the way they have to happen. This theory is blasted altogether by the sheer novelty of events: for it is true that events resemble each other in many ways, yet no two events are exactly alike. History is a mixture of chance and cause; yet we are no more justified in confusing chance and cause than we are in confusing occasion and cause. Chance is not the same as cause and never will be; indeed, respectable theories of history try to separate out the pattern of history from actual history, i.e., its underlying cause which is independent of chance. Smirnov's Hamlet, then, is a prince who emerges from the maze of history only to discover that social events have offered him two stimuli in the shape of economic alternatives which he finds equally distasteful. It could never have happened otherwise. Faced with two disagreeable opposites of feudalism and primary accumulation, Hamlet becomes a neurotic or psychotic; he retires to the insanity which inhibits purposive action. But in stating this simple answer to a difficult problem, Smirnov, like the earlier objectivist in *Hamlet* interpretation, Werder, has exchanged one knowledge end-term for another. He has rejected the subjective interpretation of *Hamlet* for an objective interpretation. But in so doing he has not got rid of the principal dilemma; for both objectivists and subjectivists view the problem of *Hamlet* as though the answer must necessarily be found in the relation between the mind of Hamlet and the world about him. Is it his mind which works on the events at least so far as he is concerned (subjective version); or is it the social events at court which work on his mind (objective version)?

Before we can answer this question, it may be wise to examine some of the other objective theories of interpretation which have been employed in the attempt to discover the true meaning of *Hamlet*. Two of these may be described, roughly, as the dramatic interpretation and the symbolic interpretation.

The dramatic interpretation of *Hamlet* rests on the assumption that the play can be totally explained as a dramatic problem; that, in other words, the meaning of *Hamlet* is to be found in the stage of presentation, and found only there. Robertson, for instance, holds that the proper explanation of *Hamlet* is to be made in terms of Shakespeare's attempt to use, and improve on, older material. All of the difficulties and special features of the play are caused by the effort of Shakespeare to create out of the somewhat intractable material of the sources in Kyd and Belleforest an aesthetic masterpiece.[17] Stoll similarly wishes to explain Hamlet's delay in carrying out his revenge solely as a stage and dramatic device.[18] And, again, Wilson in much the same vein considers that the meaning of the play is that one which it held for Shakespeare's contemporaries, more particularly for his audiences. The delay is a necessary technical device, nothing more, for the making of a play. Hamlet is a *stage* character, that explains everything; and we only come to grief in trying to pretend that there is more meaning in Hamlet than we should expect to find in a stage character.[19]

The difficulties of such a view appear to be obvious. These critics also are taking the occasion of the play for its cause. Of course, Hamlet *is* a stage character; obviously, he is not a real person, if by real person we mean one of flesh and blood. But does that limit his meaning rather than increase it? Many real flesh-and-blood persons have no particularly signi-

[17] Robertson, J. M., *The Problem of "Hamlet"* (London 1919).
[18] Stoll, E. E., *Hamlet: An historical and comparative study* (Research Publications of the University of Minnesota, VIII, no. 5 [Minneapolis 1919].)
[19] Wilson, J. D., *What Happens in Hamlet* (New York 1935).

ficant meaning, while many fictional characters have nothing else. To assume that the problem of artistic invention which presented itself to Shakespeare when he was busy adapting Kyd and Belleforest to his own purposes, or that the practical problem of putting the play on the stage successfully, constitutes and indeed exhausts whatever meaning the play may have, is to confuse the occasion with the cause. Shakespeare is dead, but *Hamlet* is not; and whatever Shakespeare may have meant by the play is probably an answer we shall never know with any certainty, while what *Hamlet* means *Hamlet* itself is still here to tell us. A work of art has a life of its own. Such a meaning may or may not correspond to that which the artist intended to give it. There are artists who have builded better than they knew, and others who have builded worse than they intended. Shakespeare's control over language would lead us to believe that he wrote exactly what he meant. But in any case—and this is the important point—we have no way of finding out what he meant except from the play itself, and there it may or may not correspond with what the play means. But, since we lack the means of distinguishing, we may still endeavor to discover what the play means and let it go at that. In other words, we should not confuse what Shakespeare meant with what *Hamlet* means. Similarly, the problem of the play as a stage production in the early seventeenth century throws no final light on the meaning of the play now. The play itself has not changed, and we may presume that therefore its meaning has not changed, either. Both these dramatic arguments are essentially historical arguments and as such unsound.

The last type of artistic theory which we shall consider is the symbolic interpretation. Unfortunately, these have been few in number. We may, however, consider one of the better known. Knight states that Hamlet is a symbol—*the* symbol, in fact, the symbol of Death. Hamlet is an impersonation of Death. Truth is evil. The climax of the play occurs in the first act, when the ghost appears. The rest of the play, contrary to the usual procedure, is a reverberation of this original explosion, and ends only with what Knight calls an "act of creative assassination."[20] There is nothing essentially wrong with this particular symbolic approach. The symbolism chosen, that of death, is a difficult one to fit into the entire play. The arguments which have been advanced in the past by the subjectivists are pertinent here. Hamlet represents the life of the intellect, an abundance of mental energy so great that it interferes with and inhibits physical action. But this is not death, it is life, albeit a life that is mental. Shakespeare was too profound a playwright to employ a symbolism so crude. Death is after all a figure allegorical in the most

[20] Knight, G. W., *The Wheel of Fire* (London 1930), pp. 34–50.

obvious sense of the term, whereas Shakespeare's characters were nothing if not human. If they had other meanings, and there were few of them which did not, those other meanings can never be explained so simply: Shakespeare is not to be explained in terms that would be sufficient for John Bunyan.

IV

The objective school, albeit its variety is greater than anything which the subjectivists have to offer, is never altogether satisfactory in any one of its branches. The subjectivists are partial, and so are the objectivists. Each tends to assume that the other is its only recognized adversary in the field of theory. Neither school has recognized that the alternatives are not exhausted by this choice, unless we assume as they assume that the choice has to be made up from the relation between Hamlet's mind and the world. This is an epistemological relation, but there is no reason why we could not just as well appeal to the higher and more inclusive relationships of ontology. As soon as we make this resolve, we are led to grasp the immediate and important fact that the subject and the object do not exhaust the alternatives in ontology as they seem to do in epistemology. For ontology has the power of contributing a third realm (just as epistemology has the power of requiring it, if the epistemologists only knew).

This third realm is that of logical and axiological possibility, a realm of real being, a whole from which actuality selects its parts, a realm of ideals and perfections, of ultimate unity and wholeness. In this realm, there is no change, no conflict, and no partiality, albeit its status is only that of possibility and not of a superior kind of actuality. *Hamlet,* in short, lends itself perhaps also to a realistic interpretation, and by realism here is meant a belief in the independence of elements in the ontological realm of being. It is the kind of realism which, in its broadest features, has been described many times by philosophers from Plato to Peirce and Whitehead. It is that kind of realism which Hamlet describes at the level of actuality or existence when he implies the animism in which all organizations display some evidence of sensitivity, however minimal, by arguing that

> Sense, sure, you have,
> Else you could not have motion ;[21]

thus insisting that all things which have motion, that is, all things which

[21] *Hamlet,* III, iv, pp. 70–71.

are actual or existent, also have sense. It is, too, the same kind of realism which Hamlet describes at the level of a being which is independent of actuality, which governs actuality to some extent, and which at least dictates the future of actuality, when he declares that

> There's a divinity that shapes our ends,
> Rough-hew them how we will.[22]

In the former case, we have a reaction-activity very close to that described by Montaigne[23] and Bacon,[24] as quoted in the contemporary value theory of Laird[25] and Whitehead,[26] the "natural election" of all bodies all of which have some degree of "perception."

The realistic interpretation of *Hamlet*, using realism in the philosophical sense rather than in that current literary sense which means its direct opposite, does not depend upon the specific reading of particular passages in the play. It is notorious that Shakespeare, like the Bible, will support almost any kind of realism. We must, however, if we wish to claim any validity for the realism of *Hamlet*, find it in the play as a whole, in the very meaning of the play, rather than in the import of those few speeches in which it appears to be stated explicitly. For the philosophy of *Hamlet* is the philosophy which underlies the play as a whole, which is to be found in it implicitly, coloring everything that is stated rather than itself being explicitly stated. What, then, is that implicit philosophy?

The Hamlet of realism is a Hamlet who understands the nature of the two ontological orders; he understands them, that is to say, as real things, and he understands them implicitly, not explicitly as philosophical concepts in the conscious minds of philosophers who merely reflect in their thoughts what has being outside of such thoughts. No; for Hamlet is no philosopher; he is rather a thoughtful prince who insists upon basing his impulsive actions upon previous rationality, by thinking about the actions which shall be expected of him a little while before they are expected. He *believes* in the two ontological orders, and that very deeply.

Let us suppose that he comprehends or, still better, that he feels the relationship between the two orders in terms of what-is and what-ought-to-be. The realm of being is the realm of what-ought-to-be; the

---

[22] *Hamlet,* V, ii, pp. 10–11.

[23] *Essays,* trans. Florio, bk. II, ch. xiv.

[24] Francis Bacon, *Silva Silvarum,* quoted in Whitehead, A. N., *Science and the Modern World* (New York 1929), p. 60.

[25] Laird, J., *The Idea of Value* (Cambridge 1929).

[26] Whitehead, A. N., *Science and the Modern World* (New York 1929).

realm of actuality or existence is the realm of what-is. Now, assuredly, what-is is not altogether what-ought-to-be. Hamlet, as a human being, lives to some extent at both levels. Reflectively, he is able to contemplate things-as-they-ought-to-be, while at the same time he lives in an actual world of things-as-they-are. The discrepancy is too great when it happens that "the times are out of joint," and Hamlet does not feel that he should have been the one born to set them right. He is delayed in his action of revenge for the murder of his father by the necessity for, and the diffi- culty of, seeing how the ideal can be made actual. In the words of one critic, "He is the prince of philosophical speculators, and because he cannot have his revenge perfect, according to the most refined idea his wish can form, he misses it altogether."[27] Hazlitt's language follows the subjectivism of his day, when ideas in the mind were confused with the universals they reflected. Hazlitt meant, of course, or at least should have meant, that Hamlet is the prince of implicit philosophical speculators, and because he cannot have his actions perfect, according to the highest ideals his thoughts can discover, he refrains altogether.

Now, that is not the end of the story. The sequel contains the tragedy. For while Hamlet is endeavoring to discover the *modus operandi* for bringing the two worlds together—the world of the perfect and the ideal on the one hand, and the world of imperfection and conflict on the other —and for making the ideal actual, events force his hand. He is driven to impulsive action by what happens around him. Having been desirous of the murder only of Claudius, he becomes willy nilly the murderer of Polonius and Laertes as well as of Claudius, to say nothing of the deaths of Ophelia and Gertrude, for which he is responsible, even though un- intentionally so. Through his absolute and uncompromising attitude and his unwillingness to accent anything less than perfection, he becomes a victim of the logic of events, just as do the characters in the tragedies of Aeschylus. "Hamlet," Dr. Johnson assured us, "is, through the whole piece, rather an instrument than an agent. After he has, by the strata- gem of the play, convicted the King, he makes no attempt to punish him; and his death is at last effected by an incident which Hamlet had no part in producing."[28]

Thus he who demanded too much of events is rewarded by becom- ing their helpless victim. Instead of directing events, he follows them blindly; and instead of a will which imposes his plans to some extent upon others, he allows chance to direct his adventures altogether. He had been unwilling to meet actuality halfway; he had refused to act in accord- ance with the nature of things which dictates that actuality shall never

---

[27] Hazlitt, *op. cit., loc. cit.*
[28] Johnson, S., *The Plays of Shakespeare,* VIII, p. 311.

be perfect and that ideals mediated in their application are yet better than no ideals at all; and so actuality, conflict, irrationality took their revenge upon him in the way in which the limitations of everything actual demand: he became not a leader but one led, not a king but a corpse, together with the corpse of that same King whose place in life he had wished to take, but wished to take only upon conditions laid down by himself to life in general, and which life in general had been unwilling to accept.

The moral is that the man of contemplation, who endeavors to carry into actual practice the absolute and uncompromising variety of idealism, will end with the worst sort of impulsive, irrational and un-considered action: undecided, immediate and arbitrary action. The tragedy of Hamlet is the tragedy of the reversal of rôles of him, who, unlike Aristotle, does not admit that while one hundred is the goal, fifty is yet nearer to one hundred than is ten, and five times more desirable, even to those who long for the hundred, and who recognize the com-promise involved in accepting anything less. There is a vast difference between intuitions which are based upon prior reasonings and those which are not. The former variety is the better; reason must guide the intuition. But, having reasoned, we must be prepared to act from the reason-dictated intuitions without hesitation, almost after the fashion of the impulsive man of action whose intuitions have not had the benefit of any prior reasonings at all. To act from reason directly is to commit the fallacy of rational dogmatism, and to aid in earning reason itself a bad name.

In offering here one more interpretation of the meaning of *Hamlet,* the intention is to make a positive contribution to interpretation, but with the equipment of philosophy rather than with that of scholarship. Hence the reference to the authorities whose names have graced the scholarly tradition has only the purpose of revealing the type of criticism which the present view would afford. The heart of this essay lies pri-marily in its constructive effort at interpretation and not in its destruc-tive criticism. In brief, this interpretation depends upon the metaphysical assumption that Hamlet is the "actual thing" *par excellence.* He has the human power of self-awareness, which all other things lack. As a con-sequence of this lack, actual things other than human beings are helpless playthings of the logic and chance of events. Human beings are, excep-tionally, to some extent masters of their destiny. When, however, they hesitate or fail to take advantage of their power of self-awareness, or ratiocination, in order to exercise the limited control over their environ-ment which as thinking beings they enjoy, they become, at the social level, the same helpless playthings of the logic and chance of events as the non-human actual things always are. To possess the power to reason constitutes the first human prerogative; and to possess the ability to apply the results of that reasoning, by means of what may be called enlightened impulse, to relevant occasions for action constitutes the second human prerogative. To deny the second is to vitiate the intention of the first, and hence to precipitate chance in events shorn of their natural logic. Such at least is one possible interpretation, a philosophical one, of the meaning of the play.

THE MODERN NOVEL AND ITS AUDIENCE

Culturally speaking, we Americans do not lack presumption, but it seems to me that self-criticism is a scarcity product. I do not expect to be thanked for attempting to supply it. It is no secret that Soviet Russia does not have a constant critic. The phrase is Will Roger's and so is the following epitaph.

> Here lies the body of Nicholas Vimsky
> He tried to criticize the leaders of the present
> regime, but they outlasted himsky.

In this country, it is true, criticism is not punished by law, but it is also not popular. However, I proceed on the theory that complacency is stifling; progress does not take place because of the recognition of achievements but rather by means of the frank facing of defects. You can only take steps to correct what you think is wrong.

My remarks will concern in particular one of the most recent of literary art forms: the novel. The thesis is simple: I will plead that great art elevates but that bad art depresses. Just as a culture is benefited by its greatest artists, so it is cheapened and degraded by its worst; and unfortunately the worst is also the most popular and successful. I shall not argue didactically but inferentially, seeking to persuade rather than to convince.

The novel as an art form is sadly in need of overhauling and reconsideration. It is new. It is not as new as the screen play; but as an art form capable of independent treatment it stands alone, because the screen play is still only a practical matter. We will not have *literary* screen plays until it is the custom to write them without thought of immediate film production. This custom will not come, perhaps, until we have acquired the habit of developing art films apart from commercial films whose expected profits run into the millions. Culturally speaking, the use of prose as an art medium does not have a very long history. The practice of relating a story in prose for its own sake is a more recent affair than the practice, pretty universal, of doing so in poetry.

Last year, in this country thousands of separate titles were published, over half of which were novels. That is quite a few novels. Some of them sell by the millions, and many by the thousands. Ours is a period in which are produced and consumed an immense number of novels. What a curious age it is, too, to be sponsoring such a development! For the times in which we live may be known to the anthropologists of the future as Neon Culture—early Neon. I have not the least doubt in the world that the advertisements are right: when better Buicks are built, we will build them. Buicks and bathtubs. Of course I don't want to sound opposed to these things; on the contrary I like them. Some day I am going to have a Buick with a bathtub built in it.

Spengler's analogy between Greece and Rome on the one hand, and Europe and the United States on the other, is better than he knew. For we do emphasize the things that Rome emphasized and neglect the things she neglected. Our Europe, like their Greece, is left holding the bag so far as the arts and pure sciences and philosophy are concerned. If we have a philosopher, like Peirce, we pass over him; and if we have a scientist, like Gibbs, we do also. It is fitting that the greatest artists in America should find themselves in arts developed by industrial technology, particularly physical technology: Chaplin in the films and Frank Lloyd Wright in architecture. Love us, love our dimensions. How striking, then, that we should finally if grudgingly come to recognize Faulkner. Of course we did not at first. Faulkner's two best novels, *The Sound and the Fury* and *As I Lay Dying,* did not sell more than their pitiful first editions of a thousand copies. Those of us who do not like the situation in which America is hostile to the fine arts and the theoretical sciences are fighting quietly to bring to the country we love the proper kind of reception for them. A public man is one engaged on a public service, and this is true whether the public takes cognizance of the fact or not.

Let us, then, look at the novel business as it is today, chiefly from the perspective of the novel as an art form.

First in the order of examination is the audience for the novel. Here the motive of interest is primarily one of entertainment. The novel is expected to be a sort of portable diversion, to be read in the automat or the cafeteria, the bus or the waiting room, as our version of bread and circuses. The reader says to the novel, "I dare you to amuse me." Well, amusement, entertainment or diversion, like everything else, has its own principles. The novel of entertainment must *be light,* which is to say not too profound. It must *move swiftly,* which is to say have plenty of action details. Proust boasted that his characters never opened doors, but in the novel of entertainment doors must be opened, entered and shut. Finally, it must *be conventional,* which is to say, sufficiently similar to previous novels so that the members of its audience are not made to feel any strain of novelty.

I once asked a friend of mine who works in Hollywood how to write a screen play for money. He said, "Why that is the easiest thing to do. Go out and see a movie and then go home and write it. Change the names and the locale for copyright reasons, but don't change too much or it won't be accepted." The members of the movie audience want to be able to say to themselves, "There but for the grace of God go I, just as I almost went last week."

What kind of an audience does this article of consumption point to? We have only to attribute the properties which people generally seek in a novel to the people who seek them, pausing only to change the signs. In place of lightness, swiftness and conventionality, we have heaviness, immobility, unconventionality. We have the prospect of a bored population, living in the chains of custom that they themselves have had manufactured, probably on a belt-line, inert but eager for some kind of compensation or relief in the form of vicarious experience. What a deplorable spectacle: so many people ready to follow something, anything; so empty and yet knowing not even how to seek. The whole continent of novel readers cannot boast of the power that is contained in a single genuine artist. It is a pathetic aggregation of shadow people: clever, chic, hurrying to nowhere like sheep, lacking spiritual content, leaderless toward the values, each one with a copy of the Book-of-the-Month Club under his, or in most cases her, arm.

The publishers come next for our consideration, and the publishers are cynical about the audience: they would tell you that what I have told you is all there is to tell. But the publishers cannot be altogether correct about this; because if they were, they would publish nothing but best sellers, which is after all their aim. The time has passed when prestige was a thing to be considered even in the publishing business. In the days of my youth the publishers liked to have items which they said "toned up their lists," books they were sure in advance would not sell but which somehow made a respectable profession of the publishing business. The publishers would like to sound like artists when talking with business men, and they succeed in being business men when dealing with artists. So, despite their cynical attitude toward the public, there must be more to the picture than what I have thus far painted. Someone should weep for the publishers, I suppose, and I am planning to do that as soon as I have found my own peace.

What is the hopeful note in the audience that seeks primarily (the publishers would say exclusively) for entertainment? It is simply that the public does build better than it knows, its tastes are eventually an improvement over its pocket book. The novels that reach the top of the best seller lists are certainly the ones that pay the food and rent bills, the light, the heat and power, for both author and publisher, but the slow starters are usually the ones that travel the farthest. Needless to say, there are notable exceptions. Dickens was a popular author in his own day and he remains so in ours. But the rule is not based on such exceptions. In general, time does attempt to approximate to the true values, and it does so no less for not always succeeding. No doubt there has been fiction that was born to blush unseen, but it is the Faulkners of the present who hold the Keyes to the future. The books that are kept in print over the centuries are the ones with the most inclusive subject matter. We shall return to this theme. Meanwhile, let us claim that the novel audience today is better than the popular novelists and their publishers are willing to admit. They, like all people, are possessed by what Einstein has called "the holy curiosity of inquiry." Their desire to know and to feel in the greatest dimensions is submerged, and when it rises to the surface it is fumbling; but nevertheless it is there. Despite themselves they want something better than what they think they want, and in the end they get it—or at least not they but their children and their children's children. For the great geniuses of their day are not writing for them but as always addressing their work to the unborn perfect audience which is to appear some day in the indefinitely remote future.

We can see the faint outlines of what they want if we examine the classifications of the current novel.

The first category is the one I have already discussed; this is the novel of entertainment. We might perhaps call it the anaesthetic novel. It can be divided into various subclasses: the mystery story, the historical novel, the religious novel, and so on. The chief characteristic of this variety of literature is its conventionality. No new insights are provided, no new feelings—nothing to enrich life. Harmless, you say? Perhaps. Merely easy forms of escape from some of the intolerable pressures of the complicated existence of modern civilization. Georges Simenon, John P. Marquand, Raymond Chandler, and many others of lesser magnitude, provide the only anodynes which your local druggist can supply you without insisting upon receiving a prescription from your doctor. This drug is habit forming, too, because it develops a kind of mechanical dullness and a craving, so that the need gets well established of giving nothing and asking everything of fiction, an attitude which can be reconciled only to this kind of slick and stereotyped variety. Consider the novels of nostalgia which place the ideal world in a past that never existed: *Gone With The Wind,* for instance; or the pornographic novels which have now come out into the open, such as O'Hara's *A Rage to Live,* worth having if only to convince the last puritans that sex is here to stay, and otherwise illegitimate because employed as a substitute, a vicarious source of experience, and guilty of the usual charges levelled against the literature of escape. Two weeks after reading the latest best seller the people who have bought it in such quantities cannot remember the name of the author or the title, and often they have forgotten even the plot. You must not overlook the fact that Harnett Kane outsells Thomas Mann two to one; as in the case of Chesterfield cigarettes, it's the mildness that satisfies.

Everything in the world leads on toward life or death; and we submit here that bad art, if we are privileged to call the anesthetic literature of entertainment art, leads on toward death: death to the spirit, death to the kind of enlightenment great art brings to us and which as cultured beings we cannot do without.

The second category of modern novel is the journalistic novel. Although as old as Defoe, it is as recent as O'Hara's *A Rage to Live* or Mailer's *The Naked and the Dead,* (which by the way the London *New Statesman and Nation* reviewed under the title of "Kinsey's Army"). Most people lead lives of obscure inexperience, and so they depend upon the contemporary novelist to tell them in the concrete what it would be like to be in a beautiful society woman's bedroom or in an island hopping campaign in the Pacific war against Japan, and what sorts of things go on in those places. The journalistic novel is not a new *genre* but its popularity has increased to an amazing degree in recent decades. There is nothing wrong with it provided that its proper claims are recognized. It does not in most cases pretend to be a work of art. It is simply a variety of painless reporting, a device for making the latest news vivid. The only damage done by the journalistic novel is its misuse as a substitute for the art novel and as a standard when we judge others by it. It falls somewhere between the art novel and the daily newspaper and is probably closer to the current type of motion picture. We tend to regard other novels as moving too slowly by comparison. But at least the journalistic novel gets around. It is not a phony like the literature of entertainment but it helps to widen the area embraced by the novel form.

The third category of modern novel is the psychological novel. This variety purports to reveal to us what goes on in people's minds; and since many of the things that go on in people's minds are things they would never tell us about voluntarily, we find the revelations interesting. The mistake here is in regarding what is subjective as essential. Some philosophers think that there is nothing in the mind that was not first in the external world, with the possible exception of error. We can watch the decline of the Greek drama played out on the highest stage, as the subject matter becomes more inward, from Aeschylus, the cosmic dramatist, to Sophocles, the tragic dramatist, to Euripides, the psychological dramatist. We could pause here long enough to wonder how much greater our O'Neill would have been had he not followed the wrong Greek.

But the greatest mistake we make in this connection is to regard all novels of ideas as psychological novels. This is to confuse the holding of the ideas with the ideas themselves. Kierkegaard, the Danish philosopher, who, incidentally, had all the ideas that Sartre ever had only a century earlier, is the prime philosopher of the contemporary novel of psychology. His philosophical position could be paraphrased in a single sentence. He said in effect, "I choose myself and accept the attendant anguish." We do not call the novelists of existentialism philosophers. We call them psychologists. When we exclaim over a novelist, "What a psychologist he is," we ought to be condemning him. To call a man a psychologist these days is to pay him a dubious compliment, but even if our psychologist were the scientist he is not, why would it be proper to call our artist a scientist? The artist must leave to the scientists the things that are the scientists'; and this is in fact precisely what the novelist of ideas does do. Philosophy is not psychology, and, as I hope to show, the great novelist is a man working on the material of art at the philosophical level.

We are now in the introduction to our fourth category, the art novel; but before we move into this area I would like to stop long enough to dismiss what I may term the degenerate art novel, a species of the literature of affection. This is the kind of novel that tries to be art and fails, that tries to do the right thing but just does not have it and so substitutes a synthetic plastic which it is hoped will never be detected. The examples we might use are—to take some extreme ones at random—Djuna Barnes, Henry Miller and Andre Gide.

Nightwood by Djuna Barnes, with an introduction by T. S. Eliot, the St. Louis royalist, is a sick book; and a sicker man to introduce it could not have been found. Eliot praises the style, good heavens! He does not seem to recognize the difference between style and an effort at style. A good style never shows the effort. This one strains continually and with the usual glowing results. The fact is of course that large cultures are filled with compromises and adjustments. It is possible to over-emphasize this feature. Drugs, homosexual deviations; the disappearance of all loyalties, of all interest in the good, the beautiful and the true—how much evidence is required in order to show that our civilization has not far to travel? A growing society is structured of loves, ours is structured of hatreds, of jealously guarded differences interpreted as virtues. When people do not like you, you are supposed to comfort yourself with the thought that after all they do not like each other any better. Then the thought that this thought is a comfort is in turn disquieting. Surrealism, existentialism, non-objective painting: a culture does not decline without such a decline being represented by the artists. When initiative is taken, the artist will take it, and this includes also the first steps downward.

Is it necessary to insist that this is not the whole story of our culture, only one side of it? Is it needful to point out that Henry Miller has never written an art novel, only fragments of pornographic autobiography which he cuts into book lengths from time to time? Andre Gide is perhaps a better case. He almost got there. If he has proved anything it is that if you hang around long enough, people will begin to take you seriously, despite the thinness of your talent. Gide deserves to be remembered chiefly for his rejection of *Swann's Way* which he has admitted in print he made as an editor of the N.R.F. on *prima facie* grounds: that is, he prejudged the book by the man, he knew Proust was a frequenter of salons and how could a fashionable butterfly do anything important? Sound reasoning in general, perhaps, but not infallible; and in this case very wrong.

Let us begin this discussion with an abstract picture of the contemporary novel as a work of art. Art is a distillation of existence, for the events it reveals in essence will disappear. Tragedy is much grander than the tragic events it depicts, comedy much greater than the episodes it mocks; for in the long run art is all that will be left of the life it describes. Nobody except William James ever claimed that in the beginning was the action, and certainly words speak louder than actions. The art novel takes off from what-is to describe what-ought-to-be. It is the attempt to bring the actual world a little closer to the ideal's desire.

The importance of the art novel has a simple criterion: how much does it include? This must not be interpreted too naively. Size is size of subject matter, and so often more can be got into the life of one unimportant character than into a whole society, innocently considered a much broader canvas. The great novelists suggest cosmic themes no matter what they are talking about, and the reforms they call for can never be altogether accomplished. The grand theme of art is the infinite strivings and yearnings of the finite creature, whatever the mode of its presentation. Of course, not just any presentation: artfulness is required, and the method is symbolic and indirect.

Art always has a moral, and the greater the work of art the more profound the moral. But the moral, which is the meaning, of the work of art is best presented indirectly. The novel as a work of art communicates values, not propositions, and connotation rather than denotation is its method. Hence morals must not be yelled at readers, but left over for them after their experience with the novel is done. It must hover in the air around the reader's head after he has finished the last page, its quality and aroma outlasting even the delight of the shock of the freshness of its novelty.

The novelist is not a time-server but a time-saver; he holds valuable only what cannot be destroyed in space-time. All men concerned with the pursuit of value ought to take the arch truth-pursuers as their models, and, like Socrates, stand fast in the face of crucial contemporary events, working like Archimedes to the last day. For the things that are manufactured in the ivory tower are among the most important products of the market place.

Santayana's essay on Proust is very much to the point. Witness Proust's affirmation of the persistence of the values, in a world of change. Proust reaffirmed the constants of essence in terms of the variables of existence. In *The Remembrance of Things Past* a device very much like the branch of mathematics known as the theory of transformations is employed: whatever can be changed is changed in order to show what is safe from change. Proust affirmed the essences by plunging into the fluxing world of existence.

Proust's philosopher was Leibniz, just as Dostoyevsky's was Hegel and Joyce's Vico. "Send me my copy of Hegel, else I die," Dostoyevsky wrote a friend from exile in Siberia. And Proust's letters are filled with references to Leibniz.

That Joyce was made possible at least partly by Vico is well known. For Joyce is almost more than a novelist, more than an artist. He is a myth-maker, which is to say a culture-maker. The tail-biting snake of the ageless *Finnegan's Wake,* the book in which Joyce left even his imitators behind, is an example of the most beautiful letters of our times, I think the greatest literary work of art composed in this generation. We are close to the book and yet it is so strange to us that we fail to see how a new kind of literature has been discovered. Neither poetry nor prose but something in between—prosetry is not as good as grult—composed in a method of deliberate but suggestive ambiguity, *Finnegan's Wake* is akin to Peirce's description of the contradictory proposition, which, as he said, is not meaningless but means too much. There is hardly a contemporary novel that does not owe something to *Ulysses,* but the effect of *Finnegan's Wake* will probably be the more tremendous for being delayed.

The nearer we get to home, in space as well as in time, the more likely we are to miss the giants and to see only their feet of clay. We watch the footprints of Faulkner in Mississippi, we judge his work as an attempt at writing journalistic novels, and we ask, Is Mississippi actually as Faulkner's novels describe it? There are two answers to this question. In the first place, whoever said it was supposed to be? Faulkner's novels are art-novels if they are anything, and art-novels are not necessarily reportorial. The difficulty here is with the audience, not with the novel. You can hear Faulkner, like Dostoyevsky before him, described as a "novelist of mental distress," a good enough phrase if applied to the members of the Anemic League, the Low Blood Pressure School of Painless Culture, and not to the powerful authors they lack the strength to appreciate or accept. And in the second place even if Mississippi were as bad as Faulkner says, the similarity would still be irrelevant. For the artist must make actuality symbolic and take off from the world of existence to the ideal world. We can with practice learn to recognize the true novel, even the minor true novel: *Miss Lonelyhearts,* for example.

The novel as an art form, as we said at the beginning of this discussion, is one of the most recent. It has hardly been explored. The great men, men like Joyce, are busy experimenting; and the experimental novel represents a courageous attempt to pioneer in human experience, to bring some additional values into men's lives in the way of an intensification of experience. The form of the novel is still soft and elastic, like the bones of all young animals. We must exercise it and stretch it before it hardens. The novel, remember, can be, if it is not often, an art form. We should listen with sympathy to those who are struggling with it to widen and deepen our lives for us. A culture is no bigger than its biggest artist, to have great cultures there must be great artists, and for this purpose, as Whitman said about the production of poets, we need great audiences, too.

THE DECLINE OF LITERARY CHAOS

It is no less a truth for being a truism to say that the artist is one who seeks for the meaning of existence, or to add that the more capable the artist the profounder the level at which he conducts his search. The artist takes delight in singular things and occurrences, but if he is a genuine artist he is delighted only to the extent to which he is able to find in them a universal import. The lesser artist is willing to settle for what is merely general, while the great artist strives onward toward the realm of that which is ubiquitous and eternal. In the field of literature, and especially of the novel, the description of persons and events without symbolic meaning remains at the stage of mere reporting, as in the regional or "realistic" novel. The book which describes, and in describing attacks, the terrible limitations imposed upon southern communities in the United States by irrational prejudice against the negro, is apt to be forgotten once the conditions of inequality which justified the attack no longer exist. Can Sinclair Lewis' *Babbitt* survive the disappearance of the *ethos* of the American business man of the nineteen-twenties, when already in the nineteen-sixties the work has begun to appear seriously dated and old-fashioned? The poorhouses and orphan asylums of nineteenth-century England have been considerably reformed, yet the novels of Dickens remain as great as ever, because the meaning which was put into them included more than a protest against the maladministration of such social institutions; it included an appeal to the sublime tragedy, and comedy, of the human predicament, a condition which is not likely to undergo any fundamental change so long as people remain people. The work of art which concentrates upon universals at the expense of singulars is apt to be sterile, a barren allegory in which the bones of the moral show through too plainly to have any effect but the opposite of the one intended. Thus the artist is constrained to emphasize neither the historical order of singulars nor the logical order of universals in the pursuit of his method. In the writings of the greatest of literary artists, the balance between the unique singularity of persons and events on the one hand and of the eternal verities on the other is maintained with a smooth blending which does not allow us to perceive how it could ever have been otherwise.

The properties of universality and singularity appear in existence under many guises, and there are many ways in which they are apprehended by the artist. We know them more familiarly, for instance, as elements of order and of chance. Order manifests itself as uniformity, regularity, law, system, consistency; while chance manifests itself as chaos, spontaneity, abundance, variety, contradiction. No description of existence, or of the symbolism suggested by what exists, could possibly be adequate were it not to contain aspects both of order, in some one of its various manifestations, and of chance. The meaning for which the artist seeks lies somehow in the relation between the two orders. The artist, needless to add, is not necessarily conscious of his problem in just these abstract terms; but the problem itself is implicit in his method and the field in which that method operates.

In addition to these two elements, then, there is a third consideration of no less importance, and this is the problem of the relationship which prevails between them. How is order related to chance, and, conversely, how is chance related to order? The American philosopher, Charles S. Peirce, admitted his failure to understand aesthetics and art; yet he invented a tremendous theory of the relation of chance to order. He said that chance begets order, a theory which occurred to him in the course of applying the new statistical method to fairly ancient moral considerations. He meant that given a sufficiently large number of instances, usually requiring a very long run of time, mere chance happening would begin to manifest some incipient kind of order. Chance, in Peirce's view, is not a product of ignorance; it is something entirely objective: the sheer randomness of great populations of events whose indefinitely large multiplicity provides that certain types of events may happen again, and in so doing occasion a tendency to repeat the process, until a habit is established and a law approximated. The argument is too long to reproduce here, but the details are interesting. Peirce failed to point out whether he believed that the law behind the uniformity of behavior was also generated by the large number of instances, or whether the latter tended to approximate law by sheer repetition; but the belief in law underlies his position even though it is only stated explicitly in other connections.

Order and chance and the relations between them characterize existence to a very large extent, and so the artist who is concerned with the discovery of artistic values in existence is naturally fascinated by both orderly and disorderly manifestations of these values. The ultimate concern of the artist is of course the graded values, that is to say values in their proper order. But there are two ways of satisfying this concern open to him. He can strive to get at the order directly, or he can strive to get at it indirectly by means of the very chance which constitutes its opposite. The first method is more that of the scientist and the philosopher than the artist. For the scientist works with particular facts to reveal universal laws, whereas the artist works with particular feelings to reveal universal values. The relation of particular fact to universal law is exemplification; the relation of particular feeling to universal value is symbolism. The method of the artist, then, is one involving mediation, and the medium of such a method is often started toward the opposite of the end sought; indirection is routed through chaos to order. This method puts the emphasis of the artist upon the relations between chance and order, both of which contain elements he is seeking. For each contains properties which must be taken into consideration by the other. The attractiveness of order is of course its consistency, while the attractiveness of chance is its abundance. Consistency and inclusiveness are coordinate criteria of the worth of any system. We alternate from time to time in the type of emphasis chosen. The greatest artists endeavor to demonstrate how much of chaos can be made to reveal its order. Put in other words, they attempt to show by means of artistic values how much of order there is in apparently confused, contradictory and chaotic existence.

The measure of this aspect of art can best be shown by submitting it to specific examples, and here of course our examples must come from the work of those artists who have been the most preoccupied with chaotic properties as such. Not all artists who have been fascinated by the material of the irrational have been equally great artists. We may see the chaotic expertly treated by Dostoyevsky, and then we may witness its successive decline at the hands of Gide and Saroyan. Of course no direct succession will be intended here except in the transition from Dostoyevsky to Gide; Gide has been heavily influenced by Dostoyevsky, a debt which he has been only too willing to acknowledge; but it is doubtful whether Saroyan has been influenced by either of the others. The examples we shall take from the work of these men will all be studies of murder, since situations involving murder, its motives and execution, contain large elements of confusion and chaos.

If it is true, as Peirce has insisted, that chance begets order, the illustrations must remain on a statistical basis. For it is only in large populations of instances that the emergence of order from chaos can be discerned. Statistical theorists are undoubtedly correct in their assertion that statistical averages can tell us nothing at all about the next single instance. Given fair throws of a coin under properly controlled conditions, the probability asserts that out of a hundred throws fifty will fall heads and fifty tails. Now if we have thrown the coin thirty-five times, say, and all thirty-five have brought tails, certainly a head is due. Yet the chances of the next throw being heads is still fifty-fifty. In the demonstration of order through chaos in art, then, how is the artist to work? For those artists who are fascinated by the spectacle of chaos, the problem is how to show that chance begets order in a single instance. Obviously this cannot be done symbolically.

It is no accident that the method of art involves symbolism. For the artist must work with single instances; he can tell only one story at a time, paint only one picture or sing one song. The story, the picture or the song, would mean nothing artistically unless it dragged in its wake a wide penumbra of meaning. Behind every concrete object of art is reflected the shadows of countless absent particulars which it affectively symbolizes. The hold upon us of a character in fiction, for instance, is its ability to remind us of all those actual people who are therein described. It is not the particularity of such a figure but rather its valuational generality which carries the appeal. We have never met Polonius nor shall we ever meet him: there is no such person. Yet we meet him every day and he lives for us because we have met so many dull, busybody, meddling bores in high places. Needless to emphasize, the abstract qualities which are embodied in a fictional character do not of themselves constitute the artistic property, and indeed they are incapable by themselves of carrying it. They require embodiment, embodiment in a particular symbolism; and it is just this step which the artist is obliged to furnish. Our problem, then, in this essay, is to illustrate with cases the symbolism of chaos, the way in which concrete instances of art are made to carry the suggestion symbolically of how chaos (or chance) begets order.

The relation of statistics to symbolism is an obscure and difficult field, as yet totally unworked. Universality is as vague as it is broad, and its vagueness is a natural consequence of its broadness; what reaches afar cannot ever be seen clearly. What, in the language of the statistical method, represents a large population does so in an abstract way, and lends itself readily to counting. But symbolic representation contains the vagueness of universality, as does all affective value. The estimation of the population of what is represented, not abstractly after the manner of logic and mathematics but affectively after the manner of all symbolism, has not yet lent itself to a successful method. But in symbolism there is an aspect from which it may be viewed as an example of statistical probability, despite the fact that the affective value of universality contains a vagueness of generality which defies simple enumeration. The mathematical approach to art is no more a matter of simple enumeration than the field of higher mathematics is confined to the real number system. Statistical symbolism is a topic for the future.

The first, and by far the greatest, example is that offered by Dostoyevsky. *Crime and Punishment* has been called by many a psychological study, and this is what to a subjectively-oriented interpretation it appears to be. Perhaps it even has a value as such, but this is a question for the psychologists to study. At any rate the psychological value of the novel is not its artistic value. The artistic value can best be approached through ontological considerations. There is a sense in which ontology has no field of interest of its own. Pure ontology is the most powerful of studies. But in connection with other fields, ontology is a mere solvent which makes the fields under consideration stand out in all their clean and glittering purity. It lays bare the foundations upon which they rest. The ontological considerations of aesthetic content force us to view *Crime and Punishment* as a study in the symbolism of the emergence of order from chaos through concentration on the chaotic. In great art such as this the characters and events remain affective in their singularity while symbolizing universal, even ontological, values.

The central event in the Russian novel we are considering is the murder of the old woman by Raskolnikov: why did he kill her? We may pass at once over the obvious motives. Alyona Ivanovna had money, but Raskolnikov did not take it. We may even be willing to admit that before the murder he *thought* that his motive was theft; yet he may have been wrong, since few if any of us are capable of understanding completely the springs of our own actions. And even if we say that his self-analysis was correct and theft was *at the time* his motive, there is much left unexplained. Certainly Raskolnikov himself is portrayed as having been none too sure. Later he tells Sonia that he wanted to have the daring, and that that was the reason he did it. The chance and the chaos in society exist at the bottom of the class hierarchy, because it is chiefly there that the ugly side of life exhibits itself most clearly; the filth, the poverty, the evil and the suffering are at that level most surely revealed. And it is there, too, of course, that the impulse toward the breaking of existing social relations finds its strongest incentive. If order exists even in chaos, then order is real, and we can expect to find it in greater abundance, at higher strata of society. Dostoyevsky, in all his novels and indeed throughout his life, was fascinated by the artistic problem presented by the necessity of looking for elements of order in chaos, or, to put it in another way, for elements of salvation in the most unmixed evil.

The point is illustrated in a particular way by Dostoyevsky's preoccupation with gambling. He was a terrific gambler and disposed of (for him) huge sums in this way. The usual motive of the gambler is quick profits; but if we view Dostoyevsky's passion for gambling in the context of his life and his other interests, we can see that he was more statistically-minded. It is not for nothing that the statistician's examples come so often from the gaming table. For when we know what the percentage relations are in any given case, we can recall that the future is just around the corner: will the next card, the next throw of the dice, the next turn of the roulette wheel, bear out the percentages predicted or will they not? We can hardly wait to see, and the profit or loss seen in this way, is merely the marker of the accuracy of the percentages as borne out by events. Gambling for the purposes of statistical method is merely a swift way of collecting relatively large populations of instances. Dostoyevsky no doubt needed the money and could have used it had he not been willing to risk it back again; but profit could hardly have been his sole interest.

The point is illustrated, this time in a general way, by the interpretation of Dostoyevsky made by Beardsley.[1] The underground is Dostoyevsky's metaphor for the lowest order of society and for the lowest characters in that order—for chaos. The way to heaven lies through the underground, the way to order through chaos. The idiot, the drunkard, the intimidated and worthless, the beaten, the murderer, these are the inhabitants of the underground, the instruments through which salvation shall come. Dostoyevsky is always looking for The Good, for an ecstatic Good, for God; but he insists on looking for it, for Him, among instances of unadulterated evil. Raskolnikov's deliberate choice of evil, a choice whose deliberateness accords well with his own chosen motives of theft, is the first step he must take on his long upward climb toward the raising of society to its Christ-like possibilities. The life of Sonia repeats the theme in a minor key, the girl turned prostitute to earn bread for her family, who appears like a far-off, shining white light, in whose name Raskolnikov finds he is forced to the confession of his crime and the willing shouldering of seven years of exile in Siberia, provided that with her at the end of that time he can initiate a new order. His identity, his emergence, in other words, from the underground, begins, as Beardsley very well understands, with the commission of the murder, since it is there that his self-consciousness begins. For an unidentified entity in the social chaos, there can be no moral conscience because there is no self-consciousness, no responsibility, to contain it. In the end Raskolnikov escapes from the chaos of the underground; he becomes differentiated and discrete, but at what a price! Only at the cost of the most intense guilt and suffering is it possible. But then, at least, he is on his way to God.

We are in a position to see now what the motive of the murder was. The psychological explanation is at this point in full flight. The book is

[1] Beardsley, Monroe C. "Dostoyevsky's Metaphor of the 'Underground'," in the *Journal of the History of Ideas,* vol. III (1942), p. 265.

not a study of crime and punishment in the police sense, either, for the
law which is being broken, the crime which is being committed, the
money which is being sought, and even in a sense the persons who are
being involved, are mere instruments in a passion play where the passion
itself and its high symbolism constitute the central characters. Why did
Raskolnikov kill the old woman if not because murder as motiveless as
that must constitute the extreme of social disorder, a fertile field for the
pursuit of the reality of the elements of order? Assuredly he had no
ordinary motive, and in the ordinary sense he had no motive at all. It is
indeed just this absence of motive which makes the theme of the novel;
the absence of motive is in this case the motive itself; to seek chaos in
search of order, to commit the most dastardly of crimes in search of
God's absolute moral law which states that thou shalt not kill: where
else shall we find a motive and a theme so pure?

The story of the raising of Lazarus which Raskolnikov compelled
Sonia to read to him, and toward the end of the book the nightmare
of a world gone mad which he experiences, are very much to the point.
In these episodes the contrast is directly indicated. The act without
apparent motive is a random act, but in the mind of the actor we see that
chaos, which Nietzsche says, in *Thus Spake Zarathustra,* we must have
within us in order to give birth to a dancing star. Only the imperfect can
give birth to the perfect; absolute evil is a limit which, once we have
touched it, is sure to turn us back on our very long journey toward the
good. This is the moral secret which lies at the heart of the actual existence of human beings. Raskolnikov reassures Sonia and explains why he
needs her when he tells her that he is glad she has committed evil deeds.

> You, too, have transgressed ... have had the strength to transgress. You
> have laid hands on yourself, you have destroyed a life ... *your own*
> (it's all the same!)[2]

We are at this point farther from the good than we ever were, but
at least we are headed in the right direction; we are facing it and striving
toward it, knowing then that there is no other path and no other avenue
we have not explored.

For the purposes of this essay, then, the important feature of Dostoyevsky's *Crime and Punishment* is the deliberate commission of a murder by one whose motive is not what he thinks it to be because his true
motive for the meaning of the tale is the deep significance imparted to his
act by the very absence of motive.

Let us turn next to a famous French novelist and admirer of

[2] Part IV, chapter IV.

Dostoyevsky, André Gide, and to his novel, *Les Caves du Vatican*. Gide wrote a book about Dostoyevsky; there can be little doubt of the strength of the influence. We shall in the study of this author and his book want to know how the motiveless murder fares, how it is executed and how interpreted.

When we turn from Dostoyevsky's young man in *Crime and Punishment* to Gide's young man in *The Vatican Swindle* (to use the title of the English translation), what a surprise awaits us. Raskolnikov had been rather serious, a character willing to commit murder yet intent upon his soul's salvation. Lafcadio Wluiki, on the other hand, is frivolous and fundamentally evil, for he is willing to commit murder while remaining intent only upon entertainment and the avoidance of boredom. The influence in Gide of Dostoyevsky is plain, a fact which does not hide its naïveté and literalness of treatment; the simple failure of Gide to understand Dostoyevsky would be pitiful if it were not so ludicrously apparent. Dostoyevsky's man commits a motiveless murder—in a way, but only in a way, as we have noted. Lafcadio commits a murder for Gide and first announces its motivelessness.

" 'A crime without a motive,' went on Lafcadio, 'what a puzzle for the police!' "[3] These are the words of the murderer, Lafcadio, speaking a few moments before the murder. Monsieur Wluiki is presented to us now as a homosexual sadist, now as an irresponsible fellow entirely lacking in the moral sense. Lafcadio is made to say that he

> could have clasped the whole of mankind to my heart in my single embrace—or strangled it, for that matter. Human life! What a paltry thing! And with what alacrity I'd risk mine if only some deed of gallantry would turn up—something really rather pleasantly rash and daring![4]

The occasion that suits him does turn up on a journey from Rome to Paris. An old man enters his compartment in the railway car, an old man who is not distinguished—or offensive—in any special way, an old man Lafcadio has never seen before. At a convenient moment crossing a bridge, Lafcadio quickly opens the door and pushes the old man out. The old man is killed, of course, and Lafcadio in order to escape detection is forced to change the plans he has laid for a sea voyage to the Orient. Lafcadio is in a sense chaos itself; he has no feeling for social order, for morals; he has no particular plans for his own future. He is capable of anything and accomplishes nothing, nothing, that is, except the utmost evil. He is not sorry, he has no regrets; he does not even have any

qualms when another man is arrested and charged with the murder, not
even when the other man proves to be Protos, his old school fellow and
chum.

What, then, is Gide's point? Is it the motiveless murder of Dostoyevsky? Hardly, for Dostoyevsky is in quest of the solution to a theological problem—one might say *the* theological problem. Gide's murder
is a motiveless murder, but there is no theology involved. As for the
distinction between chaos and order, the relationship is inverted. There is
an abundance and variety of chaos in the happenings of Dostoyevsky's
characters even though the characters themselves are orderly and good
of soul. In *The Vatican Swindle* there is the kind of tight order we are
apt to find in a well-written detective novel: the events are closely knit
together; the people we have met we meet again; clues are laid down
and picked up at exactly the right time and in the correct situation.
Yet the whole leaves an impression of going nowhere. At least that is the
kindest interpretation we can put upon it; a less kind one might lead us
to the conclusion that the effect of the whole is amoral, antisocial and
evil. Dostoyevsky, irrespective of the details of his work, we feel intends
no harm; Gide in the same fashion makes us feel that he intends no good.
Gide's characters lack the high emotionalism which prevails in *Crime
and Punishment*. The crime is premeditated murder, not murder committed in a high state of excitement. Raskolnikov acted on the spur of
the moment; Lafcadio anticipates the event and coldly calculates his
chances of getting away with it.

Dostoyevsky was in search of order through chaos; Gide is in search
of chaos through order. The orderliness of his plot is designed to this end;
but, do what he will, it defeats him. For it ends as he did not wish it to
end: in chaos. Lafcadio, the Lafcadio who as a young boy lived on
intimate terms with his mother's lovers, falls in love with his half-sister
and begins an affair with her, a (even for him) highly irregular procedure.
The plot rather trails off and does not have the neat ending which all
through the story we have been led to expect, and which we rather may
suppose Gide earnestly sought and failed to find. Somewhat pathetically,
Protos, the arch-criminal, voices Gide's disappointment for us when he
points out to Lafcadio the impossibility of escaping from "the social
framework that hems us in"[5] . . . "without at the same moment taking us
into another"[6] order of society. For there is no social group without its
laws, and this is as true of those who move without the law as of those
who move within it. Dostoyevsky rejoiced to learn that wherever he looked
in chaos there was law. Gide, who is really seeking with difficulty for the

[5] *Ibid.*, p. 255.
[6] *Ibid.*, p. 256.

chaos that Dostoyevsky had no trouble in discovering, is dismayed by the same fact.

We have taken note of the decline which the idea of chaos has suffered in the murder which is performed in Gide's *The Vatican Swindle*. Gide's account, as we have observed, rests on a misunderstanding of Dostoyevsky on the narrowly rational, coldly unemotional, side. For an account of defection of the conception of chaos on the other side, we shall be compelled to depart from our neat scheme in order to use as illustration the work of an author, William Saroyan, who has in all likelihood not been influenced by Dostoyevsky if indeed he has ever read or even heard of him.

Saroyan's work illustrates a defection from the grandeur of the conception of chaos on the sentimental side. Premeditated murder as an artistic subject-matter is somewhat out of the Saroyan line, as indeed is anything complicated or considered; Saroyan's characters are gentle people, and well worn from having passed through so many literary hands before they reached him. Saroyan wears his modesty inside out, so that fleshy parts show where the curing was not effective. This leads him to make brash and bold statements of egocentric policy which he timidly likes to think he means. His characters reflect the same kind of tentatively excessive, egocentric obsession; they are concerned exclusively with their own happiness. Saroyan's characters are thus nineteenth century English utilitarian characters, expressing a kind of Benthamite ethics: they wish to be happy, and they wish, somewhat further, happiness for their neighbors, too; and that is all.

Saroyan's work is not profound. It is the surface of things which is being reflected to us, but a surface which wears an air assumed in imitation of the depths. For we have long ago seen through the superficiality of mere personal happiness; we know that it is desirable, of course, but we also know that it is a by-product of the pursuit of more formidable and more remote if less elusive ends. We can be happy only when we are accomplishing something which is good; we certainly cannot pursue happiness directly. Therefore we may say that we have marked happiness as a state which we should like to attain but which we can only hope to reach as a secondary reward for the achievement of something primary in the way of goals.

But Saroyan is not aware of these issues; his methods are direct and his ends simple. Chaos is introduced into all of Saroyan's work, but the task of chaos is not to add to confusion; it is to eliminate complexity and organization. Chaos in the stories and plays of Saroyan has the quixotic task of keeping everything orderly and simple at the level of elemental order and simplicity. To shatter social organization, to discard established customs and institutions, to mock at folkways and mores, marks a negative approach to the human scene. To launch the attack, however, is not enough; one must also be prepared with something positive which one wishes to establish when the obstacles have been removed. Saroyan does indeed have a plan. He wishes everyone to be happy, in elementary ways; that is his plan. And when higher levels of culture are done away with, and everyone goes back to being himself (assuming that the self is quite simple and aimed at simple happiness), the world will be a better place.

Saroyan believes so firmly in this Cinderella goal of life that he is even willing to see murder committed to reach it. In his play, *The Time of Your Life,* Joe shoots Blick because Blick, who is described as a "heel," i.e., a mean and disagreeable fellow, keeps other people from being happy. Everyone, we are assured, only wants to be happy in simple, uncomplicated ways. The social milieu makes no sense at all in any other terms. There is no set of intelligible social relations in the light of which we are able to orient ourselves. The social order consists in the individual's right to be as chaotic as possible in his pursuit of lightweight, sensual happiness. Willie, the idiot who devotes all his time and money to playing an automatic marble-game, is a sympathetic character (but for his relations to the marble-game and for his naïveté, not for the marble-game's relations to him, which, Saroyan forgets, are rather complex, as those of all complicated social tools are apt to be). In the last act, everyone gets the happiness he wants, and the happy ending rests upon a firm foundation in the murder of Blick, which somehow is considered too trivial and justified to dim the desired solution which it is instrumental in bringing about. We are led to assume not only that the social order, through the law, will not interfere but also that the moral order, through the sense of responsibility or conscience, will not interfere, either. The simple life of happiness has won by means of chaos.

There is a point here which is very well worth noting. The man, Blick, is killed because he interferes with the happiness of others. By happiness, Saroyan intends to convey the notion of the individual right to random action. If the individual is to be happy, he must be free to "obey that impulse," to do whatever he feels like doing, on the assumption that what he feels like doing, will always be good and aimed at the happiness of others, although certainly in the case of Blick's own untrammeled actions, there was no such good either of intention or of effect. But Blick and evil intentions aside, it is just possible that two persons who were equally good and equally simple and equally untrammeled in their impulse to perform whatever random actions they wished to perform might come into random conflict and thus defeat the purpose of their freedom by denying them happiness. In other words, two persons, each inspired by the simple desire to be happy, and performing random actions in the pursuit of that end, might each be the innocent and unintentional cause of the unhappiness of the other. Thus the individual end sought, as elementary as we make it, still requires a social framework. This social framework, which, while capable of restricting individual freedom, is also capable of allowing it and in this way of making it possible, is viewed by Saroyan as being inevitably a restrictive force. Thus we may conclude that chaos in Saroyan's hands is an instrument aimed at the elimination of social organization in favor of the achievement of the tenuous individual salvation of personal happiness. The whole treatment is sentimental and conventional, as we should expect that it would be. The sentiment is emphasized as though it were an artistic virtue, and the conventionality is hidden behind the screen which the ingredient of chaos furnishes. Chance does not beget order and indeed is not expected to do so in the picture which Saroyan draws. Chance is the reward bestowed upon those who abandon higher order in favor of lower order, he would lead us to believe. Chance is its own excuse for being; and as for order, if we love our fellow men it must be held down to a minimum. This is the message Saroyan comes to bring us.

We have said at the beginning of this study that the artist seeks for universal significance and value among singular persons and occurrences. We have further asserted that the search for consistency and inclusiveness of such significance and value can consist in elements of order amidst the utmost in chaos and confusion. Chaos, seen in the light of the proper perspective, is nothing more than the field of population of orderly relationships; as such it has been interpreted by the very greatest artists after the fashion of a kind of statistical symbolism; lesser artists are discouraged or frightened by the evidences of power which the spectacle of chaos displays. We have sought for an illustration of the principle that chance begets order with the purpose of showing how it is presented symbolically, and we have chosen for our example three contrasted instances of literary murder as devised in fiction by a man of genius, by a man of great talent, and by a man of mere talent, respectively. Nothing more remains to be done except to draw some general conclusions.

All three literary artists have sought in chaotic and chance events for elements of some sort of order. The chaos in the work of Dostoyevsky is aimed at the improvement of the social order, at the establishment of a better society, albeit by means of individual salvation. The chaos in the work of Gide is aimed at existing society based upon amoralism. The chaos in Saroyan is aimed against existing society in favor of individual order without any social hindrances: a kind of hedonistic anarchy. All three see clearly the closely-knit relationship between chaos or chance on the one hand and order or law on the other; they differ sharply, however, in the way they evaluate this relationship. Dostoyevsky, who is anxious to include as great an abundance of existence as possible in his system, is delighted by the fact that he must encounter so much of chaos on his way toward order. Gide is dismayed, discouraged and frightened by the fact that everywhere he looks for chaos, he can only find order; and he is compelled by this fact to narrow his hold on what he can approve of in existence. Saroyan deplores the close connection between chaos and order, which he instinctively labels respectively good and bad, and he seeks to eliminate the order. Dostoyevsky is a Christian realist; Gide is a nominalistic materialist; Saroyan is a nominalistic solipsist. Dostoyevsky believes in the reality of objective ideals and values, and he finds ample evidence for his belief among the crudest of material facts and experiences. Gide believes only in those facts and experiences, and in the right of man to derive what crumbs of sensual pleasure and comfort he can from them. Saroyan believes only in the sole reality of physical particulars, in man the feelings of the individual, and denies the reality of whatever interferes with the enjoyment and expression of those feelings. At Dostoyevsky's hands the idea of chaos reaches its highest function as a literary preoccupation, almost transcending literature itself. It suffers a sharp and successive decline at the hands of his successors, until indeed it is almost meaningless: Dostoyevsky's belief in the reality of possible values makes his work great. Gide's and Saroyan's disbelief in the reality of such values in any broad social sense allows their work to degrade the very functions which it is the task of great literature to elevate.

MEMORIES OF SHERWOOD ANDERSON

A single personality is capable of transforming the perspective from which we view the world, illuminating not only unfamiliar corners of existence but familiar corners as well. Sherwood Anderson was able to do this for those of us who knew him.

When Sherwood first came to New Orleans he looked like an old mother, his face, I mean, very like that of Gertrude Stein. His was a full head with a large and almost bulbous nose. His mouth was thin and determined, a straight line cut across the clear expanse of his lower jaw.

It was the expression of a wise old woman, not effeminate but strong, a peasant woman who had raised a brood, done the washing and cooking for the family and kept her children firm in the law of her religion.

Is there anything to be learned from the study of faces alone? Because the rest of the picture changed all that. Sherwood always had his hair brushed in a line curving down over one corner of his forehead. The hair, the blackthorne stick and the clothes completely altered the first impression. He wore a corduroy shirt, a loud green one, and a finger ring for the knot in his tie. His suit was brown with a loud green pin stripe, and his woolen socks were constantly falling over the tops of his high shoes. I first caught a glimpse of him as he was climbing down from a shoeshine stand; the glimpse turned into a stare. He did not see me, was no doubt hardly disconcerted by what must have been a common occurrence: he was almost certainly a spectacle wherever he went.

I later met him and we became friends. We talked together a great deal. I had at the time recently begun my friendship with Bruce Manning. Sherwood and Bruce are the only two men I have ever known who could tell a story properly. They employed the same method, as a matter of fact. It consisted in the technique of the bedtime story for children, applied to the commonplace, an atmosphere of great mystery surrounding the most trivial of events and thereby transforming them into something greatly meaningful. The effect was tremendous; suddenly the present, everything in the present: the room in which we were sitting, the furniture, the glasses in our hands, the fire in the fireplace, even the sounds outside, became invested with enormous significance. You felt as you sat there that you were being let in on some event of tremendous importance, that you were the only one being made acquainted with happenings which were capable of changing the whole course of history.

"You know, Jim," Sherwood would begin, "I made lots of money one time and that was on a book called *Dark Laughter*. I bought a big farm in Virginia with the royalties, a place with a large stone farm house. Well, I decided that I could not write in the house, so I had a little stone cottage set up away from the main building." He leaned forward in his chair, his voice dropped, and his eyes looked away. "In the cottage there were two stone tables, I was to write on one of them." He was on the edge of his chair now. "You know, Jim, what happened? I went down to that cottage every morning and sat there pencil in hand and paper before me." Here he looked around the room apprehensively, as though to catch the murderer himself in the act of eavesdropping. I could hardly understand the hoarse and furtive whisper, spoken very slowly: "Well, I sat there and never wrote a god-damn word."

Other story-tellers could produce suspense by introducing supernatural elements, mystery, or magic. Sherwood needed only the ordinary circumstances of the everyday life of ordinary men. The magic was almost metaphysical: it was of significance to him not that a man walked strangely but that he walked at all. The metaphysician is concerned with the commonplace but he has, so to speak, an uncommon interest in it. For motion itself is the mystery: how can there be the phenomenon of motion? Now, this concern of the metaphysician is abstract and general; he is never absorbed in a particular motion; this man or that walking down the street means little or nothing to him in his capacity as a metaphysician. What does interest him is the general law or significance of motion. The interest of Sherwood was typical of the interest of the artist. He was concerned neither with the particular alone nor with the general alone but with the general *through* the particular. A man walking had no interest by itself for Sherwood; neither would the laws of motion have had if he had known about them. But a man walking somehow illuminated for him the whole value of motion, and consequently was heavy with large and powerful symbolism. Sherwood could catch that significance readily, he could catch it but he could not hold it. That is why he wrote greater short stories than novels. His was the art of the flash, the single impression: the poem, the short story, the song. But he certainly could catch it; what is more rare, he could catch it not only in writing but almost as well in speech. There is no way to describe the peculiar values elicited from something which Sherwood had apprehended in the commonplace.

Perhaps his gift came from the peculiar way in which he saw the world. He understood a certain viewpoint well, and once came very near expressing it abstractly. "You know, Jim," he said, "when we are talking there is not only you and me. There is a third." He could not explain further what the third thing was and I could not very well press him about it. Certainly, values meant more to him than facts. He was impressed by the value in the actual situation more than he was by its carrier. The significance of a passing event came up to meet him, detached itself for him from the event and rose pure and clean and immortally true and applicable, shorn of the details which while immutable would perhaps never happen in exactly the same way again.

He had gone to Europe once with a friend who was a radical lawyer. They had their trip paid for them by some wealthy woman in New York who had sympathized with the socialist cause. The trip was taken on the *Titanic,* a boat whose destination was unknown; it had sailed, he said, under sealed orders.

On the way over, the socialist passengers held a meeting in the grand salon to which the crew, in true socialist fashion, were cordially invited.

But the captain was a die-hard and forbade the crew to leave their posts. Both Sherwood and the radical lawyer grew thoroughly disgusted with the attitude of the socialists on the trip over, Sherwood explained, and once the boat reached its destination, which proved to be Rotterdam, they separated and did not attend the labor congress for which they had made the trip. Sherwood did not see again either the socialists or his radical lawyer friend. He returned home alone.

At this point in the story, beguiled somewhat by its very staid and factual presentation, I became interested in the figure of the radical lawyer as I was then in all persons who could not make up their minds once and for all on the question of radical politics. I could see what had happened to Sherwood; he had, in his own account, become an anarchist. Anarchism did not mean to him what it meant to other people; he thought the word stood for an extreme and aberrant form of individualism in which it would be possible to form a society founded on neighbor-love. Perhaps Sherwood was somewhat right that this is, or at least ought to be, the essential meaning of the word. Anyhow, I wanted to know what was the later career of the lawyer, and I accordingly asked.

Sherwood seemed a little surprised at my question. "Why, he's in New York, of course," he exclaimed, "a radical lawyer spending most of his time working for the radicals."

The point of this story is that the *Titanic* only began one trip across the Atlantic and on that trip hit an iceberg and sank. Sherwood had obviously not been on it, but he had read about it in the newspapers. It was the only name of an ocean liner that he knew which had some particularly significant story attached to it. All other ships were mere names, and it must have been on one of these others that Sherwood had actually gone to Europe; but he could not recall the exact year or the exact ship. What was more natural, then, that he should connect what he knew? The truth is that he was not trying to deceive either himself or me; his logic was not the logic of fact, it was the logic of symbolism. In the story, he had finished with the radical lawyer and was slightly annoyed with me for being so illogical as to reintroduce a figure now a superfluity into the conversation.

The career of Sherwood is the typical tragedy of the American artist, the one-book man. It is all very well to be an uneducated writer, but the absence of craft means that when inspiration fails there is no sound knowledge of procedure to take its place. We have our Whitmans, our Melvilles, our Poes; but we do not have our Dostoyevsky's, our Goethes, or our Hardys. For our writers suppose that writing is writing, that newspaper reporting, for example, is good training for the novel. Sinclair Lewis ought to be a sufficient refutation of any such wild notions. The newspaper man learns his sentimentality from his work, and acquires a nose for spot news; but he does not learn either how to write slowly or how to discover profundity. He does not learn how to think as well as feel. He learns only how to deal with what in fact the newspapers do deal: surfaces. And surfaces are where the novelist of dimensions begins, not where he stops.

Education is no end in itself; from the point of view of the artist it serves only as immunization against the devastating shock of new ideas. Regard for a moment the tragedy of Sherwood's development. He began life in a small town; he first wrote fiction as a small business man in a big city. Fortunately, he managed to get something down on paper before the literary critics and editors got hold of him. Those were the days of *Winesburg, Ohio,* and *The Triumph of the Egg.*

Then came New York and the intellectuals. Through them Sherwood discovered Freud, he discovered D. H. Lawrence. The New Yorkers began to tell him what it was he was trying to do. They made him conscious of himself, his style, his contemporaries. From that period, he began to write in the way they expected him to write, and it was bad. For of all things that could happen, they certainly did not expect him to do what they expected him to do. Sherwood began to write parodies of his own good work; *Many Marriages* came along and financially speaking proved his most successful book. The critics who were responsible for him now took charge; maybe it had been all right after all to advise the author. But when Sherwood began to parody his own parodies of his own work, the show was over and everybody prepared to go home. The critics slipped quietly off in the darkness and his public, which had never been too large or too faithful, stopped buying his books.

His friends remained with him, but it was a broken Sherwood, striving desperately to keep up the old optimism and courage and enthusiasm, that they saw. It had nothing to do with liking him, of course. One likes people or one does not for just what they are in themselves.

Sherwood and I were having lunch one afternoon in the restaurant of the St. Charles Hotel in New Orleans. An Arrowcollar-looking stockbroker of the Wall Street type came over to the table and addressed Sherwood.

"I beg your pardon, but are you Roger P. Thompson of New York? I am supposed to meet him here."

Sherwood's face fell. "No, I'm not," he said quietly; then as the man retreated after begging our pardon for disturbing us, "No, I'm not, but I wished I was."

Another time he told me that he had been a week-end guest at the home of a fox-hunting friend. He had followed the hounds all afternoon in his white Ford truck, and then listened all through dinner while the other guests talked about *Gone With the Wind*. Early in the evening he had retired.

"I wasn't sleepy, I just lay in bed and pretended that they had only been waiting for me to go upstairs so that they could discuss *my* novels without causing me embarrassment. Oh, I knew that wasn't true," he said, leaning over, "only, I had to get through the night somehow."

Is it better to hear nothing from the public than to be lifted up and then dropped? I do not know. I only know that this is what happened to Sherwood. He was famous for a brief while, an all too brief while, and then forgotten. The intellectuals stove him in. They led him to suppose that what his work did was to release the world sexually, free it from inhibitions. They made him think that the significance that he was searching for was sexual in origin. That was the day of Freud. I'm afraid that, too, was partly to blame. The others were men like Julius Friend, Roger Sergel, and Paul Rosenfeld, and there were still more. Sherwood adored intellectuals, I never knew why. Perhaps it was because he had never been educated, and so believed that they had a precious and private knowledge that was inaccessible to him but that being around them he might catch it. He certainly did receive only through his bones whatever he had in the way of ideas. Certainly little except feeling came through his conscious understanding. I do not believe that he was capable of reading a volume of what is known these days as "non-fiction," consecutively. He would try such books and put them down.

"I don't know what you fellows are after," he said once, and while he added that he did not think much of it, there was little conviction in his voice.

After the Freudian influence of the nineteen-twenties which had hurt him so badly, he almost recovered. The Marxists of the nineteen-thirties made an awful big play for him, but he was not going to get burned again. That was when he used to say that he was an anarchist. People who are very earnest about their mission in life can hardly spare the time to look for signs of the tongue in a man's cheek.

Perhaps the only one of Sherwood's early influences which remained all powerful was that of Theodore Dreiser. It was hard to tell whether it was the man or his work, but Dreiser was something that Sherwood had mistaken for leadership in American letters. We were talking about Dreiser once. I had been challenging Sherwood's estimation of his magnitude, when suddenly I remembered the wording of Sherwood's dedication in a volume of short stories entitled *Horses and Men*. I read, "To Theodore Dreiser, In whose presence I have sometimes had the same refreshed feeling as when in the presence of a thoroughbred horse."

"What did Dreiser think of your dedication?" I asked after reminding him of it.

But Sherwood was not bothered. In an exceedingly matter of fact way, he answered, "Oh, he forgave me." I had the feeling that the natural response to a dedication was forgiveness, and for a moment my evaluations were upset.

There were stories I had not heard, *Mamma Geiger,* and all the other famous ones he told so often but never wrote down. He came to New Orleans for a month almost every winter. He wrote in the morning and then I had lunch with him; often Friend would be along. In the afternoon he would go to the races or wander along the docks. At night we would frequently foregather to drink and talk. One day I brought him a copy of *Lady Chatterley's Lover* which had just appeared. He took a day off from his writing (a very unusual thing) to read it. He came to lunch after consuming the whole novel and a few drinks, in a morning. He was loud and robust about his enthusiasm, until the crowded restaurant rang with the timbre of his approval. Afterwards, he became quite sad. It was beyond a doubt the book he would like to have written, the book he had always tried to write. It was his book in a sense in which it was not Lawrence's.

The absence of an education of any formal kind has its advantages. In the process of becoming familiar with the insides of books, much is gained but something is certainly lost. The advantages may outweigh the disadvantages, but Sherwood had the other side to defend. He had what so many of us have not: a feeling for the values to be apprehended in the actual world, values which exceed the respect for their apprehension in books and other works of record.

He would often engage in expatiating upon his favorite theme: the sterilization of men by machines. The operation of the machine had robbed men of manhood, so that they had nothing to offer women. We had heard it before, but this was a brilliant example of exposition. Sherwood had been sitting before the fire, highball glass in hand. As the whiskey took effect, the monologue became more eloquent, and Sherwood reached heights he had rarely touched. As he relaxed, he observed that he had written most of what he had been saying, in a book called *Perhaps Women.*

Roger Sergel was there, a friend I owe to Sherwood. Roger was puzzled. He had read the book and could find in it few of the arguments and nothing of the conviction with which Sherwood had just presented his case, and he ventured to say so.

"You have said some things that were not in that book, Sherwood," he observed quite mildly.

Sherwood was not as much hurt as he was irritated. He objected to the bookishness of men. "Well, hell," he exploded, "I'm saying them now."

Sherwood had befriended a young writer in New Orleans. He had gone on a picnic with the man and his wife one Sunday afternoon. The man had been trying to write and sell his writings but had sold nothing. Sherwood spent the day encouraging him. On Monday I saw Sherwood, and he told me about the writer. He had met many young hopefuls in the imitation Greenwich Village parties he had occasionally attended in the *Vieux Carré,* but this was the only one with any promise.

Sherwood left town shortly afterwards, and did not return for a year. Then suddenly one day without warning he turned up at the Monteleone Hotel. The young writer heard that he was in town, and went to the hotel to call him on the house telephone. He wanted to tell Sherwood the good news: he had sold a couple of stories to magazines and was thinking of giving up his job to devote all his time to writing. Sherwood was delighted.

"Come on up," he said, "I'm glad to hear your voice."

"No," answered the young writer in a slightly different tone. "You come on down; I can talk to you more like an equal now."

The first book of philosophy that Friend and I published had just appeared and we had given Sherwood a copy. He had struggled with it a while and had given it up as a bad enterprise, but not before seeing what we had to say about Jesus. That was in the days when the influence of James' *Varieties of Religious Experience* and the work of Freud and Frazer, explaining all religion away on the basis of psychological aberration, had begun to penetrate even to those who could not read such weighty works. Sherwood was puzzled by our discussion of the God-man.

"What is the point you are trying to make about the life of Jesus?" he asked.

We endeavored to explain to him that, as opposed to the notion of a transcendental and remote God in heaven who opened a hopeless breach between this world and the other, the idea of Jesus was that of a God who had made his presence known in the actual world, thus dispelling the false notion that there is nothing divine about what we experience. Sherwood looked very puzzled for a little, and then a light appeared in his face.

"I think I get it," he said brightly. "You mean, 'Come on down; I can talk to you more like an equal now!'"

For some reason I felt very much like crying. Sherwood could do that; without effort he could evoke the beauty of the world, and, behold, it was simple, like the world of a little child.

Does anything ever exceed the enormous complexity that is required in order to support simplicity? Sherwood had never been exposed to higher education, and his small town associations early in life had persuaded him that he was very simple with the simplicity of the artists; and so he was. But the simplicity of the artist is something different from that of the ordinary person. My wife and I visited Sherwood in Marion, Virginia. We saw him in what he fancied was his natural environment, among country people. But the effect was really fantastic. Sherwood was the only one there under any illusion that he was fading against his background. To the local inhabitants, he was obviously something out of this world: an amiable eccentric with influential connections. They liked him and he liked them, but that is quite another thing from their believing that he was one of them. Sherwood was in fact a very complex individual: sensitive; warm but suspicious; and not a little given over to an optimistic love of the world, a love which he never altogether lost.

Sherwood and I once spent a weekend with friends who had an old plantation house near New Orleans. After dinner we sat on the porch and in the distance we could hear a gramophone being played, folk songs. Sherwood and I set out in search of it. The sounds were coming from a box car on a siding; there was an old Negro family living in it and they had an ancient gramophone of the horn variety which had to be wound by hand. We met them and they invited us in for a drink. They owned only one record which they played over and over—it was an early Southern folk song, entitled "You Gotta Quit Kickin' My Dog Around— it don't matter if he is a hound, you gotta quit kickin' my dog around." In ten minutes, and the second playing, Sherwood and our host were friends and he was able to talk with them as easily and as relaxed as anybody I have ever seen. It was a wonderful evening. We drank and talked and sang, and when we were tired of singing we played the record again. I had the feeling afterward that we had been somewhere.

Sherwood had a power which is exceedingly rare. He could elicit from the simplest of surroundings a kind of cosmic significance. He could make the present moment seem the greatest moment—the moment of greatest value. And he could make of life in its ordinary ways an exalted adventure. He always did, as he wrote in one of his poems, succeed in taking a bite out of the now. The world is filled with the history of men who managed to make great events significant, but Sherwood could find greatness in the commonplace, and he could catch it in his life as he did in his short stories but never in his novels. He had no secret—there was no secret method, no arcanum—by which he managed to do this: it was built into his nature and it oozed from him as naturally as he breathed.

Toward the end of his life he told stories better than he wrote them. I remember his telling me about a visit to Hoover, when Hoover was

Secretary of Commerce, and considered presidential timber. Sherwood was then running a newspaper in Marion, Virginia, and the Associated Press or the United Press (I cannot remember which) offered him $300 for an interview with Hoover. Sherwood wrote ahead and obtained an appointment. He arrived in Washington somewhat early and so went to the Freer Gallery where he sat in front of a painting of a Chinese mandarin, entitled "The Mandarin Walks in his Garden with a Concubine with Lacquered Teeth." The concubine, Sherwood told me, was sixteen years old and extremely pretty; the mandarin looked very much like Hoover. Sherwood sat in front of this painting until it was time for his appointment.

When he arrived, Hoover shook hands, offered him a seat and then said, "You've come to interview me; I will be glad to answer any questions you may wish to ask." But Sherwood said, "I don't know any questions to ask; why don't you just talk?" Hoover then launched upon a long description of a new throughway which was being built between Washington and New York which would make it possible to drive the distance in under five hours. Sherwood was puzzled. "What's the hurry," he said, "what have you got to do in New York that can't wait a couple of hours?" It was Hoover's turn to be puzzled. He thought everybody knew how much better it was to have high-speed roads and to get places faster. The conversation was at cross-purposes continually, and so finally Sherwood said very politely, "Mr. Hoover, I am sorry, but I think they've sent the wrong man to interview you. It isn't your fault, it's mine. Thank you very much for your time."

He went home to Marion and reported that he had been unable to interview Hoover because neither he nor Hoover understood each other. He then sat down and wrote an account of exactly what had happened and printed it as an editorial in his own newspaper; in it he concluded, "I don't think Hoover is the kind of man who would like to walk in his garden with a concubine with lacquered teeth."

Sherwood's paper was not copyrighted, and he told me that six metropolitan dailies had picked it up and reprinted it but out of conscience each one had sent him $50. So he made the $300 he had originally been offered, though he knew that if he had sent the article in as he wrote it, the Associated Press would have turned it down; it was not, he thought, what they wanted.

After he finished, I said "Sherwood, why don't you write this up? It's a wonderful story." And he said, "I did; it is in a book called *Hello Towns.*" As soon as he left the house that evening I rushed up to my shelf where I kept his books and read it. It had no magic; he had lost that, and could preserve it now only in the telling but not in the writing.

In an earlier year he would have written it as he talked; that was gone.

Sherwood was the voice of something in our country which is native to it: the pure heroic voice of quality, the dignity of simplicity; these things had had no other hearing, but for Sherwood Anderson they were genuine. He lived among them and at their level, and he was real.

Sherwood came down to New Orleans every spring and stayed several months. He arrived late in the winter, in fact, and remained until the end of spring. He spent his mornings writing and his afternoons wandering about. He liked to walk along the docks and talk to stevedores; he liked to sit down in bars in workingmen's neighborhoods and have a beer and talk to the workers. In one such bar a man came up to him and said, "Sir, do you mind if I bask awhile in the sunlight of your personality?" This rather amused Sherwood but I am afraid it also flattered him. He was pleased with it.

At other times he would go to the races. He did not bet on the horses, nor, so far as I could ever discover, did he watch them run. He liked to talk to the people: to race horse touts and handlers; he liked to talk to the clockers and the rubbers and the trainers. He hung around the paddocks a lot in off hours talking to the men and looking at the horses. He liked the color and the smell of life at its most concrete. He had very little use for paperwork, or for men who did the paperwork: for clerks, white collar workers. He liked hunters and fishermen and men whose labors kept them close to concrete things. He was a lover of nature but only insofar as it remained in contact with human nature. I don't think he ever wanted to be off by himself in the woods or at sea unless there were woodsmen or seamen present. He liked the life of people, in short, insofar as it brought them into close contact with non-human nature—men who worked at the edge of non-human nature, but not that nature by itself nor men far removed from it in the life of the great cities.

He was a primitivist and a naturalist but on the positive side rather than the negative; he liked the virtues of the primitive but not as part of an effort to escape from the virtues of the more complex and civilized. He was an art-intoxicated man. He had tried to paint and painted very badly—but with fancy titles and great amusement. He wrote as he painted: rapidly, without revising. He shared the religious enthusiasm of the time for the creative instincts of the artist untrammeled by hard work or revision or effort. Art was not a cumulative affair for him, but a single effort, like a lyric poem, and what could not be caught in that way need not be caught at all or was not worth catching.

The word, *American,* appears many times in Sherwood's work. It is as though he had awakened suddenly to find himself a literary artist and a stranger in his own country. The self-consciousness of the American artist is something we shall have to get over. Sherwood wanted us to get over it, for he was not the type who liked being exceptional; he was no precious artist who rejoiced in the superiority of his own sensibilities. He was surprised and he did not understand it but he knew that it was wrong to regard native products as unnatural. He was a story-teller, and what lumber camp had ever been without one? James Stephens used to say that the time of Ireland's fall dates from the first day when a poet was asked to pay for his drinks in a pub. Could a poet ever get into a bar in this country with any degree of personal safety if it was known that he was a poet? Assuredly, we shall have to change all that, if we are to grow up to our own capabilities. We shall have to make this country the kind of place that Sherwood thought it could become; for while he knew its shortcomings and felt the need for improvement, he loved it beyond anything. We shall have to take pride in our artists and acknowledge the extent of our dependence upon them, if we are to gain from them the advantage of a mature culture.

Sherwood from time to time had contemplated many vast projects. He was going to write a history of the Civil War; when he died he was working on a large volume of memoirs. He was all devoted to the future and not at all confined to the past, despite the large measure of oblivion which his later work had cost him. In the United States the artist must earn the love and gratitude of the people each time he does something. Nothing remains over for the man who has made a contribution from the admiration which was bestowed upon him at the time; he must perform his miracle again and again. But the forgetfulness did not oppress Sherwood beyond recall. When he died he was on the way to South America both to reap some adulation, which was no more than his due, and to look toward a continent which everyone thought was to count for a great deal in the world.

Sherwood Anderson was more and less than a literary man. His good work is inconsiderable in bulk and distinctly minor, but filled with an inestimably precious magic; it will survive. But he was more than a writer in that he was also a seer. He called our attention to the things which never die, things which might disappear for a while but must reappear again in the future of which the prophet speaks. He was prophetic of the reappearance of the artist in the greater America that is to come.

XVI

EDUCATION

AN ONTOLOGICAL PHILOSOPHY OF EDUCATION

There are some topics so seldom treated by philosophers that a professional can very nearly make his reputation outside his own field merely by dabbling in any one of them. Among these topics are religion, jurisprudence, and education. Now the corollary happens too often that the philosopher with a deserved reputation among professionals is seldom taken seriously when he turns to the philosophy of education. So we have the unfortunate situation of educational philosophers with nothing to say and philosophers in education to whom no one listens. This situation must not be allowed to discourage the truly earnest workers. It is possible to make the greatest of claims in theory and still to hope that, because the methods of translation into concrete applications have been indicated, if there is any residue of value lurking here, something will be done in practice.

From one point of view, education proper is the acquisition of existing knowledge on the principles of rhetoric. Rhetoric is the theory of communication. The theory of education is a branch of pure rhetoric; the practice of education, applied rhetoric. Rhetoric, like most secondary theories with a field of application, is suspended in a sort of limbo between metaphysics, on the one hand, and practical states of affairs, on the other. It must have the character of a deduction from ontology and epistemology, and it must be susceptible of serving as the conclusion to a series of inductions from actual practice. Thus continual checking in both directions is indicated; a difficult task, when we take into consideration that we are dealing with three areas in which changes are taking place.

The aim of the following pages is to set the problem, present the difficulties, and then offer a constructive hypothesis, ending with some suggestions as to how such a proposal could be put into practice.

THEORY OF UNLEARNING

For most young persons, education does not start at the beginning but in the middle. No matter at what stage formal learning is initiated, a great deal of damage has already been done. For we shall usually find that we are dealing, not with ignorance, but with false knowledge, with accepted errors and half-truths. If we take into consideration the usual procedures of education, we have to face additional difficulties instead of enlightenment. For education often reassures the ignorant by intensifying the ignorance. The less we know, the more certainly do we impart it to others. The result is not knowledge but absolute beliefs; the frozen procedures of side-tracked attention lead to the squirrel cages of deflected inquiry. In a small way, we learn to play games; in a large way, we adopt ritual cycles, e.g., religions without the concept of progress.

Most people, in other words, young as well as old, do not approach formal education with inviting ignorance but with their ignorance and its limited virtues already lost to them. Very young children ask the fundamental questions which suggest a purity of ignorance. They want to know such things as who is God and how far space extends. We hypocrites have answers ready for them. And so they lose their ignorance; grow up in a bewildering maze of formulas which are intended to satisfy them; marry; and enter the rat race of paying taxes, running for streetcars, reading the funny papers, getting to the office, shaving, and the myriad other ways of conforming to the set practices of their society. This is not the stage of wisdom and knowledge; it is merely the stage of ignorance lost.

Due to the marvels of modern universal education, most people have been trained for a life to be led in this limbo. They eke out their anomalous existence somewhere between the abstract and the concrete. Common experience is not a base line, it is a compromise, inherited in average form; the shreds of ancient knowledge and wisdom worn away at the edges by a constant rubbing against mediocrity. For intensification has come in two directions: The artists have genuine experience of concrete objects, the product of high concentration for many years; and the mathematicians and empirical scientists know what it means to move among abstractions. But the education most people receive prepares them for neither.

Historically speaking, the peasants were accustomed to dealing with concrete particulars, and the scholars with abstractions. This took place at a fairly common-sense level, however, in both cases. The extraordinary progress in mathematics and in empirical science, if not in all of the arts, has penetrated to deeper levels of analysis and has left the bulk of the population far behind. For them we have invented a new kind of thing: mass half-education. We have produced an exceedingly large population which has lost contact with the concrete particulars of the illiterate but which has not succeeded in gaining a familiarity with the abstractions afforded by the erudite.

Mass man today never reaches up to the logical structures of mathematics, physics, and metaphysics, while he has lost the ability to get down to the intensive cultivation of the active, concrete world. He has, in other words, forsaken the cultivation of his feelings without having the reward of an increased cultivation of his reason. He lives in an unreal world especially created for him by the popular press, the Hollywood movies, the big radio programs, the popular books (such as detective novels and sodden, sentimental, historical romances). Ignorance indeed has been lost in this stage of education which is yet the fate of so many that the customs and institutions of the western world have hardened around it.

A few, a very few, persons struggle on past their education and into a third stage which, for want of a better phrase, we may name "ignorance regained." Here a caution is necessary. Knowledge is power, and power is ethically neutral. The first use of a newly acquired power is its misuse. The airplane bombed in war before it carried passengers in peace, high-speed printing produces the yellow press, and soap operas are the chief ornaments of the radio. But these abuses are not inherent in the media. We cannot blame the power, only the errors which have led to its misuse. The way out, then, is not down to the primitive. We should not fall back on candlelight when the electric power fails but rather perfect the electrical system so that it will not break down. The road to the romantic past is closed; we must look forward to the true cultivation and the proper functioning of the new instruments for mass education which we in the western world have acquired. Hence, ignorance regained is not a phrase to describe a fashionable sort of primitivism. It absorbs rather than denies the techniques we have acquired.

Ignorance regained consists in the attitude of inquiry which has at its command the instruments of controlled imagination and developed logic against the background of a greater experience with fact, reluctant to accept any knowledge as final except the tools of reason and the passion for the search. Some of those who acquire this faculty are to be found among the personnel of the arts, the sciences, and philosophy. The task of the theory of education, then, is how to disclose the formal principles of theory and the interpretations of procedure which will produce these results in more students. Put otherwise, how are we to substitute aids for obstacles, the questions for the answers, the methods of research for the absolute truth?

At first glance, we appear to be cautioning skepticism; but such is not the case. It is the ignorant and the stupid and the slow whose minds are storehouses of beliefs. The intelligent know how to think and to judge; hence, a belief has a harder time getting into their minds. The process of education requires as much effort and time to unlearn the wrong beliefs as it does to indoctrinate the right ones. It is the certainty of beliefs which must be placed under attack, for the fear of false knowledge is the beginning of wisdom. Skepticism is a stage in the process of unlearning, not an end in the pursuit of knowledge. We should not accept dogma—this is what we have been saying; but we cannot remain skeptics. Socrates did not teach skepticism; he taught the limits of ignorance and assumed the existence of a true knowledge which he hoped to find, and at least intended to seek on very nearly religious grounds. The alternative to these errors in procedure is to acknowledge that the search for truth is asymptotic. The pursuit of knowledge is always a matter of approach, for we can believe that there is such a thing as the truth without thinking that we have it or even that we are very close to finding it. We are obliged, then, to employ the techniques of the asymptote, and we shall be surprised to find that they are somewhat complicated. Before we can proceed with such techniques, however, we shall have to study the nature of belief as important to the theory of unlearning.

THEORY OF BELIEF

The mind is a more complex affair than was once supposed. Indeed, so difficult is the whole business that it is no longer fashionable to refer to it as an entity but only to point to the integration of its parts in a process. Awareness is the traditional name for this entity, though behavior is the more recent one; while the unconscious is presently represented only by its malfunctioning. Other departments pertinent to our purpose must be introduced: There is memory, for instance, whose current surrogates are recall, recognition, and relearning. We shall have need here to direct attention mainly to a more recent philosophical and anthropological theory dealing with the positive content of the unconscious. Behavior in terms of responses to the stimuli set up by propositions and by combinations of propositions has yet to be sufficiently explored. It so happens that human cultures, being more or less consistent structures, exhibit in their details the implicit deductions from hidden axioms. The cultures are permeated through and through with the influence of the axioms, so that to live in the culture, to grow up in it, is to absorb the axioms without ever once becoming aware of them. The deeper the level of the unconscious, the more primitive the logical level of the structural proposition represented by belief, so that as we endeavor to think through to the elements of the unconscious, we penetrate past deductions, reach lower than theorems, and finally get down to the layer of the axioms themselves. In the sense that these are common to all individual members of a culture, they are social. Erroneous deductions may be private and individual, but the axiom-set is public.

It is also ontological, and by "ontological" here is meant concerned with basic value systems. We shall use the term "ontology" as the positive and constructive answers to metaphysical problems. Here, then, at the level of unconsciously held beliefs resides that profoundest of beliefs, the belief in what is real. By "real" here we shall mean the immediate object of the true. No human can live among his fellows for any length of time and share their interests and activities without holding in common with them some beliefs about the ultimate nature of things. These beliefs may be implicit rather than explicit, but they dominate most surely every one of our thoughts and actions; and the less we are aware of them, the more they are effective. They are the axioms dictating action. The culturally prevalent, implicit, dominant ontology is the greatest force in the life of every individual.

Most people do not do any more abstract thinking than is absolutely necessary for their simple needs; but each of us feels, if not all equally profoundly, and everyone engages in action. Unconscious beliefs are contained as consequences more clearly in feelings and actions than they are in the expression of conscious thoughts. So it is at the level of feeling and action that we readily find the phenomenon of the implicit, dominant ontology. A man may assert one belief and, under the pressure of crisis, act in the spirit of another. When we act from feeling, we act from the springs of unconscious belief. Our beliefs, so to speak, betray themselves in feelings and in actions, but they never appear candidly as what they are, and their axiomatic nature is well concealed.

The acquisition of the axioms takes place early in life. It is not absorbed at any one moment nor by any single process. We accept beliefs from our way of life, from our parents, friends, and teachers, from all contacts with other persons, and also with the folkways and artifacts of the culture of which we are to be a part. The formalization of the process of axiom-acquisition is a topic to be undertaken somewhat later in the discussion. Here we shall be concerned only with the situation as it confronts the educator. By the time formal education begins at any advanced stage, it is already late. Who can yet determine how soon we adopt those beliefs of which we are so unconscious that we question the sanity of any who may wish to examine them? Yet, all further education is in terms of those beliefs and must reckon with them.

We have praised reason only at the conscious level and feelings only at the unconscious. And this has led us to note that principles are held at the unconscious level as well, so that the reasons which underlie the conscious feelings must also be reckoned with; but there is more to the problem than that. The trouble with education in this connection may have been that it has operated in terms of an imperfect analysis of reason. It may have allowed people to be taught how to draw conclusions from axioms but not how to question axioms. Now here is an effective field of inquiry. It happens that this sort of education for reasoning may have bad effects as well as good ones. When Hitler came into power the German nation was one of the most highly educated in the world. Thus, the Germans were able to follow the logic of Naziism, once they accepted its axioms, with all the deadly deducibility that education for reasoning could bestow. The questioning of axioms is not a simple affair of reasoning; it involves some knowledge of ontology as well as of logic.

The proper kind of education, then, must consist in the eliciting of contradictions in the matter of unconsciously held beliefs, to demonstrate elements of untenability in the implicit, dominant ontology. Only when this has been done have we prepared a student for the ready reception of material furnished by the agreement between logic and fact. For to convince him that he holds contradictions is to render his present beliefs untenable and thus to put him in the way of examining others along with them.

Here, of course, we have reached the boundaries of philosophy. The professional philosophers have their own difficulties. To make the implicit explicit, to choose between alternative ontologies (including the consideration of anti-ontological positions), to seek to discover what they themselves believe (in contrast to what at first they may think they believe), and, finally, to seek to discover the truth about such matters is to be confronted with a set of almost hopeless tasks. Yet this is where education begins, not where it ends. We do not have to be in possession of more than a small part of the truth in order to know something of the method by which it might be pursued. The techniques of the asymptote are the limits of the ontological field, suggested by empirical data and defined by logical structure. Such knowledge can never be more than probabilistic, and our approach to it, tentative, exploratory, and inquisitive; and the more profound the level at which our investigations are made, the more this holds true.

THEORY OF LEARNING

The theory of education ought to have two broad divisions. The first of these might be a deduction from the theory of knowledge (epistemology). The educational process would follow theoretically from the tentatively accepted principles as to how we can know. Learning, considered in this connection, is the disciplined method of control whereby we utilize the knowledge process. The second is a deduction from the theory of reality (ontology). The educational process would follow theoretically also from the tentatively accepted body of knowledge as to what there is to be known. Learning, considered in this connection, is the disciplined method of control whereby we utilize the process of inquiry into being. In this section we must try to sketch a theory of knowledge and to give some implications to education; in the next section, to perform the same service for the theory of reality. But before we can consider the formal type of learning which this advanced stage represents, we shall be obliged to consider some earlier, yet very important, preliminary stages. Learning will be considered under three broad subdivisions: (a) preformal learning, (b) informal learning, and finally (c) formal learning.

Preformal Learning

Preformal learning is ontogenetic. We are dealing with the development of the individual as a matter of capacity. Maturation is the first indication that there are definite stages in such development. Apart from theories of inherent knowledge, such as anamnesis, the capacity for the holding of knowledge is a definite preparation for its acquisition. A mind, before knowledge, is a definite capacity, a possibility of sheer awareness. Here, no doubt, heredity plays a role; from the remote recapitulation of phylogenetic patterns to the nearer immediate antecedents from grandparents down, certain excellences of physiological equipment are handed on which are at present largely a matter of guesswork. What is it that makes one child brighter than another? Better coupling of the neurons, smoother pathways across synapses, faster connections within the hypothalamus? This will be a matter for physiology some day to decide. But that differences do exist in the degree of ability to acquire knowledge and to manipulate it once acquired, there can be little doubt, even though these differences are difficult to measure and, indeed, cannot be accurately measured by means of any existing techniques.

The mind, we shall venture at this point, is a certain capacity to acquire knowledge, to hold it, and to use it. It must be that, in addition to maturation and other ontogenetic and phylogenetic factors, there are also the accidents of chance encounters with the environment. The brain of the infant develops from birth, but he also lives in the world and has interactions with it. Thus, there arise individual peculiarities and differences quite apart from those originally present. These differences, together with the total inheritance, produce a perspective. No two individual perspectives are alike, though all largely overlap.

It would be difficult, if not impossible, to say when the perspectives become influenced by belief. Most certainly, beliefs do begin at the earliest moments. Perspectives are formed by the awareness that, for the subject, there are objects among the data of experience. We have, then, separate occasions for the development of perspectives which are phenomenological, and beliefs which are ontological. The ontological categories do not, as Kant insisted, prevent us from experiencing the real world; but, like binoculars, by intensifying our vision, they also narrow it and determine what part of the real world we shall experience. Very soon we understand that what we believe in comes to us through a perspective. Thus, there arises the notion of an implicit, dominant ontology which delimits the capacity it helps to provide.

Sheer awareness has its own structure. It has also its own selected environment. Obviously, any actual thing—in this case any organism—is affected by the total environment. But it is aware from its perspective of a more limited area, which we shall call the available environment. To this area it devotes a certain alertness, a low-grade sensitivity which is invoked when attending to something, the mildest of disturbances. Stimulus at this level is a matter of mere exposure; and response, one of elementary awareness. The structure of awareness is so primitive that the individual is, so to speak, helpless in the hands of the data and can only respond with surprise to the novelty inherent in every act of experience. The preformal development of the capacity for learning comes to this: The organism in its occupancy of a perspective, in virtue of its equipment, undertakes to be the more sensitive end-term in the relation with the environment and to store as images and generals the products of their interaction.

Informal Learning

We shall examine informal learning on the assumption that it is generally of three kinds, (a) ordinary living encounters, (b) encounters with inconsistency in knowledge held, and (c) problem-solving.

Ordinary Living Encounters. The most rudimentary kind of informal learning issues from feelings of attraction or repulsion for elements encountered in experience. Feelings of pleasure or pain could be the primary sources. Feelings of pleasure lead to attraction in the service of the desire for repetition. These feelings eventually take the crude form of imitation, which is perhaps the earliest version of learning. Feelings of repulsion are initiated in the same way, namely as a matter of encounters with resistance in experience, as the lowest variety of pain. Contrary perceptions are one instance of this resistance, since difficulty of this sort is an obstacle. Plato thought that such, indeed, was the origin of all thought.

Imitation is more active than any response produced by resistance, but the beginnings of planned activity in learning come with trial-and-error. Here we are still in the province of informal learning, but we are approaching the borders. We now sample the environment with a view to discovering whether the feelings received will be pleasurable or painful, with the anticipation only that they will tend toward the one or the other. This kind of learning still survives, although less and less, in higher types of formal learning. There is no doubt a large, logical element in trial and error. We seek to find whether the portions of the environment we encounter will prove compatible or will conflict with our feelings. This is the element which the higher types of learning have sought to save.

Encounters with Inconsistency in Knowledge Held. We have a more rigorous variety of the use of logic in the inspection of knowledge already acquired. The judgment of the inadequacy of knowledge held requires some logical estimation. We perceive a shortcoming in what we believe we know as contrasted with what we continue to experience. Logic operates on mere experience, but not to the extent to which it does when we shift our attention altogether with an increase in knowledge. Here contradiction is the only kind of resistance which it is possible to encounter. Such an event constitutes a way of learning, for it tells us that what we know is badly known or that, to some extent, it consists in false knowledge. For the first time we are leaning on purely logical elements in the learning process. Hitherto, logic had been an adjunctive component of sensory elements encountered in experience. The experience of inconsistency, while requiring more acute perceptions, is still an experience. Only now our sensations tell us of more than sensory elements; these can in fact be discriminated only with the aid of the perception of relations. Logical relations are part of the product of sense experience. We get the tools along with the raw materials and then work over the one with the other.

Problem-solving. Problem-solving must still be classified as informal learning so long as we do not employ established techniques. Let us say that in the course of our experience we have encountered obstacles; these are either of an empirical nature, such as are found among the elements of the external world, or of a logical nature, and located among the relations of our knowledge. Further, we recognize in these obstacles a generic property; we see that from time to time we shall encounter similar difficulties, or else we comprehend that the problem is of the kind that will allow us time for its solving. Thus, we are formalized in our learning procedure to a much greater extent than formerly. Problem-solving can become established as a practice, and it can lead to discovery. In problem-solving, reason begins to assume a dominance over feeling, and we are led on toward more disciplined techniques. We have, in fact, reached the borders of formal learning.

Formal Learning

There are in problem-solving some notions of generality, as contained, for instance, in what we might call an anticipation of similarity in respect to further problems yet to arise. In this anticipation there are feelings of inadequacy—the awareness of ignorance, for instance, carrying with it the necessity for training. We know that we need to acquire the equipment in terms of which future problems can be properly and perhaps successfully met. The fear of failure may often lead to the awareness of ignorance, and this is where formal learning begins.

The training, of which we have spoken, is in two parts, (a) the theoretical and (b) the practical. The theoretical training consists in learning systems of ideas and values; the practical, in deriving inferences from performance. The first category should be turned over to theorists who have worked out the techniques of communication. The second is a matter of getting hold of the principles of conditioning, after the methods followed by Pavlov and the later behaviorists.

Theoretical Training. Theoretical learning is dependent upon systems of communication. This in turn will here be subdivided into (1) communication proper, involving the learning of systems of ideas, and (2) persuasion, involving the apprehension of values.

1. Communication is conducted in terms of languages. Languages are systems of ideas expressed as sets of signs or symbols. Any system of knowledge is also a system of communication: There would be no point in the abstract organization of our knowledge of theoretical physics were there no hope of communicating it. We may, then, consider all knowledge systems as communication systems in at least one of their aspects, although this function may be indirect as well as direct. Here we are concerned with language systems which operate in terms of direct communication. Direct communication takes place by means of denotative signs: signs that directly refer to logical meanings.

There are three, and only three, kinds of signs, and as a consequence three kinds of language according to the predominant sign in use in each of them. There are axial languages, logical languages, and actual-object languages, depending upon whether value-signs, logical signs (i.e., universals or generals), or actual-object signs (i.e., particulars or individuals) prevail. There is no such thing in practice as a pure language, that is, one involving only one kind of sign, yet there are languages containing marked amounts of one element clearly dominant over the others. Most of the great world languages are combinations of all three kinds of pure language. We must remember that, although language is the greatest of cultural tools and, therefore, systematic to some extent, still it is not entirely a planned affair. We can separate out the elements.

Axial languages were devised to communicate values. The language of art is an example of an axial language. Axial languages are employed in indirect communication. There is no such thing as a direct communication of the values. Analogy is one of the more popular tools of the axial language. It seems easier for critics to talk about one art in the terms of another, when they wish to transfer feelings. Theology is another province where axial languages are employed.

Logical languages were devised to communicate abstract structures, laws, all denotative material. The language of mathematics is the prototype of all logical languages. It works by analysis, by division, and with reference to fixed principles. The bare bones of the technique of communication show through here so plainly that the deductive method itself becomes part of the communication. In logic, we communicate the system of communication as well as the subject matter communicated.

Actual-object languages were devised to communicate matters of fact. They cannot escape the use of universal signs nor the connotations dragged along by images, but their main concern is with actual situations. They work chiefly by definite description. Journalistic language and descriptive history are good examples of the use of actual-object languages.

It should perhaps be emphasized that the analysis of the elements of the three languages is difficult, because sometimes a word represents one language in one context and another in another. Consider the word "red" in three sentences. "The river ran red with blood," "Red lies near one end of the spectrum," and "The color of this tie I am wearing is red." The first red is an axial term, the second a logical term, and the third an actual-object term. The determination of what language is being employed depends upon the references involved and can sometimes be made from context. More often than not, the situation is a mixed one, containing several types of elements.

It is important to note in the theory of education that not all formal communication is in terms of written or spoken sign languages. Gestures become standardized, too. Any movement may be meaningful and even be established as such. Hence, they may become part of formal communication. The material to be communicated and the means of communication interact; ideas determine language positively, and language determines ideas negatively. Communication is on its way to becoming an empirical science, due to the work of Shannon, Wiener, and others. Eventually this could exercise an effect upon the theory of education.

2. Persuasion is a kind of communication. Just as communication proper was concerned with formal languages, including the axial language, so persuasion is concerned with indirect communication by means of values. It hopes to play upon the emotions to achieve the feeling of conviction. Communication proper works with the axial language, but in direct terms. Indirect communication or persuasion works with all languages as though they were axial languages. For it seeks to communicate the apprehension of values, which is always a matter of connotation rather than of denotation.

Here we must revert to our theory of belief, to the process of awareness. Education-wise, the important part of belief was asserted to be unconscious. We shall now be dealing with opinion, which is deliberately held belief. We are unaware of most of our beliefs, but those of which we are aware are the objects of scrutiny. We can be conscious of only one belief at a time, and this is because we wish to examine it. A belief in the presence of awareness, then, is named opinion; for it is scheduled to be more firmly accepted or else to be rejected. Hence, the stage of opinion is for a proposition a temporary one.

For the purposes of persuasion, then, a language is required. Underlying any language is an implicit ontology. It is to be found imbedded in the syntax, even if nowhere else, and so takes effect indirectly. Thus, the process of persuasion lurks in the implicit assumption carried by the didactic languages which are employed in direct communication. To enunciate any statement of sufficient importance is to convey presuppositions unwittingly; in this way we often say more than we wish to say, more, for that matter, than we know. Thus, in employing languages emotively, we are almost certain to go beyond the immediate question at hand.

To say that persuasion communicates values and so obtains its effects by indirection is not to say that it is irrational, however. We would do well to distinguish the reasons which conflict with certain of the feelings from those which are in accord with them. There is no inherent opposition between values and logic; the achievement of harmony is more a matter of arrangement. Any change of opinion finally requires reasons; it can never be brought about arbitrarily. Belief and doubt stand equally in need of arguments which at least appear to be cogent. Now it is true that, in the act of persuasion, reasons are often disguised or submerged; they may be heavily cloaked with emotion or presented in some other wrapping. No persons exist so stupid or dull as not to require reasons for changing their opinions.

Persuasion aims to communicate a change of views. This means introducing a doubt as to the truth of the proposition held which it is proposed to alter. We are all a mass of prejudices. Everyone has an opinion on every topic of which he takes cognizance; and if we admit the existence of unconscious belief, then he has opinions, too, on many topics of which he does not take cognizance. We would never deliberately change an opinion did we not acquire some misgivings as to the position we already held. Now this is never done gladly and on a purely logical basis; a change always involves some doubt together with its feelings of discomfort, often amounting to pain. Thus, persuasion involves a negative factor. Self-persuasion includes the cultivation of doubt in one's self. We must learn to doubt what we hold to be valid and true, if only in order to test its validity and truth.

Completed acts of persuasion never have been brought about by gradual stages but always take place by jumps. Looking back, we see that we have been influenced often by means of a number of small, imperceptible steps; but the actual change in opinion was a sudden affair of which perhaps we had been unaware. There is no middle ground between believing in one thing and coming to accept its contradictory, and so the shift from one to the other cannot take place by degrees. The process is no less decisive for being unobtrusive and unobserved. Reason operates with a silent method yet one which is none the less sure.

Practical Training. Formal learning as it stems from the practical business of deriving inferences from performance is an unsteady affair which presents obstacles when we attempt to reduce it to a set of principles. Conditioning experiments introduce controls into the matter of experience, and this does tell us something about how the mechanism of stimulus and response operates. But in the matter of relating experience to education, particularly with respect to formal learning, such efforts do not go far enough. The reason is that in the process of education we are dealing, not merely with controlled acts of experience, but with the whole human being. The lessons of experience must be different for an illiterate and for an intellectual. The same stimulus would not meet with the same response since the capabilities of receiving stimuli are not equal in all cases. Moreover, within each group, the lessons differ from individual to individual. What Hegel made out of his experience is quite distinct from what Kant did.

The analysis of experience in these terms reveals not one philosophy, as the philosophers of experience maintain, but many. There must be as many philosophies of experience as there are philosophers having experiences, and this includes even those who deny the cogency of experience in philosophy. Therefore, we are forced back into a more primitive analysis, we cannot talk about the lessons of experience until we have examined the structure of experience. Experience has a structure and a content. The content comes through experience but has little otherwise to do with it. In the analysis of experience, then, we discover, not what it contains, but what it is. Experience is an act, and it involves presuppositions, data, and a perspective. It is in the act that the transfer of content occurs. If by a supposed analysis we remove these, we would find ourselves left with the parts of the mechanism. It would soon be discovered, then, that the presuppositions are not logically derived from experience, since it is in terms of them that experience can take place. It would be discovered also that the data do not depend upon the experience through which their existence is first revealed. And, finally, it would be discovered that the perspective taken up was arbitrary. In this way, the analysis of experience would lead to philosophical implications which in the end have no more than an accidental connection with experience. Thus, we find that it is not experience which is our starting point but the formal structure of inquiry, a more active and at the same time a more logical affair. The principles of scientific method are being studied now under the general heading of the technique of discovery, and this should open up some very important areas to inquiry.

THEORY OF THE KNOWN

Education might be defined as the formal communication of the known. It is always a tentative affair, due to the limitations of both the methods of acquisition and the knowledge acquired. Neither process nor content should ever be regarded as more than interim affairs, for knowledge is hypothetical and only the inquiry itself is stable. Yet a theory of the known is involved, as is some organization of knowledge. This is not the place in which to undertake a survey of the whole of knowledge, though some such survey is a necessary part of every philosophy of education. It is obviously the task of the philosopher of education to get into communicable form the material which he wishes to pass on. Now since all learning takes place in terms of universals and in some order or system, it is by communicating the structure of knowledge that we render much more accessible the transfer of its details. We want to know the limits of what there is to be known, and we cannot become acquainted with the limits without some familiarity with the structure of knowledge—the form, so to speak, in which it is to be passed on.

The last structure of the whole of knowledge was the one erected by Aristotle. With certain adjustments and revisions, we employ his ideas in our practice today. The Greeks did not have experimental science, not, at least, in the modern sense of controlled experiments at deep levels of analysis, where instruments become necessary and final mathematical formulations are made of empirical findings. But such activities have been squeezed into the Aristotelian synthesis—not, of course, without some difficulty. The modern departments of a university are no longer viable. They were set up along Aristotelian lines, but, in terms of the rapid advances of modern knowledge, they have become unserviceable. Recategorization is seriously required. New crosslines of research, fresh fields of inquiry, indicate sorely needed realignments.

Several examples taken from actual practice will make this clear. Recent work in the foundations of mathematics has shown that mathematics is an extension of logic. Logic is a branch of philosophy, so that those departments require reordering. Mathematics has outgrown its origins, yet the relationship ought to be recognized and kept in the foreground. Proximity would serve this purpose well.

Again, history, philosophy, and other social studies have been pursued in a very disorganized fashion. It is becoming increasingly obvious that the parent study is social anthropology, the theory of human cultures. It has its structural subdivision in philosophy, particularly in ontology and ethics, and its developmental subdivision in history. The special social studies, such as economics and politics, must be ranged in their places, with economics as the most fundamental.

The entire business of knowledge is part of the philosophy of culture. There is no body of world knowledge which everyone is trying more or less successfully to learn. Knowledge for all cultures is not fixed or static, and the whole enterprise must be kept more or less permanently subject to revision. The implicit, dominant ontology governs what shall be worth knowing. It governs, also, how that knowledge shall be employed in practice. Since cultures are in a sense ontologies which have been applied within the limits of the given environment, the role of knowledge in a culture is a function of the orientation of that culture. Thus, knowledge differs from culture to culture and from time to time within a culture. The unconscious belief in what is real, which anchors the ontology in the culture, does not remain the same but changes very slowly. It is these very elusive influences which are the more powerful for being unacknowledged, these implicit consistencies which are the more pervasive for seeming to have no fixed center, which must be the most carefully analyzed and represented in fixed principles.

We might pause to regard one important recent shift in this area, where the belief in reality is beyond the conscious control of all of us. This is in the implicit, dominant ontology, the basic value system, of the western culture, particularly as it is reflected in the United States. Here the departure from the system of ideas established in the name of Aristotle has already been accomplished, though as yet its effects are not everywhere felt. The main shift has been one from substance to function. It can be seen in physics, for instance, in the transformation of matter into energy; it can be seen in logic in the replacement of the old subject-predicate logic by a relational logic; in legal theory by the conception of property as dynamic function substituting for that of property as static substance; and in politics by the shift from a negative democracy to a positive democracy, in which the government which operates effectively is not only the least possible but also the most necessary.

It is evident that a new synthesis is emerging, a new structure of the whole of knowledge which will not leave any department unaffected. What is actually involved is a transfer of social belief and practice from the philosophy of nominalism to that of a modified Platonic realism, underground perturbations certain to cause convulsive movements in the whole of the culture. To explore its various ramifications, therefore, requires the utmost in sensitivity and in breadth of investigative techniques. Knowledge is a by-product of the search for truth; and systems of knowledge are thrown up—and left behind—by every new and concerted cultural effort of inquiry. It is one task of the philosophy of education to call the turn on every large-scale movement in the fundamental theory of knowledge in a given culture.

There are four, and at the present time only four, grand routes of inquiry. These are: art, religion, philosophy, and science. To these must be added, in a secondary manner, practical techniques. All but one of these are so old that we know nothing of their beginnings. The arts and religion are very ancient, and very possibly philosophy is, too. The last of the four, science, at least in the sense we now intend by the term, which is experimental science, is no older than the seventeenth century. There may well be others of which we, as yet, are unaware. In historical development, now one and now another of these fields sparks the remainder. Education must reckon with all four, but only to the extent to which they possess positive communicable knowledge and viable methods of inquiry.

Nothing ought to be taught publicly and formally except in areas where there is agreement among rational investigators. This would require us to leave the teaching of the established, institutionalized religions to others and to concentrate on the problems of religion, including the whole spectrum of comparative religion from dogmatism to atheism. Each of the others has its own educative value. The sciences teach expermental skills and instrumental techniques. The arts teach the intensification of the senses. Philosophy, including mathematics, teaches rational facility in coping with formal structures. The scientist is more dextrous in dealing with empirical material, the artist is more sensitive, while the philosopher and the mathematician move more easily at the level of high abstractions.

Each of these broad fields has, of course, its own principles and practices. Thus, education cannot afford to omit any, though such omissions have been and continue to be the custom. Socrates thought that the acquisition of moral perfection was the goal of education. In the *Laws* we are told that education is instruction in perfect virtue. Today we see education more in terms of the use of technical facilities. Both are important. Knowledge is virtue, Socrates asserted, and this can be maintained even after we have broadened knowledge to include manual skills which he would never have admitted.

CONCRETE PROPOSALS

The next step will be to suggest some applications which are relevant to the foregoing pages. These will be in terms of concrete problems in education, first as to methods, next as to program, and finally as to institutions.

Methods

The methodology of teaching properly centers on the theory of the relation of theory to practice. This, it should be noted, is a theory and not a practice, even where the theory emphasizes practice over theory.

The oldest and best established tradition of education is the one which concentrates on the principles. The compulsory learning of what is believed in the way of principles is the form this tradition has taken. It has been perhaps longest the custom to teach abstract principles, on the assumption that, with a thorough grounding in their knowledge, students could easily work out for themselves how to apply them. The difficulties and limitations of this conception became evident with the increase in exact knowledge. For application itself now requires a whole new set of principles which have to do with the techniques of practice. These *modus operandi* formulas relate the highly abstract principles to the concrete practices, both of which are powerless without them.

When the reaction occasioned by the new technical knowledge occurred, it went to the other extreme, as might have been expected. Principles were to be abandoned altogether, on the plea that they were not fixed or absolute, and practices were to be taught for their own sake. Progressive education is as old as Plato but looks unfamiliar in its modern dress. Some authorities in progressive education teach that we must learn by doing, or, as some wit put it, by the theory of doing, which is translated in the modern progressive schools into "learn by watching someone else do." The assumption is that the best way to learn theory is through practice and that then, having the practice, we will not need the theory. This is an Aristotelian type of confusion of theory with practice, of which, by the way, Aristotle himself would never have been guilty. If we are to learn by doing, that should be the end of formal education: We ought merely to go out and do. For there is nothing more to learn about learning by doing; there is only the doing.

What saves progressive education at this point is that the theory of the relation of theory to practice is not a practice after all but a theory. As such, of course, it may be practiced, and we can tell in advance that such practice must prove sterile. It issued, as a matter of fact, in the improvised curriculum. Presumably the theory would be all right for a society which planned to be static, which wanted to hang on but not to advance. If education is a reorganization of experience, then we might well ask, "Experience in terms of what?" The philosophy of experience obviously teaches in terms of things as they are. It does not teach about them as they ought to be or as they might be. So much the worse, then, for certainly things are not what they ought to be. If we cannot strive even on ideal grounds to make the next generation better than ourselves, then all is lost and there is no reason to hope.

The reaction to Dewey's anti-intellectual influence has been comparatively mild but potentially dangerous. It has consisted in traditionalism with a vengeance. We are to return to metaphysics but not to speculative metaphysics; instead, we are offered an official and dogmatic metaphysics. Now if there is anything less stimulating to education than an anti-intellectual philosophy, it is an authoritative intellectual philosophy; for both are the enemies of reason. Curiously, both Dewey and the Thomists ban free speculation in metaphysics; the former by declaring metaphysics useless, the latter by making a single metaphysics official. No one seeks knowledge of the truth who thinks he has found it, and in the field of metaphysics the competing systems and theories have exploratory value to the extent to which they differ. No enterprise can hope to stay alive that does not keep its doors open. To pronounce one metaphysics imperative is as damaging to the open-mindedness which true education requires as to ostracize metaphysics altogether in terms of an unacknowledged and implicit metaphysics. Curiously, although the one emphasizes principles and the other practice, in neither case is there any progress in the knowledge of principles, and in both cases practice suffers.

Program

May there not be a third alternative to the traditional emphasis on principles and the modern proffered alternative of an emphasis on practice? For after all, what is practice if not the practice of some theory? The best type of education must teach theory as though it did not need applications (which in fact it does not, except for the sake of practice), but also it must teach practice as though it did need theory (which in fact it does). We ought to abandon the old devotion to principles alone and the new devotion to practice alone and substitute the technical practice of abstract theory. It should be made clear that we are dealing with three types of items: principles, practices, and the relations between them. These distinctions can be maintained effectively only if we teach principles and practices separately, for only things which are properly distinguished can be properly related.

When we come to apply our new doctrine to education, we find that we must begin with the problem as it faces us. Children are knowledgeable early. In terms of what their information consists, it can be said, not that they do not know, but that they know too much. At this point we ought to apply the procedure which would follow from the theory of unlearning. Children are ethically neutral until taught otherwise. Here we should have to introduce the range of the field together with some classic proposals in it. We have learned from progressive education that the young must have whatever freedom and pleasures they can be given consonant with the establishment of good habit-patterns. The behaviorists have not sufficiently generalized Pavlov's work. Establishing habit-patterns with respect to principles as well as practices is more important for students than allowing them to express themselves. Only, in contrast to what has been the most recent custom, there ought to be available an objective orientation.

It will not be enough to weave the warp of principles with the woof of practice unless we can also show that there is a whole cloth emerging. We want students to know without the aid of some dogmatism, such as an official philosophy or theology, that there is a consistency of such truths and applications as they already accept. Here there lurk dangers, unless the conception of an open system is carried along. Plato was right when he said that the end of education is insight into the harmony of the cosmos. But we must remember that, as knowledge increases, all schemes of harmony are apt to reveal their deficiencies; we think we know the whole until we learn more about the parts and learn, too, about more parts. Hence, along with the notion of integration must come that of toleration.

In the humble sense, a teacher ought finally to be one who imparts tentative knowledge and especially acts as a leader in inquiry, a more or less blind, yet intuitive, guide to the discovery of the truth. He must believe that there are truths to be known and that events, however unfavorable, cannot affect the order of their importance. The arch example is that of Comenius, the seventeenth-century Moravian textbook writer and educator, who was exiled innumerable times from various places of refuge and had the trial of watching his home burned three times in as many countries. He taught that culture was general in Europe, that truth was independent of nationality, and that humanity was universal in its good qualities. Those who exhibit the same fortitude as his but do so in terms of some set of national or institutional truths hold their mission otherwise. They have not yet learned Comenius' lesson.

Institutions

The function of the university is the communication and the advancement of inquiry into culture. Methods of teaching have their chosen content and their institutional expression. When institutions are the means by which we pass on the knowledge of the whole, we get procedures which tend to be oppressive. This can be equally damaging when it is fragmented; what undergraduate today understands anything about the connection between his various studies? The problem is how to institutionalize education conceived as the by-product of the search for truth without doing harm to the existing knowledge of principles.

There has developed gradually through recent decades an unsatisfactory type of education in our institutions of higher learning. Apart from the special empirical sciences (which stress practice over theory), most teaching is a matter of pat formulas and takes place in a limbo which lies inconveniently between theory and practice. Highly abstract speculations are neglected, along with highly concrete data, for a set of maxims and short cuts to procedures, a mixture which contains no wisdom and no genuine experiences. These practical maxims are not to be confused with the *modus operandi* principles which were mentioned in the last section. They could be better labeled as conformist devices for avoiding experiences. They are techniques for escaping from the novelty and the variety and the freshness which are life itself.

To counter these baffling influences, and in terms of the new synthesis, we might state and illustrate the aims of education as follows:

The aims of education are threefold. These are to build right thought, right feeling, and right action.

First, as to right thought: The direction of learning seems to be toward increasing objectification. First, the child thinks only of himself, then of the object in relation to himself, and finally of the object in relation to other objects. Formal education ought to follow closely and take advantage of this feature of maturation. Thus far, as we have seen, the unconscious is represented only by its malfunctioning, and objectivity is merely mental hygiene. But here is the place for the formalization of the process of axiom-acquisition, a task of gigantic proportions.

Second, as to right feeling: In elementary education, this is learning what to dislike. Pleasure is a matter of faring well and of being happy, but these must come from pursuing the best and achieving the good. Speculative morality is the standard here, leading to the same unconscious axiomatic belief with which right thought is concerned, because the holding of knowledge is a matter of feeling and, therefore, the holding of right knowledge is the basis of right feeling. We must acquire, then, the proper quality standards and a prejudice in favor of the excellent. We shall not understand how to possess knowledge until we have learned to live with a faith in its limitations.

Third, as to right action: Learning to live with faith in the limitations of knowledge is carried out in practice by the techniques of the asymptote. The development from the point of maturation ought to be met with habit-patterns to form character, which is the strength to pursue aims. We are accustomed to witnessing this only in the army and the church, not in the arts and the sciences where it might equally well exist. Discipline teaches character if it is provided with reasons and does not exist merely for its own sake. Herbart was correct in supposing that discipline should be introduced into education from the beginning and that the child not be left free to find his own path of development, as Rousseau had advocated.

Formal education ought to start, then, with the fundamental tools of communication and soon advance to the theoretical knowledge of some branch of philosophy and of mathematics, the working knowledge of one fine art, and the empirical knowledge of one laboratory science. In addition, and with a view to the larger integration, a year spent in another culture, in order to gain some perspective, ought to be an indispensable part of everyone's preparation. It is the only possible coign of vantage from which to understand the culture in which we live. The foreign culture selected for this purpose ought to be as diverse as possible from one's own.

The university could well be divided according to the triad of aims of education. Instead of the present departments in the liberal-arts college, we would have: (1) a division of philosophy and mathematics, (2) a division of the fine arts (including literature), and (3) a division of the empirical sciences, the latter subdivided into (a) formal (pure) sciences and (b) applied (practical) techniques.

A Division of Philosophy and Mathematics. It would be the business of the division of philosophy and mathematics primarily to teach ease and familiarity of movement among formal structures. This would mean to acquire the memory of a set of abstractions and then to get to know them; for it is only after knowing some such set that it becomes possible to learn about it. There are definite degrees in the acquisition of knowledge, and learning is only the first of them. Knowing something well means knowing it a long time, as Joubert pointed out; and Santayana indicates the penumbral areas with which we can become familiar, starting from a grasp of the core area. A knowledge of the history of philosophy and familiarity with logical principles and the manipulation of mathematical systems would be taught primarily from this point of view.

A Division of the Fine Arts. It would be the primary task of the division of the arts to educate the senses. It is possible to acquire an increased intensity of sense experience through the cultivation of a deliberate naïveté of perception. Through the practice of painting, for instance, the student can actually learn to see things as they are and not as he conceived them to be; he can learn to see through eyes as free as possible of preconceptions. Thus, painting requires unlearning before learning, as all other learning processes do. The arts would be available to any student, and one art would be required of each. He would have to know something of the theory of the fine arts and have a working, studio experience of at least one of them. It is not sufficiently known that the fine arts are supreme extensions of crafts and that some technical education in the craft is a necessary prerequisite to the practice of the art. Painters must know something about pigments as well as perspectives; composers must be familiar with the range and tonal quality of the instruments for which they propose to write, as well as the principles of harmony and counterpoint. Technique and knowledge of the craft is the necessary but of course not the sufficient cause for the production of an artist. It is the communicable part.

A Division of Empirical Sciences: Formal. It would be the task of the empirical sciences to teach the depths of structure inherent in the empirical world. The student would have to know something of the principles of scientific method and have a working laboratory experience with at least one of them. In addition to a firsthand knowledge acquired in the field or laboratory, a student in the division of the sciences ought to know something of the relation between the sciences, on the one hand, and the logic and presuppositions of the method, on the other. He ought to be familiar, in other words, with the area surrounding his science as well as with the details within it.

The department of applied mathematics would be located here. These would be matters of pure knowledge, not of practical experience.

A Division of Empirical Sciences: Applied Techniques. The subdivision of the practical techniques would teach the application of the pure sciences, a field which has its own abstract formulas. Education ought to prepare a man to meet his civilized problems as well as the uneducated man meets his relatively simpler problems; the needs are brought into play along with the formulas for satisfying them. It would also teach communication of skills, the practical techniques which have not yet been elevated into the position of a science or of an art, such as cooking, clothing, etc.

Finally, before leaving the student up in the air, there would be a finishing course in the learning which lies at the level of enlightened common sense but which for the present has no other home. It is not now taught as a matter of principles but is either handed on by word of mouth or learned as a matter of what is sometimes bitter experience. The subject matter here would be devoted to actually existing conditions. Some of these change from time to time while others do not. As an example of the former, there is the fact that most corporation lawyers spend a great deal of their time helping their clients legitimately to reduce their tax burden. As an example of the latter, there is the fact that most women are irritable during their menstrual period, and due allowance should be made for this emotional turmoil.

What a University Ought To Be. Hutchins deserves credit for having advertised in this country the fundamental question of what a university ought to be. His answer and Adler's, of course, are wrong, but American education owes him this: Any other answer will have to be made at the high level of the question he has asked. Fortunately, the question had already been answered in Europe. A university ought to be a community of capable teachers who are trained enthusiasts, backed by productive scholars. Some of the best teachers and textbook writers are those who do not see all the implications; they are able to turn a limitation into an institutional advantage. The greatest of the productive scholars ought not to be made to teach any more than they care to. They ought to be left alone, and the efforts of a skeleton administrative staff concentrated on the welfare and discipline of the student body.

A SLOWER PACE FOR SUPERIOR STUDENTS

The philosophers of history are fond of distinguishing between "culture" and "civilization" meaning by "culture" the small originative and productive social unit, and by "civilization" the large social organization. Cultures, so to speak, produce culture out of all proportion to their size; whereas civilizations spread culture but do not produce it.

The archetype for this distinction is, of course, Greece and Rome. Greece was extraordinarily productive, while Rome produced very little beyond law, good roads, and cement. Most of the arts of Rome are poor imitations of the arts of Greece, and there are no Roman philosophers at all. Translations and imitations abound.

It has been pointed out that a comparison can be made with our own times. European culture has given rise to two civilizations, those of the United States and of Soviet Russia. And there are parallels in many other ways. Europe, like Greece, has produced its geniuses; the United States and Soviet Russia, like Rome, have undertaken the spread of European culture. As is usual in the transition from culture to civilization, the emphasis has shifted from theoretical concerns to matters of the most immediate usefulness. Not science but applied science and technology, not works of the highest literary genius, but the greatest number of English professors, not new political ideas but the widest spread of economic benefits to the masses (and in the case of the United States, of political benefits as well).

In education we see the same forces at work: not education of a high quality but education of a tremendous quantity, more young people educated yet few if any receiving an education of the highest type. The situation is a logical consequence of the type of civilization in which it occurs. In the United States, practical issues are respected and applied science pursued, but the dependence of these on theoretical issues and pure science is not well understood. The anti-intellectual and isolationist trends persist even though the conditions which produced them no longer prevail. We no longer have the pioneers' work to do: the forest has been cut down and our cities are built. We no longer can enjoy the security of separation from the rest of the world since the invention of the airplane and—worse still—the guided missile. We shall have to abandon these attitudes as no longer realistic; we need to take our place in the world and acknowledge the leadership of the productive intellectual.

But we cannot any longer depend upon imports for this commodity. Europe is tired after its wars, economically insolvent and energetically bankrupt, no longer independent of the giants between which it finds itself caught. We shall have to develop our own scientists—yes, and our own artists—if these are to exist in our country. Our very survival may depend upon them. How are we to do this in a way which shall enable us to excel and to maintain our leadership in the world?

There are obstacles to the achievement of such a goal. The anti-intellectual philosophy, and the mass half-education that goes along with it, stand in the way. The rational and the theoretical, to say nothing of the artistic, are very much derogated in favor of the practical. Our universities reflect this by becoming trade schools in which technology and applied science are more important than pure science.

The mass half-education produced by our instructional industry has a curious result. We educate our citizens away from the cultivation of their senses, so that they no longer have the ability to perceive which was their natural gift as children and which is the professional equipment of farmers and fishermen. Yet we do not educate them up to the skilful manipulation—and discovery—of abstract structures, such as those of mathematics and philosophy. The result is that they fall between these two able extremes and plunge into a world of formulas, advertising slogans, manufactured fiction, and conventional customs. They no longer are able to judge anything for themselves and they seek comfort and protection in conformity—what the British sociologists have called the ad-mass. Now the ad-mass is a large mass and calls for manipulation.

Hence the great need for administrators and institutional men generally. In a word, our universities are run like business corporations and run so well that they do not produce the desired effects at all.

We shall have to alter these methods and their results if we are to produce leaders. But leadership of the desired sort does not consist merely nor primarily in having the right kind of political or institutional administrators. Like all civilizations, ours does this sort of thing very well. But so did Rome; there is little doubt that Rome far surpassed Greece at the business of social organization. What it could not do was to produce artists and scientists. With certain rare exceptions we have not done so, either. Have we a physicist of the class of Planck and Einstein, a psychologist of the class of Pavlov and Freud, a biologist of the class of Pasteur, a mathematician of the class of Gauss? If, for instance, one were to name the greatest novelists of recent decades, the list would have to include Gorky, Proust, and Joyce. Have we a name that could be added to this list? We have excellent writers: Hemingway, Caldwell, Steinbeck, Faulkner. Yet not one of these has produced work of the level of the Europeans.

The problem becomes that of learning how to produce producers. Our colleges are already excellently organized for the mass production of college degrees for which they were designed. But we are not so well prepared to produce educated men who can themselves produce original science and art. The society which functions so efficiently is actually an obstacle to the kind of quality production we now wish to add to it. The stretch-out system will make Buicks faster but it will not make Rolls-Royces at any rate, fast or slow.

If we are to produce producers, if we are not to waste talents, then what we need in education is not a stretch-out system but a slow-down system. Doing a quality job does not consist in doing a quantity job faster. Quality in education has the dimension of depth, whereas quantity is a surface measurement. Quantity means: how much have you memorized, how many formulas have you learned to call on, how many techniques have you mastered? Quality means: how deeply do you understand, how excellent is your knowledge, to what depths of penetration does your comprehension reach? Not how many credits do you have or even what grade average did you maintain but how fully do you comprehend what you have learned, how thoroughly are you able to think for yourself?

We need to ask our superior students to do what other students are doing but to do these same things a lot slower. We want them to think, we want the ideas to be assimilated. We want these men and women to germinate—and eventually to produce. Such results are not obtained by speeding up a mass production system nor by passing the superior students along the belt-line a little more quickly than the others. To state more concretely what such a program would mean is to defeat it at the very beginning. In the interest of origination, an atmosphere would have to be brought into existence in which it would occasion no surprise. Only the kind of men who understand what this means are capable of engendering it.

If we are not careful with our superior students, they will turn into average professors, that is to say, they will hand on to successive generations what has been handed down to them from the past. In lieu of a contribution of their own, which is allegedly required of them in the present system of higher education in the United States, they will crank out the usual number of journal articles, complete with assorted footnotes, that passes for scholarship. Scholarship *sui generis* is not origination. What we need in order to gain and maintain world leadership in all fields is original production. There is such a thing as original scholarship, but it is never at the level of original production. Gilbert Murray's study of *Aeschylus* is a magnificent performance, but even so it is not at the level of Aeschylus. The disease of the second-rate scholar consists in supposing that the existence of Aeschylus can be justified only as the basis for such a study. To be second-rate, one does not strive to be first-rate and fail; instead one deliberately strives to be second-rate and succeeds. The principles of second-ratedness are twofold: never be the first to do anything, and never do anything as well as it can be done. In short, the principles call for the failure of originality as well as the absence of excellence.

To guide superior students we need a superior faculty. To produce both, we need leisure. Nothing as profound as the production of original work in the arts and sciences was ever done in a hurry. Nature is everywhere dense and, as Heraclitus said, likes to hide. To discover what has not yet been disclosed requires knowledge, of course, but also a withdrawal and an invited contemplation. What is needed is an atmosphere of freedom in an institution devoted to transparent facilitation where the superior student can humbly pursue his studies at his own pace.

To develop artists and scientists, we shall have to cultivate the kind of attitude and interest which cannot at the present time be measured by intelligence or aptitude tests, punched on cards, or encoded. We ought, perhaps, to give up in this connection the ideal of the well-rounded man, the institutional man, and substitute the man of straight-line accomplishment. By mass-production methods it is possible to get only mass-production results. Individuals who are dealt with in terms of statistics will behave like statistics. It is time to remind ourselves that history remembers few administrators. To produce superior students, we must plan in superior ways, and these are more often indirect than direct. The talents of the superior student can only be encouraged, they cannot be compelled or disciplined. And this requires a comprehension of what is involved that surpasses in subtlety and complexity the methods recently introduced and presently employed.

What is at stake is nothing less than our safety as a nation. We cannot hope to excel in the competition with Soviet Russia by working with ideas identical with those they are using. We shall have to learn how to invest in the ideals of the future as much as we are willing to contribute to the exigencies of the present. And this means, in the case of education, building into the superior student the qualities which will make him capable of advancing the culture while others do the work of maintaining it.

COLLEGE TEACHING

In no profession, I suppose, is one more frequently asked to give advice than in teaching. In my own office, two or three times a week I can count on having a serious conversation with a serious young man about the perennially serious question: What am I going to do with my life? And the most difficult conversations of all are those about a career in college teaching. It is hard to hold a mirror to yourself in the best of times. And it is even harder when the scene is changing as rapidly as it is in college today.

THE PICTURE HAS CHANGED

Not too long ago, going into college teaching was roughly equivalent to entering a monastery or the ministry. You were propelled by a burning desire akin to religious fervor and, of course, you automatically eschewed all earthly rewards. At its best, this system produced men devoted to teaching or research—men who had given up a very great deal for the privilege. At its worst—and this was by and large the way things did actually happen—it produced a disillusioned, cynical, disappointed faculty. And good and bad alike lived with Shaw's dictum ringing in their ears: Those who can, do; those who can't, teach. It was also a proposition to which most people would have agreed. Furthermore, the universities themselves seemingly were committed to preserving the best of the past and preventing any additions in the future. They were not trying to be first rate and failing; they were trying to be second rate and succeeding.

Then World War II came, and in education, as in so many other things, a dispensation ended and a new order began gradually (because education moves very slowly and ponderously, like an old rhinoceros) to assume dominance.

Mostly it had to do with that mushroom-shaped cloud which appeared first on the Nevada desert and then over the skies of Japan. A German refugee at Princeton with the air and appearance of a tired old circus lion suddenly seemed one of the most powerful men in the world. With him appeared a new group, the users of this unbelievable power. Since this new elite was composed largely of academicians, their fame and success reflected on the rest of the college world. Everyone began to realize that the mild mannered college professor with the tweed suit and the horn rimmed glasses might just after all pack a terrific punch.

The winds of change were blowing. The technological element of our culture increased rapidly, at a pace few would have thought possible. New television sets; new data processing machines; new calculating machines; new mass production methods called automation, where machines instead of men ran production lines; and a hundred other gadgets all requiring tending. These instruments had accompanying technologies and called for more and more men with technical training.

Then there was that population explosion which everyone now knows about. More babies that would soon need a higher education. More teachers at the college level. Almost overnight college changed from a place you went to, if you felt like it, to a place where attendance was a privilege for which you competed. Education, not only undergraduate but increasingly graduate, became a must in an increasingly complex world.

All three of these developments raised the standards and the needs of the universities. They expanded rapidly in every way, both in prestige and in quantity, and the combined private and public institutions began a job that was never done before and is not yet being done anywhere in the world except in the United States: the job of giving to everyone who wants it a higher education. The result is that there are now some 1,400 accredited colleges and universities.[1] They have to be funded and staffed

---

[1] As of fall, 1962, there were 1,174 colleges and universities and 304 junior colleges which were regionally accredited in our fifty states, according to the North Central Association of Colleges and Secondary Schools.

to educate the three and a half million students who now attend college, and to prepare for the two and a half or three million additional students who will appear by 1970.

The business of universities is big business, and the university professor, a scarce and precious commodity. Today, the nation's colleges and universities have some 272,000 people of professional standing. In 1959-60 universities and colleges hired slightly over 10,000 new teachers, people who had not previously been in education. During the next ten years those institutions estimate that they will have to hire some 336,000 more people. And the trained man (the one with a Ph.D. in his chosen field) is going to be in very short supply. In the United States we are producing about 9,600 doctorates a year. Of this number only some sixty per cent enter the field of education. So we will produce 58,000 qualified people to fill the space for 336,000. Already there are vacancies cropping up on the statistic sheets. For 1960-61, for example, eleven state universities reported vacancies in their English staffs, as did five non-public universities. Forty state universities reported vacancies in their math staffs, as did thirty-one private universities. On the over-all, about half the educational institutions reported unfilled positions in one or more teaching fields.

What this augurs for the future of the universities as a whole is perhaps not so encouraging—but what it says to the individual is: there will be no shortage of jobs in the foreseeable future.

THE WAY AN ACADEMIC CAREER BEGINS
. . . AND CONTINUES

What happens then after commencement, after the velvet-striped Ph.D. robe has been returned to the rental agency and the protected, isolated graduate school days are finished? The fledgling moves on to a college or university (most usually *not* the one from which he has just graduated) with the rank of instructor or assistant professor. The difference in rank is determined by a great many things—his previous teaching experience (most graduates have had some), his recommendations, and how badly the school wants to get him.

He will have been flown out to have a look at his new job—tourist class; he is at the moment only a very junior member. He will have met the head of the department (and the dean, too, if the college is a small one) for a formal courtesy interview—after all, his record has already told them as much as they probably want to know. He will have been taken for a stroll through the campus and to lunch with other junior members of the department.

He probably will find himself teaching twelve hours (or four classes a week) which, with the proper amount of preparation and paper work, is the equivalent of a forty hour week. As a junior man he will have the last choice of class times, and so will most likely find himself teaching the eight o'clock classes. His textbooks probably will have been selected by the department or a state committee, and he will have some course outline given to him, some specific amount of work to cover. He will probably also have his classes visited once or twice by the ranking members of his department. They are trying to see what they have bought and whether his one year contract will be renewed. Incidentally, the amount of supervision decreases very rapidly. Experienced men have in most cases a great deal of freedom, both as to the choice of courses they will teach and how they will teach them.

The beginning instructor will try very hard to find the time to do some writing or research on his own, knowing that his advancement can be helped immeasurably if he can show himself to be a young man with ideas. He will have the distinctly unpleasant knowledge that he is the low man on the totem pole, with the assistant professors, associate professors, full professors, associate deans, assistant deans, and deans towering above him. He will keep his eyes and ears open, if he is an able young man, and say nothing, though he will sit in the faculty cafeteria and the faculty lounge and hear a great variety of gossip. He will begin to learn to sift it carefully for its few grains of truth. He will also try to avoid the palace revolutions and the squabbles that rage through any school.

And he will find himself beginning to engage in the most fascinating of games: watching the academic human comedy. There is the campus politician, the man who rises rapidly with a minimum of talent just by knowing where the bodies are buried, by flattering the right individuals at the right time, and by doing what seems expected. (He would be a more entertaining sight were he not a threat to the more talented.) There are the little gray folk, withered like leaves, spiritually if not physically, left over from the school's less ambitious past—patient souls secure within the tenure system, waiting to retire. There are the empire builders, the department heads who seem to get more than their share of the university budget in order to build a bigger department than the size and structure of the school warrants. There are the deans of all ranks, the teachers who have given up teaching for the lure of the higher paid administrative jobs. There is the most harried man of all—the dean of students; it is his job to handle student troubles, which include everything from parking tickets to simple pranks after a football game to robbery and murder.

And the young instructor will hear repeated so often that he may come to believe it: Publish or perish. There is no doubt that writing or research will help a man in his career, but any young man who has the wits to look about will see a great many eminent professors who have published practically nothing. In many cases, the last word they wrote was the final word in their Ph.D. dissertation. Some are academic politicians. Some are superb teachers, able to inspire almost fanatical devotion in their students. Some are superb organizers whose talent consists in their ability to select good men, to hire them, and to keep them. This is the sort of man who will brag to his friends, as I have heard one do, "I've just hired a man who's forgotten more than I'll ever know."

REMUNERATIONS AND COMPENSATIONS

It's quite conventional to say that the college professors are woefully underpaid. And so they are—for the job they do. But it is possible to make a decent, modest living. The latest information on college salaries is reported by the AAUP, a sort of teachers' union. They report that the average salary for an instructor is $5,800; for an assistant professor, $7,144; for an associate professor, $8,545; for a professor, $11,268. And the averages are steadily rising, from two hundred dollars more than last year's at the lowest level to nearly seven hundred at the highest. Contrary to popular belief, the averages at private (other than church-related) colleges and universities are a bit higher than those at their public counterparts. Teachers' colleges tend to average well below both. Averages, however, can be misleading. An able man will make more, whatever his field. In general the sciences are more highly paid than the humanities.

There are other financial possibilities. One is textbook writing. Every college teacher in the country is showered with requests to do a textbook, to do a teaching anthology. If he does, and if he is lucky, he will find that he has improved his income considerably. And for the scientist, in addition to the possibility of textbook royalties there is the possibility that he might stumble upon something in the course of his research which is of industrial significance.

But of course no man goes into college teaching for the money. He does it because it offers him the sort of life he likes, the sort of life that is becoming increasingly difficult to find today. Colleges are havens for the non-conformists. The oddball professor, the universities have learned, may also be a genius, while those who do painstakingly and conscientiously everything they are supposed to do rarely do anything else. Nowhere in the country is there the variety of opinion, dress, and personality that there is on a university faculty. And it is not just an uneasy truce. It is a real way of life.

Occasionally this gives you situations which are absolutely ridiculous. A small southern school (segregated) possesses a senior faculty man who is an avowed Marxist ... One young associate professor slept on his desk for two nights because he was working on a job and felt that going home was not worth the trouble. The only thing his fellow faculty members found strange was that such a tall man should be *able* to sleep on a desk ... Then there was the brilliant young instructor who was discovered on Easter Sunday morning walking stark naked down an empty canal. Since the bottom of the canal was littered with broken bottles, he was cut so badly that he had to be taken to a hospital before he could be transferred to a mental institution. The verdict on him the next day in the faculty lounge was merely that he had always seemed "nervous."

At its worst this attitude is a kind of stoical stolidness, an indifference to others. At its best it is a kind of genuine tolerance and acceptance of others as they are.

At its best, too, this tolerance extends to the students. Most teachers, in my experience, have a sympathy, an understanding, and a genuine patience. No teacher worth his salt will quietly let a promising student be thrown out because of an idiotic prank or even a psychiatric difficulty, and most times school authorities will overlook a great deal if a man's teachers are behind him.

Unless one has the patience to cope with some students' peculiar behavior one had better not become a teacher. There will be a lot of it. If I look back to my last academic year, I remember a steady stream of incidents, all of them demanding extra attention and time. There was the student who, with reversed collar, went knocking on doors at night in the university neighborhood, admonishing sleepy citizens to "repent before it is too late." Another student stole a double mattress—he had an immediate and pressing need of it. Another refused to attend class in one particular building "because it was aesthetically unsatisfying." Still another turned in some thirty fire alarms before he was apprehended. I've even discussed suicide with rejected suitors, finally convincing them that the presence of seven hundred other girls in a college a half mile away was sufficient inducement for living. I've been asked in the remarkable words of one of my more pompous students to find "a suitable female of my intellectual level and interest, of marriageable age." He is, I believe, still a bachelor.

Teaching at the college level takes patience, a sense of humor, and the non-committal expression of a good poker player.

The career of a faculty man is as varied as he cares to make it. His teaching load will start at fifteen or twelve hours (depending on the policy of his school) and will reduce as he advances. He may find himself eventually a full professor teaching six hours, or three, or none. In the latter case he has in reality shifted his field from teaching to research. There are plenty of opportunities for that, particularly in the sciences, if he is able and so inclined.

Teaching is also one of the most traveled of professions. There are very many opportunities—grants, fellowships, sabbaticals, transfers of all sorts—all of them giving the faculty freedom to see the world and to exchange ideas with foreign colleagues. Several years ago, from four and a half to six per cent of full-time faculty were reported on leave. As a matter of fact, a resourceful man can arrange things so that he is almost never on his home campus and yet retains his position and salary.

I don't think I've ever known a faculty member (once past the first two junior levels) to be fired for incompetence. In fact, I don't know what one would have to do to get fired if one just taught one's classes— barring certain political statements, and not always that. Life in a college is just exactly what you choose to make it. I've known men to bumble through their days, giving ten- or fifteen-year-old lectures they first heard in graduate school, following big league sports on the faculty lounge's color set. And I've known men to do the equivalent of three full-time jobs: teaching, research, writing and lecturing. A man can be a hermit, spending every free moment dug into library or laboratory, completely uninterested in the world around him. Or he can be as social as he pleases. The university apparently has room for it all.

XVII

SCHOLARSHIP

INVITATION TO LEARNING:
PLATO'S *APOLOGY*,
A BROADCAST DISCUSSION

Bryson: There have been a number of books which attempted to draw out of the legal process of judging a man's life—putting him up against accusations, unfair, unjust, unreasonable—the quality of what he did. The *Apology* was an attempt, on the part of Plato, to tell why he thought Socrates was as great a man as he was.

Morris: I think it was an attempt, Mr. Bryson, to justify the way of life and the philosophy of a teacher in a work of art. The teacher, and the philosopher, was at that time under great obloquy; he had been put to death as an enemy of the state. Plato tried to show why that condemnation was unjust through a presentation of the man's character and teaching.

Bryson: And that in the form of not a reported, but an imaginary, defense of Socrates by himself.

Feibleman: Yes, Mr. Bryson, this is not, after all, a dialogue. It's really a monologue. It's a part of a transcript of a court trial.

Bryson: That is, it seems to be.

Feibleman: It seems to be. It's set up as that—with interruptions from the court, and so on. It's set up that way, as you say, but it wouldn't have been set up that way, probably, by Xenophon, with the idealistic coloring that this has. It's an idealized version. After all, you know the authenticity of the details has been questioned.

Bryson: Well, Plato, of course is trying to do it as it should have been done.

Morris: That's right.

Bryson: But what is it that Socrates was defending himself against? What is the essence of the accusation against Socrates?

Feibleman: Well, the accusation, Mr. Bryson, was twofold. Socrates starts out by defending himself against a general charge of the corruption of youth. He was an evil-doer, according to the general charge.

Bryson: Corrupting youth how, Mr. Feibleman?

Feibleman: By trying to make the worse cause appear the better.

Bryson: That is, he was making sophistical reasoners out of youth?

Feibleman: He was trying to investigate their beliefs. And where beliefs are established by the state, this is a sort of treason. That was the charge, at any rate.

Bryson: And yet, don't we generally think of Athens at that time— more than two thousand years ago, at the beginning of her decline, but at the end of her great Periclean period—don't we think of Athens as a fairly free country? Isn't that where we get some of our ideas of freedom?

Feibleman: We think of it that way, Mr. Bryson, but there were the gods, after all. And the specific charge here is that he did not accept the gods that the state accepted.

Bryson: He corrupted youth and he was impious?

Feibleman: He was impious—an atheist.

Morris: He also was charged with making investigations in physics, which, of course, he did not. But what he was really guilty of, according to his accusers, was questioning conventional beliefs. And they were the beliefs of a business civilization, not the beliefs of what we consider a classical Greek civilization.

Bryson: Well, let's examine that business civilization a moment later. You say that he questioned the beliefs but not the physical universe. Do you mean that it was in Athens—and perhaps now—safer for a philosopher to invent a bomb that could destroy civilization than it was to invent an idea that might destroy the accepted gods?

Morris: I think it's certainly safer to invent a bomb that might destroy civilization than to question whether the use of that bomb is justified.

Bryson: So it's the ethical philosopher who gets into trouble.

Morris: The ethical philosopher who always gets into trouble.

Feibleman: Actually, Mr. Morris, Socrates was not impious, as he said. He believed in God; but he believed in the right of the individual to find God in his own way, and to search for the knowledge of God. What he was attacking, always, was the certainty of other men's beliefs —not their right to have the beliefs, but the certainty of their beliefs.

Bryson: Is that because he wanted to make people unhappy about their failure to find the truth, Mr. Feibleman? What's the essence of a man who says that everybody must be skeptical—using that word in its mildest sense?

Feibleman: I think, Mr. Bryson, that no true happiness, no ultimate happiness can be founded upon false knowledge.

Bryson: You're quoting Socrates now?

Feibleman: I'm quoting Socrates.

Bryson: But you believe it.

Feibleman: Absolutely! This is my Bible, you know. This is the New Testament of the man of good will; and I like to think myself a man of good will. Socrates did not believe in atheism at all. He was a theist. But he believed in the right of the individual. He believed in what Bertrand Russell has called "the free man's worship"—in the right of the individual to search for God in his own way, and to search for true knowledge in his own way—in a world where true knowledge is a pretty rare thing, much rarer than we think.

Morris: He was interested, actually, in wisdom, rather than in fact. And his definition of knowledge was, I think, that he was more interested in being, in conduct, than he was in achievement or results.

Feibleman: Well, Mr. Morris, don't you think that wisdom and fact are not irreconcilable? We could perhaps bring them together in what the scientists call evidence. He didn't want to accept beliefs without evidence. Of course, there are two kinds of evidence—not only factual evidence but rational evidence. And rational evidence is called wisdom.

Bryson: Let me be a weak imitator of Socrates here, Mr. Feibleman, and push this a little bit further. You say that he wanted every man to search for the truth. Did he think that every man searching for the truth would come to some truth that he, Socrates, had in his possession?

Feibleman: No! He said, Mr. Bryson, that he didn't teach any specific truth.

Bryson: So it wasn't inquiry of him that he wanted?

Feibleman: Oh no! No, he taught ignorance. He taught the limits of ignorance.

Bryson: What do you mean by that?

Feibleman: I mean that he tried to show how little we know. He said that the only advantage which he had over other men was that he knew what he didn't know; whereas other people thought they had knowledge. And the beginning of wisdom is the fear of false knowledge. That's the beginning.

Morris: Well, didn't he also teach the fact that you had to examine the meaning of what you believed?

Bryson: And what you said.

Morris: And what you said. And that your conduct should square with your profession, after you knew what your profession really meant.

Bryson: But, Mr. Morris, what's the end of this attitude? Where does a lifelong belief in its validity as a way of existing and a way of finding some kind of personal salvation lead you? My skepticism is not directed against Socrates; but I want to know what skepticism does to you. If you always search, do you ever find?

Morris: Yes, you would find as you went along.

Bryson: You mean you find the way to the next step?

Morris: The way to the next step, and you find the truth that is tomorrow's truth in the light of tomorrow's experience—as William James said, I think.

Feibleman: Well, Mr. Morris, if I may quote another friend of ours —not William James but Charles Peirce—the enemy of true knowledge is absolutism. What we find are tentative truths; and the only absolute we can accept—I think this is the big point in Socrates—the only absolute that we can accept is reason itself and man's ability to reason.

Bryson: Going back then to Athens, Mr. Feibleman, what you and Mr. Morris are saying is that the reason why Socrates was condemned to death was because he said there is no final resting place for reason. You go on looking. That makes people awfully uncomfortable.

Feibleman: It makes them uncomfortable. Whatever is good for them makes them uncomfortable, frequently. Education always makes people uncomfortable.

Morris: Like the dentist!

Feibleman: It's real, yes. The dentist is not a fellow who makes you feel very good.

Bryson: I know, but there's a point at which the dentist stops, Mr. Feibleman. That's a good Socratic analogy. The dentist finally plugs the hole in your tooth, or he pulls your tooth, and then you're quits. Then you go home. You don't have to bother about it for a while. Socrates evidently never quit.

Morris: There's no point at which reason stops, that's why. The dentist's drill has a terminal point, but reason hasn't. And there's nothing, really, that can be put beyond the limits of inquiry.

Bryson: Then it's a quest without a goal.

Morris: Well, it has a goal.

Bryson: I'm being a man who says that Socrates is just a trouble-maker; he corrupts our youth.

Feibleman: It's a quest for the real goal. The goal is the knowledge of positive reason. After all, would you search for knowledge if you didn't think there was some in the world?

Bryson: That's the question I'm asking.

Feibleman: Well, I don't think it makes any sense—I don't mean your question—I mean the search wouldn't make any sense. You wouldn't search for something you didn't think existed; and you wouldn't search for it either if you were absolutely sure that you already had it. So the position of the inquirer—and for Socrates the man of inquiry is the holy man—is that he believes in what Einstein has so superbly called, "the holy curiosity of inquiry." And you don't have that unless you believe both in your own ignorance and in the true existence of a knowledge which you hope to find, although you can't date it.

Bryson: Is that just sophism?

Morris: No, I don't believe it is. I think that is the cold truth of Socrates' quest. He was in search of what he called virtue, which was the way of life in which your beliefs and your conduct would square, and in which you would practice what you thought.

Bryson: All right. Now, let's go on. Socrates is accused here, not only on the basis of his principles, but also on what he taught other people. Did he say that everyone should live this way?

Feibleman: I think this involves a great democratic point, Mr. Bryson, in an otherwise aristocratic outlook. After all, Plato, you know, was an aristocrat, and the Greeks have been charged with being aristocrats. Karl Marx said the Greeks were children. Well, if they're children, they're the kind of children I want to be. I want to keep the kind of innocence which makes you keep on asking questions the way children ask questions. And the only hope for people is in regaining the kind of innocence that children have.

Bryson: And you think that this is democratic, in the sense that Socrates thought every man could live this way?

Feibleman: Well, he made the point explicitly. He said, "Rich and poor alike may come to me and question me and receive answers."

Bryson: That sounds, Mr. Feibleman, since we're pressing this point, as if Socrates were saying, "Look, I have the truth, but I'm denying it to no man; any Athenian can come to me, rich and poor alike, and I will tell him the truth." Is that what he meant?

Feibleman: No, Mr. Bryson, because he didn't have any truths to tell. As a matter of fact, he recognized the situation very clearly. He said he was a gadfly. He was one who stung you into thinking about fundamental things. And the only thing he had to teach was your right and your ability to reason about the questions which most ultimately and fundamentally concern you, whoever you are.

Morris: Isn't his point there, his phrase that "the unexamined life is worthless"? What he taught you was to examine not your own life, but the life of others and the life of the state. He said a man's first duty was to acquire wisdom, not to acquire wealth or reputation, and his first duty to the state was to examine the state and then only further its interests. His method was his goal.

Bryson: Did he believe, Mr. Morris, that if you thought the state was wrong you could desert it?

Morris: Not that you could desert it, but that you could oppose it. Twice in this *Apology* he points out that unjust decisions which he was ordered to carry out (once by the tyrants and once by the democracy) he refused to carry out.

Feibleman: Ah, but what about this, Mr. Morris? In the end of this so-called dialogue, he considered that the court's decision, that the court's judgment of guilt in his case, was a false judgment. But he insisted upon it being carried out. He made quite a point of it.

Bryson: Yes, and you have two other dialogues, the *Phaedo* and the *Crito,* in which that point is worked out, haven't you, Mr. Feibleman? But going on to the next point here in the *Apology,* doesn't he say that if you live the kind of life which he advocates, this life of inquiry, taking your word, Mr. Feibleman, this life of constant search for the truth— doesn't he say that you are untouchable, that the state cannot really do you any harm, that a wicked man cannot do you harm? Isn't it part of his defense?

Feibleman: Surely!

Bryson: You can't hurt me, he says, I'm a good man.

Feibleman: No harm, he said, can come to a good man either in this life or in the next.

Bryson: That wasn't a very Socratic statement. He doesn't say, "You can't hurt me; I'm a good man." He says, " ... if I'm a good man."

Feibleman: No harm can come to a good man. But he fundamentally believed that he was a good man. At the end of the dialogue, where they're talking about immortality, or, rather, where Socrates is considering the possibility of immortality and what its nature is, he makes the point that he's not worried, because no harm can come to a good man, which would imply that he thinks he is one. And he conceives it in military terms, if you remember. He says a soldier under command does not desert his post, if he's been put at a post. And he conceived the religious thing in military terms. The still, small voice of conscience which never, as he said, told him what to do, but always warned him what not to do, wouldn't let him leave the post where he'd been put, namely, the position of gadfly and inquirer into the truth.

Bryson: Doesn't that lead us, Mr. Feibleman, back to the trial again? He says, when they accuse him of corrupting youth and not believing in the gods, on the contrary, he's teaching youth how to live, and he's teaching the true search for the Good. He does believe that he has a mission. Now, what's the nature of a man who has a mission?

Morris: Well, in the first sense, he's a dedicated creature.

Bryson: That makes him difficult to live with, Mr. Morris.

Morris: Makes him extremely difficult to live with. He is also sure of whatever inner light he has. And he argues, too, for the inner light of other people.

Bryson: "Inner light"—that's a mystical phrase.

Morris: I think he was essentially a mystic who taught reason.

Bryson: A mystic who taught that one must constantly use reason to examine the good life? That he had a mystical reason for doing it?

Morris: I think he did, yes.

Bryson: Makes him a little difficult to understand, doesn't it?

Morris: Well, I think his point is that it wasn't knowledge—knowledge in the sense of factual information—that was going to save the individual or the state; it was the understanding of man's potentialities. And that is a mystical doctrine.

Bryson: Also a great assertion of democracy?

Morris: It's an assertion of democracy, which is a form of mysticism.

Feibleman: He was a prophet, Mr. Morris, wasn't he? He spoke as a prophet. And the prophet is always the enemy of the priest. It's necessary to have prophets dead in order for priests to live on their sayings. You perhaps remember the passage in *The Brothers Karamazov* by Dostoyevsky, when Jesus comes back and the Grand Inquisitor says: "This is a very embarrassing situation. You know, we had this thing all set—and you're going to gum it up for us." So, in a sense, it's always necessary to have prophets dead, and we do what we can about that; we always kill them. And Socrates received the same treatment. He was a prophet, and he had a mission, and he conceived of it in those terms. It's been pointed out that he could have escaped very easily from this thing. He wanted—he asked for—crucifixion.

Bryson: He insisted upon his own martyrdom.

Feibleman: I think the analogy between Socrates in this dialogue and Jesus is very close—very close indeed. He's falsely accused; he is given a trial; he is condemned to death; he is executed—when it's obvious, afterward, to everyone that he was the best man there, the best one present, that his motives were really very great and very unselfish. He's a disinterested man who knows that society can only live by the truth and not by its own half-truths or falsehoods; and exposing the falsehoods by which current societies always live is not a thing that increases your popularity. But it has a good motive, certainly.

Morris: Well, his motive was great, obviously. I think it's easily understood why his trial was brought about, because he was questioning the people who believed that progress is more of the same, more of the *status quo.*

Bryson: He denied that.

Morris: And he denied that. He said progress was change and greater knowledge, greater virtue, greater wisdom all the time. He also was against those intellectual conservatives—who are the Emily Posts of every civilization, who tell you what it is proper to believe.

Bryson: Who were their spokesmen, Mr. Morris? Who spoke for conventionalism as against the prophet, here?

Morris: A minor poet who was outraged because Socrates said that poets frequently spoke without understanding what they meant. And let me say that, as a frequent reviewer, I understand the exasperation, particularly, of any contemporary minor poet whom some critic tries to make intelligible.

Bryson: I thought minor poets had abandoned reason by intention, Mr. Morris.

Morris: No, they may seem to! The other one was a minor politician, and the third one had a personal grudge. He was a tanner who left Athens when the tyrants came with the democracy, but whose son wanted, instead of going into the tannery, I believe, to become an intimate of Socrates and listen to these discussions.

Bryson: He wanted to become a philosopher.

Morris: He wanted to become a philosopher.

Bryson: That's the corruption of youth—turning a good tanner into a philosopher.

Morris: Yes, certainly it's the corruption of youth.

Bryson: Isn't it interesting that in his work of art, as you called it, Mr. Morris, Plato should have chosen those three types: a minor politician, a minor poet, and a minor businessman.

Feibleman: But, as we've said, Mr. Bryson, we've really made the man in this book a scientist, a religious leader, and an artist. And I think he's all three.

Bryson: Well, the platonic Socrates is all three.

Feibleman: Yes, the platonic Socrates. But I return to the one, over the other two. I think the keynote here is religion. And I think it's never been explored. There is in this book the possibility of a finite theology, a true theology which does not go beyond the limits of reason. We've had that sort of thing before, but in very weak form. Here it is very strongly put, and put on a basis on which it can be a developing thing.

Bryson: You're saying, Mr. Feibleman, that Socrates' answer to the problems of Athens, more than two thousand years ago, would do for now?

Feibleman: I think so. I think there's the seed here for a realistic protestantism, what Russell, again, has called "a free man's worship"— a religion based on the individual conscience and not on some externally imposed doctrine of authority of a totalitarian nature of whatever sort.

Bryson: You mean protestantism as a principle?

Feibleman: Protestantism as a set of principles, yes. We have never really established in abstract and dogmatic form the framework of Protestant theology, and we've never given it its full run. It's a powerful thing. It's a very powerful thing. And it doesn't need external sanctions. It doesn't need, in a way, anything beyond the human. To think that the human being needs to find sanction to see God is wrong.

Bryson: Socrates thought so.

Feibleman: Socrates thought so. But all you really need is the human function of reasoning and the desire, the deep desire, in people to know the truth. This is from God.

Bryson: Do you think, then, Mr. Feibleman, that if we followed Socrates' principle we would get away from Socrates' own supernaturalism?

Feibleman: I think we might not stress it as much as it's stressed in organized religions.

Bryson: Would a man then have a mission?

Feibleman: Definitely.

Bryson: Can he be a mystic?

Feibleman: He would be a mystic. He'd have a mission; but he'd conceive it in terms of reason. I profess to find an analogy between Socrates and Gandhi, for instance. Gandhi said, "The only God that I know of is the God of truth." And isn't that in a sense what Socrates is saying here?

Morris: Entirely! He would be in accord with Emerson, who said the over-soul was the God of truth, practically, and that if you were in contact with the over-soul, or what Mr. Huxley today calls the ground, you would be living in accord with the principle of the universe. And that is what Socrates was teaching, it seems to me.

Feibleman: Yes, but Mr. Bryson, I think, is challenging me on the question of the transcendental elements.

Bryson: I'm not challenging you about anything, Mr. Feibleman. But you have gone out on a philosophic limb by saying that, out of Socrates, we could develop a modern type of individualistic approach to religious life, and that we could get rid of supernaturalism. I'm not saying you're wrong. I'm saying that that would have startled Socrates a little bit, because his idea of a mission was something divinely inspired.

Feibleman: Well, I don't want to get rid of the idea of God here. I don't think Socrates got rid of it, and I don't think I would want to get rid of it; but I would want to examine it, and I would want to show how in this dialogue it comes up in evidential form, you see—not in transcendental beliefs, but in evidential form. It comes up in the notion of a still, small voice of conscience; it comes up in the discussion of immortality, at the end, where Socrates makes it very plain that he isn't stating any received notion of immortality but speculating on the possibilities. And there's nothing transcendental about that.

Morris: He was prepared for any possibility, at the end. If you remember, he said: "If death is nothing but an eternal sleep, who would reject it; but if it is, on the other hand, the association with the great who have preceded you into death, who, equally, would reject it—since conversation would be good, and the pursuit of truth could be carried on?"

Feibleman: Yes, he says that the best evidence for God is the motives of a good man. In other words, he doesn't need a transcendental belief, he doesn't need irrationalism, to get belief in God. You can get it from faith and reason.

Bryson: I think he raises that question, Mr. Feibleman, but he raised another question we haven't touched on, which disturbs me—about Socrates as Plato describes him—and that is Socrates' assumption or Socrates' implication that everybody could live his way. Yet the life he described is the life of challenging all things authoritative, the life of speculative ideas, which always make trouble. In other words, he's saying we can all be prophets if we want to be. Well, in what kind of a world could all men be prophets?

Morris: They could be philosophers. We can all be philosophers, rather than prophets.

Bryson: Not go the Socratic length, then, Mr. Morris.

Morris: Only to the degree that you would be a prophet by prophesying to yourself. I don't think he meant that all men could be prophets for the state as a whole.

Bryson: No, that's not quite my point. Did he believe that all men could be prophets to the extent of challenging the beliefs around them?

Morris: Yes.

Bryson: All men?

Morris: All men.

Feibleman: Of course, Mr. Bryson, you can't get along without organization of some kind, in the state or in any other enterprise. But you can have such a thing as a tentative subscription to the existing order—the kind of thing we like to have in America, where you have a debate about a proposed course of action, and you disagree with the final decision but you go along with it; you have a voice in it; and if your voice loses out, you go along with it, but always with the right to criticize it, and to come back and in the end, perhaps, to change it through persuasion.

Bryson: Even if you have to die for it, Mr. Feibleman?

Feibleman: You still go along with it. Socrates did. And I think it's a wonderful picture of the ability of a free man in a democracy to go along and accept a fatality which ends him, while fundamentally, rationally disagreeing with it, and defending his right to disagree with it to the end.

Bryson: He'll accept death, but he won't accept silence.

Morris: Yes. He said he would not desert his mission, though the mission might be discredited and he might be put to death. His notion of inquiry was one that everybody could follow; every man could become a philosopher in that sense.

Feibleman: I think he also said something very important at the end, in a note of prophecy. He said his death would be the seed from which would spring many like him. I find an analogy between this statement and the New Testament statement, if you remember, "except a seed of corn fall to the ground and die, it abideth alone; but if it die, it giveth forth much fruit." In a sense, he's saying the same thing. He says: my crucifixion, my death, really, is going to be the seed of many like me. He is the saint of reason, this man. He's the prophet and saint of reason. And such hope as we have for progress through the scientific method depends upon reason.

Morris: Yes, I think he's the martyr to the cause that we all believe in but that few people practice.

Bryson: Isn't it true, Mr. Morris, that all the great answers to life's predicament are rather too difficult for the average man? The great teachers come and they set forth their great truths; men martyrize them and then find what they have said is great but too difficult to live up to.

REFLECTIONS AFTER WITTGENSTEIN

Every philosophy is like a man speaking a language which he has learned imperfectly. One has to determine just what it is that he wishes to say before one is in a position to decide whether he is right or wrong. In the following pages some lessons are drawn from Wittgenstein's *Philosophical Investigations* which it must be clear he himself would not have approved. It is too late for there to be any danger of subverting his influence. Each of his two books has already given rise to schools; logical positivism has come out of the first and linguistic analysis out of the second. It may be that Wittgenstein himself was not a member of either school. We could at least entertain the hypothesis that *Philosophical Investigations* is an outcome of the *Tractatus Logico-Philosophicus* and not opposed to it. In his second book he has shown a way of getting at the proposals advanced in the first, where "getting at" means literally "getting out of." *Philosophical Investigations* continues the proposition next before the last in the *Tractatus*.

Wittgenstein's *Tractatus* is a systematic ambiguity whose elements are problems. One might say that Wittgenstein began his work by picturing a world of logic, only it is such a world as logic requires. For it soon becomes plain that by logic he means the logical language, that is to say, language (the logically perfect language), and by the world only those features of it which can be depicted in logic. Thus we get the logical aspects of the concrete world and a kind of substantive view of abstractions. The world pitches us up to its representations in logic, while the logical picture not only reflects the world but indicates downward, so to speak, that it does so. In addition to the convention of existential import (which refers only to factual meanings), there is also a logical import to facts. And even so he soon gets away from the world in quest of a logically perfect language. The logic of the language carries that part of the world which it refers to around with it.

Having reached to logic by climbing up on fact, fact is next hauled up, so that we have been prepared for a second book in which the logic of language, and not the world, is the theme. But let us pursue the implications to fact here a little further. The logical import of actual things is as important as (though perhaps no more important than) the existential import of propositions. It is not at all a question of setting up a logic for propositions and then of determining whether the propositions correspond with the relevant segment of actuality. Rather things *say* their logic; the empiricist equipped with his powers of observation and his knowledge of the rules of logic is in a position to listen to what actual things say, and this gives him his correct propositions. Logic, in other words, tells us how language can say what it says correctly; how what is being said can properly represent what being says.

What is set forth here is not Wittgenstein but something of what can be done with Wittgenstein. The following discussion is aimed to develop and present some oblique inferences from Wittgenstein's second published work. When a reader who is located somewhere in the world of abstraction looks at the work of a philosopher who is somewere else, angles of reference are likely to emerge which neither of them had foreseen. Then, too, it often may be that in this case we keep up with the differences only in order to reinforce the similarities. No more apology need be made for the argument except to add that it is hoped that in this way some advances may be the result.

The work is in the main an elaboration of three theses. These are: (1) that philosophy is an activity, not a static set of beliefs; (2) that this activity consists in examining the contents of the natural languages in order to get rid of the false philosophy and so discover the logic by means of which they correspond to reality; and (3) that the categories of philosophy so discovered are again activities (or methods); they are transparent, and we look *through* them rather than *at* them. We may best begin our discussion by considering inferences from these theses taken separately.

1. The aim of philosophy is "to show the fly the way out of the flybottle" (103).[1] The use of the proper description is to get rid of explanation (47); we wish the logic to fit the facts in such a fashion that nothing stands between us and the facts. For a conception is not an object but a grammatical movement. Philosophy is something that we do, not something that we accept or reject. Just what it is that we do, or rather try to do, will be made evident as we proceed.

Meanwhile it may be instructive to point to an analogue. Did not Wittgenstein, Paul Klee and Gertrude Stein employ the same method in philosophy, painting and literature, respectively? Just what this common method is was best stated perhaps in its most general terms by Klee: "It is a great handicap and a great necessity to have to start with the smallest. I want to be as though newborn, knowing nothing absolutely

[1] All references in the text, unless otherwise noted, are to page numbers of the first edition (Oxford 1953, Blackwell).

about Europe; ignoring poets and fashions, to be almost primitive. Then I want to do something very modest; to work out by myself a tiny, formal motif, one that my pencil will be able to hold without any technique. One favorable moment is enough. The little thing is easily and concisely set down. It's already done! It is a tiny but real affair, and some day, through the repetition of such small but original deeds, there will come one work upon which I can really build."[2]

Of Wittgenstein it can be said that he has set a predicament in motion. To suffering epistemologists who feel that the interference of ways of knowing in what is known must of necessity be fatal, Wittgenstein promised a remedy. The therapy he suggested is one that can be practiced only by the patient and is, moreover, one involving a long process. Yet it offers hope at least, and is a method of working our way out of the difficulty in which Kant has reminded us we shall find ourselves. Kant wished us to embrace the forms of intuition and the categories, and to accept bravely the limitations they impose, even though they prevent us from knowing the real object. Wittgenstein wanted us to take notice of the elements of whatever philosophy we hold but only in order to banish them. To learn, in other words, what it is that constitutes our limitations is to be able to work toward getting rid of them and so to approach the real object with the minimum amount of interference.

2. Activity is to play the "language-game" (5). The language-game is also a logic game. Here Wittgenstein is advancing a thesis not too far removed from the viewpoint of Hilbert: "If anyone utters a sentence and *means* or *understands* it he is operating a calculus according to definite rules" (38). We are told explicitly that "logical investigation explores the nature of things.... It takes its rise ... from an urge to understand the basis, or essence, of everything empirical" (42). The activity of philosophy will thus consist in a grammatical investigation to uncover the nature of empirical things by means of logic.

The awareness which we have of the mechanism of language means an interference with the awareness of the world. This is evident when we know that we are using one language as opposed to another. Wittgenstein has found it necessary to back up from the problem presented by the necessity of constructing the logically perfect language, a problem set forth in his first book, to the antecedent task of doing away with the obstructions preventing its solution. The analysis of language is negative, not positive; it is neither intended to discover anything nor to create understandings but only to get rid of misunderstandings (43). The positive logic of empirical situations is hidden. The language by means of

---

[2] *Paul Klee*, Museum of Modern Art (New York 1946), p. 8.

which we get rid of misunderstandings is ordinary language (46). Our misunderstandings are ordinary ones; they are so common that we make them but do not know them. The analysis of ordinary language is the method by which we make ourselves know our ordinary, which is to say false, beliefs.

Predecessors and parallels are not wanting for the negative method which Wittgenstein proposes to the philosophical investigator. Perhaps the citation of one of each will suffice.

The predecessor is Plato. The method of Socrates which is known as *elenchus* is well described by Richard Robinson as "examining a person with regard to a statement he has made, by putting to him questions calling for further statements, in the hope that they will determine the meaning and the truth-value of the first statement."[3] Note especially, that "Most often the truth-value expected is falsehood; and so 'elenchus' in the narrower sense is a form of cross-examination or refutation."

The parallel is with Freud. The method of psychoanalysis is to make the patient who is suffering from a neurosis aware of the false or contradictory beliefs which he unconsciously holds and which dictate his emotions and perhaps also many of his overt actions, on the assumption that when he is aware of their untenability he will be able to cope with them and perhaps even to get rid of them. This covert method of eliminating error, like the overt method of Socrates, substitutes nothing affirmative or positive, though of course the preparation for the freedom to receive truth assumes its existence.

Like Socrates, Wittgenstein assumed the metaphysics of realism behind his method. This ought not to be too surprising when we consider his antecedents and influences. He belonged to the British realists, through Moore and Russell. We should expect strong affinities with Whitehead who regarded a philosophical system as a high set of abstractions which could grip us without our being aware of it. Are we indeed so very far here from one side of Whitehead? The theory on which an analogy could be based is termed by Whitehead the "Fallacy of Misplaced Concreteness" and is to be found, among other places, in the third chapter of his *Science and the Modern World*. The abstract structure by means of which we view the world is confused with the world. Other views are possible, and a more transparent one which will occasion less distortion could be discovered. In this connection, at least, Whitehead, too, regarded philosophizing as a negative function undertaken in order to get rid of mistakes. Philosophy, he said in the next chapter, was "the critic of abstractions." Whitehead went on to construct a philosophy; Wittgen-

---

[3] *Plato's Earlier Dialectic*, second edition, (London 1953, Oxford), p. 7.

stein, in the work under consideration here, makes no such attempt. Wittgenstein, however, does develop and illustrate the method more fully than Whitehead did.

It must be emphasized strongly that the investigation proposed is not psychological. Psychology is specifically ruled out. When we talk about understanding we do not intend a mental process at all (61); understanding is a state, not a mental state (59). For the unconscious we use the term, disposition (59) or intention (181); we are probing beneath the surface but by means of grammar (168); belief itself is a kind of disposition (191). There is no help for us from psychology, which is only confused and barren (232).

The escape from psychological involvement requires that we use words properly. This means that we must break through words in order to get at that to which they refer. The realist must also entertain the possibility of thinking without words. He is at the opposite pole from the Kantian-like symbolism of Cassirer, for instance. The absence of language from the highest type of thinking is illustrated in intuition or insight; here there are no steps. Even in the instance of logic, however, we are discussing possible states of affairs.

The empirical world is both what is the case and what is not the case; nothing stands still in existence. Hence the value to empiricism of logic, which can help us through thought to understand "what is not the case" (44). We must learn to distinguish between what is not the case and what is not possible or what is contradictory. The wall is now tan and we can consider it being painted blue; but it cannot be both tan and blue. The endorsement borrowed from tautology and the intent of non-trivial tautologies is required and serves to keep us within the bounds of logical security. Logic lies beneath the surface, not open to the view (43). "It is the business of philosophy, not to resolve a contradiction ... but to make it possible for us to get a clear view of ... the state of affairs before the contradiction is resolved" (50). The bulk of Wittgenstein's book, then, is devoted to the empirical test of language: can it describe the simplest feelings and actions? Is it adequate for this purpose? Wittgenstein makes innumerable samplings. These are done in two ways: one is to sort out and examine the meanings and consequences of ordinary words and phrases; the other is to imagine how things could be with respect to language (230), because "to imagine a language is to imagine a form of life" (8).

3. We may for purposes of brevity refer to the third thesis, which is the most important one, as the transparent ontology. Very pure theory must for logical reasons consist in no theory at all; only, we do not start there but instead work our way toward there, and it is in this work-

ing of our way that the activity of philosophy consists. Philosophy "leaves everything as it is" (49); we do not disturb anything, we only make pictures of how things are. Compare this, for instance, with Descartes' view of consciousness as a diaphanous medium analogous to light. Only, this time there is a vast difference, for it is by means of logic that we shall be enabled to see clearly and distinctly. And we shall obtain our view, as we shall presently note, by regarding the structure of language—its grammar—as a picture of the world.

Philosophy is the effort to see things as they are. To some extent it fails and we measure the degree of failure. In viewing nature through an ontology, we must find out the angle of distortion in order to make the proper allowances. How much surface dust should we expect on the lens, etc.? We must take account in our philosophical investigations of the fact that our own considerations are visible: to what degree do the means we employ to see the world interfere with our seeing, so that we can subtract them from the total picture. In order to be successful at this game we shall have to rid ourselves of our ontological categories. But we need to make certain before we do so that they are in need of elimination, for they constitute our main line of defense. It is only the proper ontology after all which in passing casts the least shadow.

Wittgenstein's biggest point in both of his books (though perhaps he would not have put it exactly in this way) is that when the true propositions of philosophy correspond exactly to the conditions of being, the propositions will become transparent and only the being will be evident, so that philosophy itself will seem to have disappeared. It is the ambition of Wittgenstein to establish through a very pure theory the transparent ontology. When philosophy understands other things correctly, that is because there is no philosophy in them. The philosophy of science, for instance, will consist in understanding science correctly, and not in constructing a philosophy of science to be regarded separately, after the way of philosophy. In our understanding of the external world we wish as little interference as possible occasioned by the mechanism of understanding. The problem posed in this ambition is a delicate one calling for enormous subtlety and precision.

In the meanwhile, however, this is far from a statement of the true situation. What we are faced with may be termed premature ontological systems. These we need to break up into single ideas for purposes of testing. What is required is the reduction to simple names (21). When we begin with names, we know that our procedure is empirically reliable (27) and logically primitive. For we have only chosen the counters to be employed in our logic-game (24). Every word is a name and not merely those which stand for actual physical objects or for their collection, chairs as well as this chair. In this view we are committed to the realist's assumption that relations exist externally to and independently of the knower. Prepositions, then, are names of relations; conjunctions are, too; articles are names of numbers; verbs are names of actions; and so on. "Above" describes a position; "and" refers to togetherness and is exemplified when objects are spatially juxtaposed; etc. We may find that we shall have to put them together in different ways. An analogy is the method which Peirce termed experimentation with mental graphs (the observation of abstract pictures). This is a process of necessary fragmentation and fractionation. In this way we work toward very pure theory. A consideration of the categories could be a starting point. To what extent are they mutually exclusive and exhaustive? Take the Cartesian *res cogitans* and *res extensa,* for instance; under which of these should we classify the proposition? What did Spinoza gain by following Descartes into thought and extension, when *res extensa* was a nominalizing shift from the Platonic "idea" and the Aristotelian "formal cause"? But there is another way. We can work more constructively, for example, by collecting all the information of a metaphysical nature that we need, and translating all the pieces into the same philosophical language.

The angle of distortion that we have observed in the case of Descartes is not confined to names. It is also to be observed with principles. For we find groups of distortions that bear a family resemblance. Let us consider such a one. We shall label it the axiom of pre-eminent reality. For it is found among all the philosophies which assume or admit a difference in degree of reality. Let us consider in this connection the quarrel between nominalists, idealists and realists. Wittgenstein himself attacks the nominalists for "interpreting all words as *names*" (118). It is a controversy not over the state of things but only over words (122). Wittgenstein in the last reference chooses the solipsists to represent the nominalists (he might as easily have chosen the materialists).

We could go on with the argument. Perhaps we should select one instance and do so. Take the solipsists, for instance. If one of them says, "The world is my idea," we could reply, "Very well, but tell me, what is your idea of the world?" And thenceforth we would be concerned with whether his account was true or false, complete or incomplete, adequate or inadequate, and not particularly with what is involved in his having it as an idea. We are going to be concerned, in short, with the self-consistent (and, it is hoped, empirically supported) structure, and not with the authority of its promulgation or with its genesis or history. These would all be irrelevant to its criteria and antecedent to its value, as well as beside the fact. "That is the truth," says Jurgen to the King Gorgyrvan Gawr, "whoever says it."

Wittgenstein's early influences, we have noted, were Moore and Russell. He may have acquired from them the highly sensitive and tentative version of metaphysical realism which underlies his work. This would be not a highly substantialized realm of essence but instead a range of recurrence, not a realm of existence but a range of transient elements, together with a highly elusive principle of interaction; but the whole structure so delicate that the mere names with their historic associations seem crude and misleading by comparison. Hence what we are given is not a bald philosophy but a tour around it and a view of its landscape, without once coming into contact with the delicate filaments of the theory (18). The presentation of realism becomes a matter of movement; the recurrent elements return us to the transient ones, and vice versa. Metaphysics, then, is a movement among the categories, not a fixed assembly. The categories themselves are paths, not points. They are not locations at which to stop, only places to turn. The "infinitely fine network" of the *Tractatus* has become a fluid set of points, a sort of topological philosophy required by standpointlessness.

Some philosophical systems resemble formal gardens, others are more like jungles. We make up the patterns with the simplest pieces, but the patterns after all can be too simple. We shall find that the natural ones are more complex and also more magnificent as well as invisible. In philosophy what man discovers ought to be what he himself has left untouched; that is the message Wittgenstein is trying to bring us, or, perhaps more accurately, to show us. It is a method which could be employed even in societies where the scientific method has not yet found its way of coping with the extenuating circumstances. The natural society is the cultural ideal. We shall find that man has discovered the pieces but not the secret of how they are put together. There are subtleties in the field of certainties. These occur in connection with the fitting of data corresponding to the absolutes of sensation into structures prescribed by the absolutes of mathematical tautology. In combining the two sorts of absolutes the absoluteness itself has had to be abandoned. We have left only absolute-guided probabilities. We are committed to the delicate business of the fitting.

How can this best be done? Fortunately, we have already at hand a method which has been used extensively even if never formalized. We have the study of paradigmatics, the technique of model-construction. In philosophy our metaphysical systems are models. We should observe them more carefully. We need, so to speak, a phenomenology of the paradigms —paradigmatic phenomenology. They disclose new relations and suggest novel values.

One convenient way of looking at models is to talk about systems.

In philosophy ideas have a summation in a system, although this is not always admitted by those who treat of ideas. But as Wittgenstein wrote, "the most general remarks yield at best what looks like the fragments of a system" (228). To concede ideas but not a system is as though we were to admit destinations but not destiny.

Wittgenstein's method in his second book seems to indicate the replacing of philosophy by a kind of aimed or purposive casuistry. It is overlooked by most of his followers that he is intending systematic philosophy. To play the language-game with him is to clear the ground of misunderstandings in order to make way for the proper understanding, which would require no screen at all. We want to achieve what Peirce termed the vagueness of generality without the mechanism responsible for the vagueness.

If fame consists in a sufficient number of misunderstandings, it is a mistake to read the work of a great thinker until we have got rid of some of the misunderstandings. It is perhaps the only way to save the very pure theory. One could perhaps tell best what one looked like by having children by a number of different women, and then comparing their faces after discounting what each mother had contributed individually in the way of features. It is interesting to watch Wittgenstein's emphases reflected in the work of his followers. Those who would eliminate philosophy in favor of science offer a poor tribute indeed to the man who in his first book tried to restore to philosophy a position of its own; while those who would reduce philosophy to the analysis of meaning commit an act of subreption in view of his second book since they offer an interpretation which manages to conceal behind the means which they recognize the end which he sought. He liberated philosophy from science (with which it cannot have the proper relations if it is not free), and he made the categories more permeable and movement among them more fluid.

We have returned to our starting point. It may be, in the manner of Wittgenstein, that the present interpretation, too, is to be discounted. And at the end of his book (230) has he not suggested how this might be done for all attempts to account for the world?

EMINENCE OF SCHOLARSHIP

Of all professions, that of scholarship seems to be the most thoroughly misunderstood. In the popular estimation the scholar is incompetent, lazy, unnecessary and a fool. We see little of him, fortunately, for he keeps himself from getting underfoot by remaining within the university. And not only is he secluded within those walls, but even there he is further hidden by the shelves of the library, so that he appears to be at best merely a man with a harmless and small antiquarian interest. However, since our scholar is also a professor in the college, good citizens scrape and save their pennies to make it possible for their children to study with him. He is underpaid and undervalued and most necessary to the culture. With these paradoxes in mind, we may do well to take a closer look at his functions in order more properly to evaluate them.

The scholar, according to one of the main dictionary meanings of the term, is a student in one of the schools at a university; but the term has been broadened to mean one who devotes himself to the study of the past, however and wherever that is done. The term "past" is used here as a metonymy, by the "past" we shall mean work done in the past. The functions of the scholar, then, are fourfold. He is (1) the discoverer of the past, (2) the custodian of the past, (3) the appreciator of the past, and (4) the critic of the past. Let us examine each of these functions separately and briefly.

1. The scholar is a discoverer in the sense that he is often able to recover for us old texts that were forgotten and which may otherwise have perished. The journal of Boswell found by Tinker in 1925 in an ebony cabinet in a castle owned by Lord Talbot de Malahide is a case in point. The scholar discovers books and other records which may not have been known to have survived. Another interesting case is the discovery of some of the Delphic Hymns of the second century B.C. carved on the wall of the Treasury of the Athenians at Delphi and found by Professor Theodore Reinach, of the French School of Archælogy in 1893.

The scholar's work as a discoverer is by no means confined to physical discovery. For he may find meanings as well. These may be anything from the reinterpretation of a passage to the understanding of an entire language, from a fresh reading of a phrase of Shakespeare to the deciphering of the priestly writings of the Mayans, the latter of which thus far remain unread. We could scarcely omit from this category the vast labors of the philosopher of history, the man who seeks for a pattern in history after having first devised an hypothesis in regard to it, but who, above all, must approach his problem with an enormous knowledge of the events of the past, a scholar and discoverer of the size of a Vico, a Spengler or a Toynbee. One of the lesser ways in which fresh meanings are discovered is through the study of a period or a man, a period in which some important work was done or the biographical details of the man who did it. We tend to underestimate the amount of imagination involved in the discovery of facts. Before we are able to frame an hypothesis as to how they were, we need to imagine how they could be and then and only then are able to employ our hypothesis as an instrument of discovery. The natural scientist knows this well. It is difficult indeed if not impossible to determine at what point "creation" leaves off and discovery replaces it. The artist brings something new into the actual world: new values; the scientist introduces something, too: new truths; and it is less well known that the scholar has something peculiar to add also: namely, new facts. For he alone works in a field in which what ever is actual is fixed forever. Whitehead was fond of reminding us that the past is the area of immortal fact, that nothing can change whatever has happened, though the task of learning what it is exactly that has happened is often difficult and sometimes almost impossible.

Thus the scholar is instrumental in increasing the sum of human knowledge, even though what he adds to it is quite modestly not his own. We owe him a considerable debt for the performance of this particular function. The knowledge and preparation which he needs to bring to his work, and the painstaking detail involved in its execution, are labors which the rest of us would not undertake without the promise of more of a reward than the scholar ever secures.

2. The scholar is a preserver, in the sense that he guards and protects the records of culture. We live by passing on the accumulation of past cultural achievements, and this is true to a degree that few of us would ever quickly recognize, believe or admit. The world of the present changes continually, the culture in which we are immersed progresses; yet the role played in this evolution by what was accomplished through generations which have gone before, is severely underestimated. We are constituted for the most part of whatever the past has accumulated, and we are the more powerful for knowing about it. Truth is dateless and must be preserved; and so the task of the scholar, which is to see that we do not lose even the petty gains we have made over the centuries, is a crucial one.

The preservation of records may mean anything, from getting folk songs down on tape to preserving perishable but rare and valuable codices in air-conditioned libraries. The librarians and the curators of art museums are scholars in this sense. They perform one of the functions of scholarship, which, we must bear in mind, is not confined to books but must be extended to all sorts of cultural records, of which books may be the chief sort yet remain only one. The record of the past is preserved in books, in sound recordings, in works of art, in scientific instruments, in anything old of a cultural nature which has managed to survive. And the man who devotes his professional career to the protection and safeguarding of the things of the past is a scholar. Think how much richer we might be had the scholars of the last three millennia been allowed to exercise their profession without interference. The happiness of cultivated people is an intense and complicated affair, and admits of degrees. How much would the sum of happiness be increased by the discovery of Homer's comedy or of the twenty-nine lost comedies of Aristophanes! Think how much catharsis would be discharged were we to possess again and so to be able to produce on the stage the sixty-three tragedies of Aeschylus which have perished! What would we not give for the collected works of the philosopher Democritus, of whose sixty books not one has survived?

3. The scholar is the appreciator of the past. Very often works of value remain neglected or, because of some change in the accepted values, become neglected. It then proves the duty of the scholar to point this out. He is the advocate of the worth of texts, and so enriches the heritage which makes life significant. The revival of interest in the seventeenth-century metaphysical poets, Peirce's calling to our attention the fact that the writings of the scholastic philosophers had a philosophical value apart from their religious aspects, the rise in the current estimation of the paintings of El Greco, of Piero della Francesca and of Zurbaran, are cases in point. The scholar cries to us in the exuberance of his appreciation: see what you have that you have overlooked and enjoy it afresh. We could ill afford to do without the performance of this service.

Part of the appreciation of the past is to reveal its relevance to the present. Scholarship is a labor-saving device, for we need not discover again what we have already possessed. Often the scholar as well as the inventor is able to place in our hands at the right moment exactly what we needed to solve a pressing problem. In this way the scholar is a guide and an aide to the accomplishment of present ends.

He is also a teacher of proportions. We could not go overboard for a current fad if we knew that it had been tried before and abandoned. There are lessons in the past that would keep us soberer in the present had we but sufficient knowledge of them. Thus the scholar helps us to maintain our balance. Dictatorships have been attempted and have failed, religions have endeavored to suppress all opposition by force, poets have been neglected, and all in vain. We need to be kept advised of Attila, of the Spanish Inquisition, and of the death of Chatterton at the age of eighteen.

Lastly, (4) the scholar is the critic of the past. He furnishes some of the reasons for revising accepted evaluations, he urges on historical grounds the rejection of some of the current estimations, and he eliminates meanings which have perhaps obscured others more valuable. This is the prophylactic function, often an unpleasant one yet none the less necessary. Raphael did not paint a certain picture after all; a text attributed to Aristotle was actually written by Theophrastus; and Shakespeare, not Bacon, is the author of Shakespeare's plays. These acts are often disappointments—for it seemed at one time that we had more of Aristotle than in fact we do have—yet since it is the truth alone that shall set us free, we might as well have it however much it may at times hurt.

In short, the scholar in the grand sense is the custodian of the culture. It is his task to cherish it for us, to keep it bright and ever-present, to clear away the obscuring smogs which somehow interpose themselves between us in our busy world and the best of our splendid heritage. We owe him our sense of fitness, therefore, and our breadth of perspective. If knowledge is virtue, as Socrates claimed, then we owe to the scholar also something of our virtue as the preserver of a good deal of our knowledge. We ought to accord him a position of considerably more eminence than he now enjoys.

How has the scholar consoled himself for his state of neglect? Why, just as we might have anticipated: by the assiduous nurturing of that little pride which we never fail to find prevailing in the atmosphere inside any tight profession. We would do him an injustice if we failed to score the limitations which are inherent in his class. Corresponding to every function which he performs, there are errors to which he may be prone. We shall therefore discuss them in the same order, first as to excess and then as to defect.

1. As the scholar is the discoverer of the past, so he tends to elevate the past in terms of the present. He is duty-bound to judge his own field superior. This is an easy comparison to make and certainly a necessary one. The fault lies only in the conclusions which are often drawn from it. For in choosing the past its worst aspects are omitted and only the best selected. The instantaneous present, which cannot be selected but is bluntly given, is measured, then against the best of the long past, and the conclusion is obvious: we are in a period of serious decline! But on such

a basis of comparison we always would seem to be. What else could we expect? If we compare Shakespeare's grandiloquence with Mrs. Grundy's boardinghouse lingo, the moral is obvious. We can only point out that the basis is unfair. Not even a current Golden Age could stand up to the best of *all* the past. Nor should it have to. For in the pure form in which we have distilled the past from its dross, it stands as an ideal when it is in fact not one. The scholar's lesson is invariably that the past is not to be even approached; but if we want ideals we should place them in the future, and in this way regard the past not as something to be approached but as something to be exceeded. The past exists in order to be surpassed. For nothing has ever been done perfectly, and so it is fair to say that, in this sense, at least, nothing has ever been done. The scholar mistakes the cream of his charge as a defeat for the present and even for the future. He mistakes his model for an absolute.

Just as the scholar as discoverer sometimes commits errors of excess, so he does occasionally commit those of defect. This error consists in mistaking the form of discovery for the contents discovered. It is what the writing in books means that is important, not the books. A forgotten poet rediscovered shakes hands across the centuries not with the scholar who may have turned the manuscript up in some old attic but with living poets who share his interests and perhaps, also, despite the intervening time and space, his outlook. It is the error of defect which leads the scholar to prefer an old edition to a readable one; the collector of rarities who seldom peruses the treasures which he collects, and cherishes the owning of them for their own sake is of this company.

2. Our second point of scholarly excess arises because the scholar, in his zeal to be a custodian of the past, errs in regarding all the achievements of the present as a threat. He has officially located the best in the past; how, then, can the present make claims without effrontery? One philosophical scholar has spoken for the others in denying the possibility of originality. "The only difference," he maintains, "between a historian of philosophy and an original philosopher is honesty. The original philosopher is simply one who omits his footnotes." Everything, you see, has already been done, all possibilities explored, all combinations tried; and if we think for a moment that we have got something of value we would be better off for admitting where we obtained it. Admittedly, this is an extreme case of scholarly pretension; yet are not many scholars touched with something of the same ardor? To understand is to pardon, that is true, still it would be a shame if the enthusiasm of the custodian were to hamper the productive thinker, writer or artist.

The defect of the custodian is not sufficiently to call attention to the works in his care. Some scholars withdraw into the aristocratic attitude of considering that the works they preserve are too precious for the vulgar mob and ought to be retained for the benefit of the initiated. Or they constitute themselves the censors of works in their charge, and decide *ipse dixit* what ought and what ought not to be available to others. As Pericles, according to Thucydides, declared the whole world to be the sepulchre of famous men, so the entire living population ought to be the audience of their writings and not just those chosen few selected by the custodians. The scholars fail in their duty when work saved from the past is not made available to any who wish to see it.

3. The excess of the scholar as appreciator is, of course, contained in the claim that the past has a monopoly of the best of all time. The Golden Age, he contends, lies behind us, and we look forward only to a continual recession from it; for the further we advance in time, the more we get away from the ideal. There is, and there can hardly be, any doubt as to the merit of Greek culture; and so it is a favorite for this purpose among scholars. We are told that the Golden Age lies in the period from the fifth to the fourth centuries B.C., and that nothing that will ever be done can hope to equal it. Thus the excess of the scholarly zeal lays a prohibition upon the future as to the limitations of its quality. The scholar forgets that the time to come holds unbounded possibilities; it is a time when, in Jurgen's phrase, anything is more than likely to happen. For nothing has ever been done finally or in the best way, and there is nothing that, theoretically, at least, cannot be done better.

On the side of defect, the scholar functioning as an appreciator of the past is apt to develop a natural yet regrettable conservatism. In this he identifies himself somewhat with the work that he loves and guards. At his most successful he is an intimate in circles where the artist or philosopher who was responsible for the work now entrusted to his care would never have been admitted. The creative man is to some extent uncouth, he suffers from the crudeness to which all power is susceptible. The art critic, for instance, is at home among the patrons of Van Gogh's canvases, where in many cases Van Gogh himself, the earless Van Gogh, would most certainly have been turned away at the door. Yeats' picture of the scholar is not a flattering one.

> Bald heads forgetful of their sins,
> Old, learned, respectable bald heads
> Edit and annotate the lines
> That young men, tossing on their beds,
> Rhymed out in love's despair
> To flatter beauty's ignorant ear.
> They'll cough in the ink to the world's end;
> Wear out the carpets with their shoes

Earning respect ; have no strange friends ;
If they have sinned nobody knows.
Lord, what would they say
Should their Catullus walk that way?

4. The scholar in his role of critic of the past is apt to mistake the trees for the wood. The paraphenalia of survival, the care of old manuscripts, the ingenuity of decipherment, the collation of texts, the construction of glossaries, and all the technical machinery of the practicing scholar, are likely at times to get between him and the essence of his subject-matter, between the form in which objects of value have persisted and the contents of those objects. He becomes so involved in the technique of survival that he tends to forget why it is that anyone wishes his work to survive. The error often reaches proportions so absurd that it becomes necessary to take an humorous view. How seriously otherwise could one regard the English scholar who gave the following reason for his preference of Faulkner over Hemingway as a literary artist? The novels of Faulkner, he said, were sufficiently obscure to keep scholars occupied with the task of interpretation, whereas Hemingway wrote so clearly that no commentary was necessary. In short, the greatness of a writer is to be measured by what he has left for the critic to do.

As the excess of criticism is to regard the criticism itself as more important than the work criticized, so the defect of criticism is to regard the work as perfect. Age is mistaken on this criterion as an endorsement of value: there are held to be no old works of little value and all is deemed precious in proportion to its age. The defect of criticism confuses time with value, assuming that what has survived for centuries must have done so for a good reason and never by chance. Would we have not been better off to have preserved the writings of Heraclitus and Parmenides and if necessary to have lost instead those of Statius and Frontius? Unless one undertakes a mystic view that somehow works of merit naturally survive and works of demerit as naturally perish, it is clear that chance operates as much in the past as it does in the present, and that most probably some of the things deserving of survival have been lost and trivial things, hardly worth preserving, have managed to hang on through the years.

These various complaints, though serious, are not intended to be damaging. We began by reciting the legitimate and necessary functions of the scholar; then we moved to a criticism of his excesses and defects; it will only be fair to end with words of praise. The chief purpose of this study is in fact to raise the stock of the scholar in general, to call attention to an eminence of function which has been sadly overlooked in the contemporary world. It is curious to observe in an age such as our own, when the original producer and creator is derogated and the middle man and interpreter raised to absurd heights of estimation, that the scholar is overlooked. We should expect that at a time when the actor is more highly regarded than the playwright, the conductor of a symphony orchestra lionized beyond the wildest dreams of any composer, the scholar would be deemed more estimable than the literary artist; yet such is in fact not the case. The neglect of the scholar in a period of neglect of the artist no doubt is an oversight and ought to be corrected. We should at least be consistent in our errors and not add contradiction to false evaluation.

As matters stand the scholar enjoys virtues to which he ought not to be entitled, the virtues of obscurity and anonymity. In our day these are almost the exclusive legitimate prerogative of the original mathematicians. Mathematics has made greater progress in the last hundred years than in all the previous centuries, and today the headlong advance is still on, evidenced in the work of many pure "creative" mathematicians. Yet hardly a name of the most brilliant among them is known to the public at large. Sharing their elimination from the stronger currents of popularity are the majority of scholars who seem to the publicity-hungry world to be almost as much to be derogated as teachers.

In the last analysis, scholarship, like all other fields of endeavor in a free democracy, is advanced by professionals but available to all. The amateur scholar has done something if it is only to cultivate himself when he engages in his spare time in acts of discovery, of custodianship, of appreciation, or of criticism of the past. It is said, during the last war when the Army wanted some particular work done in Zanzibar on the east coast of Africa, only one engineer could be found with the requisite knowledge of both electronics and Swahili, the acquisition of the latter language having been, among other esoteric languages, one of this man's peace-time hobbies. There is in the opinion of some no such thing as useless knowledge; and, as the career of T. E. Lawrence amply illustrates, one never knows when an unknown architectural student may through his special equipment rise to the heights of the most violent and significant action. Lawrence succeeded in demonstrating that if knowledge is not virtue at least it is power. And in parlous times we had better learn where the advantages lie which we possess without effort, and learn to cultivate them against the strains on our culture. We would be wise to acquire the strength which is needed to gaze without flinching at the highly-reflecting surface of any work well done.

ACTIVITY AS A SOURCE OF RELIABLE KNOWLEDGE

I

There is no division of human life which has not been touched upon and altered by science, and this is no less true of philosophy than it is of other concerns. The experimental method of the physical sciences in particular has been and still is the part of science which has influenced philosophy the most. Elsewhere I have tried to argue that philosophical empiricism though developed in imitation of scientific empiricism differs from it sharply.[1] Scientific empiricism is objective while philosophical empiricism is subjective. Scientific empiricism has tried to verify by means of the disclosures of sense experience the regularities which it hypothesizes in nature; philosophical empiricism has tried to verify by means of the sense experiences themselves the meanings which they have for the subject. The result is that science has begun and continues to develop a description of the world, while philosophy remains behind debating the various alternative interpretations of sense experience.

There is another point of comparison which may be relevant. While science worked with the experience of the entire man employing all of his faculties, philosophy has tried to get along with some of his faculties. It is very well known that the Continental rationalists, Descartes, Spinoza and Leibniz, for instance, sought an explanation of the world in terms of what could be constructed primarily by means of the reasoning faculty. Alternatively, the British empiricists, it is equally well known, sought to discover a source for indubitable knowledge in the isolated deliverances of sense experience.

It is difficult not to ask why such narrow efforts were undertaken. The Continental rationalists inherited the scholastic method but with a new freedom from dogma and a new empirical interest. They were in a way the closest of the philosophical enlightenment to the period which had gone before. If science touched them in a philosophical way it did

---

[1] "Philosophical Empiricism from the Scientific Standpoint," in *Dialectica,* Vol. 16, pp. 5–14 (1962).

so with a light hand. The British empiricists, on the other hand, were uncompromising in their efforts to follow the lead of the scientists. They worked hard at making primitive beginnings in sense experience, and if they did not advance as far as the scientists beyond those beginnings it was not for lack of rigorous efforts. Their enterprise was not less uncompromising because they were themselves mild fellows with no wish to upset the apple-cart, and in some cases, that of Berkeley for instance, exceedingly conservative in religious matters.

If the entire man is one who is able to think, feel and act, as we have known since Plato's *Republic* if not much earlier, then why is there assumed to be an advantage in endeavoring to found reliable knowledge upon less resources than the entire man has to call on? Why try to get along with one faculty: reason or sense experience—there is little to choose? Common experience, which is able to operate only at the gross level of ordinary objects, still refutes such specialized appeals, and it is significant that one protest to the method of single faculties came from the Scotch common sense school, led by Thomas Reid.

Hume working with the experiences of the senses alone (and neglecting the importance of the fact that he was thinking about them in so doing) posed the most serious problems to the pursuit of reliable knowledge. He himself has been misinterpreted, and it is one of his ablest commentators who makes the point that Hume's conclusion is not necessarily a sceptical one. N. Kemp Smith has contended that for Hume the source of reliable knowledge is to be found in belief rather than reason, and that it was this positive source in belief which was what Hume had maintained rather than the purely negative scepticism with regard to knowledge which is usually attributed to him.[2] As Hume himself remarked, "The great subverter of Pyrrhonism, or the excessive principle of sceptism, is action, and employment, and the occupations of common life."[3] Belief is yet to receive its due of analysis either from the philosophers or the psychologists. But it remains true that the refutation of Hume properly consists in a consideration of the grounds he adopted for forming his conclusions. The failure to discover a genuine external world and a self was based upon sense experience alone. Had he included action as a source of knowledge, he might have found the external world to be real. For if knowledge is to be derived from experience, as most philosophers as well as all experimental scientists now pretty well agree that it is, then it must be the whole of experience, experience in all of its parts rather than only in some, that is meant. Action must be included as well as thought and sensation.

[2] N. Kemp Smith, *The Philosophy of David Hume*, London, 1941. Macmillan.
[3] David Hume, *An Inquiry Concerning Human Understanding*, XII, II.

II

A complete empirical philosophy must await a complete use of all of the faculties of entire man engaging together in the pursuit of reliable knowledge. Perhaps this is yet to be formulated. It could not be accomplished through an assemblage of the component parts, as we know from other discoveries, for that is not how discoveries are made. They are made by single inductive leaps to the knowledge of systems which can then painstakingly be tested against the relevant data. They are made by first making hypotheses and then testing them. Two sorts of philosophers are required for this task, just as in science two sorts of scientists. The great synthesizer is necessary, the man whose dreaming is of possible systems, and then the patient investigator must go to work. Neither can do much without the other, even though the terms of mutual respect based on a common complementarity have not yet been agreed upon.

In the meanwhile, however, the consequences of adopting certain principles of procedure must first run their course. It has been for some time the practice to assume that some single human capacity holds the key to reliable knowledge, first rationalism and then sense experience or philosophical empiricism. But there is a third human capacity which has not yet been included in the catalogue of the method of single inference from single capacities. This is: action. It would have to be true that some school of philosophy would have had to take its turn in the succession of exploring how much reliable knowledge could be obtained employing the human capacity for action alone. Then it might be possible that philosophy would make a new start more in keeping with the actual procedure of science and try the united and integrated capacities of the entire man.

The American pragmatists have not often been looked at in this way. They have not ordinarily been supposed to have explored activity as a source of knowledge. Rather have they been thought of in other ways, and the relationship has been turned around. The pragmatists have been interpreted, not without some reason, as having concerned themselves with the verification of meaning in terms of practice. If you wish to understand propositions, they tell us, then consider what practical effects such propositions would have, and this is their meaning.

But suppose we do look at the pragmatists in the way I have suggested, namely, as having tried to explore activity as a source of reliable knowledge. It does not necessarily follow that such a thesis was deliberate or conscious with them or that they understood in this fashion their place in the history of philosophy. I assume that philosophers for all their strenuous efforts to understand what they are taking for granted are like all other people in not being able to attain to the degree of detachment necessary in order to comprehend the first principles from which their thinking proceeds. Moreover, philosophy, unlike other disciplines, has the additional problem of the meta-axioms. Its adherents understand very well the axioms from which its theorems are deduced, and even the rules of inference by which such deductions are made. But what it often if not usually misses is the existence of a set of meta-axioms by which its axioms themselves could be established; or, if the very absence of procedure is entailed here in the terms of the existence of a philosophy, then of the inferential existence of meta-axioms. The existence of meta-axioms in mathematics belongs to an allied discipline: the study of the foundations of mathematics; but to what discipline does the study of the foundations of philosophy belong? That there is such a discipline dimly discerned has been noted, as for instance in Aristotle and by Boas.[4]

It will be the aim of this study, then, to examine briefly some of the writings of the American pragmatists, Peirce, James, Dewey and Mead in order to determine whether they can be interpreted together as having endeavored to found reliable knowledge upon activity. All were philosophers, all concerned themselves with action, all were related, and all wished to understand the relation between propositions and the relevant practices.

III

The greatest of American philosophers was also the founder of pragmatism, Charles S. Peirce. It is too often forgotten that Peirce was a metaphysician as well as a practicing physicist and an empirically-minded man, and the reason for this is the failure to recognize empiricism as a metaphysics. Metaphysics has been identified with one particular metaphysics, that of idealism, although generically there is no warrant for such an exclusiveness.

Peirce had a philosophical system. His ontological categories were: firstness, secondness and thirdness, or, in other words, quality, reaction and representation. In secondness or reaction he recognized the bruteness of the hard fact of resistance and effort, and gave it a prominent place

---

[4] George Boas, *Some Assumptions of Aristotle,* Philadelphia, 1959. American Philosophical Society.

in his theory of reality.[5] He did not distinguish altogether between a fact and an activity; facts are, among other things, activities (CP 1.427–440). Secondness is force (CP 1.487). It is the prime characteristic of all existence, whose very nature consists in opposition (CP 1.458).

When Peirce came to pronounce his methodological doctrine of pragmatism, however, the relations between concepts and activities got somehow turned around, so that pragmatism became a theory of meaning rather than a doctrine of activity as a source of reliable knowledge. Peirce gave seven definitions of pragmatism. I will quote the most familiar. "Consider what effects, that might conceivably have practical bearings, we conceive the object of our conception to have. Then our conception of these effects is the whole of our conception of the object" (CP 5.2).

Pragmatism has been more generally associated with the name of James than with that of Peirce. But James himself freely acknowledged his debt. The term and the conception of pragmatism had their points of origin in the thoughts and writings of Charles S. Peirce. For Peirce, pragmatism was a method of determining the meaning of those concepts which are peculiarly concerned with objective fact (CP 5.467).

Pragmatism was designed by Peirce to be a method of logic (CP 5.14, 5.465). It is framed in terms of conceptions and of practical effects, and states that conceptions of the practical effects of an object constitute the whole conceptions of the object (CP 5.2).[6] There is activity implied as a source of reliable knowledge, but it is certainly not explicitly stated. There is no such thing as practical effects without activity, but the pure experience or the abstract conception of activity is missing. It could be elicited from the pragmatic conception and is very close to it but cannot be identified with it. The consequences of a conception and their part in the defining of the conception is, one might almost say, logically adjacent to the derivation of reliable knowledge from activity; but the connection is too close between conception and consequences. Activity must first be conceived independently of its role as a source of reliable knowledge, if it is to be productively thought of in that connection. Activity does not exist because it is a source of reliable knowledge; it is a source of reliable knowledge because of its independence from its effects upon knowledge. And just in that and in nothing else lies its value to knowledge. Peirce repudiated the Kantian epistemology from which he had learned so many of the problems of philosophy.[7] The relativism

[5] *Collected Papers of Charles Sanders Peirce.* Cambridge, 1931–58. 8 vols. References indicated in terms of volume and hereinafter referred to as CP. CP, 1.322–325.
[6] See also CP 5.9; 5.18; 5.467; 5.438; 6.490; 5,412.
[7] See the reference in James Feibleman, *An Introduction to Peirce's Philosophy.* New York, 1946. Harper. Chapter II.

of knowledge in a way cancels the authenticity of the claim of pure activity to be a source of reliable knowledge because of the extent to which in that relativism the activity itself is tied in with the process by which the knowledge is elicited.

For the promise which Peirce had made in his metaphysics, in which activity was one of the three primary ontological categories, is not fulfilled in his methodological theory of pragmatism. There is no room in pragmatism for quality, and reaction is inextricably intertwined with representation. Toward the end of his life, Peirce specifically repudiated any interest in activity for its own sake, and insisted that he had meant pragmatism all along to be a theory of meaning. Not "doing" but "rational purport" must be considered as the product at which pragmatism is aiming (CP 5.429).

Let us revert now to the categories of Peirce's metaphysics. These are, we may remember, firstness or quality, secondness or reaction, and thirdness or representation; subjectively: feeling, effort and thought. Strictly speaking, reaction (resistance or force) is not the same as activity though belonging to the same generic category. But even without this conception there is a discrepancy between Peirce's metaphysics and his pragmatism. Peirce's doctrine remains a theory of meaning, not a method of deriving reliable knowledge from experience. It was, however, as we shall see, suggestive in this connection to others.

IV

In an address to psychologists on radical empiricism, James sought most vigorously to place activity upon a respectable philosophical footing.[8] In an earlier essay in the same volume, James had described radical empiricism in terms of pure experience, without the emphasis on activity (RE Ch. II). In his celebrated pragmatic maxim, James had laid the foundation for a theory of practice. "To attain perfect clearness in our thoughts of an object, we need only consider what effects of a practical kind the object may involve—what sensations we are to expect from it, and what reactions we must prepare. Our conception of these effects, whether immediate or remote, is then for us the whole of our conception of the object."[9] The closeness of James' formulation of pragmatism to that of Peirce is painfully obvious. To be perfectly fair, it is one which

[8] Williams James, *Essays in Radical Empiricism*. London, 1938. Longmans, Green. Chapter VI. Hereinafter referred to as RE.

[9] William James, *Pragmatism*. London, 1940. Longmans, Green. pp. 46–7. Hereinafter referred to as P.

James himself freely acknowledged. The practical effects of an object can hardly be construed as otherwise than an activity. And so it is from the activity of an object that we are instructed to gather its meaning.

James was an epistemological realist, as he asserted more than once. He "posited reality *ab initio*"[10] and insisted that he meant that "ideas should be true in advance of and apart from their utility, that, in other words, their objects should be really there" (MT 207). However, he did say that by "practical experience" he meant that the experience must be particular rather than active (MT 210). Agreement with reality: that touchstone of epistemological realism, stood James in good stead. Truth means agreement with reality; agreement with reality means verifiability; verifiability means ability to guide us through experience. Thus "the possession of true thoughts means everywhere the possession of invaluable instruments of action" (P 202).

But the presence of activity is pervasive in his thinking never the less, and he returns to it again and again. James more than the other pragmatists saw in activity an important philosophical category.[11] He was concerned with it as a pure experience and he was concerned with it for its connections with the pragmatic method.

James the philosopher is a familiar figure in philosophy, but it must be remembered by philosophers that he was also and often primarily a psychologist. In discussing the types of decision under the general heading of the will, James wrote—in italics—*"In action as in reasoning, the great thing is the quest of the right conception."*[12] He came closer than most pragmatists to enunciating a theory of truth in terms of activity because he saw the intimate connection between statements regarding the truth and the relevant activities. His conception of the correspondence theory was a dynamic one. However, he was as much concerned with meaning and particulars as he was with statements and activities, and he wavered between the various combinations of these four interests. The practical man cognizant of affairs and the psychologist took precedence over the detached concerns of the scientifically-minded philosopher in search of a source for reliable knowledge. The result was that he sought primarily a workable theory of meaning as it applied to practice. "Pragmatic method asserts that what a concept means is its consequences."[13]

---

[10] William James, *The Meaning of Truth*. New York, 1932. Longmans, Green. p. 195. Hereinafter referred to as MT.

[11] *A Pluarlistic Universe*. New York, 1932. Longmans, Green. Appendix B.

[12] *The Principles of Psychology*. New York, 1931. Holt, 2 vols. Vol. II, p. 531.

[13] Ralph Barton Perry, *The Thought and Character of William James*. Boston, 1935. Little Brown. 2 vols. Vol. II, p. 444.

It happened as often in James' thinking that conceptions were selected in order to bring about practical results as that practical results were employed in order to derive reliable knowledge. The effort to influence action is practical; the effort to employ action in order to determine truth is theoretical. Theory has more far-reaching effects on practice than practice itself approached immediately and directly. That is certainly the practical lesson to be learned from "pure" science. And so James did not formulate as precisely as he might have a verification theory for statements in terms of activity.

V

Of the pragmatists, Mead perhaps best understood the nature of activity as a source of reliable knowledge, and he set up the most adequate model for it. His shortcoming was that he never followed through with an examination of concrete experience in terms of his model, and so he never succeeded in completing the projected ambition and in illuminating knowledge in this way. He left behind him, however, an intriguingly suggestive conceptual scheme.

His model is best explained by beginning with its sources. He proposed to consider a human individual as suggested by the psychological behaviorism of John Watson in a world as outlined by Minkowski. The link between them, as we shall presently note, was what Mead called "contact experience."

Let us begin with the behaviorism. This is best outlined under the heading of social behaviorism. The conduct of the human individual studied within the behavior of the social group[14] and not confined to that part which can be externally observed is what Mead meant by his "social behaviorism." But the role is not merely a passive one, for the "organism goes out and determines what it is going to respond to" (MSS 25). The "bodily structure can be stated in terms of behaviorism—à la Watson."[15] As we shall see, Mead intended a stimulus-response system but with the emphasis upon the dynamic response.

Now let us turn to the model of the world as Mead envisaged it. Here he relied almost entirely upon the *a priori* character of the four-dimensional continuum of space-time and events as set forth by Herman Minkowski. The Minkowski world, according to Mead, is important in

[14] George H. Mead, *Mind, Self and Society*. Chicago, 1934. University Press. p. 6. Hereinafter referred to as MSS.
[15] George Herbert Mead, *The Philosophy of the Act*. Chicago, 1938. University Press. p. 659. Hereinafter referred to as PA.

the human context because it is a stable world "back of our action, even hurried action" . . . "a world that hypothetically endures both in its structure and in its rhythms of recurrence" (PA 179–180). It is paradoxically "a world lying beyond any possible experience" (PA 609), but in which "we have the experience of continuous passage" (PA 635), "a world that assimilates space and time" (PA 524) but which also is, through "space-time . . . the condition of the change" (PA 63).

The Minkowski world, for Mead, is a "world where all stimuli are spatio-temporally away from them (i.e., those who live in it)" (PA 143). It is, in short, "a world of stimuli and responses" (PA 147). We now have a description of characteristic human behavior and of the world in Mead's model. We have now to describe the conduct which connects them in order to complete the model. But the stimuli are not present in any contiguous sense. Mead recognized that the individual lives in a larger world than he can ever comprehend, and that the effects of this world upon the individual are far greater than the effects of the individual upon the world (PA 21). The perceived object is a distant object. Perception thus leads to action, for experience of the object certainly involves a closer approach to it (PA 12). For "distance experience of any sort is of a different sort from that of ultimate contact" and so "the ultimate reality of the distance experience is to be found in that of contact experience" (PA 16).

Our exploration of experience, then, means either that we can move around the object or that we can move the object around by manipulating it (PA 16–17). Reliable knowledge may be considered a by-product of the adaptation of the human organism to its environment (PA 312), through a kind of adaptation which consists in substituting "contact observation" (PA 22) for distance (PA 144). And so it is not surprising to learn from Mead that "the ultimate experience involves not only contact, but it also involves manipulation" (PA 226).

"The act is an impulse that maintains the life-process by the selection of certain sorts of stimuli it needs" (MSS 6). "The distant object has a reality which waits upon the completion of the act" (PA 175–176). Acts become conduct by means of various degrees of deliberation, until conduct becomes the key even to the knowledge of the self (PA 65).

The act becoming conduct for the individual in a social world in which he must move toward the material object in order to establish "contact experience" with it makes the sense of touch the important one for Mead. "If we present a distant planet, its matter is presented as we would actually sense it if we could place our hands upon it" (PA 20). He emphasizes the point again and again. "The round solid coin in the hand is the ultimate fact of every oval of vision" (PA 281). "Things," he confidently assured us, "are not real as seen or heard or smelled; they are real as actually or potentially experienced through contact" (PA 364).

The objects with which we have "contact experience" are material objects. "From the standpoint of the perceptual judgment of reality, that of manipulatory contact, these physical objects are there in independence of the acts, and they were there before the organism arose and will continue after its disappearance" (PA 453). "That which appears in contact experience is matter" (PA 287), "matter as effectively occupying space, its resistance, its inertia, its mobility, as we experience these characters" (PA 15).

And so now he has his model complete, an abstract, geometric, material world, as designed by Minkowski, a behaviorist model arrived at by elaborating Watsonian behaviorism, together with the movements of activity and conduct designed to achieve contact experience on the part of the individual. A good place to start, assuming that the next step would be the interpretation of the concrete world with its living human individuals in terms of the model. But this is not only where Mead started, it is also where he stopped. And so he missed the possibilities of translating his model into the terms of experience which make it possible to interpret activity as a source of reliable knowledge. The champion, who would raise his candidate for priority of dependence in the method of inquiry—"contact experience"—to a place of eminence on a par with the reason of the Continental rationalists and the sense experience of the British empiricists, failed at the very last. He did not fail, however, without indicating a direction in which success could be achieved.

VI

Dewey was a pragmatist; that is to say, he sought an instrumental method for testing the meaning of ideas in the light of their consequences. His emphasis, however, was practical rather than theoretical. What he advocated was a way of testing meaning by means of the practical approach through broad and immediate social consequences. The direction of conduct by beliefs was to be decided in this way.

Dewey was very anxious to bring together again what the Greeks had sundered: pure knowledge and practical activity. For the Greeks, he observed, Doing was not intellectually respectable in the way that Knowing and Being was.[16] But in this effort Dewey managed somehow to reduce

[16] John Dewey, *The Quest for Certainty*. New York, 1929, Milton Balch. pp. 16–18. Hereinafter referred to as QC. *Logic*. New York, 1938. Holt. pp. 57, 73. Hereinafter referred to as L.

knowledge to the status of an instrument for accomplishing the practical without raising practice to the level of a source for reliable knowledge. His aim was practical rather than knowledgeable, but being a philosopher rather than a man of affairs the result was an instrumental theory of meaning. "The existentialist basis of a universal proposition is a mode of action" (L 271). Dewey was thus the last of the philosophers who endeavored to settle technical matters at the common sense level by "formulating a theory of knowledge and of mind in relation to nature" (QC 86).

Dewey noted that "action is at the heart of ideas" (QC 167). Hypotheses are always intended to be "tried in action" (QC 194). But he confused ideas with action by his insistence that "knowing is a form of doing" (QC 205). And he let the emphasis of the "theory in which knowing and doing are intimately connected" (QC 214) become shifted so that "the final import of the conclusions as to knowledge resides in the changed idea it enforces as to action" (QC 245). "Thought ... is a mode of directed overt action" (QC 166), and "a question is a demand for action on someone's part" (L 169). Like James, Dewey was concerned with the influence of thought over action, as well as with the verification of thought by action. He thought of ideas as the instruments of action. If "reflective knowledge as such is instrumental" (QC 218) and "the only means of regulation" (QC 219), it was because they were both incomplete parts of the same enterprise, the solving of a problem in which the object is as much involved as the subject (QC 233f).

There is some reason to suspect that Dewey thought of the scientific method as a practical tool rather than as a method for seeking the knowledge of abstract laws capable of application. Science has a method in which activity is central, the experimental method in which controlled observations by means of instruments furnishes the leading edge, but with thought and feeling involved: thought involved in calculations and feelings involved intuitively in the choosing of hypotheses—all very far from Dewey's conception. With small changes, he might have discovered the usefulness of activity as a source of reliable knowledge, but as matters stood, like his predecessors in pragmatism, he missed. His accomplishments were of course considerable, but not in this direction.

VII

The American pragmatists more than most philosophers were concerned with practice. But they thought of it in some tangential way. Either it was concerned with meaning as a matter of clarification and limitation, or it was a practical effort to hold down speculation to what was considered feasible, or it was a model for constructing a theory of activity which was never completed, or it was a plain man's rule of thumb for getting on with the job. It is possible to look on activity as an elucidation of meaning in a perfectly legitimate fashion, but that is not a philosophical endeavor in any way comparable to the scientific method. The experimental method in philosophy would have to consider activity as a way of verifying or falsifying any hypothesis, which is an altogether different consideration from the theory of meaning. Moreover, it has little or nothing to do directly with practice. The scientific method is not concerned with improving practice, it is concerned with discovering the laws of nature; and if its results can be employed in practice with astonishing success, that is still only a by-product of the method and not its principal aim. The pragmatists walked all round the problem of how to develop a philosophical correlate of the experimental method of the physical sciences but they never did turn to approach it directly.

A hidden assumption may have vitiated all the attempts of the American pragmatists to found activity on reliable knowledge. The hidden assumption underlying most fundamental inquiry of a philosophical nature is the rationalist assumption: that reason by itself is competent adequately to represent reality. This was Hegel's assumption, and it can be made legitimately if and only if reality itself is altogether rational. Only Bergson among the philosophers has openly challenged it. Thanks to Bergson we know of an alternative. One can take the intellectualist point of view from which it appears necessary to tame activity by reducing it to a formula suitable for inclusion in a conceptual scheme (the pragmatists). Or one can take the action point of view according to which philosophy has the task of deriving its valid statements by making them strictly in accordance with concrete events (the scientists). James did undertake the latter attempt for philosophy even though on the whole he was unsuccessful. That is why Whitehead said that he was anxious to rescue the thought of Bergson, James and Dewey from "the charge of anti-intellectualism, which rightly or wrongly [sic] has been associated with it."[17]

I have tried to show in this study that thanks to the pragmatists we now know there is such a problem as the hidden assumption. And in philosophy it often happens that a problem fully recognized is a problem well on its way to solution. In philosophy, it has been further argued,

[17] Alfred North Whitehead, *Process and Reality* New York, 1941. Macmillan. p. vii.

progress consists not in answering a question in any final way but only in refining the question. Thanks to the pragmatists, then, we have begun the process of refining the question of how activity can be a source of reliable knowledge.

XVIII

CONCLUSION

SAMPLES OF APPLICATIONS

The writing of this book has been prompted by the belief that there are no inapplicable true theories. Some theories will work better than others, and we proceed on the assumption that the widest and most integrated will also be the most applicable. The terrible difficulty is that we cannot always tell in advance which theory will work (because we do not always know which is valid) or, if we can, then we still may be unable to tell which one will work best. At this point we are entirely in the hands of practice, and lessons of practice are not easy lessons. We are not always given the opportunity to apply what we have learned.

If individual investigators did not have their favorite hypotheses, there would probably be no investigators. The ideal of inquiry is detached inquiry, and this to some extent does exist; but complete detachment is an ideal toward which we strive, not an end we have already gained. The reason for this is the point over which Dewey has made so much, that the instrument of inquiry is itself involved in the inquiry, and disturbs to some extent the subject-matter into which we are inquiring. We are never investigating anything which is altogether free of our investigation, so that we are partly inquiring into our own inquiry whenever we examine anything. This may be so; but far from erecting it into a virtue, we should regard it as a vice. The fact that we must to some extent stand in our own light should not deter us from striving to stand in our own light as little as possible. We must learn how to cultivate that amateur approach to life in which we want only the best, and retain a prejudice in favor of the excellent. Meanwhile, we know of the failure of men to adhere to their ideals in practice. We know, too, that objectivity is the proper kind of mental hygiene and that we must live with problems until they can be solved.

There are times when the ideal of the detached devotion to truth is considered so remote that we identify it with the saints, with Socrates, Buddha, or Jesus, or the contemporary Gandhi, as something whose very nature involves a degree of purity and strength for self-sacrifice denied to the ordinary mortal, so far removed that its very pursuit is idle. Yet such an ideal is implicit in the nature of the scientific method, it is implicit in art, and it should be equally implicit in philosophy. The pretension is there as a matter of course; but that the ideal itself is missing is a significant failure which has vitiated most philosophical inquiry. If other inquiries are bound to preserve an attitude of detachment, how much more of a responsibility is placed upon the philosopher to do so! His is the widest of inquiries, the most generalized of knowable goals.

However, it does remain true that the philosopher himself is involved in the culture from which he is endeavoring to elicit the implicit dominant ontology. For if this i. d. o. is as crucial as we have asserted it to be, then he is working near the cultural vortex, a dangerous occupation for an observer who wishes to remain free and impartial and personally unaffected. We may compare the philosopher's task in this regard with the observation airplanes which gather data for the weather bureau, and which fly into the center of a hurricane in order to record its breadth and intensity and direction. In general, a safe guide for the theorizer is to be suspicious of any argument which bolsters his own material advantage. Men who profess to examine theoretical questions are human enough to have a tendency to emerge from the inquiry with answers conformable with what they themselves would like to see true. Thus the old Roman challenge, *cui bono?* is a good working principle. We ought to be suspicious of the degree of detached truth involved when he who has discovered it is the one who stands most to benefit. For prejudices do exist in every one of us, and we tend without knowing it to seek out just those arguments which will secure to us the gains we have already made. Thus for purposes of arriving at the truth, the government of the U.S.S.R. ought to be suspicious of arguments which seem to make communism the best political and economic system, and capitalists ought to be suspicious of arguments in favor of individual enterprise. The philosopher living under the i. d. o. of nominalism ought to be suspicious of any argument in favor of the sole reality of actual physical particulars, on the grounds that it defends what he already profoundly accepts and so involves no necessity for change on his part. Any unconscious belief is of the nature of a vested intellectual interest, valuable in the sense of a property but capable of acting as a stubborn obstacle where progress toward truth is concerned.

Someone could write a good book on the topic of the therapeutic half-truths which have consoled humanity. These consist in subjectivisms of all sorts, religious ones mainly, the crutches of those whom the society itself has failed to bear up. Just as men in various cultures have employed drugs to obtain pleasure and to escape from the pain of the consciousness of pain, of their own shortcomings, of goals not reached and ambitions forgotten, so they have fallen back upon limited systems in the same vein, and sought in pitiful little explanations some escape and relief from the doubts and questions they found insupportable. So few human beings have the stamina to face the larger ignorances without flinching that therapeutic half-truths are popular.

We are not always busy defending a theory we already accept. In addition to the pure and detached search for truth, which is one alternative, we often resort to another which consists in attacking a position we do not find valid. But attacking a false position is not identical in character with defending a true one. The negative approach works from universal to particular; for in attempting to refute a false position we bring to bear upon the particular argument all the relevant universal principles we are able to find. In contrast, the positive works from particular to universal: we are anxious to defend some general thesis with singular cases. This distinction between the positive and negative approaches holds true even where the appearances seem to indicate otherwise. As examples we may instance a polemic which is couched in general terms but is actually aimed at one man, and a love ostensibly aimed at one woman but actually spread out to embrace the whole world.

Ontological postulates are assumed everywhere and by everyone, but we regard as illogical those whose postulates depart from our own. We simply take it for granted that since their postulates cannot be different, it must be in their deductions that they have gone wrong. That is because we can no more perceive their postulates than we can ours. Common sense, as we have noted earlier, is the name for that part of the rational process which is concerned with the implicitly held, socially acquired postulates for immediate practical action. We cannot conceive of our common sense shifting, but of course it does. For there are times like the present when social change moves faster than the shifts in the implicit dominant ontology. Consider the rapidity of developments in recent physical technology. Consider the devious and (as it is called) diabolical cleverness that goes into the making of the controls of contemporary social power, as in the large machinery of politics and economics, where the furies live. In this holocaust our sanity is challenged if we are well along in years, or at the very least all our conservatism is strongly invoked.

Moral considerations apart, however, the fact is that the function of disorder has an important role to play in inquiry. The fact that empirical investigations turn up so many unrelated things, that, in a certain sense, the scientific systems seem impossible to close, is a necessary thing if progress is to continue. In other words, a certain amount of disorder is a function of continuing inquiry.

But the fact is that ever since Socrates we have been formally inquisitive, and ever since Descartes we have substituted an infallible method of inquiry for infallible conclusions. The genius of contemporary philosophy insures that from now on we shall be able to incorporate in a system which is not infallible the results of our inquiries. Fallibilism is Peirce's principle, and Whitehead's; and the open system of the tentatively held metaphysical theory is the latest and perhaps the most valuable of human discoveries. One major contention of this approach is that the open system of axiologic realism, the positivism of the ontological philosophy, has not been tried in practice and has rarely been held even in theory. Of course, realism as a practicing philosophy is an ideal to be striven toward, not an attitude which can be easily assumed and maintained without further ado. Men slip noiselessly into idealism or nominalism according as they reject the culture in which they find themselves or wish to enshrine it untouched and unamended, fearful of improvements because any change might involve possible retrogression. But the delicate balance of realism, walking on tiptoe between the rejection of all generalizations and the abject worship of mythologized universals, is not easy to hold; it requires a constant vigil.

THE CATAPLEXY OF HUMANISM

Cataplexy: the term is defined in the *Oxford English Dictionary* as "the temporary paralysis or hypnotic state in animals when 'shamming death.'" Life is a kind of running away from death, and there is no other kind; life is the stupefaction which follows upon the prospect of death.

To some extent we do enjoy the journey toward death, which is life. The aim at final ends is immersed in detail, and we are forever taking the next tiny step toward ultimate goals. Hence our subjective fears, hopes and desires become translated into their objective counterparts; and "what can we hope to feel?" "what should we think?" and "what must we do?" turn into "what values should be actualized?" "what is the truth?" and "what can be achieved in the world?"

The postulate of humanism demands that the results of speculation shall never reach the stage where the conclusions demand that harm shall come to any speculating creature. Thus the protection of reasoning is the logical truth residual in humanism. There is virtue and happiness in mere understanding, as Spinoza claimed, and perhaps this is, as he says, the highest form of human existence. We would have to abate these claims somewhat while still insisting that their limited truth has been sadly overlooked. Humanism is true within limits, and it can be set for the goal of the individual in a world where social organizations that he could respect and wish to contribute to have been disrupted. Certainly it is a better goal for the individual than the desire to reconcile him to his own nausea.

It is a fact that the postulates for existence must include some mention of the furies. But there are several kinds of madness, as Plato insists in the *Phaedrus*. One is a kind of inspired ecstasy in the soul of the philosopher, which is mistaken for frenzy by the multitude, he says. It is the task of reason to work the two kinds of feeling together, the disciplined with the undisciplined.

Man is the center for the actualization of values which, however, do not owe their existence to man. Humanism is a safeguard against absolutism, and a guarantee that all vital questions shall be kept open. Yet it, too, cannot be allowed to be absolute, lest the vital questions themselves in this way be set aside altogether. Man, we might say, was clearly designed to strain with all his energy against the natural limitations set upon his achievements. Nothing was ever devised less native to human beings than that brand of humanism which assumes that men like to refer everything to themselves, and to limit voluntarily all effort to what is certain of accomplishment beforehand. Looking down, it is easy to see that all theology, all philosophy, every discipline in which man aspires toward the perfect good, are defeated by the fact that he cannot sustain life without the death of other organisms, plants if not animals—in any case, other life. The highest problems are settled at the lowest levels. That is why the seeker after truth must be humbler than the dust, as Gandhi said. It is more human to want the moon. False magic and astrology and pseudo-sciences apart, we may say that from the point of view advanced here there can be little doubt that astronomy is a social science.

For the human race is doomed to this paradox: that men are destined to speculate about ultimate questions such as the nature of God, immortality and the justification of evil in the world; and they are equally destined evidently not to find the answers to these questions. A million years of life on the earth, and yet we know something of only seven thousand; a half million galaxies and billions of planets, and yet we know only one of each. If we can derive any personal attitude from the vastness of this field, it ought to be that of humility, a profound humility for the human species and for ourselves individually, though not necessarily the self-effacement of the ontological idealist. Yet the problems here are larger than the capacities of those condemned to attempt their solutions. Small wonder, then that they do

> grow sick of dripping in the well
> of knowledge ; clawing the walls of the knowable.

The prime factor in knowledge is ignorance. We must teach people not how much we know but how little. They have been endowed with reasoning powers capable of dealing with cosmic problems but incapable of solving them. Hence we cannot in practice get away from the limited range of human values, and by human values here is meant not the values appertaining *to* the human but the values ascertainable *from* the human.

Eighteenth-century Europe was devastatingly aware of this, and its truth overwhelmed Chinese philosophy and reduced it to a kind of practical ethics. It would be possible theoretically to draw up a list of practical facts of commonplace wisdom, among others, for instance, the following: that no men are entirely consistent in their actions and few in their thoughts, that women do not have the same postulates as men though they do have the same deductive logic, that men rarely forgive those who have put them under an obligation by doing them a good turn, and so forth. The human range of possibilities runs all the way from Birkenau to Calvary. Yet the vast majority of human values tend to cluster about a limited center of small human goods and evils. The curve is a peaked one which dies away swiftly, with a densely-packed central frequency distribution.

The same conflict that attends the distinction between aims and achievements turns up in the gap between theories and practices. The cave analogy of Plato's *Republic* will not do for the relation between universals and singulars, but it will do excellently well for the relation between theory and practice. The so-called practical man sees only the shadows that constitute his world as they fall from the operations of the theorists with their theories. Atomic bombs, wars, medical aids to therapy —the practical man deals with these things only as they happen. Hence they are all irrational and haphazard, having no apparent cause, no antecedents and no foreseeable consequences. The practical man who has no interest in or knowledge of theory is a prisoner in Plato's cave.

Conversely, the man who is concerned with theory alone is left out of the actual world to an alarming degree. Each of the basic needs: feeding, breeding, inquiring, all have their attendant makings, each has its practice as well as its theory. Man may not be the only productive animal but he is the most productive. And he produces dreams, too, dreams of what would be better; he dreams about order. Lastly, then, he has his own conflicts, because what he will settle for is always something more than what he thinks he is entitled to. When he becomes wholly aware of this paradox he becomes man the maker in the grand sense. Then he takes up the wager supplementary to Pascal's: the chances are that we had better look around—now; we may not ever be able to do so again. In other words, in addition to our duties and obligations of an individual and institutional nature, we had better find the time to be lazy, to "loaf and invite the soul" as Whitman said, and had better do so quickly, for there is not much time, there never is.

What shall we do with this fact that nothing actual lasts forever? Philosophy here reduces not to cataplexy but to cataplexis, the meaning of which is "to threaten with misfortune." It is certain that what will happen is more important than what has happened, although nothing that ever happens can alter the list of important things. The philosopher can never wholly approve anything actual, for nothing is perfect. He is always opposed to the office-holders among his contemporaries, for they have set their endorsement upon things-as-they-are, while he stands always for things-as-they-ought-to-be. Like Diogenes, he has two missions: to warn men of the truth, and to set slaves free. Yet he is not a Cynic.

QUOD FORTASSE INCERTUM EST

PHILOSOPHICAL WRITINGS OF JAMES K. FEIBLEMAN

1933

Science and the Spirit of Man. London. Allen and Unwin (with J. W. Friend).

1936

The Unlimited Community. London. Allen and Unwin (with J. W. Friend).

1937

What Science Really Means. London. Allen and Unwin (with J. W. Friend).
Christianity, Communism and the Ideal Society. London. Allen and Unwin.

1938

"The Meaning of Comedy," *The Journal of Philosophy*, XXXV, 16:421-432.
"Democracy and the Middle-Class Rule of Reason," *Ethics*, XLVII, 4:536-542.

1939

In Praise of Comedy. London. Allen and Unwin.
"Une Philosophie Americaine," *Revue Metaphysique et de Morale*, pp. 443-459.
"Toward the Recovery of Giambattista Vico," *Social Science*, 14, 1:31-40.

1940

Positive Democracy. Chapel Hill. University of North Carolina Press.
"Toynbee's Theory of History," *T'ien Hsai Monthly*, XI, 1:9-29 and 2:140-173.

1941

"The Logical Value of Objects of Art," *Journal of Aesthetics and Art Criticism*,
  Fall, 70-85.
"Biological Analysis in Allergy," *International Correspondence Club of Allergy*.

1942

"The Scientific Outlook of Cézanne," *Philosophy of Science*, 9, 3:275-280.

1943

"A Systematic Presentation of Peirce's Ethics," *Ethics*, LII, 2:98-109.
"A Theory of Social Belief," *Journal of Psychology*, 16:219-237.
"How to Read a Word," *Philosophy and Phenomenological Research*, III, 4:478-486.
"Therapy of the Dialectic," *Journal of Philosophy*, XL, 21:566-575.
"Preventive Psychiatry," December 15.

1944

"The Role of Philosophy in a Time of Troubles," *Philosophical Review*, LIII:69-75.
"Reid and the Origins of Modern Realism," *Journal of the History of Ideas*, V,
  1:113-120.
"The Ethical Basis of Chinese Unity," *Ethics*, LIV, 3:223-225.
"The Mythology of Science," *Philosophy of Science*, 11, 2:117-121.
"Have We Exhausted Greek Culture?" *Social Science*, 19, 3:132-138.
"Individual Psychology and the Ethics of Peirce," *Journal of General Psychology*,
  31:293-295.
"The Relation of Peirce to New England Culture," *American Journal of Economics
  and Sociology*, 4, 1:99-107.
"A Reply to Bertrand Russell's Introduction to the Second Edition of *The Principles
  of Mathematics*," in *The Philosophy of Bertrand Russell*. Evanston, Ill. The
  Library of Living Philosophers. Ch. 4:157-174.

1945

"The Theory of the Ethos," *Journal of Legal and Political Sociology*, pp. 83-99.
"The Psychology of the Artist," *Journal of Psychology*, 19·165-189.
"The Structure and Function of Organization," *Philosophical Review*, LIV:19-44
  (with J. W. Friend).

"Pragmatism and Inverse Probability," *Philosophy and Phenomenological Research*, V, 3:309-319.
"Science from the Standpoint of Realism," *Journal of Higher Education*, XVI, 3:127-138.
"Normative Organization and Empirical Fields," *Philosophy of Science*, 12, 2:52-56.
"Peirce's Use of Kant," *Journal of Philosophy*, 14, 5:365-377.
"The Influence of Peirce on Dewey's Logic," *Education*, pp. 1-7.
"The Hypothesis of Aesthetic Measure," *Philosophy of Science*, 12, 3:194-217.

1946

The Theory of Human Culture. New York. Duell, Sloan and Pearce.
The Revival of Realism. Chapel Hill. University of North Carolina Press.
An Introduction to Peirce's Philosophy. New York. Harper and Bros.
"The Theory of *Hamlet*," *Journal of the History of Ideas*, VII, 2:131-150.
"The Psychology of Art Appreciation," *Journal of General Psychology*, 35:43-57.
"The Decline of Literary Chaos," *Sewanee Review*, October, pp. 3-20.

1947

"The Master-Myth and the Modern Artist," *Ethics*, LVII, 2:131-136.
"La Place d'Art dans la Culture," *Les Etudes Philosophiques*, 2, 3 and 4:148-157 and 262-270.

1948

"A Set of Postulates and a Definition for Science," *Philosophy of Science*, 15, 1:36-38.
"The Genesis of the Dialectic," *Philosophy and Phenomenological Research*, VIII, 4:668-678.

1949

Aesthetics. New York. Duell, Sloan and Pearce.
"An Ontology of Art," *The Personalist*, XXX, 2:129-141.
"The Art of the Dance," *Journal of Aesthetics and Art Criticism*, VIII, 1:47-52.
"A Defense of Ontology," *Journal of Philosophy*, XLVI, 2:41-51.

1950

"Class-Membership and the Ontological Problem," *Philosophy of Science*, 17, 3:254-259.

1951

Ontology. Baltimore. John Hopkins University Press.
"Was Spinoza a Nominalist?" *Philosophical Review*, LX, 3:386-389.

"Culture as Applied Ontology," *Philosophical Quarterly*, 1, 5:416-422.
"The Metaphysics of Logical Positivism," *Review of Metaphysics*, V, 1:55-82.
"The Modern Novel and Its Audience," *Education*, 71:1-8.

1952

Philosophers Lead Sheltered Lives. London. Allen and Unwin.
"The Analysis of Perception," *Sophia*, XX, 2:153-159.
"Propositions and Facts," *Tulane Studies in Philosophy*, I:71-85.
"On the Future of Some of Peirce's Ideas," in *Studies in the Philosophy of Charles Sanders Peirce*. Cambridge. Harvard University Press. pp. 325-334.

1953

"Eminence of Scholarship," *Education*, 73:1-7.
"The History of Dyadic Ontology," *Review of Metaphysics*, VI, 3:351-367.
"Aristotle as Finite Ontologist," *Tulane Studies in Philosophy*, II:39-58.
"Freedom and Authority in the Structure of Cultures," in *Freedom and Authority in our Time*. New York. Conference on Science, Philosophy and Religion. Ch. XXVI:309-316.
"The Problem of the Meta-Axiom," *The Southern Philosopher*, 2, 4:5-8.

1954

"On the Topics and Definitions of the Categories," *Philosophical Quarterly*, 4, 14:45-59.
"The Range of Dyadic Ontology," *Journal of Philosophy*, LI, 4:117-124.
"On the Theory of Induction," *Philosophy and Phenomenological Research*, XIV, 3:332-343.
"Theory of Integrative Levels," *British Journal for the Philosophy of Science*, V, 17:59-66.
"Toward an Analysis of the Basic Value System," *American Anthropologist*, 56, 3:421-432.
"Le Domaine de l'Ontologie Finie," *Les Etudes Philosophiques*, 3:338-351.
"Kant and Metaphysics," *Tulane Studies in Philosophy*, III:55-87.
"The Place of Science in Human Culture," *Annals of Allergy*, 12:555-560.

1955

"An Introduction to an Objective, Empirical Ethics," *Ethics*, LXV, 2:102-115.
"The Rational Unconscious," *Journal of General Psychology*, 52:157-162.
"A Esfera da Epistemologia Sensista, *Revista Portuguesa de Filosofia*, I:59-63.
"On Substance," *Review of Metaphysics*, VIII, 3:373-378.
"Un'Ontologia della Conoscenza," *Rivista di Filosofia*, LXVI, 3:247-260.
"Reflections After Wittgenstein," *Sophia*, XXIII, 3 and 4.
"Viennese Positivism in the United States," *Tulane Studies in Philosophy*, IV:31-47.
"Knowing About Semipalatinsk," *Dialectica*, 9, 3 and 4:279-286.

"An Ontological Philosophy of Education," in *Modern Philosophies and Education,* Chicago. National Society for the Study of Education. 54th Yearbook, Part I, Ch. X:342-369.

1956

The Institutions of Society. London. Allen and Unwin.
"Mathematics and Its Applications in the Sciences," *Philosophy of Science,* 23, 3:204-215.
"Some Problems in the Philosophy of Education," *Harvard Educational Review,* XXVI, 2:150-153.
"On the Universal and On the Individual," *Tulane Studies in Philosophy,* V:25-53.
"On Quality," *Journal of Philosophy,* LIII, 21:625-634.

1957

"An Introduction to Metaphysics for Empiricists," *Giornale di Metafisica,* I:1-14.
"Institutions, Law and Morals," *Tulane Law Review,* XXXI:503-516.
"Ethical Variations on a Theme by Rosmini-Serbatti," *Tulane Studies in Philosophy,* VI:53-66.
"Language and Metaphysics," *Rivista Methodos,* pp. 1-20.

1958

The Pious Scientist. New York. Bookman Associates.
Inside the Great Mirror. The Hague. Martinus Nijhoff.
"A Conversation with Einstein," *The Personalist,* 39:15-18.
"An Explanation of Philosophy," *Tulane Studies in Philosophy,* VII:35-68.
"L'Etica dell'Azione," *Rivista di Filosofia,* XLIV, 3:359-378.
"Superior Students," *College Board Review,* 36:21-22.
"On the Connections Between the Two Worlds," *Rivista Mexicana de Filosofia,* 1, 2:109-123.

1959

Religious Platonism. London. Allen and Unwin.
"The Logical Structure of the Scientific Method," *Dialectica,* 13, 3 and 4:208-225.
"Aristotle's Religion," *Hibbert Journal,* LVII:124-132.
"The Education of the Administrator," *Journal of Educational Sociology,* 32:2-12.
"On Relations," *Journal of Philosophy,* LVI, 4:165-173.
"The Role of Hypotheses in the Scientific Method," *Perspectives in Biology and Medicine,* II, 3:335-346.
"Darwin and the Scientific Method," *Tulane Studies in Philosophy,* VIII:3-14.

1960

An Introduction to Peirce's Philosophy, 2nd edition. London. Allen and Unwin.

"The Social Adaptiveness of Philosophy," *Ethics*, LXX, 2:146-154.
"The Genius versus the University," *Journal of Higher Education*, XXXI, 3:139-142.
"The Psychology of the Scientist," *Synthese*, XII, 1:79-113.
"Testing Hypotheses by Experiment," *Perspectives in Biology and Medicine*, IV, 1:91-122.
"Hegel Revisited," *Tulane Studies in Philosophy*, IX:16-49.
"The Principle of Indeterminancy Re-Examined," *Ratio*, German: Heft 11:119-134; English: 111, 2:133-151.

1961

"Transfer-Matching: A New Method in Psychotherapy," *Journal of Psychology*, 51:411-420.
"Philistines on the Faculty," *School and Society*, 89, 2187:82-84.
"The Well-Rounded Graduate," *Journal of Educational Sociology*, 34, 9:417-421.
"The Cultural Circuit in Psychology and Psychiatry," *Journal of Nervous and Mental Disease*, 132, 2:127-145.
"The Condition of the Humanities," *Educational Theory*, XI, 2:71-75.
"The Scientific Philosophy," *Philosophy of Science*, 28, 3:238-259.
"Notes for a Commentary on Whitehead's *Science and the Modern World*," *Darshana*, 1, 3:44-55.
"Pure Science, Applied Science, Technology, Engineering: An Attempt at Definitions," *Technology and Culture*, 2, 4:305-317.
"The Nature of Hypotheses," *Nuring Forum*, I, 1.
"Ontology and Ideology," *Rivista Methodos*, XIII, 51 and 52:1-8.
"Ecological Factors in Human Maladaptation," *American Journal of Psychiatry*, 118, 2:118-124.

1962

In Praise of Comedy. 2nd edition. New York. Russell and Russell.
Foundations of Empiricism. The Hague. Martinus Nijhoff.
Biosocial Factors in Mental Illness. Springfield, Ill. Charles C. Thomas.
"An Illustration of Retention Schemata," *Psychological Record*, 12, 1:1-8.
"Concreteness in Painting: Abstract Expressionism and After," *The Personalist*, 43, 1:70-83.
"Behavior as Response," *Psychiatric Research Report No. 14*:15-28.
"The Stressed Conditioning of Psychotics," *Journal of Psychology*, 53:295-299.
"The Hidden Philosophy of Americans," *Saturday Review*, March 10:15-16 and 55.
"Memories of Sherwood Anderson," *Shenandoah*, XIII, 3:32-45.
"The Impact of Science on Society," *Tulane Studies in Philosophy*, XI:39-75.
"A Logically Primitive and Empirically Verifiable Ontology," *Revue Philosophique*, 4:497-514.
"What Happens in College," *Saturday Review*, October 20:74-76.
"Philosophical Empiricism from the Scientific Standpoint," *Dialectica*, 16, 1:5-14.
"Formal Materialism Reconfirmed," *Philosophy and Phenomenological Research*, XXIII,1:62-70.

1963

Mankind Behaving: Human Needs and Material Culture. Springfield, Ill. Charles C. Thomas.

"Plato versus the Atomists in Aristotle," *Sophia*, XXXI, 1 and 2:68-75.

"The Uses of Thinking," *Saturday Review*, March 2:18-19 and 48.

"A Behaviorist Theory of Art," *British Journal of Aesthetics*, 3, 1:3-14.

"Camus and the Passion of Humanism," *Kenyon Review*, XXV:281-292.

"Beginning College Teaching," *Association of College Admissions Counselors Journal*, 9:6-9.

"Activity as a Source of Knowledge in American Pragmatism," *Tulane Studies in Philosophy*, XII:92-105.

"Childhood: A Study in Philosophical Psychology," *Psychological Record*, 13, 3:329-340.

"Biosocial Adaptation and Mental Illness," *International Journal of Social Psychiatry*, IX, 2:94-101.

1964

"Sexual Behavior, Morality and the Law," in *Sexual Behavior and the Law*, Springfield, Ill. Charles C. Thomas. pp. 171-190.

"A Philosophic Analysis of Pleasure," in *The Role of Pleasure in Behavior*. New York. Hoeber Medical Division of Harper and Row. pp. 251-256.

"Human Nature and Institutions," in *Dr. S. Radhokrishnan Souvenir Volume*. Moradabad, India. Darshana International. Ch. 17:113-122.

"God, Man and Matter," *The Personalist*, 45, 1:80-89.

"Knowing, Doing and Being," *Ratio*, English: VI, 1:12-27; German: Heft 1, 6:11-25.

"Institutional Conditioning," *Indian Journal of Social Research*, 2:99-110.

"Material Objects and the Reference of Signs," *Synthese*, XV, 4:424-435.

"Aggression: The Muscle and Alterable Objects," *Tulane Studies in Philosophy*, XIII:3-26.

1965

"Literary New Orleans Between World Wars," *Southern Review*, 1, 3:702-719.

"Artifactualism," *Philosophy and Phenomenological Research*, XXV, 4:544-559.

"The Integrative Levels in Nature," in *Focus on Information and Communication*. London. Aslib. pp. 27-41.

"How Abstract Objects Survive," *Philosophy Today*, IX, 2/4:79-85.

"Infancy—A Study in Philosophical Psychology," *The Philosophical Journal*, 2, 2:104-122.

"Artistic Imagining," *The Personalist*, 46, 4:468-484.

"Falsity in Practice," *Tulane Studies in Philosophy*, Vol. XIV: 19–43.

Index of Names

Index of Topics